The
Guide to
Cooking
Schools

2005

The Guide to Cooking Schools

Seventeenth Edition

ShawGuides
NEW YORK

Inquiries concerning this book should be addressed to: Editor, ShawGuides, P.O. Box 231295, New York, New York 10023, Phone: (212) 799-6464, Fax: (212) 724-9287, E-mail: info@shawguides.com, URL: www.shawguides.com.

Please note that the information herein has been obtained from the listed cooking schools and organizations and is subject to change. The editor and publisher accept no responsibility for inaccuracies. Schools should be contacted prior to sending money and/or making travel plans.

Library of Congress Catalog Card Number 88-92516
ISSN 1040-2616
ISBN 0-945834-32-2

Printed in the United States of America by
Bookmasters, Inc.

Introduction

First published, in 1989, *The Guide to Cooking Schools is the only comprehensive resource to career and recreational culinary and wine education programs worldwide. This 17ᵗʰ annual edition contains descriptions of 509 career and 708 recreational cooking and wine programs worldwide, The number of programs and students has increased every year as has the interest in food, cooking, and wine education. The opportunities for employment as a cook or chef in the foodservice industry continue to exceed the supply of qualified individuals. Experienced chefs in top restaurants can become celebrities, star in reality television shows, and earn an income commensurate with their status.*

If you love to cook and are eager to learn new techniques, replicate the dishes you've enjoyed in fine dining establishments, try new foods and equipment, and meet interesting people, a local cooking course or a cooking vacation will expand your knowledge and widen your circle of friends. Cooking is a chance to be creative, to experiment, to share a special and memorable meal with the people you care for.

Looking for the right gift for a friend or relative who enjoys cooking, good food, and fine wine? ShawGuides Cooking and Wine School Gift Certificates make it easy for you to give a thoughtful, useful gift of lasting value. Perfect for any occasion, a ShawGuides Gift Certificate eliminates guesswork and transfers decision-making to the recipient, who can use your gift to purchase a cooking or wine class, course, vacation, or product at any one of dozens of cooking and wine schools worldwide. Certificates are available in any amount with a $50 minimum. They are mailed and/or e-mailed worldwide at no additional cost. For more information or to purchase a certificate, call 212-799-6464, e-mail info@shawguides.com or visit our website at http://cookforfun.shawguides.com.

CHOOSING A CAREER SCHOOL

1. How long is the program? Career programs range from a few weeks to four years or more. Curricula for programs of a year or less consist primarily of culinary courses that prepare you for an entry level position. College degree programs include general education courses and electives that provide a more well-rounded education. The 3-year apprenticeship program sponsored by the American Culinary Federation (ACF) offers paid on-the-job training in a foodservice establishment and the opportunity to earn a college degree.

2. Is it affordable? Tuition ranges from a few hundred dollars at community colleges to over $10,000 per program or year at trade schools that offer a specialized curriculum. If cost is an obstacle, inquire about scholarships or loans, which are offered by many schools and some culinary organizations.

3. What are the scheduling options? If you're unable to attend classes full-time, consider programs that permit you to enroll part-time or offer flexible schedules.

4. How qualified is the faculty? Instructor credentials should include certification by the American Culinary Federation, college degree, and/or industry experience.

5. Is the school accredited? A school in operation for five years or more should be accredited. Colleges are accredited by one of six regional associations, private and trade schools by three organizations.

6. Is real-world experience part of the program? Some schools have student-staffed foodservice facilities on-campus where students are required to work as part of the program. Others offer intern- or externships in an off-campus setting.

7. What courses, textbooks, and course materials are provided? Has the school's curriculum adapted to today's healthier lifestyles with emphasis on fresh ingredients, nutrition, and a variety of international cuisines. Do they offer specialized courses in the subjects that interest you?

8. What kind of job offers can you expect? Will the school's placement office be able to find you a position in the setting you desire? Obtain the names of graduates and contact them to determine whether the school met their expectations for training and placement.

CHOOSING A COOKING VACATION

1. What can you expect to learn? Are the dishes appealing and suited to your expertise? Will you be learning the how's and why's of cooking, rather than just following recipes?

2. Will classes be demonstration or hands-on? Hands-on classes are necessary for learning techniques. Demonstrations are appropriate for experienced cooks and those who prefer observing to participating. Most vacation programs combine both.

3. What are the cooking and lodging facilities like? For hands-on classes will you have your own work station and utensils? Are appliances modern and in good working condition? Is the space large enough for everyone to move about comfortably? For demonstrations, is there an overhead mirror and is seating close enough that you'll be able to see clearly? Is lodging part of a chain or rated by a recognized travel guide? Do the rooms have private baths?

4. What are the qualifications of the instructor? If the teacher has written a cookbook, obtain a copy to determine whether the recipes appeal to you. If the teacher is a chef, will the recipes be adapted to a home kitchen? Request copies of some of the recipes that will be prepared and speak with the instructor to get a sense of his or her teaching style and communication skills.

5. What is scheduled during non-cooking time? Some vacation programs emphasize cooking over other activities, some offer a few classes with more time devoted to sightseeing, visiting food-related sites, shopping, dining out, or at leisure. Obtain a detailed itinerary so you'll know what to expect.

6. What is covered by the cost? The cost always covers classes and the meals prepared, usually covers sightseeing, most other meals, and ground transportation, and sometimes covers lodging and airfare. Find out what your payment covers and how much you should budget for the rest.

7. Request the names of recent participants and contact them. Did the program meet their expectations, does it offer the features you desire, would they would recommend it?

Although we strive to make each listing accurate, changes do occur. For updates and new listings, check our web site – http://www.shawguides.com – which contains the unabridged contents of this directory, updated daily and accessible at no charge.

May you find pleasure and success in all your culinary endeavors.

*Shaw**Guides***

ACCREDITING AGENCIES

ACCET	Accrediting Council for Continued Education and Training
ACCSCT	Accrediting Commission of Career Schools/Colleges of Technology
ACF	American Culinary Federation
ACICS	Accrediting Council for Independent Colleges and Schools
COE	Council on Occupational Education
MSA	Middle States Association of Colleges and Schools
NASC	Northwest Association of Schools and Colleges
NCA	North Central Association of Colleges and Schools
NEASC	New England Association of Schools and Colleges
SACS	Southern Association of Colleges and Schools
WASC	Western Association of Schools and Colleges

Contents

1

Career and Professional Programs

ALABAMA

ACF BIRMINGHAM CHAPTER
Birmingham
Sponsor: ACF chapter. Program: 3-yr apprenticeship, degree program through Jefferson State Community College. Curriculum: culinary, core. Total enrollment: 25.
Costs: $3,500 in-state, $5,000 out-of-state. Beginning salary $5/hr, $0.40 increases every 6 mos. Housing $350-$500/mo.
Contact: Doug Allen, CEC, Acting Coordinator, ACF Birmingham Chapter, 750 Lakeshore Parkway, Birmingham, AL 35211; 205-328-ROUX, E-mail doug_allen@saksinc.com, URL http://www.acfbirmingham.org.

BISHOP STATE COMMUNITY COLLEGE
Mobile/Year-round
Sponsor: 2-yr college. Program: 6-qtr, 90 cr-hr certificate/114 cr-hr (or 2-sem+summer term/74 cr-hr) AAS degree in Commercial Food Service. Established: 1963. Accredited by ACF, SACS. Calendar: semester. Curriculum: culinary, core. Admission dates: Aug, Jan. Total enrollment: 25. 100% of applicants accepted. 75% receive financial aid. 25% enrolled part-time. Student to teacher ratio 10:1. 100% of graduates employed within six months. Facilities: Fully equipped kitchen.
Faculty: 2 certified chefs.
Costs: $50/cr-hr in-state, $100/cr-hr out-of-state. Admission requirements: HS diploma or GED.
Contact: Levi Ezell, Director, Commercial Food Service, Bishop State Community College-Carver Campus, 414 Stanton St., Mobile, AL 36617; 334-473-8692, Fax 334-473-7915, E-mail cfs@bscc.cc.al.us, URL http://www.bscc.cc.al.us.

CULINARD – THE CULINARY INSTITUTE OF VIRGINIA COLLEGE
Birmingham/Year-round   *(See also page 175) (See display ad page 3)*
Sponsor: Virginia College, a private institution of higher education. Program: 24-mo (106 cr-hr) AOS degree in Culinary Arts; 27-mo (118 cr-hr) AOS degree in Pastry, Baking & Confectionary Arts; 18-mo (40 cr-hr) wkend diploma program in Culinary Arts. Established: 2000. Accredited by ACICS, Culinary Arts AOS program ACF accredited. Calendar: quarter. Curriculum: core. Admission dates: Oct, Jan, Apr, Jul. 96 each admission period. Student to teacher ratio 16:1. Facilities: 7 instructional kitchens, full-service restaurant, full-service bakery, 10 classroom lecture facility, conferencespace. Courses: Food Production, Bake Shop & Patisserie, Garde Manger, Computer Fundamentals, Marketing & Menu Planning, Cost Controls, Mixology & Viniculture, Purchasing, Dining Room Service, Human Relations, Nutrition, Advanced Patisserie, Confiserie & Center Pieces.
Faculty: Faculty is selected for academic qualifications & business experience. Credentials include advanced degrees & industry certifications.
Costs: $325/cr-hr. Total cost for Culinary Arts is $34,450+$995 tools/uniform fee. Total cost for Pastry, Baking & Confectionary Arts is $38,350+$1,125 tools/uniform fee. Admission requirements: HS diploma or equivalent, admissions interview, assessment exam, letters of recommendation, personal statement, deposit. Scholarships: yes. Loans: yes.
Contact: Bibbi McLaughlin, Vice President of Admissions, CULINARD The Culinary Institute of Virginia College, 65 Bagby Drive, Suite 100, Birmingham, AL 35209; 205-802-1200, 877-429-CHEF (2433), Fax 205-802-7045, E-mail admissions@culinard.com, URL http://www.culinard.com.

FAULKNER STATE COMMUNITY COLLEGE
Gulf Shores/Year-round
Sponsor: 2-yr college. Program: 1-yr/26 sem-hr certificate & 2-yr/75-76 sem-hr AAS degree in Culinary Arts. Established: 1994. Accredited by SACS, ACF, CHRIE. Calendar: semester. Curriculum: culinary, core. Admission dates: Aug, Jan, May. Total enrollment: 90. 25 each admis-

sion period. 90% of applicants accepted. 80% receive financial aid. 10% enrolled part-time. Student to teacher ratio 15:1. 100% of graduates employed within six months. Facilities: New 18,000-sq-ft building.

Faculty: Gerhard Brill, CEC, pastry chef Jim Hurtubise, Ron Koetter, CEC, CCE, CMB, AAC, Program Coordinator.

Costs: $72/sem-hr, in-state; $144/sem-hr, out-of-state. Admission requirements: HS diploma or GED & entrance exam. Scholarships: yes. Loans: yes.

Contact: Ron Koetter, Program Coordinator, Faulkner State Community College, 3301 Gulf Shores Pkwy, Gulf Shores, AL 36542; 251-968-3108, Fax 251-968-3120, E-mail rkoetter@faulknerstate.edu, URL http://www.faulknerstate.edu.

JEFFERSON STATE COMMUNITY COLLEGE
Birmingham/Year-round

Sponsor: 2-yr college. Program: 34-hour Culinary Apprentice Option leading to an AAS degree (requires 6,000-hour on-the-job internship), 28-hour Food Service mgmt option. Established: 1988. Accredited by ACF. Calendar: semester. Curriculum: culinary, core. Student to teacher ratio 10:1. 100% of graduates employed within six months.

Costs: $59/cr-hr. Admission requirements: HS diploma or GED, essay, references. Scholarships: yes. Loans: yes.

Contact: George White, Program Coordinator, Jefferson State Community College, 2601 Carson Rd., Birmingham, AL 35215-3098; 205-853-1200, Fax 205-815-8499, E-mail gwhite@jscc.cc.al.us, URL http://www.jscc.cc.al.us.

LAWSON STATE COMMUNITY COLLEGE
Birmingham/September-May

Sponsor: College. Program: 21-mo certificate in Culinary Arts. Established: 1949. Accredited by SACS. Admission dates: Qtrly. Student to teacher ratio 23:1. 50% of graduates employed within 6 mos.

Faculty: 2 full-time.

Costs: $39/cr-hr in-state, $78/cr-hr out-of-state. Admission requirements: HS diploma or equivalent and admission test.

Contact: Deborah Harris, Lawson State Community College, Commercial Food Preparation, 3060 Wilson Rd., SW, Birmingham, AL 35221-1717; 205-925-2515, E-mail dharris@cougar.ls.cc.al.us, URL http://www.ls.cc.al.us.

TRENHOLM STATE TECHNICAL COLLEGE
Montgomery/Year-round

Sponsor: 2-yr technical college. Program: 42-cr-hr (12-mo) certificate in Culinary Arts, 64-cr-hr (24-mo) associate degree in Culinary Arts Applied Technology, 6,000-hr Chef Apprenticeship-Mgmt option, 74-cr-hr Hospitality Mgmt associate degree option. Established: 1980. Accredited by COE, ACF. Calendar: trimester semester. Curriculum: culinary, core. Admission dates: Jan, May, Aug. Total enrollment: 101. 80+ each admission period. 90% of applicants accepted. 50% receive financial aid. 10% enrolled part-time. Student to teacher ratio 8:1. 100% of graduates employed within six months. Facilities: Free-standing Culinary Arts Ctr, fully-equipped kitchen, classrooms, dining rooms, conference room, computer lab, library.

Faculty: ACF-certified executive chef instructors, members of the American Academy of Chefs.

Costs: $84/sem-cr-hr, ~$300/sem for uniforms, books, insurance. Admission requirements: 17 yrs of age, HS diploma or GED. Scholarships: yes. Loans: yes.

Contact: Mary Ann Campbell, Director of Culinary Arts/Hospitality Mgmt., Trenholm State Technical College, 1225 Air Base Blvd., Montgomery, AL 36108; 334-420-4495, Fax 334-420-4491, E-mail mcampbell@trenholmtech.cc.al.us, URL http://www.Trenholmtech.cc.al.us.

CULINARD. WHERE BREAD IS BROKEN AND CAREERS ARE BUILT.

The preparation of good food is both a science and an art. There is more to preparing food than knowledge, the mastery of skills, and technique. At Culinard, we believe that in order to develop dishes that enrich as well as sustain life, you must develop a passion for food, a deep understanding of the science of food preparation, and an instinct for the culinary arts. Turn your passion for food into a rewarding career at Culinard.

The Culinary Institute of Virginia College

65 Bagby Drive / Birmingham, AL 35209
205.802.1200 / **1-877-CULINARD** */ www.culinard.com*

(FINANCIAL AID IS AVAILABLE FOR THOSE WHO QUALIFY.)

WALLACE STATE COMMUNITY COLLEGE
Hanceville/Year-round

Sponsor: 2-yr college. Program: 18-mo diploma in Commercial Food Technology, 24-mo degree in Commercial Foods. Established: 1979. Accredited by SACS. Calendar: semester. Curriculum: culinary, core. Admission dates: Aug, Jan, Jun. Total enrollment: 18. 100% of applicants accepted. 80-90% receive financial aid. 5% enrolled part-time. Student to teacher ratio 15:1. 98% of graduates employed within six months. Facilities: Classroom & lab.

FACULTY: 2 full-time.

COSTS: $1,100-$1,300 in-state. Admission requirements: HS diploma or equivalent.

CONTACT: Donna Jackson, Dept. Chair, Wallace State Community College, Commercial Foods & Nutrition, Box 2000, Hanceville, AL 35077; 256-352-8227, Fax 256-352-8228, URL http://www.wallace.edu.

ALASKA

ALASKA VOCATIONAL TECHNICAL CENTER (AVTEC)
Seward/August-June

Sponsor: Trade-technical school. Program: Professional Cooking and Baking program consisting of 4 certificates (1,470 hrs): Food Service Worker, Culinary Baker, Cooks Helper/Prep Cook, Cook/Culinarian. Established: 1972. Accredited by ACF, COE. Curriculum: culinary. Admission dates: Aug, Oct. Total enrollment: 30. 16 each admission period. Student to teacher ratio 10:1. 80% of graduates employed within six months. Facilities: 3rd Street Café open-to-the-public restaurant, full service volume kitchen,full service bakery, two dining rooms,classrooms.

FACULTY: Dept. Head Robert E. Wilson, Elizabeth K. Fackler, Kevin M. Lane.

CONTACT: Robert E. Wilson, Dept. Head, Alaska Vocational Technical Center (AVTEC), Culinary Arts, P.O. Box 889, 809 2nd Ave., Seward, AK 99664; 800-478-5389, 907-224-4152, Fax 907-224-4143, E-mail robert_wilson@labor.state.ak.us, URLhttp://www.avtec.alaska.edu/culinary.htm.

UNIVERSITY OF ALASKA – ANCHORAGE
Anchorage/Year-round

Sponsor: University. Program: 2-yr AAS degree in Culinary Arts, BA degree in Hospitality & Restaurant mgmt. Curriculum: core.

CONTACT: Nancy Overpeck, University of Alaska-Anchorage, 3211 Providence Dr. - Cuddy 126, Anchorage, AK 99508; 907-786-1487, Fax 907-786-1402, E-mail afnlo@uaa.alaska.edu, URL http://www.uaa.alaska.edu.

UNIVERSITY OF ALASKA – FAIRBANKS
Fairbanks/August-April

Sponsor: University. Program: 2-yr certificate & 2-yr AAS degree in Culinary Arts. Established: 1879. Accredited by NASC, ACCSCT. Calendar: semester. Curriculum: culinary, core. Admission dates: Fall, spring. Total enrollment: 30-45. 85% of applicants accepted. Student to teacher ratio 8-10:1. 95% of graduates employed within six months.

FACULTY: 3 full-time, 7 part-time.

COSTS: Annual tuition in-state $77/cr-hr, out-of-state $241/cr-hr. Admission requirements: HS diploma or equivalent. Scholarships: yes.

CONTACT: Program Coordinator, University of Alaska - Tanana Valley Campus, Culinary Arts, PO Box 758080, Fairbanks, AK 99775; 907-474-5240, E-mail fycah@uaf.edu, URL http://www.tvc.uaf.edu/programs/cah-info.html#Facilities.

ARIZONA

ARIZONA CULINARY INSTITUTE
Scottsdale/Year-round   *(See display ad page 7)*
Sponsor: Private school. Program: Professional 9-mo diploma program in Culinary Arts, Baking & Restaurant mgmt. Established: 2001. Accredited by Arizona State Board for Private Postsecondary Education. Curriculum: culinary. Admission dates: Every 6 wks. Total enrollment: ~240. ~18-36 each admission period. 75% of applicants accepted. ~70% receive financial aid. Student to teacher ratio 7:1. 98% of graduates employed within six months. Facilities: New 18,000-ft facility with 5 kitchens, 2 classrooms & a student-run du Jour restaurant. Courses: Basic Culinary Arts I & II, Saucier & Meat Fabrication, Baking, Restaurant Mgmt, Wines & Spirits, Advanced Baking, Pastry & Showpieces, Restaurant Operations, Intl Cuisine/du Jour Restaurant, Internship.

FACULTY: 11 full-time faculty with formal culinary education, ~6 yrs teaching experience plus industry work experience.

COSTS: $15,045 tuition, $1,140 fee (knives, uniforms, books), $25 application fee. Admission requirements: HS diploma, GED, essay, 3 personal references. Scholarships: yes. Loans: yes.

CONTACT: Keith Herron, Admissions Director, Arizona Culinary Institute, 10585 N. 114th St., #401, Scottsdale, AZ 85259; 480-603-1066, 866-294-CHEF (2433) toll free, Fax 480-603-1067, E-mail info@azculinary.com, URL http://www.azculinary.com. Darren Leite, President & Co-Founder.

ARIZONA WESTERN COLLEGE
Yuma/August-June
Sponsor: State-supported community college. Program: 1-yr (2-sem, 25-cr) program. Established: 1996. Accredited by NCA. Calendar: semester. Curriculum: culinary. Admission dates: Aug, Jan. Total enrollment: 30. 15 each admission period. 100% of applicants accepted. 50% receive financial aid. 20% enrolled part-time. Student to teacher ratio 15:1. 50% of graduates employed within six months. Facilities: Fully-equipped kitchen/lab & dining room.

FACULTY: 1 full-time registered dietitian with master's degree, 2 part-time chef instructors with 25 yrs experience.

COSTS: $1,800/yr. Admission requirements: Open enrollment. Placement tests in reading & math recommended. Scholarships: yes. Loans: yes.

CONTACT: Nancy Meister, Coordinator, Arizona Western College, Culinary Arts Program, Box 929, Yuma, AZ 85366; 928-344-7779, Fax 928-317-6119, E-mail Nancy.Meister@azwestern.edu, URL http://www.azwestern.edu.

THE ART INSTITUTE OF PHOENIX – CULINARY ARTS
Phoenix/Year-round   *(See display ad page 11)*
Sponsor: Private school. Program: 18-mo AAS degree in Culinary Arts (24-mo in the evening), certification in Sanitation & Safety & Nutrition, 2- to 9-mo diploma programs in The Art of Cooking & Baking & Pastry. Established: 1996. Accredited by ACICS. Calendar: quarter. Curriculum: core. Admission dates: Oct, Jan, Apr, Jul. Total enrollment: 200+. 40 each admission period. 90% of applicants accepted. 70% receive financial aid. 7% enrolled part-time. Student to teacher ratio 18:1. 100% of graduates employed within six months. Facilities: 3 production kitchens, dining lab, 3 computer labs, learning resource center, student lounge & restaurant.

COSTS: AAS degree in Culinary Arts: $305/cr-hr, $5,440/qtr. Application fee $150, supply kit $700, lab fee $300/qtr, (total $34,590). Admission requirements: HS diploma or equivalent, 150-word essay, interview. Scholarships: yes. Loans: yes.

CONTACT: Director of Admissions, Art Institute of Phoenix-Culinary Arts Program, 2233 W. Dunlap Ave., Phoenix, AZ 85021; 800-474-2479, Fax 602-216-0439, E-mail aipxadm@aii.edu, URL http://www.aipx.edu.

CENTRAL ARIZONA COLLEGE
Coolidge/Year-round

Sponsor: 2-yr college. Program: AAS degrees in Culinary Apprenticeship and Hotel/Restaurant mgmt, 18-credit Cook's Certificate, 17-credit certificate in Restaurant Mgmt. Accredited by NCACS, ACF. Calendar: semester. Curriculum: culinary. Total enrollment: 800. 60 each admission period. Student to teacher ratio 10:1. FACULTY: 2 full-time faculty.

COSTS: In-state $40/credit, $48/special lab credit; non-resident $80/credit, internship fee $43/credit.

CONTACT: Glenna McCollum, Dietetic Education Program Director, Central Arizona College, 8470 N. Overfield Rd., Coolidge, AZ 85228; 800-465-1016 X4497/520-426-4497, Fax 520-426-4476, E-mail nutrition@python.cac.cc.az.us, URL http://www.cac.cc.az.us/dep.

CULINARY BUSINESS ACADEMY
Phoenix/Year-round

Sponsor: Private school. Program: Home Study, 16-hr Quick Start, & 50-hr (5-day) Undergraduate Program. Established: 1996. Accredited by Approved by the Arizona Board of Post-Secondary Education. Curriculum: culinary. Admission dates: Ongoing. 100% of applicants accepted. Student to teacher ratio 4:1. FACULTY: Working Certified Professional Chefs.

COSTS: $895-$2495.

CONTACT: Culinary Business Academy LLC, 4150 W. Peoria, #220, Phoenix, AZ 85029; 800-747-2433, Fax 602-938-4644, E-mail info@culinarybusiness.com, URL http://www.culinarybusiness.com.

MARICOPA SKILL CENTER
Phoenix/Year-round

Sponsor: Community college division. Program: 14- to 27-wk certificates in Cook's Apprentice, Kitchen Helper, Baker's Helper, Pantry Goods Maker. Established: 1962. Accredited by NCA. Curriculum: culinary. Admission dates: Any Monday. Total enrollment: 25. open each admission period. 100% of applicants accepted. 80% receive financial aid. 10% enrolled part-time. Student to teacher ratio 7:1. 80% of graduates employed within six months. Facilities: Commercial kitchen. FACULTY: 3 full-time: Dan Bochicchio, CWC, and 2 assistants.

COSTS: ~$2,835, $225 lab fee. Admission requirements: at least 16 yrs old. Scholarships: yes.

CONTACT: Richard Sandoval, Instructor, Maricopa Skill Center, 1245 E. Buckeye Rd., Phoenix, AZ 85034-4101; 602-238-4378, Fax 602-238-4307, E-mail sandisandoval@aol.com, URL http://www.gwc.maricopa.edu/msc/clusters/fp.html.

PHOENIX COLLEGE
Phoenix/ August-May

Sponsor: 2-yr college. Program: AAS degree & 16-wk certificate of completion programs in Culinary Studies & Foodservice Administration. Established: 1972. Accredited by NCA. Calendar: semester. Curriculum: culinary, core. Admission dates: Aug & Jan. Total enrollment: 38. 40 each admission period. 98% of applicants accepted. 20% receive financial aid. 60% enrolled part-time. Student to teacher ratio 18:1. 95% of graduates employed within six months. Facilities: 5,000-sq-ft of teaching facilities, the latest equipment, on-site 40-seat restaurant.

COSTS: ~$3,200. Admission requirements: GED, previous transcripts, application. Scholarships: yes. Loans: yes.

CONTACT: Scott Robinson, Program Director, Phoenix College, 1202 W. Thomas Rd., Phoenix, AZ 85013; 602-285-7901/7765, Fax 602-285-7705, E-mail scott.robinson@pcmail.maricopa.edu, URL http://www.pc.maricopa.edu/departments/aahs/culinary/index.html.

PIMA COMMUNITY COLLEGE
Tucson/Year-round

Sponsor: State-supported college. Program: 2-sem certificate & 2-yr AAS in Culinary Arts. Established: 1972. Accredited by NCA. Admission dates: Jan, May, Aug. Total enrollment: 36. 36 each admission period. 95% of applicants accepted. 5% enrolled part-time. Student to teacher ratio 18:1. 90% of graduates employed within six months. Facilities: 1 kitchen, 1 classroom. Faculty: 1 full-time, 10 adjunct.

Costs: $2,000 for certificate & lab fees; ~$500 for uniform, books, knives. Admission requirements: Interview, 8th grade education, 2 employer recommendations, experience in field suggested.

Contact: Misty Lorien, Pima Community College, Desert Vista Campus, 5901 S. Calle Santa Cruz, Tucson, AZ 85709; 800-860-7462, 520-206-5164, Fax 520-206-5143, E-mail misty.lorien@pima.edu, URL http://dv.pima.edu/~culinary.

SCOTTSDALE COMMUNITY COLLEGE
Scottsdale/August-May

Sponsor: State-supported college. Program: 9-mo certificate, 2-yr AAS degree in Culinary Arts. Established: 1985. Accredited by NCA. Calendar: semester. Curriculum: culinary, core. Admission dates: Aug, Jan. Total enrollment: 72. 36 each admission period. 60% of applicants accepted. 80% receive financial aid. Student to teacher ratio 12:1. 100% of graduates employed within six months. Facilities: 10,000-sq-ft kitchen, 2 classrooms, 2 student-run dining rooms. Faculty: 4 full-time, 6 part-time.

Costs: Annual tuition in-state $1,800, out-of-state $5,600, includes course fee of $350/sem. Admission requirements: HS diploma and application/interview. Scholarships: yes. Loans: yes.

Contact: Karen Chalmers, Director, Scottsdale Community College, Culinary Arts Program, 9000 E. Chaparral Rd., Scottsdale, AZ 85256; 480-423-6241, Fax 480-423-6091, E-mail karen.chalmers@sccmail.maricopa.edu, URL http://www.sc.maricopa.edu.

Scottsdale Culinary Institute, Le Cordon Bleu

SCOTTSDALE CULINARY INSTITUTE
Scottsdale/Year-round   *(See display ad page 9)*

Sponsor: Culinary & Baking Arts College. Program: 15-mo AOS degree in Le Cordon Bleu Culinary Arts, 9-mo certificate in Le Cordon Bleu Patisserie & Baking. Established: 1986. Accredited by ACCSCT, ACF. Curriculum: culinary. Admission dates: Jan, Feb, Apr, May, Jul, Aug, Oct, Nov. Total enrollment: 1,000+. 80-140 each admission period. 70% of applicants accepted. 70% receive financial aid. Student to teacher ratio 16:1. 98% of graduates employed within six months. Facilities: 45,000-sq-ft main campus facility: 7 kitchens, bakery, meat fabrication shop, student-run restaurant, classrooms, student resource center, library; 53,000-sq-ft Sky Bridge campus facility: teaching & demo kitchens, classrooms, student-run restaurant. Courses: Degree program: Classic French techniques, international cuisine, traditional & contemporary trends, nutrition, restaurant management. Certificate program: Artisan Bread Production, Sugar & Chocolate Work, European Pastries, Wedding Cakes.

Faculty: 60+ full-time American & European-trained professionals.

Costs: $34,000 for degree program, $16,000 for certificate program. add'l $2,200 fee for textbooks & supplies & $95 application fee/program. Admission requirements: HS diploma or GED & application. Scholarships: yes. Loans: yes.

Contact: Director of Admissions, Scottsdale Culinary Institute, Le Cordon Bleu, 8100 E. Camelback Rd., Suite 1001, Scottsdale, AZ 85251; 800-848-CHEF (2433), Fax 480-990-0351, E-mail admissions@scichefs.com, URL http://www.chefs.com.

ARKANSAS

ARKANSAS CULINARY SCHOOL OF APPRENTICESHIP
Little Rock/August-May
Sponsor: ACF Central Arkansas Chapter. Program: 3-yr apprenticeship program with 198 classroom-hrs/yr & 2,000 hrs/yr of paid, supervised on-the-job training. Established: 1993. Accredited by ACF. Curriculum: culinary. Admission dates: Aug. Total enrollment: 65. 40 each admission period. 90% of applicants accepted. 50% receive financial aid. Student to teacher ratio 15:1. 100% of graduates employed within six months. Facilities: Classroom training at Technology Center. Apprenticeship training in hotels, hospitals, owner-operated restaurants, catering companies, bakeries.
FACULTY: 1 full-time & 8 adjunct faculty with certification in coursework &/or masters degree.
COSTS: $2,000/yr + books, uniform, knife kit. Beginning salary $7/hr min. Admission requirements: HS diploma or equivalent, 17 yrs oldmin, writing skills & math proficiency exam, interview with Board of Directors. Scholarships: yes.
CONTACT: Will Hutchison C.S.C., Executive Director, Arkansas Culinary School of Apprenticeship, Box 3275, Little Rock, AR 72203; 501-831-CHEF (2433), Fax 501-255-2108, E-mail arkansaschef@aristotle.net, URL http://www.arkansaschef.com.

OZARKA COLLEGE CULINARY ARTS PROGRAM
Melbourne/August-May
Sponsor: Public 2-yr college. Program: 9-mo technical certificate program, 2-yr AAS General Technology degree option. Established: 1975. Accredited by Higher Learning Commission. Calendar: semester. Curriculum: culinary, core. Admission dates: Aug, Jan. Total enrollment: 15. 6 each admission period. 60% of applicants accepted. 80% receive financial aid. 10% enrolled part-time. Student to teacher ratio 15:1. 80% of graduates employed within six months. Facilities: Culinary lab with adjoining classroom.
FACULTY: 1 instructor.
COSTS: $1,500/yr, fees $250/yr. Admission requirements: HS graduate or GED. Scholarships: yes. Loans: yes.
CONTACT: Richard Tankersley, Chef, Ozarka College Culinary Arts Program, PO Box 10, 218 College Dr., Melbourne, AR 72556; 870-368-7371/800-821-4335, Fax 870-368-4733, E-mail rtankersley@ozarka.edu, URL http://www.ozarka.edu/d_cularts.cfm.

CALIFORNIA

AMERICAN RIVER COLLEGE
Sacramento/Year-round
Sponsor: 2-yr college. Program: 1-yr/39 unit certificate & 2-yr AA degree in Culinary Arts/Restaurant Mgmt. Established: 1976. Accredited by NRA. Calendar: semester. Curriculum: culinary, core. Admission dates: Jan, Jun, Aug. Total enrollment: 200. 100% of applicants accepted. Student to teacher ratio 15:1. Facilities: Lab classrooms & commercial kitchen.
FACULTY: 2 full-time, 4 part-time.
COSTS: $12/unit in-state, $138/unit out-of-state. Admission requirements: College level reading & writing. Scholarships: yes. Loans: yes.
CONTACT: Brian Knirk, Program Coordinator, American River College, 4700 College Oak Dr., Sacramento, CA 95841; 916-484-8656, Fax 916-484-8880, E-mail KnirkB@arc.losrios.edu, URL http://www.arc.losrios.edu/~chef.

baked alaska

THE ART INSTITUTE OF CALIFORNIA – LOS ANGELES
Santa Monica/Year-round   *(See display ad page 11)*
Sponsor: Private college. Program: 77-wk (2-yr) AS degree in Culinary Arts, 132-wk (3-yr) BS degree in Culinary mgmt. Established: 1997. Accredited by ACICS. Calendar: quarter. Curriculum: core. Admission dates: Jul, Oct, Jan, Apr. Total enrollment: 340. 40-120 each admission period. 90% of applicants accepted. 75% receive financial aid. 32% enrolled part-time. Student to teacher ratio 20:1. 90% of graduates employed within six months. Facilities: 4 kitchens, classrooms, dining lab room. FACULTY: Includes Joe Zoellin CEC, CCE, Kurt Struwe CEC, CCE, Dan Drumlake CCE, CEC. COSTS: $5,680/qtr. Fees $150, supply kit $655, lab fees $300/qtr. Admission requirements: Interview, proof of HS graduation, final transcripts or GED. Scholarships: yes. Loans: yes. CONTACT: Joe Zoellin, Culinary Arts Director, The Art Institute of Los Angeles, 2900-31st St., Santa Monica, CA 90405; 888-646-4610, 310-752-4700, Fax 310-752-4708, E-mail zoellinj@aii.edu, URL http://www.aicala.artinstitutes.edu.

THE ART INSTITUTE OF CALIFORNIA-ORANGE COUNTY
Santa Ana/Year-round   *(See display ad page 11)*
Sponsor: Visual & practical arts school. Program: AS degree (112 qtr-cr) in Culinary Arts;BS degree (192 qtr-cr) in Culinary Mgmt. Established: 2001. Accredited by ACICS. Calendar: quarter. Curriculum: culinary, core. Admission dates: Rolling. Total enrollment: 247. Student to teacher ratio 24:1. Facilities: 55,000 sq-ft facility.
FACULTY: 7 culinary instructors.
COSTS: $42,031 for AS program, $74,199 for BS program; $373/cr-hr. Admission requirements: Personal interview, essay. Scholarships: yes. Loans: yes.
CONTACT: Ken Post, Director of Admissions, The Art Institute of California-Orange County, 3601 W. Sunflower Ave., Santa Ana, CA 92704-9888; 888-549-3055, 714-830-0200, Fax 714-556-1923, E-mail aicaocadm@aii.edu, URL http://www.aicaoc.aii.edu.

THE ART INSTITUTE OF CALIFORNIA – SAN DIEGO
San Diego/Year-round   *(See display ad page 11)*
Sponsor: Private college. Program: AS degree program in Culinary Arts consisting of seven 11-wk qtrs, 112 credits, 1,969 hours. Established: 2002. Accredited by ACCSCT. Calendar: quarter. Curriculum: culinary. Admission dates: Jul, Oct, Jan, Apr. Total enrollment: 80. Facilities: New 76,000-sq-ft building with 3 kitchens, classrooms, labs.
COSTS: $5,680/qtr, application fee $50, enrollment fee $100, starting kit $860, lab fee $300/qtr. Admission requirements: Interview, HS graduate, GED accepted. Scholarships: yes. Loans: yes.
CONTACT: Sandy Park, Director of Admissions, The Art Institute of California-San Diego, 7650 Mission Valley Rd., San Diego, CA 92108; 858-598-1399, 800-591-2422, Fax 858-457-0903, E-mail parks@aii.edu, URL http://www.aicasd.artinstitutes.edu.

BAUMAN COLLEGE NATURAL CHEF TRAINING PROGRAM
Penngrove, Santa Cruz/Year-round
Sponsor: Vocational school. Program: 5-mo course, Certified Natural Chef,Nutrition Consultant. Established: 1984. Accredited by California Bureau for Private Postsecondary & Vocational Ed. Calendar: semester. Curriculum: culinary. Admission dates: Ongoing. 60 each admission period. 99% of applicants accepted. Student to teacher ratio 15-20:2. 95% of graduates employed within six months. Facilities: Classrooms with professional kitchens.
FACULTY: Includes Edward Bauman, Ph.D.,Catherine McConkie, N.C., Marcy Roth, N.C.
COSTS: $6,950. Admission requirements: HS diploma or equivalent.
CONTACT: Marsha McLaughlin, Marketing, Bauman College, PO Box 940, Penngrove, CA 94951; 800-987-7530, 707-795-1284, Fax 707-795-3375, E-mail inquiry@baumancollege.com, URL http://www.baumancollege.org.

CABRILLO COLLEGE
Aptos/Year-round

Sponsor: Community college. Program: 30-unit certificate & 60 unit AS degree in Culinary Arts & Hospitality Mgmt. AS degree in Baking. Established: 1972. Calendar: semester. Curriculum: core. Admission dates: Aug, Jan. Total enrollment: 200+. 150-200 each admission period. 100% of applicants accepted. 70% enrolled part-time. 100% of graduates employed within six months. Facilities: Restaurant kitchen, quantity foods kitchen, bake shop, lecture/demo room, student-run restaurant.

FACULTY: 3 full-time 5 part-time.

COSTS: Annual tuition for full-time students $464 in-state, $4,820 out-of-state. Admission requirements: HS diploma or equivalent. Scholarships: yes. Loans: yes.

CONTACT: Katherine Niven, Director of Culinary Arts, Cabrillo College, Culinary Arts & Hospitality Mgmt., 6500 Soquel Dr., Aptos, CA 95003; 831-479-5749, E-mail kaniven@cabrillo.cc.ca.us, URL http://www.cabrillo.cc.ca.us/divisions/has/cahm/index.html.

CALIFORNIA CAPITOL CHEFS ASSOCIATION
Granite Bay/Year-round

Sponsor: ACF chapter. Program: 3-yr apprenticeship; degree program through Sierra College. Curriculum: culinary. Total enrollment: 43.

COSTS: $15 for books & materials. Beginning salary is $5.40/hr with increases every 6 mos. Housing $425/mo.

CONTACT: Donald Dickinson, CEC, California Capitol Chefs Association, PO Box 214171, Sacramento, CA 95821; 916-326-5020, E-mail chefdoncec@cs.com.

CALIFORNIA CULINARY ACADEMY
San Francisco/Year-round   *(See also page 180) (See display ad page 13)*

Sponsor: Culinary & hospitality career academy. Program: 60-wk AOS degree program in Le Cordon Bleu Culinary Arts; 30-wk certificate program in Baking & Pastry Arts; 45-wk AOS degree program in Le Cordon Bleu Hospitality & Restaurant Mgmt. Established: 1977. Accredited by ACF, ACCSCT. Curriculum: culinary, core. Total enrollment: 1900. 95% of applicants accepted. 85% receive financial aid. Student to teacher ratio 16:1. 98% of graduates employed within six months. Facilities: 75,000+ sq-ft historic building with professional production & garde manger kitchens, baking & pastry kitchens, butchery, confiseries, lecture classrooms & labs, retail shop, student-staffed restaurant. Courses: Sequential learning curriculum includes nutrition, food prep & presentation, wine studies, baking & pastry, butchery, purchasing, restaurant & hotel mgmt/operations, mixology/beverage, externship.

FACULTY: 85+ chef instructors including Master Chefs, Executive Chefs; qualified & experienced in global cuisine, baking & pastry, hospitality; guest professionals.

COSTS: Admission requirements: Proof of HS graduation or GED/equivalency; personal interview. Scholarships: yes. Loans: yes.

CONTACT: Nancy Seyfert, V.P. of Admissions, California Culinary Academy, Admissions Dept., 625 Polk St., San Francisco, CA 94102; 800-229-CHEF (2433), 415-771-3500, Fax 415-771-2194, E-mail admissions@baychef.com, URL http://www.baychef.com.

CALIFORNIA SCHOOL OF CULINARY ARTS
Pasadena/Jan Feb Apr May Jul Aug Oct Nov   *(See display ad page 15)*

Sponsor: Culinary & Hospitality career school. Program: Le Cordon Bleu programs: 15-mo Culinary Arts AOS degree; 12-mo Hospitality & Restaurant Mgmt diploma; 30-wk (48-wkend) Patisserie & Baking diploma. Established: 1994. Accredited by ACICS. Calendar: quarter. Curriculum: culinary, core. Admission dates: Jan, Feb, Apr, May, Jul, Aug, Oct, Nov. Total enrollment: 1700. 220 each admission period. 90% of applicants accepted. 80% receive financial aid. Student to teacher ratio 16:1. Facilities: 80,000-sq-ft space includes fine dining restaurant, 30 kitchen labs, learning resource center. Courses: Includes Food History, Sanitation, Purchasing,

Nutrition, Wine & Beverage, Supervision.

FACULTY: 100.

COSTS: $44,400 for degree program, $27,500 for Hospitality & Restaurant Mgmt diploma program, $24,250 for Patisserie & Baking diploma; off-campus lodging ~$600-$800/mo. Admission requirements: Interview, HS diploma or equivalent, entrance test for Hospitality & Restaurant Mgmt Program and Patisserie & Baking Program. Scholarships: yes. Loans: yes.

CONTACT: Dominick Miciotta, V.P., Admissions, California School of Culinary Arts, 521 E. Green St., Pasadena, CA 91101; 888-900-2433, 626-403-8490, Fax 626-403-4835, E-mail info@scsca.com, URL http://www.calchef.com.

CALIFORNIA SUSHI ACADEMY
Venice/Year-round

Sponsor: Private school. Program: 12-wk certificate course (250 class hrs, 100 internship hrs); 20-wk professional program. Calendar: quarter. Curriculum: culinary. Admission dates: Yr-round. 30 each admission period. 100% of applicants accepted. 100% enrolled part-time. Student to teacher ratio 7:1 max. 100% of graduates employed within six months.

COSTS: $5,500/certificate course, $3,500/professional course, $80-$85/one-day courses.

CONTACT: Phil Yi, Director, California Sushi Academy, 1611 Pacific Ave., Venice, CA 90291; 310-581-0213, Fax 310-306-2605, E-mail email@sushi-academy.com, URL http://www.sushi-academy.com.

CHAFFEY COLLEGE
Alta Loma/Year-round

Sponsor: Public 2-yr community college. Program: 1-yr certificate in Culinary Arts, 2-yr associate degree in Culinary Arts & Foodservice mgmt. Established: 1986. Accredited by WASC. Calendar: semester. Curriculum: culinary. Admission dates: Jan, Jun, Aug. Total enrollment: 52. 20+ each admission period. 100% of applicants accepted. 85% receive financial aid. 80% enrolled part-time. Student to teacher ratio 18:1. 98% of graduates employed within six months.

FACULTY: 2 full- & 17 part-time.

COSTS: $12/unit, books $150/sem. Admission requirements: HS diploma preferred. Scholarships: yes. Loans: yes.

CONTACT: D. Suzanne Johnson, Dept. Chair, Chaffey College-Hotel & Foodservice Management, 5885 Haven Ave., Alta Loma, CA 91737-3002; 909-941-2711, Fax 909-466-2831, E-mail sjohnson@chaffey.cc.ca.us, URL http://www.chaffey.cc.ca.us.

CHARLES A. JONES SKILLS & BUSINESS EDUCATION CENTER
Sacramento/Year-round

Sponsor: Public vocational school. Program: 24- & 42-wk certificate programs in Culinary Arts. 75% of time is spent in production serving the public & students. Established: 2002. Accredited by WASC. Admission dates: Every 6 wks. Total enrollment: 35. 20 each admission period. 85% of applicants accepted. 80% receive financial aid. Student to teacher ratio 10:1. 50% of graduates employed within six months. Facilities: Production kitchen & 2 classrooms.

FACULTY: 3 instructors with 60+ yrs experience in industry, school's principal is an ACF CEC & CE.

COSTS: $804 includes books, uniforms, knives & materials fees.

CONTACT: David Edgar, Culinary Arts Program Coordinator, Charles A. Jones Education Center, 5451 Lemon Hill Ave., Sacramento, CA 95824; 916-433-2600 x1101, Fax 916-433-2640, E-mail David-Edgar@sac-city.k12.ca.us, URL http://www.scusd.edu/adult_education/Vocational_Training_Schedule.htm.

CHEF ERIC'S CULINARY CLASSROOM
Los Angeles/Year-round

Sponsor: Private school. Program: 40-hr (10-wk) & 80-hr (20-wk) Culinary Chef & Culinary Baking certificate programs. Established: 2003. Curriculum: culinary. Admission dates: Yr-round. Total enrollment: 38272. 100% of applicants accepted. Student to teacher ratio 2-12:1. Facilities:

Classroom with display mirror area, professionally designed kitchen with new equipment.
FACULTY: Owner Chef Eric Jacques Crowley, an honors graduate of The CIA; Chef Julia Stein has 3 yrs of culinary training.
COSTS: $2,000 for Culinary Chef I; $1,000 each for Culinary Chef II, III; $950 for Culinary Baking I.
CONTACT: Eric Crowley, President, Chef Eric's Culinary Classroom, 2366 Pelham Ave., Los Angeles, CA 90064; 310-470-2640, Fax 310-470-2642, E-mail cheferic@culinaryclassroom.com, URL http://www.CulinaryClassroom.com.

CHEFS DE CUISINE ASSOCIATION OF CALIFORNIA
Los Angeles/Year-round
Sponsor: ACF chapter. Program: 3-yr appenticeship; degree program through California Polytechnic is completed by 100%. Curriculum: culinary. Total enrollment: 15.
COSTS: $150. Beginning salary is variable with increases every 6 mos.
CONTACT: LeRoy Blanchard, CEC, AAC, Chairman, Chefs de Cuisine Association of California, Culinary Arts Dept., 400 W. Washington Blvd., Los Angeles, CA 90015; 213-744-9489, Fax 213-748-7334, E-mail LeRoy_S._Blanchard@laccd.cc.ca.us.

CITY COLLEGE OF SAN FRANCISCO – CULINARY ARTS
San Francisco/August-May
Sponsor: 2-yr community college. Program: 4-sem AS degree in Culinary Arts, Food Service Mgmt or Hotel Mgmt; Award of Achievement & ACF certificate. Established: 1935. Accredited by WASC, ACF. Calendar: semester. Curriculum: culinary, core. Admission dates: Aug, Jan. Total enrollment: 240. 86 each admission period. 90% of applicants accepted. Student to teacher ratio 20:1. 100% of graduates employed within six months. Facilities: 5 kitchens, 3 classrooms, student-run fine dining restaurant, cafeteria, quick service cafe.
FACULTY: 11 full-time, 6 part-time.
COSTS: Annual tuition in-state $390, out-of-state $3,720. Admission requirements: Age 18 or HS diploma, CCSF English placement test. Scholarships: yes. Loans: yes.
CONTACT: Lynda Hirose, Advisor/Placement Counselor, City College of San Francisco, CAHS, 50 Phelan Ave. SW156, San Francisco, CA 94112; 415-239-3152, Fax 415-239-3913, E-mail lhirose@ccsf.edu, URL http://www.ccsf.edu/cahs.

COLLEGE OF THE DESERT
Palm Desert/Year-round
Sponsor: 2-yr college. Program: 20-unit certificate in Basic Culinary Arts, 62-unit AA degree in Culinary mgmt. Calendar: semester. Curriculum: culinary, core.
COSTS: $13/unit in-state, $140.25/unit out-of-state.
CONTACT: Steve Beno, Professor of Culinary Arts, College of the Desert, 43500 Monterey Ave., Palm Desert, CA 92260; 760-776-7384, E-mail SBeno@collegeofthedesert.edu, URL http://www.desert.cc.ca.us.

COLLEGE OF THE SEQUOIAS
Visalia/August-May
Sponsor: 2-yr college. Program: 11- to 13-unit certificate in Food Service, 28-unit certificate in Food Service mgmt, 20-unit certificate in Dietetic Service Supervisor, AS degree in Food Service. Established: 1993. Calendar: semester. Curriculum: culinary. Admission dates: Aug, Jan. Total enrollment: 100. 50 each admission period. 100% of applicants accepted. 40% receive financial aid. 60% enrolled part-time. Student to teacher ratio 20:1. Facilities: Commercial food lab.
FACULTY: 3 full- and 4 part-time instructors (R.D.s and chef).
COSTS: Enrollment fee $12/unit for all students, non-resident tuition $118/unit. Loans: yes.
CONTACT: Barbara Reynolds, Consumer/Family Instructor, College of the Sequoias, 915 S. Mooney Blvd., Visalia, CA 93277; 559-730-3717, Fax 559-737-4810, E-mail barbarar@cos.edu, URL http://www.sequoias.cc.ca.us.

COLUMBIA COLLEGE
Sonora/August-May

Sponsor: California community college. Program: 2-yr AS degree in Culinary Arts/Hospitality mgmt; 10 culinary certificates. Established: 1977. Accredited by WASC, ACF. Calendar: semester. Curriculum: culinary. Admission dates: Aug, Jan. Total enrollment: 125. 30 each admission period. 99% of applicants accepted. 40% receive financial aid. 40% enrolled part-time. Student to teacher ratio 10-15:1. 90% of graduates employed within six months. Facilities: 2 kitchens, 4 classrooms, 3-star restaurant.

FACULTY: 2 full-time, 7 part-time. Qualifications: full-time: lifetime teaching credential and industry experience; part-time: A.S. degree + 6 yrs industry experience.

COSTS: Annual tuition in-state $312, out-of-state $3,144. Health & student fees $30/sem. On-campus housing $300/mo. Housing $500/mo. Admission requirements: Admission test. Scholarships: yes. Loans: yes.

CONTACT: Gene Womble, Hosp. Mgmt. Program Coordinator, Columbia College, Hospitality Mgmt., 11600 Columbia College Dr., Sonora, CA 95370; 209-588-5135, Fax 209-588-5316, E-mail wombleg@yosemite.cc.ca.us, URL http://columbia.yosemite.cc.ca.us/hospmgmt.html.

CONTRA COSTA COLLEGE
San Pablo/September-May

Sponsor: College. Program: 2-yr certificate. Established: 1962. Calendar: semester. Curriculum: culinary. Admission dates: Aug, Jan. Total enrollment: 75-100. 90% of applicants accepted. Student to teacher ratio 20-25:1. 90% of graduates employed within six months.

FACULTY: 2 full-time, 2 part-time.

COSTS: $11/unit enrollment fee in-state, non-resident tuition; $155/unit tuition + $11/unit enrollment fee out-of-state. Admission requirements: Admission test. Loans: yes.

CONTACT: David Rosenthal, Culinary Instructor, Contra Costa College, Culinary Arts, 2600 Mission Bell Dr., San Pablo, CA 94806; 510-235-7800 x4320, E-mail drosenthal@contracosta.cc.ca.us, URL http://www.contracosta.cc.ca.us.

THE CULINARY INSTITUTE OF AMERICA AT GREYSTONE
Napa Valley/Year-round   *(See also pages 90, 182, 224) (See display ad page 89)*

Sponsor: The CIA's Greystone campus, a continuing ed center for food & wine professionals. Program: Fundamental to advanced 2- to 5-day courses for foodservice professionals; 30-wk Baking & Pastry Arts Certificate Program; 30-wk Advanced Culinary Arts Certificate program. Established: 1995. Accredited by MSA, ACCSCT. Curriculum: culinary. Admission dates: Ongoing. Total enrollment: 3,500/yr. 18/class session each admission period. Student to teacher ratio 18:1. Facilities: 15,000-sq-ft open teaching kitchens that include Bonnet Cooking Suites & Bongard Hearth ovens, 125-seat Ecolab Theatre, Rudd Center for Professional Wine Studies with two 36-seat classrooms, on-campus vineyards & gardens. Courses: Culinary skill development, world cuisines, garde manger, advanced culinary programs, professional baking & pastry, baking & pastry arts certificate program, wine programs, executive chef seminars, certification offered for culinary and wine professionals.

FACULTY: 22 full- & part-time instructors, visiting instructors include chef/owners of fine restaurants, also drawn from the 140 instructors at the Hyde Park, NY, campus.

COSTS: From $850 for 30 hrs of instruction to $21,000 for the Baking & Pastry Arts and Advanced Culinary Arts Certificate Program. Lodging available at the on-campus Guest House. Admission requirements: For cooking production classes, a min of 6 mos experience in a professional kitchen. Scholarships: yes. Loans: yes.

CONTACT: Baking & Pastry Coordinator, The Culinary Institute of America, 2555 Main St., St. Helena, CA 94574; 800-888-7850, E-mail ciaprochef@culinary.edu, URL http://www.ciaprochef.com.

CYPRESS COLLEGE
Cypress/Year-round
Sponsor: College. Program: 1-yr certificate, 2-yr AS degree in Food Service mgmt, Hotel Operations, & Culinary Arts. Established: 1975. Accredited by WASC. Calendar: semester. Curriculum: culinary, core. Admission dates: Aug, Jan. Total enrollment: 100. 30 each admission period. 90% of applicants accepted. 45% receive financial aid. 70% enrolled part-time. Student to teacher ratio 16:1. 85% of graduates employed within six months. Facilities: 1 kitchen, 4 classrooms, student-run dining room.

FACULTY: 2 full-time, 12 part-time.

COSTS: In-state $12/unit, out-of-state $114/unit. $5/lab fee. Housing ~$250-$750/mo. Admission requirements: HS diploma or equivalent. Scholarships: yes. Loans: yes.

CONTACT: Michael Bird, Department Chair, Cypress College, Hospitality Mgmt./Culinary Arts, 9200 Valley View, Cypress, CA 90630; 714-826-2220 #208, Fax 714-527-8238, E-mail mbird@cypress.cc.ca.us, URL http://cypresscollege.org.

DIABLO VALLEY COLLEGE
Pleasant Hill/Year-round
Sponsor: College. Program: Program in Culinary Arts, Baking & Patisserie, Restaurant mgmt & Hotel Administration. Established: 1971. Accredited by ACF, WASC. Calendar: semester. Curriculum: core. Admission dates: Aug, Jan. Total enrollment: 750. 50 each admission period. 100% enrolled part-time. Student to teacher ratio 24:1. 100% of graduates employed within six months. Facilities: Include a fully-equipped food production kitchen, demonstration laboratory, 130-seat open-to-the-public restaurant.

FACULTY: 5 full-time, 14 part-time. Qualifications: BA degrees and 7 yrs industry experience.

COSTS: In-state tuition for first sem is $225. Fees & deposits: $11/unit for residents, $127/unit for non-residents, $135/unit for international students. Housing $500/mo. Admission requirements: HS diploma or equivalent. Scholarships: yes. Loans: yes.

CONTACT: Nader Sharkes, Department Chair, Diablo Valley College, Hotel & Restaurant Management Dept., 321 Golf Club Rd., Pleasant Hill, CA 94523; 925-685-1230 x2252, Fax 925-825-8412, E-mail NSharkes@dvc.edu, URL http://www.dvc.edu.

EPICUREAN SCHOOL OF CULINARY ARTS
Los Angeles/Year-round
Sponsor: Private school. Program: 9-mo Professional Chef certificate program (Pro Chef I & Pro Chef II). Established: 1985. Calendar: semester. Curriculum: culinary. Admission dates: yr-round. Total enrollment: 15. 50 each admission period. 100% of applicants accepted. 100% enrolled part-time. Student to teacher ratio 15:1. Facilities: Teaching kitchen with 5 work stations.

FACULTY: 4 part-time instructors are CIA and CCA graduates.

COSTS: $2,800 for Pro Chef I & II. Admission requirements: None.

CONTACT: Diana Tracy, Epicurean School of Culinary Arts, 8759 Melrose Ave., Los Angeles, CA 90069; 310-659-5990, Fax 310-659-0302, E-mail epicurean5@aol.com, URL http://www.epicureanschool.com.

GLENDALE COMMUNITY COLLEGE
Glendale/August-May
Sponsor: College. Program: 2-yr certificates in Culinary Arts, Restaurant mgmt, Hotel mgmt, & Dietary Services. Established: 1974. Accredited by State. Calendar: semester. Curriculum: culinary. Admission dates: Aug. Total enrollment: 338. 95% of applicants accepted. 50% enrolled part-time. Student to teacher ratio 35:1.

FACULTY: 1 full-time, 5 part-time. Qualifications: BS or MS degree, at least 6 yrs experience.

COSTS: Annual tuition in-state $13/unit, out-of-state $130/unit. Admission requirements: HS diploma or equivalent.

CONTACT: Yeimei Wang, Prof. of Food & Nutrition and Coordinator, Glendale Community College, Culinary Arts Dept., 1500 N. Verdugo Rd., Glendale, CA 91208; 818-240-1000 x5597, Fax 818-549-9436, E-mail ywang@glendale.edu, URL http://www.glendale.cc.ca.us.

GROSSMONT COLLEGE
El Cajon/Year-round
Sponsor: Two-yr college regional occupational program. Program: 1-yr certificate in Culinary Arts, 2-yr associate degree in Culinary Arts. Established: 1988. Calendar: semester. Curriculum: culinary, core. Admission dates: Aug, Jan, Jun. Total enrollment: 350. 150 each admission period. 100% of applicants accepted. 35% receive financial aid. 40% enrolled part-time. Student to teacher ratio 25:1. 95% of graduates employed within six months. Facilities: Classroom, lab, cafeteria, internships in fine restaurants.

FACULTY: 11 instructors: 3 executive chefs (2 Culinary Olympic Gold Medal Winners/team members), 2 professors (master's degrees), 4 instructors (master's degree).

COSTS: $12/unit in-state ($180/sem), $121/unit out-of-state ($1,815/sem). Admission requirements: Ability to read and write. Loans: yes.

CONTACT: Joseph Orate, Professor, Coordinator of Culinary Arts Program, Grossmont College, 8800 Grossmont College Dr., El Cajon, CA 92020; 619-644-7469/7550, Fax 619-644-7190, E-mail joe.orate@gcccd.net, URL http://grossmont.gcccd.cc.ca.us/culinaryarts.

HIGH SIERRA CHEFS ASSOCIATION
South Lake Tahoe/Year-round
Sponsor: ACF chapter. Program: 3-yr apprenticeship; degree program through Lake Tahoe & Truckee Meadows Community Colleges. Established: 1978. Accredited by Community colleges are institutionally accredited. Curriculum: culinary, core. Admission dates: Ongoing. Total enrollment: 12. Student to teacher ratio 12:1. 100% of graduates employed within six months. Facilities: Community college classrooms, labs & sponsoring property kitchens.

FACULTY: 3 full-time, ACF certified.

COSTS: $185 dues, $500-$1,000 over 3 yrs. Beginning salary is ~$7/hr with annual increases. Housing $300-$500/mo. Admission requirements: HS diploma or equivalent, essay. Scholarships: yes.

CONTACT: Steve Fernald, Culinary Arts Instructor/Apprenticeship Coord., High Sierra Chefs Association, One College Drive, South Lake Tahoe, CA 96150; 530-541-4660 x334, Fax 530-541-7852, E-mail fernald@ltcc.cc.ca.us.

INSTITUTE OF TECHNOLOGY
Roseville/Year-round
Sponsor: Private school. Program: 8-mo diploma in Culinary Arts. Established: 2002. Accredited by California Private Post Secondary, ACCSCT. Curriculum: culinary, core. Admission dates: Every 5 wks. Total enrollment: 130. 15 each admission period. 95% of applicants accepted. 90% receive financial aid. Student to teacher ratio 15:1. 100% of graduates employed within six months.

FACULTY: 4 part-time instructors, 1 full-time director.

COSTS: 9800. Loans: yes.

CONTACT: Kelly Jean Galvin, Andmissions, Institute of Technology, 333 Sunrise Ave., #400, Roseville, CA 95661; 916-797-6337, Fax 916-797-6338, E-mail davalos@it-email.com, URL http://www.it-colleges.com.

LAGUNA CULINARY ARTS PROFESSIONAL CHEF PROGRAM
Laguna Beach/Year-round
Sponsor: Private school. Program: 6-mo full-time Professional Chef Program. Established: 2002. Calendar: quinmester. Curriculum: culinary. Admission dates: Mar, Sep. 8 each admission period. 75% of applicants accepted. Student to teacher ratio 8:1. 90% of graduates employed within six months. Facilities: Industry-current kitchen.

FACULTY: Chef Laurent Brazier, chef/owner of Picayo Restaurant.

COSTS: $25,000 includes uniforms, tools, supplies. $7,500 discount for tuition paid in advance. Admission requirements: HS diploma or equivalent.

CONTACT: Laguna Culinary Arts, 550 South Coast Hwy., #7, Laguna Beach, CA 92651; 949-494-0745, 888-288-0745, Fax 949-494-0136, E-mail nancy@lagunaculinaryarts.com, URL http://www.lagunaculinaryarts.com/pages/ProfChefProg.html.

LAKE TAHOE COMMUNITY COLLEGE
South Lake Tahoe/Year-round

Sponsor: Part of California Community College System. Program: 33-wk certificate in Culinary Arts, advanced certificate in Culinary Arts, AA degree in Culinary Arts. Established: 1999. Accredited by WSA. Calendar: quarter. Curriculum: culinary, core. Admission dates: Sep, Jan, Apr. Total enrollment: 60. 24 each admission period. 100% of applicants accepted. 50% enrolled part-time. Student to teacher ratio 12:1. 50% of graduates employed within six months. Facilities: Newly-equipped culinary arts facilities constructed in 2002.

FACULTY: One full-time, Certified Chef de Cuisine, former ACF Director of Education.

COSTS: ~$300/yr tuition & fees, ~$300/yr for books, uniforms, tools, $300-$500/mo housing expense. Admission requirements: HS diploma or equivalent. Scholarships: yes.

CONTACT: Stephen C. Fernald, CCC, Instructor, Lake Tahoe Community College, One College Dr., South Lake Tahoe, CA 96150; 530-541-4660 x334, Fax 530-541-7852, E-mail fernald@ltcc.cc.ca.us, URL http://www.ltcc.cc.ca.us/depts/culinary%5Farts.htm.

LANEY COLLEGE
Oakland/Year-round

Sponsor: Community college. Program: 2-yr AA degree in Culinary Arts, 2-yr certificate in Retail Baking. Established: 1948. Accredited by WASC. Admission dates: Aug, Jan. Total enrollment: 200. 60 each admission period. 80% of applicants accepted. 70% receive financial aid. 10% enrolled part-time. Student to teacher ratio 12:1. 100% of graduates employed within six months. Facilities: Include 7 kitchens & classrooms, a student-run restaurant, retail bakery.

FACULTY: 5 full-time, 4 part-time.

COSTS: In-state $12/unit, out-of-state $138/unit.

CONTACT: Wayne Stoker, Culinary Arts Co-Dept. Chair, Laney College, Culinary Arts Dept., 900 Fallon St., Oakland, CA 94607; 510-464-3407, Fax 510-464-3240, E-mail wstoker@peralta.cc.ca.us, URL http://laney.peralta.cc.ca.us.

LONG BEACH CITY COLLEGE
Long Beach/Year-round

Sponsor: 2-yr college. Program: 1-1/2-yr certificate & 2-yr AS degree in culinary arts and commercial baking & pastry. Certificate programs in institutional cooking, cake decorating, food prep, gourmet cooking. Established: 1949. Accredited by WASC. Total enrollment: ~480. 75% enrolled part-time. Student to teacher ratio 1:30. Facilities: Include 4 demo labs, 4 food production kitchens, gourmet dining room, bake shops.

FACULTY: 5 full-time, 16 part-time.

COSTS: $11/cr in-state, $129/cr out-of-state. Scholarships: yes.

CONTACT: Frank Madrigal, Chef, Long Beach City College, 4901 E. Carson St., Long Beach, CA 90808; 562-938-4471, URL http://www.lbcc.cc.ca.us/cg/pdf/culinaryarts.pdf.

LOS ANGELES MISSION COLLEGE
Sylmar/Year-round

Sponsor: 2-yr college. Program: 2-yr/60-64 unit AAS degree in Culinary Arts. Calendar: semester. Curriculum: core.

COSTS: $13/unit in-state, $128/unit out-of-state.

CONTACT: Sandra Lampert, Los Angeles Mission College, Culinary Arts, Instructional Building, Sylmar, CA 91342; 818-364-7696, Fax 818-364-7755, E-mail sandilampert@sbcglobal.net, URL http://www.lamission.edu/culinary.

LOS ANGELES TRADE-TECHNICAL COLLEGE
Los Angeles/September-May
Sponsor: College. Program: 2-yr (48-unit) certificates and AA degrees in Culinary Arts and Professional Baking. Established: 1927. Accredited by WASC, ACF. Calendar: semester. Curriculum: culinary, core. Admission dates: Jul/Aug, Dec/Jan. Total enrollment: 280. 90 each admission period. 95% of applicants accepted. 70% receive financial aid. Student to teacher ratio 26:1. 95% of graduates employed within six months. Facilities: Include 3 kitchens, 6 classrooms.
FACULTY: 11 full- & 6 part-time. Qualifications: AA degree, ACF certification, industry experience.
COSTS: Annual tuition in-state $300+, out-of-state $500+. $600 for tools, uniforms, books. Total expense for 4 sems is ~$1,500 minimum. Admission requirements: HS graduate or 18 yrs of age. Scholarships: yes. Loans: yes.
CONTACT: Steven Lee Kasmar, Dept. Chair, Los Angeles Trade-Technical College, Culinary Arts Dept., 400 W. Washington Blvd., Los Angeles, CA 90015; 213-763-7331, E-mail culinary@lattc.edu, URL http://www.lattc.cc.ca.us.

NAPA VALLEY COOKING SCHOOL
St. Helena/Year-round   *(See also page 186) (See display ad page 23)*
Sponsor: Napa Valley College. Program: 14-mo certificate (Professional Training for Fine Restaurants) that consists of 9 mo's of school & 5 mo's of externship. Established: 1996. Curriculum: culinary. Admission dates: Aug. Total enrollment: 18. 18 each admission period. 75% of applicants accepted. 50% receive financial aid. Student to teacher ratio 9:1. 100% of graduates employed within six months. Facilities: Modern teaching kitchen. Courses: Basic to advanced techniques, food & wine education. Special emphasis on skills for entry & advancement in fine restaurants.
FACULTY: Northern California chef-instructors. Guest lecturers include area chefs, growers, specialty food producers, viticulturists, & winemakers. Includes Executive Chef Barbara Alexander & Chef Christopher Mazzanti.
COSTS: ~$15,500 tuition includes uniforms, materials & books. Off-campus housing ~$600/mo. Admission requirements: HS diploma or equivalent & industry experience recommended. Scholarships: yes. Loans: yes.
CONTACT: Barbara Alexander, Executive Chef, Napa Valley Cooking School, 1088 College Ave., St. Helena, CA 94574; 707-967-2930, Fax 707-967-2909, E-mail balexander@napavalley.edu, URL http://www.napavalley.edu/cookingschool.

MODESTO JUNIOR COLLEGE
Modesto/August-May
Sponsor: Public 2-yr college. Program: 1-yr certificate & 2-yr AS degree in Culinary Arts. Established: 1998. Accredited by WASC. Calendar: semester. Curriculum: culinary. Admission dates: Aug. Total enrollment: 30. 30 each admission period. 20% of applicants accepted. Student to teacher ratio 15:1. Facilities: Food production kitchen, bake shop, classroom, lecture room.
FACULTY: 1 full-time, 2 part-time.
COSTS: $19/unit, 14 units/sem. $125 lab fee. Scholarships: yes. Loans: yes.
CONTACT: Bob Glatt, Chef Instructor, Modesto Junior College – Culinary Arts, 435 College Ave., Modesto, CA 95350; 209-575-6975, Fax 209-575-6989, E-mail glattb@yosemite.cc.ca.us, URL http://mjc.yosemite.cc.ca.us.

NATIONAL CULINARY & BAKERY SCHOOL
San Diego/Year-round

Sponsor: Private school. Program: Accelerated certificate programs in Culinary & Baking Arts. Established: 1994. Curriculum: culinary. Admission dates: Open enrollment all yr. 10 max each admission period. 95% of applicants accepted. 5% receive financial aid. Student to teacher ratio 10:1. 100% of graduates employed within six months. Facilities: 2 commercial culinary kitches, 1 bakery kitchen, classroom, restaurant & banquet facilities.

FACULTY: Professional Certified Executive Chefs by the ACF, Professional Chef Assn. & Les Toques Blanch Intl. 30+ yrs of professional experience.

CONTACT: National Culinary & Hospitality School, 8400 Center Dr., San Diego, CA 92108; 888-321-CHEF, 619-283-0200, E-mail natlschools@nationalschools.com, URL http://www.nationalschools.com.

THE NEW SCHOOL OF COOKING
Los Angeles/Year-round

Sponsor: Private school. Program: 20- & 30-wk part-time professional chef's training, 10-wk part-time professional pastry training, recreational classes, kid's camp. Established: 2000. Curriculum: culinary. Admission dates: Yr-round. 12/class each admission period. 100% of applicants accepted. 100% enrolled part-time. Student to teacher ratio 12:1. Facilities: 1,400-sq-ft professional kitchen classroom with instructor demo area & hands-on student work area.

FACULTY: Includes CCA graduate Carol Cotner Thompson & Tracy Callahan.

COSTS: $2,400 Pro 1, $1,200 Pro 2, $1,200 Pro Baking.

CONTACT: Anne Smith, Director, The New School of Cooking, 8690 Washington Blvd., Culver City, CA 90232; 310-842-9702, E-mail annesmith@newschoolofcooking.com, URL http://www.newschoolofcooking.com.

ORANGE COAST COLLEGE
Costa Mesa/August-May

Sponsor: College. Program: 1-yr certificate, 2-yr AA degree. Established: 1964. Accredited by WASC, ACF. Calendar: semester. Curriculum: culinary. Admission dates: Jan, Aug. Total enrollment: 350. 100-125 each admission period. 100% of applicants accepted. 40% enrolled part-time. Student to teacher ratio 15:1. 100% of graduates employed within six months. Facilities: Full-service cafeteria (seats 300), 80-seat restaurant, full-service bakery.

FACULTY: 15 full-time.

COSTS: In-state $120/yr, out-of-state $102/unit. Admission requirements: HS diploma or equivalent. Scholarships: yes. Loans: yes.

CONTACT: Bill Barber, Program Coordinator for Culinary Arts, Orange Coast College, Hospitality Dept., 2701 Fairview Blvd., Box 5005, Costa Mesa, CA 92628-5005; 714-432-5835 x2, Fax 714-432-5609, E-mail wbarber@mail.occ.cccd.edu, URL http://www.occ.cccd.edu.

OXNARD COLLEGE
Oxnard/August-May

Sponsor: College. Program: 2-yr certificate, 2-yr degree. Established: 1985. Accredited by WASC. Calendar: semester. Curriculum: culinary, core. Admission dates: Aug, Jan. Total enrollment: 75-125. 30 each admission period. 100% of applicants accepted. 20% receive financial aid. 40% enrolled part-time. Student to teacher ratio 12:1. 95% of graduates employed within six months. Facilities: Training kitchen with dining room.

FACULTY: 1 full-time, 5 part-time.

COSTS: In-state $11/unit, out-of-state $130/unit. Admission requirements: HS diploma or equivalent. Scholarships: yes. Loans: yes.

CONTACT: Frank Haywood, Instructor, Oxnard College, Hotel & Restaurant Mgmt., 4000 S. Rose Ave., Oxnard, CA 93033; 805-986-5869, Fax 805-986-5865, E-mail fhaywood@vcccd.net, URL http://www.oxnardcollege.edu.

QUALITY COLLEGE OF CULINARY CAREERS
Fresno/Year-round

Sponsor: Private career school. Program: 30-wk Culinary Chef, 12-wk Culinary Arts, 12-wk Advanced Baking & Pastry Arts, 40-wk Food & Beverage Mgr certificate. Established: 2000. Curriculum: culinary, core. Admission dates: Every Monday. Total enrollment: ~40. 82% of applicants accepted. 100% receive financial aid. 10% enrolled part-time. Student to teacher ratio 10:1. 99% of graduates employed within six months. Facilities: 8,000-sq-ft building with 3 classrooms, 3 labs, full service restaurant.

FACULTY: 5 instructors, 3 CEC, 1 CEC & CCE, 1 Certified Baker.

CONTACT: Lon Edwards, Director, Quality College of Culinary Careers, 1776 N. Fine Ave., Fresno, CA 93727; 559-497-5050, Fax 559-264-4454, E-mail director@qualityschool.com, URL http://www.qualityschool.com.

SAN DIEGO CULINARY INSTITUTE, INC.
La Mesa/Year-round

Sponsor: Private postsecondary vocational school. Program: 352-hr certificate in Basic Professional Culinary Skills (full- or part-time).1150-hr (30-wk) certificate in Baking & Pastry Arts. Established: 2000. Accredited by California Bureau for Private Postsecondary & Vocational Ed. Curriculum: culinary. Admission dates: Rolling. Total enrollment: 120/yr. 50-60 each admission period. 100% enrolled part-time. Student to teacher ratio 1:16 max. 98% of graduates employed within six months. Facilities: 5000-sq-ft facility with 2 fully-equipped kitchen class rooms, central kitchen, library, lecture room.

FACULTY: Must have 5 yrs minimum executive chef experience & teaching skills. Includes founder Harold Meyberg.

Costs: Basic Professional Culinary Skills tuition, books, uniforms, knife kit: $10,130. Baking & Pastry Arts tuition, books, uniforms, tool kit: $18,000. Admission requirements: HS diploma or GED. Scholarships: yes. Loans: yes.

Contact: Harold Meyberg, Founder/President, San Diego Culinary Institute, Inc., 8024 La Mesa Blvd., La Mesa, CA 91941; 619-644-2100, Fax 619-644-2106, E-mail info@sdci-inc.com, URL http://www.sdci-inc.com.

SAN FRANCISCO BAKING INSTITUTE
San Francisco/Year-round

Sponsor: Private school. Program: 14-wk diploma program in Professional Bread & Pastry, includes 2 wks in France. Established: 1991. 12-15 max each admission period. 100% of applicants accepted. Facilities: Bakery/classroom with up-to-date production equipment.

Faculty: Head Instructor Didier Rosada; Baking & Pastry Instructors Jeffrey Yankellow & Erin Quinn.

Costs: $17,500; $22,300 with housing. Includes all expenses, except airfare, for 2 wks in France.

Contact: Evelyne Suas, Administrator, San Francisco Baking Institute, 480 Grandview Dr., South San Francisco, CA 94080; 650-589-5784, Fax 650-589-5729, E-mail contact@sfbi.com, URL http://www.sfbi.com.

SAN FRANCISCO CULINARY/PASTRY PROGRAM
San Francisco/Year-round

Sponsor: Hotel & Restaurant Employees Local 2 Union. Program: State of California Div of Apprenticeship Standards: Certification as Journeyman Cook. Established: 1976. Curriculum: culinary.

Costs: Beginning salary is 55% of journeyman wage with 5% increases every 6 mos. Admission requirements: Age 16, HS diploma or GED.

Contact: Joan Ortega, Director, San Francisco Culinary/Pastry Program, 760 Market St., #1066, San Francisco, CA 94102; 415-989-8726, Fax 415-989-2920, E-mail joanlortega@aol.com.

SAN JOAQUIN DELTA COLLEGE
Stockton/August-May

Sponsor: 2-yr college. Program: 1-sem certificate in Basic Culinary Arts, 3-sem certificate in Advanced Culinary Arts, 4-sem AS degree in Culinary Arts, 2-sem certificate in Dietetic Services Supervisor. Established: 1979. Accredited by ACF, WASC. Calendar: semester. Curriculum: core. Admission dates: Rolling. Total enrollment: 80. 20-30 each admission period. 100% of applicants accepted. 40% receive financial aid. 40% enrolled part-time. Student to teacher ratio 15:1. 90% of graduates employed within six months. Facilities: 2 kitchens, 2 classrooms, student-run restaurant.

Faculty: 2 full-time, 1 part-time. Qualifications: Master's degree.

Costs: In-state $12/unit, out-of-state $125/unit. Housing $400/mo. Admission requirements: HS graduate or age 18. Scholarships: yes.

Contact: John Britto, Program Coordinator, San Joaquin Delta College, Culinary Arts Dept., 5151 Pacific Ave., Stockton, CA 95207; 209-954-5582, Fax 209-954-5600, E-mail jbritto@deltacollege.edu, URL http://www.deltacollege.org/div/fchs/cularts.html.

SANTA BARBARA CITY COLLEGE
Santa Barbara/August-May

Sponsor: College. Program: 2-yr certificate, 2-yr AS degree in Culinary Arts & Restaurant-Hotel mgmt. Established: 1970. Accredited by WASC, ACF. Calendar: semester. Curriculum: culinary. Admission dates: Fall, spring. Total enrollment: 120. 50 each admission period. 80% of applicants accepted. 60% receive financial aid. Student to teacher ratio 10-15:1. 100% of graduates employed within six months. Facilities: Include 6 kitchens & classrooms, a gourmet dining room, coffee shop, bake shop, lecture/lab room, cafeteria, & snack shop.

Faculty: 3 full-time, 6 part-time, and 11 lab teaching assistants.

Costs: Annual tuition in-state $500, out-of-state $3,360. Housing $350/mo. Admission requirements: HS diploma or equivalent. Scholarships: yes. Loans: yes.

CONTACT: Randy Bublitz, Chairperson, Santa Barbara City College, Hotel/Restaurant & Culinary Dept., 721 Cliff Dr., Santa Barbara, CA 93109-2394; 805-965-0581 #2457, Fax 805-963-7222, E-mail bublitz@sbcc.edu, URL http://www.sbcc.net.

SANTA ROSA JUNIOR COLLEGE
Santa Rosa

Sponsor: College. Program: 1-yr certificate. Accredited by WASC. Total enrollment: 25-40. Student to teacher ratio 100. 100% of graduates employed within six months.

FACULTY: 3 full-time, 10 part-time.

COSTS: In-state $12/unit, out-of-state $121/unit + $12/unit enrollment fee.

CONTACT: Harriett Lewis, Santa Rosa Junior College, Consumer & Family Studies Dept., 1501 Mendocino Ave., Santa Rosa, CA 95401; 707-527-4395, E-mail msalinge@floyd.santarosa.edu, URL http://www.santarosa.edu.

SHASTA COLLEGE
Redding

Sponsor: 2-yr college. Program: 1-yr certificate, 2-yr AA program. Established: 1966. Calendar: semester. Curriculum: culinary, core. Admission dates: Jun, Dec, Aug. Total enrollment: 35. 35 each admission period. 100% of applicants accepted. 50% receive financial aid. 50% enrolled part-time. Student to teacher ratio 35:1. 100% of graduates employed within six months.

FACULTY: 1 instructor, Mike Piccinino, CEC, CCE.

COSTS: $11/sem-cr in-state, $116/sem-cr non-resident. Admission requirements: HS diploma or GED.

CONTACT: Michael Piccinino, Culinary Arts Instructor, Shasta College, 11555 N. Old Oregon Trail, Redding, CA 96003; 530-225-4829, Fax 530-225-4829, E-mail mpiccinino@shastacollege.edu, URL http://www.shastacollege.edu.

SUSHI CHEF INSTITUTE
Los Angeles/Year-round

Sponsor: Japanese cooking school. Program: 4-wk basic, professional & advanced sushi chef certificate programs; 1-wk intensive & 1-day wkend classes; 4-hr private class. Established: 2002. 15 max each admission period.

FACULTY: Chef Andy Matsuda was head sushi chef at a restaurant in Kobe for 4 yrs.

COSTS: 4-wk courses $2,900 + $100 fee; 1-wk intensive $1,500; 1-day class $80; private class $400. Admission requirements: Basic class completion required for professional class. Professional class completion & 1+ yrs experience as a chef required for advanced class.

CONTACT: Sushi Chef Institute, 927 Deep Valley Dr., #299, Rolling Hills Estate, CA 90274; 310-544-0863, Fax 310-541-3087, E-mail andy@sushischool.net, URL http://www.sushischool.net.

TANTE MARIE'S COOKING SCHOOL
San Francisco/Year-round

Sponsor: Small private school. Program: 6-mo certificate programs in culinary arts (full-time) & pastry (part-time), nonvocational evening & wkend courses, cooking vacations & parties. Established: 1979. Curriculum: culinary. Admission dates: Apr, Oct. Total enrollment: 24-28. 14 each admission period. 95% of applicants accepted. 50% enrolled part-time. Student to teacher ratio 14:1. 95% of graduates employed within 6 mos. Facilities: Tile floors, wooden counters, 6 ovens, 20 burners.

FACULTY: Founder Mary Risley studied at Le Cordon Bleu & La Varenne. Guest instructors.

COSTS: $16,500 for the 6-mo culinary certificate course, $6,500 for the 6-mo part-time pastry course. Admission requirements: HS diploma. Scholarships: yes. Loans: yes.

CONTACT: Peggy Lynch, Administrative Director, Tante Marie's Cooking School, 271 Francisco St., San Francisco, CA 94133; 415-788-6699, Fax 415-788-8924, E-mail peggy@tantemarie.com, URL http://www.tantemarie.com.

WESTLAKE CULINARY INSTITUTE
Westlake Village/Year-round

Sponsor: Private school. Program: 24-session professional series, 5-session baking series, 3-session catering series, certificate granted upon completion. Established: 1988. Curriculum: culinary. Admission dates: Variable. Total enrollment: 36. 12 each admission period. 80% of applicants accepted. 5% receive financial aid. 100% enrolled part-time. Student to teacher ratio 12:1. 90% of graduates employed within six months. Facilities: 1,500-sq-ft combination demonstration/participation facilities with 2 kitchens, cookware store.

FACULTY: Cecilia DeCastro, CCP, and guest instructors.

COSTS: $2,750 for the professional series, $595 for the baking series, $295 for the catering series. Admission requirements: Commitment, written application, basic skills, attitude.

CONTACT: Phyllis Vaccarelli, Owner/Director, Let's Get Cookin', 4643 Lakeview Canyon Rd., Westlake Village, CA 91361; 818-991-3940, Fax 805-495-2554, E-mail lgcookin@aol.com, URL http://www.letsgetcookin.com.

COLORADO

ACF CULINARIANS OF COLORADO
11 cities/Year-round

Sponsor: ACF Chapter. Program: 3-yr apprenticeship; degree program through any Colorado community college with 42 sem cr-hrs earned. Established: 0. Accredited by Emily Griffith Opportunity School. Curriculum: culinary. Admission dates: Jan through May. Total enrollment: 39. 30 each admission period. 100% of applicants accepted. 75% receive financial aid. 100% of graduates employed within six months. Facilities: Related instruction classes are located at Warren Tech Center in Lakewood, Colorado. Students are responsible for transportation to/from work & class.

COSTS: $2,100/three yrs. Admission requirements: HS diploma or equivalent, age 17 or older. Scholarships: yes.

CONTACT: Tiffany Brewster, Director of Apprenticeship, ACF Culinarians of Colorado Apprenticeship Program, 1937 Market Street, Denver, CO 80202; 303-308-1611, Fax 303-308-9400, E-mail cochefs@prodigy.net, URL http://www.acfchefs.org/chapter/co013.html.

THE ART INSTITUTE OF COLORADO – CULINARY ARTS
Denver/Year-round   *(See display ad page 11)*

Sponsor: Private school. Program: 12-mo Diploma in The Art of Cooking, 21-mo AAS degree in Culinary Arts, 21-mo AAS degree in Catering & Banquet Operations, 39-mo BA degree in Culinary Mgmt. Established: 1994. Accredited by ACICS, ACFAC. Calendar: quarter. Curriculum: culinary, core. Admission dates: All yr. Total enrollment: 450. 100 each admission period. 98% of applicants accepted. 75% receive financial aid. 90% enrolled part-time. Student to teacher ratio 20:1. 97% of graduates employed within six months. Facilities: Include 5 kitchens, classrooms, computer lab,Assignments Restaurant.

FACULTY: 16 full-time, 14 part-time; professional certification, BA degree, 20 yrs experience.

COSTS: $360/cr-hr, $50 application & $100 enrollment fee, $300/qtr lab fee, $1,010 supply kit. Admission requirements: HS diploma or equivalent & essay. Scholarships: yes. Loans: yes.

CONTACT: Brian Parker, Director of Admissions, Art Institute of Colorado-Culinary Arts, 1200 Lincoln St., Denver, CO 80203; 800-275-2420, Fax 303-860-8520, E-mail aicinfo@aii.edu, URL http://www.aic.aii.edu.

COLORADO MOUNTAIN CULINARY INSTITUTE
Keystone & Vail/Year-round   *(See display ad page 28)*

Sponsor: Colorado Mountain College with Keystone Resort & foodservice operations in Vail. Program: 3-yr (68 sem credit) program: AAS in Culinary Arts & ACF Certificate of Apprenticeship. Established: 1993. Accredited by NCA. Calendar: semester. Curriculum: culinary, core. Admission

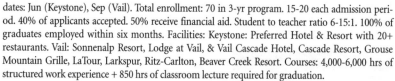
dates: Jun (Keystone), Sep (Vail). Total enrollment: 70 in 3-yr program. 15-20 each admission period. 40% of applicants accepted. 50% receive financial aid. Student to teacher ratio 6-15:1. 100% of graduates employed within six months. Facilities: Keystone: Preferred Hotel & Resort with 20+ restaurants. Vail: Sonnenalp Resort, Lodge at Vail, & Vail Cascade Hotel, Cascade Resort, Grouse Mountain Grille, LaTour, Larkspur, Ritz-Carlton, Beaver Creek Resort. Courses: 4,000-6,000 hrs of structured work experience + 850 hrs of classroom lecture required for graduation.

FACULTY: Keystone: Director is Chef Kevin Clarke, CEC; Vail: Director is Todd Rymer, CEC. Each program has 6-10 part-time instructors, all with industry experience.

COSTS: Annual tuition in-district $41/cr, in-state $69/cr, out-of-state $220/cr. $850 initial program fee. Housing $350-$550/mo. Admission requirements: 6 mos work experience, interview, essay, hs/college transcripts, college level reading, writing & math. Scholarships: yes. Loans: yes.

CONTACT: Chef Kevin Clarke or Chef Todd Rymer, Directors of Culinary Education, Colorado Mountain Culinary Institute, Admissions, PO Box 10001SG, Glenwood Springs, CO 81602; 800-621-8559, Fax 970-947-8324, E-mail JoinUs@coloradomtn.edu, URL http://www.coloradomtn.edu.

COOK STREET SCHOOL OF FINE COOKING
Denver/Year-round   *(See also page 190) (See display ad above)*

Sponsor: Private culinary school. Program: 6-mo Food & Wine Career Program with 3 wks of travel & culinary education in France & Italy & a sponsored Externship. Short courses & specialty classes also offered. Established: 1999. Accredited by Licensed by the Colorado Private Occupational School Board. Calendar: trimester. Curriculum: culinary. Admission dates: Day: Jan, May, Aug. Night: Jul. Total enrollment: 24. 24 each admission period. 85% of applicants accepted. 85% receive financial aid. Student to teacher ratio 8:1. 90% of graduates employed within six months. Facilities: 5,000-sq-ft facility includes 3,000-sq-ft teaching kitchen with commercial-grade equipment & custom-built wood-fired bread oven. Courses: Menu-based curriculum explores the principles & techniques of classical European cuisine, including bread & pastry work.

FACULTY: Michael Comstedt, CEC, formerly of the Greenbriar; Dale Eiden, CIA graduate; Shellie Kark, formerly of La Folie; Mary Cech, one of Top Ten Pastry Chefs in America by Chocolatier; Bette Smith, CWE, Certified Sommelier.

Costs: $20,000 includes trip to Europe & externship. Application fee $150. Admission requirements: HS diploma or GED, application, essay, interview. Scholarships: yes. Loans: yes.
Contact: Chris Caldes, Director of Admissions, Cook Street School of Fine Cooking, 1937 Market St., Denver, CO 80202; 303-308-9300 x106, Fax 303-308-9400, E-mail info@cookstreet.com, URL http://www.cookstreet.com.

CULINARY INSTITUTE OF COLORADO SPRINGS
Colorado Springs/Year-round
Sponsor: Division of Pikes Peak Community College. Program: 2-yr AAS degree in Culinary Arts; 1-yr certificates in Culinary Arts, Baking, & Food Service Mgmt. 3-yr apprenticeship program. Established: 1986. Accredited by The Higher Learning Commission. Calendar: semester. Curriculum: culinary, core. Admission dates: Aug, Jan, Jun. Total enrollment: Culinary 210, baking 40. 250 each admission period. 100% of applicants accepted. 70% receive financial aid. 50% enrolled part-time. Student to teacher ratio 15:1. 80% of graduates employed within six months. Facilities: Includes industrial kitchen & classrooms.
Faculty: 1 full-time, 5 part-time, ACF-certified.
Costs: In-state $2,500/yr, out-of-state $10,000/yr. Housing $400+. Admission requirements: Admission test. Scholarships: yes. Loans: yes.
Contact: Rob Hudson, Dept. Chair, CEC, CCE, Culinary Institute of Colorado Springs, BSBS Div., PPCC, 5675 S. Academy Blvd., Colorado Springs, CO 80906; 719-540-7371, Fax 719-540-7453, E-mail rob.hudson@ppcc.edu, URL http://www.ppcc.edu.

CULINARY SCHOOL OF THE ROCKIES
Boulder/Year-round
Sponsor: Private school. Program: Full-time 6-mo Professional Culinary Arts diploma program featuring 4 wks study in France. Part-time, evening 24-wk Chef Track program. 23-day Professional Pastry Arts diploma program covers pastry & baking. Established: 1996. Accredited by ACCET; Dept. of Higher Education of the State of Colorado. Calendar: semester. Curriculum: culinary. Admission dates: All. Total enrollment: 16. 16 each admission period. 50% receive financial aid. Student to teacher ratio 8:1. 90% of graduates employed within six months. Facilities: Modern, fully-equipped professional kitchen.
Faculty: 10-16 chef/instructors.
Costs: $22,850 tuition for full-time culinary program (includes airfare, rm & bd in France); $4,485 for mo-long Pastry Program; $8,650 for 24-wk, part-time Chef Track program. Admission requirements: HS diploma, personal essay, interview. Loans: yes.
Contact: Abigail VanDeventer, Director of Admissions and Placement, Culinary School of the Rockies, 637 S. Broadway, Suite H, Boulder, CO 80305; 303-494-7988, 877-249-0305, Fax 303-494-7999, E-mail abigail@culinaryschoolrockies.com, URL http://www.culinaryschoolrockies.com.

JOHNSON & WALES UNIVERSITY AT DENVER
Denver/Year-round *(See also page 37, 124) (See display ad page 124)*
Sponsor: Private nonprofit career institution. Program: 1-yr accelerated AAS degree in Culinary Arts for those with a bachelor's degree or higher, 2-yer AAS degree in Culinary Arts, 4-yr BS degree in Food Service Mgmt. Established: 2000. Accredited by NEASC, ACICS-CCA. Calendar: quarter. Curriculum: culinary. Admission dates: Sep, Dec, Mar. Total enrollment: 539 full time, 14 part time. 98% of graduates employed within six months. Facilities: 17,000-sq-ft kitchen & restaurant, 4 hot kitchens, bake shop, beverage lab, dining room, computer center, classroom. Courses: Lab courses, professional development, menu planning, nutrition, sanitation, cost control, garde manger, advanced patisserie/dessert, advanced dining room procedures, intl, classical French, & American regional cuisines, stocks & sauces.
Faculty: Includes Christine Stamm, MS, CWE & James Griffin, MS, CEC, CEC.
Costs: Tuition $19,182, general fee $810. Admission requirements: HS diploma or equivalent.

Scholarships: yes. Loans: yes.

CONTACT: Dave McKlveen, Director of Admissions, Johnson & Wales University at Denver, 7150 Montview Blvd., Denver, CO 80220; 303-256-9300, Fax 303-256-9333, E-mail admissions@jwu.edu, URL http://www.jwu.edu/denver/index.htm.

PUEBLO COMMUNITY COLLEGE
Pueblo/Year-round
Sponsor: 2-yr college. Program: 5 certificates (15-16 cr) & 69.5 cr-hr AAS degree programs in Culinary Arts & Hospitality Studies. Degree students choose from mgmt, production or hospitality tracks. Established: 1984. Accredited by ACF, Pro-Management Partner. Calendar: semester. Curriculum: core. Admission dates: All. Total enrollment: 95. Open each admission period. 100% of applicants accepted. 85% receive financial aid. 35% enrolled part-time. Student to teacher ratio 10:1. 95% of graduates employed within six months. Facilities: College's kitchen, dining areas, classrooms; computers in Library Learning Ctr.

FACULTY: Dept. Chair Carol Himes, M.Ed., FMP, CHE.

COSTS: ~$85/cr-hr in-state, $364/cr-hr out-of-state. Admission requirements: HS diploma or GED. Scholarships: yes. Loans: yes.

CONTACT: Carol Himes, M.Ed., Dept. Chair, Pueblo Community College, 900 West Orman Ave., Pueblo, CO 81004-1499; 719-549-3071, Fax 719-543-7566, E-mail carol.himes@pueblocc.edu, URL http://www.pueblocc.edu.

SCHOOL OF NATURAL COOKERY
Boulder
Sponsor: Private trade school. Program: Certificate courses: 3-mo Foundation, 2-mo Personal Chef Training, 3-wk Vegan Gastronomy, 3-wkCommercial Baking (vegan), Teacher Training. Established: 1991. Calendar: semester. Curriculum: culinary. Total enrollment: 20. 10 each admission period. 95% of applicants accepted. 10% receive financial aid. Student to teacher ratio 5/10/1:1. 98% of graduates employed within six months. Facilities: Modern residential-style kitchen, herb garden, composting; clients' homes. commerical bakery.

FACULTY: 6 instructors, certified chef, cookbook authors, doctor of natural medicine.

COSTS: Foundation Course $9,800, Vegan Gastrononmy $3,250, Personal Chef Training (includes gastronomy) $5600, Commercial Baking $7,200. Admission requirements: HS grad or equivalent, written essay & personal or phone interview. Loans: yes.

CONTACT: Joanne Saltzman, Director, School of Natural Cookery, P.O. Box 19466, Boulder, CO 80308; 303-444-8068, E-mail info@naturalcookery.com, URL http://www.naturalcookery.com.

WARREN OCCUPATIONAL TECHNICAL CENTER
Golden/August-May
Sponsor: Public institution. Program: 1-sem (options for 2nd & 3rd sems) certificate in Restaurant Arts. Established: 1974. Accredited by State, NCA. Calendar: semester. Curriculum: culinary. Admission dates: Aug, Jan. Total enrollment: 60. 45 each admission period. 98% of applicants accepted. 2% receive financial aid. 25% enrolled part-time. Student to teacher ratio 20:1. 95% of graduates employed within six months. Facilities: Kitchen, 60-student classroom, 2 dining rooms & a restaurant.

FACULTY: 3 full-time with master's degree in vocational education.

COSTS: In-state $1,600/sem, out-of-state $2,464/sem. Parking fee $50, materials $10. Housing $350/mo. Admission requirements: Diploma or GED. Scholarships: yes. Loans: yes.

CONTACT: David Bochmann, Warren Occupational Technical Center, 13300 W. 2nd Place, Lakewood, CO 80228-1256; 303-982-8600, Fax 303-982-8547, E-mail dbochman@jeffco.k12.co.us, URL http://jeffco.k12.co.us.

CONNECTICUT

CENTER FOR CULINARY ARTS
Cromwell/Year-round

Sponsor: Private school. Program: 15-mo diploma in Culinary Arts, 6-mo certificate in Baking & Pastry Arts. Established: 1997. Accredited by ACCSCT. Calendar: trimester. Curriculum: culinary. Admission dates: Sep, Jan, Apr: Culinary Arts. Oct, Jan: Baking & Pastry Arts. Total enrollment: 110. 36 each admission period. 75% of applicants accepted. 85% receive financial aid. 50% enrolled part-time. Student to teacher ratio 9:1. 95% of graduates employed within six months. Facilities: Kitchens with the latest professional equipment & cookware, dining room, classrooms. **Faculty:** 5 full-time & 12 adjunct, all schooled in the latest cooking trends & classic French cuisine. **Costs:** $14,300-$16,400 for Culinary Arts, $3,800 for Baking & Pastry Arts. Admission requirements: Interview, passion for cooking. Scholarships: yes. Loans: yes.

Contact: Mike Frechette, Admissions Representative, Center for Culinary Arts, 106 Sebethe Drive, Cromwell, CT 06416; 860-613-3350, Fax 860-613-3353, E-mail frechettem@netimail.net, URL http://www.centerforculinaryarts.com.

CONNECTICUT CULINARY INSTITUTE
Farmington and Suffield/Year-round   *(See display ad above)*

Sponsor: Private culinary school. Program: Advanced Culinary Arts Program (15 mos full-time/22 mos part-time), Professional Pastry & Baking Program (8 mos full-time/11 mos part-time). Established: 1987. Accredited by ACCSCT, Connecticut Commission of Higher Education. Calendar: semester. Curriculum: core. Admission dates: Continuous enrollment. Total enrollment:

400+. 90 each admission period. 88% of applicants accepted. 75% receive financial aid. 38% enrolled part-time. Student to teacher ratio 15:1. 95% of graduates employed within six months. Facilities: Multiple modernized teaching kitchens with the schools restaurant, Cafe Mise en Place; live ChefCam; 2,500-volume culinary library. Courses: Hands-on, small class size. Students practice techniques in classroom kitchens, school-run restaurants & in paid externship.

FACULTY: 24 full-time chefs, 5 adjunct. Industry experience ~10+ yrs with awards & honors.

COSTS: Advanced Culinary Arts Program $19,400, Professional Pastry & Baking Program $13,200. Registration fee $100; materials, uniforms, textbooks $1,395-$1,545. Admission requirements: HS diploma or GED or ATB test given by an independent agent; program evaluation test, personal interview. Scholarships: yes. Loans: yes.

CONTACT: Mike Phelps, Admissions Director, Connecticut Culinary Institute, Talcott Plaza, 230 Farmington Ave., Farmington, CT 06032; 860-677-7869, 800-762-4337, Fax 860-676-0679, E-mail ct.culinary.inst@snet.net, URL http://www.ctculinary.com. Branch Campus, 1760 Mapleton Ave., Suffield, CT 06078.

GATEWAY COMMUNITY COLLEGE
New Haven/Year-round

Sponsor: College. Program: 1-yr certificate in Culinary Arts, 2-yr degree in Food Service Mgmt. Established: 1987. Accredited by State, NEASC. Calendar: semester. Curriculum: culinary. Admission dates: Sep, Jan. Total enrollment: 80. 20-30 each admission period. 100% of applicants accepted. 40% receive financial aid. 60% enrolled part-time. Student to teacher ratio 15:1. 100% of graduates employed within six months. Facilities: Include1 lab, classrooms, restaurant.

FACULTY: 2 full-time, 4 part-time.

COSTS: Annual tuition in-state $2,406 full time, out-of-state $7,178. Housing ~$500/mo. Admission requirements: HS diploma or equivalent. Loans: yes.

CONTACT: Stephen Fries, Director, Gateway Community College, Hospitality Mgmt., 60 Sargent Dr., New Haven, CT 06511; 203-285-2175, E-mail sfries@gwcc.commnet.edu, URL http://www.gwctc.commnet.edu/culinary.html.

MANCHESTER COMMUNITY COLLEGE
Manchester/September-May

Sponsor: 2-yr college. Program: 1-yr certificate in Culinary Arts, AS degree in Foodservice Mgmt, 12-cr Professional Bakers certificate. Established: 1977. Accredited by ACF, NEASC. Calendar: semester. Curriculum: culinary, core. Admission dates: Sep, Jan. Total enrollment: 200. 200 each admission period. 100% of applicants accepted. 75% receive financial aid. 80% enrolled part-time. Student to teacher ratio 15:1. 100% of graduates employed within six months. Facilities: 2 commercial kitchens, classrooms, 100-seat dining room.

FACULTY: 6 full-time with master's degree or equivalents.

COSTS: In-state $1,650/sem (full time, 12 credits), Culinary Arts certificate $3,500. Application fee $20. Admission requirements: HS diploma or equivalent. Scholarships: yes. Loans: yes.

CONTACT: Jayne Pearson, Hospitality Program Chairperson, Manchester Community College, Div of Hospitality Mgmt, Great Path, M.S.#4, Box 1046, Manchester, CT 06040-1046; 860-512-2785, Fax 860-512-2621, E-mail jpearson@mcc.commnet.edu, URL http://www.mcc.commnet.edu.

NAUGATUCK VALLEY COMMUNITY COLLEGE
Waterbury/September-May

Sponsor: 2-yr college. Program: AS degree (4 sem full-time) in Foodservice mgmt & in Hotel mgmt. Established: 1982. Accredited by NEASC. Calendar: semester. Curriculum: culinary, core. Admission dates: Sept, Jan. Total enrollment: 100. 100% of applicants accepted. 30% receive financial aid. 40% enrolled part-time. Student to teacher ratio 12:1. 100% of graduates employed within six months. Facilities: Commercial kitchen lab, formal dining room, modern computer labs & classrooms; wine & viticulture lab.

FACULTY: 7 full- & part-time faculty with advanced degrees & industry experience.

COSTS: $1,155/sem in-state full-time (12 cr or more). $309/3-cr course. Admission requirements: Open. Scholarships: yes. Loans: yes.

CONTACT: Todd Jones, Program Coordinator, Naugatuck Valley Community-Technical College, E-519B, 750 Chase Pkwy., Waterbury, CT 06708; 860-575-8175, E-mail tjones@nvcc.commnet.edu, URL http://155.43.16.5/hospman.

NORWALK COMMUNITY COLLEGE
Norwalk/August-May

Sponsor: 2-yr community college. Program: 6-mo & 1-yr 30-credit certificate programs in Culinary Arts, associate degree in Restaurant/Foodservice mgmt. Established: 1992. Accredited by NEASC. Calendar: semester. Curriculum: culinary, core. Admission dates: Aug, Sep, Jan. Total enrollment: 190. 95 each admission period. 100% of applicants accepted. 50% receive financial aid. 75% enrolled part-time. Student to teacher ratio 16:1. 100% of graduates employed within six months. Facilities: High-tech fully-equipped kitchen.

FACULTY: 2 full- & 9 part-time instructors.

COSTS: $1,1980/yr tuition & fees, $600 other expenses. Admission requirements: HS diploma & placement test. Scholarships: yes. Loans: yes.

CONTACT: Tom Connolly, Coordinator, Hosp. Mgmt. & Culinary Arts, Norwalk Community College, 188 Richards Ave., Norwalk, CT 06854-1655; 203-857-7355, Fax 203-857-3327, E-mail nk_connolly@commnet.edu, URL http://www.ncc.commnet.edu.

DELAWARE

DELAWARE TECHNICAL & COMMUNITY COLLEGE
Newark/September-May

Sponsor: College. Program: 2-yr AAS degree in Culinary Arts, 2-yr AAS degree in Foodservice mgmt. Established: 1994. Accredited by MSA. Calendar: semester. Curriculum: culinary. Admission dates: Aug. Total enrollment: 45. 24 each admission period. 80% of applicants accepted. 50% receive financial aid. 80% enrolled part-time. Student to teacher ratio 12:1. 100% of graduates employed within six months. Facilities: One training kitchen & dining room.

FACULTY: 3 full-time (2 are CEC), 4 part-time (1 is FMP).

CONTACT: David Nolker, CEC, Dept. Chair, Delaware Technical & Community College, 400 Stanton-Christiana Rd., Newark, DE 19713; 302-453-3757, Fax 302-368-6620, E-mail dnolker@hopi.dtcc.edu, URL http://www.dtcc.edu.

UNIVERSITY OF DELAWARE, HRIM
Newark

Sponsor: University. Program: One 30-session wine course/yr. Established: 1995. Admission dates: Spring. 30 each admission period.

CONTACT: Fred DeMicco, Ph.D., Chair, University of Delaware, HRIM, Amy Rextrew House, 321 S. College Ave., Newark, DE 19716-3365; 302-831-6077, Fax 302-831-6395, E-mail fdemicco@udel.edu, URL http://www.udel.edu/HRIM.

FLORIDA

ACF CENTRAL FLORIDA CHAPTER – APPRENTICESHIP
Orlando/Year-round

Sponsor: ACF chapter. Program: 3-yr ACF Apprenticeship graduates earn Certified Culinarian from ACF. Accredited by ACF, SACS, COE. Calendar: quinmester. Curriculum: culinary. Admission dates: Aug, Oct, Jan, Mar. Total enrollment: 35. 100% of applicants accepted. Student to teacher ratio 15:1. 100% of graduates employed within six months. Facilities: Kitchen facility with up-to-date equipment, separate bakery & garde manger areas, classroom/dining room.

FACULTY: David W. Weir, Apprenticeship Coordinator, full time instructor; part-time instructors.

COSTS: $300. Beginning salary is $6.50/hr with 25 cent increases annually. Admission requirements: HS diploma or GED, age 17 min.

CONTACT: David Weir, CEC, CCE, Culinary Apprenitceship Coordinator, ACF Central Florida Chapter, Mid Florida Tech, Culinary Arts, 2900 W. Oak Ridge Rd., Orlando, FL 32809; 407-855-5880 #2286, Fax 407-251-6197, E-mail weird@ocps.k12.fl.us, URL http://mft.ocps.k12.fl.us.

ACF FIRST COAST CHAPTER
Ponte Vedra/Year-round
Sponsor: ACF chapter. Program: 3-yr apprenticeship; degree program through St. Augustine Technical Center. Curriculum: culinary. Total enrollment: 25.

COSTS: $300/yr. Beginning salary is $7.50/hr. Housing $400/mo.

CONTACT: Noel Ridsdale, CEC, ACF First Coast Chapter, Ponte Vedra Inn & Club, 200 Ponte Vedra Blvd., Ponte Vedra, FL 32082; 904-633-2286, E-mail chefnoel@bellsouth.net.

ACF GULF TO LAKES CHEFS CHAPTER
Eustis/Year-round
Sponsor: ACF chapter. Program: 2-yr apprenticeship; diploma program through Lake Technical Center. Accredited by ACF. Curriculum: culinary. Total enrollment: 45.

CONTACT: Ken Koenig, CCC, CCE, Chef Instructor, ACF Gulf to Lakes Chefs Chapter, 2001 Kurt St., Eustis, FL 32726-0616; 352-589-2250 x212, E-mail koenigk@lake.k12.fl.us, URL http://www.gulftolakeschefs.com.

ACF PALM BEACH COUNTY CHEFS
Palm Beach Gardens/Year-round
Sponsor: ACF chapter. Program: 3-yr apprenticeship; degree program through Palm Beach Community College is completed by 80%. Curriculum: culinary. Total enrollment: 28.

COSTS: $300/yr. Beginning salary is $6/hr with 50 cent increases every 6 mos. Housing $400/mo.

CONTACT: Dominick Laudia, CEC, ACF Palm Beach County Chefs, PO Box 970206, Boca Raton, FL 33497-0206; 561-712-3426, E-mail Chefnooch@aol.com, URL http://www.acfpalmbeach.com.

ACF TREASURE COAST CHAPTER
Stuart/Year-round
Sponsor: ACF chapter. Program: 3-yr apprenticeship. Curriculum: culinary. Total enrollment: 30.

COSTS: $160+texts & materials. Beginning salary is $5-$6/yr with increases every 3 mos.

CONTACT: E. Scott Sibley, President, ACF Treasure Coast Chapter, 321 Shady Lane, Port Saint Lucie, FL 34952; 772-340-0339, E-mail tcchefs@hotmail.com, URL http://www.acfchefs.org/presidents_portal/ACFChapter.cfm?ChapterChoice=FL121.

ART INSTITUTE OF FT. LAUDERDALE – SCHOOL OF CULINARY ARTS
Ft. Lauderdale/Year-round   *(See display ad page 11)*
Sponsor: Proprietary school. Program: 12-mo diploma in The Art of Cooking, 18-mo AS degree program in Culinary Arts, 36-mo program in Culinary mgmt. Established: 1991. Accredited by ACCSCT, ACF. Calendar: quarter. Curriculum: culinary, core. Admission dates: Jan, Apr, Jul, Oct. Total enrollment: 350. 60-100 each admission period. 90% of applicants accepted. 80% receive financial aid. Student to teacher ratio 19:1. 98% of graduates employed within six months. Facilities: 4 kitchens & classrooms, student-run restaurant.

FACULTY: 10 full-time ACF-certified instructors.

COSTS: $350/cr. Application fee $50. On-campus housing $1,395/qtr. Housing $600/mo. Admission requirements: HS diploma or equivalent. Scholarships: yes. Loans: yes.

CONTACT: Klaus Friedenreich, Master Chef, Art Institute of Ft. Lauderdale-School of Culinary Arts, 1799 S.E. 17th St., Ft. Lauderdale, FL 33316; 954-463-3000 x708/800-275-7603 x708, Fax 954-728-8637, E-mail friedenk@aii.edu, URL http://www.aifl.artinstitutes.edu.

ATLANTIC TECHNICAL CENTER OF GREATER FT. LAUDERDALE
Coconut Creek/Year-round
Sponsor: Public institution. Program: 1,050-hour certificate in Culinary Arts. Established: 1976. Accredited by COE, ACF. Calendar: quarter. Curriculum: core. Admission dates: Open. Total enrollment: 80. 65 each admission period. 90% of applicants accepted. 35% receive financial aid. 35% enrolled part-time. Student to teacher ratio 12:1. 95% of graduates employed within six months. Facilities: Student-run restaurant, private function room, cafeteria, 3 kitchens, computer lab, 2 classrooms, media center.

FACULTY: 6 full-time, 1 CEC & CCE, 1 CMB.

COSTS: $2,052; books, uniforms $145. Admission requirements: Admission test & basic academic skills. Scholarships: yes. Loans: yes.

CONTACT: Martin Wilcox, CEC. CCE., Department Head, Atlantic Technical Center, Culinary Arts, 4700 N.W. Coconut Creek Pkwy., Coconut Creek, FL 33066; 954-977-2066, Fax 954-977-2019, E-mail wilcox_m@firn.edu, URL http://www.atlantictechcenter.com.

CAPITAL CULINARY INSTITUTE OF KEISER COLLEGE
Melbourne & Tallahassee/Year-round
Sponsor: 4-yr private college. Program: 2-yr AS degree in Culinary Arts. Continuing ed courses. Established: 1977. Accredited by SACS, ACF. Calendar: trimester. Curriculum: culinary, core. Admission dates: Rolling admissions every 4 wks. 18 each admission period. 80% of applicants accepted. 90% receive financial aid. Student to teacher ratio 13:1. 90% of graduates employed within six months. Facilities: 4 full kitchens, 115-seat banquet room.

FACULTY: 4 full & 3 part-time faculty, 1 full-time Dean.

COSTS: $5,060 for day students, $4,220 for night students. Admission requirements: HS completion or GED, entrance exam & interview. Scholarships: yes. Loans: yes.

CONTACT: Guy Pierce, Director of Admissions, Capital Culinary Institute of Keiser College, 1700 Halstead Blvd., Tallahassee, FL 32308; 850-906-9494, 877-CHEF-123, Fax 850-906-9497, E-mail admissions-tal@keisercollege.edu, URL http://www.capitalculinaryinstitute.com.

CHARLOTTE TECHNICAL CENTER
Port Charlotte/August-June
Sponsor: Technical post-secondary school. Program: Certificate of completion (1,500 hrs, 5 qtrs) in Commercial Foods & Culinary Arts. Established: 1980. Accredited by COE. Calendar: quarter. Curriculum: culinary. Admission dates: Jul, Oct, Jan, Mar. Total enrollment: 15. 99% of applicants accepted. 50% receive financial aid. 5% enrolled part-time. Student to teacher ratio 5-1. 93% of graduates employed within six months. Facilities: Fully equipped kitchen, lab, classroom.

FACULTY: 3 full-time faculty, 1 part-time aide.

COSTS: ~$600/qtr. Admission requirements: T.A.B.E. assessment. Scholarships: yes.

CONTACT: Dick Santello, Admissions Counselor, Charlotte Technical Center, 18300 Toledo Blade Blvd., Port Charlotte, FL 33948-3399; 941-255-7500, Fax 941-255-7509, E-mail Richard_Santello@ccps.k12.fl.us, URL http://CharlotteTechCenter.ccps.k12.fl.us.

DAYTONA BEACH COMMUNITY COLLEGE
Daytona Beach/Year-round
Sponsor: 2-yr college. Program: AAS degree in Culinary mgmt, 18- to 24-mo program. Established: 1997. Accredited by SACS. Calendar: semester. Curriculum: culinary, core. Admission dates: Aug (Fall) and Jan (Spring). Total enrollment: 80. 20-30 each admission period. 99% of applicants accepted. 80% receive financial aid. 25% enrolled part-time. Student to teacher ratio

12:1. 85% of graduates employed within six months. Facilities: Production, baking & lab kitchen.Banquet facility & student-run gourmet restaurant.

FACULTY: 3 full-time & 5 part-time. All faculty are credentialed & have industry experience.

COSTS: $50/cr-hr FL residents, $187/cr-hr non-resident. Uniform/tools $400, lab fees $50/food prod. class. Admission requirements: HS diploma or equivalent. Scholarships: yes. Loans: yes.

CONTACT: Jeff Conklin, CEC, Program Manager, Daytona Beach Community College, P.O. Box 2811; Bldg #39, Room #149, Daytona Beach, FL 32120-2811; 904-255-8131 #3735, Fax 904-254-3063, E-mail conklij@dbcc.cc.fl.us, URL http://www.dbcc.cc.fl.us.

THE FCTI SCHOOL OF CULINARY ARTS
St. Augustine/Year-round

Sponsor: Division of First Coast Technical Institute. Program: 18-mo (1,500-hr) certificate & diploma program. Established: 1970. Accredited by ACF, COE, SACS. Calendar: quinmester. Curriculum: culinary, core. Admission dates: Every 9 wks. Total enrollment: 600+. 15-20 each admission period. 95% of applicants accepted. 40% receive financial aid. 20% enrolled part-time. Student to teacher ratio 15-20:1. 99% of graduates employed within six months. Facilities: Modern commercial kitchens, demo theater, labs & classrooms.

FACULTY: 15 instructors, all ACF-certified or pending; 5 part-time instructors.

COSTS: $5,000 in-state, $15 registration fee, $415/quinmester fee, $600 for supplies. Off-campus lodging $400/mo. Admission requirements: 16 yrs or older, HS diploma or equivalent. Scholarships: yes.

CONTACT: Chef David S. Bearl, CCC, CCE, Program Coordinator/Division Head, The FCTI School of Culinary Arts, 2980 Collins Ave., St. Augustine, FL 32094-9970; 904-829-1060, 904-829-1061, Fax 904-824-6750, E-mail bearld@fcti.org.

FLORIDA CULINARY INSTITUTE
West Palm Beach/Year-round

Sponsor: Proprietary institution. Program: 18-mo AS degree programs in Culinary Arts, International Baking & Pastry, and Food & Beverage mgmt. Established: 1987. Accredited by ACF, COE. Calendar: quarter. Curriculum: culinary, core. Admission dates: Jan, Apr, Jul, Oct. Total enrollment: 600. 200 each admission period. 95% of applicants accepted. 75% receive financial aid. Student to teacher ratio 18:1. 100% of graduates employed within six months. Facilities: Include 8 kitchens & 9 classrooms, Cafe Protege gourmet restaurant.

FACULTY: 20 full-time.

COSTS: $16,000/academic yr. Housing ~$350-$500/mo. Admission requirements: HS diploma or equivalent. Scholarships: yes. Loans: yes.

CONTACT: Kevin Cassidy, Director of Admissions, Florida Culinary Institute, 2400 Metrocentre Blvd., West Palm Beach, FL 33407-9985; 800-TOP-CHEF (867-2433), 561-842-8324, Fax 561-842-9503, E-mail info@floridaculinary.com, URL http://www.floridaculinary.com.

GULF COAST COMMUNITY COLLEGE
Panama City/Year-round

Sponsor: 2-yr college. Program: 2-yr AS degree in Culinary mgmt. Established: 1988. Accredited by SACS, ACF. Calendar: semester. Curriculum: core. Admission dates: Fall, spring. Total enrollment: 70. 20 each admission period. 100% of applicants accepted. Student to teacher ratio 16:1. Facilities: Includes a student-run restaurant.

FACULTY: 2 full-time, 1 part-time.

COSTS: In-state $49/credit, out-of-state $183/credit. Lab fees $8-$9. Admission requirements: HS diploma or equivalent. Scholarships: yes. Loans: yes.

CONTACT: Richard Stewart, Chair/Coordinator, Business/Culinary, Gulf Coast Community College, Culinary Mgmt., 5230 W. U.S. Hwy 98, Panama City, FL 32401; 850-872-3850, Fax 850-913-3319, E-mail rstewart@ccmail.gc.cc.fl.us, URL http://www.gc.cc.fl.us.

HILLSBOROUGH COMMUNITY COLLEGE
Tampa/Year-round
Sponsor: Community college. Program: 2-yr (64-cr-hr) AS degree in Culinary Arts. Established: 1984. Accredited by ACF, SACS. Calendar: semester. Curriculum: core. Admission dates: Aug, Jan, May, Jul. Total enrollment: 51. Varies each admission period. 98% of applicants accepted. 60% receive financial aid. 85% enrolled part-time. Student to teacher ratio 12:1. 100% of graduates employed within six months.
FACULTY: 1 full-time, 3 part-time.
COSTS: $48.50/cr-hr. Admission requirements: HS diploma or equivalent. Scholarships: yes. Loans: yes.
CONTACT: George Pastor, Ed.D., CEC, CCE, Dept. Chair, Hillsborough Community College, 4001 Tampa Bay Blvd., Tampa, FL 33614; 813-253-7316, E-mail GPastor@hcc.cc.fl.us, URL http://www.hcc.cc.fl.us.

INSTITUTE OF THE SOUTH FOR HOSPITALITY & CULINARY ARTS
Jacksonville/Year-round
Sponsor: 2-yr college. Program: 2-yr AS degree. Established: 1990. Accredited by SACS, ACF, CHRIE. Calendar: semester. Curriculum: culinary, core. Admission dates: Aug, Jan. Total enrollment: 130. 40 each admission period. 98% of applicants accepted. 30% receive financial aid. 80% enrolled part-time. Student to teacher ratio 15:1. 98% of graduates employed within six months. Facilities: 3 kitchens, 4 classrooms, 2 restaurants.
FACULTY: 4 full-time, 6 part-time.
COSTS: Annual tuition in-state $832, out-of-state $3,328. Admission requirements: HS diploma or equivalent. Scholarships: yes. Loans: yes.
CONTACT: Richard Donnelly, Instructional Program Manager, Florida Community College at Jacksonville, Inst. of the South for Hospitality & Culinary Arts, 4501 Capper Rd., Jacksonville, FL 32218; 904-766-5572, Fax 904-713-4858, E-mail bwright@fccj.org, URL http://www.fccj.org.

JOHNSON & WALES UNIVERSITY AT NORTH MIAMI
North Miami/Year-round *(See also page 29, 124) (See display ad page 124)*
Sponsor: Private nonprofit career institution. Program: 2-yr AS in Culinary Arts and Baking & Pastry Arts, 4-yr BS in Culinary Arts. Established: 1992. Accredited by NEASC. Calendar: quarter. Curriculum: culinary, core. Admission dates: Rolling. Total enrollment: 2,073 full time. ~80% receive financial aid. Student to teacher ratio 20:1. 98% of graduates employed within six months. Facilities: Lab kitchens, academic classrooms, library, computer lab, conference center. Courses: Culinary fundamentals, advanced culinary technologies, culinary principles. Other required courses: professional studies & academic courses.
FACULTY: 27 full-time, 5 part-time.
COSTS: Annual tuition $18,444. Other costs: $750 general fee, $200 orientation fee, on-campus housing $6,777. Admission requirements: HS diploma or equivalent. Scholarships: yes. Loans: yes.
CONTACT: Jeffrey Greenip, Director of Admissions, Johnson & Wales University at North Miami, Admissions Office, 1701 N.E. 127th St., North Miami, FL 33181; 800-232-2433, Fax 305-892-7020, E-mail admissions@jwu.edu, URL http://www.jwu.edu/florida.

LE CORDON BLEU – ORLANDO CULINARY ACADEMY
Orlando/Year-round *(See display ad page 101)*
Sponsor: Career culinary academy. Program: 15-mo AAS degree in Le Cordon Bleu Culinary Arts and Le Cordon Bleu Patisserie & Baking. Established: 2002. Accredited by ACICS. Calendar: quarter. Curriculum: culinary, core. Admission dates: Every 6 wks. Total enrollment: 800. 95% receive financial aid. Student to teacher ratio 16:1. 96% of graduates employed within six months. Facilities: 60,000+ sq-ft modern facility with student-operated fine dining restaurant & cafe, computer lab, retail store.
FACULTY: 45 full-time with professional industry experience.

CONTACT: Amber Stenbeck, VP Admissions, Orlando Culinary Academy, 8511 Commodity Circle, Orlando, FL 32819; 866-OCA-CHEF (866-622-2433) or 407-888-4000, Fax 407-888-4019, E-mail astenbeck@orlandoculinary.com, URL http://www.orlandoculinary.com.

MARCHMAN TECHNICAL EDUCATION CENTER
New Port Richey/September-June
Sponsor: Private trade-technical school. Program: 1-yr (6 hours/day) and 2-yr (3 hours/day) certificate programs in Commercial Foods. Established: 1984. Accredited by Pasco County Public Schools. Calendar: semester. Curriculum: culinary, core. Admission dates: Aug, Jan. Total enrollment: 60. 60 each admission period. 90% of applicants accepted. 10% receive financial aid. Student to teacher ratio 30:2. 90% of graduates employed within six months. Facilities: Full commercial kitchen & classroom, 300-seat dining facility.
FACULTY: 1 instructor.
CONTACT: Peter Kern, Commercial Foods Instructor, Marchman Technical Education Center, 7825 Campus Dr., New Port Richey, FL 34653; 727-774-1700, Fax 727-774-1791, E-mail jwhitake@pasco.k12.fl.us, URL http://mtec.pasco.k12.fl.us.

McFATTER SCHOOL OF CULINARY ARTS
Davie/Year-round
Sponsor: Public, post-secondary occupational educational facility. Program: 1-yr certificate. Established: 1996. Accredited by COE. Calendar: quarter. Curriculum: culinary, core. Admission dates: Each 9-wk term. Total enrollment: 50. 10-20 each admission period. 100% of applicants accepted. 50-75% receive financial aid. 10% enrolled part-time. Student to teacher ratio 20:1. 100% of graduates employed within six months. Facilities: Cafeteria, cafe, dining room.
FACULTY: 2 full-time, 2 part-time.
COSTS: $501/9-wk term (270 hrs) full time. Other costs include books, uniforms, supplies. Admission requirements: Basic skills testing. Scholarships: yes.
CONTACT: V. Paul Citrullo, Jr., CEC, Exec. Chef/Director of Culinary Arts, McFatter Vocational Tech Center, 6500 Nova Dr., Davie, FL 33317; 954-382-6543, Fax 954-370-1647, E-mail chefpaul2@yahoo.com, URL http://www.mcfattertech.com.

MIAMI LAKES EDUCATIONAL CENTER
Miami Lakes/Year-round
Sponsor: Trade-technical high school. Program: 13- to 14-mo (1,500-hr) diploma in Culinary Arts, including Cooking (750 hrs) & Baking (750 hrs). Transfers to other area institutions receive 1-yr credit. Established: 1978. Accredited by COE,SACS. Calendar: trimester. Curriculum: culinary, core. Admission dates: Jan, Apr, Jul, Oct. Total enrollment: 100. 8-10 each admission period. 80% of applicants accepted. 40% receive financial aid. Student to teacher ratio 16:1. Facilities: Full kitchen & bake shop. Large classrooms with modern equipment.
FACULTY: 3 certified instructors, 1 for baking & 2 for cooking.
COSTS: ~$600/trimester (3 mos). Students must buy at least 2 sets of uniforms & textbooks. Admission requirements: Orientation class. Scholarships: yes. Loans: yes.
CONTACT: Manny Delgado, CCE, CEC, CFE, Chef Instructor, Miami Lakes Educational Center, 5780 N.W. 158th St., Miami Lakes, FL 33014; 305-557-1100, x2264, Fax 305-557-7391, E-mail delgadom@mlec.dadeschools.net, URL http://mlec.dadeschools.net/culinary_arts.html.

PENSACOLA JR. COLLEGE CULINARY MANAGEMENT PROGRAM
Pensacola/Year-round
Sponsor: College. Program: 2-yr (64-cr-hrs) AAS degree. Established: 1995. Accredited by SACS, ACF. Calendar: semester. Curriculum: culinary, core. Admission dates: Fall, spring, summer. Total enrollment: 75. Student to teacher ratio 14:1. Facilities: Enlarged, updated culinary & baking labs, student-run restaurant.

FACULTY: Chef Travis Herr CEC,CCE, & Chef Bill Hamilton CEC,CCE.

CONTACT: Travis Herr CEC,CCE, Pensacola Jr. College, Culinary Management, 1000 College Blvd., Pensacola, FL 32504; 850-484-2506, E-mail therr@pjc.edu, URL http://www.pjc.edu.

PINELLAS TECHNICAL EDUCATIONAL CENTER
N. Clearwater/Year-round
Sponsor: Technical center. Program: 13-mo diploma in Culinary Arts. Established: 1965. Accredited by ACF, COE. Calendar: trimester. Curriculum: culinary. Admission dates: moly. Total enrollment: 50. 6-10 each admission period. 100% of applicants accepted. 75% receive financial aid. Student to teacher ratio 15:1. 100% of graduates employed within six months. Facilities: Include 2 kitchens, 2 classrooms & a student-run restaurant.

FACULTY: 4 full-time.

COSTS: In-state $1.25/student contact hour, ~$375/trimester. Housing ~$350/mo. Admission requirements: Admission test. Scholarships: yes. Loans: yes.

CONTACT: Vincent Calandra CCE, Dept. Chair, Pinellas Technical Educational Center, Culinary Arts Dept., 6100 154th Ave., N. Clearwater, FL 33760; 813-538-7167 x1140, Fax 813-538-7203, E-mail vcalandra@ptecclw.pinellas.k12.fl.us, URL http://www.ptecclw.pinellas.k12.fl.us.

PINELLAS TECHNICAL EDUCATIONAL CENTER
St. Petersburg/Year-round
Sponsor: Trade school. Program: 1,800-hour diploma in Culinary Arts. Accredited by SACS. Admission dates: Open. Total enrollment: 52. 10 each admission period. 100% of applicants accepted. 60% receive financial aid. Student to teacher ratio 17:1. 95% of graduates employed within six months. Facilities: Include kitchen, baking lab & classroom.

FACULTY: 2 full-time, 1 part-time.

COSTS: Annual tuition $495 resident. Books $42. Admission requirements: Admission test.

CONTACT: Victoria Butler, Pinellas Technical Educational Center, Culinary Arts Dept., 901 34th Street South, St. Petersburg, FL 33711; 727-538-7167 x1020, E-mail VButler@ptec.pinellas.k12.fl.us, URL http://www.ptecclw.pinellas.k12.fl.us.

ROBERT MORGAN VOC TECH INSTITUTE
Miami/Year-round
Sponsor: Public school. Program: Two 15-wk trimester courses in Commercial Cooking (800 hrs) & Commercial Baking (700 hrs), 212-hr course in Cake Decoration. Established: 1979. Accredited by SACS, COE. Calendar: trimester. Curriculum: culinary. Admission dates: Open. Total enrollment: 220-250. 50 each admission period. 100% of applicants accepted. 30% receive financial aid. 30% enrolled part-time. Student to teacher ratio 15:1. 95% of graduates employed within 6 mos.

FACULTY: 3 full- and 2 part-time Florida certified instructors.

COSTS: $1.20/hr in-state, $3.25/hr out-of-state, $5.25/hr part-time. Admission requirements: 10th grade. Scholarships: yes. Loans: yes.

CONTACT: Giorgio Moro, Food Services Coordinator, Robert Morgan Vocational Technical Institute, Culinary Arts Program-18180 SW 122nd Ave., Miami, FL 33177; 305-253-9920 x197, Fax 305-253-3023, E-mail gmoro@dadeschools.net, URL http://www.dade.k12.fl.us/8911.

SARASOTA COUNTY TECHNICAL INSTITUTE
Sarasota
Sponsor: Institution. Program: 2 yr/1,485-hour certificate. Established: 1967. Accredited by SACS. Admission dates: Open. 90% of applicants accepted. 100% of graduates employed within 6 mos.

FACULTY: 1 full-time.

COSTS: $2,055/yr in-state, $10,080/yr out-of-state.

CONTACT: Dee Zulauf, Sarasota County Technical Institute, Culinary Arts, 4748 Beneva Rd., Sarasota, FL 34233; 941-924-1365 x312, E-mail dee_zulauf@sarasota.k12.fl.us, URL http://www.sarasotatech.org.

SOUTH FLORIDA COMMUNITY COLLEGE
Avon Park/August-June

Sponsor: College. Program: Vocational certificate in Food mgmt, Production, & Services. AS degree in Hospitality mgmt. Established: 1965. Accredited by SACS. Calendar: semester. Curriculum: culinary. Admission dates: Aug, Dec. Total enrollment: 15-30. Varies each admission period. 50% enrolled part-time. Student to teacher ratio 12:1. Facilities: College-owned historic Hotel Jacaranda, in downtown Avon Park.

FACULTY: 1 full- and 2 part-time.

CONTACT: Professor of Hospitality Management, South Florida Community College, 600 W. College Dr., Avon Park, FL 33825; 941-453-6661 x337, Fax 941-453-8023, E-mail info@sfcc.cc, URL http://www.sfcc.cc.fl.us.

WALT DISNEY WORLD AT VALENCIA COMMUNITY COLLEGE
Orlando/Year-round

Sponsor: Valencia Community College. Program: 2-yr (64 cr-hr) AS degree in Culinary Mangement, three separate 2-yr degrees in Hospitality mgmt, 2-yr degree in Restaurant mgmt. Established: 1997. Accredited by SACS. Calendar: semester. Curriculum: culinary. Admission dates: Jan, May, Aug. Total enrollment: 330. 5 each admission period. 100% of applicants accepted. 30% receive financial aid. 77% enrolled part-time. Student to teacher ratio 18:1. 85% of graduates employed within six months. Facilities: Audio-visually equipped demo studio kitchen, baking & pastry kitchen, modern restaurant kitchen, computer lab with 30 computers, classrooms.

FACULTY: Swiss-trained Certified Executive Chef is program manager; area chefs are adjunct faculty.

COSTS: $5.000 in-state, $13.000 out-of-state for 64 cr-hrs (~2 yrs). Admission requirements: HS diploma or equivalent. Scholarships: yes. Loans: yes.

CONTACT: Pierre Pilloud, CEC, Program Director, Walt Disney World Center for Hospitality & Culinary Art, Valencia Community College, W. Campus, 1800 S. Kerkman Rd., Orlando, FL 32811; 407-582-1880, Fax 407-273-9754, E-mail ppilloud@valencia.cc.fl.us, URL http://valencia.cc.fl.us.

GEORGIA

ART INSTITUTE OF ATLANTA – CULINARY ARTS
Atlanta/Year-round   *(See display ad page 11)*

Sponsor: Private college of creative professional studies. Program: 7-qtr AA degree in Culinary Arts, 8-qtr AA degree in Culinary Arts (concentration in baking & pastry), 5-qtr BS degree in Culinary Arts Mgmt. Established: 1991. Accredited by ACF, SACS. Calendar: quarter. Curriculum: culinary, core. Admission dates: Jan, Apr, Jul, Oct. Total enrollment: 470. 85% receive financial aid. Student to teacher ratio 20:1. 100% of graduates employed within six months. Facilities: 15,000-square-foot facility with 5 teaching kitchens, purchasing lab, sanitation lab, classrooms, computer labs, full-service teaching dining room, library, student lounge.

FACULTY: 15 full-time & 10 part-time instructors, many of whom are also working chefs.

COSTS: $5,520/qtr, application fee $50, lab fee $285/qtr. College-sponsored housing $2,215/qtr, culinary kit $800 (1st qtr only for AA degree). Admission requirements: HS diploma or equivalent, essay, SAT/ACT or COMPASS test scores. BS degree applicants require AA degree in Culinary Arts or Baking & Pastry Arts and 2000 hrs culinary work experience. Scholarships: yes. Loans: yes.

CONTACT: Admissions Office, Art Institute of Atlanta-Culinary Arts, 6600 Peachtree Dunwoody Rd., 100 Embassy Row, Atlanta, GA 30328; 800-275-4242, 770-394-8300, Fax 770-394-0008, E-mail aiaadm@aii.edu, URL http://www.aia.artinstitutes.edu.

ATLANTA AREA TECHNICAL SCHOOL
Atlanta

Sponsor: Career institution. Program: 18-mo diploma. Established: 1967. Accredited by SACS. Admission dates: Qtrly. Student to teacher ratio 12:1. 92% of graduates employed within 6 mos. **FACULTY:** 6+ full-time. **COSTS:** $296/qtr full-time, $23/credit part-time. Admission requirements: HS diploma or equivalent and admission test. **CONTACT:** Andrew G. Phillips, Director, Atlanta Area Technical School, Culinary Arts Program, 1560 Stewart Ave. S.W., Atlanta, GA 30310; 404-756-3715, Fax 404-756-0932, E-mail aphillip@admin1.atlanta.tec.ga.us, URL http://www.atlantatech.org/Programs_Credit/human_serv.htm.

AUGUSTA TECHNICAL INSTITUTE
Augusta/Year-round

Sponsor: State technical school. Program: 4-qtr certificate program in Food Service, 6-qtr diploma in Culinary Arts. Established: 1985. Accredited by SACS. Calendar: quarter. Curriculum: culinary. Admission dates: Sep, Mar. Total enrollment: 36. 15 each admission period. 90% of applicants accepted. 100% receive financial aid. 3% enrolled part-time. Student to teacher ratio 18:1. 100% of graduates employed within six months. Facilities: Include 1 kitchen, 2 classrooms, & local restaurants. **FACULTY:** 2 full-time. **COSTS:** $274/qtr in-state, $548/qtr out-of-state. Application fee $15. Housing $500/mo. Admission requirements: HS diploma or GED. Scholarships: yes. **CONTACT:** Augusta Technical Institute, Culinary Arts, 3116 Deans Bridge Rd., Augusta, GA 30906; 706-771-4028, Fax 706-771-4034, E-mail bcrobert@augusta.tec.ga.us, URL http://www.augusta.tec.ga.us/Catalog/CULINARY%20ARTS.htm.

CHATTAHOOCHEE TECHNICAL COLLEGE
Decatur/Year-round

Sponsor: Technical college. Program: AAT degree (109 credits) in Culinary Arts, diploma (92 credits) in Culinary Arts, certificate programs (16-17 credits) in Culinary Skills & Culinary-Stewarding. Accredited by SACS, ACF. Calendar: quarter. Admission dates: Spring, summer, fall, winter. **FACULTY:** Michael Bologna, CEC. **COSTS:** In-state: $312/qtr full-time (12 or more credits), $26/credit part-time (less than 12 credits); Out-of-state: $624/qtr full-time, $52/credit part-time. **CONTACT:** Michael Bologna, Chattahoochee Technical College, 980 South Cobb Dr., Marietta, GA 30060; 770 -528-4545, Fax 770-528-4465, E-mail mbologna@chattcollege.com, URL http://www.chat-tec.com.

LE CORDON BLEU COLLEGE OF CULINARY ARTS ATLANTA
Tucker/Year-round   *(See display ad page 42)*

Sponsor: Private school. Program: 15-mo AOS degree in Culinary Arts. Established: 2003. Accredited by ACCSCT. Curriculum: culinary. Admission dates: Jan, Feb, Apr, May, Jul, Aug, Oct, Nov. 70-80 each admission period. Student to teacher ratio 32:1. Facilities: 60,000-sq-ft facility with up–to-date well- equipped kitchens & classrooms, computer labs, library, bookstore. Courses: Le Cordon Bleu skill set, culinary fundamentals, purchasing & cost control, nutrition, baking, pastry, wines, restaurant mgmt. **COSTS:** $34,300 includes tuition & fees. Admission requirements: HS diploma or equivalent. Scholarships: yes. Loans: yes. **CONTACT:** Janice Davidson, Director of Admissions, Le Cordon Bleu College of Culinary Arts Atlanta, 1927 Lakeside Parkway, Tucker, GA 30084; 770-938 4711, Fax 770-938- 4571, E-mail info@atlantaculinary.com, URL http://www.atlantaculinary.com.

SAVANNAH TECHNICAL COLLEGE
Savannah/Year-round

Sponsor: Public institution. Program: 6-qtr diploma & 2-yr AAA degree in Culinary Arts. Established: 1981. Accredited by SACS, ACF. Calendar: quarter. Curriculum: culinary, core. Admission dates: Spring & fall. Total enrollment: 75. 24 each admission period. 100% of applicants accepted. 85% receive financial aid. 75% enrolled part-time. Student to teacher ratio 24:1. 100% of graduates employed within six months. Facilities: Include kitchen, classroom, student-run restaurant.

FACULTY: 2 full-time.

COSTS: In-state $312/qtr, out-of-state $624/qtr. Fees ~$79, uniforms, tools $400, books ~$150/qtr. Admission requirements: HS diploma or equivalent & placement test or SAT. Scholarships: yes.

CONTACT: Marvis Hinson, Department Head, Savannah Technical College, Culinary Arts, 5717 White Bluff Rd., Savannah, GA 31405-5594; 912-303-1833, Fax 912-303-1760, E-mail mhinson@savtec.org, URL http://www.savtec.org.

THE WINE SCHOOL
Atlanta/August-June

Sponsor: Wine professional. Program: Three 6-wk Diploma courses/yr, advanced classes, wkend courses at client venues, online courses. Established: 1978. Diploma course approved by ACF.

FACULTY: Anita Louise LaRaia, member SWE, author of Wine FAQs, former online wine expert CNN.com.

COSTS: $350 for diploma course.

CONTACT: Anita Louise LaRaia, Director, The Wine School, P.O. Box 52723, Atlanta, GA 30355; 770-901-9433, Fax 770-901-9969, E-mail anitalaraia@msn.com, URL http://www.anitalaraia.com.

HAWAII

CULINARY INSTITUTE OF THE PACIFIC
Pearl City/Year-round

Sponsor: 2-yr college. Program: 2-yr AAS in Food Service, 1.5-yr certificate in Food Service, 1-sem certificate in Food Preparation, 2-sem certificates in Baking & Dining Room. Established: 1974. Accredited by WASC, ACF. Calendar: semester. Curriculum: core. Admission dates: Aug, Jan. Total enrollment: 80-100. 25-30 each admission period. 100% of applicants accepted. 40% receive financial aid. 20% enrolled part-time. Student to teacher ratio 15-20:1. 90% of graduates employed within six months. Facilities: 3 kitchens, 5 classrooms, 1 restaurant, 2 cafe/dining rooms.

FACULTY: 5 full-time with 15-20 yrs industry experience, 3 part-time.

COSTS: Sem tuition in-state $468, out-of-state $2,856. Admission requirements: Age 18 or 17 with HS diploma. Scholarships: yes. Loans: yes.

CONTACT: Tommylynn Benavente, Program Coordinator, Leeward Community College, Food Service, 96-045 Ala Ike, Pearl City, HI 96782; 808-455-0298/808-455-0300, Fax 808-455-0471, E-mail tlbenave@hawaii.edu, URL http://alaike.lcc.hawaii.edu/FoodService/default.htm.

KAPI'OLANI COMMUNITY COLLEGE
Honolulu/Year-round

Sponsor: 2-yr college. Program: 2-yr AS degrees in Culinary Arts & Patisserie, 18-mo certificate in Culinary Arts, 1-yr certificate in Culinary Arts & Patisserie. Established: 1947. Accredited by ACF, CAHM, WASC. Calendar: semester. Curriculum: culinary, core. Admission dates: Fall, spring, summer. Total enrollment: 500. 100% of applicants accepted. 40% receive financial aid. 50% enrolled part-time. Student to teacher ratio 20:1. 98% of graduates employed within six months. Facilities: 9 kitchens, 7 classrooms, 1 demo auditorium, 5 restaurants.

FACULTY: 14 full-time, 6 part-time, all with industry experience.

COSTS: Annual tuition in-state $47/cr, out-of-state $242/cr. $30 fee/sem. Housing ~$600/mo. Admission requirements: Age 18, or age 17 with HS diploma or GED. Scholarships: yes. Loans: yes.

CONTACT: Lori Maehara, Assistant Professor/Counselor, Kapiolani Community College, Food Service & Hospitality Education, 4303 Diamond Head Rd., Honolulu, HI 96816; 808-734-9466, Fax 808-734-9212, E-mail lmaehara@hawaii.edu, URL http://www.kcc.hawaii.edu.

KAUAI COMMUNITY COLLEGE
Lihue/August-May

Sponsor: 2-yr college. Program: 1-yr certificate and 2-yr AAS degree in Culinary Arts. Calendar: semester. Curriculum: core.

COSTS: $41.50/credit in-state, $240.50/credit out-of-state.

CONTACT: Clarence Nishi, Chief, Kauai Community College, 3-1901 Kaumualii Hwy., Lihue, HI 96766; 808-245-8311 x265, Fax 808-245-8297, E-mail cnishi@mail.kauaicc.hawaii.edu, URL http://www.kauaicc.hawaii.edu.

MAUI CHEFS ASSOCIATION
Kahului/Year-round

Sponsor: ACF chapter. Program: 3-yr apprenticeship; degree program through Maui Community College is completed by 50%. Established: 1975. Accredited by ACF. Calendar: semester. Curriculum: culinary, core. Admission dates: Open. Total enrollment: 6. 35 each admission period. 80% of applicants accepted. 50% receive financial aid. 20% enrolled part-time. Student to teacher ratio 15:1. 100% of graduates employed within six months.

FACULTY: 5 full-time instructors.

COSTS: $525 in-state, $2,913 out-of-state/sem. Beginning salary is $10-$11.50/hr with increases every 6 mos. Housing $600-$800/mo. Scholarships: yes. Loans: yes.

CONTACT: Christopher Speere, Culinary Educator, Maui Chefs Association, Maui Community College, 310 Kaahumanu Ave., Box 1284, Kahului, HI 96732; 808-984-3479, Fax 808-984-3314, E-mail speere@hawaii.edu, URL http://www.mauicc.hawaii.edu.

MAUI COMMUNITY COLLEGE/CULINARY ARTS PROGRAM
Kahului/August-May
Sponsor: 2-yr college. Program: 1-yr certificate, 2-yr AAS degree-Culinary; 2-yr AAS degree-Baking. Established: 1969. Accredited by ACF. Calendar: semester. Curriculum: culinary, core. Admission dates: Aug, Jan. Total enrollment: 140. 45 each admission period. 100% of applicants accepted. 40% receive financial aid. 30% enrolled part-time. Student to teacher ratio 15:1. 98% of graduates employed within six months. Facilities: New facility, industry-current equipment. Includes bakeshop, hotel-style kitchens, ocean-view restaurant, skills kitchen.

FACULTY: 8 full-time, 5 part-time.

COSTS: Annual tuition in-state $47.50/cr, out-of-state $246.50/cr. 2-bedroom lodging $997/sem. Admission requirements: Min. 18 yrs, HS graduate or transfer. Scholarships: yes. Loans: yes.

CONTACT: Robert Santos, Program Coordinator, Maui Community College, Culinary Arts, 310 Kaahumanu Ave., Kahului, HI 96732; 808-984-3225, Fax 808-984-3314, E-mail santosro@hawaii.edu.

IDAHO

BOISE STATE UNIVERSITY
Boise/August-May
Sponsor: University. Program: 6-mo, 1-yr, & 18-mo certificates; 2-yr AAS degree. Established: 1969. Accredited by ACF, NCA. Calendar: semester. Curriculum: culinary. Admission dates: Aug, Jan. Total enrollment: 35-50. 25/sem each admission period. 5% enrolled part-time. Student to teacher ratio ~10:1. 97% of graduates employed within six months.

FACULTY: 3 full-time & 4 adjunct chefs.

COSTS: In-state $1,995/sem, out-of-state $3,360/sem + $1,995 fee. Admission requirements: HS diploma or equivalent & admission assessment. Scholarships: yes. Loans: yes.

CONTACT: Vern Hickman, Chef Instructor, Boise State University, Culinary Arts, 1910 University Dr., Boise, ID 83725; 208-426-4199, Fax 208-426-1948, E-mail vhickman@boisestate.edu.

COLLEGE OF SOUTHERN IDAHO
Twin Falls/September-May
Sponsor: Community college. Program: 2-yr AAS, 1-yr technical certificate. Established: 1986. Calendar: semester. Curriculum: core. Admission dates: Open. Total enrollment: 20. 12 each admission period. 32% of applicants accepted. 90% receive financial aid. Student to teacher ratio 10:1. 90% of graduates employed within six months.

FACULTY: 2 full-time, 6 part-time.

COSTS: In-state $615/sem, out-of-state $1,615/sem. On-campus rm & bd is $1,625; Housing $350/mo. Admission requirements: HS diploma or equivalent. Scholarships: yes.

CONTACT: Pamela Namer, Program Coordinator, College of Southern Idaho, Hotel-Restaurant Mgmt., P.O. Box 1238, 315 Falls Ave., Twin Falls, ID 83303-1238; 208-733-9554 x2380, 800-680-0274 x2380, Fax 208-736-2136, E-mail pnamer@csi.edu, URL http://www.csi.edu/l4.cfm?chef.

IDAHO STATE UNIVERSITY SCHOOL OF APPLIED TECHNOLOGY
Pocatello/Year-round
Sponsor: University. Program: 2.5-sem certificate program in Culinary Arts Technology, AAS degree in Culinary Arts Technology. Calendar: semester. Curriculum: core. Admission dates: Aug, Jan, May. Total enrollment: 20. 15 each admission period. 100% of applicants accepted. Student to teacher ratio 14:01. 100% of graduates employed within six months.

COSTS: $992/sem (resident). Supplies $556.

CONTACT: David K. Hanson, Dept. Chair, Idaho State University School of Applied Technology, Campus Box 8380, Pocatello, ID 83209-8380; 208-236-3327, Fax 208-236-4641, E-mail hansdavi@isu.edu, URL http://www.isu.edu.

NORTH IDAHO COLLEGE
Coeur d'Alene/Year-round
Sponsor: College. Program: 36.5 cr-hr certificate in Culinary Arts. Calendar: semester. Curriculum: culinary.

COSTS: Annual tuition is $1,128-$1,687/credit in-state, $3,884-$4,443/credit out-of-state. Room and board $3,510/yr. Books & supplies $225-$2,300/yr.

CONTACT: Richard Schultz, North Idaho College, 1000 W. Garden Ave., Coeur d'Alene, ID 83814; 208-769-3458, E-mail rick_schultz@nidc.edu, URL http://www.nidc.edu.

ILLINOIS

BELLEVILLE AREA COLLEGE
Granite City/Year-round
Sponsor: College. Program: 1-yr certificate programs in Culinary Arts (15 cr-hrs), Foodservice (16 cr-hrs), & Hospitality Food Service (31 cr-hrs); 2-yr AAS degree in Hospitality Food Service mgmt (71 cr-hrs). Accredited by ACF. Calendar: semester.

COSTS: $44/cr-hr in-district, $107/cr-hr out-of-district, $150 for uniforms & supplies.

CONTACT: Steven Nigg, Program Coordinator, Belleville Area College, 4950 Maryville Rd., Granite City, IL 62040-2699; 618-235-2700 x5436, E-mail steve.nigg@swic.edu.

COLLEGE OF DUPAGE
Glen Ellyn/Year-round
Sponsor: College. Program: 1-yr certificate & 2-yr AAS degree in Food Service Administration & Culinary Arts, 1-yr certificate in Pastry Arts. Established: 1966. Accredited by NCA, RBA, NRA, ACF. Calendar: quarter. Curriculum: culinary, core. Admission dates: Sep, Jan, Mar, Jun. Total enrollment: 200. 50-125 each admission period. 100% of applicants accepted. 25% receive financial aid. 30% enrolled part-time. Student to teacher ratio 15:1. 100% of graduates employed within six months. Facilities: Include kitchen, pastry shop, classrooms, restaurant, dining room.

FACULTY: 4 full-time, 12 part-time.

COSTS: In-district $35/cr-hr. Admission fee $10. Texts, uniforms, tools & fees vary. Off-campus housing ~$500/mo. Admission requirements: HS diploma or equivalent. Scholarships: yes. Loans: yes.

CONTACT: George Macht, Coordinator/Professor, College of DuPage, Culinary Arts/Pastry Arts, 425 Fawell Blvd., Glen Ellyn, IL 60137; 630-942-3663, Fax 630-858-9399, E-mail machtg@cdnet.cod.edu, URL http://www.cod.edu/Catalog/F/FoodServ.htm.

COLLEGE OF LAKE COUNTY
Grayslake, Vernon Hills & Waukegan/Year-round
Sponsor: 2-yr community college. Program: 1-yr certificate in Culinary Arts, Food Service Mgmt or Professional Cooking; AAS in Food Service Mgmt. Established: 1987. Accredited by NCA. Calendar: semester. Curriculum: culinary, core. Admission dates: Aug, Jan, Jun. Total enrollment: 50. 20 each admission period. 95% of applicants accepted. 10% receive financial aid. 50% enrolled part-time. Student to teacher ratio 10:1. 98% of graduates employed within six months. Facilities: Include 2 kitchens & 3 classrooms.

FACULTY: 1 full-time, 7 part-time.

COSTS: $64/cr-hr. Admission requirements: Math & language proficiency exam or GED, ACT, Military. Scholarships: yes. Loans: yes.

CONTACT: Cliff Wener, Instructor, College of Lake County, Food Service Program, 19351 W. Washington St., Grayslake, IL 60030-1198; 847-543-2823, Fax 847-543-3823, E-mail crwener-fsm@clcillinois.edu.

THE COOKING AND HOSPITALITY INSTITUTE OF CHICAGO
Chicago/Year-round   *(See display ad above)*
Sponsor: Private institution. Program: 12-mo/3-sem/65-cr-hr + externship (up to 4 mos to complete) AAS degree in the Le Cordon Bleu Culinary Program, & in the Le Cordon Bleu Patisserie & Baking Program. Established: 1983. Accredited by ACCSCT, ACF, NCA. Calendar: semester. Curriculum: core. Admission dates: 6 times/yr. Total enrollment: 900. 90% of applicants accepted. 80% receive financial aid. Student to teacher ratio 16:1. 98% of graduates employed within six months. Facilities: 13 fully-equipped instructional kitchens, on-site restaurant. Courses: Combines classical French techniques & American technology. Courses cover qualitative & quantitative cooking, menu planning, recipe development, sanitation. Baking/pastry courses cover production techniques, food as art form, yeast breads, decoration.
FACULTY: Instructors are ACF certified & accomplished in their fields of expertise.
COSTS: $12,250/sem. Registration fee $150. Books & supplies ~$3,200 for entire program. Admission requirements: HS diploma or equivalent. Scholarships: yes. Loans: yes.
CONTACT: Alan Schultz, VP of Admissions, The Cooking and Hospitality Institute of Chicago, 361 W. Chestnut, Chicago, IL 60610; 312-944-0882, 877-828-7772, Fax 312-944-8557, E-mail chic@chicnet.org, URL http://www.chic.edu.

ELGIN COMMUNITY COLLEGE
Elgin/Year-round
Sponsor: College. Program: 2-yr AAS in Culinary Arts, Restaurant Mgmt and Baking & Pastry. Established: 1972. Accredited by Illinois Community College Board, ACF. Calendar: semester. Curriculum: culinary, core. Admission dates: Aug, Jan. Total enrollment: 325. 40-50 each admission period. 80% of applicants accepted. 30% enrolled part-time. Student to teacher ratio 15-30:1.

100% of graduates employed within six months. Facilities: 2 culinary & 2 baking labs, kitchen, 160-seat dining room with chefs stage, retail store.

FACULTY: 5 full- & 8 part-time, ACF-certified.

COSTS: $70/cr-hr in-district, $260/cr-hr out-of-district. Books & uniforms ~$200. Housing ~$400-$600/mo. Admission requirements: HS diploma or equivalent. Scholarships: yes. Loans: yes.

CONTACT: Michael Zema, Director, Elgin Community College, Hospitality Dept., 1700 Spartan Dr., Elgin, IL 60123; 847-214-7461, Fax 847-214-7510, E-mail admissions@mail.elgin.edu, URL http://www.elgin.cc.il.us.

FRENCH PASTRY SCHOOL
Chicago/Year-round

Sponsor: Pastry school. Program: 24-wk certificate in Pastry Arts focusing on classic French methods, contemporary aesthetics & production techniques. Established: 1996. Accredited by ICCB (24-wk program), ACF (Guest Chef program). Calendar: semester. Curriculum: culinary. Admission dates: Jan & Jul. 16 students in 2 classes/day each admission period. Student to teacher ratio 16:1. 90% of graduates employed within six months. Facilities: Purpose-built pastry kitchens with the latest equipment including KOMA freezers, Bongard ovens, Spring induction stoves, Kitchen Aid mixers.

FACULTY: Chef Jacquy Pfeiffer co-founder/instructor, has 25+ yrs experience, named one of the Top Ten Pastry Chefs in the U.S. by Chocolatier & Pastry Art and Design. Chef Sebastien Canonne, M.O.F. & coach of 2002 winning World Pastry Championship team in Las Vega.

COSTS: $16,400 includes books, uniforms, supplies, knife/tool kit. Admission requirements: HS diploma or equivalent. Scholarships: yes. Loans: yes.

CONTACT: Renee Bohus, French Pastry School, 226 W. Jackson Blvd., Chicago, IL 60606; 312-726-2419, Fax 312-726-2446, E-mail info@frenchpastryschool.com, URL http://www.frenchpastryschool.com.

THE ILLINOIS INSTITUTE OF ART CHICAGO – CULINARY ARTS
Chicago/Year-round *(See display ad page 48)*

Sponsor: 2-yr college. Program: 18-mo AAS degree in Culinary Arts, 4-yr BAS degree in Culinary Mgmt.1-yr certificates in Professional Baking & Pastry, Professional Cooking, and Professional Catering. Established: 2000. Accredited by ACCSCT, ACF. Calendar: quarter. Curriculum: culinary, core. Total enrollment: 300. 65 each admission period. 95% of applicants accepted. 98% receive financial aid. 30% enrolled part-time. Student to teacher ratio 19:1. 98% of graduates employed within six months. Facilities: 48,000-sq-ft new facility with 5 complete kitchens & a restaurant; 2 more kitchens planned. Courses: Baking & Pastry; Garde Manger; Food Production; Dining Room Services; Nutritional Cooking; Safety & Sanitation; Intl Cuisine; Menu Mgmt & Facilities Design; Restaurant Kitchen; Purchasing & Cost Control.

FACULTY: 7 full-time, 10 part-time, all with industry experience.

COSTS: $360/cr-hr. Admission requirements: HS diploma or GED. Personal or phone interview. Scholarships: yes. Loans: yes.

CONTACT: Janis Anton, Director of Admissions, The Illinois Institute of Art Chicago-Culinary Arts, 180 N. Wabash, Chicago, IL 60601; 800-351-3450, 312-280-3500, Fax 312-364-9451, E-mail antonj@aii.edu, URL http://www.ilic.artinstitutes.edu.

THE INSTITUTE OF CULINARY ARTS AT ROBERT MORRIS COLLEGE
Aurora/Year-round

Sponsor: Private college. Program: AAS degree in Culinary Arts, BBA degree in Hospitality mgmt. Established: 2003. Accredited by NCA. Calendar: quarter. Curriculum: culinary, core. Admission dates: Jul, Sep, Feb. Total enrollment: 60. 60 each admission period. 90% of applicants accepted. 90% receive financial aid. Student to teacher ratio 18:1. Facilities: Newly constructed, modern facilities.

FACULTY: 2 full- & 4 part-time faculty, AAS in Culinary, Bachelors in related field.

Costs: $4,550/qtr. Admission requirements: 2.0 HS GPA or GED. Scholarships: yes. Loans: yes.

Contact: Nancy Rotunno, Director, The Institute of Culinary Arts at Robert Morris College, DuPage Campus, 905 Meridian Lake Dr., Aurora, IL 60504; 877-Cook RMC (877-266-5762), Fax 312-935-6819, E-mail nrotunno@robertmorris.edu, URL http://www.robertmorris.edu/culinary.

JOLIET JUNIOR COLLEGE
Joliet/Year-round

Sponsor: College. Program: 2-yr certificate/AAS degree in Culinary Arts and Baking & Pastry Certificate. 2-yr AAS in Hospitality Mgmt or 3-yr dual AAS degrees in Culinary Arts & Hospitality Mgmt. Established: 1970. Accredited by NCA, ACF. Calendar: semester. Curriculum: culinary. Admission dates: Aug, Jan, May, Jun. Total enrollment: 200. 100 each admission period. 98% of applicants accepted. 40% receive financial aid. 10% enrolled part-time. Student to teacher ratio 16:1. 95% of graduates employed within six months. Facilities: Include 3 kitchens, demo kitchen, 3 classrooms, pastry shop.

Faculty: 7 full-time.

Costs: $50/cr-hr in-state. Admission requirements: HS diploma or equivalent & admission test. Scholarships: yes. Loans: yes.

Contact: Michael McGreal, Department Chair, Joliet Junior College, Culinary Arts/Hotel-Restaurant Mgmt., 1215 Houbolt Ave., Joliet, IL 60431-8938; 815-280-2255, E-mail mmcgreal@jjc.edu, URL http://www.jjc.edu.

KENDALL COLLEGE, THE SCHOOL OF CULINARY ARTS
Evanston/Year-round   *(See also page 202) (See display ad page 49)*

Sponsor: Private college. Program: 4-yr BA degrees in Culinary Arts, Culinary mgmt, & Food & Beverage mgmt; 5- & 6-term AAS degrees in Culinary Arts; 6-term AAS degree in Baking & Pastry Arts; 24 qtr-hr certificates in Baking & Pastry, Professional Catering, Professional Personal Chef, & P. Established: 1985. Accredited by NCA, ACF, Illinois Board of Higher Education. Calendar: quarter. Curriculum: culinary, core. Admission dates: Rolling. Total enrollment: ~350. 75-90 each admission period. 85% of applicants accepted. 87% receive financial aid. 30% enrolled part-time. Student to teacher ratio 15:1. 99% of graduates employed within six months. Facilities: Up to 20 industry-current kitchens. Courses: Include fundamental & advanced culinary skills. Business mgmt courses include Menu & Facilities Planning, Dining Room Service, Professional Ethics. **FACULTY:** 18 full-time.

COSTS: Culinary Arts $6,120/term, $24,4800/yr (4 qtrs). Admission requirements: 2.0 GPA or above, 18 ACT or above. Scholarships: yes. Loans: yes.

CONTACT: Office of Admissions, Kendall College, The School of Culinary Arts, 900 N. North Branch St., Chicago, IL 60622; 877-588-8860, Fax 312-752-2021, E-mail admissions@kendall.edu, URL http://www.kendall.edu.

LEXINGTON COLLEGE
Chicago/August-May

Sponsor: Private, 4-yr college for women. Program: 129 cr-hr BAS degree & 66 cr-hr AAS degree in Hospitality Mgmt. Established: 1977. Accredited by NCA. Calendar: semester. Curriculum: culinary, core. Admission dates: Aug, Jan. Total enrollment: 45. 20 each admission period. 85% of applicants accepted. 90% receive financial aid. 10% enrolled part-time. Student to teacher ratio 8:1. 95% of graduates employed within six months. Facilities: Include culinary & demo labs,classrooms, library, computer lab, bookstore, student commons. **FACULTY:** 4 full-time, 12 part-time.

COSTS: $7,245/sem; books, fees, equipment $875/sem; culinary lab fees $132/sem. Admission requirements: HS diploma or equivalent, ACT or SAT, letter of recommendation, essay. Transfers: transcripts, letter of recommendation, essay. Scholarships: yes. Loans: yes.

CONTACT: Giselle Castillo, Director of Admissions, Lexington College, 310 S. Peoria St., Chicago, IL 60607; 312-226-6294, Fax 312-226-6405, E-mail adm@lexingtoncollege.edu, URL http://www.lexingtoncollege.edu.

LINCOLN LAND COMMUNITY COLLEGE
Springfield/Year-round   .

Sponsor: Community college. Program: 2-yr diploma, 1-yr certificate, specialty classes. Established: 1994. Accredited by NCA, Pro-Management National Restaurant Assn., Dietary Manager Assn. Calendar: semester. Curriculum: culinary, core. Admission dates: yr-round. Total enrollment: 50. 50 each admission period. 100% of applicants accepted. 35% receive financial aid. 50% enrolled part-time. Student to teacher ratio 15:1. 100% of graduates employed within six months. Facilities: Training kitchen. **FACULTY:** 12 instructors, 6 certified by the ACF, 1 instructor MSRD.

COSTS: $52/cr-hr. Scholarships: yes. Loans: yes.

CONTACT: Jay Kitterman, Director, Hospitality Management, Lincoln Land Community College, Hospitality Management, 5250 Shepherd Rd., Springfield, IL 62794; 217-786-2772, Fax 217-786-2495, E-mail jay.kitterman@llcc.cc.il.us, URL http://www.llcc.cc.il.us.

MORAINE VALLEY COMMUNITY COLLEGE
Palos Hills/Year-round

Sponsor: Community college. Program: Certificate programs in Culinary Arts mgmt, Baking/Pastry Arts, Beverage mgmt, and Restaurant/Hotel mgmt. AAS degree programs in

Culinary Arts mgmt and Restaurant/Hotel mgmt. Established: 1967. Calendar: semester. Curriculum: culinary, core. **Costs:** In-district (out-of-district, out-of-state) $44 ($179, $204)/cr-hr. Scholarships: yes. Loans: yes. **Contact:** Anne Jachim, Moraine Valley Community College, 10900 S. 88th Ave., Palos Hills, IL 60465; 708-974-5320, Fax 708-974-1184, E-mail jachim@morainevalley.edu, URL http://www.morainevalley.edu/hospitality.

REND LAKE COLLEGE
Ina/Year-round
Sponsor: College. Program: One-yr/32 cr-hr occupational certificate in Culinary Arts mgmt. Calendar: semester. Curriculum: culinary. **Costs:** In-district $36/cr-hr, out-of-district $124/cr-hr, out-of-state $160/cr-hr. **Contact:** Eddie Billinglsey, Dept. Chair / AAA, Rend Lake College, 468 N. Ken Gray Pkwy., Ina, IL 62846; 618-437-5321 x 260/800-369-5321 x260, Fax 618-437-5677, E-mail billingsley@rlc.cc.il.us, URL http://www.rlc.cc.il.us.

TRITON COLLEGE
River Grove/Year-round
Sponsor: College. Program: 2-yr AAS degree in Culinary mgmt, AAS degree in Hotel mgmt. Established: 1970. Accredited by NCA. Calendar: semester. Curriculum: culinary, core. Admission dates: Aug, Jan. Total enrollment: 150. 30 each admission period. 90% of applicants accepted. 20% receive financial aid. 30% enrolled part-time. Student to teacher ratio 12:1. 97% of graduates employed within six months. Facilities: 2 kitchens & classrooms, demonstration kitchen, ice carving facility, & student-run restaurant. **Faculty:** 3 full-time, 10 part-time. **Costs:** $43/cr-hr in-district, $128.25/cr-hr out-of-district. Application fee $25. Other fees approximately $100/sem. Housing $300/mo. Admission requirements: HS diploma or equivalent. Scholarships: yes. Loans: yes. **Contact:** Jerome J. Drosos, Coordinator, Triton College, Hospitality Industry Administration, 2000 Fifth Ave., River Grove, IL 60171; 708-456-0300 #3624, Fax 708-583-3108, E-mail jdrosos@triton.cc.il.us, URL http://www.triton.cc.il.us.

WASHBURNE CULINARY INSTITUTE
Chicago/Year-round
Sponsor: City colleges of Chicago. Program: 80-wk certificate in Chef Training. Established: 1937. Accredited by City Colleges of Chicago. Curriculum: culinary. Admission dates: Sep, Jan, May. Total enrollment: 150. 25 each admission period. 100% of applicants accepted. 75% receive financial aid. Student to teacher ratio 21:1. 98% of graduates employed within six months. Facilities: 6 kitchens, 6 classrooms. **Faculty:** 7 full-time. **Costs:** Annual tuition of $4,600 includes cutlery, books, & uniforms. Admission requirements: HS diploma or equivalent and admission test. Scholarships: yes. **Contact:** Dean Jaramillo, Department Program Director, Washburne Culinary Institute, Chef Training Program, 6800 S. Wentworth Ave., Chicago, IL 60621; 773-602-5487, Fax 773-602-5452, URL http://www.ccc.edu/washburne.

WILLIAM RAINEY HARPER COLLEGE
Palatine/August-May
Sponsor: Community college. Program: 1-yr certificates in Culinary Arts, Baking, Hotel mgmt, & Restaurant mgmt. 2-yr AAS degree in Hospitality mgmt. Established: 1970. Accredited by NCA. Calendar: semester. Curriculum: culinary, core. Admission dates: Yr-round; sems begin Aug, Jan, Jun. Total enrollment: 180. 60 each admission period. 95% of applicants accepted. 60% receive

financial aid. 65% enrolled part-time. Student to teacher ratio 15:1. 100% of graduates employed within six months. Facilities: 3 kitchens including a production bakery & production kitchen, demo lab, dedicated classrooms. **FACULTY:** 2 full-time, 10 part-time. Certified chefs & bakers, most with a master's degree. **COSTS:** $67/cr in-district (+ $5.25/hr), $280/cr out-of-district; application fee $25, $50 fee/lab class, books $60/class. Housing ~$500-$800/mo. Admission requirements: Open admissions, assesment testing required for full-time students & students taking math classes. Scholarships: yes. Loans: yes. **CONTACT:** Michael Held, Director of Admissions, William Rainey Harper College, 1200 W. Algonquin Rd., Palatine, IL 60067-7398; 847-925-6506, Fax 847-925-6044, E-mail pbeach@harpercollege.edu, URL http://www.harpercollege.edu/catalog/2000/career/hosp/index.htm.

WILTON SCHOOL OF CAKE DECORATING
Woodridge/Year-round
Sponsor: Private school. Program: Career-oriented 1- to 10-day cake decoration & candy making diploma courses. Established: 1929. Admission dates: Open. Total enrollment: 350. 20/class max each admission period. 100% of applicants accepted. Student to teacher ratio 15:1. Facilities: The 2,200-sq-ft school includes a classroom, teaching kitchen, student lounge, & retail store. **FACULTY:** 2 full-time, 10 part-time instructors with 2-23 yrs teaching experience. **COSTS:** From $80 for 1 day to $775 for a 10-day course. **CONTACT:** School Coordinator, Wilton School of Cake Decorating and Confectionery Art, 2240 W. 75th St., Woodridge, IL 60517; 630-810-2211, Fax 630-810-2710, E-mail cweeditz@wilton.com, URL http://www.wilton.com.

INDIANA

ACF SOUTH BEND CHEFS & COOKS ASSOCIATION
Notre Dame/Year-round
Sponsor: ACF chapter. Program: 3-yr apprenticeship; degree program through Ivy Tech State College. Established: 1992. Calendar: semester. Curriculum: culinary, core. Admission dates: Jan through Dec. Total enrollment: 12. 24 each admission period. 90% of applicants accepted. Student to teacher ratio 1:12. 100% of graduates employed within 6 mos. Facilities: Full service kitchens. **COSTS:** $4,446/3 yrs (6,000 hrs). Beginning salary is $8.50/hr with 8% increases every 1,000 hrs. add'l $1,780 for AOS degree. Admission requirements: College placement test, references, hand written essay, interview. Scholarships: yes. Loans: yes. **CONTACT:** Denis F. Ellis, CEC, AAC, ACF South Bend Chapter, 1043 University of Notre Dame, 213 South Dining Hall, Notre Dame, IN 46556-1043; 219-631-5416, Fax 219-631-7994, E-mail denis.f.ellis.1@nd.edu.

IVY TECH STATE COLLEGE
East Chicago, Gary, Valparaiso, Michigan City/Year-round
Sponsor: Public state 2-yr college. Program: 2-yr AAS degree & 1-yr technical certificate in Hospitality Administration. Established: 1981. Accredited by NCA, ACF. Calendar: semester. Curriculum: culinary, core. Admission dates: OpenrRolling. Total enrollment: 100. 15 each admission period. 90% of applicants accepted. 50% receive financial aid. 30% enrolled part-time. Student to teacher ratio 12:1. 100% of graduates employed within six months. Facilities: Include full kitchen at 3 locations, catering facilities, restaurant, bakeshop. **FACULTY:** 2 full-time, 7 part-time. **COSTS:** $73.80/cr-hr in-state, $148.75/cr-hr out-of-state. Admission requirements: HS diploma or equivalent. Scholarships: yes. Loans: yes. **CONTACT:** Bob Forster, Ivy Tech State College, Hotel & Restaurant Mgmt./Culinary Arts, 1440 E. 35th Ave., Gary, IN 46409; 219-981-1111, Fax 219-981-4415, E-mail rforster@ivytech.edu, URL http://www.gary.ivytech.edu.

IVY TECH STATE COLLEGE
Fort Wayne/Year-round

Sponsor: College. Program: 2-yr AAS degree in Hospitality Administration with Culinary Arts or Pastry Arts Specialty. Established: 1981. Accredited by NCA, ACF. Calendar: semester. Curriculum: culinary. Admission dates: Yr-round. Total enrollment: 140. 75 each admission period. 100% of applicants accepted. 75% receive financial aid. 42% enrolled part-time. Student to teacher ratio 10-12:1. 100% of graduates employed within six months. Facilities: Include 5 kitchens & classrooms, pastry arts lab, large full service kitchen.

FACULTY: 2 full-time, 12 part-time.

COSTS: Annual tuition $1,835 in-state, $3,335 out-of-state. Admission requirements: HS diploma or equivalent & admission test. Scholarships: yes. Loans: yes.

CONTACT: Alan Eyler, CCE, CFBE, Program Chair, Ivy Tech State College, Hospitality Administration, 3800 N. Anthony Blvd., Fort Wayne, IN 46805; 219-480-4240, Fax 219-480-4171, E-mail aeyler@ivy.tec.in.us, URL http://www.ivytech.edu/catalog/hospitality.pdf.

IVY TECH STATE COLLEGE
Indianapolis/Year-round

Sponsor: College. Program: 2-yr AAS degree in Culinary Arts, Baking & Pastry Arts, & Hotel Restaurant mgmt, Certification Dietary mgmt. Established: 1986. Accredited by NCA, ACF, CAHM, DMA, RBA. Calendar: semester. Admission dates: Aug, Jan, May. Total enrollment: 225. 60 each admission period. 100% of applicants accepted. 75% receive financial aid. 50% enrolled part-time. Student to teacher ratio 10:1. 100% of graduates employed within six months. Facilities: 2 kitchens, classrooms, cafeteria.

FACULTY: 3 full-time, 15 part-time.

COSTS: Annual tuition $3,000 in-state, $4,650 out-of-state. Housing $300/mo. Admission requirements: HS diploma or equivalent & admission test. Scholarships: yes. Loans: yes.

CONTACT: Chef Vincent Kinkade, Chair, Ivy Tech State College, Hospitality Administration, One W. 26th St., Indianapolis, IN 46208; 317-921-4619, Fax 317-921-4753, E-mail vkinkade@ivy.tec.in.us, URL http://www.ivytech.edu.

VINCENNES UNIVERSITY
Vincennes/August-May

Sponsor: Public institution. Program: 2-yr AS degree in Culinary Arts. Established: 1983. Accredited by NCA. Calendar: semester. Curriculum: culinary, core. Admission dates: Open. Total enrollment: 60. 30+ each admission period. 100% of applicants accepted. 90% receive financial aid. 5% enrolled part-time. Student to teacher ratio 12:1. 100% of graduates employed within six months. Facilities: Include kitchen, 3 classrooms, hands-on lab & restaurant.

FACULTY: 2 full-time, 1 part-time.

COSTS: Annual tuition $2,000 in-state, $5,200 out-of-state. Application fee $20. Student activities fee $18. Admission requirements: HS diploma or equivalent. Scholarships: yes. Loans: yes.

CONTACT: Phyllis Richardson, Vincennes University, Culinary Arts, Hoosier Hospitality Center, Vincennes, IN 47591; 812-888-5741, Fax 812-888-4586, E-mail prichardson@indian.vinu.edu, URL http://www.vinu.edu/factsheets.asp?ctid=188.

IOWA

CHEF DE CUISINE/QUAD CITIES
Bettendorf/Year-round

Sponsor: ACF chapter. Program: 3-yr apprenticeship; degree program through Scott Community College. Curriculum: culinary. Total enrollment: 25.

COSTS: $4,500 for 3 yrs. Beginning salary is $5/hr with 25 cent increases every 6 mos.

CONTACT: Jennifer Cook-DeRosa, Culinary Arts/Apprenticeship Facilitator, ACF Chef de Cuisine/Quad Cities, Scott Community College, 500 Belmont Rd., Bettendorf, IA 52722; 319-359-7531 #278.

DES MOINES AREA COMMUNITY COLLEGE
Ankeny/Year-round
Sponsor: College. Program: 2-yr AAS degree in Culinary Arts. Established: 1975. Accredited by NCA, ACF. Calendar: semester. Curriculum: culinary, core. Admission dates: Fall, spring. Total enrollment: 100. 50 each admission period. 100% of applicants accepted. 60% receive financial aid. 25% enrolled part-time. Student to teacher ratio 15:1. 90% of graduates employed within six months. Facilities: Include 2 kitchens, demonstration lab, several classrooms & restaurant.
FACULTY: 3 full-time, ACF-certified.
COSTS: $59.40/cr-hr in-state, $112.40/cr-hr out-of-state. Application fee $10. Housing ~$300/mo. Admission requirements: HS diploma or equivalent and admission test.
CONTACT: Robert Anderson, Program Chair, Des Moines Area Community College, Culinary Arts, 2006 S. Ankeny Blvd., #7, Ankeny, IA 50021; 515-964-6532, Fax 515-965-7129, E-mail RLAnderson@dmacc.cc.ia.us, URL http://www.dmacc.cc.ia.us.

INDIAN HILLS COMMUNITY COLLEGE
Ottumwa/Year-round
Sponsor: 2-yr college. Program: 18-mo AAS in Culinary Arts, 9-mo diploma in Culinary/Baking Assistant. Established: 1969. Accredited by NCA. Calendar: semester. Curriculum: culinary. Admission dates: Fall, spring. Total enrollment: 35. 15-20 each admission period. 100% of applicants accepted. 85% receive financial aid. Student to teacher ratio 12:1. 97% of graduates employed within 6 mos. Facilities: 2 kitchens, fully equiped bakery lab, 3 classrooms, student-run dining room.
FACULTY: 2 full-time.
COSTS: $57/cr-hr in-state, $82/cr-hr out-of-state. On-campus housing: 472 spaces. Housing $350/mo. Admission requirements: HS diploma or equivalent and admission test. Scholarships: yes.
CONTACT: Mary Kivlahan, Program Director, Indian Hills Community College, Culinary Arts Dept, 525 Grandview, Bldg. #7, Ottumwa, IA 52501; 515-683-5196, Fax 515-683-5184, E-mail jsapp@ihcc.cc.ia.us, URL http://www.ihcc.cc.ia.us.

IOWA LAKES COMMUNITY COLLEGE
Emmetsburg/Year-round
Sponsor: College. Program: 2-yr AAS degree in Culinary Arts and/or Hotel, Motel, Restaurant Mgmt. Established: 1974. Accredited by NCA, NRA, AHLA, DMA. Calendar: semester. Curriculum: core. Admission dates: Sep, Jan. Total enrollment: 30-40. 95% of applicants accepted. 70% receive financial aid. Student to teacher ratio 10-12:1. 95% of graduates employed within six months. Facilities: 3 kitchens, 3 classrooms, 1 restaurant, 1 banquet facility.
COSTS: Annual tuition $5,000 in-state, $3,500 out-of-state. Dormitory spaces available on campus. Admission requirements: HS diploma or equivalent & admission test. Scholarships: yes. Loans: yes.
CONTACT: Robert Halverson, Professor/Coordinator, Iowa Lakes Community College, So. Attendance Ctr., Culinary Arts, 3200 College Dr., Emmetsburg, IA 50536; 712-852-5256, Fax 712-852-2152, E-mail rhalverson@iowalakes.edu, URL http://www.ilcc.cc.ia.us/programs_study/business/hotel_restaurant.htm.

IOWA WESTERN COMMUNITY COLLEGE
Council Bluffs/August-May
Sponsor: College. Program: 2-yr AAS degree in Culinary Arts. Established: 1974. Accredited by NCA, ACF. Admission dates: Fall, spring. Total enrollment: 30-40. 10-20 each admission period. 95% of applicants accepted. 80% receive financial aid. 1% enrolled part-time. Student to teacher ratio 10-12:1. 95% of graduates employed within six months. Facilities: Include kitchen & 2 classrooms.

FACULTY: 2 full-time, 3 part-time.

COSTS: In-state $58/cr-hr, out-of-state $81/cr-hr. Room and board $1,500-$2,000/sem. Admission requirements: HS diploma or equivalent and admission test. Scholarships: yes.

CONTACT: Robert Graunke, Professor, Iowa Western Community College, Food Service Mgmt./Culinary Arts, 2700 College Rd., Box 4-C, Council Bluffs, IA 51502; 712-325-3238/712-325-3398, Fax 712-325-3335, E-mail bgraunke@iwcc.edu, URL http://iwcc.cc.ia.us.

KIRKWOOD COMMUNITY COLLEGE
Cedar Rapids/August-April

Sponsor: 2-yr community college. Program: 1-yr Bakery certificate, 2-yr AAS degrees in Culinary Arts & Restaurant mgmt, 1-yr Food Service Training Diploma. Established: 1972. Accredited by NCA, ACF. Calendar: semester. Curriculum: culinary, core. Admission dates: Fall, spring. Bakery admission in fall only. Total enrollment: 190. 64/fall, 32/spring each admission period. 100% of applicants accepted. 60-70% receive financial aid. 25% enrolled part-time. Student to teacher ratio 16:1. 95% of graduates employed within six months. Facilities: Includes 1 kitchen with 2 food labs & a bakery lab, 4 classrooms, restaurant.

FACULTY: 5 full-time, 2 part-time. Qualifications: college degrees & industry experience.

COSTS: In-state $78/cr-hr, out-of-state $156/cr-hr. Housing ~$325-$425/mo. Admission requirements: HS diploma or equivalent, placement test, program conference. Scholarships: yes. Loans: yes.

CONTACT: Mary Jane German, Asst. Professor/Coordinator, Kirkwood Community College, 6301 Kirkwood Blvd. S.W., PO Box 2068, Cedar Rapids, IA 52406; 319-398-4981, Fax 319-398-5667, E-mail mgerman@kirkwood.cc.ia.us, URL http://www.kirkwood.edu/businessdept/programs/culinar.htm.

SCOTT COMMUNITY COLLEGE
Bettendorf/Year-round

Sponsor: College. Program: 3-yr AAS degree & 6,000-hour apprenticeship in sanitation & cook certification from ACF. Established: 1991. Admission dates: Fall. Total enrollment: 30. 10-15 each admission period. 60% of applicants accepted. 75% receive financial aid. 5% enrolled part-time. Student to teacher ratio 10:1. 100% of graduates employed within six months.

FACULTY: 1 full-time, 8 part-time.

COSTS: $58.50/cr-hr in-state. Other costs: application fee $25, books, uniform, knives, ACFEI registration $650 (one-time). Housing $300-$400/mo. Admission requirements: Admission test.

CONTACT: Bradley Scott, Scott Community College, Culinary Arts, 500 Belmont Rd., Bettendorf, IA 52722-6804; 563-441-4246, Fax 563-344-0384, E-mail bscott@eicc.edu, URL http://www.eicc.edu.

KANSAS

AMERICAN INSTITUTE OF BAKING
Manhattan/Year-round

Sponsor: Nonprofit educational & research institution. Program: 20-wk Baking Science & Technology course, 10-wk Bakery Maintenance Engineering program. Established: 1919. Accredited by NCA. Calendar: semester. Curriculum: culinary. Admission dates: Jul & Feb. ~55-60 each admission period. 90% of applicants accepted. 25% receive financial aid. Student to teacher ratio 15:1. 95% of graduates employed within six months. Facilities: Bread shop with 1,500 loaves/hr capacity oven, cake shop with carbon dioxide freezer, in-store bakery, cookie & cracker pilot plant.

FACULTY: 7 full-time.

COSTS: 20-wk program is $5,000+. Registration fee is $45. Admission requirements: HS diploma or equivalent & min 2 yrs bakery experience (or completion of Science of Bakingcorrespondence course). Scholarships: yes. Loans: yes.

CONTACT: Ken Embers, Registrar, American Institute of Baking, 1213 Bakers Way, Manhattan, KS 66505-399; 800-633-5137/785-537-4750, Fax 913-537-1493, E-mail info@aibonline.org, URL http://www.aibonline.org.

JOHNSON COUNTY COMMUNITY COLLEGE
Overland Park/Year-round

Sponsor: College. Program: 2- to 3-yr AOS degree. Established: 1975. Accredited by NCA, ACF. Calendar: semester. Admission dates: Jul, Nov. Total enrollment: 500. 140 each admission period. 80% of applicants accepted. 100% enrolled part-time. Student to teacher ratio 20:1. 100% of graduates employed within six months.
FACULTY: 10 full-time.

COSTS: Annual tuition $1,700 in-state, $5,100 out-of-state. Housing $500/mo. Admission requirements: HS diploma or equivalent and admission test. Scholarships: yes. Loans: yes.

CONTACT: Lindy Robinson, Academic Director, Johnson County Community College, 12345 College Blvd, Overland Park, KS 66210-1299; 913-469-8500, Fax 913-469-2560, E-mail lrobinsn@jccc.net, URL http://www.jccc.net/cat/courses/hmgt.htm.

KANSAS CITY KANSAS AREA VOCATIONAL TECHNICAL SCHOOL
Kansas City/August-May

Sponsor: Public institution. Program: 720-hour certificate in Professional Cooking, certificate in Cooking & Baking. Established: 1975. Accredited by State. Calendar: quarter. Curriculum: culinary. Admission dates: Open. Total enrollment: 20. 99% of applicants accepted. 60% receive financial aid. 50% enrolled part-time. Student to teacher ratio 5:1. 88% of graduates employed within 6 mos. Facilities: Include working kitchen, classroom, cafeteria, child care center, banquet facilities.
FACULTY: 4 full-time.

COSTS: Annual tuition $780. Application fee $25. Other fees: $50. Admission requirements: Admission test.

CONTACT: Matt Miller, Program Director, Kansas City Kansas Area Vocational Technical School, 2220 W. 59th St., Kansas City, KS 66104; 913-627-4149, Fax 913-627-4109, E-mail mamille@gw.kckps.k12.ks.us, URL http://www.kckats.com.

NORTHEAST KANSAS AREA VOCATIONAL TECHNICAL SCHOOL
Atchison/August-May

Sponsor: Trade & technical college. Program: 2-yr (67 credit) diploma & AAS degree (83-85 credits) in Food and Beverage mgmt. Established: 1969. Accredited by State. Admission dates: Open. Total enrollment: 12. 90% receive financial aid. 30% enrolled part-time. Student to teacher ratio 15:1. 100% of graduates employed within six months. Facilities: Include student-run kitchen facility, off site catering.
FACULTY: 1 full-time.

COSTS: ~$945/sem.

CONTACT: Marianne Estes, Northeast Kansas Area Vocational Technical School, 1501 West Riley, Atchison, KS 66002; 913-367-6204, Fax 913-367-3107, E-mail mestes@nekatech.net, URL http://www.nektc.net/op_fabm.html.

KENTUCKY

BOWLING GREEN TECHNICAL COLLEGE
Bowling Green/Year-round

Sponsor: Career institution. Program: 2-yr AAT degree in Culinary Arts. Certificate in Catering and diplomas in Professional Baking and Kitchen mgmt available. Established: 1998. Accredited by COE. Calendar: semester. Curriculum: culinary, core. Admission dates: Jan, May, Aug. Total enrollment: 15. 5 each admission period. 100% of applicants accepted. 80% receive financial aid. 4% enrolled part-time. Student to teacher ratio 7:1. Facilities: Include commercial kitchen, banquet facilities, dining room, & classroom.

FACULTY: Two full-time.

COSTS: $760 per sem. Admission requirements: 18 ACT, HS diploma or equivalent. 16 ACT, HS diploma or equivalent for certificate and diploma programs. Scholarships: yes. Loans: yes.

CONTACT: Lisa Hunt or Mike Riggs, Senior Instructors, Bowling Green Technical College, 1845 Loop Drive, Bowling Green, KY 42101; 270-746-7461, E-mail lisaa.hunt@kctcs.net, URL http://www.bgtc.net.

ELIZABETHTOWN TECHNICAL COLLEGE
Elizabethtown/August-May

Sponsor: Public institution (formerly Kentucky Tech Elizabethtown). Program: 1-yr Restaurant Cook diploma, 18-mo Kitchen Supervisor & Food Service Healthcare diploma,2-yr AAS degree. Established: 1966. Accredited by COE. Calendar: semester. Curriculum: culinary, core. Admission dates: Aug, Jan, Jun. Total enrollment: 18. 18 each admission period. 95% of applicants accepted. 60% receive financial aid. Student to teacher ratio 10:1. 95% of graduates employed within six months. Facilities: Kitchen, classroom & restaurant.

FACULTY: 1 full-time (Brenda Harrington, CCE), 2 part-time.

COSTS: $725/sem in-state, $2,175/sem out-of-state plus books & uniforms. Housing ~$2500. Admission requirements: HS diploma or equivalent and admission test. Scholarships: yes.

CONTACT: Brenda Harrington, Instructor, Elizabethtown Technical College, Culinary Arts, 505 University Dr., Elizabethtown, KY 42701; 270-766-5133 x3128, Fax 270-766-5224, E-mail brenda.harrington@kctcs.net.

JEFFERSON COMMUNITY COLLEGE
Louisville/August-May

Sponsor: 2-yr college. Program: 2-yr AAS degree. Certificate option (no general ed requirements). Established: 1974. Accredited by ACF, SACS. Calendar: semester. Curriculum: culinary, core. Admission dates: Apr, May, Aug, Dec, Jan. Total enrollment: 86. 22 each admission period. 90% of applicants accepted. 80% receive financial aid. 40% enrolled part-time. Student to teacher ratio 11:1. 96% of graduates employed within six months. Facilities: Commercial kitchen with new equipment installed 2000. Teaching lab, kitchen, executive dining room, library, computer labs, research learning center, classrooms.

FACULTY: 2 full-time, 2 part-time.

COSTS: Annual tuition $1,450 in-state, $4,350 out-of-state. Admission requirements: HS diploma or equivalent and admission test. Scholarships: yes. Loans: yes.

CONTACT: Gail Crawford, Program Coordinator, Jefferson Community College, Downtown Campus, 109 E. Broadway, Louisville, KY 40202; E-mail gail.crawford@kctcs.net.

KENTUCKY TECH-DAVIESS COUNTY CAMPUS
Owensboro/August-June

Sponsor: Independent institution. Program: 4- to 5-sem certificate/diploma in Culinary Arts. Established: 1971. Accredited by SACS. Calendar: semester. Curriculum: culinary. Admission dates: Aug. Total enrollment: 24. 2-6 each admission period. 100% of applicants accepted. 90% receive financial aid. 50% enrolled part-time. Student to teacher ratio 18:1. 85% of graduates employed within six months. Facilities: Include kitchen & classroom.

FACULTY: One full-time, Dudley Mitchell.

COSTS: $175/qtr. Application fee $25. Admission requirements: TABE test, HS diploma or equivalent. Scholarships: yes. Loans: yes.

CONTACT: Kaye Evans, Counselor, Kentucky Tech-Daviess County Campus, Student Services, 15th and Frederica St., Owensboro, KY 42301; 502-687-7260, Fax 502-687-7208, E-mail kay.evans@kctcs.net.

SULLIVAN UNIVERSITY'S NATIONAL CENTER FOR HOSPITALITY STUDIES
Louisville/Year-round *(See display ad page 58)*

Sponsor: Division of Sullivan University. Program: 18-mo AS degree programs in Culinary Arts, Baking & Pastry Arts, Hotel/Restaurant Mgmt, &Professional Catering; 36-mo BS/BA in Hospitality Studies; 9-12 mo diplomas in Professional Cooking & Professional Baking. Established: 1987. Accredited by SACS, ACF. Calendar: quarter. Curriculum: culinary, core. Admission dates: Jan, Mar, Jun, Sep. Total enrollment: 700. 50-250 each admission period. 85% of applicants accepted. 93% receive financial aid. 20% enrolled part-time. Student to teacher ratio 18:1. 100% of graduates employed within six months. Facilities: A la carte cafe, 5 bakery labs, 2 garde manger, 2 basic skills labs, catering, computer labs, retail bakery, fine dining restaurant, catering company. Courses: Include theory & skills, regional & intl cuisine & pastry, business mgmt, sanitation, nutrition & meal planning, menu design. Students in each program also participate in a related practicum.

FACULTY: 26-member resident faculty & 2-member adjunct faculty.

COSTS: Tuition $26,520. Supplies fee $990/qtr. Nearby apartments $410/mo. Admission requirements: HS diploma or equivalent & satisfactory basic test scores. Scholarships: yes. Loans: yes.

CONTACT: Greg Cawthon, Director of Admissions, Sullivan University's National Center for Hospitality Studies, 3101 Bardstown Rd., Louisville, KY 40205; 800-844-1354, 502-456-6505, Fax 502-456-0040, E-mail admissions@sullivan.edu, URL http://www.sullivan.edu.

WEST KENTUCKY TECHNICAL COLLEGE
Paducah/Year-round

Sponsor: Career institution. Program: 18-mo diploma/AAS degree in Culinary Arts; degrees in Food & Beverage Mgmt and Catering; certificates in Culinary Arts, Fundamentals, Catering, Advanced Catering, Beverage Mgmt, Advanced Culinary Arts. Established: 1979. Accredited by SACS. Calendar: semester. Curriculum: culinary, core. Admission dates: Jan, May, Aug. Total enrollment: 36. Student to teacher ratio 20:1. 80% of graduates employed within six months.

FACULTY: 2 full- & part-time instructors.

COSTS: In-state $1,185/sem, out-of-state $3,555. Admission requirements: HS diploma or equivalent & admission test. Scholarships: yes. Loans: yes.

CONTACT: Vicki Koehler, Culinary Arts Director, West Kentucky Technical College, Culinary Arts, 5200 Blandville Rd., Box 7408, Paducah, KY 42002-7408; 502-554-4991 ext 232, Fax 502-554-9754 x221, E-mail vicki.koehler@kctcs.net, URL http://www.westkentucky.kctcs.edu.

LOUISIANA

ACF NEW ORLEANS CHAPTER
New Orleans/Year-round

Sponsor: ACF chapter. Program: 3-yr apprenticeship; degree program through Delgado Community College completed by 90%. Curriculum: culinary. Total enrollment: 190.

COSTS: $3,600. Housing $350-$550/mo.

CONTACT: Dr. M. Bartholomew, ACF New Orleans Chapter, Delgado Community College, 615 City Park Ave., Bldg. 11, New Orleans, LA 70119-4399; 504-483-4208, Fax 504-483-4893, E-mail mbarth@dcc.edu.

BOSSIER PARISH COMMUNITY COLLEGE
Bossier City

Sponsor: College. Program: 9-mo certificate. Established: 1986. Accredited by ACF. Admission dates: Aug. Total enrollment: 25. 98% of applicants accepted. Student to teacher ratio 13:1. 100% of graduates employed within six months.

FACULTY: 2 full-time, 4 part-time.

COSTS: $3,100/yr. Admission requirements: HS diploma or equivalent & admission test.

Scholarships: yes. Loans: yes.

CONTACT: Elizabeth Dickson, Chef/Coordinator, Bossier Parish Community College, Culinary Arts, 2719 Airline Drive North, Bossier City, LA 71111; 318-747-4567, Fax 318-742-8664, E-mail edickson@bpcc.cc.la.us, URL http://www.bpcc.cc.la.us.

CHEF JOHN FOLSE CULINARY INSTITUTE
Thibodaux/Year-round

Sponsor: Regional university. Program: 2-yr AS degree in Culinary Arts, 4-yr BS degree in Culinary Arts. Established: 1994. Accredited by SACS. Calendar: semester. Curriculum: culinary, core. Admission dates: Rolling. Total enrollment: 200. 40-50 each admission period. 90% of applicants accepted. 44% receive financial aid. 14% enrolled part-time. Student to teacher ratio 15:1. 100% of graduates employed within six months. Facilities: 2 newly-equipped teaching kitchens, 2 demo classrooms.

FACULTY: 5 full- & 1 part-time.

COSTS: $1,184/sem in-state, $3,752/sem out-of-state. Add'l fees & equipment $650 + $250/lab course. Admission requirements: HS GPA 2.5+ or ACT score of 19 or top 50% of HS class. Scholarships: yes. Loans: yes.

CONTACT: Dr. Robert Harrington, Dean, Chef John Folse Culinary Institute, Nicholls State University, P.O. Box 2099, Thibodaux, LA 70310; 985-449-7100, 877-NICHOLLS, Fax 985-449-7089, E-mail jfci-info@nicholls.edu, URL http://www.nicholls.edu/jfolse.

CULINARY INSTITUTE OF NEW ORLEANS
New Orleans/Year-round

Sponsor: Private school. Program: 900-hr (7-mo) certificate & 1,800-hr (14-mo) diploma/AOS degree in Culinary Arts; 180-hr (6-wk) certificate in Professional Baking. Established: 1984. Accredited by COE. Curriculum: culinary. Admission dates: Continuous. Total enrollment: 250/yr. 18/mo each admission period. 90% of applicants accepted. 82% receive financial aid. Student to teacher ratio 18:1. 100% of graduates employed within six months. Facilities: 3 bake shops, 2 cafeterias, 3 catering services, 3 demo labs, 3 food prodkitchens, 8 classrooms, 3 gourmet dining rooms, 2 public restaurants.

FACULTY: 8 full-time.

COSTS: Certificate (diploma/degree) programs: tuition $9,000 ($18,000), textbooks/clothing/equipment $730 ($1,114), fees $1,550 ($3,025). Scholarships: yes. Loans: yes.

CONTACT: Bob Koehl, Director, Culinary Institute of New Orleans, 2100 St. Charles Ave., #1, New Orleans, LA 70140; 504-525-2433, Fax 504-525-2466, E-mail cino2100@aol.com, URL http://www.ci-no.com.

DELGADO COMMUNITY COLLEGE
New Orleans/Year-round

Sponsor: 2-yr college. Program: 2-yr/6,000-hr Culinary Arts Apprenticeship AAS degree & Pastry Arts certificate. Established: 1926. Accredited by ACF. Calendar: semester. Curriculum: core. Admission dates: Aug. Total enrollment: 200. 75 each admission period. 90% of applicants accepted. 50% receive financial aid. Student to teacher ratio 15:1. 100% of graduates employed within six months. Facilities: 2 labs & 9 lecture rooms.

FACULTY: 4 full-time, all ACF-certified; 2 part-time.

COSTS: $800/sem in-state, $2,000 out-of-state. Admission requirements: GED or HS diploma, 2 reference letters. Scholarships: yes. Loans: yes.

CONTACT: Dr. Mary P. Bartholomew, Culinary Arts Director, Delgado Community College-Culinary Arts Dept., 615 City Park Ave., New Orleans, LA 70119; 504-483-4208, Fax 504-483-4893, E-mail mbarth@dcc.edu, URL http://www.dcc.edu.

LOUISIANA CULINARY INSTITUTE
Baton Rouge/Year-round

Sponsor: Private school. Program: 48-wk (1200-hr) diploma in Professional Cooking & Culinary Arts. Established: 2003. Curriculum: culinary. Admission dates: Feb, May, Aug, Nov. Total enrollment: 25. 15 each admission period. 90% of applicants accepted. Student to teacher ratio 6:1. 100% of graduates employed within six months. Facilities: 7,100-sq-ft facility includes bakery, classrooms, library, food production & teaching kitchens, banquet room, demo lab.

FACULTY: 3 full- & 1 part-time, includes 1 CCP, 50 yrs culinary experience total.

COSTS: $15,000 + $100 registration fee. Admission requirements: HS diploma or GED, placement test, 4 interviews, 3 letters of recommendation.

CONTACT: Whitney Jolliff, Admissions, Louisiana Culinary Institute, 5837 Essen Lane, Baton Rouge, LA 70820; 877-769-8820, Fax 225-769-8792, E-mail admissions@louisianaculinary.com, URL http://www.louisianaculinary.com.

LOUISIANA TECHNICAL COLLEGE – BATON ROUGE
Baton Rouge/Year-round

Sponsor: Public institution. Program: 1-yr diploma/certificate in Culinary Arts. Established: 1974. Calendar: quarter. Curriculum: culinary. Admission dates: yr-round. Total enrollment: 38275. 6 each admission period. 95% of applicants accepted. 45% receive financial aid. 20% enrolled part-time. Student to teacher ratio 12:1. 95% of graduates employed within six months. Facilities: Include 2 kitchens.

FACULTY: 1 full-time. Michael Travasos. Qualifications: bachelor's degree, industry experience.

COSTS: Annual tuition $420. Application fee $9.50. Books, uniforms, equipment $215. Housing $300/mo.

CONTACT: Michael Travasos, Louisiana Technical College-Baton Rouge Campus, Admissions, 3250 N. Acadian Throughway, Baton Rouge, LA 70805; 225-359-9202, Fax 225-359-9296, E-mail mtravasos@brti.tec.la.us, URL http://www.brti.tec.la.us.

LOUISIANA TECHNICAL COLLEGE – LAFAYETTE CAMPUS
Lafayette

Sponsor: Technical college. Program: 18-mo (1800-clock-hr) diploma program in Culinary Arts & Occupations. Established: 1979. Accredited by ACF, COE. Calendar: quarter. Curriculum: culinary. Admission dates: Aug, Nov, Feb-Mar, May. Total enrollment: 45. 20 each admission period. 100% of applicants accepted. 25% receive financial aid. Student to teacher ratio 15:01. 100% of graduates employed within six months.

FACULTY: 3 instructors.

COSTS: $105/qtr. Admission requirements: 16 yrs. of age, interest in culinary field, HS diploma or GED by date of completion of program.

CONTACT: Chef Earline Thomas, Louisiana Technical College, Lafayette Campus, 1101 Bertrand Dr., Lafayette, LA 70506-4909; 318-262-5962, Fax 318-262-5122, E-mail earlinet@lafayette.tec.la.us, URL http://ltcl.lafayette.tec.la.us/diploma/personal/culinary1.html.

LOUISIANA TECHNICAL COLLEGE – SIDNEY N. COLLIER CAMPUS
New Orleans/Year-round

Sponsor: Career institution. Program: 18-mo certificate. Established: 1957. Accredited by SACS. Admission dates: Open. Total enrollment: 20. 100% of applicants accepted. Student to teacher ratio 20:1. 80% of graduates employed within six months.

FACULTY: 30 full-time, 1 part-time.

COSTS: $105/qtr, $630 for program (6 qtrs/18 mos).

CONTACT: Edward James, Instructor, Louisiana Technical College - Sidney N. Collier Campus, Culinary Arts, 3727 Louisa St., New Orleans, LA 70126; 504-942-8333 x147, Fax 504-942-8337, E-mail ejames@theltc.net, URL http://www.angelfire.com/la2/collier.

LOUISIANA TECHNICAL COLLEGE – SLIDELL CAMPUS
Slidell/September-July

Sponsor: Technical College. Program: 14-mo diploma in Culinary Arts & Occupations. Accredited by COE. Calendar: semester. Curriculum: culinary. Total enrollment: 20. 15 each admission period. 100% of applicants accepted. 75% receive financial aid. 10% enrolled part-time. Student to teacher ratio 10:1. 95% of graduates employed within six months. Facilities: Classroom & lab, herb garden, demonstration area, computer lab.

FACULTY: 1 fulltime & 1 adjunct.

COSTS: $336/sem, $300 books, $100 uniforms, $65 ACF Junior dues. Admission requirements: TABE placement test. Scholarships: yes. Loans: yes.

CONTACT: Jan Rost, Chef Instructor, Louisiana Technical College, 1000 Canulette Rd., Slidell, LA 70460; 985-646-6430 x134, Fax 985-646-6442, E-mail queenjanxxii@yahoo.com, URL http://www.theltc.net/slidell.

NUNEZ COMMUNITY COLLEGE
Chalmette/Year-round

Sponsor: 2-yr college. Program: 1-yr/33-cr-hr certificate and 2-yr/68-cr-hr AAS degree in Culinary Arts and Occupations. Calendar: semester. Curriculum: culinary, core.

COSTS: For 12+ cr-hrs: in-state $488, out-of-state $1,523 plus technology fee.

CONTACT: Donna Clark, Nunez Community College-Culinary Arts, 3700 LaFontaine St., Chalmette, LA 70043; 504-680-2457, E-mail dclark@nunez.cc.la.us, URL http://www.nunez.cc.la.us.

SCLAFANI'S COOKING SCHOOL, INC.
Metairie/Year-round

Sponsor: Post-secondary proprietary school. Program: 4-wk (120-hr) certificate in commercial cooking/baking. Established: 1987. Accredited by Licensed by Louisiana State Board of Regents. Calendar: quarter. Curriculum: culinary. Admission dates: Moly. Total enrollment: 120. 10-15 each admission period. 90% of applicants accepted. 60% receive financial aid. Student to teacher ratio 10:1. 98% of graduates employed within six months. Facilities: Classroom/dining room, commercial kitchen prep room, storage area.

FACULTY: 4 full-time. Includes Frank P. Sclafani, Sr., CEC, FMP; chef Angelique Connors.

COSTS: $2,995 total. Housing $50+/day. Admission requirements: Age 18 +; 7th grade level reading/math.

CONTACT: Frank P. Sclafani, Sr., President, Sclafani's Cooking School, Inc., 107 Gennaro Pl., Metairie, LA 70001-5209; 504-833-7861, 800-583-1282, Fax 504-833-7872, E-mail info@sclafani-cookingschool.com, URL http://www.sclafanicookingschool.com.

MAINE

EASTERN MAINE TECHNICAL COLLEGE
Bangor/Year-round

Sponsor: 2-yr college. Program: 66-hr AAS degree in Culinary Arts, 33-hr Food Service Specialist certificate. Calendar: semester. Curriculum: culinary. Total enrollment: 55. 20% enrolled part-time. Student to teacher ratio 10:1. Facilities: Include food production kitchen, bakeries & bake shop, dining room, computer labs.

FACULTY: 2 full-time, 4 part-time.

COSTS: $1,122/sem in-state, $3,283/sem out-of-state. Scholarships: yes.

CONTACT: Elizabeth Russell, Director of Admissions, Eastern Maine Technical College, Culinary Arts Dept., 354 Hogan Rd., Bangor, ME 04401; 207-941-4680, Fax 207-941-4683, E-mail erussell@emtc.org, URL http://www.emtc.org/Technologies/culinary_arts.

SOUTHERN MAINE COMMUNITY COLLEGE
South Portland/September-May

Sponsor: State-owned institution. Program: 2-yr associate degree in Culinary Arts. Established: 1958. Accredited by NEASC. Calendar: semester. Curriculum: culinary, core. Admission dates: Rolling. Total enrollment: 70. 80 each admission period. 75% of applicants accepted. 65% receive financial aid. 10% enrolled part-time. Student to teacher ratio 16:1. 90% of graduates employed within six months. Facilities: Include 8 kitchens & classrooms, restaurant.

FACULTY: 6 full-time with college degrees &/or ACF certification.

COSTS: In-state $3,100/yr, out-of-state $5,800/yr. On-campus housing: 140 spaces; rm & bd $4,800. Admission requirements: HS diploma or equivalent & admission test. Scholarships: yes. Loans: yes.

CONTACT: Odilia Harmon, Director of Admissions, Southern Maine Community College, 2 Fort Rd., South Portland, ME 04106; 207-741-5802, E-mail oharmon@smccME.edu, URL http://www.smccme.edu/programs/culinaryarts.htm.

YORK COUNTY COMMUNITY COLLEGE
Wells/Year-round

Sponsor: 2-yr college. Program: 68-cr AAS degree in Culinary Arts, 1-yr Food Service Specialist certificate. Established: 1995. Accredited by NEASC. Calendar: semester. Curriculum: core. Admission dates: Sep, Jan, May. Total enrollment: 52. 99% of applicants accepted. 80% receive financial aid. 50% enrolled part-time. Student to teacher ratio 12:1. Facilities: Demo lab, food production & teaching kitchens, computer lab.

FACULTY: 1 full-time, 7 part-time.

COSTS: $2,312/yr in-state, $5,066/yr out-of-state. Program fees $350. Admission requirements: HS or GED completion. Scholarships: yes.

CONTACT: Leisa Collins, Director of Admissions, York County Community College, 112 College Dr., Wells, ME 04090; 207-646-9282, 800-580-3820, Fax 207-641-0837, E-mail lcollins@YCCC.edu, URL http://www.yccc.edu/student_services/courses/culinary.htm.

MARYLAND

ALLEGANY COLLEGE OF MARYLAND
Cumberland/Year-round

Sponsor: 2-yr college. Program: 2-yr AS degree in Culinary Arts. Established: 1998. Curriculum: culinary. Admission dates: Jan, Aug. Total enrollment: 26. 48% enrolled part-time. Student to teacher ratio 10:1. Facilities: Food production kitchen, teaching kitchen, computer lab.

FACULTY: 2 full-time, 5 part-time.

COSTS: $3,060/yr in-state, $5,984/yr out-of-state. Scholarships: yes.

CONTACT: David Sanford II, Allegany College of Maryland, Culinary Arts, 12401 Willowbrook Rd., SE, Cumberland, MD 21502; 301-784-5308, E-mail dsanford@ac.cc.md.us, URL http://www.ac.cc.md.us/careers/hospitality/chef.

ANNE ARUNDEL COMMUNITY COLLEGE
Arnold/Year-round

Sponsor: 2-yr public community college. Program: AAS degree in Chef Apprentice, Pastry Apprentice, Hospitality Mgmt., Culinary; Certificate programs in Hospitality Mgmt., Culinary, Baking & Pastry, Catering. Established: 1988. Accredited by MSA. Calendar: semester. Curriculum: culinary, core. Admission dates: Sep, Jan, May. Total enrollment: 150. 60 each admission period. 100% of applicants accepted. 45% enrolled part-time. Student to teacher ratio 16:1. 90% of graduates employed within six months. Facilities: Modern training facilities & 5 dedicated smart classrooms; 2 campuses.

FACULTY: 4 full-time, 15 part-time.

Costs: $62/cr-hr. Admission requirements: Open enrollment. Apprentice students must submit application, 2 letters of reference, essay, & transcripts. Scholarships: yes. Loans: yes.
Contact: Scott Strong, Director, Anne Arundel Community College, 101 College Pkwy., Arnold, MD 21012; 410-777-2398, Fax 410-777-1143, E-mail wsstrong@aacc.edu, URL http://www.aacc.edu.

BALTIMORE INTERNATIONAL COLLEGE
Baltimore/Year-round   *(See display ad page 65)*

Sponsor: Independent college offering specialized degree & certificate programs through its School of Culinary Arts and School of Hospitality Mgmt. Program: BS in Culinary Mgmt, Culinary Mgmt/Food Mgmt, Hospitality Mgmt, Hospitality Mgmt/Marketing. AAS in Prof. Cooking, Prof. Baking & Pastry, Prof. Cooking & Baking, Food & Beverage Mgmt. Certificate in Culinary Arts. Established: 1972. Accredited by MSA. Calendar: semester. Curriculum: culinary, core. Admission dates: Jan, May, Sep. Total enrollment: 850. 100-270 each admission period. 95% of applicants accepted. 90% receive financial aid. Student to teacher ratio 13:1. 98% of graduates employed within six months. Facilities: Baltimore Campus includes 19 buildings; Virginia Park Campus is an historic, 100-acre campus in County Cavan, Ireland. Courses: Each program builds from a basic foundation to advanced theories, techniques & special projects. Core courses include math, science, English, nutrition, history, & psychology.
Faculty: 45-member faculty with degrees through the doctorate level. European-trained chefs at the campus in Ireland hold credentials from the City & Guilds of London.
Costs: $7,024/sem (15 wks) for degree students, $7,024/sem for certificate students. Student activity fee $101/sem, comprehensive fees $116-$2,870/sem. Admission requirements: HS diploma or equivalent & satisfactory SAT, ACT, or college admissions test score required. Scholarships: yes. Loans: yes.
Contact: Brain Booher, Director of Admissions, Baltimore International College, 17 Commerce St., Baltimore, MD 21202; 800-624-9926 ext 120, 410-752-4710 ext 120, Fax 410-752-3730, E-mail admissions@bic.edu, URL http://www.bic.edu.

INTERNATIONAL SCHOOL OF CONFECTIONERY ARTS, INC.
Gaithersburg/Year-round

Sponsor: Proprietary school. Program: 2-day to 1-wk certificate courses in confectionery arts. Established: 1982. Admission dates: wkly. Total enrollment: 400/yr. 12-16 each admission period. 100% of applicants accepted. 3% receive financial aid. Student to teacher ratio 4:1. 100% of graduates employed within six months. Facilities: 2,400-sq-ft area with 16 individual work stations, overhead mirrors, marble tables, decorating & candy-making equipment.
Faculty: Ewald Notter has won gold medals in intl competitions.
Costs: $275-$950 includes breakfast & lunch. Nearby lodging ~$64/night. Admission requirements: Courses are for professionals & culinary students only.
Contact: Petr Nepozitek, Admissions, International School of Confectionery Arts, Inc., 9209 Gaither Rd., Gaithersburg, MD 20877; 301-963-9077, Fax 301-869-7669, E-mail ESNotter@aol.com, URL http://www.notterschool.com.

L'ACADEMIE DE CUISINE
Gaithersburg/Year-round

Sponsor: Proprietary vocational school. Program: 48-wk full-time Culinary Career Training program, 30-wk full-time Pastry Arts program, part-time professional & certificate courses. Established: 1976. Accredited by ACCET & approved by the Maryland Higher Education Commission. Calendar: semester. Curriculum: culinary. Admission dates: Jan, Mar, Jul, Oct. Total enrollment: 60 culinary, 60 pastry. 30 culinary, 15 pastry each admission period. 85% of applicants accepted. 61% receive financial aid. Student to teacher ratio 15:1. 100% of graduates employed within six months. Facilities: 35-station practice & pastry kitchen & 35-seat demo classroom.
Faculty: 5 full-, 3 part-time. School President Francois Dionot, graduate of L'Ecole Hoteliere de la Societe Suisse des Hoteliers, IACP founder.

Costs: Full-time Culinary Career program $19,420 + $885 fees. Pastry Arts program $12,000 + $600 fees. Certificate course $1,400-$2,645. Continuing ed $1,400-$2,550. Admission requirements: HS diploma or equivalent & 18 yrs of age. Completed application, 2 letters of reference & an interview. Scholarships: yes. Loans: yes.

Contact: Barbara Cullen, Admissions, L'Academie de Cuisine, 16006 Industrial Dr., Gaithersburg, MD 20877-1414; 301-670-8670, 800-664-CHEF, Fax 301-670-0450, E-mail info@lacademie.com, URL http://www.lacademie.com.

MASSACHUSETTS

BERKSHIRE COMMUNITY COLLEGE
Pittsfield

Sponsor: College. Program: 1-yr certificate, 2-yr AAS degree. Established: 1977. Accredited by NEASC. Calendar: semester. Curriculum: culinary, core. Admission dates: Fall, spring. Total enrollment: 15/sem. Facilities: Full kitchen lab, use of local hotel kitchen/dining room for quantity food dinners. **Faculty:** 2 full-time, 2 part-time.

Costs: $88/cr-hr in-state, $105/cr-hr out-of-state. Admission requirements: HS diploma or equivalent and learning skills assessment. Loans: yes.

Contact: Nancy Simonds-Ruderman, Professor of Hotel & Restaurant Management, Berkshire Community College, Culinary Arts, 1350 West St., Pittsfield, MA 01201-5786; 413-499-4660 #229, Fax 413-447-7840, E-mail nruder@cc.berkshire.org, URL http://cc.berkshire.org.

BOSTON UNIVERSITY'S CULINARY ARTS PROGRAM
Boston/Year-round

Sponsor: Boston University. Program: 4-mo certificate in Culinary Arts, Master of Liberal Arts with concentration in Gastronomy, certificates in Wine Studies & Cheese Studies, Personal Chef Certification. Established: 1986. Calendar: semester. Curriculum: culinary. Admission dates: Rolling. Total enrollment: 24. 12 each admission period. 50% of applicants accepted. 20% receive financial aid. Student to teacher ratio 6:1. 100% of graduates employed within six months. Facilities: Demo room with overhead mirror, classroom, 8 restaurant stations in the lab kitchen. **Faculty:** 1 full-time, 30 part-time.

Costs: Culinary certificate tuition $11,500, application fee $50. Admission requirements: Some foodservice experience preferred. Loans: yes.

Contact: Rebecca Alssid, Director, Boston University's Culinary Arts Program, 808 Commonwealth Ave., Boston, MA 02215; 617-353-9852, Fax 617-353-4130, E-mail ralssid@bu.edu, URL http://www.bu.edu/lifelong/culinary.

BRISTOL COMMUNITY COLLEGE
Fall River/September-May

Sponsor: College. Program: 2-yr AAS degree with options in Culinary Arts & Baking/Pastry Arts. Established: 1985. Accredited by NEASC. Calendar: semester. Curriculum: core. Admission dates: Sep/Jan. Total enrollment: 88-100. 44-50 each admission period. 80% of applicants accepted. 70% receive financial aid. 20% enrolled part-time. Student to teacher ratio 6:1. 75% of graduates employed within six months. Facilities: Fully eqipped kitchen, bakeshop, 36-seat dining room with bar, dedicated C/A classroom. **Faculty:** 2 full-time, 2 part-time.

Costs: In-state & R.I. $109/cr, out-of-state $349/cr. Admission requirements: HS diploma or GED, personal interview & assessment testing. Scholarships: yes. Loans: yes.

Contact: John Caressimo, CCE, Culinary Director, Bristol Community College, Culinary Arts, 777 Elsbree St., Fall River, MA 02720; 508-678-2811 #2111, Fax 508-730-3290, E-mail jcaressi@bristol.mass.edu, URL http://www.bristol.mass.edu.

BUNKER HILL COMMUNITY COLLEGE
Boston/Year-round

Sponsor: 2-yr college. Program: 1-yr/29-cr certificate & 2-yr/62-cr AS degree in Culinary Arts. Established: 1979. Calendar: semester. Curriculum: culinary, core. Admission dates: Sep, Jan. Total enrollment: 180. 30-50 each admission period. 100% of applicants accepted. 70% receive financial aid. 10% enrolled part-time. Student to teacher ratio 12:1. 60% of graduates employed within six months. Facilities: New kitchen, bakeshop, POS system, dining room/restaurant, storeroom.

FACULTY: 3 full-time & 2 part-time.

COSTS: MA residents (non-residents) tuition $100/cr ($300/cr), applic. fee $10 ($30). Admission requirements: HS diploma. Scholarships: yes. Loans: yes.

CONTACT: Cheryl Senato, Professor, Bunker Hill Community College, 250 New Rutherford Ave., Boston, MA 02129-2991; 617-228-2336, Fax 617-228-2082, E-mail csenato@bhcc.mass.edu, URL http://www.bhcc.mass.edu/degreeandcetprog/hospitality.htm.

THE CAMBRIDGE SCHOOL OF CULINARY ARTS
Cambridge/Year-round

Sponsor: Proprietary school. Program: 37-wk Professional Chef diploma program, 15 wk certificate program, continuing ed classes, culinary tours to Europe. Established: 1974. Accredited by ACCSCT, licensed by the Commonwealth of Mass. Dept. of Education. Calendar: quarter. Curriculum: culinary. Admission dates: Sep, Jan, May. Total enrollment: 339. 113 each admission period. 90% of applicants accepted. Student to teacher ratio 12-15:1. 90% of graduates employed within six months. Facilities: 3 lecture spaces & adjacent practice kitchens professionally equipped with commercial grade equipment, culinary library.

FACULTY: 6 full- & 5 part-time instructors approved by the Commonwealth of Mass. Dept. of Education. President Roberta Avallone Dowling, CCP, holds diplomas from Julie Dannenbaum, Marcella Hazan, & Madeleine Kamman.

COSTS: 37-wk program $18,300, certificate program $8,500, $45 application fee/program, $300-$1,100 for equipment, books, & fees. Admission requirements: Min. age 18 & have a HS diploma or equivalent. Loans: yes.

CONTACT: Gwenn Legters, Director of Admissions, The Cambridge School of Culinary Arts, 2020 Massachusetts Ave., Cambridge, MA 02140-2104; 617-354-2020, Fax 617-576-1963, E-mail info@cambridgeculinary.com, URL http://www.cambridgeculinary.com.

DELPHIN'S GOURMANDISE SCHOOL OF PASTRY
Marblehead/August-June

Sponsor: Private school. Program: 240-hr (6-mo) part-time Certificate Pastry Program that emphasizes the basics. 1- to 3-day workshops & evening classes. Established: 2000. Accredited by Licensed by state of MA. Calendar: trimester. Curriculum: culinary. Admission dates: Jan-Jun, Aug-Dec. Total enrollment: 24. 6 each admission period. 90% of applicants accepted. 100% enrolled part-time. Student to teacher ratio 6:1. 95% of graduates employed within six months. Facilities: Kitchen/class room.

FACULTY: Master Pastry Chef Delphin Gomes, co-owner of Delphin's Gourmandise Fine French Patisserie.

COSTS: $6,000/certificate, $295-$840/workshop, $85/class. Admission requirements: HS diploma.

CONTACT: Tone Gomes, Program Director, Delphin's Gourmandise School of Pastry, 258 Washington St., Marblehead, MA 01945; 781-639-2311, Fax 781-631-2311, E-mail DGschoolofpastry@aol.com, URL http://www.delphins.com.

EPICUREAN CLUB OF BOSTON
Boston/Year-round

Sponsor: ACF chapter. Program: 3-yr apprenticeship; degree program through Bunker Hill Community College is completed by 60%. Curriculum: culinary. Total enrollment: 5.

Costs: Housing $700+.

Contact: Americo DiFronzo, CEC, Epicurean Club of Boston, 29 Johnson Street, Saugus, MA 01906-1745; 781-231-1115, E-mail DiFronzoA@aol.com, URL http://www.theEpicureanClubofBoston.com.

ESSEX AGRICULTURAL AND TECHNICAL INSTITUTE
Hathorne/September-May

Sponsor: Career institution. Program: 2-yr AAS degree in Culinary Arts & Food Service. Established: 1968. Accredited by NEASC. Calendar: semester. Curriculum: culinary. Admission dates: Sep, Jan. Total enrollment: 65. 40 each admission period. 50% of applicants accepted. 20% receive financial aid. 12% enrolled part-time. Student to teacher ratio 15:1. 60% of graduates employed within six months. Facilities: Include 6 kitchens & classrooms, bakery & restaurant.
Faculty: 4 full-time.
Costs: Annual tuition $2,400. Acceptance fee $30. Other fees approximately $1,830. Admission requirements: HS diploma or equivalent. Scholarships: yes. Loans: yes.
Contact: Admissions Coordinator, Essex Agricultural and Technical Institute, Admissions, 562 Maple St., Box 362, Hathorne, MA 01937-0362; 978-774-0050 #210, Fax 978-774-6530, E-mail admin@agtech.org, URL http://www.agtech.org.

HOLYOKE COMMUNITY COLLEGE
Holyoke/September-May

Sponsor: 2-yr community college. Program: 10-mo certificate in Culinary Arts, AS degree in Hospitality Mgmt. Established: 1991. Accredited by NEASC. Calendar: semester. Curriculum: culinary, core. Admission dates: Sep, Jan. Total enrollment: 50. 50 each admission period. 100% of applicants accepted. 50% receive financial aid. 20% enrolled part-time. Student to teacher ratio 12:1 lab. 90% of graduates employed within 6 mos. Facilities: Include 2 kitchens, bakeshop, dining room.
Faculty: 4 full-time, 4 part-time.
Costs: In-state $2,605/yr, out-of-state $6,275/yr. Fees ~$40. Admission requirements: HS diploma or equivalent, math competency test. Scholarships: yes. Loans: yes.
Contact: Kristine Ricker Choleva, Department Chair, Holyoke Community College, Hospitality Management & Culinary Arts, 303 Homestead Ave., Holyoke, MA 01040; 413-552-2408, Fax 413-534-8975, E-mail kcholeva@hcc.mass.edu, URL http://www.hcc.mass.edu.

INTERNATIONAL INSTITUTE OF CULINARY ARTS
Fall River/September-June
(See display ad page 69)

Sponsor: Private 2-yr culinary institute. Program: 2-yr Grande Diploma in Culinary Arts/Restaurant Hospitality; 1-yr Culinary Certificate program; 1-yr Diploma in Baking/Pastry Arts. Established: 1997. Calendar: semester. Curriculum: culinary, core. Admission dates: Open. Total enrollment: 50. Open each admission period. 61% of applicants accepted. Student to teacher ratio 8:1. 100% of graduates employed within six months. Facilities: Bake shop, 2 catering services, classrooms, lecture rooms, food prod kitchen, 4 gourmet dining rooms, library, 6 public restaurants, 6 teaching kitchens. Courses: Incl Baking & Pastry, Beverage Mgmt, Buffet Catering, Confectionery, Cost Control, Culinary Skills, Food Prep, Garde Manger, Intl Cuisine, Meal & Hospitality Planning, Meat Cutting, Menu Design, Nutrition.
Faculty: 5 full-time instructors: 3 industry professionals & 1 Master Chef.
Costs: $19,000/yr for 2-yr Culinary program; $19,000/1-yr Culinary certificate program; $19,000/1-yr Baking/Pastry Arts.Each student receives $5,000 scholarship upon entering the IICA (for each yr); certain standards must be met & maintained. Admission requirements: HS diploma or GED with 2.0 GPA. Scholarships: yes. Loans: yes.
Contact: Theodore Karousos, Director of Admissions, International Institute of Culinary Arts, 100 Rock St., Fall River, MA 02720; 508-675-9305, 888-383-2665, Fax 508-678-5214, E-mail info@iicaculinary.com, URL http://www.iicaculinary.com.

MASSASOIT COMMUNITY COLLEGE
Brockton
Sponsor: College. Program: 2-yr degree. Established: 1982. Accredited by State. Admission dates: Sep. Total enrollment: 60. Student to teacher ratio 20-35:1. 93.5% of graduates employed within 6 mos.
FACULTY: 3 full-time, 2 part-time.
COSTS: In-state $72/credit, out-of-state $204/credit. Admission requirements: HS diploma or equivalent.
CONTACT: David Portesi, Department Chair, Massasoit Community College, Culinary Arts, 1 Massasoit Blvd., Brockton, MA 02402; 508-588-9100 x1697, E-mail dportesi@massasoit.mass.edu, URL http://www.massasoit.mass.edu/acad_depts/human/culinary/culinary_home.htm.

MINUTEMAN REGIONAL VOCATIONAL TECHNICAL SCHOOL
Lexington/Year-round
Sponsor: Independent trade school. Program: 3-yr diploma, 2-yr post-graduate course, 90-day retraining courses in Culinary, Baking, Hotel & Restaurant mgmt. Established: 1973. Calendar: quarter. Curriculum: culinary, core. Total enrollment: 150. 25 each admission period. 95% of applicants accepted. Student to teacher ratio 10:1. 99% of graduates employed within six months. Facilities: Include 6 kitchens & classrooms.
FACULTY: 10 certified full-time vocational educators.
COSTS: Annual tuition in-state $6,200. Uniform fee: $100. Admission requirements: Admission test. Scholarships: yes.
CONTACT: John Fitzpatrick, Director, Minuteman Tech, Foodservice/Hospitality Mgmt., 758 Marrett Rd., Lexington, MA 02173; 781-861-6500 #200, Fax 781-863-1254, E-mail jfitzpatrick@minuteman.org, URL http://www.minuteman.org.

NEWBURY COLLEGE
Brookline/Year-round

Sponsor: 2- & 4-yr independent college. Program: BS in Culinary Mgmt, AS in Culinary Arts and Food Service Mgmt. Established: 1981. Accredited by NEASC. Calendar: semester. Curriculum: culinary, core. Admission dates: Sep, Jan. Total enrollment: 240. 140 each admission period. 86% of applicants accepted. 80% receive financial aid. 20% enrolled part-time. Student to teacher ratio 14:1. 99% of graduates employed within six months. Facilities: Include 7 production kitchens & the Weltman Dining Room Restaurant.

FACULTY: 10 full- & 6 part-time.

COSTS: Annual tuition $15,325, culinary program fee $1,170. On-campus shared lodging & board $7,575. Admission requirements: HS diploma or GED & 2.0 GPA. Scholarships: yes. Loans: yes.

CONTACT: Francois Nivaud, Dean of School of Hotel & Restaurant Mgt., Newbury College, Office of Admission, 129 Fisher Ave., Brookline, MA 02445; 617-730-7007, 800-NEWBURY, Fax 617-731-9618, E-mail fnivaud@newbury.edu, URL http://www.newbury.edu.

NORTH SHORE COMMUNITY COLLEGE
Danvers/Year-round

Sponsor: 2-yr college. Program: 2-yr associate degree in Culinary Arts & Food Service. Established: 1965. Admission dates: Jan, Sep. Total enrollment: 52. 25% enrolled part-time. Student to teacher ratio 14:1. Facilities: Include 3 demo labs, food production kitchen, teaching kitchen, bake shop.

FACULTY: 4 full-time, 2 part-time.

COSTS: $2,190/yr in-state, $8,610/yr out-of-state; program fees $250. Scholarships: yes.

CONTACT: George Anbinder, Dept. Chair, North Shore Community College, Hathorne Campus Berry Hall, Room 103, Danvers, MA 01923; 781-762-4000, ext. 1537, Fax 978-762-4021, E-mail ganbinde@northshore.edu, URL http://www.northshore.edu.

MICHIGAN

ACF MICHIGAN CHEFS DE CUISINE ASSOCIATION
Farmington Hills/September-July

Sponsor: ACF chapter. Program: 3-yr apprenticeship; degree program through Oakland Community College. Established: 1978. Accredited by ACF. Calendar: semester. Curriculum: culinary. Total enrollment: 65. 20 each admission period. Facilities: 3 floors including labs & production kitchen.

FACULTY: 8 chefs. Certified Executive Pastry Chefs, Certified Executive Chefs.

COSTS: $1,500/yr. Beginning salary is $7/hr with increases every 6 mos. Admission requirements: Interview. Scholarships: yes. Loans: yes.

CONTACT: John McCormack, CEC, CCE, AAC, ACF Michigan Chefs de Cuisine Association, 1240 Muirwood Court, Rochester Hills, MI 48306; 248-377-9032, E-mail john@gatewayfood.com.

ACF OF NORTHWESTERN MICHIGAN
Bellair/Year-round

Sponsor: ACF chapter. Program: 3-yr apprenticeship; degree program Lake Michigan College. Curriculum: culinary. Total enrollment: 36.

COSTS: $2,800 for 3 yrs. Beginning salary is $6/hr with increases every 6 mos. Housing $280/mo.

CONTACT: Lucille House, CCC, ACF of Northwestern Michigan, 6285 Swamp Road, Frankfort, MI 49635; 231-995-7196, Fax 231-995-1134, E-mail lhouse@nmc.edu.

BAKER COLLEGE CULINARY ARTS
Muskegon/Year-round

Sponsor: Private 2- & 4-yr college. Program: 2-yr AB in Culinary Arts; 2-yr AB & 4-yr BBA in Food & Beverage Mgmt. Certificate in Baking & Pastry Arts. Established: 1997. Accredited by AB in Culinary Arts accredited by ACF. Calendar: quarter. Curriculum: culinary, core. Admission dates:

Sep, Jan, Apr, Jun. Total enrollment: 200. ~25 each admission period. 99% of applicants accepted. 70% receive financial aid. 100% enrolled part-time. Student to teacher ratio 12:1. 100% of graduates employed within 6 mos. Facilities: Main culinary arts kitchen, new industry-current baking & pastry kitchen, student-run fine-dining restaurant, student center grill, classrooms, library.

FACULTY: 2 full-time, 4 part-time. Program director & full-time faculty are ACF-accredited.

COSTS: Annual tuition $7,560. Application fee $20. Uniforms, books, cutlery $1,200. Admission requirements: HS diploma or GED. Scholarships: yes. Loans: yes.

CONTACT: Kathy Jacobson, Director of Admissions, Baker College Culinary Arts, 1903 Marquette Ave., Muskegon, MI 49442; 231-777-5200, Fax 231-777-5201, E-mail jacobs_k@muskegon.baker.edu, URL http://www.baker.edu.

CULINARY STUDIES INSTITUTE/OAKLAND COMMUNITY COLLEGE
Farmington Hills/September-June

Sponsor: 2-yr college. Program: 2-yr AAS program in Culinary Arts, Food Service Mgmt, Hotel Mgmt, Chef Apprentice; Pastry Arts certificate. Established: 1978. Accredited by ACF. Calendar: semester. Curriculum: culinary, core. Admission dates: Sep, Jan, May. Total enrollment: 260. 98% of applicants accepted. 35% receive financial aid. 25% enrolled part-time. Student to teacher ratio 12:1. 90% of graduates employed within six months. Facilities: Include 3 floors of kitchens, labs & classrooms & 2 student-operated restaurants.

FACULTY: 8 full-time, 6 part-time.

COSTS: In-county $51/cr-hr, out-of-county $83/cr-hr. Lab fee ~$50/course. Admission requirements: Open. Students must successfully complete Intro to Culinary Arts to enter program. Scholarships: yes. Loans: yes.

CONTACT: Susan Baier, Program Coordinator, Oakland Community College, Culinary Studies Institute 27055 Orchard Lake Rd., Farmington Hills, MI 48334; 248-522-3700, Fax 248-522-3706, E-mail smbaier@oaklandcc.edu, URL http://www.oaklandcc.edu.

GRAND RAPIDS COMMUNITY COLLEGE
Grand Rapids/August-May
(See display ad page 73)

Sponsor: 2-yr college. Program: 2-yr AAAS degree in Culinary Arts & AAAS degree in Culinary Mgmt, certificate in Baking & Pastry Arts. Established: 1980. Accredited by ACF, NCA. Calendar: semester. Curriculum: culinary, core. Admission dates: Jan, Aug. Total enrollment: 400. 80 each admission period. 95% of applicants accepted. 60% receive financial aid. 30% enrolled part-time. Student to teacher ratio 18:1. 99% of graduates employed within six months. Facilities: Include 8 kitchens, 6+ classrooms, beverage lab, 3 bakeries, bistro, banquet rooms, food/beverage library, auditorium, 2 storerooms; student-run restaurant & deli-bakery, open to the public. Courses: Basic & advanced culinary, vegan cuisine & baking skills, ice carving, banquets & catering, garde manger, restaurant operations, intl studies.

FACULTY: 12 full-time, 7 part-time. Qualifications: equivalent of a bachelor's degree & min 6 yrs industry experience in mgmt. Most have master's degrees or are master chefs.

COSTS: Culinary Arts: $8,778 resident, $14,630 non-resident, $19,950 out-of-state. Culinary Management slightly less. Baking & Pastry Arts ~50%. Application fee $20. Books, uniforms, cutlery kit $1,450. Admission requirements: HS diploma or equivalent & admission test. Scholarships: yes. Loans: yes.

CONTACT: Marcia Arp, Grand Rapids Community College, Hospitality Education, 151 Fountain, N.E., Grand Rapids, MI 49503-3263; 616-234-3690, Fax 616-234-3698, E-mail marp@grcc.edu, URL http://www.grcc.edu.

GREAT LAKES CULINARY INSTITUTE
Traverse City/Year-round

Sponsor: College. Program: 2-yr AAS degree in Culinary Arts. Established: 1978. Accredited by ACF. Calendar: semester. Curriculum: culinary, core. Admission dates: Open. Total enrollment: 90.

75 each admission period. 100% of applicants accepted. 65% receive financial aid. 45% enrolled part-time. Student to teacher ratio 15:1. 98% of graduates employed within six months. Facilities: Include 6 kitchens, restaurant, classrooms, bake shop, computer labs.

FACULTY: 5 full- & 10 part-time.

COSTS: In-county $65/cr-hr, out-of-county $110/cr-hr, application fee $15. On-campus housing:120 spaces, ~$2,200 with meal plan. Admission requirements: HS diploma or equivalent. Scholarships: yes. Loans: yes.

CONTACT: Fred Laughlin, CCE, Director, Great Lakes Culinary Institute, 1701 E. Front St., Traverse City, MI 49686; 231-995-1197, Fax 231-995-1134, E-mail Flaughlin@nmc.edu, URL http://www.nmc.edu/culinary.

HENRY FORD COMMUNITY COLLEGE
Dearborn/Year-round

Sponsor: 2-yr college. Program: AA degree. Established: 1972. Accredited by ACF. Calendar: semester. Curriculum: culinary. Total enrollment: 200. 40 each admission period. 100% of applicants accepted. 80% receive financial aid. 60% enrolled part-time. Student to teacher ratio 16:1. 90% of graduates employed within six months. Facilities: 2 kitchens, student-run dining room.

FACULTY: 4 full-time, 6 part-time.

CONTACT: Dennis Konarski, CFE, CCE, Culinary Director, Henry Ford Community College, Culinary Arts, 5101 Evergreen Rd., Dearborn, MI 48128; 313-845-9651, Fax 313-845-9784, E-mail dennis@hfcc.net, URL http://www.henryford.cc.mi.us.

MACOMB COMMUNITY COLLEGE – CULINARY INSTITUTE
Clinton Township/September-May

Sponsor: 2-yr college. Program: 2-yr AAS degree in Culinary Arts, ACF-Certified Culinarian, NRA diploma, certificatein Culinary Mgmt & Pastry Arts, Skill-specific certificates in Asst. Baker & Prep Cook, ACF Apprenticeship program. Established: 1972. Accredited by ACF. Calendar: semester. Curriculum: culinary. Admission dates: Fall, winter, spring/summer. Total enrollment: 223. 100% of applicants accepted. 35% enrolled part-time. Student to teacher ratio 16:1. 99% of graduates employed within six months. Facilities: 4 full-service kitchen labs, demo kitchen, confectionary kitchen, beverage lab, public dining room.

FACULTY: 3 full-time, 9 part-time.

COSTS: In-county $60/cr-hr, out-of-county $88/cr-hr. Admission requirements: U.S. citizen or permanent resident whose HS class has graduated or is at least age 18. Scholarships: yes. Loans: yes.

CONTACT: David Schneider, CEC, CCE, Dept. Coordinator, Macomb Culinary Institute at Macomb Community College, 44575 Garfield Rd., Clinton Township, MI 48038; 586-286-2088, Fax 586-286-2250, E-mail schneiderd@macomb.edu, URL http://www.macomb.edu.

MONROE COUNTY COMMUNITY COLLEGE
Monroe/September-May

Sponsor: Independent 2-yr college. Program: 2-yr AOC degree/certificate in Culinary Skills & Mgmt. Established: 1981. Accredited by NCA, ACF. Calendar: semester. Curriculum: core. Admission dates: Sep. Total enrollment: 36. 20 each admission period. 80% of applicants accepted. 25% receive financial aid. 25% enrolled part-time. Student to teacher ratio 18:1. 87% of graduates employed within six months. Facilities: Include 2 kitchens, classroom, restaurant.

FACULTY: 2 full-time.

COSTS: $47/cr-hr in-county, $75/cr-hr out-of-county, $83/cr-hr out-of-state. Technology fee $3/cr-hr, application fee $21. Housing ~$400/mo. Admission requirements: HS diploma or equivalent & admission test. Scholarships: yes. Loans: yes.

CONTACT: Kevin Thomas, Instructor of Culinary Skills, Monroe County Community College, Culinary Arts, 1555 S. Raisinville Rd., Monroe, MI 48161; 734-384-4150, E-mail kthomas@monroeccc.edu, URL http://www.monroeccc.edu.

MOTT COMMUNITY COLLEGE
Flint/Year-round

Sponsor: 2-yr college. Program: 66 cr-hr/83 contact-hour AAS degree in Culinary Arts, 65 cr-hr/80 contact-hour AAS degree in Food Service mgmt.

COSTS: $56/contact-hr in-state, $82/contact-hr out-of-district, $109/contact-hr out-of-state.

CONTACT: Grace Alexander, Instructor/coordinator, Mott Community College, 1401 E. Court St., Flint, MI 48503; 810-232-7845, E-mail galexand@mcc.edu, URL http://www.mcc.edu.

NORTHERN MICHIGAN UNIVERSITY
Marquette/August-April

Sponsor: University. Program: 1-yr certificate, 2-yr AAS degree, 4-yr BS degree, program in Culinary Arts, Restaurant & Institutional mgmt. Established: 1970. Accredited by NCA. Calendar: semester. Admission dates: Sep, Jan. Total enrollment: 74. 36 each admission period. 100% of applicants accepted. 80% receive financial aid. 25% enrolled part-time. Student to teacher ratio 18:1. 100% of graduates employed within six months. Facilities: Include 1 kitchen & 4 classrooms, computer lab, restaurant & meat-cutting room.

FACULTY: 4 full-time. Qualifications: bachelor's or master's degrees.

COSTS: In state $1,493/sem full-time, out-of-state $2,633/sem full-time. Application fee $50. Housing $2,300/yr. Admission requirements: HS diploma or equivalent. Scholarships: yes. Loans: yes.

CONTACT: Kathy Solka, Northern Michigan University, College of Technology & Applied Sciences, D.J. Jacobetti Center, Room 123, Marquette, MI 49855; 906-227-2135, Fax 906-227-2156, E-mail ksolka@nmu.edu, URL http://www.nmu.edu/technology.

SCHOOLCRAFT COLLEGE
Livonia/August-April

Sponsor: 2-yr college. Program: 1-yr certificate/2-yr AAS in Culinary Arts & Culinary Mgmt; 1-yr certificate in Baking & Pastry; post-grad Brigade Advanced Culinary Arts certificate. Established: 1964. Accredited by NCA. Calendar: semester. Curriculum: core. Admission dates: Jan, Aug. Total enrollment: 232. 12-90 each admission period. 100% of applicants accepted. Student to teacher ratio 16:1. 100% of graduates employed within six months. Facilities: Include 6 industry-current kitchens, public restaurant & retail outlet.

FACULTY: 6 full-time, 12 part-time, ACF-certified.

COSTS: $61/cr-hr resident, $91/cr-hr non-resident. Lab fees $35-$120. Admission requirements: HSdiploma or equivalent, admission test, completion of CAP 090. Scholarships: yes. Loans: yes.

CONTACT: Cathy McCardle, Admissions/Culinary Arts, Schoolcraft College, Culinary Arts, 18600 Haggerty Rd., Livonia, MI 48152-2696; 734-462-4426, Fax 734-462-4531, E-mail culinary@schoolcraft.edu, URL http://www.schoolcraft.edu.

WASHTENAW COMMUNITY COLLEGE
Ann Arbor/September-June

Sponsor: 2-yr college. Program: 1-yr certificate in Food Service Production Specialist and a 2-yr AAS degree in Culinary Arts and Hotel & Restaurant mgmt. Established: 1975. Accredited by NCA, ACF. Calendar: semester. Curriculum: culinary. Total enrollment: 80-120. 50 each admission period. 90% of applicants accepted. 10% receive financial aid. 60% enrolled part-time. Student to teacher ratio 16-25:1. 95% of graduates employed within six months. Facilities: Include kitchen, bake shop, & student-run dining room.

FACULTY: 4 full-time. Qualifications: bachelor's or master's degree and ACF certification.

COSTS: $52/cr-hr in-district, $77/cr-hr out-of-district, $98/cr-hr out-of-state. $23 registration fee/sem. Housing $400-$600/mo. Admission requirements: HS diploma or equivalent and admission test. Scholarships: yes.

CONTACT: Don Garrett, Department Chair, Washtenaw Community College, Culinary Arts & Hospitality Management, 4800 E. Huron River Dr., Ann Arbor, MI 48106-0978; 734-973-3601, Fax 734-677-5414, E-mail dgarrett@wccnet.org, URL http://www.washtenaw.cc.mi.us.

MINNESOTA

THE ART INSTITUTES INTERNATIONAL MINNESOTA
Minneapolis/Year-round   *(See display ad page 75)*

Sponsor: Private school. Program: 12-qtr BS in Culinary Mgmt, 7-qtr AAS in Culinary Arts, two 4-qtr certificate programs in Art of Cooking and Baking & Pastry. Established: 1998. Accredited by ACICS, ACF. Calendar: quarter. Curriculum: culinary, core. Admission dates: yr-round. Total enrollment: 180. 94% receive financial aid. Student to teacher ratio 20:1. 100% of graduates employed within six months. Facilities: Specialized educational kitchens, dining lab. Courses: Basic skills & techniques, purchasing & cost control, kitchen mgmt, intl cuisine, nutrition, dining room procedures, garde manger, baking, a la carte kitchen.

FACULTY: 12 instructors.

CONTACT: Director of Admissions, The Art Institutes International Minnesota, 15 S. 9th St., Minneapolis, MN 55402; 612-332-3361, Fax 612-332-3934, E-mail aimadm@aii.edu, URL http://www.aim.artinstitutes.edu.

HENNEPIN TECHNICAL COLLEGE
Brooklyn Pk, Eden Prairie/August-May

Sponsor: Career college. Program: 64-cr AAS degree in Culinary Arts, 50-cr diploma/certificate in Culinary Arts. Established: 1972. Accredited by NCA, ACF. Calendar: semester. Curriculum: culinary. Admission dates: Fall, spring. Total enrollment: 60. 24 each admission period. 100% of applicants accepted. 40% receive financial aid. 10% enrolled part-time. Student to teacher ratio 15:1. 98% of graduates employed within 6 mos. Facilities: Include 3 kitchens, 3 classrooms & restaurant. FACULTY: 4 full-, 3 part-time; ACF certified or certifiable.

COSTS: Annual tuition $2,228 in-state, $4,456 out-of-state. ~$550 for supplies. $20 application fee. Admission requirements: Placement test & application. Scholarships: yes. Loans: yes.

CONTACT: Carlo Castagneri, Lead Instructor, Hennepin Technical College-Brooklyn Park Campus, Culinary Arts, 9000 Brooklyn Blvd., Brooklyn Park, MN 55445; 612-425-3800 x2116, Fax 612-550-2119, E-mail Carlo.Castagneri@htc.mnscu.edu, URL http://www.htc.mnscu.edu.

HIBBING COMMUNITY COLLEGE
Hibbing/Year-round

Sponsor: 2-yr college. Program: 103-credit diploma and 113-credit AAS degree programs in Food Service mgmt. Calendar: semester. Curriculum: culinary.

COSTS: $66/credit in-state, $132/credit out-of-state plus fees.

CONTACT: Dan Lidholm, Department Head, Hibbing Community College, 2900 E. Beltline, Central Campus, Hibbing, MN 55746; 800-224-4422 #7228, Fax 218-262-7222, E-mail dan.l@ins.hcc.mnscu.edu, URL http://www.hibbing.tec.mn.us.

LE CORDON BLEU PROGRAMS AT BROWN COLLEGE
Mendota Heights/Year-round   *(See display ad page 77)*

Sponsor: Private 2-yr culinary college. Program: Three 60-wk/90-credit AAS degree Le Cordon Bleu Programs (Culinary; Patisserie & Baking; Hospitality & Restaurant Mgmt). Each ends in a 6-wk externship. Emphasis is on hands-on teaching of skills & providing training for cooks & apprentice chefs. Established: 1999. Accredited by ACCSCT. Calendar: quarter. Curriculum: culinary, core. Admission dates: Continuous. Total enrollment: 890. 200/6 wks each admission period. 90% of applicants accepted. 85% receive financial aid. Student to teacher ratio ~16:1. 98% of graduates employed within six months. Facilities: Includes 6 instructional kitchens, restaurant, deli. Courses: Include: Intro to the Culinary Arts, Purchasing & Cost Control, Hotel & Restaurant Butchery, Basic Soups, Garde Manger, A La Carte Kitchen, Dietetics, Sanitation, Baking & Pastry, Intl Cuisine.

FACULTY: 40 faculty members with a combined 600 yrs experience in the culinary arts field.

COSTS: 39765. Admission requirements: HS diploma or GED. Scholarships: yes. Loans: yes.

CONTACT: Darice Norton, Vice President of Admissions, Le Cordon Bleu Programs at Brown College, 1440 Northland Dr., Mendota Heights, MN 55120; 800-528-4575, Fax 651-675-4700, E-mail lcb-info@browncollege.edu, URL http://www.chef-bc.com.

MINNESOTA STATE COMMUNITY AND TECHNICAL COLLEGE
Moorhead/September-May

Sponsor: 2-yr college. Program: 2-yr diploma in Chef Training. Established: 1966. Accredited by NCA. Calendar: semester. Curriculum: core. Total enrollment: 40-50. 25 each admission period. 80% receive financial aid. 10% enrolled part-time. Student to teacher ratio 20-25:1. 89% of graduates employed within six months. Facilities: 2 kitchens, 1 classroom, 2 restaurants.

FACULTY: 2 full-time.

COSTS: Annual tuition in-state $1,996, out-of-state $3,840. $150/sem meal fee, $105/sem uniform fee, $20 admission application fee. Housing $250/mo. Admission requirements: HS diploma or equivalent. Loans: yes.

CONTACT: Kim Brewster, Dept. Chairperson, Minnesota State Comm & Tech College, Chef Training, 1900 28th Ave. S., Moorhead, MN 56560; 800-426-5603 x572, Fax 218-236-0342, E-mail kim.brewster@minnesota.edu, URL http://www.minnesota.edu.

ST. CLOUD TECHNICAL COLLEGE CULINARY ARTS
St. Cloud/August-May

Sponsor: College. Program: 32-wk diploma. Established: 1972. Accredited by NCA. Calendar: semester. Curriculum: culinary, core. Admission dates: Open. Total enrollment: 20. 24 each admission period. 100% of applicants accepted. 90% receive financial aid. Student to teacher ratio 24:1. 80% of graduates employed within six months. Facilities: 2 kitchens.

FACULTY: 1 full-time.

COSTS: $2,695 plus $390 for books and supplies. Admission requirements: HS diploma or GED. Scholarships: yes. Loans: yes.

CONTACT: Diane Wysoski, Assistant to the President, St. Cloud Technical College, Culinary Arts, 1540 Northway Dr., St. Cloud, MN 56303-1240; 320-654-5000, Fax 320-654-5981, E-mail dmw@cloud.tec.mn.us, URL http://sctconline.com.

ST. PAUL TECHNICAL COLLEGE
St. Paul/Year-round

Sponsor: Career college. Program: 3-sem (55 credits) diploma program, 2-yr (72 credits) AAS degree, short order cooking certificate (25 credits). Established: 1967. Accredited by NCA, ACF. Calendar: quarter semester. Curriculum: culinary. Admission dates: Aug, Jan. Total enrollment: 40-50. 25 each admission period. Student to teacher ratio 16:1. 95% of graduates employed within 6 mos.

FACULTY: 3-1/2 full-time.

COSTS: Tuition in-state $76.57/cr-hr, out-of-state $145/cr-hr. Admission requirements: HS diploma or equivalent and admission test. Scholarships: yes. Loans: yes.

CONTACT: Manfred Krug, Culinary Director, St. Paul Technical College, Culinary Arts, 235 Marshall Ave., St. Paul, MN 55102; 612-221-1300/1398, Fax 612-221-1416, E-mail Manfred.Krug@sptc.mnscu.edu, URL http://www.sptc.mnscu.edu.

SOUTH CENTRAL TECHNICAL COLLEGE
North Mankato/September-July

Sponsor: Career college. Program: 15-mo, 52-cr diploma & 2-yr, 72-cr AAS degree in Hotel, Restaurant & Institutional Cooking. Established: 1968. Accredited by NCA. Calendar: semester. Curriculum: culinary. Admission dates: Aug, Jan, May. Total enrollment: 25. 7-8 each admission period. 100% of applicants accepted. 90% receive financial aid. 10% enrolled part-time. Student to teacher ratio 17:1. 95% of graduates employed within 6 mos. Facilities: Include 2 kitchens, bakery & classroom.
FACULTY: 1 full-time.
COSTS: In-state $74/sem-cr, out-of-state $148/sem-cr. Books & uniforms $520. Housing $300/mo. Admission requirements: HS diploma or equivalent. Scholarships: yes. Loans: yes.
CONTACT: Jim Hanson, Instructor, South Central Technical College, Culinary Arts, 1920 Lee Blvd., P.O. Box 1920, North Mankato, MN 56003; 507-389-7229, Fax 507-388-9951, E-mail JimH@tc-mankato.scm.tec.mn.us, URL http://www.sctc.mnscu.edu.

MISSISSIPPI

Earn a B.S. Degree in Culinary Arts!

Prepare for a lifetime - a liberal arts core, a classic culinary curriculum and four specialty areas of study:

• entrepreneurship • food art (photography/styling)
• food journalism • nutrition & wellness

Mississippi University for Women
www.muw.edu/interdisc • (662) 241-7472

MISSISSIPPI UNIVERSITY FOR WOMEN CULINARY ARTS INSTITUTE
Columbus/Year-round *(See display ad above)*

Sponsor: Public university. Program: 4-yr BS (52 sem-hrs): required minor (18-21 sem-hrs) in Entrepreneurship/Small Business Development, Food Journalism, Food Art, Nutrition/Wellness; minor (22 sem-hrs) in Culinary Arts. Established: 1997. Accredited by SACS. Calendar: semester. Curriculum: culinary, core. Admission dates: Aug, Jan. Total enrollment: 65. Open each admission period. Student to teacher ratio 12:1. 100% of graduates employed within 6 months. Facilities: 5 kitchens, classrooms in renovated building listed in National Register of Historic Places. Courses: Classic cooking techniques, small quantity food prep. Correlate minor required, culinary entrepreneurship studies.
FACULTY: 4 full-time; 3 part-time. Chef/Director, nutritionist/RD, chef-instructors.
COSTS: $1,649 ($3,982.50)/sem in-state (out-of-state), Academic Common Market available; $1,689 living expenses; $100 fee for food prep classes. Admission requirements: College prep curriculum with 2.0 GPA/850 SAT, 2.5 GPA/760 SAT, or 3.2 SAT. Scholarships: yes. Loans: yes.
CONTACT: Sarah Labensky, CCP, Director, Mississippi University for Women, 1100 College St., W-1639, Columbus, MS 39701; 877-GO-2-THE-W x7472, 662-241-7472, Fax 662-241-7627, E-mail cularts@muw.edu, URL http://www.muw.edu/interdisc.

HINDS COMMUNITY COLLEGE
Jackson/August-May

Sponsor: 2-yr college. Program: 1-yr certificate & 2-yr AAS degree program in Culinary Arts. Accredited by SACS. Calendar: semester. Curriculum: culinary, core. Admission dates: Jan, Aug. Total enrollment: 50. 20 each admission period. 100% of applicants accepted. 80% receive financial aid. 15% enrolled part-time. Student to teacher ratio 16:1. 100% of graduates employed within six months. Facilities: Full-scale commercial kitchen with all major equipment.

FACULTY: 3 faculty.

COSTS: $515 for full-time students (12-19 hrs), $25 registration fee. Deferred payment plan. Admission requirements: HS diploma or GED. Scholarships: yes. Loans: yes.

CONTACT: Kathleen Bruno, Chef/Instructor, Hinds Community College, Culinary Arts Program, 3925 Sunset Dr., Jackson, MS 39213; 601-987-8130, Fax 601-982-5804, E-mail Gata1967@aol.com, URL http://www.hinds.cc.ms.us.

MISSOURI

ST. LOUIS COMMUNITY COLLEGE – FOREST PARK
St. Louis/August-May

Sponsor: 2-yr college. Program: 2-yr AAS degree, apprenticeship leading to ACF certification. Established: 1976. Accredited by NCA. Calendar: semester. Curriculum: culinary. Admission dates: Aug, Jan. Total enrollment: 150. 50 each admission period. 100% of applicants accepted. 40% enrolled part-time. Student to teacher ratio 20:1. 98% of graduates employed within six months. Facilities: 30,000-sq-ft facility: 4 kitchens, student-operated restaurant, classrooms.

FACULTY: 4 full-time, 25 part-time. Qualifications: masters degree and industry experience.

COSTS: Annual tuition: $1,200 in-state, $1,700 out-of-state. Parking $16. Housing $450/mo. Admission requirements: HS diploma or equivalent & admission test. Scholarships: yes. Loans: yes.

CONTACT: Kathy Schiffman, Dept. Chair, St. Louis Community College-Forest Park, Culinary Mgmt., 5600 Oakland Ave., St. Louis, MO 63110; 314-644-9747, Fax 314-644-9992, E-mail kschiffman@stlcc.edu, URL http://www.stlcc.cc.mo.us/fp/hospitality/hospitality.html.

MONTANA

UNIVERSITY OF MONTANA – COLLEGE OF TECHNOLOGY
Missoula/Year-round

Sponsor: Public career institution. Program: 1-yr certificate & 2-yr AAS degree in Food Service mgmt. Established: 1973. Accredited by ACF, NASC. Calendar: trimester. Curriculum: culinary, core. Admission dates: Aug, Jan. Total enrollment: 62. 25 each admission period. 90% of applicants accepted. 30% receive financial aid. 5% enrolled part-time. Student to teacher ratio 15:1. 90% of graduates employed within six months. Facilities: 1 kitchen, classrooms, 1 restaurant.

FACULTY: Qualifications: CEC, CPC, CC.

COSTS: Annual tuition $2,400 resident, $5,000 non-resident. Application fee $30. Other fees $400. Housing $300/mo. Admission requirements: HS or equivalent and admission test. Scholarships: yes. Loans: yes.

CONTACT: Ross Lodahl, Interim Program Director, University of Montana-College of Technology, Culinary Arts, 909 S. Avenue West, Missoula, MT 59801-7910; 406-243-7816, E-mail Ross.Lodahl@mso.umt.edu, URL http://www.cte.umt.edu.

NEBRASKA

ACF PROFESSIONAL CHEFS OF OMAHA
Omaha/Year-round

Sponsor: ACF chapter. Program: 3-yr apprenticeship; degree program through Metro Community College is completed by 80%. Curriculum: culinary. Total enrollment: 20.

COSTS: $3,300. Beginning salary is $7/hr with variable increases annually.

CONTACT: Chris Zeeb, CEC, ACF Professional Chefs of Omaha, Metropolitan Community College, Bldg. 10, Box 3777, 30th & Fort Sts., Omaha, NE 68103-0777; 402-449-3397, E-mail cmzeeb@msn.com, URL http://www.acfchefs.org/presidents_portal/ACFChapter.cfm?ChapterChoice=NE032.

CENTRAL COMMUNITY COLLEGE
Hastings/September-June

Sponsor: 2-yr college. Program: 2-yr certificate/AAS degree in Culinary Arts. Established: 1971. Accredited by NCA. Calendar: semester. Curriculum: core. Admission dates: Open. Total enrollment: 40. 10 each admission period. 100% of applicants accepted. 80% receive financial aid. Student to teacher ratio 8:1. 95% of graduates employed within six months. Facilities: 1 kitchen, 4 classrooms, restaurant.

Faculty: 2 full-time.

Costs: Annual tuition in-state $1,440, out-of-state $1,920. Uniform & supplies $50. Admission requirements: HS diploma or equivalent. Scholarships: yes. Loans: yes.

Contact: Jaye Kieselhorst, Program Supervisor, Central Community College, Hotel, Motel, Restaurant Mgmt., P.O. Box 1024, Hastings, NE 68902; 402-461-2572, Fax 402-461-2454, E-mail jkieselhorst@cccneb.edu, URL http://www.cccneb.edu.

THE INSTITUTE FOR CULINARY ARTS AT MCC
Omaha/Year-round

Sponsor: 2-yr college. Program: 1- to 2-yr AAS degree programs in Culinary Arts, Foodservice mgmt, Chef Apprentice, Culinology (TM), Bakery Arts, Culinary mgmt. Established: 1975. Accredited by ACF, CAHM. Calendar: quarter. Curriculum: culinary, core. Admission dates: Sep, Dec, Mar, Jun. Total enrollment: 425. 75 each admission period. 50% receive financial aid. 45% enrolled part-time. Student to teacher ratio 18:1. 97% of graduates employed within six months. Facilities: Kitchens, classrooms, restaurant.

Faculty: 5 full-time, all certified or certified eligible; 20+ adjunct faculty.

Costs: In-state ~$35/cr-hr, out-of-state ~$50/cr-hr. Admission requirements: At least age 17 or HS diploma or equivalent. Scholarships: yes. Loans: yes.

Contact: Jim Trebbien, Chef, The Institute for Culinary Arts at MCC, PO Box 3777, 30th & Fort Sts., Omaha, NE 68103-0777; 402-457-2510, Fax 402-457-2515, E-mail jtrebbien@mccneb.edu, URL http://business.mccneb.edu/culinaryarts.

SOUTHEAST COMMUNITY COLLEGE
Lincoln/Year-round

Sponsor: 2-yr college. Program: 18-mo AS degree in Culinary Arts. Established: 1988. Accredited by NCA, ACF. Calendar: quarter. Curriculum: core. Admission dates: Sep, Mar. Total enrollment: 140. 36 each admission period. 100% of applicants accepted. 30% enrolled part-time. Student to teacher ratio 15:1. Facilities: Include kitchen & 3 classrooms.

Faculty: 2 full-time, 2 part-time. Qualifications: associate degree.

Costs: Annual tuition in-state $36/cr-hr, out-of-state $43.50/cr-hr. Fees $37. Admission requirements: HS diploma or equivalent. Scholarships: yes. Loans: yes.

Contact: Jo Taylor, Program Chair, Southeast Community College, Food Service, 8800 'O' St., Lincoln, NE 68520-9989; 402-437-2465, Fax 402-437-2404, E-mail jtaylor@southeast.edu, URL http://www.southeast.edu/Programs/Curriculum/FOOD.htm.

NEVADA

THE ART INSTITUTE OF LAS VEGAS
Las Vegas/Year-round *(See display ad page 11)*

Sponsor: Private career school. Program: 21-mo (112 cr-hr, 7 qtr) AS degree program in Culinary Arts. Established: 2002. Accredited by ACCSCT, Nevada Commission on Postsecondary Education. Calendar: quarter.

Faculty: Includes one Certified Master Chef.

Costs: $316/cr-hr, application & enrollment fee $150.

CONTACT: Suzanne Noel, Director of Admissions, The Art Institute of Las Vegas, 2350 Corporate Circle, Las Vegas, NV 89074; 800-833-2678, E-mail noels@aii.edu, URL http://www.ailv.artinstitutes.edu.

COMMUNITY COLLEGE OF SOUTHERN NEVADA – CHEYENNE
North Las Vegas/Year-round

Sponsor: 2-yr college. Program: 1-yr certificate and 2-yr AAS degree in Hotel, Restaurant, and Casino mgmt with Culinary Arts emphasis. Established: 1990. Accredited by NASC, ACF. Calendar: semester. Curriculum: culinary, core. Admission dates: Open. Total enrollment: 400. 100% of applicants accepted. Student to teacher ratio 15:1. 100% of graduates employed within 6 mos.

FACULTY: 4 full-time, 18 part-time.

COSTS: $42.50/credit in-state. Out-of-state tuition is $63.50/credit for 1-6 credits and $42.50/credit plus $2,075/sem for 7 credits or more.

CONTACT: Jill Mora, Culinary Director, Community College of Southern Nevada, Culinary Arts, 3200 E. Cheyenne Ave., Z1A, North Las Vegas, NV 89030; 702-651-4656, Fax 702-651-4116, E-mail jill_mora@ccsn.nevada.edu, URL http://www.ccsn.nevada.edu.

CREATIVE COOKING SCHOOL OF LAS VEGAS
Las Vegas/Year-round

Sponsor: Creative Cooking School of Las Vegas & University of Nevada, Las Vegas (UNLV). Program: 20-wk (600-hr) Professional Chef certificate program. Established: 2004. Facilities: 2,000 sq-ft kitchen with the latest equipment.

CONTACT: Catherine Margles, President/Founder, Creative Cooking School of Las Vegas, 7385 W. Sahara Ave., Las Vegas, NV 89117; 702-562-3900, Fax 702-562-3939, E-mail catherine@creative-cookingschool.com, URL http://www.creativecookingschool.com/ProfessionalChef.asp.

FRATERNITY OF EXECUTIVE CHEFS OF LAS VEGAS
N. Las Vegas/Year-round

Sponsor: ACF chapter. Program: 3-yr apprenticeship; degree program through University of Las Vegas. Curriculum: culinary. Total enrollment: 11.

COSTS: $165. Beginning salary is 80% of cook's helper's wages with increases annually. Housing $350-$500.

CONTACT: Robert O'Brien, Fraternity of Executive Chefs of Las Vegas, PO Box 93933, Las Vegas, NV 89193; 702-734-0410, E-mail bobrien@mrgmail.com, URL http://www.acfchefs.org/chapter/nv013.html.

LE CORDON BLEU CULINARY ARTS LAS VEGAS
Las Vegas/Year-round   *(See display ad page 101)*

Sponsor: Private school. Program: 15-mo AOS degree program in Culinary Arts. Established: 2003. Accredited by ACCSCT. Curriculum: culinary. Admission dates: Every 6 wks. Total enrollment: 80. 80 each admission period. Student to teacher ratio 16-40:1. Facilities: New 60,000-sq-ft facility includes 6 production kitchens, 4 demo kitchens, computer classroom, library, bookstore, student-staffed fine dining restaurant.

FACULTY: Chef and associate chef instructor for each production & demo class.

COSTS: $37,800 includes supplies & fees. Admission requirements: Personal interview & essay. Scholarships: yes. Loans: yes.

CONTACT: Tyka Burton, Director of Admissions, Le Cordon Bleu Culinary Arts Las Vegas, 1451 Center Crossing Rd., Las Vegas, NV 89144; 702-365-7690, Fax 702-851-5299, E-mail tyburton@VegasCulinary.com, URL http://www.VegasCulinary.com.

TRUCKEE MEADOWS COMMUNITY COLLEGE
Reno/September-May

Sponsor: 2-yr college. Program: 2-yr AAS degree in Culinary Arts, 1-yr certificate in Culinary Arts or Baking & Pastry. Established: 1980. Accredited by State, NCA, ACF. Calendar: semester.

Curriculum: culinary, core. Admission dates: Aug, Jan. Total enrollment: 130. 75 each admission period. 95% of applicants accepted. 30% receive financial aid. 70% enrolled part-time. Student to teacher ratio 16:1. 75% of graduates employed within six months. Facilities: Include 8 kitchens & classrooms, student-run restaurant.

FACULTY: 1 full-time, 10 part-time.

COSTS: In-state $49/cr-hr, out-of-state $1,995 + $61/cr-hr unless eligible for good neighbor tuition. Application fee $15. Housing $500-600/mo. Admission requirements: HS diploma or equivalent. Scholarships: yes. Loans: yes.

CONTACT: Karen Cannan, Culinary Arts Instructor, Program Coordinator, Truckee Meadows Community College, Culinary Arts, 7000 Dandini Blvd., RDMT-207-L, Reno, NV 89512-3999; 775-674-7917, Fax 775-674-7980, E-mail info@tmcc.edu, URL http://www.tmcc.edu.

UNIVERSITY OF NEVADA LAS VEGAS CULINARY ARTS MANAGEMENT
Las Vegas/Year-round

Sponsor: 4-yr college. Program: 4-yr BS degree in Culinary Arts Mgmt designed for community college transfers; freshmen are accepted. Established: 1998. Accredited by NACS. Calendar: semester. Curriculum: culinary, core. Admission dates: Aug, Jan. Total enrollment: 187. 16-20 each admission period. Student to teacher ratio 25:1. Facilities: Lab, demo & production kitchens, dining room, full bar.

FACULTY: 10 full-time, 4 part-time.

COSTS: Resident $72/cr-hr; nonresident $150/cr-hr for 1-6 credits or $72/cr-hr + $3,174 for 7+ credits. Admission requirements: SAT, 2.5 GPA for upperclassmen. Scholarships: yes. Loans: yes.

CONTACT: Claude Lambertz, Program Director, University of Nevada Las Vegas Culinary Arts Management, 4505 Maryland Pkwy., Las Vegas, NV 89154-6022; 702-895-4466, Fax 702-895-4871, E-mail clambertz@ccmail.nevada.edu, URL http://www.unlv.edu/Tourism/culinary.html.

NEW HAMPSHIRE

ATLANTIC CULINARY ACADEMY – LE CORDON BLEU
Dover/Year-round   *(See display ad page 83)*

Sponsor: Two-yr private college. Program: 12-mo program leading to an associate degree in Culinary Arts and Le Cordon Bleu diploma. Established: 1996. Accredited by NEASC. Calendar: semester. Curriculum: culinary, core. Admission dates: moly. Total enrollment: 100+. 16 each admission period. 86% of applicants accepted. 85% receive financial aid. Student to teacher ratio 16:1. 94% of graduates employed within six months. Facilities: Newly renovated 20,000-sq-ft facility featuring 4 modern kitchens, 1 restaurant, pastry shop & coffee shop. Courses: Le Cordon Bleu curriculum covers such areas as: A la Carte Fine Dining, Baking & Pastry, Flavors of the World, and Business Management.

FACULTY: Full-time instructors and local area chefs who are on staff as part time instructors.

COSTS: ~$27,000 includes books, supplies, uniforms and tuition for both degree and diploma programs. Admission requirements: HS diploma, interview, letters of recommendation, application with fee. Scholarships: yes. Loans: yes.

CONTACT: Heather McBreen, Director of Admissions, Le Cordon Bleu @ Atlantic Culinary Academy, 181 Silver St., Dover, NH 03820; 877-628-1222, Fax 603-749-0837, E-mail hmcbreen@mcintoshcollege.com, URL http://www.atlanticculinary.com.

THE BALSAMS CULINARY APPRENTICESHIP SCHOOL
Dixville Notch/Year-round

Sponsor: Cooking school in a privately owned, 4-star resort hotel. Program: 3-1/2 yr program granting certification with the ACF & an AOS degree. Calendar: quarter. Curriculum: culinary, core. Admission dates: Jun. Total enrollment: 20. 10 each admission period. 50% of applicants accepted. 80% receive financial aid. Student to teacher ratio 1.5:1. 100% of graduates employed

within six months. Facilities: The Balsams hotel kitchens, garde manger & full bakery. Hotel also has a butcher shop, 3 outlets & main dining room. Apprenticeship center with lodging, demo kitchen & banquet area.

FACULTY: 13 chef-supervisors, 5-7 instructors from New Hampshire Technical College.

COSTS: ~$3,000/yr + equipment & textbooks. Admission requirements: HS diploma or equivalent, min 1 yr experience in the cooking industry or participation in a culinary arts program at HS level or greater. Scholarships: yes. Loans: yes.

CONTACT: Steven Learned, Executive Chef, The Balsams Culinary Apprenticeship School, Rt. 26, Dixville Notch, NH 03576; 603-255-3861, 603-255-2661, Fax 603-255-4670, E-mail plearned@ncia.net, URL http://www.thebalsams.com.

NEW HAMPSHIRE COMMUNITY TECHNICAL COLLEGE
Berlin/Year-round

Sponsor: Career college. Program: 2-yr AAS degree & 1-yr diploma in Culinary Arts, 24-cr certificate in Food Service Production. Established: 1966. Accredited by NEASC. Calendar: semester. Curriculum: core. Admission dates: Open. Total enrollment: 30. 20 each admission period. 76% of applicants accepted. 89% receive financial aid. 10% enrolled part-time. Student to teacher ratio 15:1. 100% of graduates employed within six months. Facilities: 3 kitchens, classrooms.

FACULTY: 2 full-time. Includes K. Hohmeister & S. Griffiths.

COSTS: Annual tuition $3,500 in-state, $$4,950 New England regional, $7,590 out-of-state. Summer externship $110/cr in-state, $165/cr New England, out-of-state $253/cr. Other fees: $90. Admission requirements: HS diploma or equivalent. Scholarships: yes. Loans: yes.

CONTACT: Kurt Hohmeister, Department Chair, New Hampshire Community Technical College, Culinary Arts, 2020 Riverside Dr., Berlin, NH 03570; 800-445-455, 603-752-1113, Fax 603-752-6335, E-mail khohmeister@tec.nh.us, URL http://comet.berl.tec.nh.us/courses/cook.html.

SOUTHERN NEW HAMPSHIRE UNIVERSITY CULINARY PROGRAM
Manchester/September-May   *(See display ad page 85)*

Sponsor: University. Program: 2-yr AAS degree in Culinary Arts; can be transferred into 4-yr BS degree in a hospitality mgmt program. Established: 1983. Accredited by ACFEI. Calendar: semester. Curriculum: culinary. Admission dates: Rolling - Sept. entrance only. Total enrollment: 120. 75 each admission period. 75% of applicants accepted. 90% receive financial aid. 10% enrolled part-time. Student to teacher ratio 15:1. 100% of graduates employed within six months. Facilities: New facility with the latest equipment: 2 bakeshop labs, 2 production labs, 75-seat restaurant open to the public, demo classroom, computer center, 5 classrooms. Courses: Include culinary skills, bakeshop, food production, garde manger, nutrition, general ed courses, menu & facilities planning, cost control, dining room mgmt, classical, regional, intl cuisine.

FACULTY: 5 full-time, 6 part-time, all with industry experience & teaching credentials.

COSTS: Tuition $18,984/yr. Knife set $300, books $500, uniforms $120, fees $330. On-campus rm & bd $7,866/yr. Admission requirements: HS diploma or equivalent, SAT scores, essay, letters of recommendation. Transfer credit may be awarded. Scholarships: yes. Loans: yes.

CONTACT: Steve Soba, Director of Admission, Southern New Hampshire University Culinary Program, Office of Admission, Manchester, NH 03106; 800-642-4968, Fax 603-645-9693, E-mail admission@snhu.edu, URL http://www.snhu.edu.

NEW JERSEY

ACADEMY OF CULINARY ARTS – ATLANTIC CAPE COMM. COLLEGE
Mays Landing/August-May

Sponsor: 2-yr college. Program: 2-yr AAS in Culinary Arts, Baking & Pastry, and Food Service Mgmt; 1-yr certificate in Baking & Pastry, Catering, Hot Food, and Food Service Mgmt. Established: 1981. Accredited by MSA. Calendar: semester. Curriculum: culinary. Admission dates: Aug, Jan. Total enrollment: 343. 150 each admission period. 100% of applicants accepted. 60% receive financial aid. 48% enrolled part-time. Student to teacher ratio 20:1. 100% of graduates employed within six months. Facilities: 5 teaching kitchens; restaurant, pastry & baking kitchen; 4 lecture rooms; computer lab; 70-seat gourmet & 35-seat garden dining rooms; banquet room; pastry/baking retail store.
FACULTY: 18 full-time international faculty with professional designations.
COSTS: ~$4,500/sem, in-state. Admission requirements: HS diploma or equivalent, College Placement Test. Scholarships: yes. Loans: yes.
CONTACT: Linda McLeod, Asst. Director for College Recruitment, Academy of Culinary Arts - Atlantic Cape Community College, Admissions, 5100 Black Horse Pike, Mays Landing, NJ 08330-2699; 609-343-5000, 800-645-CHEF, Fax 609-343-4921, E-mail accadmit@atlantic.edu, URL http://www.atlantic.edu/aca.

BERGEN COMMUNITY COLLEGE
Paramus/August-May

Sponsor: College. Program: 1-yr (18-30 cr) certificate in Culinary Arts, 2-yr (64-cr) degree in Hotel/Restaurant/Hospitality. Established: 1974. Accredited by MSA. Calendar: semester.

Curriculum: culinary, core. Admission dates: Sep, Jan. Total enrollment: 125. 40-50 each admission period. 25% of applicants accepted. 10% receive financial aid. 20% enrolled part-time. Student to teacher ratio 25:1. 100% of graduates employed within six months. Facilities: 2 cooking labs, 2 dining rooms, 1 computer lab.

FACULTY: 4 full- time. All master's level & industry trained.

CONTACT: Prof. David Cohen, Prof. Don Delnero, Bergen Community College-Hotel/Restaurant/Hospitality, 400 Paramus Rd., Paramus, NJ 07652; 201-447-7192, Fax 201-612-5240, E-mail dcohen@bergen.cc.nj.us, URL http://www.bergen.edu/ecatalog/subcrslist.asp?type.cbn=27.

CULINARY EDUCATION CENTER OF MONMOUTH COUNTY
Lincroft/Year-round

Sponsor: Brookdale Community College. Program: 1-yr (34.5-credit) certificate and 2-yr (69.5-credit) AAS degree programs in Culinary Arts, 2-yr AAS degree in Food Service mgmt. Established: 1998. Accredited by MSA. Calendar: semester. Curriculum: culinary, core. Admission dates: Sep, Jan. Total enrollment: 320. 50-85 each admission period. 100% of applicants accepted. 30% enrolled part-time. Student to teacher ratio 16:1. Facilities: Include 3 kitchens, 2 baking kitchens, 2 dining rooms, computer lab, classrooms.

FACULTY: 10 full- and part-time faculty with advanced degrees & work experience.

COSTS: ~$3,500/ sem in-county. Total 2-yr program cost ~$14,000 (includes tuition, fees, books, knife kit, uniforms). Admission requirements: HS diploma or equivalent, successful completeing of college placement test. Scholarships: yes. Loans: yes.

CONTACT: Shirley Sesler, Enrollment Specialist, Brookdale Community College, 765 Newman Springs Rd., Lincroft, NJ 07738-1597; 732-224-2371, Fax 732-842-0203, E-mail cberg@brookdale.cc.nj.us, URL http://www.brookdale.cc.nj.us.

HUDSON COUNTY COMMUNITY COLLEGE
Jersey City/September-May

Sponsor: 2-yr public college. Program: 2-yr AAS degrees & 1-yr certificates in Culinary Arts & Hospitality Mgmt. Specialized proficiency certificates in Hot Foods, Baking, & Garde Manger. Established: 1983. Accredited by MSA, State Commission on Higher Education, ACF. Calendar: semester. Curriculum: core. Admission dates: Aug, Jan. Total enrollment: 325. 125 each admission period. 90% of applicants accepted. 60% receive financial aid. 20% enrolled part-time. Student to teacher ratio 15:1. 99% of graduates employed within six months. Facilities: 4 instructional kitchens, 3 classrooms, instructional bar/lounge, formal dining room.

FACULTY: 9 full-time, 24 part-time.

COSTS: AAS degree $12,344 in-county, $17,384 out-of-county, $22,424 out-of-state, includes fees, supplies, uniforms, books, insurance. Admission requirements: Open. HS diploma, GED, or 18+ yrs of age. Scholarships: yes. Loans: yes.

CONTACT: Dennis Baumeyer, Executive Director, Hudson County Community College-Culinary Arts Institute, 161 Newkirk St., Jersey City, NJ 07306; 201-714-2193, Fax 201-656-1522, E-mail dbaumeyer@hccc.edu, URL http://www.hccc.edu.

MIDDLESEX COUNTY COLLEGE
Edison/Year-round

Sponsor: 2 yr college. Program: Certificate in Culinary Arts; 2-yr AAS in Hotel Restaurant, & Institution Mgmt with Culinary Arts Mgmt Option. Established: 1987. Accredited by MSA. Calendar: semester. Curriculum: culinary, core. Admission dates: Jan, May, Sep. Total enrollment: 70. 10 (summer), 30 (spring, fall) each admission period. 100% of applicants accepted. 88% receive financial aid. 40% enrolled part-time. Student to teacher ratio 16:1. 95% of graduates employed within six months. Facilities: Includes 1 kitchen, 3 classrooms.

FACULTY: 5 full-time, 3 part-time.

COSTS: Annual tuition in-state $3,500, out-of-state $7,000. Application fee $25. Admission requirements: HS diploma or equivalent. Scholarships: yes. Loans: yes.

CONTACT: Marilyn Laskowski-Sachnoff, Department Chair, Middlesex County College, Hotel Restaurant & Institution Mgmt., 2600 Woodbridge Ave., P.O. Box 3050, Edison, NJ 08818-3050; 732-906-2538, Fax 732-906-7745, E-mail M_Laskowski_Sachnoff@middlesexcc.edu, URL http://www.middlesexcc.edu.

MORRIS COUNTY SCHOOL OF TECHNOLOGY
Denville/September-June

Sponsor: Trade-technical school. Program: 1- or 2-yr sequential program in Culinary Arts offering certificates in Hospitality Mgmt, Food Prep/Production, & ServSafe Sanitation. Established: 1977. Accredited by Dept. of Vocational Ed. Curriculum: culinary, core. Admission dates: Sept. Total enrollment: 90. 45-50 each admission period. 100% of applicants accepted. 10% receive financial aid. 90% enrolled part-time. Student to teacher ratio 15:1. 95% of graduates employed within six months. Facilities: 2 high-tech commercial kitchens, including a bakeshop in one.

FACULTY: 3 instructors with culinary degrees, teaching degrees, & industry experience.

COSTS: $1,050/yr part-time, $2,100/yr full-time. Admission requirements: Jr/sr level in HS, HS graduate. Scholarships: yes. Loans: yes.

CONTACT: MaryAnne Regan, Supervisor of Curriculum, Morris County School of Technology, 400 E. Main St., Denville, NJ 07834; 973-627-4600 x224, Fax 973-627-6979, E-mail reganm@mcvts.org, URL http://www.mcvts.org.

PASSAIC COUNTY TECHNICAL INSTITUTE
Wayne/September-June

Sponsor: Vocational high school. Program: High school diploma in Culinary Arts. Established: 1970. Accredited by NJ State Dept. of Education. Calendar: semester. Curriculum: core. Admission dates: Sep. Total enrollment: 90+. 90+ each admission period. Student to teacher ratio 10:1. Facilities: 3 kitchens, 3 student cafeterias faculty cafeteria, full service restaurant, bakeshop.

FACULTY: 9 culinary arts teachers.

CONTACT: Michael W. Adams, Passaic County Technical Institute, 45 Reinhardt Rd., Wayne, NJ 07470; 973-389-4296, E-mail madams@pcti.tec.nj.us, URL http://www.pcti.tec.nj.us.

SALEM COUNTY VOCATIONAL TECHNICAL SCHOOLS
Woodstown

Sponsor: Career institution. Program: 2-yr certificate in Culinary Arts. Established: 1976. Accredited by MSA. Admission dates: Sep, Jan. Total enrollment: 30. 75% of applicants accepted. Student to teacher ratio 15:1. 85% of graduates employed within six months.

FACULTY: 20 full-time.

COSTS: Annual tuition $3,000.

CONTACT: Eva Hoffman, Culinary Arts Instructor, Salem County Vocational Technical Schools, Culinary Arts, Box 350, Woodstown, NJ 08098; 856-769-0101, Fax 856-769-4214, E-mail Info@scvts.org, URL http://www.scvts.org.

NEW MEXICO

ALBUQUERQUE TECHNICAL VOCATIONAL INSTITUTE
Albuquerque/Year-round

Sponsor: Community college/career institution. Program: Baking certificate, Professional Cooking certificate, Food Service Mgmt certificate, AAS degree in Culinary Arts. Established: 1965. Accredited by ACF. Calendar: trimester. Curriculum: culinary, core. Admission dates: yr-round. Total enrollment: 150. 130 each admission period. 100% of applicants accepted. 65% receive financial aid. 33% enrolled part-time. Student to teacher ratio 16:1. 100% of graduates employed within six months. Facilities: 1 commercial baking lab & retail bakery, 2 commercial kitchens, student-operated buffet, catering, bistro, fine dining restaurant, computer labs.

FACULTY: 10 full- & part-time.

COSTS: $1,097/term for full-time students. $30 reg fee + equipment & uniforms. Admission requirements: Age 18+, HS diploma, GED or concurrent HS. Scholarships: yes. Loans: yes.

CONTACT: Carmine J. Russo, CCC, CCE, Program Chair, Albuquerque Technical Vocational Institute-TVI Community College, Culinary Arts, 525 Buena Vista SE, Albuquerque, NM 87106; 505-224-3755, Fax 505-224-3781, E-mail crusso@tvi.cc.nm.us, URL http://www.tvi.edu.

SANTA FE COMMUNITY COLLEGE
Santa Fe/Year-round

Sponsor: 2-yr college. Program: 2-yr certificate/AAS degree in Culinary Arts, 1-yr certificate. Established: 1985. Accredited by NCA. Calendar: quarter. Curriculum: culinary, core. Admission dates: Aug 20, Jan 10, Jun 1. Total enrollment: 190. 30 each admission period. 100% of applicants accepted. 20% receive financial aid. 20% enrolled part-time. Student to teacher ratio 14:1. 100% of graduates employed within six months. Facilities: Include 2 kitchens & classrooms, culinary lab, banquet facilities, restaurant.

FACULTY: 1 full-time, 8 part-time. Qualifications: working executive chef.

COSTS: Annual tuition in-county $20/cr-hr, out-of-county $25/cr-hr, out-of-state $45/cr-hr plus lab fees. Admission requirements: HS diploma or equivalent. Scholarships: yes. Loans: yes.

CONTACT: Director of Culinary Arts, Santa Fe Community College, 6401 Richards Ave., Santa Fe, NM 87502; 505-428-1600, Fax 505-428-1237, URL http://www.santa-fe.cc.nm.us.

NEW YORK

ACF OF GREATER BUFFALO
Lewiston/Year-round

Sponsor: ACF chapter. Program: 3-yr apprenticeship; degree program through Niagara County Community College or Erie Community College is completed by 100%. Curriculum: culinary. Total enrollment: 3.

CONTACT: Cornelia Walmsley, ACF of Greater Buffalo, PO Box 61, Buffalo, NY 14207; 716-688-5646, E-mail walmsley@pcom.net.

ADIRONDACK COMMUNITY COLLEGE
Queensbury/September-May

Sponsor: Proprietary college. Program: 1-yr certificate & 2-yr AAS degree in Food Service. Established: 1969. Accredited by MSA. Admission dates: Fall, spring. Total enrollment: 25. 70-80% receive financial aid. 75% enrolled part-time. Student to teacher ratio 10:1. 90% of graduates employed within six months. Facilities: Include 3 kitchens, classroom & restaurant.

FACULTY: 1 full-time, 3 part-time.

COSTS: $1,075/sem in-state, $2,150/sem out-of-state. Admission requirements: HS diploma.

CONTACT: William Steele, Program Coordinator, Adirondack Community College, Commercial Cooking, Bay Rd., Queensbury, NY 12804; 518-743-2200 x374, Fax 518-743-2317, E-mail info@acc.sunyacc.edu, URL http://www.suny.edu.

ALFRED STATE COLLEGE – CULINARY ARTS
Wellsville/August-May

Sponsor: 2-yr college. Program: 2-yr AOS degree. Established: 1966. Accredited by MSA. Calendar: semester. Curriculum: culinary. Admission dates: Jan, Aug. Total enrollment: 60. 65/71 each admission period. 75% of applicants accepted. 87% receive financial aid. Student to teacher ratio 8:1. 95% of graduates employed within 6 mos. Facilities: Comparative with the food industry.

FACULTY: 142.

COSTS: $3,200 in-state, $5,000 out-of-state; books, uniforms, tools ~$300/sem; rm & bd $5,668.

Admission requirements: HS average of C or better. Scholarships: yes. Loans: yes.

CONTACT: Deborah Goodrich, Director of Admissions, Alfred State College, Upper College Dr., Alfred, NY 14802; 800-4AL-FRED, Fax 607-587-4299, E-mail admissions@alfredstate.edu, URL http://www.alfredstate.edu.

THE ART INSTITUTE OF NEW YORK CITY
New York/Year-round   *(See display ad page 11)*

Sponsor: Private college, formerly New York Restaurant School. Program: 6-qtr/8-qtr full-time/part-time AOS degree in Culinary Arts & Restaurant Mgmt, 4-qtr/6-qtr certificate in Culinary Arts, 3-qtr/4-qtr certificates in Pastry Arts & Restaurant Mgmt. Established: 1980. Accredited by ACICS. Calendar: quarter. Curriculum: culinary. Admission dates: Jan, Apr, Jul, Oct. Total enrollment: 1484. 400 each admission period. 80% of applicants accepted. 85% receive financial aid. 35% enrolled part-time. Student to teacher ratio 21:1. 90% of graduates employed within six months. Facilities: 42,000-sq-ft recently renovated facility, 9 newly-equipped kitchens, new classrooms, restaurant.

FACULTY: 60 full- & 8 part-time faculty, all with a minimum 5 yr's experience, many with 4-yr degrees & prior teaching background.

COSTS: $22,561 for Culinary Arts, $17,398 for Pastry Arts, $15,664 for Restaurant Mgmt, $41,546 for AOS degree program. $50 application fee, $100 registration fee. Admission requirements: HS diploma or GED. Scholarships: yes. Loans: yes.

CONTACT: Michell Clark-Boyd, Admissions, The Art Institute of New York City, Admissions, 75 Varick St., New York, NY 10013; 212-226-5500/800-654-CHEF, Fax 212-226-5664, E-mail mclark-boyd@edmc.edu, URL http://www.ainyc.aii.edu.

THE CULINARY INSTITUTE OF AMERICA
Hyde Park/Year-round   *(See also page 18, 182, 224) (See display ad page 89)*

Sponsor: Independent, not-for-profit educational institution. Program: 38-mo bachelor's degree programs in Culinary Arts Mgmt and Baking & Pastry Arts Mgmt, 21-mo associate degree programs in Culinary Arts and Baking & Pastry Arts, continuing ed & nonvocational courses. Established: 1946. Accredited by MSA, ACCSCT, curricula registered with NY State Education Dept. Curriculum: culinary. Admission dates: 4 enrollment seasons with 16 entry dates/yr. Total enrollment: 2404. 90/50 assoc./bachelor's degree each admission period. 70% of applicants accepted. 85% receive financial aid. Student to teacher ratio 18:1. Facilities: 41 kitchens & bakeshops, 69,000-volume library, 4,000 instructional videos & DVDs, learning resource & nutrition centers, bookstore, 5 student-staffed restaurants, student recreation center. Courses: Associate & Bachelor's degree programs give students comprehensive, hands-on experience in the theory & techniques of foodservice. Bachelor's degree programs provide add'l managerial & conceptual skills.

FACULTY: 130+ chefs & instructors from more than 15 countries.

COSTS: $18,620/yr for freshman/sophomore, $13,860/yr for junior/senior. Admission requirements: HS diploma or equivalent & min 6 mos foodservice experience, including work in a professional kitchen. Scholarships: yes. Loans: yes.

CONTACT: Drusilla Blackman, Dean of Enrollment Management, The Culinary Institute of America, 1946 Campus Dr., Hyde Park, NY 12538; 800-CULINARY (800-285-4627), Fax (845) 451-1068, E-mail Admissions@culinary.edu, URL http://www.ciachef.edu.

ERIE COMMUNITY COLLEGE – CITY CAMPUS
Buffalo/September-May

Sponsor: 2-yr community college. Program: 2-yr AOS degree in Culinary Arts Technology; 1-yr certificate in Baking & Pastry Arts. Established: 1985. Accredited by MSA. Calendar: semester. Curriculum: culinary. Admission dates: Fall & Jan./spring. Total enrollment: 80. 80 each admission period. 60% of applicants accepted. 70% receive financial aid. 10% enrolled part-time. Student to teacher ratio 20:1. 75% of graduates employed within six months. Facilities: Include 5 kitchens &

Congratulations. You've decided to be a chef. This is where many people blow it.

Choosing the right culinary school can make a big difference in your success. There are many reasons students choose The French Culinary Institute: Our fast-paced six or nine month career courses taught by accomplished chef-instructors get you out and working long before other schools. Our Total Immersion℠ method of teaching means you're cooking and learning your very first day. A curriculum designed and directed by culinary masters and respected professionals: Alain Sailhac, Jacques Pépin, André Soltner, Jacques Torres, Alice Waters,

Alan Richman and Andrea Immer. Our New York City location, the center of the culinary world, surrounded by the brightest in the business, introduces you to a variety of career paths and culinary experiences. Our career services office provides ongoing job placement assistance and guidance. A career in the culinary world is exciting and rewarding, so your education should be too. ***To be your best, learn from the best.***

Career Courses at The FCI
  • Classic Culinary Arts
  • Classic Pastry Arts
  • Art of International Bread Baking

Culinary Business Courses
  • Essentials of Restaurant Management
  • Fundamentals of Wine
  • Craft of Food Writing

Call for a free information packet or to arrange a complete tour.

The French Culinary Institute
N E W   Y O R K   C I T Y

1-888-FCI-CHEF • www.FrenchCulinary.com/shaw
462 Broadway • New York, NY 10013 • Admission@FrenchCulinary.com

Financial assistance & scholarships are available for those who qualify.

classrooms, computer lab, student-operated fine dining restaurant.

FACULTY: 6 full-time, 7 part-time.

COSTS: Annual tuition: county resident $1,450, out-of-state/county $2,700. Fees $100. Admission requirements: HS diploma or equivalent & placement test. Scholarships: yes. Loans: yes.

CONTACT: Richard Mills, Professor, Erie Community College, Culinary Arts Technology, 121 Ellicott St., Buffalo, NY 14203-2698; 716-851-1034, Fax 716-851-1129, E-mail millsr@ecc.edu, URL http://www.ecc.edu.

THE FRENCH CULINARY INSTITUTE
New York/Year-round   *(See also page 225) (See display ad page 91)*

Sponsor: Proprietary institution founded by Dorothy Cann Hamilton. Program: 600-hr 6-mo full-time & 9-mo part-time Grande Diplôme programs in Classic Culinary or Pastry Arts; 6-wk Diplôme du Boulanger program in the Art of International Bread Baking; Culinary Business courses in catering, restaurateuring, wine merchandising. Established: 1984. Accredited by ACCSCT. Curriculum: culinary. Admission dates: Rolling. Total enrollment: 850. 24 each admission period. 90% of applicants accepted. 75% receive financial aid. 60% enrolled part-time. Student to teacher ratio 12:1. 98% of graduates employed within six months. Facilities: 30,000-sq-ft facility with newly equipped culinary, pastry & bread kitchens, demo amphitheater, L'Ecole restaurant (open to the public; all food prepared by students). Courses: Classic Culinary Arts emphasizing French Techniques. Classic French pastry technique, traditional dessert composition. Classic artisanal breads, restaurant breads. Fundamentals of Catering, Fundamentals of Wine, Essentials of Restaurant Mgmt.

FACULTY: 41 teachers & culinary staff, including Dean of Studies Alain Sailhac, Dean of Special Programs Jacques Pépin, Master Chef André Soltner, Dean of Pastry Arts Jacques Torres, Dean of Wine Studies Andrea Immer, Visiting Dean Alice Waters, Marcella Hazen.

COSTS: $28,500/$33,500 for Classic Culinary Arts full-time /part-time, $32,500 for Classic Pastry Arts, $6,150 for International Bread Baking, $895 for Fundamentals of Wine, $6,900 for Essentials of Restaurant Management. Admission requirements: HS diploma or equivalent, 150-word essay, personal interview. Scholarships: yes. Loans: yes.

CONTACT: David Waggoner, Dean of Enrollment, The French Culinary Institute, 462 Broadway, New York, NY 10013-2618; 888-FCI-CHEF/212-219-8890, Fax 212-431-3054, E-mail admission@french-culinary.com, URL http://www.frenchculinary.com/landings/culinary0604_b.php?r=INTERS.

FULTON-MONTGOMERY COMMUNITY COLLEGE
Johnstown/Year-round

Sponsor: Public 2-yr college. Program: 1-yr certificate in Quantity Food, 2-yr associate degree in Food Service Administration. Established: 1964. Accredited by MSA. Calendar: semester. Curriculum: culinary. Admission dates: Jan, Sep. Total enrollment: 15. 75% of applicants accepted. 25% enrolled part-time. Student to teacher ratio 7:1. Facilities: Food production kitehcn, gourmet dining room.

FACULTY: 1 full-time, 3 part-time.

COSTS: $1,115/sem full-time, $93/cr-hr part-time. Application fee $40. Scholarships: yes.

CONTACT: Alexandra Henderson, Professor, Food Service Administration, Fulton-Montgomery Community College, Route 67, Johnstown, NY 12095; 518-762-4651 x6104, Fax 518-762-4334, E-mail ahenders@fmcc.suny.edu, URL http://fmcc.suny.edu.

ICE CREAM UNIVERSITY
Riverdale

Sponsor: Ice cream, dairy & food consultants. Program: 3- to 5-day seminars for prospective & current ice cream business owners, annual gelato tour of Italy.

FACULTY: Includes Malcolm Stogo, founder of an ice cream consulting firm with 25 yrs experience.

COSTS: ~$225-$995/seminar.

CONTACT: Ice Cream University, 2727 Palisade Ave., #11H, Riverdale, NY 10463; 718-884-5086, 914-588-2002 (cell), Fax 718-884-2255, E-mail mstogo@aol.com, URL http://www.icecreamuniversity.org.

THE INSTITUTE OF CULINARY EDUCATION
New York/Year-round   *(See also page 226) (See display ad above & pages 93, 226)*
Sponsor: Private institute, formerly known as Peter Kump's New York Cooking School. Program: 26- to 39-wk diploma programs in Culinary Arts, Pastry & Baking Arts, & Culinary mgmt. Flexible schedules. Continuing education & business courses, programs for professionals & non-professionals. Established: 1975. Accredited by ACCSCT, licensed by NY State Dept. of Education. Curriculum: culinary. Admission dates: moly. Total enrollment: 750. 75% of applicants accepted. 70% receive financial aid. Student to teacher ratio 13:1. 96% of graduates employed within six months. Facilities: 27,000-sq-ft facility includes 9 kitchens, wine studies center, confectionery lab, reference library. Courses: In addition to theory & hands-on training in the preparation & presentation of classic cuisines, culinary arts courses cover Italian & Asian cuisine, kitchen management, garde manger, pastry & baking, wine.
FACULTY: 45 chef-instructors. Founder Peter Kump was founding president of The James Beard Foundation. Dir. of Pastry & Baking Nick Malgieri is one of Pastry Art & Design's Top 10 Pastry Chefs. Advisory board includes chefs Daniel Boulud, Marcus Samuelsson, Lidia.
COSTS: Culinary Arts program $19,300, Pastry & Baking Arts program $18,750, Culinary Management $11,000. Admission requirements: HS diploma or GED plus proof of 1 yr college or 1 yr professional work experience (any profession). Scholarships: yes. Loans: yes.
CONTACT: Stephen Tave, Director/Vice President, The Institute of Culinary Education, 50 W. 23rd St., New York, NY 10010; 800-522-4610, 212-847-0770, Fax 212-847-0726, E-mail stave@iceculinary.com, URL http://www.iceculinary.com.

INTERNATIONAL SOMMELIER GUILD
Australia, Bahamas, Canada, China, New Zealand, Singapore, South Africa, US
Sponsor: Wine organization. Program: 23-wk Sommelier Diploma Program, 24-hr Wine Fundamentals Certificate Level 1 & 45- or 48-hr Certificate Level 2. Established: 1984. Calendar: semester. Total enrollment: 24 max. 24 each admission period. 100% enrolled part-time. Student to teacher ratio 24:1.

FACULTY: 25 instructors, all with hospitality & adult ed experience, Sommelier certification.

COSTS: $1,500-$3,100. Admission requirements: Legal drinking age, HS diploma or GED.

CONTACT: Daria Rozik, Administrator, International Sommelier Guild, 363 Lang Blvd., Grand Island, NY 14072; 866-412-0464, 302-622-3811, 905-858-1217, 416-699-3666, Fax 905-858-3440, E-mail info@internationalsommelier.com, URL http://www.internationalsommelier.com.

INTERNATIONAL WINE CENTER
New York/Year-round
Sponsor: Private wine school. Program: 8-session Intermediate Certificate Course, 15-session Advanced Certificate Course, 2-yr Diploma Course. Home study. Established: 1982. Admission dates: Yr-round. 30-50 each admission period.

FACULTY: Master of Wine Mary Ewing Mulligan; all instructors with WSET diploma.

COSTS: $448-$1,875.

CONTACT: Linda Lawry, Int'l Wine Center, 1133 Broadway, Ste. 520, New York, NY 10010; 212-627-7170, Fax 212-627-7116, E-mail IWCNY@aol.com, URL http://www.internationalwinecenter.com.

JEFFERSON COMMUNITY COLLEGE
Watertown
Sponsor: 2-yr college. Program: 2-yr certificate/AAS degree. Established: 1975. Accredited by MSA. Admission dates: Aug, Jan. Total enrollment: 120. 100% of applicants accepted. Student to teacher ratio 25:1. 95% of graduates employed within six months.

FACULTY: 4 full-time.

COSTS: Annual tuition in-state $1,250 full-time, $84/cr part-time; out-of-state $2,318/sem, $168/cr. Admission requirements: HS diploma or equivalent.

CONTACT: Deborah McGloine, Assistant Professor, Jefferson Community College, Hospitality & Tourism, Outer Coffeen St., Watertown, NY 13601; 315-786-2333, E-mail dmcgloine@sunyjefferson.edu, URL http://www.sunyjefferson.edu.

L'ECOLE DES CHEFS RELAIS GOURMANDS
Locations Worldwide/Year-round
Sponsor: Relais & Chateaux Relais Gourmands. Program: 2- & 5-day internship programs with Michelin & Mobil-starred chefs. Program is offered to amateur cooks & culinary students only. Certificate upon completion. Established: 1999. Curriculum: culinary. Admission dates: Yr-round. Total enrollment: 1 per chef/restaurant. Based upon chef availability each admission period. 80% of applicants accepted. Student to teacher ratio 1:1. Facilities: On-site in the kitchens of noted restaurants in 17 countries.

FACULTY: Master chefs with 156 Michelin & 58 Mobil-starred chefs.

COSTS: 2-day (5-day) programs $1,100-$1,400 ($1,900-$2,950). Admission requirements: Resume & application.

CONTACT: L'Ecole des Chefs Relais Gourmands, 11 E. 44th St., #707, New York, NY 10017; 877-334-6464, Fax 212-856-0193, E-mail info@ecoledeschefs.com, URL http://www.ecoledeschefs.com.

MOHAWK VALLEY COMMUNITY COLLEGE
Rome/August-May
Sponsor: 2-yr community college. Program: AOS Degree in Culinary Arts Mgmt & in Culinary Arts Mgmt with Baking & Pastry emphasis, AAS Degree in Restaurant Mgmt, Chef Training

Certificate. Established: 1946. Accredited by MSA. Calendar: semester. Curriculum: culinary, core. Admission dates: Aug, Jan. Total enrollment: 110. 45-55 FT, 20 PT, 18+ on-line each admission period. 94% of applicants accepted. 90% receive financial aid. 40% enrolled part-time. Student to teacher ratio 14:1. 99% of graduates employed within 6 mos. Facilities: Cuisine & baking labs, 7 classrooms, demo kitchen, conference room, 110-seat dining room, computer lab, culinary library. FACULTY: 3 full-time, 6 adjunct. Includes Director Mark Waldrop, MS.
COSTS: N.Y State Residents: $1,400/sem full-time, $115/cr-hr part-time. Admission requirements: HS Diploma or GED. Scholarships: yes. Loans: yes.
CONTACT: Mark Waldrop, Director of Hospitality, Mohawk Valley Community College, Hospitality Programs, 1101 Floyd Ave., Rome, NY 13440; 315-334-7710, Fax 315-334-7762, E-mail mwaldrop@mvcc.edu, URL http://www.mvcc.edu/catalog/hospitality.

MONROE COLLEGE
New York & Westchester/Year-round
Sponsor: Private college. Program: AAS degree in Hospitality mgmt and the Culinary Arts. Established: 2002. Accredited by MSA. Calendar: semester. Admission dates: Sep, Jan, Apr. Total enrollment: 150. 80/30/30 each admission period. 50% of applicants accepted. 95% receive financial aid. 5% enrolled part-time. Student to teacher ratio 16:1. 95% of graduates employed within six months. Facilities: Full-service white tablecloth restaurant at the New Rochelle campus.
FACULTY: Experienced professors, 95% full time.
COSTS: $4,680/sem, administrative fee $300, housing $2,300-$3,00/sem. Admission requirements: Essay, HS diploma, interview. Scholarships: yes. Loans: yes.
CONTACT: Craig Rutman, Monroe College, 2501 Jerome Ave., Bronx, NY 10468; 718-933-6700, 800-55-MONROE, E-mail crutman@monroecollege.edu, URL http://www.monroecollege.edu/academics/hospitality_culinary.html.

MONROE COMMUNITY COLLEGE
Rochester/September-May
Sponsor: 2-yr college. Program: 2-yr certificate/AAS degree. Established: 1967. Accredited by MSA. Calendar: semester. Curriculum: core. Admission dates: Fall, spring. Total enrollment: 175. 60 each admission period. 80% of applicants accepted. 60% receive financial aid. 20% enrolled part-time. Student to teacher ratio 18:1. 96% of graduates employed within six months. Facilities: 4 kitchens, computer lab, dining room.
FACULTY: 8-10 full- and part-time.
COSTS: $1,205/sem in-state full-time, $105/cr-hr part-time. Out-of-state tuition is double. Admission requirements: HS diploma or equivalent.
CONTACT: Eddy Callens, Chairperson, Monroe Community College - Brighton Campus, Food, Hotel, & Tourism Mgmt., Bldg. 3, Rm. 155, Rochester, NY 14623; 585-292-2542/2586, E-mail ecallens@monroecc.edu, URL http://www.monroecc.edu.

THE NATURAL GOURMET COOKERY SCHOOL
New York/Year-round   *(See also page 229) (See display ad page 97)*
Sponsor: Proprietary school devoted to health supportive, natural foods cooking & theory. Program: 600+-hr, 4-mo full-time/10-mo part-time Culinary Arts Program, individual nonvocational courses for the public. Established: 1977. Accredited by Chef's Training Program curriculum licensed by NY State Dept. of Education & accredited by ACCET. Curriculum: culinary. Admission dates: CTP begins 9 times/yr. 16 each admission period. 33% enrolled part-time. Student to teacher ratio 16:1. 80% of graduates employed within six months. Facilities: Include 2 newly renovated kitchens, classroom, & bookstore. Courses: Vegetarian focus, emphasis on natural foods, health supportive cooking, contemporary presentation, preparation, techniques, knife skills, limited poultry & fish, baking & desserts, career opportunities, theoretical approaches to diet & health.

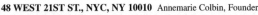

FACULTY: 15 full/part-time faculty, incl founder Annemarie Colbin, MA, Certified Health Education Specialist, author of Food and Healing, The Book of Whole Meals, The Natural Gourmet; President Jenny Matthau, a graduate of the school.

COSTS: $15,850 tuition includes books. $100 application fee. Nearby lodging begins at $500/mo. Admission requirements: HS diploma or equivalent. Scholarships: yes. Loans: yes.

CONTACT: Merle Brown, Director of Admissions, The Natural Gourmet Cookery School, 48 W. 21st St., 2nd Floor, New York, NY 10010; 212-645-5170, 212-627-COOK, Fax 212-989-1493, E-mail admissions@naturalgourmetschool.com, URL http://www.naturalgourmetschool.com.

NEW SCHOOL CULINARY ARTS
New York/Year-round

Sponsor: New School University. Program: Master class certificate courses in Cooking (25 sessions), Baking (15), Professional Catering (10), Italian Cooking (10), Restaurant mgmt (12). Established: 1919. Calendar: trimester. Curriculum: culinary. Total enrollment: 12 maximum in each Master class. 100% enrolled part-time. Student to teacher ratio 12:1. Facilities: Bed & breakfast new instructional kitchen equipped with a mix of professional & high-end home equipment.

FACULTY: 50+ faculty headed by Gary Goldberg, co-founder Martin Johner, incl Bruce Beck, Miriam Brickman, James Chew, Richard Glavin, Arlyn Hackett, Micheal Krondl, Harriet Lembeck, Lisa Montenegro, Robert Posch, Dan Rosati, Stephen Schmidt, Carole Walter.

COSTS: Master Class $2,510 (+$475 materials fee) for Cooking, $1,505 (+$215) for Baking, $995 (+$205) for Catering.

CONTACT: Gary A. Goldberg, Executive Director, New School Culinary Arts, 131 West 23rd St., New York, NY 10011; 212-255-4141/800-544-1978, Fax 646-336-6317, E-mail NSCulArts@aol.com, URL http://www.nsu.newschool.edu/culinary.

NEW YORK CITY TECHNICAL COLLEGE
Brooklyn/September-May

Sponsor: Career college. Program: 2-yr AAS degree & 4-yr BS degree in Hospitality mgmt. Established: 1947. Accredited by MSA, state, ACPHA. Calendar: semester. Curriculum: core. Admission dates: Sep, Feb. Total enrollment: 600. 125 each admission period. 50% receive financial aid. 50% enrolled part-time. Student to teacher ratio 15:1. 90% of graduates employed within six months. Facilities: Include 5 kitchens, dining room, 3 classrooms, restaurant.

FACULTY: 13 full-time, 20-40 part-time.

COSTS: Annual tuition in-state $3,200, out-of-state $6,400. CUNY fee is $35. Textbooks $1,000, materials fee $10, uniforms $120. Housing $800/mo. Admission requirements: HS diploma or equivalent and admission test. Scholarships: yes. Loans: yes.

CONTACT: Francisco Betancourt, Chair, New York City Technical College, Hospitality Mgmt., 300 Jay St., #N220, Brooklyn, NY 11201; 718-260-5630, Fax 718-260-5997, E-mail fbetancourt@citytech.cuny.edu, URL http://www.nyctc.cuny.edu.

NEW YORK FOOD AND HOTEL MANAGEMENT SCHOOL
New York/Year-round
Sponsor: Proprietary institution. Program: 9-mo certificate in Commercial Cooking & Catering.
Established: 1935. Accredited by ACCST. Curriculum: culinary. Admission dates: Every 4 to 6 wks.
Total enrollment: 90. 20 each admission period. 80% of applicants accepted. Student to teacher ratio
16:1. 89% of graduates employed within 6 mos. Facilities: Include 4 kitchens, 5 classrooms, restaurant.
FACULTY: 10 full-time & part-time.
COSTS: Annual tuition $7,515. Registration fee $100. Books $235, food lab fee $1,490, kits & uni-
forms $155. Admission requirements: HS diploma or equivalent or admission test.
CONTACT: Harold Kaplan, Vice-President, New York Food and Hotel Management School,
Admissions, 154 W. 14th Street, New York, NY 10011; 212-675-6655, Fax 212-463-9194, E-mail
nyfood@hotmail.com, URL http://www.nyfoodandhotelschool.com.

NEW YORK INSTITUTE OF TECHNOLOGY – CULINARY ARTS CENTER
Central Islip & Old Westbury/Year-round
Sponsor: Independent institution. Program: 19-mo AOS degree in Culinary Arts. Certificate in
Culinary Arts & certificate in Pastry & Baking. Established: 1984. Accredited by MSA, ACF.
Calendar: semester. Curriculum: culinary, core. Admission dates: Fall, spring. Total enrollment:
140. 80/20 each admission period. 90% of applicants accepted. 85% receive financial aid. 15%
enrolled part-time. Student to teacher ratio 15:1. 99% of graduates employed within six months.
Facilities: Include 6 kitchens, bakery, 2-10 classrooms, computer software, 2 restaurants, ISDN lab.
FACULTY: 9 full-time, 3 part-time.
COSTS: Annual tuition $16,000. On-campus housing: 150 spaces, average cost $2,500/sem.
Admission requirements: HS diploma or equivalent. SAT preferred. Scholarships: yes. Loans: yes.

CONTACT: New York Institute of Technology-Culinary Arts Center, Culinary Arts, 300 Carleton Ave., #66-118, PO Box 9029, Central Islip, NY 11722-9029; 631-348-3290, Fax 631-348-3247, E-mail admissions@nyit.edu, URL http://iris.nyit.edu/culinary.

NEW YORK UNIVERSITY
New York/September-July
(See also page 229) (See display ad page 98)
Sponsor: Dept. of Nutrition, Food Studies and Public Health, The Steinhardt School of Education. Program: Bachelor's, master's, & doctoral degree programs in Food Studies, Food mgmt, Nutrition, and Community Public Health. Established: 1986. Accredited by MSA. Curriculum: core. Admission dates: Sep, Jan, Summer. Total enrollment: 60 in food program, many part-time. Student to teacher ratio 10-15:1. 100% of graduates employed within six months. Facilities: New teaching kitchen & library, computer, academic resources. Courses: Over 50 in food science & management, food culture & history, food writing, nutrition.

FACULTY: 9 full-time academic, 45 part-time academic & professional.

COSTS: $30,094 flat rate/yr for full-time undergraduates includes fees. rm & bd $12,000. $12,259/sem for for full-time graduate students includes fees. Some housing available. Scholarships: yes. Loans: yes.

CONTACT: Program Director, NYU Dept. of Nutrition, Food Studies and Public Health, 35 W. Fourth St., New York, NY 10012-1172; 212-998-5580, 800-771-4NYU, Fax 212-995-4194, E-mail nutrition@nyu.edu, URL http://www.education.nyu.edu/foodshaw.

NIAGARA COUNTY COMMUNITY COLLEGE
Sanborn/Year-round
Sponsor: 2-yr college. Program: 2-yr/66 cr-hr AOS degree in Food Service with Professional Chef emphasis. Calendar: semester. Curriculum: core.

COSTS: $88/cr-hr in-state.

CONTACT: Sam Sheusi, Coordinator/Instructor, Niagara County Community College, 3111 Saunders Settlement Rd., Sanborn, NY 14132; 716-731-3271 #248, Fax 716-731-4053, E-mail sheusi@niagaracc.suny.edu, URL http://www.sunyniagara.cc.ny.us.

ONONDAGA COMMUNITY COLLEGE
Syracuse
Sponsor: 2-yr college. Program: 1-yr certificate, 2-yr AAS degree. Established: 1979. Accredited by State. Admission dates: Fall, spring. Total enrollment: 90-100. Student to teacher ratio 16:1.

COSTS: In-state $1,225/sem, out-of-state $3,675/sem. Scholarships: yes.

CONTACT: Jillann Neely, Curriculum Chairperson, Onondaga Community College, Culinary Arts, Onondaga Hill, Syracuse, NY 13215; 315-498-2622 x2232, E-mail occinfo@sunyocc.edu, URL http://www.sunyocc.edu.

PAUL SMITH'S COLLEGE
Paul Smiths/Year-round
(See display ad page 100)
Sponsor: College. Program: 2-yr AAS degree in Culinary Arts, 1-yr Baking certificate, 4-yr BPS degree in Culinary Arts & Service mgmt. Established: 1946. Accredited by MSA, ACF. Calendar: semester. Curriculum: culinary, core. Admission dates: Sep, Jan. Total enrollment: 229 Sept. 116 each admission period. 85% of applicants accepted. 90% receive financial aid. 10% enrolled part-time. Student to teacher ratio 14:1. 99% of graduates employed within six months. Facilities: Include 6 campus Foods Laboratories, an a la carte kitchen, & a 60-seat dining room in addition to a fine dining restaurant in the college-owned Hotel Saranac. Courses: Baking certificate curriculum covers journeyman skills, including advertising, merchandising, & management. Students produce goods for an on-campus bakery.

FACULTY: 66 full-time, 12 part-time. Includes Robert Brown, CM, & Paul Sorgule, CCE, 1988 Culinary Olympics gold medalist.

COSTS: Annual tuition $14,050. Culinary Arts program comprehensive fee is $545/sem. $30 application fee. Housing averages $3,000/yr; board is $3,000/yr. Admission requirements: HS completion or GED. SAT or ACT. Scholarships: yes. Loans: yes.

CONTACT: Paul Smith's College, Admissions, P.O. Box 265, Paul Smiths, NY 12970; 800-421-2605, 518-327-6227, Fax 518-327-6016, E-mail admiss@paulsmiths.edu, URL http://www.paulsmiths.edu.

PROJECT RENEWAL
New York

Sponsor: Non-profit job training program. Program: 3-mo classroom training & 3-mo externship in Culinary Arts or Baking & Pastry. Established: 1992. Calendar: quarter. Curriculum: culinary. Admission dates: 4 cycles/yr. Total enrollment: 250/yr. 40 culinary/40 baking each admission period. 100% of applicants accepted. 100% receive financial aid. Student to teacher ratio 20:1. 89% of graduates employed within six months. Facilities: Modern training kitchen with 4 gas ranges, industrial equipment & utensils.

FACULTY: 1 full-time culinary instructor. 2 part-time pastry/baking instructors.

CONTACT: Project Renewal, 200 Varick St., New York, NY 10014; 212-620-0340, Fax 212-243-4868, E-mail BarbaraH@projectrenewal.org, URL http://www.projectrenewal.org.

SCHENECTADY COUNTY COMMUNITY COLLEGE
Schenectady/Year-round

Sponsor: 2-yr college. Program: 2-yr degree, 1-yr certificate. Established: 1980. Accredited by MSA, ACF. Calendar: semester. Curriculum: culinary. Admission dates: Sep, Jan, Jun. Total enrollment: 340. 100 each admission period. 86% of applicants accepted. 22% enrolled part-time. Student to teacher ratio 20:1. 88% of graduates employed within six months. Facilities: 7 kitchens, restaurant, 2 dining rooms, banquet room.

FACULTY: 13 full-time, 22 part-time.

COSTS: $2,500 in-state, $5,000 out-of-state. Admission requirements: HS diploma or equivalent & placement testing. Scholarships: yes. Loans: yes.

CONTACT: Toby Strianese, Chair and Professor, Schenectady County Community College, Hotel, Culinary Arts, 78 Washington Ave., Schenectady, NY 12305; 518-381-1391, Fax 518-346-0379, E-mail strianaj@gw.sunysccc.edu, URL http://www.sunysccc.edu/academic/cularts/index.html.

SUNY COLLEGE OF AGRICULTURE & TECHNOLOGY
Cobleskill/August-May

Sponsor: 2- & 4-yr College of Technology. Program: 2-yr AOS degree in Culinary Arts, AAS degrees in Restaurant mgmt & Institutional Foods, Certificate in Commercial Cooking. Established: 1971. Accredited by MSA, ACF. Calendar: semester. Curriculum: culinary, core. Admission dates: Aug & Jan. Total enrollment: 120. 60 each admission period. 85% of applicants accepted. 80% receive financial aid. 5% enrolled part-time. Student to teacher ratio 15:1. 99% of graduates employed within six months. Facilities: Includes 5 kitchens, on-campus restaurant, catering facilities, USDA-certified meat cutting lab.

FACULTY: 10 full-time.

COSTS: $3,200/yr in-state, $5,000/yr out-of-state. Admission requirements: HS diploma or equivalent, good preparation in English, math, & lab science. Scholarships: yes. Loans: yes.

CONTACT: Clayton Smith, Director of Admissions, SUNY College of Agriculture & Technology at Cobleskill, Knapp Hall, Route 7, Cobleskill, NY 12043; 518-255-5525 or 800-295-8988, Fax 518-255-6769, E-mail admissions@cobleskill.edu, URL http://www.cobleskill.edu.

SUNY DELHI
Delhi/August-May

Sponsor: 2- & 4-yr public college. Program: AAS & BBA in Culinary Arts. Established: 1994. Accredited by MSA. Calendar: semester. Curriculum: culinary, core. Admission dates: Sep. Total enrollment: 100. 70 each admission period. Student to teacher ratio 10:1. Facilities: Hospitality center with catering & restaurant kitchens, catering facility, beverage lounge, on-site restaurant.

FACULTY: 3 certified executive chefs, bachelor's degrees.

COSTS: $3,200/yr in-state, $5,000/yr out-of-state. Admission requirements: HS graduate with 1 yr gen'l biology. Scholarships: yes. Loans: yes.

CONTACT: Rosalie Higgins, Dean, Business & Hospitality, SUNY Delhi College of Technology, 2 Main St., Delhi, NY 13753; 607-746-4550, Fax 607-746-4104, E-mail elwellja@delhi.edu, URL http://www.delhi.edu.

SULLIVAN COUNTY COMMUNITY COLLEGE
Loch Sheldrake/September-May

Sponsor: 2-yr college. Program: 2-yr AAS degree in Professional Chef & Hotel Technology. Established: 1965. Accredited by MSA, ACF. Calendar: semester. Curriculum: culinary. Admission dates: Sep, Jan. Total enrollment: 126. 75 each admission period. 95% of applicants accepted. 90% receive financial aid. 22% enrolled part-time. Student to teacher ratio 14:1. 100% of graduates employed within six months. Facilities: Include 7 kitchens & classrooms, restaurant.

FACULTY: 8 full-time. Qualifications: bachelor's or master's degree.

COSTS: ~$2,500 in-state, ~$4,500 out-of-state. Application fee $25. On-campus housing: 300 spaces. Housing: $4,600. Admission requirements: HS diploma or equivalent and admission test. Scholarships: yes. Loans: yes.

CONTACT: Mark Sanok, Chairperson, Sullivan County Community College, Hospitality, 1000 LeRoy Rd., Box 4002, Loch Sheldrake, NY 12759-4002; 914-434-5750, Fax 914-434-4806, E-mail msanok@sullivan.suny.edu, URL http://www.sullivan.suny.edu.

WESTCHESTER COMMUNITY COLLEGE
Valhalla/September-May
Sponsor: 2-yr college. Program: 2-yr AAS in Food Service Admin. Established: 1946. Accredited by MSA. Calendar: semester. Curriculum: culinary. Admission dates: All yr. Total enrollment: 100. 50 each admission period. 20% receive financial aid. 25% enrolled part-time. Student to teacher ratio 15:1. 100% of graduates employed within six months. Facilities: Include lab/demo kitchen, baking kitchen, production kitchen, bar/beverage management lab, instructional dining room.

FACULTY: 4 full-time. Qualifications: MS required.

COSTS: Annual tuition in-state $1,075/sem. Lab fees $15. Admission requirements: HS diploma or equivalent. Scholarships: yes.

CONTACT: Daryl Nosek, FMP, Curriculum Chair, Westchester Community College, Restaurant Mgmt., 75 Grasslands Rd., Valhalla, NY 10595-1698; 914-785-6765, Fax 914-785-6423, E-mail info@sunywcc.edu, URL http://www.wcc.co.westchester.ny.us.

NORTH CAROLINA

ALAMANCE COMMUNITY COLLEGE
Graham/Year-round
Sponsor: Public 2-yr college. Program: 6-mo certificate in Culinary Specialist, 12-mo diploma in Culinary Professional, 24-mo associate degree in Culinary Technology. Established: 1959. Accredited by SACS. Calendar: semester. Curriculum: culinary, core. Admission dates: Jan, May, Aug. Total enrollment: 70. 30 each admission period. 100% of applicants accepted. 50% receive financial aid. 40% enrolled part-time. Student to teacher ratio 15:1. 99% of graduates employed within six months. Facilities: Bake shop, catering service, classroom, food production kitchen, gourmet dining room, computer & food labs, lecture room, teaching kitchen.

FACULTY: 2 full-time, 1 part-time.

COSTS: In-state: $496/sem full-time, $31/cr part-time. Out-of-state: $2,716/sem full-time, $169.75/cr part-time. $150 for uniforms/knives. Admission requirements: Open door policy. Remedial math & English may be required based on entrance exam scores. Scholarships: yes. Loans: yes.

CONTACT: Doris Schomberg, Dept. Head, Culinary Technology, Alamance Community College, PO Box 8000, Graham, NC 27253-8000; 336-506-4241, Fax 336-578-1987, E-mail schombed@alamance.cc.nc.us, URL http://www.alamance.cc.nc.us.

THE ART INSTITUTE OF CHARLOTTE – CULINARY ARTS
Charlotte/Year-round   *(See display ad page 11)*
Sponsor: Private college. Program: 21-mo (7-qtr, 108-credit) AAS degree in Culinary Arts. Established: 2002. Accredited by ACICS. Calendar: quarter. Facilities: Industry-standard kitchens.

COSTS: $315/credit ($300/credit before 11/02). $50 application fee, $100 enrollment fee.

CONTACT: David Laughry, Director of Admissions, The Art Institute of Charlotte-Culinary Arts, Three LakePointe Plaza, 2110 Water Ridge Pkwy., Charlotte, NC 28217; 704-357-8020, Fax 704-357-1133, E-mail laughryd@aii.edu, URL http://www.aich.artinstitutes.edu.

ASHEVILLE-BUNCOMBE TECHNICAL COMMUNITY COLLEGE
Asheville/Year-round
Sponsor: 2-yr community college. Program: 2-yr AAS degrees in Culinary Technology, Baking & Pastry Arts, and Hotel & Restaurant Mgmt. Established: 1968. Accredited by SACS. Calendar: semester. Curriculum: core. Admission dates: Begins Sept. of yr prior to official enrollment. Total enrollment: 70. 35 each admission period. 100% of applicants accepted. 25% receive financial aid. 55% enrolled part-time. Student to teacher ratio 11:1. 100% of graduates employed within six months. Facilities: Include 2 kitchens, 4 classrooms, restaurant 1 day/wk, 2 dining rooms.

FACULTY: 4 full-time, 5 part-time.

COSTS: $1,172 in-state, $6,500out-of-state. Activity fee $8-$10. Housing $300/mo. Admission

requirements: HS diploma or equivalent & admission test. Scholarships: yes. Loans: yes.
CONTACT: Sheila Tillman, Chairperson, Asheville-Buncombe Technical Community College, Dept. of Hospitality Education, 340 Victoria Rd., Asheville, NC 28801; 828-254-1921 x232, Fax 828-281-9783, E-mail stillman@abtech.edu, URL http://www.abtech.edu.

CAPE FEAR COMMUNITY COLLEGE
Wilmington/Year-round
Sponsor: Public 2-yr college. Program: 1-sem diploma, 1-yr certificate, and 2-yr associate degree in Culinary Technology. Established: 1959. Accredited by SACS. Calendar: semester. Curriculum: culinary. Admission dates: Jan, Aug. Student to teacher ratio 15:1. Facilities: Food production & teaching kitchens, gourmet dining room & public restaurant, bake shop, classroom.
FACULTY: 2 full-time, 5 part-time.
COSTS: In-state: $280/sem full-time, $20/cr-hr part-time. Out-of-state: $2,282/sem full-time, $163/cr-hr part-time. Scholarships: yes.
CONTACT: Valerie Mason, Lead Instructor, Culinary Arts, Cape Fear Community College, 411 N. Front St., Wilmington, NC 28401; 910-251-5960, E-mail vmason@capefear.cc.nc.us, URL http://cfcc.net.

CENTRAL PIEDMONT COMMUNITY COLLEGE
Charlotte/Year-round
Sponsor: 2-yr college. Program: 2-yr AAS degree in Culinary Arts. Certificate programs in baking, culinary, garde manger, hot foods. Established: 1974. Accredited by SACS. Calendar: semester. Curriculum: culinary, core. Admission dates: Fall, winter, spring, summer. Total enrollment: 500. 100-150 each admission period. 75% of applicants accepted. 10% receive financial aid. 25% enrolled part-time. Student to teacher ratio 15:1. 98% of graduates employed within 6 mos. Facilities: Include 4 kitchens, 3 classrooms, baking lab, small quantities lab, computer lab, restaurant.
FACULTY: 3 full-time C.I.A. graduates, 5 part-time.
COSTS: Annual tuition in-state $800, out-of-state $4,800. Housing $400-$500/mo. Admission requirements: HS diploma or equivalent and admission test.
CONTACT: Robert G. Boll, FMP, CFE, Department Head, Central Piedmont Community College, Culinary Arts, P.O. Box 35009, Charlotte, NC 28235; 704-330-6721, Fax 704-330-6581, E-mail bob_boll@cpcc.cc.nc.us, URL http://www.cpcc.cc.nc.us.

DURHAM COMMUNITY COLLEGE & CHEZ BAY COOKING SCHOOL
Raleigh-Durham-Chapel Hill/Year-round
Sponsor: Community college. Program: 6-session certificate in Culinary Arts. Established: 2002. Accredited by SACS. Admission dates: Jan-May, Jul-Nov. Total enrollment: 25. 25 each admission period. 95% of applicants accepted. Student to teacher ratio 15:1. Facilities: 1,500-sq-ft Chez Bay culinary arts center with prep area & 6 cooking stations.
FACULTY: Chez Bay Gourmet instructors.
COSTS: $935 for 6-course program. Admission requirements: HS diploma (req. may be waived).
CONTACT: Joel Goldfarb, President/Executive Chef, Chez Bay Gourmet Cooking School, 1921 North Pointe Dr., Durham, NC 27705; 919-477-7878, 800-477-7857, Fax 919-882-9129, E-mail dt@chezbaygourmet.com, URL http://www.chezbaygourmet.com/dt.htm.

GUILFORD TECHNICAL COMMUNITY COLLEGE
Jamestown/Year-round
Sponsor: 2-yr community college. Program: 1-yr & 2-yr program in Culinary Technology, Hotel/Restaurant mgmt. Established: 1989. Accredited by ACF. Calendar: semester. Curriculum: culinary, core. Admission dates: yr-round. Total enrollment: 130. 45 each admission period. 90% of applicants accepted. 50% receive financial aid. 50% enrolled part-time. Student to teacher ratio 15:1. 98% of graduates employed within six months. Facilities: New facility with latest technology.
FACULTY: 4 full-time, 5 part-time.

Costs: In-state $26.75/cr-hr, out-of-state $69.75/cr-hr. Admission requirements: Placement exam. Scholarships: yes.

Contact: Keith Gardiner CEC, CFE, Department Chair, Guilford Technical Community College, Culinary Technology, Box 309, Jamestown, NC 27282; 336-334-4822 #2347, Fax 336-841-4350, E-mail gardinerk@gtcc.cc.nc.us, URL http://technet.gtcc.cc.nc.us.

SANDHILLS COMMUNITY COLLEGE
Pinehurst/Year-round

Sponsor: 2-yr college. Program: 2-yr/70 sem-hr degree in Culinary Technology and in Baking & Pastry Arts. Calendar: semester. Curriculum: culinary, core. Total enrollment: 75. 30 each admission period. 50% receive financial aid. Student to teacher ratio 10:1. 95% of graduates employed within six months.

Costs: Full-time students $426/sem in-state, $2,364/sem out-of-state. Scholarships: yes. Loans: yes.

Contact: Ted Oelfke, Sandhills Community College, 2200 Airport Rd., Pinehurst, NC 28374; 910-695-3756, Fax 910-695-1823, E-mail oelfket@email.sandhills.cc.nc.us, URL http://www.sandhills.cc.nc.us.

SOUTHWESTERN COMMUNITY COLLEGE
Sylva/Year-round

Sponsor: Two-yr college. Program: Two-yr AAS degree in Culinary Technology, 16 cr-hr NCCCS certificate. Facilities: Classroom & teaching kitchen.

Faculty: Program Coordinator Ceretta Davis.

Costs: In-state $440/sem full time, $27.50/cr-hr.

Contact: Ceretta Davis, Program Coordinator, Southwestern Community College, 447 College Dr., Sylva, NC 28779; 800-447-4091 x 256, 828-586-4091, x 256, Fax 828-586-3129, E-mail ceretta@southwest.cc.nc.us, URL http://www.southwest.cc.nc.us/cul/index.htm.

WAKE TECHNICAL COMMUNITY COLLEGE
Raleigh/Year-round

Sponsor: 2-yr community college. Program: 2-yr associate degree in Culinary Arts. Established: 1985. Accredited by SACS. Calendar: semester. Curriculum: culinary, core. Admission dates: yr-round. Total enrollment: 105. 60 each admission period. 75% of applicants accepted. 10% receive financial aid. 15% enrolled part-time. Student to teacher ratio 10:1. 98% of graduates employed within six months. Facilities: Include kitchen & restaurant.

Faculty: 6 full-time, 1 part-time.

Costs: Annual tuition in-state $2,300. Housing $500+/mo. Admission requirements: HS diploma or equivalent. Scholarships: yes. Loans: yes.

Contact: Alice Downum, Administrative Asst., Wake Technical Community College, Culinary Technology, 9101 Fayetteville Rd., Raleigh, NC 27603; 919-662-3537, Fax 919-779-3360, E-mail agdownum@gwmail.wake.tec.nc.us, URL http://www.wake.tec.nc.us/catalog/associates/culinary.html.

WILKES COMMUNITY COLLEGE
Wilkesboro/August-May

Sponsor: Two-yr college. Program: Two-yr degree in Culinary Technology. Established: 1965. Accredited by SACS. Calendar: semester. Curriculum: core. Admission dates: Aug & Jan. Total enrollment: 30. 100% of applicants accepted. 60% receive financial aid. 10% enrolled part-time. Student to teacher ratio 10:1. 90% of graduates employed within six months. Facilities: Kitchen one updated as needed, kitchen two constructed in 2001, oe dining room seating 30, lecture room.

Faculty: 1 full-time chef graduate of & former instructor at The CIA. 2 part-time instructors.

Costs: $35.50/cr-hr in-state, $197/cr-hr out-of-state. Admission requirements: Open-door policy; all students welcome. Scholarships: yes. Loans: yes.

Contact: Jeanne Griffin, Dept. Chair, Wilkes Community College, PO Box 120, Wilkesboro, NC 28697; 336-838-6164, Fax 336-838-6277, E-mail griffinj@wilkes.cc.nc.us, URL http://www.wilkes.cc.nc.us.

NORTH DAKOTA

NORTH DAKOTA STATE COLLEGE OF SCIENCE
Wahpeton/August-May

Sponsor: 2-yr post-secondary institution. Program: Three 18-mo programs: associate degree in Chef Training & mgmt Technology, diploma in Chef Training & mgmt Technology, associate degree in Restaurant mgmt. Established: 1903. Accredited by NCACS. Calendar: semester. Curriculum: culinary, core. Admission dates: Aug, Jan. Total enrollment: 30-35. 18 each admission period. 95% of applicants accepted. 88% receive financial aid. 5% enrolled part-time. Student to teacher ratio 18:1. 100% of graduates employed within six months. Facilities: Modern, on-campus kitchen facilities & classrooms.

FACULTY: 2 full-time, each with formal training & practical industry experience.

COSTS: Annual tuition $1,768.50 in-state, $4,467.50 out-of-state. On-campus housing ~$1,000, 1,700 spaces. Admission requirements: HS diploma or equivalent. Scholarships: yes. Loans: yes.

CONTACT: Mary Uhren, Director, North Dakota State College of Science, Culinary Arts, 800 N. 6th St., Wahpeton, ND 58076; 701-671-2842, 800-342-4325, Fax 701-671-2774, E-mail mary.uhren@ndscs.nodak.edu, URL http://www.ndscs.nodak.edu/instruct/cularts.

OHIO

CINCINNATI STATE TECHNICAL & COMMUNITY COLLEGE
Cincinnati/Year-round

Sponsor: 2-yr career college. Program: 2-yr AAB degree in Chef Technology, Restaurant mgmt, Hotel mgmt, 36-hour Culinary Arts Certificate program. Established: 1980. Accredited by ACF, NRA. Calendar: quinmester. Curriculum: core. Admission dates: Open. Total enrollment: 180. 60 each admission period. 100% of applicants accepted. 50% receive financial aid. 30% enrolled part-time. Student to teacher ratio 15:1. 100% of graduates employed within six months. Facilities: Include commercial kitchen.

FACULTY: 4 full-time.

COSTS: Annual tuition $3,350 in-state, $6,000 out-of-state. Housing $350/mo. Admission requirements: HS diploma or equivalent and admission test. Scholarships: yes.

CONTACT: Jeff Sheldon, Dept. Chair, Cincinnati State Technical & Community College, Business Division, 3520 Central Pkwy., Cincinnati, OH 45223; 513-569-1637, Fax 513-569-1467, E-mail sheldonj@cinstate.cc.oh.us, URL http://www.cinstate.cc.oh.us/btd%2Dhm.htm.

COLUMBUS STATE COMMUNITY COLLEGE
Columbus/Year-round

Sponsor: 2-yr college. Program: 3-yr AAS degree in Chef Apprenticeship (Journeyman Chef), 2-yr AAS degree in Foodservice/Restaurant Mgmt. Established: 1978. Accredited by ACF, CAHM, NCA. Calendar: quarter. Admission dates: Sep, Mar. Total enrollment: 200. ~60 each admission period. 80% enrolled part-time. Student to teacher ratio 15:1. 100% of graduates employed within six months. Facilities: Classrooms, food labs, computer labs, off-site industry training sites.

FACULTY: 4 full-time, 3-5 part-time industry professionals.

COSTS: $73/cr-hr in-state, $161/cr-hr out-of-state. Lab fees add'l. Admission requirements: HS diploma, 2 letters of reference, essay, interview. Scholarships: yes. Loans: yes.

CONTACT: Carol Kizer, CCE, FMP, RD, Chairperson, Columbus State Community College, Hospitality Mgmt., 550 E. Spring St., Columbus, OH 43215; 614-287-5126, Fax 614-287-5973, E-mail hospitality@cscc.edu, URL http://www.cscc.edu/hospitality.

CUYAHOGA COMMUNITY COLLEGE
Cleveland/Year-round
Sponsor: 2-yr community college. Program: 2-yr AAB degree in Culinary Arts & Restaurant Food Service mgmt. Pro mgmt courses & certification, ACF Apprentice Program (220 hrs for degree). 1-yr Baking Certificate. Established: 1969. Accredited by NCA. Calendar: semester. Curriculum: culinary, core. Admission dates: Aug, Jan. Total enrollment: 175. 60-80 each admission period. 95% of applicants accepted. 60% receive financial aid. 60% enrolled part-time. Student to teacher ratio 10:1. 95% of graduates employed within six months. Facilities: Include 3 kitchens, 2 classrooms, computer lab, restaurant.
FACULTY: 6 full-time, 9 part-time.
COSTS: Annual tuition in-state (out-of-county, out-of-state) $58 ($77, $160)/sem-hr. Lab fees $300. Housing $500/mo. Admission requirements: Testing in English/math. Scholarships: yes. Loans: yes.
CONTACT: Jan DeLucia, Program Manager, Cuyahoga Community College, Hospitality Mgmt., 2900 Community College Ave., Cleveland, OH 44115; 216-987-4081, Fax 216-987-4086, E-mail julia.patterson@tri-c.edu, URL http://www.tri-c.cc.oh.us.

HOCKING COLLEGE
Nelsonville/Year-round
Sponsor: Career college. Program: 2-yr certificate/AAS degree. Established: 1979. Accredited by NCA, ACF. Calendar: quarter. Curriculum: culinary. Admission dates: Sep, Jan, Mar, Jun. Total enrollment: 198. 100% of applicants accepted. 65% receive financial aid. Student to teacher ratio 15:1. 98% of graduates employed within six months.
FACULTY: 6 full-time, includes Tom Landusky CEC.
COSTS: Annual tuition in-state $2,151, out-of-state $4,302. Admission requirements: HS graduate, GED, or ability to benefit. Scholarships: yes. Loans: yes.
CONTACT: Tom Lambrecht, Executive Director, Hocking College, 3301 Hocking Pkwy., Nelsonville, OH 45764; 740-753-3531, 800-282-4163, Fax 740-753-5286 Attn: Lisa, E-mail admissions@hocking.edu, URL http://www.hocking.edu.

INTERNATIONAL CULINARY ARTS & SCIENCES INSTITUTE
Chesterland/Year-round
Sponsor: Proprietary culinary school. Program: Certificate & diploma programs in Culinary Arts & Pastry Arts. Established: 1989. Calendar: quarter. Curriculum: culinary. Admission dates: Jan, Apr, Sep. Total enrollment: 100. 90% of applicants accepted. 50% enrolled part-time. Student to teacher ratio 12:1. 80% of graduates employed within six months. Facilities: 2 fully-equipped 600-sq-ft professional kitchens, library, dining room, culinary garden.
FACULTY: 14 full- & part-time, all graduates of professional programs.
COSTS: Certificate $6,000, diploma $13,000. Admission requirements: HS Diploma or GED, entrance exam. Loans: yes.
CONTACT: Ruthann Kostadinov, Student Services Director, Loretta Paganini School of Cooking, 8623 Mayfield Rd., Chesterland, OH 44026; 440-729-7340, Fax 440-729-4546, E-mail icasi@lpscinc.com, URL http://www.icasi.net.

OWENS COMMUNITY COLLEGE
Toledo/August-May
Sponsor: 2-yr college. Program: 2-yr AAB degree in Food Service Mgmt. Established: 1968. Accredited by NCA. Calendar: semester. Curriculum: core. Admission dates: Aug, Jan, Jun. Total enrollment: 75. 100% of applicants accepted. 75% receive financial aid. 45% enrolled part-time. Student to teacher ratio 18:1. 95% of graduates employed within six months. Facilities: Production kitchen & dining room.
FACULTY: 1 full-time, 9 part-time.
COSTS: $110/cr-hr in-state, $205/cr-hr out-of-state. Admission requirements: Assessment of reading,

writing & math skills. Scholarships: yes. Loans: yes.

CONTACT: Tekla Madaras, Dept. Chair, Owens Community College, HRI, P.O. Box 10,000 - Oregon Rd., Toledo, OH 43699-1947; 419-661-7214, Fax 419-661-7251, E-mail tmadaras@owens.edu, URL http://www.owens.edu.

SINCLAIR COMMUNITY COLLEGE
Dayton/Year-round

Sponsor: 2-yr college. Program: 2-yr Associate Degree in Hospitality mgmt/Culinary Arts Option. Established: 1993. Accredited by ACF. Calendar: quarter. Curriculum: culinary, core. Admission dates: Yr-round. Total enrollment: 200. 100% of applicants accepted. 30% receive financial aid. 40% enrolled part-time. Student to teacher ratio 15:1. 100% of graduates employed within six months. Facilities: 3 kitchens, 150-seat dining room, classrooms.

FACULTY: 3 full-time, 8 part-time.

COSTS: In-county $29.50, in-state $49, uniforms & knife kit $300, lab fees $50-$100. Admission requirements: HS diploma or GED. Scholarships: yes. Loans: yes.

CONTACT: Steven Cornelius, Dept. Chair, Sinclair Community College, Hospitality Mgmt., 444 W. Third St., Dayton, OH 45402-1460; 937-512-5197, Fax 937-512-5396, E-mail scorneli@sinclair.edu, URL http://www.sinclair.edu.

UNIVERSITY OF AKRON
Akron/September-April

Sponsor: University. Program: 1-yr certificate & 2-yr AAS degree in Culinary Arts. Established: 1968. Accredited by State & regional. Calendar: semester. Curriculum: culinary, core. Admission dates: Fall, spring. Total enrollment: 130. 30+ each admission period. 100% of applicants accepted. 50% receive financial aid. 50% enrolled part-time. Student to teacher ratio 15:1. 95% of graduates employed within six months. Facilities: Working restaurant & kitchen.

FACULTY: 4 full-time.

COSTS: $140 ($338)/cr-hr in-state (out-of-state). Admission requirements: HS diploma or equivalent. Scholarships: yes. Loans: yes.

CONTACT: Larry Gilpatric, Assoc. Prof., University of Akron, Hospitality Mgmt., Gallucci Hall #102, Akron, OH 44325-7907; 330-972-5370, 800-221-8308, Fax 330-972-8876, E-mail gilpatric@uakron.edu, URL http://www.uakron.edu.

OKLAHOMA

ACF CULINARY ARTS OF OKLAHOMA
Oklahoma City/Year-round

Sponsor: ACF chapter. Program: 3-yr apprenticeship; degree program through Oklahoma State University. Curriculum: culinary. Total enrollment: 12.

CONTACT: Geni Thomas, CEPC, CEC, ACF Culinary Arts of Oklahoma, 4337 Dahoon Dr., Okalhoma City, OK 73120; 405-340-1010, Fax 405-340-1267, URL http://www.acfchefs.org/presidents_portal/ACFChapter.cfm?ChapterChoice=OK032.

MERIDIAN TECHNOLOGY CENTER
Stillwater/August-May

Sponsor: Career institution. Program: 1,050-hour certificate. Established: 1975. Accredited by State. Calendar: semester. Curriculum: core. Admission dates: Aug and Jan. Total enrollment: 36. Student to teacher ratio 18:1. 85% of graduates employed within six months. Facilities: 1 kitchen, 1 classroom, 2 restaurants.

FACULTY: 3 full-time.

COSTS: Annual tuition in-district $1,500, out-of-district $3,000. Admission requirements: Assessment, interview.

CONTACT: Meridian Technology Center, 1312 South Sangre Road, Stillwater, OK 74074; 405-377-3333, Fax 405-377-9604, E-mail info@meridian-technology.com, URL http://www.meridian-technology.com/full_time/culinary_arts.asp.

METRO TECH
Oklahoma City/Year-round
Sponsor: Adult technical high school. Program: Two-yr (1,050-hr) program in Culinary Arts. COSTS: $1,050. CONTACT: Metro Tech, 4901 S. Bryant Ave., Oklahoma City, OK 73129; 405-424-8324, Fax 405-424-9403, E-mail mhammond@metrotech.org, URL http://www.metrotech.org/full-time/cd-cf.html.

OKLAHOMA STATE UNIVERSITY
Okmulgee/Year-round
Sponsor: University. Program: 24-mo AAS degree in Food Service mgmt, Culinary Arts. Established: 1946. Accredited by NCA. Calendar: trimester. Curriculum: culinary, core. Admission dates: Aug, Jan, Apr. Total enrollment: 170. 50 each admission period. 90% of applicants accepted. 80% receive financial aid. 10% enrolled part-time. Student to teacher ratio 12:1. 90% of graduates employed within six months. Facilities: Include 4 kitchens & 8 classrooms.

FACULTY: 7 full-time each with 10-35 yrs experience, college level culinary arts, ACF certification. COSTS: In-state $70/cr-hr, out-of-state $150/cr-hr. Housing $1,300-$1,600/sem. Admission requirements: Admission test. Scholarships: yes. Loans: yes. CONTACT: Judy Achemire, Sr. Adm. Asst., Oklahoma State University, Hospitality Services Technology, 1801 E. 4th St., Okmulgee, OK 74447; 918-293-5030, Fax 918-293-4618, E-mail judy-ach@osu-okmulgee.edu, URL http://www.osu-okmulgee.edu/hosp.

PIONEER TECHNICAL CENTER
Ponca City
Sponsor: Career institution. Program: 1-yr certificate. Established: 1972. Accredited by NCA. Total enrollment: 36. Student to teacher ratio 6:1. 100% of graduates employed within six months. FACULTY: 3 full-time.

COSTS: Annual tuition $962 for residents, $1,924 for non-residents. Admission requirements: HS diploma or equivalent. CONTACT: Dee Price, Instructor, Pioneer Technical Center, Commercial Foods, 2101 N. Ash, Ponca City, OK 74601; 580-762-8336 x242, Fax 580-765-5101, E-mail deep@pioneertech.org, URL http://www.pioneertech.org.

TRI COUNTY TECHNOLOGY CENTER
Bartlesville
Sponsor: Trade-technical school. Program: 1050-hr diploma in Culinary Arts. 525 core hrs + 525 hrs in either culinary arts courses or baking & pastry courses. 600-hr Sous Chef & Baking Sous certificates. Calendar:quarter. Curriculum: culinary. Admission dates: Aug. Facilities: Students rotate through the stations in the school's Osage Room restaurant. FACULTY: Tiffany Poe, Philippe Garmy. CONTACT: Tiffany Poe, Tri County Technology Center, Culinary Arts Dept., 6101 Nowata Rd., Bartlesville, OK 74006; 918-331-3250, E-mail tpoe@tctc.org, URL http://www.tctc.org/fulltime/cul.html.

OREGON

CASCADE CULINARY INSTITUTE
Bend/September-June
Sponsor: Central Oregon Community College. Program: Certificate of completion in Culinary Arts. Established: 1993. Calendar: quarter. Curriculum: culinary. Admission dates: Dec, Mar, Sep.

Total enrollment: 18. 18 each admission period. 100% of applicants accepted. 90% receive financial aid. Student to teacher ratio 16:1. 100% of graduates employed within six months. Facilities: Kitchen, dining room, deli operation.

FACULTY: 2 full- and 4 part-time CEC, CCE.

COSTS: $3,410 in district, $9,485 out of state, $500 knife kit. Dorm & meals $5,772/yr. Admission requirements: HS diploma or GED. Scholarships: yes. Loans: yes.

CONTACT: Julian Darwin, Cascade Culinary Institute, 2600 NW College Way, Bend, OR 97701; 541-318-3780, Fax 541-383-7508, E-mail jdarwin@cocc.edu, URL http://culinary.cocc.edu.

INTERNATIONAL SCHOOL OF BAKING
Bend/Year-round   *(See display ad above)*

Sponsor: Private school. Program: 1- to 20-day customized courses that focus on European breads & pastries. Established: 1986. Curriculum: culinary. Total enrollment: 1 or 2/course. Student to teacher ratio 1: 2. Facilities: Modern baking facility. Courses: Cover ingredient function, bakery start-up, troubleshooting, all types of European artisan breads and pastries. Students can select their own curriculum. Schedule: 8-hour daily hands-on sessions.

FACULTY: Director Marda Stoliar has taught European bread making since 1965, owned a French bakery, and is a baking consultant in China, Hong Kong, and Macau for U.S. Wheat Associates.

COSTS: From $500/day/student includes ingredients. Nearby lodging list provided on request.

CONTACT: Marda Stoliar, Director, International School of Baking, 1971 NW Juniper Ave., Bend, OR 97701; 541-389-8553, Fax 541-389-3736, E-mail marda@schoolofbaking.com, URL http://www.schoolofbaking.com.

LANE COMMUNITY COLLEGE
Eugene/September-June

Sponsor: Independent college. Program: 2-yr AAS degree in Culinary Arts & Food Service Mgmt. Established: 1976. Calendar: quarter. Curriculum: core. Admission dates: Fall term only. Total enrollment: 80-100. 52 each admission period. 90% of applicants accepted. 60-70% receive financial aid. 10% enrolled part-time. Student to teacher ratio 24:1. 95% of graduates employed within six months. Facilities: Include 4 kitchens, 1 student-run restaurant, deli/bake shop, classrooms, conference center facilities.

FACULTY: 5 full-time, 2 part-time, ACF-certified with BS, AAS degrees & training from European cooking schools.

COSTS: Annual tuition $63/cr-hr in-state, $216/cr-hr out-of-state. Housing ~$350-$800/mo. Admission requirements: Students must meet minimum placement test scores in reading, writing & math. Scholarships: yes. Loans: yes.

CONTACT: Annie Caredio, Administrative Support Specialist, Lane Community College, Culinary Arts & Hospitality Management, Eugene, OR 97405-0640; 541-463-3503, Fax 541-463-4738, E-mail caredioa@lanecc.edu, URL http://www.lanecc.edu/culinary.

LINN-BENTON COMMUNITY COLLEGE
Albany/September-June

Sponsor: 2-yr college. Program: 2-yr AAS degree in Culinary Arts/Hospitality Services with Chef Training Option; 2-yr AAS degree in Wine & Food Dynamics (must be 21 yrs old). Established: 1973. Accredited by NASC. Calendar: quarter. Curriculum: core. Admission dates: Sep, Jan, Mar. Total enrollment: 30. 15 each admission period. 100% of applicants accepted. 50% receive financial aid. 5% enrolled part-time. Student to teacher ratio 5:1. 100% of graduates employed within six months. Facilities: Include bakery production facility, restaurant.

FACULTY: 6 full-time.

COSTS: $43/cr in-state, $130/cr out-of-state. Application fee $20, tools & uniforms ~$300, Housing ~$250/mo. Admission requirements: HS diploma or equivalent.

CONTACT: Scott Anselm, Linn-Benton Community College, Culinary Arts, 6500 SW Pacific Blvd., Albany, OR 97321; 541-917-4388, Fax 541-917-4395, E-mail anselms@linnbenton.edu, URL http://www.linnbenton.edu/programs/cheftraining.html.

OREGON COAST CULINARY INSTITUTE
Coos Bay/Year-round

Sponsor: Southwestern Oregon Community College. Program: 1-yr Chef Training certificate, 2-yr Culinary Arts mgmt Training associates degree. Established: 2001. Accredited by NASC. Calendar: quarter. Curriculum: culinary. Admission dates: Sep. Total enrollment: 20. 90% receive financial aid. Student to teacher ratio 16:1. Facilities: Food production & teaching kitchens, classroom, computer lab, dining room.

FACULTY: 2 full-time. Director Robert Gregson CEC has 35+ yrs experience & previously taught at the Florida Culinary institute.

COSTS: Degree $12,000/yr full-time, Certificate$6,600/yr full time. Degree application fee $250. Textbooks, knife set, uniforms included. Admission requirements: HS diploma or GED.

CONTACT: Robert Gregson CEC, Director, Oregon Coast Culinary Institute, 1988 Newmark, Coos Bay, OR 97420; 877-895-CHEF, 541-888-7195,541-751-1862, Fax 541-888-7194, E-mail rgregson@occi.net, URL http://www.occi.net.

WESTERN CULINARY INSTITUTE, LE CORDON BLEU
Portland/Year-round   *(See display ad page 112)*

Sponsor: Private school. Program: Le Cordon Bleu programs: 14-mo AOS degree in Culinary Arts, 9-mo diploma or 12-mo AOS degree in Pâtisserie & Baking, 14-mo AOS degree in Hospitality & Restaurant Mgmt. Established: 1983. Accredited by ACF, ACCSCT.Curriculum: culinary.

Admission dates: Every 6 wks. Total enrollment: 1000. 150 each admission period. 90% of applicants accepted. 80% receive financial aid. Student to teacher ratio 16-35:1. 98% of graduates employed within six months. Facilities: Up-to-date, well-equipped kitchens, classrooms, open-to-the-public restaurant & café. Courses: Curriculum is based on the principles of Escoffier with emphasis on modern techniques & trends. Courses include culinary fundamentals, intl. cuisines, nutrition, baking, pastry, wines, restaurant mgmt. **FACULTY:** Culinary professionals with international experience & training. **COSTS:** $20,000+/yr. Admission requirements: HS diploma or equivalent. Scholarships: yes. Loans: yes. **CONTACT:** Janine Carnel, VP of Admissions & Marketing, Western Culinary Institute, 921 SW Morrison St., #400, Portland, OR 97205; 888-848-3202, 503-223-2245, Fax 503-223-5554, E-mail info@wci.edu, URL http://www.wci.edu. LCB Hospitality & Restaurant Management Program, 1717 S.W Madison St., Portland, OR 97205.

PENNSYLVANIA

ACF LAUREL HIGHLANDS CHAPTER – CHEF APPRENTICESHIP
Youngwood/Year-round
Sponsor: ACF Chapter. Program: 3-yr chef apprenticeship; degree program through Westmoreland County CC. Established: 1981. Accredited by ACF, MSA. Calendar: semester. Curriculum: culinary, core. Admission dates: Aug, Jan. Total enrollment: 48. 48 each admission period. 100% of applicants accepted. 37% receive financial aid. 78% enrolled part-time. Student to teacher ratio 17:1. 100% of graduates employed within six months. Facilities: Industry-standard kitchens feature 6 individual test kitchens; specialty pastry & confection area; quantity foods prod area; mixology area & retail sales outlet. **FACULTY:** 4 full-time, 18 part-time. **COSTS:** In-county resident tuition $52/cr. Fees: $2/cr, lab fee $20/culinary course. Admission requirements: HS diploma or equivalent & admission test. Scholarships: yes. **CONTACT:** Mary Zappone, CCE, ACF Laurel Highlands Chapter, Westmoreland County Community College, Culinary Arts, Armbrust Rd., Youngwood, PA 15697-1895; 724-925-4016, Fax 724-925-4293, E-mail zapponm@astro.westmoreland.cc.pa.us, URL http://www.wccc-pa.edu.

ACF PITTSBURGH CHAPTER
Whitacre/Year-round
Sponsor: ACF chapter. Program: 3-yr apprenticeship; degree program through Community College of Allegheny County completed by 80%. Curriculum: culinary. Total enrollment: 60. **COSTS:** $4,000. Beginning salary is negotiable with 25 cent increases every 6 mos. **CONTACT:** Jeffrey P. Ward, CEC, CCE, Secretary, ACF Pittsburgh Chapter, 412-566-2593 x4801, E-mail jward49921@aol.com.

THE ART INSTITUTE OF PHILADELPHIA – CULINARY ARTS
Philadelphia/Year-round *(See display ad page 11)*
Sponsor: Proprietary school. Program: 6-qtr/18-mo AST degree program in Culinary Arts. Established: 1997. Accredited by ACCSCT. Calendar: quarter. Curriculum: culinary. Admission dates: Oct, Jan, Apr, Jul. Total enrollment: 150. 50 each admission period. Facilities: New 33,000-sq-ft facility. Three kitchens: baking & pastry, a la carte, skills. **FACULTY:** Chef director is Joseph Shilling, AOS degree from the CIA. **COSTS:** $4,425/qtr. Admission requirements: HS diploma or GED, interview. **CONTACT:** Tim Howard, Director of Admissions, The Art Institute of Philadelphia-Culinary Arts, 1622 Chestnut St., Philadelphia, PA 19103; 800-275-2474, 215-567-7080, Fax 215-246-3358, E-mail howardt@aii.edu, URL http://www.aiph.artinstitutes.edu.

THE ART INSTITUTE OF PITTSBURGH – CULINARY ARTS
Pittsburgh/Year-round *(See display ad page 11)*

Sponsor: Private college. Program: 12-mo (39-credit) diploma in The Art of Cooking, 21-mo (116-credit) AS degree in Culinary Arts, 36-mo (179-credit) BS degree in Culinary mgmt. Established: 2002. Accredited by ACICS, Penn. Dept. of Education. Admission dates: Yr-round. Student to teacher ratio 15:1. Facilities: Three kitchens (skills, a la carte, baking, pastry, garde manger) covering 10,000 square feet.

FACULTY: Includes one Certified Executive Chef.

COSTS: $326-$373/credit, $50 application fee, $100 enrollment fee.

CONTACT: Elaine Cook-Bartolie, Director of Admissions, The Art Institute of Pittsburgh-Culinary Arts, 420 Blvd. of The Allies, Pittsburgh, PA 15219; 800-275-2470, E-mail bartolie@aii.edu, URL http://www.aip.artinstitutes.edu.

BUCKS COUNTY COMMUNITY COLLEGE
Newtown/Year-round

Sponsor: 2-yr college, 3-yr registered Apprenticeship Program. Program: 3-yr degree/apprenticeship/culinary program. Established: 1968. Accredited by MSA. Calendar: semester. Curriculum: culinary, core. Admission dates: yr-round. 40 each admission period. 80% enrolled part-time. Student to teacher ratio 15-18:1. 95% of graduates employed within six months. Facilities: Include 2 kitchens, dining room, lab, computer labs.

FACULTY: 3 full-time, 4 part-time. ACF-certif & assoc. degree for part-time; ACF-certif with BS/BA or masters degree for full-time.

COSTS: $85/cr-hr in-county, $170/cr-hr out-of-county. Admission requirements: HS diploma or equivalent, college placement tests, essay/interview. Scholarships: yes. Loans: yes.

CONTACT: Earl R. Arrowood, Jr., Professor, Chef Apprenticeship & Culin. Coordin., Bucks County Community College, Business Dept., 275 Swamp Rd., Newtown, PA 18940; 215-968-8241, Fax 215-504-8509, E-mail arrowood@bucks.edu, URL http://www.bucks.edu.

COMMONWEALTH TECHNICAL INSTITUTE
Johnstown/Year-round

Sponsor: Proprietary school. Program: 8-mo diploma in Kitchen Helper, & 16-mo AST degree in Culinary Arts. Established: 1975. Accredited by ACCSCT. Calendar: trimester. Curriculum: core. Admission dates: Every 4 mos. Total enrollment: 45. 12-15 each admission period. 40% receive financial aid. Student to teacher ratio 15:1. 100% of graduates employed within six months. Facilities: Include 3 kitchens & classrooms & a part-time restaurant.

FACULTY: 3 full-time.

COSTS: $16,836. Admission requirements: HS diploma or equivalent.

CONTACT: Adele Sternberg, Commonwealth Technical Institute, Culinary Arts, 727 Goucher St., Johnstown, PA 15905-3092; 814-255-8233, Fax 814-255-3406, E-mail asternberg@dli.state.pa.us, URL http://www.universities.com/Schools/C/www.Commonwealth_Technical_Institute.asp.

COMMUNITY COLLEGE OF ALLEGHENY COUNTY
Monroeville

Sponsor: 2-yr college. Program: 2-yr certificate/AAS degree. Established: 1967. Accredited by MSA.Admission dates: Open. Total enrollment: 175. Student to teacher ratio 15:1. 100% of graduates employed within six months.

FACULTY: 2 full-time, 5 part-time.

COSTS: Annual tuition in-state $68/credit, out-of-county $136/credit, out-of-state $204/credit. Admission requirements: HS diploma or equivalent.

CONTACT: Timothy Sullivan, Professor, Community College of Allegheny County, Hospitality Mgmt., 595 Beatty Rd., Monroeville, PA 15146; 724-325-6736, E-mail tsullivan@ccac.edu, URL http://www.ccac.edu.

COMMUNITY COLLEGE OF ALLEGHENY COUNTY
Pittsburgh

Sponsor: 2-yr college. Program: 2-yr AAS degree in Culinary Arts. Established: 1974. Accredited by MSA.Admission dates: Fall, spring. Total enrollment: 60. 20-15 each admission period. 25% of applicants accepted. 50% receive financial aid. 50% enrolled part-time. Student to teacher ratio 2:1. 90% of graduates employed within six months.

FACULTY: 12 faculty members with bachelor's degree or CEC.

COSTS: $68/credit in-state, $136/credit out-of-county, $204/credit out-of-state.

CONTACT: Community College of Allegheny County, Culinary Arts, 808 Ridge Ave., Jones Hall, Rm. 012, Pittsburgh, PA 15212; 412-237-2698, Fax 412-237-4678, URL http://www.ccac.edu.

COMMUNITY COLLEGE OF BEAVER COUNTY
Monaca/Year-round

Sponsor: 2-yr college. Program: 2-sem/22 cr-hr certificate in Culinary Arts, 4-sem/34 cr-hr mastery certificate in Culinary Arts, 2 yr/64 cr-hr AAS in Culinary Arts.Calendar: semester. Curriculum: culinary, core.

COSTS: Full time/12 cr: $876 in-county, $1.872 in-state, $2,868 out-of-state.

CONTACT: Community College of Beaver County, 1 Campus Dr., Monaca, PA 15061-2588; 800-335-0222, 724-775-8561, x330, E-mail admissions@ccbc.edu, URL www.ccbc.edu.

COMMUNITY COLLEGE OF PHILADELPHIA
Philadelphia/Year-round

Sponsor: 2-yr college. Program: 63 cr-hr AAS degree in Culinary Arts-Chef, ACF-approved chef-apprenticeship program. Calendar: semester. Curriculum: core.

COSTS: $75/cr-hr in-state, $225/cr-hr out-of-state.

CONTACT: Mark Kushner, Community College of Philadelphia, 1700 Spring Garden St., Philadelphia, PA 19130; 215-751-8000/8797, E-mail mkushner@ccp.cc.pa.us, URL http://www.ccp.cc.pa.us.

DREXEL UNIVERSITY
Philadelphia/Year-round

Sponsor: Private 4-yr university. Program: 4-yr BS degree in Culinary Arts & 4-yr BS degree in Hospitality mgmt. Established: 1894. Accredited by MSA. Calendar: quarter. Curriculum: culinary, core. Admission dates: Rolling. Total enrollment: 170. 65% of applicants accepted. 80% receive financial aid. 20% enrolled part-time. Student to teacher ratio 10:1. 99% of graduates employed within six months. Facilities: 10,000 sq-ft of facilities, including 4 kitchens & a restaurant.

FACULTY: 7 full-time, 20 part-time.

COSTS: $18,842/yr + fees. Admission requirements: SAT score req'd. Scholarships: yes. Loans: yes.

CONTACT: Francis McFadden, Program Director, Drexel University-Hospitality Management Department, Academic Building, 33rd & Arch Streets, # 110, Philadelphia, PA 19104; 215-895-4919, Fax 215-895-2426, E-mail chef-fran@drexel.edu, URL http://www.drexel.edu/hospitality.

HARRISBURG AREA COMMUNITY COLLEGE
Harrisburg/Year-round

Sponsor: 2-yr college. Program: 2-yr certificate/AA program in Culinary Arts. Established: 1965. Accredited by MSA, ACBSP. Calendar: semester. Curriculum: culinary, core. Admission dates: Aug, Jan, May. Total enrollment: 200. 48 each admission period. 76% of applicants accepted. 50% receive financial aid. 50% enrolled part-time. Student to teacher ratio 15-20:1. 100% of graduates employed within six months. Facilities: Include production kitchen, demonstration kitchen, culinary classroom, wkly luncheons.

FACULTY: 3 full-time, 3 part-time. Qualifications: bachelor's degree, master's preferred, certifiable by ACF.

Costs: Annual tuition in-state $150/cr-hr, out-of-state $222.50/cr-hr. $30 to enroll. Equipment & uniforms about $300. Admission requirements: Admission test and portfolio. Scholarships: yes. Loans: yes.

Contact: Marcia W. Shore, M.S.Ed., CCE, AssociateProfessor, Coordinator Culinary Arts Prog, Harrisburg Area Community College, One HACC Dr., Harrisburg, PA 17110-2999; 717-780-2674, Fax 717-231-7670, E-mail mwshore@hacc.edu, URL http://www.hacc.edu.

INDIANA UNIVERSITY OF PENNSYLVANIA – CULINARY ARTS
Punxsutawney/Year-round   *(See display ad above)*
Sponsor: University. Program: Culinary Arts, Culinary Arts/Hospitality mgmt BS, Culinary Arts/Food & Nutrition BS and Baking & Pastry Arts (advanced training). Established: 1989. Accredited by MSA, ACF. Calendar: semester. Curriculum: culinary. Admission dates: Sep. Total enrollment: 100. 100 each admission period. 75% of applicants accepted. 90% receive financial aid. Student to teacher ratio 14:1. 99% of graduates employed within six months. Facilities: Include 5 production & 2 lecture/demo classrooms & computer lab. Courses: Include cuisine & pastry prep, purchasing, nutrition, wine appreciation, international cuisine, and menu & facility design.
Faculty: 8 full-time.
Costs: Tuition $5,963/sem. Application fee is $30. A $192 activity fee is required each sem. On-campus lodging is $1,133/sem for a double room. Admission requirements: HS diploma or equivalent. Scholarships: yes. Loans: yes.
Contact: Enid Maggiore, Director of Administrative Services, IUP Academy of Culinary Arts, Office of Admissions, Punxsutawney, PA 15767; 800-438-6424, Fax 814-938-1158, E-mail culinary-arts@iup.edu, URL http://www.iup.edu/culinary.

JNA INSTITUTE OF CULINARY ARTS
Philadelphia/Year-round   *(See display ad page 117)*
Sponsor: Private culinary institute. Program: 60-wk associate degree in Culinary Arts/Restaurant Mgmt; 30-wk diploma in Food Service Training (Professional Cooking);20-wk diploma in Specialized Food Service Mgmt. Established: 1988. Accredited by ACCSCT. Curriculum: culinary. Admission dates: Rolling. Total enrollment: 60. 15 each admission period. 70% of applicants accepted. 90% receive financial aid. 10% enrolled part-time. Student to teacher ratio 10:1. 98% of graduates employed within six months. Facilities: 2 commercial kitchens, 1 demo kitchen, 1 demo area, classrooms. Courses: Courses are a combination of hands-on labs, demos, & projects. Lectures are a part of training.
Faculty: 6 full- & 4 part-time, all with formal training &/or experience.
Costs: $4,500-$14,000. $75 registration fee. Admission requirements: HS diploma or equivalent. Scholarships: yes. Loans: yes.
Contact: Robert Fox, Director of Admissions, JNA Institute of Culinary Arts, 1212 S. Broad St., Philadelphia, PA 19146; 215-468-8800, Fax 215-468-8838, E-mail admissions@culinaryarts.com, URL http://www.culinaryarts.com.

KEYSTONE COLLEGE
La Plume/September-May
Sponsor: Private college. Program: 2-yr AAS degree in Culinary Arts, dual major with Hotel/Restaurant mgmt. Established: 1996. Accredited by MSA. Calendar: semester. Curriculum: culinary, core. Admission dates: Aug. Total enrollment: 35. 35 each admission period. 100% of applicants accepted. 90% receive financial aid. 20% enrolled part-time. Student to teacher ratio 6-12:01. 90% of graduates employed within six months.

FACULTY: 3 full-time, 1 part-time.

COSTS: $13,180/yr, rm & bd is $6,800/yr. Admission requirements: HS diploma or GED, SAT/ACT, 1 letter of recommendation. Scholarships: yes. Loans: yes.

CONTACT: Sarah Keating, Director of Admissions, Keystone College, One College Green, La Plume, PA 18440-1099; 570-945-6953, Fax 570-945-7916, E-mail admissns@keystone.edu, URL http://www.keystone.edu.

LEHIGH COUNTY VOCATIONAL-TECHNICAL SCHOOL
Schnecksville/August-May
Sponsor: Lehigh County Vocational-Technical School. Program: 20-wk certificate program offering both front and back of house training. Established: 1979. Calendar: semester. Curriculum: culinary. Admission dates: Aug & Jan. Total enrollment: 12 students. 12 students each admission period. 90% of applicants accepted. 50% receive financial aid. Student to teacher ratio 6:1. 95% of graduates employed within six months. Facilities: 80-seat restaurant with professional kitchen.

FACULTY: 1 Certified Executive Chef, 2 state certified educators/consultants.

COSTS: 2510. Admission requirements: Interview, basic math skills, 18 yrs or over.

CONTACT: Gary Fedorcha, Lehigh County Vocational-Technical School, 4500 Education Park Dr., Cedar Eatery/Chef Training, Schnecksville, PA 18078; 610-799-1318, Fax 610-799-1314, E-mail FedorchaG@cliu.org, URL http://www.lcti.org/home.htm.

MERCYHURST NORTH EAST – THE CULINARY & WINE INSTITUTE
North East/September-May *(See display ad page 118)*
Sponsor: Private 2-yr college. Program: 2-yr AS degree in Hotel, Restaurant & Institutional mgmt with a concentration in Culinary Art;1-yr Culinary Art Certificate. Established: 1995. Accredited by MSA. Calendar: trimester. Curriculum: culinary, core. Admission dates: Sep, Nov, Mar. Total enrollment: 70. 40 each admission period. 97% of applicants accepted. 100% receive financial aid. 18% enrolled part-time. Student to teacher ratio 15:1. 100% of graduates employed within six months. Facilities: 3 professional kitchens, bake shop, 30-seat dining room, receiving & storage area. Courses: Specialized courses in wines & wine-making; traditional culinary courses emphasizing management & thinking skills.

FACULTY: 3 full-time, 5 part-time, with industry experience & educational background.

COSTS: Tuition $11,967/yr, culinary fee $400. On-campus dorms $5,504/yr including board. Admission requirements: HS graduate or equivalent, math & English placement test. Scholarships: yes. Loans: yes.

CONTACT: Director of Admissions, Mercyhurst College-North East, The Culinary & Wine Institute, North East, PA 16428; 800-825-1926, 814-725-6144, Fax 814-725-6251, E-mail neadmiss@mercyhurst.edu, URL http://northeast.mercyhurst.edu.

NORTHAMPTON COMMUNITY COLLEGE
Bethlehem/Year-round
Sponsor: 2-yr college. Program: 45-wk specialized diploma in Culinary Arts, AAS degree in Culinary Arts. Established: 1993. Accredited by MSA. Calendar: trimester. Curriculum: culinary, core. Admission dates: Mar, Sep. Total enrollment: 52. 26 each admission period. 100% of applicants accepted. 30% receive financial aid. Student to teacher ratio 26:1. 98% of graduates employed within six months. Facilities: 4,000-sq-ft modern multi-function kitchen & bakery.

FACULTY: 4 full-time. Qualifications: culinary degree & 20+ yrs of professional experience.

COSTS: Annual tuition in-county $3,735, out-of-county $7,695, out-of-state $11,745. Other fees $1,000. On-campus housing $2,944/yr. Off-campus housing $450/mo. Meal plan $1,900/yr. Admission requirements: HS diploma or equivalent. Must place at English one level. Scholarships: yes. Loans: yes.

CONTACT: Duncan Howden, Assoc. Professor, Northampton Community College, Culinary Arts, 3835 Green Pond Rd., Bethlehem, PA 18017; 610-861-5593, Fax 610-861-5093, E-mail dhowden@northampton.edu, URL http://www.northampton.edu.

ORLEANS TECHNICAL INSTITUTE
Philadelphia
Sponsor: Career institution. Program: 30-wk specialized diploma in Food Preparation. Established: 1978. Admission dates: Open. 85% of graduates employed within six months.

FACULTY: 1 to 2 full-time.

COSTS: $2,550 (Food Service) for the 480-hour class. Admission requirements: Admission test.

CONTACT: Shirley Randall, Orleans Technical Institute, Culinary Arts, 1330 Rhawn St., Philadelphia, PA 19111; 215-728-4175, E-mail srandall1017@yahoo.com, URL http://www.jevs.org/schools_jobs.asp.

degrees that work.

Culinary Arts (B.S. & A.A.S.)

Baking & Pastry Arts (A.A.S.)

Hospitality Management (A.A.S.)

1-866-811-1511

Apply online at

www.pct.edu/shaw

Pennsylvania College of Technology

PENNSTATE

An affiliate of The Pennsylvania State University

Penn College operates on a nondiscriminatory basis.

PENNSYLVANIA COLLEGE OF TECHNOLOGY
Williamsport/Year-round   *(See display ad above)*

Sponsor: 2/4-yr college. Program: 2-yr AAS degree in Hospitality mgmt, Baking & Pastry Arts, Culinary Arts; BS degree in Culinary Arts. Established: 1981. Accredited by ACF, CAHM. Calendar: semester. Curriculum: culinary, core. Admission dates: Fall, spring & summer. Total enrollment: 165. 72 each admission period. 95% of applicants accepted. 86% receive financial aid. 15% enrolled part-time. Student to teacher ratio 12:1. 100% of graduates employed within six months. Facilities: Include 10 kitchens & classrooms, fine-dining restaurant, catering & meeting facilities, theater lounge, B&B, conference & retreat center. Courses: Cooking, baking, service, sanitation, supervision, mgmt skills, & nutrition. Emphasis on problem-solving, communications, math applications, teamwork, leadership skills.

FACULTY: 8 full-time, 12 part-time; college degrees, 70% ACF-certified, 100% certifiable.

COSTS: Annual tuition in-state $295/cr-hr, out-of-state $372/cr-hr. Application fee $50, other fees $47. Housing $250-$450/mo. Admission requirements: HS diploma or equivalent, admission test. Scholarships: yes. Loans: yes.

CONTACT: Chet Schuman, Director of Admissions, Pennsylvania College of Technology, School of Hospitality, One College Ave., Williamsport, PA 17701-5799; 570-326-3761, ext. 4761, 1-800-367-9222, Fax 570-320-5260, E-mail admissions@pct.edu, URL http://www.pct.edu.

PENNSYLVANIA CULINARY INSTITUTE
Pittsburgh/Year-round *(See display ad page 121)*

Sponsor: Private career training institution. Program: 16-mo AST degree programs in Le Cordon Bleu Culinary Arts & Le Cordon Bleu Pastry Arts. 16-mo ASB degree program in Le Cordon Bleu Hospitality & Restaurant Mgmt. Established: 1986. Accredited by ACCSCT, ACFEI. Calendar: semester. Curriculum: culinary. Admission dates: Rolling. Total enrollment: 991. 90% receive financial aid. Student to teacher ratio 24:1. 99% of graduates employed within six months. Facilities: Include 10 kitchens, 18 classrooms, full-service dining room lab & mixology lab, library resource center & computer lab. Courses: Include food prep & skill development, advanced classical & intl cuisine, garde manger, nutrition, wines & spirits, menu planning, dining room mgmt. FACULTY: 33 chef instructors, ACF-certified as Culinary Educators & Certified Chefs; 17 mgmt faculty. COSTS: Tuition $8,500/sem (programs typically 4 sem's), enrollment fee $100, books & supplies ~$4,070. Admission requirements: Enrollment fee, application, interview, HS diploma or GED. Scholarships: yes. Loans: yes. CONTACT: Robert P. Cappel, Vice President of Admissions & Marketing, Pennsylvania Culinary Institute, 717 Liberty Ave., Pittsburgh, PA 15222; 800-432-2433 or 412-566-2433, Fax 412-566-2434, E-mail info@paculinary.com, URL http://www.pci.edu.

PHILLYWINE.COM
Philadelphia/Year-round

Sponsor: Private wine education school. Program: Entry-level Intermediate Certificate through the 2-yr WSET Diploma. Shorter courses & one-night tastings also offered. Established: 1988. Accredited by The UK's Qualification & Curriculum Authority. Calendar: semester. Admission dates: Certificate: Jan & Sept. Shorter classes & tastings: yr-round. Total enrollment: WSET 85/yr, tastings 1,000/yr. 25/course max each admission period. 95% of applicants accepted. 100% enrolled part-time. Student to teacher ratio 15:1. 90% of graduates employed within six months. FACULTY: 10 part-time instructors, all holding at least the WSET Advanced Certificate. COSTS: $498 for Intermediate Certificate, $798 for Advanced Certificate, $3,500 for Diploma. Admission requirements: Advanced Certificate is prerequisite for Diploma, Intermediate Certificate is strongly recommended for Advanced Certificate. CONTACT: Neal Ewing, Director, Phillywine.com, PO Box 1478, Havertown, PA 19083; 610-649-9936, Fax 610-649-9936, E-mail neal@phillywine.com, URL http://www.phillywine.com.

READING AREA COMMUNITY COLLEGE
Reading/Year-round

Sponsor: Two-yr college. Program: Two-yr AAS degree in Culinary Arts. Accredited by MSA. COSTS: $54/credit. CONTACT: Dennis Moyer, Reading Area Community College, 10 S. Second St., Reading, PA 19603; 610-372-4721 x6214, Fax 610-372-4264, E-mail admissions@email.racc.cc.pa.us, URL http://www.racc.cc.pa.us/index.html.

THE RESTAURANT SCHOOL AT WALNUT HILL COLLEGE
Philadelphia/Year-round *(See display ad page 122)*

Sponsor: 4-yr private college. Program: 2-yr AS & 4-yr BS degree programs in Culinary Arts, Pastry Arts, Restaurant mgmt. Established: 1974. Accredited by ACCSCT. Calendar: quarter. Curriculum: culinary, core. Admission dates: Sep, Nov, Jan, May. Total enrollment: ~500. 200 each admission period. 87% of applicants accepted. 85% receive financial aid. 20% enrolled part-time. Student to teacher ratio 18:1. 98% of graduates employed within six months. Facilities: Include 5 classroom kitchens, two 85-seat demo kitchens, 3 classrooms, pastry shop, 4 student-run restaurants, computer lab, wine lab, library. Courses: Culinary Arts combines classroom instruction with apprenticeship; includes business mgmt, dining room svc, wines, 7 certification courses. Pastry Arts covers culinary & baking skills, baking science, chocolate, candies, 6 certification courses.

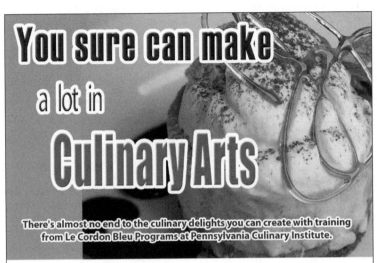

FACULTY: The 18-member professional faculty have a minimum of 12 yrs experience in the restaurant, foodservice, & hotel industry. 5 ACF-certified chefs, 1 master pastry chef.

COSTS: The $20,975 cost of each program includes trip to France. Other fees $1,000. On-campus dorm & apartments are available. Admission requirements: HS diploma or equivalent, reference letters, basic achievement test. Scholarships: yes. Loans: yes.

CONTACT: Karl D. Becker, Director of Admissions, The Restaurant School at Walnut Hill College, 4207 Walnut St., Philadelphia, PA 19104; 877-925-6884, 215-222-4200, Fax 215-222-4219, E-mail info@walnuthillcollege.com, URL http://www.walnuthillcollege.com.

WESTMORELAND COUNTY COMMUNITY COLLEGE
Youngwood/Year-round

Sponsor: 2-yr college. Program: 2- & 3-yr AAS degree in Culinary Arts and 2- & 3-yr Baking & Pastry degree, both with apprenticeship option; 16-mo Culinary Arts degree; 1-sem Culinary Arts certificate and 1-sem Baking/Pastry certificate. Established: 1981. Accredited by ACF, MSA. Calendar: semester. Curriculum: culinary, core. Admission dates: Aug, Jan. Total enrollment: 207. 207 each admission period. 100% of applicants accepted. 37% receive financial aid. 71% enrolled part-time. Student to teacher ratio 17:1. 100% of graduates employed within six months. Facilities: Industry-standard kitchens feature 6 individual test kitchens; specialty pastry & confection area; quantity foods production area; mixology area & retail sales outlet.

FACULTY: 4 full-time, 18 part-time.

COSTS: In-county tuition $52/cr. Admission requirements: HS diploma & admission test.

CONTACT: Mary Zappone, Professor, Westmoreland County Community College, Hospitality Dept., Armbrust Rd., Youngwood, PA 15697; 724-925-4016, Fax 724-925-4293, E-mail zapponm@astro.westmoreland.cc.pa.us, URL http://www.wccc-pa.edu.

THE WINE SCHOOL OF PHILADELPHIA
Philadelphia & Manayunk/Year-round

Sponsor: Private wine school. Program: Certificate of Wine Knowledge, Advanced Wine Degree, Master of Vinology Degree; wkly wine classes. Established: 2002. Calendar: semester. Admission dates: Yr-round. Total enrollment: 500. 95% of applicants accepted. 100% enrolled part-time. Student to teacher ratio 18-1. 100% of graduates employed within six months.

FACULTY: President & CEO Keith Wallace, a wine industry veteran.

COSTS: $350-$1,000.

CONTACT: Keith Wallace, Owner, The Wine School of Philadelphia, 2006 Fairmount Ave., Philadelphia, PA 19130; 267-307-9220, E-mail wineclass@winelust.com, URL winelust.com.

WINNER INSTITUTE OF ARTS & SCIENCES
Transfer/Year-round

Sponsor: Private school affiliated with Youngstown State University. Program: 50-wk diploma program in Culinary Arts. Students can take credit classes at Youngstown towards an associates degree. Established: 1997. Accredited by Registered with PA State Board of Private Schools. Calendar: trimester. Curriculum: culinary. Admission dates: Jan, Mar, Jul, Sep. Total enrollment: 36. Up to 30 each admission period. 98% of applicants accepted. 90% receive financial aid. Student to teacher ratio 7-16:1. 100% of graduates employed within six months. Facilities: Kitchen with the latest equipment, banquet room, 4 classrooms, fully-equipped computer lab & library.

FACULTY: 3 full-time chef instructors.

COSTS: $12,180, fees $1,650. Admission requirements: HS diploma or GED & passing score on entrance exam. Loans: yes.

CONTACT: Director, Winner Institute of Arts & Sciences, One Winner Place, Transfer, PA 16154; 888-414-CHEF, 724-646-2433, Fax 724-646-0218, E-mail info@winner-institute.com, URL http://www.winner-institute.com.

YORK TECHNICAL INSTITUTE
York & Mt.Joy/Year-round

Sponsor: Private proprietary 2-yr institution. Program: Culinary Arts/Restaurant mgmt (21 mos), Pastry Arts (12 mos), Associate Degree in Specialized Business. Established: 1998. Accredited by ACCST. Candidate for MSA accreditation. Calendar: quarter. Curriculum: culinary, core. Admission dates: Jan, Jul, Oct. Total enrollment: 175. 48/18 each admission period. 80% of applicants accepted. 90% receive financial aid. Student to teacher ratio 20:1. 100% of graduates employed within six months.

FACULTY: 6.

CONTACT: York Technical Institute, 1405 Williams Road, York, PA 17402; 717-757-1100, 800-227-9675, E-mail morrd@yti.edu, URL http://chefs.yti.edu.

YORKTOWNE BUSINESS INSTITUTE SCHOOL OF CULINARY ARTS
York/Year-round

Sponsor: 2-yr private school. Program: ~16-mo Associate in Specialized Technology in Culinary Arts (includes externship), ~8-mo diploma in Professional Baking & Pastry. Established: 1998. Accredited by ACICS. Calendar: trimester. Curriculum: culinary, core. Admission dates: Every 4 mos. Total enrollment: 130. 50-60 each admission period. 95% receive financial aid. 25% enrolled part-time. Student to teacher ratio 10-20:1. Facilities: 5,000-sq-ft culinary arts center includes commercial teaching kitchens, presentation area, classroom, dining area. Student-run restaurant.

FACULTY: 12 chef instructors. Chef David Haynes, CEC, program director.

COSTS: Culinary courses $330/cr-hr, business/mgmt courses $196/cr-hr. Admission requirements: HS diploma or GED, interview, entrance exam, tour. Loans: yes.

CONTACT: Admissions, Yorktowne Business Institute, Culinary Arts, West 7th Ave., York, PA 17404; 800-840-1004, 717-846-5000, Fax 717-848-4584, E-mail chef@ybi.edu, URL http://www.yorkchef.com.

RHODE ISLAND

JOHNSON & WALES UNIVERSITY/COLLEGE OF CULINARY ARTS
Providence/Year-round *(See also page 29, 37) (See display ad above)*

Sponsor: Private nonprofit career institution. Program: 2-yr AAS & 4-yr BS degree programs in Culinary Arts and Baking & Pastry Arts. 4-yr BS in Culinary Nutrition. Other degrees offered at different campuses. Established: 1973. Accredited by NEASC. Calendar: quarter. Curriculum: culinary, core. Admission dates: Sep, Dec, Mar. Total enrollment: 2,362 full-, 219 part-time. ~80% receive financial aid. 9% enrolled part-time. Student to teacher ratio 18:1. 98% of graduates employed within six months. Facilities: Modern teaching facilities, including 5 student-run restaurants. Courses: Culinary arts includes basic cooking & baking, classic & intl cuisines, food prep, nutrition, communication, menu design. Baking & Pastry includes ingredients, production techniques, pastries, desserts, chocolate & sugar artistry.

FACULTY: 79 full-time.

COSTS: $19,182/yr, general fee $810, rm & bd $7,185-8,985/yr + $891 for optional wkend meal plan. Admission requirements: HS diploma or equivalent. Scholarships: yes. Loans: yes.

CONTACT: Amy O'Connell, Asst. Director of Culinary Admissions, Johnson & Wales University, College of Culinary Arts, 8 Abbott Park Place, Providence, RI 02903; 800-342-5598, Fax 401-598-4787, E-mail ShawGuides@jwu.edu, URL http://www.jwu.edu.

SOUTH CAROLINA

GREENVILLE TECHNICAL COLLEGE
Greenville/Year-round

Sponsor: Career college. Program: 2-yr degree in Food Service mgmt, and 1-yr certificates in Baking & Pastry, Catering, Culinary Education. Established: 1977. Accredited by ACF, SACS, ACBSP. Calendar: semester. Curriculum: culinary, core. Admission dates: Sems (3). Total enrollment: 175. 45 each admission period. 75% of applicants accepted. 100% receive financial aid. 5.5% enrolled part-time. Student to teacher ratio 15:1. 100% of graduates employed within six months. Facilities: Include kitchen & 3 classrooms.

FACULTY: 3 full-time, 5 part-time.

COSTS: $996/sem in-county resident,$1,080/sem out-of-county, $25 application fee. Admission requirements: HS diploma or equivalent & admission test. Scholarships: yes.

CONTACT: Denise Bishop, Greenville Technical College, Info Center Dept., P.O. Box 5616, Station B, Greenville, SC 29606-5616; 864-250-8272, Fax 864-250-8689, E-mail bishop@gvltec.edu, URL http://www.greenvilletech.com.

HORRY-GEORGETOWN TECHNICAL COLLEGE
Conway/Year-round

Sponsor: Career college. Program: 2-yr degree in Culinary Arts Technology, certificate in Food Service, certificate inPastry Arts, personal ACF certification. Established: 1985. Accredited by SACS, ACF. Calendar: semester. Curriculum: core. Admission dates: Aug, Jan, May. Total enrollment: 105. 40 each admission period. 100% of applicants accepted. 60% receive financial aid. 10% enrolled part-time. Student to teacher ratio 10:1. 100% of graduates employed within six months. Facilities: Include 4 kitchens, 3 dining rooms, 3 restaurants.

FACULTY: 12 full- & part-time.

COSTS: In-state $600/sem, out-of-state $1,431/sem. Application fee $15. Housing ~$250-$350/mo. Admission requirements: HS diploma or equivalent & admission test. Scholarships: yes. Loans: yes.

CONTACT: Carmen Catino, Dept. Head, Horry-Georgetown Technical College, Culinary Arts, P.O. Box 1966, 2050 Hwy. 501 East, Conway, SC 29526; 803-347-3186, Fax 803-347-4207, E-mail catino@hor.tec.sc.us, URL http://www.hor.tec.sc.us.

TRIDENT TECHNICAL COLLEGE
Charleston/Year-round

Sponsor: Career college. Program: 2-sem certificate & 4-sem diploma programs & associate degree in Culinary Arts. Established: 1986. Accredited by SACS, ACF. Calendar: semester. Curriculum: culinary. Admission dates: Open. Total enrollment: 85. 75-85 each admission period. 93% of applicants accepted. 40% receive financial aid. 5% enrolled part-time. Student to teacher ratio 15:1. 100% of graduates employed within six months. Facilities: Includes 10 kitchens & classrooms, student-run restaurant.

FACULTY: 4 full- & 4 part-time.

COSTS: Annual tuition $1,572 in-county, $1,836 out-of-county, $3,266 out-of-state. Application fee $20. Housing $400/mo. Admission requirements: HS diploma or equivalent & admission test. Scholarships: yes. Loans: yes.

CONTACT: Frankie Miller, Dean, Trident Technical College, Division of Hospitality & Tourism, P.O. Box 118067, HT-P, Charleston, SC 29423-8067; 843-722-5542, Fax 843-720-5614, E-mail frankie.miller@tridenttech.edu, URL http://www.tridenttech.edu.

SOUTH DAKOTA

MITCHELL TECHNICAL INSTITUTE
Mitchell/July-May

Sponsor: 2-yr public technical college. Program: 13-mo diploma in Culinary Arts. Established: 1968. Accredited by NCA & National Restaurant Assn. Calendar: semester. Curriculum: culinary. Total enrollment: 24. 24 each admission period. 95% of applicants accepted. 85% receive financial aid. Student to teacher ratio 8:1. 100% of graduates employed within six months. Facilities: Include 3 kitchens, 3 classrooms, 54-seat restaurant, library, computer labs.
FACULTY: 3 full-time.

COSTS: $60/cr-hr in-state & out-of-state. Annual fees excluding tuition ~$2,400. Annual cost of living ~$4,200. Admission requirements: HS diploma or equivalent & admission test. ACT recommended. Scholarships: yes. Loans: yes.

CONTACT: Randy Doescher, Department Head, Mitchell Technical Institute, 821 N Capital, Mitchell, SD 57301; 605-995-3030, Fax 605-996-3299, E-mail questions@mti.tec.sd.us, URL http://www.mitchelltech.com.

TENNESSEE

GAYLORD OPRYLAND CULINARY INSTITUTE
Nashville/Year-round

Sponsor: ACF chapter. Program: 3-yr Culinary apprenticeship, 3-yr Baking & Pastry apprenticeship, AS degree in Culinary Arts through Nashville State Community College. Established: 1987. Accredited by ACF, SACS. Calendar: semester. Curriculum: culinary, core. Admission dates: Aug. Total enrollment: 36 max. 12 each admission period. 50% of applicants accepted. Student to teacher ratio 12:1. 100% of graduates employed within six months. Facilities: Gaylord Opryland Resort & Convention Center, with 2,881 rooms, 5 major restaurants & 12 add'l food & beverage outlets.
FACULTY: Coordinator Dina Starks, BS, MS, RD; Executive Chef Peter D'Andrea.

COSTS: $78/cr-hr in-state (8-9 hrs/sem + applicable college fees). $500 admission fee. Admission requirements: HS diploma or GED, foodservice experience preferred.

CONTACT: Dina Starks, Culinary Apprenticeship Coordinator, Gaylord Opryland Culinary Institute, 2800 Opryland Dr., Nashville, TN 37214; 615-458-2776, 615-889-1000, Fax 615-871-7872, E-mail dstarks@gaylordhotels.com, URL http://www.gaylordopryland.com.

MEMPHIS CULINARY ACADEMY
Memphis/Year-round

Sponsor: Private trade school. Program: 10-wk certificate program offered 4 times/yr. Established: 1984. Accredited by TN Higher Education Commission. Calendar: quarter. Curriculum: culinary. Admission dates: Jan, Apr, Jun, Sep. Total enrollment: 40. 10 each admission period. Student to teacher ratio 6:1. 95% of graduates employed within six months.

COSTS: 3750. Admission requirements: HS diploma. Scholarships: yes.

CONTACT: Elaine Wallace, Memphis Culinary Academy, 1252 Peabody Avenue, Memphis, TN 38104; 901-722-8892, E-mail ewallacechef@hotmail.com.

NASHVILLE STATE TECHNICAL INSTITUTE
Nashville/Year-round

Sponsor: 2-yr college. Program: 2-yr associate degree in Culinary Science. Accredited by SACS.
COSTS: $710/sem, $56/cr-hr.

CONTACT: Ken Morlino, Asst. Prof., Nashville State Technical Institute, 120 White Bridge Rd., Nashville, TN 37209; 615-353-3783, E-mail morlino_k@nsti.tec.tn.us, URL http://www.nscc.edu/catalog/dcul.html.

WALTERS STATE COMMUNITY COLLEGE CULINARY ARTS SCHOOL
Sevierville & Morristown/Year-round

Sponsor: 2-yr community college. Program: 2-yr AAS degree & 1-yr certificate program in Culinary Arts. 1-yr Personal Chef certificate program. Established: 1997. Accredited by SACS, ACF. Calendar: semester. Curriculum: culinary, core. Admission dates: Aug, Jan, May. Total enrollment: 125. 12-15/class each admission period. 100% of applicants accepted. 50-100% receive financial aid. 43% enrolled part-time. Student to teacher ratio 12-15:1. Facilities: Open-to-the-public instructional dining room. Full campus services for the core courses.

FACULTY: 1 full-time, 4 adjunct. All are culinary school graduates or 15+ yrs on-the-job experience.

COSTS: ~$1,600/yr in-state + books, uniforms, knives. Admission requirements: 2-yr program requires HS diploma or GED, 1-yr program does not. Scholarships: yes. Loans: yes.

CONTACT: Sheila Morris, Enrollment Development Dept., Walters State Community College, 500 S. Davy Crockett Parkway, Morristown, TN 37813-6899; 423-585-2664, Fax 423-585-6786, E-mail Sheila.Morris@ws.edu, URL http://www.ws.edu/businessdiv/culinary%20arts/default.asp.

TEXAS

THE ART INSTITUTE OF DALLAS – CULINARY ARTS
Dallas/Year-round   *(See display ad page 11)*

Sponsor: 2-yr private college. Program: Professional 18-mo curriculum leading to an AAS degree in Culinary Arts & AAS degree in Restaurant and Catering mgmt. Established: 1999. Accredited by SACS. Calendar: quarter. Curriculum: culinary, core. Admission dates: Every 11 wks. Total enrollment: ~230. 25-80 each admission period. 50% of applicants accepted. 70% receive financial aid. Student to teacher ratio 20:1. 100% of graduates employed within six months. Facilities: 2 kitchens, 1 bake shop, 1 restaurant with kitchen.

FACULTY: Full-time 5, part-time 4.

COSTS: $37,000. Admission requirements: Assessment test and essay. Scholarships: yes. Loans: yes.

CONTACT: Keith Petrovello, Director of Admissions, The Art Institute of Dallas-Culinary Arts, 8080 Park Lane, Dallas, TX 75291; 800-275-4243, 214-692-8080, Fax 214-750-9460, E-mail petrovek@aii.edu, URL http://www.aid.artinstitutes.edu.

THE ART INSTITUTE OF HOUSTON – CULINARY ARTS
Houston/Year-round   *(See display ad page 11)*

Sponsor: Proprietary school. Program: 21-mo AAS degree in Culinary Arts, 18-mo AAS degree in Restaurant & Catering Mgmt, diploma program in Culinary Arts. Established: 1992. Accredited by ACF, SACS. Calendar: quarter. Curriculum: culinary, core. Admission dates: Jan, Apr, Jul, Sep. Total enrollment: ~450. 40-80 each admission period. 75% receive financial aid. 10% enrolled part-time. Student to teacher ratio 24:1. 90% of graduates employed within six months. Facilities: Include 5 teaching kitchens, bakery, deli, open-to-the-public restaurant.

FACULTY: 12 full- & part-time.

COSTS: $5,808/qtr or $363/cr-hr. Application fee $50, lab fee $300/qtr, supply kit $800. Housing $1,515/qtr. Admission requirements: HS diploma or equivalent & interview, COMPASS test. Scholarships: yes. Loans: yes.

CONTACT: Director of Admissions, Art Institute of Houston-Culinary Arts, 1900 Yorktown, Houston, TX 77056; 800-275-4244, 713-623-2040, Fax 713-966-2797, E-mail aihadm@aii.edu, URL http://www.aih.artinstitutes.edu.

AUSTIN COMMUNITY COLLEGE
Austin/Year-round

Sponsor: Public 2-yr college. Program: 2-yr AAS degree in Culinary Arts, 22-cr Culinarian certificate, 34-cr certificate in Culinary Arts. Accredited by ACF. Calendar: semester. Curriculum: core. Student to teacher ratio 1:12.

Faculty: Brian Hay, MS, ACF; Chef Brian McCormick.

Contact: Brian Hay, Associate Professor, Austin Community College-Eastview Campus, 3401 Webberville Rd., Rm 3159, Austin, TX 78702; 512-223-5173, Fax 512-223-5191, E-mail bhay@austincc.edu, URL http://www.austincc.edu/hospmgmt.

CULINARY ACADEMY OF AUSTIN
Austin/Year-round
Sponsor: Private career school. Program: 1-yr Professional Culinary Arts, 6-wk Intro to Culinary Arts, 6-mo Pastry Arts, exchange programs in Italy. Established: 1998. Accredited by Texas Workforce Commission, COE, V.A.,Texas Rehab Commission. Calendar: quarter. Curriculum: culinary. Admission dates: Jan, Apr, Jul, Oct. Total enrollment: 35. 10-12 each admission period. 70% of applicants accepted. 50-75% receive financial aid. 20% enrolled part-time. Student to teacher ratio 8:1. 100% of graduates employed within six months. Facilities: Well-equipped commercial kitchen, bakeshop, catering operation, 2 classrooms, dining room, demo area, resource/computer room.

Faculty: 3 full-time instructors with 20+ yrs of industry experience.

Costs: $3,632-$22,415 includes uniforms, chef tool kit, textbooks, lab fees. Admission requirements: Application, HS diploma or equivalent. Scholarships: yes. Loans: yes.

Contact: Elizabeth Falto-Mannion, Office Administrator, Culinary Academy of Austin, Inc., 2823 Hancock Dr., Austin, TX 78731; 512-451-5743, Fax 512-467-9120, E-mail jhenig@culinaryacademyofaustin.com, URL http://www.culinaryacademyofaustin.com.

CULINARY INSTITUTE ALAIN & MARIE LENÔTRE
Houston/Year-round   *(See display ad above)*
Sponsor: Proprietary institution. Program: 20-wk day or 40-wk eve (748-hr) Sous-Chef Cooking/Catering or Baking/Pastry diploma. 30-wk day or 60-wk eve (1,122-hr) Culinary Arts diploma. Established: 1998. Accredited by ACCSCT, Texas Workforce Commission. Calendar: quinmester. Curriculum: culinary. Admission dates: yr-round. Total enrollment: 320. 37 each admission period. 85% of applicants accepted. 70% receive financial aid. 30% enrolled part-time. Student to teacher ratio 12:1 max. 95% of graduates employed within six months. Facilities: 15,000-sq-ft newly-equipped baking, pastry, bread, chocolate, sugar, ice-cream, cuisine, catering labs, lounge, cafeteria, conference room, amphitheater, cookware boutique. Courses: Restaurant cooking, catering, professional baking/pastry, breads, ice cream, chocolate, sugar, decor, international topics.

Faculty: Technical Director Alain LeNotre, 5 full-time French chefs.

Costs: Program A or B: $17,450 + tools, uniforms & fees. Program C: $21,100 + tools, uniforms & fees. Enrollment by the wk available. Admission requirements: HS diploma or GED, medical affidavit, picture ID. Scholarships: yes. Loans: yes.

Contact: Alain LeNotre, CEO, Culinary Institute Alain & Marie LeNôtre, 7070 Allensby St., Houston, TX 77022; 888-LeNotre/713-692-0077, Fax 713-692-7399, E-mail lenotre@wt.net, URL http://www.ciaml.com.

DEL MAR COLLEGE
Corpus Christi/Year-round

Sponsor: State-supported institution. Program: 1-yr certificate, 2-yr AAS degree in Culinary Arts (ACF-accredited), Hotel/Motel Mgmt, Restaurant Mgmt. Established: 1963. Accredited by SACS. Calendar: semester. Curriculum: culinary, core. Admission dates: Jun, Aug, Jan. Total enrollment: 175. ~60 each admission period. 100% of applicants accepted. 40% receive financial aid. 30% enrolled part-time. Student to teacher ratio 15:1. 90% of graduates employed within six months. Facilities: Restaurant, 4 classrooms, 2labs, herb garden.

Faculty: 4 full-time, 8 part-time.

Costs: In-state $3,100/2 long sems. Out-of-state/intl student $4,600/long sems. Housing ~$700-$900. Admission requirements: HS diploma or equivalent, admission test. Scholarships: yes. Loans: yes.

Contact: Bob Ard, Professor & Chair, Del Mar College, Dept. of Hospitality Mgmt., 101 Baldwin, Corpus Christi, TX 78404-3897; 361-698-1734, Fax 361-698-1829, E-mail bard@delmar.edu, URL http://www.delmar.edu.

EL CENTRO COLLEGE
Dallas/Year-round

Sponsor: College. Program: A.A.S. and certificate programs in Food & Hospitality Services, Baking/Pastry, and Culinary Arts. Established: 1971. Accredited by SACS. Calendar: semester. Curriculum: culinary, core. Admission dates: Jan, Aug, May-Jun. Total enrollment: 400. 350-400 each admission period. 100% of applicants accepted. 40% receive financial aid. 65% enrolled part-time. Student to teacher ratio 20-35:1. 98% of graduates employed within six months. Facilities: Include 3 kitchens, 4 classrooms, pastry/bakery labs, computer lab.

Faculty: 4 full-time, 12 part-time.

Costs: Annual tuition in-county $500, out-of-county $900. Admission requirements: HS diploma or equivalent and admission test. Scholarships: yes. Loans: yes.

Contact: Beth Sonnier, Director Food & Hospitality Institute, El Centro College, Main and Lamar, Dallas, TX 75202; 214-860-2368, E-mail bbs5531@dcccd.edu, URL http://www.dcccd.edu/cat0001/programs/culi.htm.

EL PASO COMMUNITY COLLEGE
El Paso/Year-round

Sponsor: Two-yr public college. Program: 1-yr certificate, 2-yr AAS degree in Food Service, Culinary Arts. Established: 1992. Accredited by SACS. Calendar: semester. Curriculum: culinary, core. Admission dates: Jul/Aug, Dec/Jan, Apr/May. Total enrollment: 40. 15 each admission period. 90% of applicants accepted. 70% receive financial aid. 50% enrolled part-time. Student to teacher ratio 18:1. 100% of graduates employed within six months. Facilities: Full kitchen.

Faculty: 1 full-time, 1 part-time.

Costs: $75 ($200-$250)/1 cr-hr + $24 ($50) ea add'l + $29 fees + $9 ($29+$9) ea add'l hr after 6 cr-hrs. Admission requirements: HS diploma, GED, TASP exam. Scholarships: yes. Loans: yes.

Contact: El Paso Community College, 919 Hunter Dr., El Paso, TX 79915; 915-831-5148, Restaurant 915-831-5061, Fax 915-831-5146, E-mail ClaudiaG@epcc.edu, URL http://www.epcc.edu.

GALVESTON COLLEGE – CULINARY ARTS ACADEMY
Galveston/Year-round

Sponsor: 2-yr community college. Program: 1-yr certificates in Culinary Arts & Culinary/Hospitality Mgmt, 2-yr AAS degree in Culinary Arts/Hospitality Mgmt. Established: 1987. Accredited by SACS. Calendar: semester. Curriculum: culinary, core. Admission dates: Jan, Jun, Jul, Aug. Total enrollment: 50-60. 30-40 each admission period. 95% of applicants accepted. 100% receive financial aid. 10% enrolled part-time. Student to teacher ratio 20:1. 97% of graduates employed within six months. Facilities: Include kitchen, bakeshop & classroom.

Faculty: Leslie Bartosh, CEC, FMP; Cheryl Lewis.

Costs: Annual tuition $2,600 in-state, $3,300 out-of-state. Admission requirements: HS diploma or equivalent & admission test. Scholarships: yes. Loans: yes.

Contact: Leslie Bartosh, CEC, FMP, Director of Culinary Arts, Galveston College-Culinary Arts Academy, 4015 Ave. Q, Galveston, TX 77550; 409-944-1304, Fax 409-944-1501, E-mail chef@gc.edu, URL http://www.gc.edu/chef.

HOUSTON COMMUNITY COLLEGE SYSTEM
Houston/Year-round

Sponsor: College. Program: Certificate in Culinary Arts, certificate in Pastry & Baking. Established: 1972. Accredited by SACS. Calendar: semester. Curriculum: culinary. Total enrollment: 200. 25 each admission period. 60% receive financial aid. 25% enrolled part-time. Student to teacher ratio 15-20:1. 95% of graduates employed within six months.

Faculty: 3 full-time, 2 part-time.

Costs: Annual tuition $1,176/in-district, $1,974 out-of-district, $4,284 out-of-state, includes fees. Admission requirements: HS/GRE. Scholarships: yes. Loans: yes.

Contact: Eddy VanDamme, Dept. Chair, Houston Community College System, Culinary Services, Houston, TX 77002; 713-718-6046, Fax 713-718-6044, E-mail eddy.vandamme@hccs.edu, URL http://www.hccs.cc.tx.us.

THE NATURAL EPICUREAN ACADEMY OF CULINARY ARTS
Austin/Year-round

Sponsor: Proprietary school. Program: 2-yr Natural Foods Training certificate program consisting of 1-3 evening & wkend classes/wk. Established: 1994. Calendar: trimester. Curriculum: culinary, core. Admission dates: Jan, Apr/May, Aug/Sep. Total enrollment: 45. 25 max each admission period. 100% of applicants accepted. 10% receive financial aid. Student to teacher ratio 10:1. 95% of graduates employed within six months. Facilities: Includes teaching kitchen, organic restaurant, herb garden, natural foods store.

Faculty: 2 full-time instructors; guest teachers & chefs.

Costs: 7100. Admission requirements: Application, statement of intent, personal interview.

Contact: Dawn Steinborn, Director, The Natural Epicurean Academy of Culinary Arts, 1701 Toomey Rd., Austin, TX 78704; 512-476-2276, Fax 512-692-1845, E-mail info@naturalepicurean.com, URL http://www.NaturalEpicurean.com.

ODESSA COLLEGE
Odessa/Year-round

Sponsor: College. Program: 2-yr certificate/AAS degree. Established: 1990. Accredited by SACS. Calendar: semester. Curriculum: culinary, core. Admission dates: Open. Total enrollment: 35-50. 35-50 each admission period. 75% of applicants accepted. 65% receive financial aid. 38275% enrolled part-time. Student to teacher ratio 10-15:1. 100% of graduates employed within six months. Facilities: Training kitchen/laboratory, dining room.

Faculty: 2 full-time.

Costs: $207 for first three cr-hrs, $19 for each add'l cr-hr. Admission requirements: HS diploma or equivalent and admission test. Scholarships: yes.

Contact: Peter Lewis, Dept. Chair, Odessa College, Culinary Arts, 201 W. University, Odessa, TX 79764; 915-335-6320, Fax 915-335-6860, E-mail plewis@odessa.edu, URL http://www.odessa.edu/dept/culin.

ST. PHILIP'S COLLEGE
San Antonio/Year-round

Sponsor: College. Program: 2-yr AAS. Established: 1979. Accredited by SACS, ACF. Calendar: semester. Curriculum: culinary. Admission dates: Aug, Jan, Jun. Total enrollment: 335. 335 each admission period. 80% receive financial aid. 50% enrolled part-time. Student to teacher ratio 15:1 lab. 90% of graduates employed within 6 mos. Facilities: 3 kitchens, classrooms, computer lab, restaurant.

FACULTY: 5 full-time.

COSTS: Annual tuition in-district $504, out-of-district $966, out-of-state $1,932. Admission requirements: HS diploma or equivalent & admission test. Scholarships: yes. Loans: yes.

CONTACT: William Thornton, Associate Professor FMP,CCE, St. Philip's College, Tourism,Hospitality,and Culinary Arts 1801 ML KING Dr., San Antonio, TX 78203; 210-531-3315, Fax 210-531-3351, E-mail wthornton@accd.edu, URL http://www.accd.edu.

SAN JACINTO COLLEGE CENTRAL
Pasadena/Year-round

Sponsor: Public 2-yr college. Program: 18-mo certificate in Culinary Arts, 2-yr associate degree in Culinary Arts. Established: 1961. Accredited by SACS. Calendar: semester. Curriculum: culinary. Admission dates: Jan, Jun, Sep. Total enrollment: 90. 55% enrolled part-time. Student to teacher ratio 15:1. Facilities: Food production kitchen, 4 classrooms, library, cafeteria.

FACULTY: 2 full-time, 6 part-time. Includes Leonard Pringle DTR, Cynthia Lundberg.

COSTS: In-state: $16/cr-hr. Out-of-district: $30/cr-hr. Out-of-state: $60/cr-hr. Fees ~$200.

CONTACT: Leonard Pringle, Dept. Chair, Culinary Arts, San Jacinto College - Central Campus, 8060 Spencer Hwy., Pasadena, TX 77501-2007; 281-542-2099, Fax 281-478-2790, E-mail leonard.pringle@sjcd.edu, URL http://www.sjcd.edu.

SAN JACINTO COLLEGE NORTH-CULINARY ARTS
Houston/September-July

Sponsor: College. Program: 2-yr & 3-yr AAS degree. Established: 1986. Accredited by SACS. Calendar: semester. Curriculum: culinary. Admission dates: Sep, Jan. Total enrollment: 20-30. 25 each admission period. 90% of applicants accepted. 50% receive financial aid. Student to teacher ratio 12:1. 70% of graduates employed within six months.

FACULTY: 3 full-time. 2 ACF chefs, CEC/CCE.

COSTS: $262/sem in-district, $430/sem out-of-district. Admission requirements: H.S. diploma-GED. Scholarships: yes. Loans: yes.

CONTACT: Arthur Ramirez, San Jacinto College North, Culinary Arts, 5800 Uvalde, Houston, TX 77049; 281-459-7150, Fax 281-459-7132, E-mail arthur.ramirez@sjcd.edu, URL http://www.sjcd.edu.

SUSHI SENSEI
Dallas/Year-round

Sponsor: Private school/corporate consultants. Program: Short courses in Japanese cuisine, particularly the art & construction of sushi & sashimi. 2 programs/yr include a culinary tour of Japan. Established: 1986. Curriculum: culinary. 20 each admission period. Facilities: At the client's site.

FACULTY: 2 CECs, 1 CE. Assistants are former students.

CONTACT: Anita B. Frank, Executive Chef, Sushi Sensei, 10204 Faircrest Dr., Dallas, TX 75238; 214-357-0960, E-mail help@on-site-services.org.

TEXAS CHEFS ASSOCIATION
Dallas or Houston/Year-round

Sponsor: ACF chapter. Program: 3-yr apprenticeship in Dallas or Houston. Associate's degree. Established: 1968. Curriculum: culinary. Admission dates: Aug/Sept or Dec/Jan. Total enrollment: 120. Facilities: San Jacinto College in Houston, El Centro Community College in Dallas.

CONTACT: Chris LaLonde CEC, Apprenticeship Chair, Texas Chefs Association, El Centro College, Dallas, TX 75202; 214-860-2209, Fax 214-860-2049, E-mail crl5531@dcccd.edu.

TEXAS CULINARY ACADEMY
Austin/Year-round

Sponsor: Private school. Program: AAS in Le Cordon Bleu Culinary Arts. Established: 1981. Accredited by COE. Calendar: trimester. Curriculum: culinary, core. Admission dates: Continuous.

Total enrollment: 700. 95% of applicants accepted. 90% receive financial aid. Student to teacher ratio 12:1. 96% of graduates employed within six months. Facilities: 36-station culinary lab, 6 lecture rooms, learning center, computer lab, conf. room, student lounge, library, on-site restaurants & store. **COSTS:** $37,500 tuition, $100 non-refundable registration fee, $2,500 books & uniforms. Admission requirements: HS diploma or GED. Scholarships: yes. Loans: yes. **CONTACT:** Paula M. Paulette, V.P. of Marketing and Admissions, Texas Culinary Academy, 11400 Burnet Rd., Ste. 2100, Austin, TX 78758; 888-553-2433, 512-837-2665, Fax 512-977-9753, E-mail admissions@txca.com, URL http://www.tca.edu.

TEXAS STATE TECHNICAL COLLEGE
Waco/Year-round
Sponsor: 2-yr technical-vocational college. Program: 1-yr certificate & 2-yr AAS degree programs in Food Service/Culinary Arts. Established: 1965. Accredited by SACS. Calendar: semester. Curriculum: culinary, core. Admission dates: Sep, Jan. Total enrollment: 75. 25 each admission period. 100% of applicants accepted. 75% receive financial aid. 10% enrolled part-time. Student to teacher ratio 12-15:1. 100% of graduates employed within six months. Facilities: Former Air Force base Officers' Club.
FACULTY: 5 full-time.
COSTS: $47.50/cr-hr in-state. Admission requirements: CPT. Scholarships: yes. Loans: yes.
CONTACT: Dr. Debby DeFee, Dept. Chair, Texas State Technical College, Food Service/Culinary Arts, 3801 Campus Dr., Waco, TX 76705-1696; 800-792-8784, 254-867-4868, Fax 254-867-3663, E-mail webmaster@tstc.edu, URL http://culinaryartcollege.com.

UTAH

BRIDGERLAND APPLIED TECHNOLOGY CENTER
Logan/Year-round
Sponsor: State applied technology center. Program: 1100-hr program consisting of basic food preparation courses. Established: 1989. Calendar: quarter. Curriculum: culinary. Admission dates: Open admission. 100% of applicants accepted. 80% receive financial aid. 90% enrolled part-time. Student to teacher ratio 7-10:1. 100% of graduates employed within six months. Facilities: 2 classrooms, large production lab, on-site cafeteria.
FACULTY: 2 full time.
COSTS: $330/qtr. Loans: yes.
CONTACT: Anne Parish, Bridgerland Applied Technology Center, 1301 N. 600 West, Logan, UT 84321; 435-750-3021, Fax 435-752-2016, E-mail aparish@m.batc.tec.ut.us, URL http://www.batc.tec.ut.us.

SALT LAKE COMMUNITY COLLEGE
Salt Lake City/Year-round
Sponsor: 2-yr college. Program: 2-yr full-time & 3-yr part-time Apprentice Chef program. Established: 1984. Accredited by NASC, ACF. Calendar: semester. Curriculum: culinary, core. Admission dates: Rolling. Total enrollment: 50. 70-80 each admission period. 95% of applicants accepted. Student to teacher ratio 15:1. 100% of graduates employed within six months. Facilities: Include kitchen, 8 classrooms, video & reference library.
FACULTY: 2 full-time, 8 part-time.
COSTS: $1,087/sem in-state, $2,427/sem out-of-state; $30 application fee. Housing ~$400/mo. Admission requirements: HS diploma or equivalent & admission test. Scholarships: yes. Loans: yes.
CONTACT: Joe Mulvey, Apprenticeship Director, Salt Lake Community College, P.O. Box 30808, Salt Lake City, UT 84130-0808; 801-957-4066, Fax 801-957-4612, E-mail mulveyjo@slcc.edu, URL http://www.slcc.edu.

UTAH STATE UNIVERSITY
Logan/Year-round

Sponsor: University. Program: 4-yr BS degree in Culinary Arts & Foodservice mgmt, major in culinary arts and minor in a business discipline. Established: 1994. Accredited by NASC. Calendar: semester. Curriculum: culinary, core. Admission dates: Ongoing. Total enrollment: 40. 100% of applicants accepted. 50% receive financial aid. Student to teacher ratio 12:1. 100% of graduates employed within six months. Facilities: On campus facilties include classrooms, labs, campus foodservice outlets.

FACULTY: 2 full-time faculty, one with masters & one with PhD degree, one CEC; part-time faculty.

COSTS: Plateau (12-18 credits) tuition is $1,122.62 in-state, $3,400.88 out-of-state. Admission requirements: HS diploma or equivalent. Scholarships: yes. Loans: yes.

CONTACT: Jeffrey Miller, CEC, CCE, Co-Director, CA/FSM Program, Utah State University, 8700 Old Main Hill, Logan, UT 84322-8700; 435-797-0897, Fax 435-797-2379, E-mail chefjeff@cc.usu.edu, URL http://www.usu.edu/~famlife/nfs/culinaryarts.

UTAH VALLEY STATE COLLEGE
Orem/August-April

Sponsor: College. Program: 2-yr AAS degree in Culinary Arts. Established: 1992. Accredited by NASC. Admission dates: Open. Total enrollment: 35. 15 each admission period. 90% of applicants accepted. 80% receive financial aid. 10% enrolled part-time. Student to teacher ratio 12:!. 100% of graduates employed within six months. Facilities: Include 3 kitchens, 3 classrooms, restaurant & food service operation.

FACULTY: 3 full-time; certified chefs, work experience.

COSTS: In-state $1,036/sem, out-of-state $3,626/sem; $100 class fee, $300 supplies fee. Housing ~$200/mo. Admission requirements: HS diploma.

CONTACT: Julie Slocum, CA Academic Advisor, Utah Valley State College, 800 W. University Parkway, Orem, UT 84058; 801-863-8914, Fax 801-863-7112, E-mail slocumju@uvsc.edu, URL http://www.uvsc.edu/ca.

VERMONT

NEW ENGLAND CULINARY INSTITUTE
Montpelier & Essex/Year-round   *(See display ad page 134)*

Sponsor: Private career institution. Program: 2-yr AOS degree programs in Culinary Arts and Food & Beverage mgmt, upper level 1-1/2-yr Bachelors degree in Food & Beverage mgmt, 10-mo certificate program in Basic Cooking. Established: 1979. Accredited by State of Vermont, ACCSCT. Calendar: semester. Curriculum: culinary. Admission dates: Sep, Dec, Mar, Jun. Total enrollment: 700. 168 each admission period. 90% of applicants accepted. 80% receive financial aid. Student to teacher ratio 7:1. 98% of graduates employed within six months. Facilities: 12 kitchens, 14 classrooms. Each campus offers a variety of restaurants, bakery, catering operation & banquet dept. Courses: Integration into real restaurant operation. In culinary arts program 75% of class time is spent preparing food for the public. Remaining classes cover cooking theory, food & wine history, wine & beverage mgmt, tableservice, purchasing.

FACULTY: 63-member faculty, 19-member administrative staff, 3 advisory boards.

COSTS: AOS in Culinary Arts: $25,975/yr includes room, board, knives, uniforms. BA: $41,210/2 academic yrs includes room, board, uniforms. Admission requirements: HS diploma or equivalent, reference letters, essay, interview. Advanced placement students must pass a written exam & practical. Scholarships: yes. Loans: yes.

CONTACT: Dawn Hayward, Director of Admissions, New England Culinary Institute, Admissions Dept., 250 Main St., Montpelier, VT 05602; 877-223-6324, Fax 802-225-3280, E-mail info@neci.edu, URL http://www.neci.edu.

VIRGINIA

THE ART INSTITUTE OF WASHINGTON
Arlington/Year-round   *(See display ad page 11)*
Sponsor: Private college. Program: 7-qtr AA degree in Culinary Arts. Established: 2000. Accredited by ACF, SACS. Calendar: quarter. Curriculum: culinary, core. Admission dates: Jul, Oct, Jan, Apr. Facilities: 14,000-sq-ft facility with 4 teaching kitchens, classrooms, full-service teaching dining room.
CONTACT: Ann Marie Drucker, Director of Admissions, The Art Institute of Washington, 1820 N Fort Myer Dr., Ground Floor, Arlington, VA 22209; 703-358-9550, 877-303-3771, Fax 703-358-9759, E-mail druckera@aii.edu, URL http://www.aiw.artinstitute.edu.

J. SARGEANT REYNOLDS COMMUNITY COLLEGE
Richmond/Year-round
Sponsor: Community college. Program: 68 cr-hr AAS degree in Culinary Arts. Established: 1973. Accredited by SACS. Calendar: semester. Curriculum: culinary, core. Admission dates: Ongoing. Total enrollment: 140. 40 each admission period. 100% of applicants accepted. 40% receive financial aid. 80% enrolled part-time. Student to teacher ratio 18:1. 100% of graduates employed within six months. Facilities: Classrooms, culinary labs, commercial production kitchen, food service & conference space, computer technology labs.
FACULTY: 12 instructors. Include Certified Hotel Administrator, Registered Dietitian & Ph.D.
COSTS: Full degree program $4,760 in-state, $14,552 out-of-state. Lodging ~$400/mo. Admission requirements: HS graduate or GED. Scholarships: yes. Loans: yes.
CONTACT: David Barrish, Director, J. Sargeant Reynolds CC, Box 85622, Richmond, VA 23285-5622; 804-786-2069, Fax 804-786-5465, E-mail dbarrish@jsr.vccs.edu, URL www.jsr.vccs.edu/hospitality.

NORTHERN VIRGINIA COMMUNITY COLLEGE
Annandale/Year-round
Sponsor: 2-yr college. Program: 1-yr certificate in Culinary Arts. Established: 1997. Accredited by SACS. Calendar: semester. Curriculum: culinary. Admission dates: Fall, spring sems. Total enrollment: 40. 40 each admission period. 100% of applicants accepted. 30% receive financial aid. 80% enrolled part-time. Student to teacher ratio 20:1. 90% of graduates employed within six months. Facilities: Include 2 classrooms, computer lab, fully-equipped commercial kitchen & dining room.
FACULTY: 6 full-time, 1 part-time.
COSTS: $57/cr-hr in-state, $202/cr-hr out-of-state. Scholarships: yes. Loans: yes.
CONTACT: Benita Wong, CCC, CCE, Culinary Arts Instructor, Northern Virginia Community College, 8333 Little River Tpk., Annandale, VA 22003-3796; 703-323-3457, Fax 703-323-3509, E-mail bwong@nvcc.edu, URL http://www.nvcc.edu.

STRATFORD UNIVERSITY – SCHOOL OF CULINARY ARTS
Falls Church/Year-round
Sponsor: Private University. Program: 30-mo BA degree in Hospitality Mgmt.,15-mo AAS degree in Culinary Arts and in Baking & Pastry Arts,12-mo diploma in Culinary Arts. Established: 1990. Accredited by ACICS, ACF, SCHEV. Calendar: quarter. Curriculum: core. Admission dates: Every 5 wks. Total enrollment: 300. 40 each admission period. 85% of applicants accepted. 80% receive financial aid. 1% enrolled part-time. Student to teacher ratio 16:1. 95% of graduates employed within six months. Facilities: 5 kitchens with latest equipment, 5 classrooms, 1 dining rooms, cafe.
FACULTY: 11 full-time & 4 part-time ACF-certified chefs.
COSTS: $275/cr-hr. Nonrefundable application fee $100. Housing & food costs ~$1,000/mo. Admission requirements: HS diploma or GED. Entrance exam. Scholarships: yes. Loans: yes.
CONTACT: Admissions, Stratford University, Culinary Arts, Falls Church, VA 22043-2403; 800-444-0804, 703-821-8570, Fax 703-556-9892, E-mail culinary@stratford.edu, URL www.stratford.edu.

TIDEWATER COMMUNITY COLLEGE CULINARY ARTS
Norfolk

Sponsor: 2-yr community college. Program: AAS degree in Culinary Arts. Established: 1997. Accredited by SACS. Calendar: semester. Curriculum: culinary, core. Admission dates: May, Aug, Dec. Total enrollment: 45. 100% of applicants accepted. 70% receive financial aid. 60% enrolled part-time. Student to teacher ratio 20:1. 100% of graduates employed within six months.

CONTACT: Chef John Cappellucci, Tidewater Community College Culinary Arts, 300 Granby St., Norfolk, VA 23510-9956; 757-822-1350, 757-822-1111, E-mail jcappellucci@tcc.edu, URL http://www.tc.cc.va.us/culinary/index.htm.

VIRGINIA CHEFS ASSOCIATION
Richmond/Year-round

Sponsor: Community college. Program: Degree program through J. Sargeant Reynolds CC. Established: 1992. Accredited by SACS. Calendar: sem. Curriculum: culinary, core. Admission dates: yr-round. Total enrollment: 140. 40 each admission period. 100% of applicants accepted. 40% receive financial aid. 80% enrolled part-time. Student to teacher ratio 18:1. 100% of graduates employed within 6 mos. Facilities: Classrooms, culinary & computer labs, production kitchen.

FACULTY: 12 instructors including Certified Hotel Administrator, Registered Dietician & Ph.D.

COSTS: $4,760 in-state + $1,250 for books & materials. Admission requirements: HS diploma or equivalent. Scholarships: yes. Loans: yes.

CONTACT: David Barrish, Director, Virginia Chefs Assn., PO Box 85622, Richmond, VA 23285-5622; 804-786-2069, Fax 804-786-5465, E-mail dbarrish@jsr.vccs.edu, URL http://www.jsr.vccs.edu//hospitality.

VIRGINIA INTERMONT COLLEGE – CULINARY ARTS
Bristol/Year-round   *(See display ad above)*

Sponsor: Private college. Program: AS in Culinary Arts; BA in Culinary Arts, Pastry Arts & Restaurant Mgmt. Established: 2002. Accredited by SACS. Calendar: semester. Curriculum: culinary, core. Admission dates: Rolling. Total enrollment: 64. 64 each admission period. 59% of applicants accepted. 74% receive financial aid. 19% enrolled part-time. Student to teacher ratio 12:1. Facilities: On-campus facility, teaching kitchens, college-owned/operated bakery. Courses: American regional & intl cuisines, baking & pastry, nutrition, sanitation & safety, hospitality law, a la carte, garde manger, entrepreneurship.

FACULTY: Full-time: Chefs Scott Lovorn & Kami Smith. Part-time: Chefs Armand Celentano, Rob McMahon, Michael Poore. Local industry chefs.

COSTS: Tuition $14,500, fees $700, rm & bd $5,650. Admission requirements: HS GPA of 2.0+, 800 SAT, 18 ACT. Scholarships: yes. Loans: yes.

CONTACT: Joe Deel, Chef, Virginia Intermont College - Culinary Arts, 1013 Moore St., Bristol, VA 24201; 276-619-4373, Fax 276-619-4309, E-mail joeldeel@vic.edu, URL http://www.vic.edu.

WASHINGTON

THE ART INSTITUTE OF SEATTLE
Seattle/Year-round   *(See display ad page 11)*

Sponsor: 2-yr college. Program: 7-qtr AAA degree in Culinary Arts, 4-qtr diploma in Baking & Pastry, 4-qtr diploma in The Art of Cooking. Established: 1996. Accredited by NASC, ACF. Calendar: quarter. Curriculum: core. Admission dates: Rolling. Total enrollment: 300. 60 each admission period. 65% of applicants accepted. 75% receive financial aid. 13% enrolled part-time. Student to teacher ratio 19:1. 95% of graduates employed within six months. Facilities: Kitchens & classroom space, dining room overlooking Puget Sound.

FACULTY: 18 culinary instructors with industry experience.

COSTS: $13,680/academic yr for AAA degree programs, $8,208/academic yr for Diploma programs. Admission requirements: HS diploma & admissions interview. Scholarships: yes. Loans: yes.

CONTACT: Lori Murray, Associate Director of Admissions, Art Institute of Seattle, Admissions Dept., 2323 Elliott Ave., Seattle, WA 98121; 800-275-2471, 206-448-6600, Fax 206-448-2501, E-mail aisadm@aii.edu, URL http://www.ais.artinstitutes.edu.

BATES TECHNICAL COLLEGE
Tacoma/Year-round

Sponsor: Two-yr college. Program: 22-mo AST degree in Culinary Arts. Accredited by ACCSCT. Calendar: quarter.

FACULTY: Roger Knapp, Ricardo Saenz.

COSTS: $720/qtr.

CONTACT: Ricardo Saenz, Bates Technical College, 1101 S. Yakima Ave., Tacoma, WA 98405; 253-680-7247, Fax 253-680-7211, E-mail rsaenz@bates.ctc.edu, URL http://www.bates.ctc.edu.

BELLINGHAM TECHNICAL COLLEGE
Bellingham/September-July

Sponsor: 2-yr technical college. Program: Certificates of completion & AAS degrees in Culinary Arts & Baking, Pastry, & Confections. Established: 1957. Accredited by ACF, NACS. Calendar: quarter. Curriculum: culinary, core. Total enrollment: 40. 40 each admission period. 90% of applicants accepted. 30% receive financial aid. 20% enrolled part-time. Student to teacher ratio 20:1. 94% of graduates employed within six months. Facilities: Instructional space, industrial kitchen/bakeshop, fine dining restaurant, deli/baking, demo kitchen.

FACULTY: Michael S.Baldwin, CEC, & William Pifer, CMB.

COSTS: Qtrly tuition & fees are $769 for Culinary Arts, $769 for Baking, Pastry & Confections. Admission requirements: 16 yrs or older, HS graduate, basic skills. Scholarships: yes. Loans: yes.

CONTACT: Michael Baldwin, Culinary Arts instructor, Bellingham Technical College, Culinary Arts, 3028 Lindbergh Ave., Bellingham, WA 98225; 360-715-8350 #400, Fax 360-676-2798, E-mail mbaldwin@belltc.ctc.edu, URL http://www.beltc.ctc.edu/index.html.

CLARK COLLEGE CULINARY ARTS PROGRAM
Vancouver/Year-round

Sponsor: Community college. Program: 1- & 2-yr certificate or AAS degree programs in cooking, baking, and bakery & restaurant mgmt. Established: 1958. Accredited by NWACC. Calendar: quarter. Curriculum: culinary, core. Admission dates: Jan, Mar, Jun, Sep. Total enrollment: 80. 15 (cooking), 10 (baking) each admission period. 80% of applicants accepted. 50% receive financial aid. Student to teacher ratio 5:1. 95% of graduates employed within six months. Facilities: Modernized facility operates like a hotel kitchen. Students make all foods sold on-campus. Baking students operate the campus' retail bakery.

FACULTY: 12-member faculty.

COSTS: 1-yr program is $3,000 in-state, $3,500 out-of-state. 2-yr program is $6,000 in-state, $7,000 out-of-state. Admission requirements: HS diploma or equivalent. Scholarships: yes. Loans: yes.
CONTACT: Larry Mains, Director, Culinary Arts, Clark College, Culinary Arts, 1800 E. McLoughlin Blvd., Vancouver, WA 98663-3598; 360-992-2143, Fax 360-992-2839, E-mail lmains@clark.edu, URL http://www.clark.edu.

EDMONDS COMMUNITY COLLEGE
Lynwood/September-June
Sponsor: Community college. Program: 6-qtr ATA, 3-qtr Advanced Commercial Cooking Certificate, 2-qtr Basic Commercial Cooking Certificate, 1-qtr Professional Food Server Certificate. Established: 1988. Accredited by State. Calendar: quarter. Curriculum: core. Admission dates: Fall, winter, spring. Total enrollment: 45. 15 each admission period. 90% of applicants accepted. 25% receive financial aid. Student to teacher ratio 20:1. 100% of graduates employed within six months. Facilities: 1 kitchen, 1 classroom, 1 restaurant.
FACULTY: 2 full-time, 2 part-time.
COSTS: Annual tuition in-state $505/qtr, out-of-state $1,987/qtr. Admission requirements: HS diploma or equivalent. Scholarships: yes. Loans: yes.
CONTACT: Nancy Lindaas, Dept. Chair, Edmonds Community College, Culinary Arts, 20000 - 68th Ave. West, Lynnwood, WA 98036; 425-640-1239, E-mail nlindaas@edcc.edu, URL www.edcc.edu.

LAKE WASHINGTON TECHNICAL COLLEGE
Kirkland/October-August
Sponsor: Public 2-yr college. Program: Three-qtr certificate & six-qtr associate degree in Culinary Arts. Established: 1983. Accredited by State of Washington. Calendar: quarter. Curriculum: culinary, core. Admission dates: Jan, Apr, Jul, Oct. Total enrollment: 50. 100% of applicants accepted. Available% receive financial aid. Student to teacher ratio 17:1. 95% of graduates employed within six months. Facilities: Food production & teaching kitchens, demo lab, computer lab, bake shop, dining room, public restaurant.
FACULTY: 1 full-time, 2 part-time.
COSTS: $1,750/certificate, $3,750/degree. Materials fee ~$650. Scholarships: yes. Loans: yes.
CONTACT: Alan Joynson, Chef Instructor, Culinary Arts, Lake Washington Technical College, 11605 132nd Ave. NE, Kirkland, WA 98034-8506; 425-739-8310, Fax 425-739-8298, E-mail alan.joynson@lwtc.ctc.edu, URL http://www.lwtc.ctc.edu.

NORTH SEATTLE COMMUNITY COLLEGE
Seattle/September-June
Sponsor: College. Program: 1-yr certificate & 2-yr AAS degree in Culinary Arts, Hospitality & Restaurant Cooking. Established: 1970. Accredited by NASC, ACF. Calendar: quarter. Curriculum: core. Admission dates: qtrly. Total enrollment: 80. 25 each admission period. 90% of applicants accepted. 25% receive financial aid. Student to teacher ratio 18:1. 90% of graduates employed within six months. Facilities: Include 2 kitchens & classrooms, restaurant, bakery.
FACULTY: 4 full-time.
COSTS: Annual tuition $1,750 in-state, $6,000 out-of-state. Uniform, supplies $750. Housing $750/mo. Admission requirements: HS diploma or equivalent and admission test.
CONTACT: Darrell Mihara, Associate Dean, Culinary Arts & Hospitality, North Seattle Community College, Culinary Arts, 9600 College Way North, Seattle, WA 98103-3599; 206-528-4402, Fax 206-527-3635, E-mail dmihara@sccd.ctc.edu, URL http://www.gonorth.org.

OLYMPIC COLLEGE
Bremerton/September-May
Sponsor: College. Program: 3-qtr certificate, 2-yr ATA degree. Advanced US Navy Food Service training also offered. Established: 1978. Accredited by State. Calendar: trimester. Curriculum: culi-

nary. Admission dates: Continuous. Total enrollment: 38. 28-35 each admission period. 85% of applicants accepted. 60% receive financial aid. 15% enrolled part-time. Student to teacher ratio 14:1. 90% of graduates employed within 6 mos. Facilities: Central kitchen, 2 classrooms, 2 restaurants. **FACULTY:** 2 full-time, 2 part-time.

COSTS: Annual tuition: in-state $1,545, out-of-state $5,991. $50 lunch fee/qtr. Housing ~$375/mo. Admission requirements: HS diploma or equivalent. Scholarships: yes. Loans: yes.

CONTACT: Steve Lammers, Chef Instructor C.C.E., Olympic College, Commercial Cooking/Food Service, 16th & Chester, Bremerton, WA 98310-1688; 360-475-7571, Fax 360-475-7575, E-mail slammers@oc.ctc.edu, URL http://www.olympic.ctc.edu.

RENTON TECHNICAL COLLEGE
Renton/Year-round
Sponsor: Career college. Program: 1,620-hr certificate in Culinary Arts/Chef, AAS degree available; 1,260-hr certificate in Professional Baking. Established: 1968. Accredited by ACF, RBA. Calendar: quarter. Curriculum: culinary. Admission dates: Open. Total enrollment: 25. 10-30 each admission period. 100% of applicants accepted. 30% receive financial aid. Student to teacher ratio 12:1. 100% of graduates employed within six months. Facilities: Industry-current kitchen, full bakery, demo classroom, 3 outlet restaurants.

FACULTY: 2 instructors & 1 assistant full-time.

CONTACT: John Fisher, Executive Chef Instructor, Renton Technical College, Culinary Arts, 3000 N.E. Fourth St., Renton, WA 98056; 425-235-2352 x5708, Fax 425-235-7832, E-mail jfisher@rtc.ctc.edu, URL http://www.renton-tc.ctc.edu.

SEATTLE CULINARY ACADEMY
Seattle/Year-round
Sponsor: 2-yr college. Program: 6-qtr Culinary Arts certificate, 2-yr Culinary AAS degree, a 5-qtr Specialty Desserts & Breads certificate. Established: 1942. Accredited by ACF. Calendar: quarter. Curriculum: culinary. Admission dates: qtrly. Total enrollment: 100-150. 25-30 each admission period. 85% of applicants accepted. 30% receive financial aid. 2% enrolled part-time. Student to teacher ratio 18:1. 97% of graduates employed within six months. Facilities: Include 5 kitchens, 8 classrooms, bistro restaurant, gourmet restaurant, lunch buffet.

FACULTY: 8 full-time, 2 part-time.

COSTS: In-state tuition $579/qtr, out-of-state $2,284/qtr. Housing $400-$600/mo. Total tuition $5,400. Admission requirements: Admissions test or college transcripts for English & Math skills. Scholarships: yes. Loans: yes.

CONTACT: Joy Gulmon-Huri, Program Manager, Seattle Central Community College, Seattle Culinary Academy, 1701 Broadway, Mailstop 2BE2120, Seattle, WA 98122; 206-587-5424, Fax 206-344-4323, E-mail jgulmo@sccd.ctc.edu, URL http://seattleculinary.com.

SKAGIT VALLEY COLLEGE
Mt. Vernon/September-May
Sponsor: College. Program: 1-yr certificate & 2-yr ATA degree in Culinary Arts/Hospitality mgmt. Established: 1979. Accredited by State, ACF. Calendar: quarter. Curriculum: core. Admission dates: Open. Total enrollment: 60. 6 each admission period. 100% of applicants accepted. 60% receive financial aid. Student to teacher ratio 15:1. 100% of graduates employed within six months. Facilities: Include kitchen, classrooms restaurant.

FACULTY: 3 full-time, 1 part-time.

COSTS: Annual tuition in-state $1,584, out-of-state $6,234. Admission requirements: HS diploma or equivalent. Scholarships: yes. Loans: yes.

CONTACT: Lyle Hildahl, Director, Skagit Valley College, Culinary Arts/Hospitality Mgmt., 2405 College Way, Mt. Vernon, WA 98273; 360-416-7618, Fax 360-416-7890, E-mail hildahl@skagit.ctc.edu, URL http://www.skagit.edu.

SOUTH PUGET SOUND COMMUNITY COLLEGE
Olympia/September-June

Sponsor: 2-yr college. Program: 2-yr ATA degree, Food Service Tech. and Food Service mgmt, 1-yr Com. Baking Tech. Established: 1989. Accredited by State. Calendar: quarter. Curriculum: culinary. Admission dates: Sep, Jan, Apr. Total enrollment: 45. 12 each admission period. 90% of applicants accepted. 70% receive financial aid. 10% enrolled part-time. Student to teacher ratio 12-15:1. 95% of graduates employed within six months. Facilities: Bake shop, institutional foods, gourmet cooking, table-side cooking.

FACULTY: 3 full-time, 5 part-time.

COSTS: Annual tuition in-state $48/cr-hr, out-of-state $192/cr-hr. Admission requirements: HS diploma or equivalent and admission test. Scholarships: yes. Loans: yes.

CONTACT: Debbie Van Camp, Food Service Director, South Puget Sound Community College, Food Service Technology, 2011 Mottman Rd., SW, Olympia, WA 98512; 360-754-7711 #5347, Fax 360-664-0780, E-mail admissions@spscc.ctc.edu, URL http://www.spscc.ctc.edu.

SOUTH SEATTLE COMMUNITY COLLEGE
Seattle/Year-round

Sponsor: 2-yr college. Program: 18-mo certificate/AAS degrees in Culinary Arts/Food Service Production and Pastry/Specialty Baking. Established: 1975. Accredited by ACF, NASC. Calendar: quarter. Curriculum: culinary, core. Admission dates: Sep, Jan, Mar, Jun. Total enrollment: 130-160. 25 - 30 each admission period. 100% of applicants accepted. 25% receive financial aid. Student to teacher ratio 15:1. 98% of graduates employed within six months. Facilities: Include new kitchen & classroom with French cooking suite, 4 lab kitchens, 6 classrooms, 2 dining rooms.

FACULTY: 7 full-time, 8 part-time with industry experience.

COSTS: Annual tuition in-state $3,800. Housing $400-$500/mo. Scholarships: yes. Loans: yes.

CONTACT: Stephen Sparks, Instructor, South Seattle Community College, Hospitality & Food Science Div., 6000 16th Ave. S.W., Seattle, WA 98106-1499; 206-764-5344, Fax 206-768-6728, E-mail ssparks@sccd.ctc.edu, URL http://www.chefschool.com.

SPOKANE COMMUNITY COLLEGE
Spokane/September-June

Sponsor: 2-yr college. Program: 2-yr AAS degree in Culinary Arts, 2-yr AAS degree and 1-yr certificate in Commercial Baking. Established: 1962. Accredited by NASC, ACF. Calendar: quarter. Curriculum: culinary, core. Admission dates: Sep, Jan, Mar. Total enrollment: 60-65 culinary, 20-30 baking. 20 culinary, 12 baking each admission period. 95% of applicants accepted. 50% receive financial aid. Student to teacher ratio 15:1. 85% of graduates employed within six months. Facilities: Include 2 kitchens, bakeshop, pastry shop, 6 classrooms, restaurant.

FACULTY: Chef Douglas A. Fisher, CEC, CCE, Chef Peter Tobin, CEC, CCE, Greg Richards, Chef Robert Lombardi, CEC, CEPC, CCE.

COSTS: $627/qtr resident, $759/qtr nonresident US citizen. Knife kit $220, chef uniform set $225. Admission requirements: HS diploma or equivalent & admission test. Scholarships: yes. Loans: yes.

CONTACT: Doug Fisher, Program Coordinator, Spokane Community College, Culinary Arts, 1810 N. Greene St., Spokane, WA 99217-5399; 509-533-7283, Fax 509-533-8108, E-mail dfisher@scc.spokane.edu, URL http://www.scc.spokane.edu/go/cularts.

WEST VIRGINIA

SHEPHERD COMMUNITY COLLEGE
Shepherdstown/Year-round

Sponsor: 2-yr college. Program: 2-yr AAS degree in Culinary Arts. Calendar: semester. Curriculum: core.

COSTS: Annual tuition is $2,228 in-state, $5,348 out-of-state. Room and board is $4,139/yr.

CONTACT: Judy Stains, Shepherd Community College, 315 W. Stephen St., Martinsburg, WV 25401; 304-754-7925, Fax 304-754-7933, E-mail jstains@shepherd.edu, URL http://www.shepherd.edu.

WEST VIRGINIA NORTHERN COMMUNITY COLLEGE
Wheeling/August-May
Sponsor: 2-yr state community college. Program: 1-yr certificate, 2-yr AAS degree in Culinary Arts. Established: 1975. Accredited by NCA, ACF. Calendar: semester. Curriculum: culinary, core. Admission dates: Open. Total enrollment: 45. 20 each admission period. 100% of applicants accepted. 75% receive financial aid. 15% enrolled part-time. Student to teacher ratio 12:1. 95% of graduates employed within six months. Facilities: Modern.
FACULTY: 2 full-time, 3 part-time.
COSTS: In-state $1,500/yr, out-of-state $2,039/yr + books. Admission requirements: HS diploma or equivalent & admission test. Scholarships: yes. Loans: yes.
CONTACT: Marian Grubor, Program Director, West Virginia Northern Community College, 1704 Market Street, Wheeling, WV 26003; 304-233-5900, Fax 304-233-5837, E-mail mgrubor@northern.wvnet.edu, URL http://www.northern.wvnet.edu.

WISCONSIN

ACF CHEFS OF MILWAUKEE, INC.
Milwaukee/Year-round
Sponsor: ACF chapter. Program: 3-yr apprenticeship; degree program through Milwaukee Area Technical College or Waukesha County Technical College is completed by 60%. Established: 1980. Accredited by ACF. Calendar: semester. Curriculum: culinary. Total enrollment: 38. 12-15 each admission period. Student to teacher ratio 10:1. 100% of graduates employed within six months.
FACULTY: 16 instructors.
COSTS: $2,200. Beginning salary is $6-$7/hr with 5%-10% increases every 6 mos. Admission requirements: HS or equivalent. Scholarships: yes.
CONTACT: Greg Abbate, President, ACF/Chefs of Milwaukee, Inc., PO Box 0894, Germantown, WI 53022; 414-353-8800 x16, Fax 414-353-5905, E-mail chefbrynwood@aol.com, URL http://www.acfchefs.org/chapter/wi012.html.

BLACKHAWK TECHNICAL COLLEGE
Janesville/Year-round
Sponsor: College. Program: 1-yr/34 cr-hr certificate & 2-yr/68 cr-hr AS degree in Culinary Arts. Established: 1972. Accredited by ACF. Calendar: semester. Admission dates: Aug, Jan. Total enrollment: 82. 32 each admission period. 43% receive financial aid. 25% enrolled part-time. Student to teacher ratio 8:1. 98% of graduates employed within six months. Facilities: Modern, well-equipped facility, student-run gourmet restaurant.
FACULTY: 2 full-time, 10 part-time.
COSTS: $4,450/yr in-state + books & uniforms. Scholarships: yes. Loans: yes.
CONTACT: Joe Wollinger, CEC, CCE, Program Coordinator, Blackhawk Technical College, 6004 Prairie Rd., P.O. Box 5009, Janesville, WI 53547; 608-757-7696, Fax 608-743-4407, E-mail jwolling@blackhawk.tec.wi.us, URL http://www.blackhawk.edu.

FOX VALLEY TECHNICAL COLLEGE
Appleton/Year-round
Sponsor: 2-yr college. Program: 2-yr associate degree in Culinary Arts. Accredited by NACS, ACF.
COSTS: $1,300/sem, $80/credit.
CONTACT: Jeffrey Igel, Dept. Chair, Fox Valley Technical College, 1825 N. Bluemound Dr., Box 2277, Appleton, WI 54912; 920-735-5643, Fax 920-735-5655, E-mail chefjeff@foxvalleytech.com, URL http://www.fvtc.edu/tp2.asp?ID=Associate+Degrees&pix=017.

MADISON AREA TECHNICAL COLLEGE
Madison/August-May

Sponsor: Career college. Program: 2-yr AAS degree in Culinary Arts. Established: 1950. Accredited by ACF. Calendar: semester. Curriculum: core. Admission dates: Aug, Jan. Total enrollment: 60. 36 each admission period. 75% of applicants accepted. 50% receive financial aid. 20% enrolled part-time. Student to teacher ratio 15:1. 100% of graduates employed within six months. Facilities: Include 3 large labs & classrooms.

FACULTY: Qualifications: certified by state and ACF.

COSTS: In-state $59.25/cr-hr. Advanced registration fee $50. Application fee $25. Housing $400-$870. Admission requirements: HS diploma or equivalent, assessment test. Scholarships: yes. Loans: yes.

CONTACT: Mary G. Hill, Associate Dean, Madison Area Technical College, Culinary Trades Dept., 3550 Anderson St., Madison, WI 53704; 608-243-4455, Fax 608-246-6316, E-mail mhill@madison.tec.wi.us, URL http://www.madison.tec.wi.us/matc.

MILWAUKEE AREA TECHNICAL COLLEGE
Milwaukee/August-May

Sponsor: 2-yr public technical college. Program: 2-yr (67-cr, 4-sem) AAS degree; 3-yr culinary apprenticeship. Established: 1955. Accredited by ACF, NCA. Calendar: semester. Curriculum: culinary, core. Admission dates: Aug, Jan. Total enrollment: 120. 40 each admission period. Student to teacher ratio 18:1. 98% of graduates employed within six months. Facilities: 6 labs for hands-on learning, including dining room service & baking, & industry-standard demo kitchen.

FACULTY: 9 full-time instructors with 300+ yrs of combined culinary experience.

COSTS: $73/cr in-state; $586/cr out-of-state. Admission requirements: HS diploma or equivalent, admission test. Scholarships: yes. Loans: yes.

CONTACT: Patricia Whalen, Instructional Chair, Hospitality Programs, Milwaukee Area Technical College, 700 W. State St., Milwaukee, WI 53233; 414-297-7897, Fax 414-297-7990, E-mail whalenp@matc.edu, URL http://www.matc.edu/utility/clas/prog/food/culi.htm.

MORAINE PARK TECHNICAL COLLEGE
Fond du Lac/Year-round

Sponsor: 2-yr Technical College. Program: 2-yr associate degree in Culinary Arts, 1-yr technical diploma in Food Service Production, certificates in Culinary Basics, Deli/bakery, Food Production, School Food Service. Established: 1980. Accredited by NCA, ACF. Calendar: semester. Curriculum: core. Admission dates: Jul-Aug, Nov-Dec, flexible. Total enrollment: 63. 24 each admission period. 90% of applicants accepted. 40% receive financial aid. 30% enrolled part-time. Student to teacher ratio 12:1. 95% of graduates employed within 6 mos. Facilities: Include 3 kitchens, 2 classrooms.

FACULTY: 3 full-time.

COSTS: $5,755/yr degree, $3,004 diploma, $2,548 certificate, $684 Culinary Basics, $1,840 Food Production, $1,126 Deli/bakery, $718 School Food Service. Admission requirements: HS diploma, placement test, & interview. Scholarships: yes. Loans: yes.

CONTACT: Patricia Olson, Moraine Park Technical College, 235 N. National Ave., PO Box 1940, Fond du Lac, WI 54936-1940; 920-924-3333, E-mail polson@morainepark.edu, URL http://www.morainepark.edu.

NICOLET AREA TECHNICAL COLLEGE
Rhinelander/August-May

Sponsor: Career college. Program: 1-yr diploma in Food Service Production, 2-yr associate degree in Culinary Arts, certificate in Baking, Catering, Kitchen Assistant, Food Service mgmt, School Food Service Assistant. Accredited by NCA. Calendar: semester. Curriculum: core. Admission dates: Fall/Aug, Winter/Jan. Total enrollment: 15/program. 15 each admission period. 85% receive financial aid. 10% enrolled part-time. Student to teacher ratio 10:1. 90% of graduates employed within six months. Facilities: Fully-equipped kitchen laboratory, restaurant dining room & classrooms.

CONTACT: Linda Arndt, Culinary Instructor, Nicolet Area Technical College, Culinary Arts, P.O. Box 518, Rhinelander, WI 54501; 715-365-4649, Fax 715-365-4596, E-mail larndt@nicoletcollege.edu, URL http://www.nicoletcollege.edu.

SOUTHWEST WISCONSIN TECHNICAL COLLEGE
Fennimore/Year-round

Sponsor: Public 2-yr college. Program: 2-yr associate degree in Culinary mgmt. Established: 1994. Accredited by NCA, DMA. Calendar: semester. Curriculum: culinary. Admission dates: Aug. Total enrollment: 20. 20 each admission period. 100% of applicants accepted. 80% receive financial aid. 20% enrolled part-time. Student to teacher ratio 10:1. 100% of graduates employed within six months. Facilities: Food production kitchen, bake shop, computer lab, gourmet dining room, learning resource center.

FACULTY: 2 full-time:.

COSTS: $6,100/degree, $84.60/credit part-time. Application fee $30. Admission requirements: Application, application fee, transcripts, testing, interview, physical exam 6 wks prior to admission. Scholarships: yes. Loans: yes.

CONTACT: Kathy Kruel, Admissions Registration, Southwest Wisconsin Technical College, 1800 Bronson Blvd., Culinary Management, Fennimore, WI 53809; 608-822-3262 x2355, Fax 608-822-6019, E-mail kkreul@southwest.tec.wi.us, URL http://www.southwest.tec.wi.us.

WAUKESHA COUNTY TECHNICAL COLLEGE
Pewaukee/August-May

Sponsor: Technical college. Program: 1-yr diploma in Culinary Arts, 2-yr AAS degree in Culinary mgmt, Baking Certificate. Established: 1971. Accredited by NCA, ACF. Calendar: quarter. Curriculum: core. Admission dates: Aug, Jan. Total enrollment: 80. 50-60 each admission period. 60% enrolled part-time. Student to teacher ratio 12:1. 95% of graduates employed within six months. Facilities: Includes 2 kitchens, demo kitchen, classrooms, restaurant lab, computer lab.

FACULTY: 4 full-time, 5 part-time, all with college degrees & industry experience.

COSTS: In-state $70/cr-hr, cutlery $307, uniform $70 purchase + $80 rental/sem. Scholarships: yes. Loans: yes.

CONTACT: Timothy J. Graham, Associate Dean, Waukesha County Technical College, Hospitality & Culinary Arts Department, 800 Main St., Pewaukee, WI 53072; 262-691-5322, Fax 262-691-5155, E-mail tgraham@wctc.edu, URL http://www.wctc.edu.

ARGENTINA

THE BUE TRAINERS
Buenos Aires/March-December

Sponsor: Private culinary training center. Program: 2-part, 3-yr culinary training program. Degree as Commis de Cuisine after 2nd yr, degree as Chef de Partie after 3rd yr. Established: 1987. Accredited by Dept of Culture & Education of the state of Buenos Aires. Curriculum: culinary, core. Admission dates: Mar &/or Aug for sems. Total enrollment: 300 max. 100 each admission period. 100% of applicants accepted. Student to teacher ratio 17:1. 75% of graduates employed within six months. Facilities: Auditorium for demos, 3 fully-equipped classrooms, computer classroom, 2 professional kitchens, 60-seat dining room, library.

FACULTY: 20 instructors including 4 fully-qualified chefs.

COSTS: $400 enrollment fee + $4,000/yr tuition including uniforms & meals on class days. Admission requirements: 16 yrs old, EGB degree (General Basic Ed), interview. Scholarships: yes. Loans: yes.

CONTACT: María Cecilia García, Secretary, The BUE Trainers, Avda. Tte. Gral. Morillas s/n, Aeropuerto Intenacional de Ezeiza, Buenos Aires, B1802EZE Argentina; (54) 11 54 80 92 34, (54) 11 54 80 90 11, x250/1/2, Fax (54) 11 54 80 92 34, E-mail buetrain@gategourmet.com.ar, URL www.thebuetrainers.com.

COLEGIO DE COCINEROS GATO DUMAS
Buenos Aires/Year-round

Sponsor: Private professional culinary arts school. Program: 2-yr degree in Cuisine & Pastry. 2-mo courses in Pastry, Wine, Bakery, Sushi, Beverages. Established: 1998. Accredited by Education Secretarie from Goubernment of Buenos Aires. Curriculum: core. Admission dates: yr-round. Total enrollment: 800. 100% of applicants accepted. Student to teacher ratio 32:1. 100% of graduates employed within 6 mos. Facilities: professional kitchens, conference room, pastry/oenology rooms.

FACULTY: 20 instructors, 3 from Europe.

COSTS: 2-yr course $1,750. Admission requirements: 17 yrs of age. Scholarships: yes. Loans: yes.

CONTACT: Student Department, Colegio de Cocineros Gato Dumas, Olazabal 2836, Boulevard Oroño 355 - Rosario, Provincia de Santa Fe, Buenos Aires, C1428DGS Argentina; (54) 11 4783-3357/1337, Fax (54) 11 4783-1197 x26, E-mail info@gatodumas.com, URL http://www.gatodumas.com.

INSTITUTO DE GASTRONOMIA PROFESIONAL MAUSI SEBESS
Buenos Aires/Year-round

Sponsor: Private professional culinary arts institute. Program: Occupational studies degree program in Cuisine & Pastry. 1-wk (45 hrs) basic-advanced courses in cuisine & pastry for foreigners leading to a professional degree. 5-mo courses for residents. Established: 1994. Accredited by Buenos Aires Ministry of Education. Calendar: quinmester. Curriculum: culinary. Admission dates: Jan-Feb for foreigners. Mar & Jul for residents. Total enrollment: 780. 780 each admission period. 100% of applicants accepted. Student to teacher ratio 10:1. 100% of graduates employed within six months. Facilities: 4 professional kitchens with latest equipment; pastry lab.

FACULTY: 12 full-time instructors graduated in France, Spain, Italy, U.S. & Thailand.

COSTS: $600-$700/course. Lodging ~$120/wk, week-end meals not included. Admission requirements: 16+ yrs old & min 8 yrs schooling.

CONTACT: Mariana Sebess, Executive Chef, Instituto de Gastronomia Profesional Mausi Sebess, Av. Maipù 594/6. Vicente Lopez 1638., Buenos Aires, 1638 Argentina; (54) 11-4791-4355, (54) 11-4796-5681, Fax (54) 11-4791-9132, E-mail mausisebess@hotmail.com, URL http://www.mausisebess.com.

ARUBA

COLEGIO EPI (ARUBA HOTEL SCHOOL)
Oranjestad, Aruba/August-June

Sponsor: Public school. Program: 3-yr Immediate Employment (I.E.) AAS degree in Culinary Arts; theoretical program; professional certificates. Established: 1997. Accredited by Government of Aruba. Calendar: semester. Curriculum: culinary. Admission dates: Aug. Total enrollment: 75. 35 each admission period. 100% of applicants accepted. Student to teacher ratio 10:1. 100% of graduates employed within six months. Facilities: Modern facility built in 1983.

FACULTY: 11 full-, 4 part-time. All faculty are formally educated with at least a bachelor's degree.

COSTS: $4,000/yr includes uniforms, textbooks, cooking utensils, local excursions. Admission requirements: Fluency in English, HS diploma or equivalent.

CONTACT: Tony A.D. Green, Director, Colegio EPI) Aruba Hotel School Hospitality Sector, I.E. Major, L.G. Smith Blvd. 35, P.O. Box 5019, Oranjestad, Aruba, DWI; (297) 8-38600, Fax (297) 8-35157, E-mail ahs@setarnet.aw, URL http://www.aruba4you.com/aruba_hotel_school.htm.

AUSTRALIA

AUSTRALIAN SCHOOL OF TOURISM AND HOTEL MANAGEMENT
Perth/Year-round

Sponsor: Private hotel management & culinary arts school. Program: 1-yr certificate III in Hospitality (Commercial Cookery), 2 yr Diploma of Hospitality Mgmt. Established: 1989.

Accredited by Training Accreditation Council. Calendar: semester. Curriculum: culinary. Admission dates: Feb, Apr, Jul, Oct. Total enrollment: 240. 60 each admission period. 98% of applicants accepted. Student to teacher ratio 16:1. 95% of graduates employed within six months. Facilities: 10 lecture rooms, information technology center, 2 commercially equipped kitchens, library/reference center, student cafe.

FACULTY: 15 full time, 18 part time.

COSTS: AU$9,800 for 1-yr program, AU$19400 for 2-yr program, A$200 enrollment fee, ~A$1,132 supplies & insurance. Admission requirements: Age 17 min, Australian HS or equivalent, yr 10, upper intermed English level (IELTS 5.5).

CONTACT: Dianne Leslie, Director of International Admissions, Australian School of Tourism and Hotel Management, 641 Wellington St., Perth, 6000 Western Australia; (618) 9322 3202, Fax (618) 9321 3698, E-mail info@asthm.com.au, URL http://www.asthm.com.au.

CANBERRA INSTITUTE OF TECHNOLOGY
Canberra City/Year-round
Sponsor: Career institute. Program: 6-mo certificate, 3-yr diploma & 3-yr part-time trade certificate. Established: 1992. Calendar: semester. Curriculum: culinary, core. Admission dates: Feb, Jul. Total enrollment: 450. 75 each admission period. 50% of applicants accepted. 50% enrolled part-time. Student to teacher ratio 15:1. 100% of graduates employed within six months. Facilities: 6 kitchens, 4 restaurants, computer lab, butchery, bakery, bars.

FACULTY: 30 full-time, 50 part-time. Qualifications: industry and educational.

CONTACT: John Wardrop, Head, Culinary Skills, Canberra Institute of Technology, School of Tourism & Hospitality, P.O. Box 826, Canberra City, 2601 Australia; (61) 2-62073184, Fax (61) 2-62073209, E-mail john.wardrop@cit.act.edu.au, URL http://www.cit.act.edu.au.

CHISHOLM INSTITUTE OF TECHNICAL & FURTHER EDUCATION
Dandenong/Year-round
Sponsor: Institute. Program: 8-wk certificate one, 20-wk certificate two, 3-yr certificate three. Established: 1986. Accredited by National. Calendar: semester. Curriculum: culinary, core. Admission dates: Feb, Jul. Total enrollment: 250. 40 each admission period. 80% of applicants accepted. 75% enrolled part-time. Student to teacher ratio 15-20:1. 100% of graduates employed within six months. Facilities: 4 kitchens, including 1 fully-equipped commercial kitchen.

FACULTY: 25 full-time, 15 part-time.

COSTS: A$500 in-state, A$7,000 out-of-state. Admission requirements: Apprentice cook to undertake Certificate III,Certificate I & II interview & short test.

CONTACT: Centre Manager, Chisholm Institute of Technical and Further Education, School of Hospitality & Tourism, PO Box 684, Dandenong, Victoria, 3175 Australia; (61) (0)3-9212-5410, Fax (61) (0)3-9212-5459, E-mail hospitality@chisholm.vic.edu.au, URL http://www.chisholm.vic.edu.au.

LE CORDON BLEU – AUSTRALIA
Adelaide/Year-round   *(See display ad page 161)*
Sponsor: Private school offering advanced management & business studies for culinary graduates. Program: 2.5-yr BBA degree in International Restaurant & Catering mgmt, MBA degree in International Hotel & Restaurant mgmt, MA degree in Gastronomy for 1 yr add'l course work. Established: 1998. Accredited by Australian Recognition Council (ARC) and La Fondation Le Cordon Bleu. Calendar: semester. Curriculum: core. Admission dates: Jan & Jul. Total enrollment: 300/yr. 150 each admission period. 98% of applicants accepted. Student to teacher ratio 15:1. 100% of graduates employed within six months. Facilities: New facilities include 3 training restaurants, 10 commercial cookery kitchens, 10 computer suites, industry-standard wine tasting rooms, food science labs, conference rooms, auditorums. Courses: Include business finance, sales & marketing, information technology and human resources pertaining to the hospitality & tourism industry.

COSTS: Freshman: Stage 1-5 (2.5 yrs) A$54,000. Holding previous qualifications in a recognized hospitality program: Stage 3-5 (1.5 yrs) A$36,000. Admission requirements: Freshman: age 18+, HS certificate, command of English, basic math, computer knowledge. Advanced placement: graduate of recognised institutions. Scholarships: yes.

CONTACT: Elizabeth Daniels, Public Relations, Le Cordon Bleu Australia, Days Road, Regency Park, Adelaide, SA, 5010 Australia; (61) 6 8348.3022, Fax (61) 8 8346.7202, E-mail australia@cordonbleu.edu, URL http://www.lecordonbleu.com.edu. Rodger Griffiths (General Manager), Lindon Price (Marketing Director).

LE CORDON BLEU – SYDNEY
Sydney/Year-round *(See display ad page 161)*
Sponsor: Private school located on the campus of Northern Sydney Institute of TAFE, Ryde Campus. Program: 9-mo program consisting of 10-wk courses in Basic, Intermediate & Superior levels of Cuisine & Patisserie leading to Le Cordon Bleu Grand Diplome for completion of all six courses. Established: 1996. Accredited by Le Cordon Bleu Award and Australian National Qualification. Calendar: quarter. Curriculum: culinary, core. Admission dates: Jan, Apr, Jul, Oct. Total enrollment: 110. 50 each admission period. 98% of applicants accepted. Student to teacher ratio 12:1. 99% of graduates employed within six months. Facilities: Professionally-equipped kitchens, individual workspaces, demo kitchen with video. Courses: Principles, theory & techniques of classical French cuisine.

FACULTY: School Director Lynley Houghton. Staff consists of French & Australian Master Chefs from international restaurants & fine hotels.

COSTS: Basic Cuisine A$7,500, Intermediate Cuisine A$7,700, Superior Cuisine A$9,500. Basic Patisserie A$7,500, Intermediate Patisserie A$7,700, Superior Patisserie A$8,500. Tool Kit A$1,005-A$1,300. Admission requirements: International students must be at least age 18. Overseas students are required to have achieved a minimum level of English fluency of IELTS 5.5.

CONTACT: Lynley Houghton, Course Director, Le Cordon Bleu Sydney Culinary Arts Institute, 250 Blaxland Rd, Ryde, Sydney, 2112 Australia; (61) 2-9448-6307, Fax (61) 2-9807-6541, E-mail australia@cordonbleu.edu, URL http://www.lecordonbleu.com.au. Liz Daniels (61) (8) 8348-3022, Marketing & Public Relations.

NORTHERN SYDNEY INSTITUTE – CROWS NEST COLLEGE
Sydney/February-November
Sponsor: State government. Program: 2-yr certificate level III (part time) in Asian cookery. Established: 1989. Accredited by National, with vocational training board & TAFE Commission. Calendar: semester. Curriculum: culinary. Admission dates: Jan, Jul. Total enrollment: 150. 50 each admission period. 90% of applicants accepted. 5% receive financial aid. 100% enrolled part-time. Student to teacher ratio 15:1. 90% of graduates employed within six months. Facilities: Include 2 kitchens, classrooms & dining room, coffee shop, computer labs, library, learning resource ctr.

FACULTY: 3 full-time, 3 part-time; trade qualifications & education degrees.

COSTS: A$350/yr. Admission requirements: Education certificate.

CONTACT: Geoff Tyrrell, Asian Commercial Cookery, Northern Sydney Institute - Crows Nest College, Tourism & Hospitality, 149 West St., Crows Nest, Sydney, NSW, 2065 Australia; (61) (0)2-9448 4433, Fax (61) (0)2-9448 4408, E-mail geoff.tyrrell@tafensw.edu.au, URL www.tafensw.edu.au.

WILLIAM ANGLISS INSTITUTE
Melbourne/Year-round
Sponsor: Career institute. Program: Certificate program in Commercial Cookery, diploma & advanced diploma in Hospitality. Students can link to degree courses at Victorian universities. Established: 1940. Accredited by National, state, and local. Calendar: semester. Curriculum: core. Total enrollment: 4000. varies each admission period. Student to teacher ratio 15:1. 91% of graduates employed within six months. Facilities: $25 million teaching facility with 4 well-equipped bakeries, 6 kitchens, 3 restaurants, bars, computer rooms, butchery & confectionery centers.

FACULTY: More than 100 full-time.

CONTACT: William Angliss Institute Information Centre, 555 La Trobe St., P.O. Box 4052, Melbourne, 3000 Australia; (61) (0)3-96062111, Fax (61) (0)3-96701330, E-mail info@angliss.vic.edu.au, URL http://www.angliss.vic.edu.au.

CANADA

ALGONQUIN COLLEGE
Ottawa/Year-round
Sponsor: College. Program: 2-yr diploma in Culinary mgmt, 1-yr certificate in Chef Training, 40-wk certificate in Baking Techniques,2-yr diploma in Hotel & Restaurant Mgmt. Established: 1960. Calendar: semester. Curriculum: culinary, core. Admission dates: Sep, Jan. Total enrollment: 650. 380 & 270 each admission period. 50% of applicants accepted. Student to teacher ratio 15-20:1. 98% of graduates employed within 6 mos. Facilities: Include 2 production kitchens, 3 demo labs. FACULTY: 7 full-time, 12 part-time.
COSTS: Annual tuition in-state C$1,600/sem, out-of-state C$5,800/sem. Books, uniforms: C$1,200. Admission requirements: Secondary school diploma or 19 yrs of age. Scholarships: yes. Loans: yes.
CONTACT: Michael Durrer, Coordinator, Cook/Culinary Programs, Algonquin College, Admissions Office, 1385 Woodroffe Ave., Ottawa, ON, K2G 1V8 Canada; 613-727-4723 Ext 5223, Fax 613-727-7670, E-mail durrerm@algonquincollege.com, URL http://www.algonquincollege.com.

CANADORE COLLEGE OF APPLIED ARTS & TECHNOLOGY
North Bay/September-April
Sponsor: College. Program: 2-yr diploma in Culinary mgmt, 3-yr diploma in Culinary Administration, 1-yr certificate in Chef Training. Established: 1984. Accreditation for the in-school portion of the Cook Apprenticeship Program. Calendar: sem. Curriculum: culinary. Admission dates: Sep. Total enrollment: 64. 64 1st yr, 25 2nd yr, 25 3rd each admission period. 100% of applicants accepted. 75% receive financial aid. 10% enrolled part-time. Student to teacher ratio 22:1. Facilities: Production & experimental kitchens with specialized equipment, 120-seat restaurant. FACULTY: 12 full-time.
COSTS: In-state C$2,400/yr, foreign C$9,020/yr. Admission requirements: HS diploma or equivalent. Scholarships: yes. Loans: yes.
CONTACT: Daniel Esposito, Professor/Advisor, Canadore College, School of Hospitality & Tourism, 100 College Dr., P.O. Box 5001, North Bay, ON, P1B 8K9 Canada; 705-474-7600, Fax 705-494-7462, E-mail espositd@canadorec.on.ca, URL http://www.canadorec.on.ca.

COLLEGE OF THE ROCKIES
Cranbrook BC/September-June
Sponsor: 2-yr college. Program: 40-wk program in Professional Cook Training, Levels 1-2-3. Established: 1990. Admission dates: May, Sep, Jan. Facilities: Fully equipped training kitchen, classroom area, formal dining room.
CONTACT: Chris Wuthrich, Chef, College of the Rockies, 2700 College Way, Cranbrook, BC, V1C 5L7 Canada; 877-489-2687 x368, Fax 250-489-1790, E-mail info@cotr.bc.ca, URL www.cotr.bc.ca.

THE CULINARY ARTS SCHOOL OF ONTARIO
Etobicoke, Mississauga & Toronto/Year-round
Sponsor: Private career college. Program: 15-wk Culinary Arts diploma, 15-wk Culinary Mgmt diploma. Established: 2002. Accredited by Registered with the Ministry of Education Colleges & Universities for the Province of Ontario. Curriculum: culinary. Admission dates: Continuous. Total enrollment: 110. 12 -14/program each admission period. 75% of applicants accepted. 50% receive financial aid. 15% enrolled part-time. Student to teacher ratio 14:1. 95% of graduates employed within six months. Facilities: Professional learning environment.

FACULTY: CECs, CCE, masters in education candidate.

COSTS: $4,990/diploma program; texts, knife kits, uniforms add'l. Admission requirements: Entrance assessment. Scholarships: yes. Loans: yes.

CONTACT: David Buchanan, Admissions Dept, The Culinary Arts School of Ontario, 95 Dundas St. West, 3rd Fl., Mississauga, ON, L5B 1H7 Canada; 905-273-5588, Fax 905-273-5589, E-mail info@chefschool.ca, URL http://www.chefschool.ca.

CULINARY INSTITUTE OF CANADA
Charlottetown, PEI/Year-round   *(See display ad above)*

Sponsor: 2-yr career school, an institute of Holland College. Program: 80-wk diploma in Culinary Arts, 40-wk certificate in Pastry Arts. Established: 1983. Calendar: trimester. Curriculum: culinary, core. Admission dates: Sep, Mar. Total enrollment: 200. 80 September, 30 March each admission period. 60% of applicants accepted. 70% receive financial aid. 5% enrolled part-time. Student to teacher ratio 16:1. 98% of graduates employed within six months. Facilities: Include 7 training kitchens, 14 classrooms, 6 labs, 2 restaurants. Courses: 75% practical courses include Stocks, Soups & Sauces, Meat, Game & Poultry, Fish & Seafood, Baking, Cold Cuisine, International & Canadian Cuisine, Classical Cuisine, Menu Planning, Wine Appreciation.

FACULTY: 40 including 12 full-time chef Instructors with international experience.

COSTS: C$8,955 (US$8,500) per yr, off-campus housing ~C$500/mo. Admission requirements: HS diploma. Scholarships: yes.

CONTACT: David Harding, Culinary Programs Manager, Culinary Institute of Canada, 4 Sydney St., Charlottetown, PEI, C1A 1E9 Canada; 902-894-6805, 800-446-5265, Fax 902-894-6801, E-mail dharding@athi.pe.ca, URL http://www.hollandcollege.com/cic.

DUBRULLE INTERNATIONAL CULINARY & HOTEL INSTITUTE
Vancouver, BC/Year-round

Sponsor: Private school. Program: Full-time diploma: Bus. Mgmt. & Culinary Operations (2 yrs), Supervisory Devel & Applied Culinary/Pastry & Desserts (1 yr ea), Culinary/ Pastry & Desserts/Business Mgmt (4 mos ea), Breadmaking (13 wks). Part-time Culinary diploma (1 yr). Established: 1982. Accredited by Canadian Ed & Training Commission/Private Post-Secondary Ed Commission. Calendar: trimester. Curriculum: culinary. Admission dates: Jan, May, Sep. Total enrollment: 700. 225 each admission period. 90% of applicants accepted. Student to teacher ratio 12:1. 100% of graduates employed within six months. Facilities: 9,000-sq-ft facility, 5 classrooms, 6 teaching kitchens, student-operated dining facility.

FACULTY: 14 credentialed full- & part-time, all with intl experience & competition awards.

COSTS: Culinary & Pastry programs C$7,650 each. Admission requirements: Grade 10, 17 yrs of age. Scholarships: yes. Loans: yes.

CONTACT: Robert Sung, Director of Admissions, Dubrulle International Culinary & Hotel Institute of Canada, 1522 W. 8th Ave., Vancouver, BC, V6J 4R8 Canada; 604-738-3155/800-667-7288, Fax 604-738-3205, E-mail cooking@dubrulle.com, URL http://www.dubrulle.com.

GEORGE BROWN CHEF SCHOOL
Toronto/Year-round

Sponsor: College. Program: 2-yr diploma in Culinary Mgmt, 1-yr certificates in Chef Training, Baking & Pastry Arts, and Advanced Pastry Arts Mgmt, 1-yr post-diploma in Italian Culinary Arts. Established: 1965. Accredited by Ontario College Standards & Accreditation. Calendar: sem. Curriculum: culinary, core. Admission dates: Sep, Jan. Total enrollment: 2,800 full-time, 3,500 part-time. 22% of applicants accepted. 50% receive financial aid. 10% enrolled part-time. Student to teacher ratio 24:1. 95% of graduates employed within six months. Facilities: 12 specialty cooking labs, mixology & wine labs, 120-seat in-house restaurant, demo labs, classrooms, bake shop, student lounge.

FACULTY: 40+ full-time internationally-trained chef & pastry professors, former hotel gen'l mgrs and food & beverage professionals.

COSTS: Resident (nonresident) tuition for diploma programs ~C$3,000 (C$10,000) for 2 sems; certificates ~C$2,400-$3,000/program. Admission requirements: Min. for a diploma program is Ontario Secondary School Diploma or equivalent from within N. America. Scholarships: yes.

CONTACT: George Brown College, 300 Adelaide St. E., P.O. Box 1015, Station B, Toronto, ON, M5T 2T9 Canada; 416-415-5000 x2225, E-mail info@gbrownc.on.ca, URL http://www.gbrownc.on.ca/chefschool.

GEORGIAN COLLEGE OF APPLIED ARTS AND TECHNOLOGY
Barrie/September-April

Sponsor: College. Program: 2-yr diploma in Culinary Mgmt. Established: 1988. Curriculum: core. Admission dates: Aug. Total enrollment: 110. 60 each admission period. 50% of applicants accepted. Student to teacher ratio 24:1. 100% of graduates employed within six months. Facilities: Include 1 large- & 2 small-quantity kitchens, bake lab, classrooms, student-run restaurant.

FACULTY: 4 full-time, 8 part-time.

COSTS: Annual tuition in-country C$3,034, out-of-country C$10,000. Application fee C$50. Housing on-campus (252 spaces) ~C$540/mo, off-campus ~C$400-C$800/mo. Admission requirements: HS diploma or equivalent. Scholarships: yes. Loans: yes.

CONTACT: David Jones, Coordinator, Georgian College, Dept. of Hospitality & Tourism, One Georgian Dr., Barrie, ON, L4M 3X9 Canada; 705-728-1968 #1145, Fax 705-728-5123, E-mail djones@georgianc.on.ca, URL http://www.georgianc.on.ca.

HUMBER COLLEGE OF APPLIED ARTS & TECHNOLOGY
Etobicoke/August-May

Sponsor: Career college. Program: 1-yr certificate, 2-yr diploma, 3-yr AS degree. All with integrated Industry Traineeship. Established: 1975. Accredited by Ontario Diploma, Cooks Red Seal certification. Calendar: semester. Curriculum: culinary. Admission dates: Sep, Jan. Total enrollment: 220. 220 each admission period. 35% of applicants accepted. 85% receive financial aid. 3% enrolled part-time. Student to teacher ratio 20:1. 95% of graduates employed within six months. Facilities: 4 culinary labs with the latest equipment, new Learning Catering Ctr with 120-seat dining room, bar/wine lab.

FACULTY: 5 full-time, 10 part-time.

COSTS: In-state C$1,530/yr, foreign C$9,600/yr + C$292 fees. Admission requirements: HS diploma or equivalent & admission test. Scholarships: yes. Loans: yes.

CONTACT: Mike Mcfadden, Coordinator-Culinary Programs Chairman, Humber College, HRT Alliance, Tourism Industries Training, T, 205 Humber College Blvd., Toronto, ON, M9W 5L7 Canada; 416-675-6622 x 4474, Fax 416-675-3062, E-mail mcfaddem@admin.humberc.on.ca, URL http://www.humberc.on.ca.

LAMBTON COLLEGE
Sarnia, ON/August-April
Sponsor: College. Program: 2-yr cook apprenticeship program. Established: 1967. Accredited by Ministry of Training, Colleges and Universities, Ontario. Calendar: semester. Curriculum: culinary. Admission dates: Sep. Total enrollment: 20. 35 each admission period. 75% of applicants accepted. 100% receive financial aid. Student to teacher ratio 12:01. 100% of graduates employed within six months. Facilities: Teaching kitchen, 35-seat restaurant, labs, classrooms, computer facilities.

FACULTY: 1 full- & 5 part-time instructors, all certified chefs with both North American and European training.

CONTACT: Cindy Buchanan, Marketing Director, Lambton College, Culinary Programs, 1457 London Rd., Sarnia, ON, N7S 6K4 Canada; 519-542-7751 x3503, Fax 519-541-2418, E-mail info@lambton.on.ca, URL http://www.lambton.on.ca.

LE CORDON BLEU – OTTAWA
Ottawa, Ontario/Year-round *(See display ad page 161)*
Sponsor: Private vocational school. Program: 11-wk certificate courses in French cuisine & pastry at Basic, Intermediate, & Superior levels. 1-day to 1-mo drop-in sessions, specialized short programs. Established: 1988. Calendar: quarter. Curriculum: culinary. Admission dates: Jan, Mar, Jun, Oct. Total enrollment: 400-600. 100-150 each admission period. 95% of applicants accepted. Student to teacher ratio 16:1 max. 85% of graduates employed within six months. Facilities: Include demo room, professional kitchens with individual workstations, specialized equipment, observation restaurant. Courses: Basic, Intermediate & Superior Cuisine and Pastry; Cuisine and Pastry diplomas; Le Grand Diplôme de Cuisine et de Pâtisserie. Credits transferable to Le Cordon Bleu Paris, London, Mexico, Sydney, or Tokyo.

FACULTY: Classically-trained professional chefs, experienced in French culinary & pâtisserie techniques.

COSTS: Basic Cuisine C$6,095, Intermediate Cuisine C$6,602, Superior Cuisine C$7,125, Basic Pastry C$5,527, Intermediate Pastry C$6,095, Superior Pastry C$6,602. Admission requirements: Min 18 yrs old & HS diploma or equivalent. Scholarships: yes.

CONTACT: Andrea Smith, Registrar, Le Cordon Bleu Ottawa Culinary Arts Institute, 453 Laurier Ave. East, Ottawa, ON, K1N 6R4 Canada; 613-236-CHEF, Fax 613-236-2460, E-mail ottawa@cordonbleu.edu, URL http://www.lcbottawa.com.

LIAISON COLLEGE – CULINARY ARTS TRAINING
6 Ontario locations/Year-round
Sponsor: Private post-secondary college. Program: 300-hr basic and/or advanced diploma in Culinary Arts. Part time recreational & baking programs. 100 hrs theory, 200 hrs practical, hands-on. Established: 1996. Accredited by Ontario's Ministry of Education & Training & Apprenticeship Board. Curriculum: culinary, core. Admission dates: moly. Total enrollment: 18 students/class. 15-18 each admission period. 90% of applicants accepted. 30% receive financial aid. 33% enrolled

part-time. Student to teacher ratio 18:1 max. 90% of graduates employed within six months. Facilities: Latest equipment with work stations for each student.

FACULTY: Instructors meet the min standards that include teaching & 10+ yrs industry experience, professional designation.

COSTS: Cook Basic C$5,995, Cook Advanced C$5,995. Uniforms, equipment, textbook $695. Admission requirements: Grade 12 diploma, mature student, prior learning assessment. Scholarships: yes. Loans: yes.

CONTACT: Susanne Mikler, Admissions, Liaison College, P.O. Box 358, Campbellville, ON, L0P 1B0 Canada; 800-854-0621, 905-854-4600, Fax 905-854-4601, E-mail liaisonhq@liaisoncollege.com, URL http://www.liaisoncollege.com.

MALASPINA UNIVERSITY-COLLEGE – CULINARY ARTS
Duncan, Nanaimo & Powell River, BC/Year-round

Sponsor: University college. Program: 12-mo certificate in Culinary Arts. Established: 1968. Calendar: semester. Curriculum: culinary. Admission dates: Jan, Mar, May, Aug, Oct, Nov. Total enrollment: 130. 18 each admission period. 95% of applicants accepted. 25% receive financial aid. Student to teacher ratio 18:1. 100% of graduates employed within six months. Facilities: New food lab & 2 kitchens.

FACULTY: Chefs with experience in Canada & abroad.

COSTS: C$4,032 tuition, C$30 application fee, C$321 student fee, C$560 supplies. Admission requirements: Grade 12 or equivalent, min age 17, interview, assessment test, Foodsafe level 1 certificate. Scholarships: yes. Loans: yes.

CONTACT: Alex Rennie, Coordinator, Malaspina University-College Culinary Arts Certificate Program, 900 Fifth St., Nanaimo, BC, V9R 5S5 Canada; 250-740-6137, Fax 250-740-6455, E-mail renniea@mala.bc.ca, URL http://www.mala.bc.ca.

McCALL'S SCHOOL OF CAKE DECORATION, INC.
Etobicoke/September-May

Sponsor: Trade school. Program: Full-time certificate courses in baking, commercial cake decorating (10 days each), Swiss chocolate techniques (5 days), gum paste (3 days). Established: 1976. Student to teacher ratio 10/class. Facilities: 1,000 sq ft of teaching space with overhead mirrors & two 20-seat classrooms.

FACULTY: Includes school director Nick McCall, and Kay Wong.

COSTS: Professional courses range from C$300-C$850.

CONTACT: Nick McCall, President, McCall's School of Cake Decoration, Inc., 3810 Bloor St. West, Etobicoke, ON, M9B 6C2 Canada; 416-231-8040, Fax 416-231-9956, E-mail decorate@mccalls-cakes.com, URL http://www.mccalls-cakes.com.

NIAGARA CULINARY INSTITUTE
Niagara Falls, Ontario/September-June

Sponsor: Niagara College of Applied Arts & Technology. Program: Chef Training, Culinary Mgmt Co-op, Cook & Baker Apprenticeship, Hotel & Restaurant Mgmt Co-op. Established: 1989. Calendar: semester. Curriculum: culinary. Admission dates: Sep, Jan. Total enrollment: 96/Culinary Mgmt. 72 & 24 each admission period. 50% of applicants accepted. 60% receive financial aid. Student to teacher ratio 24:1. 80% of graduates employed within six months. Facilities: Bake shop, cafeteria, catering service, 7 classrooms, 2 computer labs, demo lab, food prod kitchen, restaurant, 3 teaching kitchens.

FACULTY: Of 13 faculty members, 9 have received culinary certification, 7 are certified as Chef de Cuisine, 1 is an industry professional.

COSTS: C$2,600 for post-secondary, C$3,200 for post-graduate, C$8,900 for intl students. Housing ~C$400/mo. Admission requirements: Ontario Secondary School Diploma or equivalent. Scholarships: yes. Loans: yes.

CONTACT: Info Centre, Niagara College, 300 Woodlawn Rd., Welland, ON, L3C 7L3 Canada; 905-735-2211 x7559, Fax 905-736-6000, E-mail infocentre@niagarac.on.ca, URL www.niagarac.on.ca.

NIAGARA-ON-THE-LAKE CULINARY SCHOOL
Niagara-on-the-Lake /Year-round

Sponsor: Private vocational school. Program: 2-yr Chef Diploma program consisting of two 6-mo classroom training segments, & two 6-mo paid internship training modules. Accredited by Registered with the Ontario Ministry of Training & Education. Curriculum: culinary. Facilities: 2,000-sq-ft purpose-built training & demo kitchen comprising a two-tiered gallery, 5 cooking stations & baking area. Facilities of 7 on-site restaurants, hotels & wineries.

FACULTY: Executive, sous & pastry chefs in upscale food & beverage establishments.

COSTS: 1st yr program C$7,902 includes uniforms, knives; 2nd yr C$7,502. Loans: yes.

CONTACT: Geoffrey Bray-Cotton, President, Niagara-on-the-Lake Culinary School, 290 John St. East, R.R.#1, Niagara-on-the-Lake, ON, L0S 1J0 Canada; Fax 905-684-2926, E-mail g.bc@sympatico.ca, URL http://notlculinaryschool.com.

NORTHERN ALBERTA INSTITUTE OF TECHNOLOGY – CULINARY ARTS
Edmonton, Alberta/September-April

Sponsor: Technical college. Program: 2-yr Culinary Arts diploma, Hospitality Mgmt diploma (continuing ed).5-mo Retail Meatcutting certificate, 1-yr certificate in Baking, Culinary Arts, Apprentice Cook, Baker. Established: 1963. Calendar: semester. Curriculum: culinary. Admission dates: Sep & Jan. Total enrollment: 168 Culin Arts, 24 Baking, 18 RMC. 42 Culin Arts each admission period. 50% of applicants accepted. 50% receive financial aid. Student to teacher ratio 15:1. 85% of graduates employed within six months. Facilities: 9 commerical kitchens, retail meat cutting lab, commercial bakery, common market, dining room.

COSTS: Culinary Arts or Baking ~$3,050/yr (two 16-wk sems), Meat Cutting ~$1,600. Books/supplies ~$700-$1,200, fees $133. Admission requirements: Transcript, resume, career investigation. Scholarships: yes. Loans: yes.

CONTACT: Sheila Ouellet, Administrative Support, Northern Alberta Institute of Technology Culinary Arts, 11762 106 St., Edmonton, AB, T5G 2R1 Canada; 780-471-7655, Fax 780-471-8914, E-mail webmaster@nait.ab.ca, URL http://www.nait.ab.ca/schools/hospitality/default.htm.

NORTHWEST CULINARY ACADEMY OF VANCOUVER
Vancouver, BC/September-July

Sponsor: Private culinary school. Program: Chef's training in 3 independent, 15-wk programs; Professional Culinary, Pastry/Bread & Practicum. Established: 2003. Calendar: trimester. Curriculum: culinary. Admission dates: Jan, Apr, Sep. Total enrollment: 48/yr. 32 each admission period. 90% of applicants accepted. Student to teacher ratio 8-16:1. Facilities: 2,500-sq-ft new facility includes demo station/ chef's table/ pastry lab, European-style cooking island.

FACULTY: 3 full-time accredited instructors, each with 20 yrs North American & European culinary experience + 5 yrs teaching.

COSTS: C$5,950 for Professional Culinary, C$5,950 for Pastry/Bread, C$975 for Practicum; C$11,900/full yr. Admission requirements: HS diploma or equivalent, negative TB test, good written/spoken English (min 520 Toffel). Scholarships: yes.

CONTACT: Tony Minichello, Owner/Chef, Northwest Culinary Academy of Vancouver, 2725 Main St., Vancouver, BC, V5T 3E9 Canada; 604-876-7653 or 866-876-2433 US/Canada, Fax 604-876 7023, E-mail chefs@nwcav.com, URL http://www.nwcav.com.

PACIFIC INSTITUTE OF CULINARY ARTS
Vancouver/Year-round

Sponsor: Private school. Program: 2 full-time programs: Culinary Arts and Baking & Pastry Arts (each 6 mos). Established: 1996. Accredited by Private Post-Secondary Education Commission of

British Columbia. Calendar: trimester. Curriculum: culinary. Admission dates: Jan, Apr, Jul, Sep. Total enrollment: 300/yr. 12 each admission period. 90% of applicants accepted. 10% receive financial aid. Student to teacher ratio 9-12:1. 90% of graduates employed within six months. Facilities: 8 commercial training kitchens, on-site white linen teaching restaurant & bakeshop.

FACULTY: 15 full-time chef instructors, all with international experience; 2 restaurant instructors.

COSTS: C$11,000 for each 6-mo program.Lodging assistance provided, ranges from C$400-C$1,000/mo. Admission requirements: HS diploma or equivalent. Scholarships: yes. Loans: yes.

CONTACT: Sue Singer, Director of Admissions, Pacific Institute of Culinary Arts, 1505 W. 2nd Ave., Vancouver, BC, V6H 3Y4 Canada; 604-734-4488, 800-416-4040, Fax 604-734-4408, E-mail info@picachef.com, URL http://www.picachef.com.

RED RIVER COLLEGE
Winnipeg, Manitoba/Year-round
Sponsor: 2-yr college. Program: 1-yr certificate & 2-yr diploma programs in Culinary Arts consisting of seven 3-mo terms: 5 on campus & 2 off-campus cooperative education work experience in hotels, restaurants, or private clubs. Established: 1997. Calendar: trimester. Curriculum: culinary. Admission dates: Sept, Mar. Total enrollment: 70. 35 each admission period. Student to teacher ratio 15:1. 90% of graduates employed within six months. Facilities: Prairie Lights Restaurant, a full-service open-to-the-public restaurant serving lunch & dinner + 5 other kitchen training labs.

FACULTY: Dept. Chair David Rew & 9 instructors.

COSTS: C$3,918 (C$1,070) first yr tuition (books/supplies), C$3,006 (C$850) second yr tuition (books/supplies). $35 application fee. Admission requirements: Manitoba Senior 3 or equivalent secondary school prep or adult 11B. Scholarships: yes. Loans: yes.

CONTACT: David Rew, Chair, Hospitality Dept., Red River College, 2055 Notre Dame Ave., Rm. B185, Hospitality Dept., Winnipeg, MB, R3H 0J9 Canada; 204-632-2309/2285, Fax 204-633-3176, E-mail drew@rrc.mb.ca, URL http://www.rrc.mb.ca.

RIVERSIDE PARK TECHNOLOGY CENTRE
LaSalle, Quebec/Year-round
Sponsor: Vocational training Institute. Program: 45-wk Professional Cooking, 40-wk Pastry Making, 30-wk Butchery, 30-wk Restaurant Services, 30-wk Contemporary Cuisine. Established: 1977. Accredited by Sponsored by Ministry of Education of Quebec. Calendar: semester. Curriculum: culinary. Admission dates: Aug, Jan. Total enrollment: 230. 15-25/specialty, 115 total each admission period. 80% of applicants accepted. 20% receive financial aid. Student to teacher ratio 25:1. 98% of graduates employed within six months. Facilities: Modern facility with 60-seat dining room, kitchens & labs.

FACULTY: 18 instructors with provincial, national and international experience. Majority of instructors are bilingual (English/French).

COSTS: ~C$450/yr per program. Admission requirements: Legal Quebec resident, HS leaving certificate, successful interview. Scholarships: yes. Loans: yes.

CONTACT: Richard Oliver, Assistant Centre Director, Food Services, Riverside Park Technology Centre, 8310 George St., LaSalle, Quebec, H8P 1E5 Canada; 514-363-6213, Fax 514-364-1953, E-mail roliver@lbpsb.qc.ca.

ST. CLAIR COLLEGE
Windsor/September-April
Sponsor: College. Program: 4-sem diploma in Culinary mgmt, 2-sem certificate in Chef Training, 4-sem diploma in Hotel & Restaurant Mgmt. Established: 1993. Accredited by Province of Ontario. Calendar: semester. Curriculum: culinary, core. Admission dates: Sep. Total enrollment: 80. 60 each admission period. 75% of applicants accepted. 50% receive financial aid. 10% enrolled part-time. Student to teacher ratio 18:1. 98% of graduates employed within six months. Facilities: Include 2 kitchens, classrooms, student run restaurant & kiosk.

FACULTY: 2 full-time chef instructors. All have C.C.C. designation.

COSTS: Annual tuition in-state C$2,090, out-of-state C$11,506.88. Admission requirements: HS diploma (OSSD) with grade 12 English & grade 10 math. Scholarships: yes. Loans: yes.

CONTACT: Rainer Schindler, St. Clair College, Hospitality & Media Dept., 2000 Talbot Rd. W., Windsor, ON, N9A 6S4 Canada; 519-972-2727 x4614, E-mail rschindler@stclaircollege.ca, URL http://www.stclaircollege.ca.

SOUTHERN ALBERTA INSTITUTE OF TECHNOLOGY
Calgary/Year-round

Sponsor: Post-secondary technical institution. Program: 56-wk Professional Cooking diploma, 2-yrBaking & Pastry Arts diploma, 24-wkRetail Meat Cutting certificate. Established: 1949. Calendar: semester. Curriculum: culinary. Admission dates: Sep, Jan, Mar. Total enrollment: 500. 160 PC, 65 BPA, 30 RMC each admission period. 50% of applicants accepted. 50% receive financial aid. 20% enrolled part-time. Student to teacher ratio 15:1. 98% of graduates employed within six months. Facilities: Test kitchen, 4 cooking labs, 2 baking/pastry labs,11 demo labs & lecture classrooms, computer labs, dining room, cafeteria.

FACULTY: 36 full-time: Journeymans & Red Seal in Cooking, Chef de Cuisine certification, Master Baker & Master Chef.

COSTS: Professional Cooking $$6,182; Baking/Pastry Arts ~$4,053/1st yr, ~$4,632/2nd yr; Retail Meat Cutting ~$3,046. Admission requirements: Transcript, resume, career goals statement, Student for a Day attendance. Scholarships: yes. Loans: yes.

CONTACT: June MacKinnon, Marketing Specialist, Southern Alberta Institute of Technology, Business & Tourism, 1301 16th Ave. NW, Calgary, AB, T2M 0L4 Canada; 403-284-8952, Fax 403-284-7034, E-mail june.mackinnon@sait.ca, URL http://www.sait.ca.

STRATFORD CHEFS SCHOOL
Stratford/November-March

Sponsor: Nonprofit training school. Program: 2-sem full-time diploma. Established: 1983. Accredited by Province of Ontario. Calendar: semester. Curriculum: culinary. Admission dates: Nov. Total enrollment: 70. 35-40 each admission period. 25% of applicants accepted. Student to teacher ratio 12:1. 100% of graduates employed within six months.

FACULTY: 15 full-time. Founders/directors are restaurateurs Eleanor Kane & James Morris.

COSTS: Annual tuition C$6,550 (1st yr), C$5,850 (2nd yr) for Canadian citizens, C$12,500 out-of country. Housing ~C$300-C$400/mo.

CONTACT: Elisabeth Lorimer, Program Administrator, Stratford Chefs School, 68 Nile St., Stratford, ON, N5A 4C5 Canada; 519-271-1414, Fax 519-271-5679, E-mail elorimer@stratfordchef.on.ca, URL http://www.stratfordchefsschool.ca.

UNIVERSITY COLLEGE OF THE CARIBOO
Kamloops/September-May

Sponsor: 4-yr degree granting institution. Program: Certificate in Culinary Arts. 3 levels, 4 mos each. Established: 1972. Curriculum: culinary. Admission dates: Last wk of Aug, first wk of Jan. Total enrollment: 60. 20 each admission period. 80% of applicants accepted. 40% receive financial aid. Student to teacher ratio 12:1. 80% of graduates employed within six months. Facilities: Includes 4 kitchens (cafeteria, meatcutting lab, bakery, satellite kitchen), classrooms, public dining room.

FACULTY: 7 full-time instructors totaling 171 yrs of experience.

COSTS: Canadian citizen C$690/sem, Intl students C$3,731/sem; tools & texts C$570, uniform deposit C$150. Housing ~C$400/mo. Admission requirements: HS diploma or equivalent. Scholarships: yes. Loans: yes.

CONTACT: Mark Perry, Chairperson, University College of the Cariboo, Food Training/Tourism, Box 3010, 900 McGill Rd., Kamloops, BC, V2C 5N3 Canada; 250-828-5357, Fax 250-371-5677, E-mail FTC@cariboo.bc.ca, URL http://www.cariboo.bc.ca/psd/foodtrai/foodho.htm.

CHINA

CHOPSTICKS COOKING CENTRE
Kowloon, Hong Kong/September-June

Sponsor: Private trade school. Program: 1-day to 12-wk programs, tailored for individuals & groups. Established: 1971. Calendar: quarter. Curriculum: culinary. Admission dates: Yr-round. Total enrollment: 15/class max. 99% of applicants accepted. 60% enrolled part-time. Student to teacher ratio 1-10:1. 90% of graduates employed within six months. Facilities: Kitchen with full facilities for practical sessions.

FACULTY: School principal Cecilia J. Au-Yang, domestic science graduate & author of a 40 cookbook series; Director Caroline Au-yeung, graduate of HCIMA.

COSTS: 1-wk course $1,500/person, 2nd-5th person less 25%; 4-wk course $3,000 basic, $4,000 intermediate; short courses & classes $50-$900. Housing ~$400-$600/wk.

CONTACT: Cecilia Au-Yang, Managing Director, Chopsticks Cooking Centre, 8A Soares Avenue, Ground Floor, Kowloon, Hong Kong, China; (852) 2336-8433, Fax (852) 2338-1462, E-mail chopsticks1971@netvigator.com.

ENGLAND

THE ASIAN AND ORIENTAL SCHOOL OF CATERING
Hackney/Year-round

Sponsor: Private school. Program: Short courses & full-time programs designed to address training & development issues within the catering industry. Facilities: Modern facilities & a student-run restaurant/kitchen open to the public.

FACULTY: Overseen by key individuals from the Asian & Oriental restaurant sector.

CONTACT: The Asian and Oriental School of Catering, Hackney Community College, London, N1 6HQ England; (44) (0) 20 7613 9292, Fax (44) (0) 20 7613 9382, URL http://www.spice-train.com.

COOKERY AT THE GRANGE
Frome/Year-round

Sponsor: Private school. Program: 4-wk The Essential Cookery Course. Established: 1981. Accredited by Certificate with Reference. Curriculum: culinary. Admission dates: Rolling. Total enrollment: 192/yr. 14-24 each admission period. 100% of applicants accepted. Student to teacher ratio 6:1. 90% of graduates employed within six months. Facilities: 2 kitchens, cold kitchen, herb garden, game room, tennis court, satellite TV room.

FACULTY: Jane & William Averill (Grange-trained) & teaching staff.

COSTS: £2,290-£2,690 includes meals & shared housing. Single room supp. £50/wk.

CONTACT: Jane and William Averill, Cookery at The Grange, The Grange, Frome, Somerset, BA11 3JU England; (44) (0)1373-836579, Fax (44) (0)1373-836579, E-mail info@cookery-grange.co.uk, URL http://www.cookery-grange.co.uk.

CORDON VERT COOKERY SCHOOL
Altrincham/Year-round

Sponsor: The Vegetarian Society UK. Program: Four 1-wk Foundation courses leading to the Cordon Vert diploma; 4-day Professional Certificate in Vegetarian Catering; wkend & day courses. Established: 1982. Curriculum: culinary. Student to teacher ratio 12:1.

FACULTY: Lyn Weller, Principal & 10 part-time tutors.

COSTS: Resident (non-resident) tuition is £450 (£350) for 1-wk Foundation courses, £575 + VAT for Catering course.

CONTACT: Maureen Surgey, Cookery School Administrator, Cordon Vert Cookery School, The Vegetarian Society, Parkdale, Dunham Rd., Altrincham, Cheshire, WA14 4QG England; (44) (0)161-925-2000, Fax (44) (0)161-926-9182, E-mail cordonvert@vegsoc.org, URL http://www.vegsoc.org/cordonvert.

LE CORDON BLEU – LONDON
London/Year-round *(See display ad page 161)*

Sponsor: Private school acquired by Le Cordon Bleu Paris in 1990. Program: Standard 10 wk Classic Cycle Certificate courses in French Cuisine & Pâtisserie leading to the Grand Diplome. Intensive version also available. Established: 1933. Calendar: quarter. Curriculum: culinary. Admission dates: Jan, Feb, Mar, Apr, Jun, Jul, Aug, Sep, Oct. Total enrollment: 150/qtr. 120-150 each admission period. 100% of applicants accepted. 15% receive financial aid. 30% enrolled part-time. Student to teacher ratio 10:1. 95% of graduates employed within six months. Facilities: Professionally equipped kitchens; individual workspaces with refrigerated marble tops; demo rooms with video & tilted mirrors. Courses: Classic Cycle consists of 3 cuisine & 3 patisserie courses, taken consecutively. Covers basic to complex technique, classic, ethnic & contemporary cuisines, planning, presentation, decoration & execution.

FACULTY: All staff full time. Chefs all professionally qualified with experience in Michelin-starred & fine quality culinary establishments. President is Andre Cointreau, School Director is Lesley Gray.

COSTS: £145-£395 for a short course. Classic Cycle Professional Diploma courses begin at £4,191 for Basic Cuisine, including uniform. Students are assisted in finding lodging. Scholarships: yes.

CONTACT: Natalia Whale, Enrollment Supervisor, Le Cordon Bleu, 114 Marylebone Lane, London, W1U 2HH England; 0800-980-3503(freephone within UK), (44) 20-7-935-3503, Fax (44) 20-7-935-7621, E-mail london@cordonbleu.edu, URL cordonbleu.edu. US toll-free: 800-457-CHEF.

LEITHS SCHOOL OF FOOD AND WINE
London/Year-round

Sponsor: Private school. Program: 1-yr or 2-term diploma consisting of 2 or 3 consecutive 10- to 11-week Food & Wine certificate courses, foundation & beginner's cookery certification, certificate course in wine. Established: 1975. Calendar: trimester semester. Admission dates: Oct or Jan (for diploma), Apr. Total enrollment: 96. 96 each admission period. 99% of applicants accepted. Student to teacher ratio 8:1. 99% of graduates employed within six months. Facilities: Include 3 kitchens, demo theater, library, changing room.

FACULTY: 13 full-, 2 part-time. School founder & cookbook author Prue Leith.

COSTS: £4,600-£5,800/term; cost for all 3 is £13,300. Equipment fee £400. Housing £80-£120/wk.

CONTACT: Judy Wilkinson, Registrar, Leiths School of Food and Wine, 21 St. Alban's Grove, London, W8 5BP England; (44) (0) 20-7229-0177, Fax (44) (0) 20-7937-5257, E-mail info@leiths.com, URL http://www.leiths.com.

THE MANOR SCHOOL OF FINE CUISINE
Widmerpool/Year-round

Sponsor: Proprietary institution. Program: 4-wk Cordon Bleu certificate, 6-wk Advanced Cordon Bleu certificate. Established: 1988. Accredited by Cookery & Food Assn., Craft Guild of Chefs. Curriculum: culinary. Admission dates: Rolling. Total enrollment: 12. 8 each admission period. 90% of applicants accepted. 5% receive financial aid. 60% enrolled part-time. Student to teacher ratio 6:1. 100% of graduates employed within six months. Facilities: Include 7 kitchens, lecture room, large dining room, cooking library, culinary video library.

FACULTY: Principal Claire Tuttey, Cordon Bleu Diploma, head chef of noted restaurants, member of Cookery & Food Association.

COSTS: Resident (nonresident) tuition is £1,162.07 (£1,044.57).

CONTACT: Claire Tuttey, The Manor School of Fine Cuisine, Old Melton Road, Widmerpool, Nottinghamshire, NG12 5QL England; (44) (0)1949-81371, Fax (44) (0)1949-81371.

MOSIMANN'S ACADEMY
London/Year-round

Sponsor: Private school. Program: 4-day certificate course (Anton Mosimann Food Experience) that covers all aspects of food & beverage production & the culinary arts. Established: 1996. Curriculum: culinary. Student to teacher ratio 22-60:1. Facilities: Seminar & demo theater, library of Anton Mosimann's 6,000 cookery books.

FACULTY: Academy chef & manager Simon Boyle, assisted by 2 full- & 2 part-time staff.

COSTS: £1,200/4-day course. Admission requirements: Background as professional chef advisable.

CONTACT: Elizabeth St. Clair George, Librarian, Mosimann's Academy, 5 William Blake House, The Lanterns, Bridge Lane, London, SW11 3AD England; (44) (0) 20 7326 8366, Fax (44) (0) 20 7326 8360, E-mail academy@mosimann.com, URL http://www.mosimann.com.

PAUL HEATHCOTE'S SCHOOL OF EXCELLENCE
Manchester/Year-round

Sponsor: Private school. Program: Apprenticeships, supervisory and mgmt training to NVQ level 4. Established: 1997. Curriculum: culinary. Facilities: Professionally-equipped kitchen with 6 individual work spaces, demonstration auditorium with projector & screen.

FACULTY: Paul Heathcote, chef and owner of four restaurants, and his staff of instructors.

CONTACT: Administration Office, Paul Heathcote's School of Excellence, Jacksons Row, Deansgate, Manchester, M2 5WD England; (44) (0)161-839-5898, Fax (44) (0)161-839-5897, E-mail cookeryschool@heathcotes.co.uk, URL http://www.heathcotes.co.uk.

ROSIE DAVIES
Nunney/January-July, September-November

Sponsor: Culinary professional Rosie Davies. Program: 4-wk Basics Plus course for professionals, with emphasis on training for chalet or yacht chefs. Established: 1996. Curriculum: culinary. 4-5 each admission period. Student to teacher ratio 5:1. Facilities: Farmhouse-style kitchen.

FACULTY: Rosie Davies trained at Oxford in Catering & Hotel Mgmt, is a freelance cookery writer/editor & has 20+ yrs teaching experience.

COSTS: £2,450/4-wk course includes meals & lodging.

CONTACT: Rosie Davies, Penny's Mill, Nunney, Frome, Somerset, BA11 4NP England; (44) 1373-836210/836665, Fax (44) 1373-836018, E-mail rosiedavies@btconnect.com, URL http://www.rosiedavies.co.uk.

SQUIRES KITCHEN INTERNATIONAL SCHOOL
Farnham, Surrey/Year-round

Sponsor: Private school. Program: Part-time 1-wk school certificate in sugarcraft & cake decorating. Established: 1987. Calendar: trimester. Curriculum: core. Admission dates: Rolling. 100% of applicants accepted. 100% enrolled part-time. Student to teacher ratio 12:1/1:1. Facilities: Kitchen with specialized equipment & materials.

FACULTY: 17 full- & part-time. Members of the British Sugarcraft Guild.

COSTS: From £65/day.

CONTACT: Course Coordinator, Squires Kitchen Intl. School of Sugarcraft & Cake Decorating, 3 Waverley Lane, Farnham, Surrey, GU9 8BB England; (44) (0)1252-711749, Fax (44) (0)1252-714714, E-mail school@squires-group.co.uk, URL http://www.squires-group.co.uk.

TANTE MARIE SCHOOL OF COOKERY
Surrey/September-July

Sponsor: Private school. Program: 36- or 24-wk Tante Marie Cordon Bleu diploma or Intensive Diploma. 11-wk Certificate courses. 4-wk Essential Skills courses. 1-or 2-wk Beginners courses. Established: 1954. Accredited by BACIFHE (British Accreditation Council). Calendar: trimester. Curriculum: culinary. Admission dates: Jan, Apr, Sep. Short courses throughout the yr. Total enrollment: 84. 24-72 each admission period. 100% of applicants accepted. 5% receive financial aid. Student to teacher ratio 12:1. 100% of graduates employed within six months. Facilities: Include 5 modern teaching kitchens, a mirrored demo theatre, & a lecture room.

FACULTY: 12 full- & part-time, qualified to teach; many have held catering positions & all undergo teacher training.

COSTS: 36-wk course £12,600, 24-wk course £9,500, 12-wk certificate course £4,500, 1-mo course £1,800-£1,950. Uniform & equipment from £145. Admission requirements: English language intermediate. Scholarships: yes. Loans: yes.

CONTACT: Marcella O'Donovan, Principal, Tante Marie School of Cookery, Woodham House, Carlton Rd., Woking, Surrey, GU21 4HF England; (44) (0)1483-726957, Fax (44) (0)1483-724173, E-mail info@tantemarie.co.uk, URL http://www.tantemarie.co.uk.

THAMES VALLEY UNIVERSITY
Ealing-London/Year-round

Sponsor: University. Program: Chef/Restaurant Diploma BSc in International Culinary Arts. Established: 1992. Accredited by University. Calendar: semester. Curriculum: culinary, core. Admission dates: Sep. Total enrollment: 400. 40 each admission period. 70% of applicants accepted. 10% receive financial aid. 70% enrolled part-time. Student to teacher ratio 15:1. 100% of graduates employed within six months. Facilities: Include 7 kitchens, demo kitchen, 2 science labs, 2 restaurants, computer lab.

FACULTY: 60 full-time.

COSTS: £5,000/yr GBP + fees & certificate costs. Scholarships: yes.

CONTACT: David Foskett, Professor, Thames Valley Univ-London School of Tourism, Hospitality, Leisure, St. Mary's Rd., Ealing, London, W5 5RF England; (44) (0)1753 697603/697604, Fax (44) (0)7553 677682, E-mail david.foskett@tvu.ac.uk, URL http://www.tvu.ac.uk.

FRANCE

THE ALAIN DUCASSE TRAINING CENTER
Argenteuil/Year-round

Sponsor: School for professional chefs, seminars for non-professionals. Program: 1-wk training sessions ranging from 16-40 hrs; 5- to 10-wk seminars, 39 hrs of instruction/wk. Instruction in French, translation available for a fee. Non-professionals: 3 days/wk, 8 hrs of dedicated sessions. Established: 1999. Accredited by French continuing ed accreditation. Admission dates: Training sessions wkly, seminars moly. Total enrollment: 6-12/class. 24 max each admission period. Student to teacher ratio 8-10:1. Facilities: 3,250-sq-ft lab contains kitchens with the latest culinary technology, video equipment, computer center with Internet access.

FACULTY: Executive Chefs Bruno Caironi, Philippe Duc for pastry; Jean-François Piège, Franck Cerutti for wine studies.

COSTS: From €688 for micro-formations to €1,548 for all other formations, €3,000 for Alain Ducasse's French Trilogy. 5 wks €5,000, 10 wks €10,000. €290/day for non-professionals. Admission requirements: Restaurant & catering professionals, members of food- & wine-related fields.

CONTACT: Laure Frances, Client Contact, The Alain Ducasse Training Center, ADF, 41 rue de l'Abbé Ruellan, Argenteuil, 95100 France; (33) 1.34.34.19.10, Fax (33) 1.34.34.04.40, E-mail adf@ad-formation.com, URL http://www.ad-formation.com.

BELLOUET CONSEIL ECOLE GASTRONOMIQUE DE PARIS
Paris/Year-round

Sponsor: Private pastry school. Program: 6-mo course consisting of 28 two- to five-day practical classes that can be taken individually. Instruction in French. Established: 1989. Curriculum: culinary.

FACULTY: 8 instructors include Joël Bellouet, Gold Medal, M.O.F; Jean-Michel Perruchon, Gold Medal M.O.F.

Costs: From €484,95 for a 2-day class to €1212,38 for a 5-day class.

Contact: G.J. Bellouet, Bellouet Conseil Ecole Gastronomique de Paris, 304-306, rue Lecourbe, Paris, 75015 France; (33) 1 40 60 16 20, Fax (33) 1 40 60 16 21, E-mail bellouet.conseil@wanadoo.fr, URL http://bellouet.web.com.

ÉCOLE DES ARTS CULINAIRES ET DE L'HOTELLERIE, DE LYON
Lyon/Ecully/Year-round

Sponsor: Private school. Program: 8- or 16-wk Cuisine & Culture program (taught in English), 2- or 3-yr Culinary Arts & Mgmt program (taught in French), 3-yr Food Service & Hospitality Mgmt program (taught in French). Established: 1990. Calendar: semester. Admission dates: Apr, Oct. Total enrollment: 100. 50 each admission period. 55% of applicants accepted. 5% receive financial aid. Student to teacher ratio 12:1. 100% of graduates employed within six months. Facilities: 13 seminar rooms, 2 computer labs, 8 teaching kitchens, pastry/pantry facilities, video-equipped amphitheatre, sensory analysis lab, restaurants, bakery.

Faculty: In addition to the Board of Trustees, headed by Paul Bocuse, the permanent teaching staff includes 1 Meilleur Ouvrier de France.

Costs: 16-wk program is 46,200 FF including lunch. 2- & 3-yr programs are 59,000 FF/yr. Lodging 2,300 FF. Admission requirements: Students who complete the 16-wk program & pass an exam may take the longer programs. Loans: yes.

Contact: Florence Galy, Communication Dept., Ecole des Arts Culinaires et de l'Hotellerie, de Lyon, Chateau du Vivier, B.P. 25, Ecully, Cedex, 69131 France; (33) (0)4-72-18-02-20, Fax (33) (0)4-78-43-33-51, E-mail fgaly@each-lyon.com, URL http://www.each-lyon.com.

ÉCOLE LENOTRE
Plaisir Cedex/Year-round

Sponsor: Advanced cooking school for professionals & future professionals. Program: 6-mo intensive professional culinary training diploma course & ~50 four-day certificate courses. Established: 1970. Calendar: semester. Curriculum: culinary. Admission dates: 6-mo program: Jan & Sep. Total enrollment: 3,000/yr. 50/5 classes each admission period. 95% of applicants accepted. Student to teacher ratio 10:1. Facilities: Part of Lenotre, the school covers 170 acres with 5 specialized classrooms, a meeting room & boutique.

Faculty: 4 instructors are recipients of the Meilleur Ouvrier de France in cooking, pastry & confectionery, ice cream, & bakery-Viennese pastries.

Costs: Tuition (non-French students) including breakfasts & lunches, from ~$1,260 (€1,200)/wk-$1,485 (€1,350)/wk. Lodging ~$23-$62/night. Admission requirements: Some experience in the culinary field & a knowledge of the basics of French gastronomy. Scholarships: yes.

Contact: Marie-Anne Dufeu, Directrice de Clientèle, Ecole Lenotre, 40, rue Pierre Curie - BP 6, Plaisir Cedex, 78375 France; (33) (0)1-30-81-46-34, Fax (33) (0)1-30-54-73-70, E-mail ecole@lenotre.fr, URL http://www.lenotre.fr.

ÉCOLE RITZ-ESCOFFIER
Paris/Year-round

Sponsor: Culinary school in the Ritz Paris. Program: 30-wk Superior Diploma course for future professionals. Segments: 1- to 6-wk Cesar Ritz (beginner), 10-wk Ritz-Escoffier (int-advanced), 1- to 12-wk Art of French Pastry (beginner-advanced), Master Ritz Escoffier, 2 wks (pro). Established: 1988. Calendar: semester. Curriculum: core. Admission dates: Cesar Ritz & French Pastry courses begin wkly. Student to teacher ratio 8-10:1. Facilities: 2,000-sq-ft custom-designed facility includes a main kitchen, pastry kitchen, conference room/library, changing rooms.

Faculty: 4 full-time instructors.

Costs: One-wk classes start at €85/wk, 6-wk Cesar Ritz €5,336, 10-wk Ritz-Escoffier €10,825, 12-wk Art of French Pastry €10,215.75, Master 2-wk Professional Course €2,140, 30-wk Superior Diploma €27,100. Admission requirements: Ritz Escoffier course students must have Cesar Ritz diploma or equivalent experience.

CONTACT: M. Jean-Philippe Zahm-Holbecq, Director, Ecole Ritz-Escoffier Paris, 15, Place Vendôme, Paris Cedex 01, 75041 France; 888-801-1126, (33) (0)1-43-16-30-50, Fax (33) (0)1-43-16-31-50, E-mail ecole@ritzparis.com, URL http://www.ritzparis.com.

ÉCOLE SUPERIEURE DE CUISINE FRANCAISE GROUPE FERRANDI
Paris/September-June

Sponsor: Professional restaurant & culinary school. Program: Bilingual 9-mo (1200-hr) Art and Technique of French Cuisine & 1092-hr Classic French Pastry and Bread Baking programs, each awarding a diploma issued by Paris Chamber of Commerce. Established: 1986. Accredited by French Ministry of Education, US Dept. of Education for Student Aid Programs. Calendar: trimester. Curriculum: culinary. Admission dates: Sep. Total enrollment: 200. 25 each admission period. 50% receive financial aid. Student to teacher ratio 12:1. Facilities: Include more than 12 professional kitchens, tasting laboratory, auditorium, classrooms, 2 working restaurants.

FACULTY: The curriculum is supervised by a Board of Advisors including French chefs Alain Ducasse, Pierre Gagnaire & Antoine Westermann.

COSTS: Art and Technique of French Cuisine €16,700, Classic French Pastry and Bread Baking €14,300, including uniforms & equipment. Housing $500-$800/mo. Admission requirements: Proof of full medical and accident coverage, long-term student visa, certified birth certificate, and undergraduate transcript. Loans: yes.

CONTACT: Stephanie Curtis, Coordinator, ESCF Groupe Ferrandi, Bilingual Program, 10 rue Poussin, Paris, 75016 France; (33) (0)1-45-27-09-09, Fax (33) (0)1-45-25-21-37, E-mail stecurtis@aol.com, URL http://www.egf.ccip.fr/ENGLISH/index.htm.

LE CORDON BLEU – PARIS
Paris/Year-round   *(See display ad page 161)*

Sponsor: Private school acquired by Andre J. Cointreau in 1984, at present location since 1988. Program: 9-mo Classic Cycle in Cuisine & Pastry at the basic, intermediate & superior levels leading to Le Grand Diplome; 3- & 5-wk Intensive Cuisine & Pastry Classic Cycle courses, 3-wk Intro to Catering: Buffet Techniques programs. Established: 1895. Calendar: trimester. Curriculum: culinary. Admission dates: 6 times/yr. Total enrollment: 550+. 180-200 each admission period. 100% of applicants accepted. 10% receive financial aid. Student to teacher ratio 12:1. 90% of graduates employed within six months. Facilities: Professionally equipped kitchens, demo rooms with video & overhead mirrors. Courses: Basic to complex techniques; classic, regional, ethnic, & contemporary cuisines; presentation, decoration, execution.

FACULTY: 10+ full-time Master Chefs, international staff. French Master Chefs from leading restaurants & fine hotels.

COSTS: 10-wk certificate courses range from €4,750 in Pastry to €6,850 in Cuisine. 9-mo Grand Diplome €29,550. Admission requirements: Personal statement, resume, application fee. Scholarships: yes.

CONTACT: Director of Admissions, Le Cordon Bleu, 8, rue Leon Delhomme, Paris, 75015 France; 800-457-CHEF (North America), (33) 1-53-68-22-50 (Paris), Fax (33) 1-48-56-03-96, E-mail info@cordonbleu.edu, URL http://cordonbleu.edu.

ROBERT REYNOLDS APPRENTICESHIP IN FRANCE
Agen, Niort or Orange (Provence)/Spring & Fall

Sponsor: Private school. Program: 7-wk advanced certificate course, 1-wk option for addt'l travel. Established: 1987. Curriculum: culinary. Admission dates: Oct.-Mar. (France). Total enrollment: 6. 6 each admission period. 25% of applicants accepted. Student to teacher ratio 6:1. 100% of graduates employed within six months. Facilities: Restored farmhouse with home kitchen facility.

FACULTY: Robert Reynolds, French-trained chef/instructor, proprietor chef for 15 yrs of Le Trou restaurant in SF.

Costs: $8,000/7-wk course, $4,750/1-mo course, $2,250/wk;payment in . Admission requirements: Interview.

Contact: Robert Reynolds, Chef Instructor, Robert Reynolds Apprenticeship in France, 222 SE 18th Ave., Portland, OR 97214; 503-233-1934, E-mail rowbear@attglobal.net, URL http://www.nwculinaryforum.org.

WINE MBA
Davis, CA; Adelaide, Australia; Santiago, Chile; Bordeaux, France; Tokyo /Year-round
Sponsor: Bordeaux Business School. Program: 13-mo part-time program alternating travel to 5 wine-producing countries with students' work commitments. Established: 2001. 20 each admission period.

Faculty: Faculty of the Bordeaux Business School, U. of California-Davis, Universidad Catolica de Chile, Keio Business School, U. of South Australia.

Costs: $30,000 + airfare.

Contact: Isabelle Dartigues, Wine MBA Manager, Bordeaux Business School, 680, Cours de la Liberation, Talence Cedex, 33405 France; (33) (0) 5-56-84-22-29, Fax (33) (0) 5-56-84-55-00, E-mail isabelle.dartigues@bordeaux-bs.edu, URL http://www.winemba.com.

GREECE

ALPINE CENTER FOR HOTEL & TOURISM MANAGEMENT STUDIES
Glyfada, Athens/October-April
Sponsor: Swiss-managed Associate Institute of IHTTI School of Hotel Management. Program: 3-yr BA (Hons) Culinary Arts Mgmt,2-yr Swiss Diploma in Culinary Arts. Established: 1987. Calendar: trimester. Curriculum: culinary. Admission dates: May-Sep.

Faculty: 6 instructors.

Contact: Sybil Hofmann, President, Alpine Center for Hotel & Tourism Management, PO Box 70235, 70 Possidonos Ave., Glyfada, GR-166 10 Greece; (30) 010 898 3022/3210, Fax (30) 010 898 1189, E-mail services@alpine.edu.gr, URL http://www.alpine.edu.gr.

IRELAND

BALLYMALOE COOKERY SCHOOL
Midleton, County Cork/September-July
Sponsor: Private cookery school on a working organic farm. Program: 12-wk certificate course in Food & Wine, offered 3 times/yr; short courses. Established: 1983. Accredited by IACP. Calendar: quarter. Curriculum: culinary. Admission dates: Sep, Jan, Apr. Total enrollment: 150. 56 each admission period. 90% of applicants accepted. Student to teacher ratio 6:1. 100% of graduates employed within six months. Facilities: Specially designed kitchens with gas & electric cookers, mirrored demo area with TV monitors, gardens & farm that supply fresh organic produce.

Faculty: 4 full- & 4 part-time. Includes Principal Darina Allen, IACP-certified Teacher & Food Professional & Rory O'Connell.

Costs: 12-wk course is 7,650. Self-catering, shared cottage lodging is 95/wk, 115/wk single.

Contact: Darina Allen, Owner/Teacher, Ballymaloe Cookery School, Shanagarry, County Cork, Midleton, Ireland; (353) (0)21-4646-785, Fax (353) (0)21-4646-909, E-mail enquiries@ballymaloe-cookery-school.ie, URL http://www.ballymaloe-cookery-school.ie.

IRISH COOKERY SCHOOL OF IRELAND
Cork/Summer
Sponsor: Private School. Program: 2-wk short-term certificate courses. Specializing in Irish cooking. Food service, catering, food safety, hygiene. Established: 2000. Curriculum: culinary. Admission dates: Jun, Jul, Aug. Total enrollment: 5/class. 5 each admission period. Student to

teacher ratio 5 to 2. Facilities: Audio Visual equipment. Lecture Studio. Visits to food producers in the South of Ireland.

FACULTY: 1.

COSTS: IR£400/wk, IR£800/2 wk residency course. Includes single lodging & meals.

CONTACT: Mary Casey O'Carroll, Director, Irish Cookery School of Ireland, Ballincollig, Cork., Kilnaglory, Ballincollig, Cork, Ireland; (353) 21 4972646, Fax (353) 21 4877655.

ITALY

---

www.Apicius.it - Via Guelfa 85, Firenze Italia Tel.055/2658135 Fax 055/2656689

APICIUS THE ART OF COOKING
- Professional Programs
- Culinary Arts
- Wine Expertise
- Hospitality Management

- Monthly Courses
- Customized Programs
- Culinary Excursions
- Restaurant Internships

APICIUS – THE CULINARY INSTITUTE OF FLORENCE
Florence/Year-round   *(See also page 297) (See display ad above)*

Sponsor: Private school, member of the Federation of European Schools & IACP. Program: 1-yr diploma & 2-yr program in Culinary Arts. 1-yr programs: Master in Italian Cuisine, Hospitality mgmt, Wine Expertise, Italian Baking & Pastry, Food Communication, Design and Marketing for the Food Industry. Combination programs of Italian language, ar. Established: 1973. Accredited by Authorized by the region of TuscanyAffiliations: Eastern Illinois University, Robert Morris College, Texas Tech University, University of South Florida, Washington State University. Calendar: semester. Curriculum: culinary, core. Admission dates: Jan, Aug for sem & yr-long programs. Total enrollment: 150. 40 each admission period. 80% of applicants accepted. 5% receive financial aid. 20% enrolled part-time. Student to teacher ratio 12:1. 30% of graduates employed within six months. Facilities: New facility consisting of 2 kitchens with individual workstations, wine tasting room, conference room, reading room & lounge. Courses: Culinary arts, hospitality & restaurant mgmt, wine, Renaissance culture, regional Italian cooking, food resources, Italian & Jewish food traditions, bakery, pastry & confectionery.

FACULTY: Includes professional chefs Gennaro Napolitano, Stefano Innocenti, Pierluigi Campi & Andrea Bianchini, & food historian Gabriella Ganugi, Director.

COSTS: Tuition €5,240/sem, courses from €150. Scholarships: yes.

CONTACT: Dr. Gabriella Ganugi, Director, Apicius - The Culinary Institute of Florence, Via Guelfa 85, Florence, 50129 Italy; (39) 0552658135, Fax (39) 0552656689, E-mail info@apicius.it, URL http://www.apicius.it. U.S. contact: Study Abroad Italy, 339 S. Main St., Sebastopol, CA 95472; 707-824-8965, Fax 707-824-0198, e-mail mail@tuscancooking.com, http://www.tuscancooking.com.

ITALIAN CULINARY INSTITUTE FOR FOREIGN PROFESSIONALS
Piedmont region, Italy/Spring & Fall

Sponsor: Professional culinary institute (ICIF). Program: 2-mo certificate program, 6-mo diploma program, 2-wk certificate programs in olive oil studies & wine studies. Established: 1991. Curriculum: culinary. Admission dates: Ongoing. 20 each admission period. 90% of applicants accepted. Student to teacher ratio 12:1. 100% of graduates employed within six months. Facilities: High-tech equipment in an 18th-century castle, olive oil & wine tasting room, bakery, dining room.

FACULTY: In-house instructors & visiting professional chefs.

Costs: $4,500/2-mo program, $9,000/6-mo program; both include room in student housing facility, board, & roundtrip airfare NYC-Italy (must travel in group).

Contact: Enrico Bazzoni, Director of Programs, ICIF-USA, 126 Second Place, Brooklyn, NY 11231; 718-875-0547, Fax 718-875-5856, E-mail Eabchef@aol.com, URL http://www.icif.com.

SCUOLA DI ARTE CULINARIA 'CORDON BLEU'
Florence/Year-round
Sponsor: Private school. Program: Professional curriculum consists of 11-21 one- to nine-session hands-on courses, a total of 150-230 hrs of instruction. Established: 1985. Accredited by AICI (Italian Assn of Culinary Teachers). Calendar: quinmester quarter trimester semester. Curriculum: culinary. Admission dates: Jul & Nov for intensive programs; yr-round for others. Total enrollment: 150. 50-70 each admission period. 90% of applicants accepted. 90% enrolled part-time. Student to teacher ratio 8:1. Facilities: 40-sq-meter teaching kitchen + library & tasting room.
Faculty: 2 full- & 2 part-time instructors. Cristina Blasi & Gabriella Mari, 18 yrs teaching experience.
Costs: €3,820 (€4,660) for the Fall (Spring) program, €6,000 for both.
Contact: Emilia Onesti, Secretary, Scuola di Arte Culinaria 'Cordon Bleu', Via di Mezzo, 55/R, 50121 Firenze-Florence, Italy; (39) 055-2345468, Fax (39) 055-2345468, E-mail info@cordonbleu-it.com, URL http://www.cordonbleu-it.com.

SLOW FOOD – MASTER ITALIAN COOKING PROGRAM
Jesi, Italy/Year-round
Sponsor: The Higher Institute of Gastronomy & School of Regional Cooking. Program: 11-wk Slow Food - Master Italian Cooking certificate program. Established: 2003. Curriculum: culinary. Admission dates: Jan, Mar, Jun, Oct. Total enrollment: 60/yr. 15 each admission period. 90% of applicants accepted. 15% receive financial aid. Student to teacher ratio 7:1. 95% of graduates employed within six months. Facilities: New teaching kitchen facility, classroom & food/wine tasting room, student-run open-to-the-public dining room.
Faculty: Experts selected by the Slow Food Master Italian Cooking board of regional governors.
Costs: €12,300 includes course materials, uniforms, meals, lodging in newly-renovated apartments, insurance, wkend gastronomic excursions, stage up to 12 mos. Admission requirements: Culinary experience with culinary degree preferred. Designed for professionals outside of Italy in food & related fields. Scholarships: yes.
Contact: Francesco Tonelli, United States Representative, Slow Food - Master Italian Cooking Program, 46 Riverview, Port Ewen, NY 12466; 845-340-1799, Fax 845-340-1799, E-mail francesco@francescotonelli.com, URL http://www.italcook.it.

UNIVERSITY OF GASTRONOMIC SCIENCES
Pollenzo & Colorno/Year-round
Sponsor: Private school founded by the Slow Food organization. Program: Three-yr degrees in Gastronomy and Agro-ecology; two-yr specialized master's degrees in Food & Gastronomy Communications and Food mgmt. Established: 2004. Admission dates: Oct. Total enrollment: 60. 60 each admission period. Facilities: On-site training includes visits to farms & dairies, vineyards & wine cellars, factories & traditional workshops, markets & kitchens.
Faculty: Experts in agro-ecology & gastronomy.
Costs: €19,000/yr includes lodging, meals, textbooks, computer; €14,000/yr without lodging. Admission requirements: HS diploma or equivalent, entrance exam, knowledge of English & Italian. Scholarships: yes. Loans: yes.
Contact: Head Office, University of Gastronomic Sciences, Piazza Vittorio Emanuele, 9, Pollenzo - Bra (Cuneo), 12042 Italy; (39) (0)172 458511, E-mail info@unisg.it, URL http://www.unisg.it.

JAPAN

LE CORDON BLEU – JAPAN
Tokyo, Yokohama & Kobe/Year-round　　　　*(See display ad page 161)*

Sponsor: Private school, sister school of Le Cordon Bleu Paris. Program: 9-mo diploma programs in Basic, Intermediate, Superior levels for Pastry; 12-mo diploma programs in Basic, Intermediate, Advanced, Superior levels for Cuisine. Intro courses in cuisine, pastry, catering, bread baking. Established: 1991. Accredited by Through international hospitality mgmt schools. Calendar: quarter. Curriculum: culinary. Admission dates: qtrly. Facilities: Professionally-equipped kitchens, individual work spaces with refrigerated marble tables, convection ovens, specialty appliances. Courses: Diploma & Certificate core curriculum consists of 4 levels of cuisine & 3 levels of pastry, taken consecutively or together. Covers basic to complex techniques, wine & food pairing, catering, presentation.

FACULTY: 10 full-time French & Japanese Master Chefs from Michelin-star restaurants & fine hotels.

COSTS: Basic Cuisine 610,050 yen, Intermediate Cuisine 630,000 yen, Advanced Cuisine 647,850 yen, Superior Cuisine 696,150 yen, Basic Pastry 573,300 yen,Intermediate Pastry 595,350 yen, Superior Pastry 599,550 yen, Basic Bakery 546,000 yen, Intermediate Bakery 5.

CONTACT: Okabe Taeko, Student Service & Sales Manager, Le Cordon Bleu Japan, Roob-1, 28-13 Sarugaku-cho, Daikanyama, Shibuya-ku, Tokyo, 150-0033 Japan; (81) 3 5489 0141, Fax (81) 3 5489 0145, E-mail tokyo@cordonbleu.edu, URL http://www.cordonbleu.co.jp. Toll-free in the U.S. & Canada: 800-457-CHEF. http://www.cordonbleu.edu (English).

MEXICO

LE CORDON BLEU MEXICO
Mexico City/Year-round　　　　*(See display ad page 161)*

Sponsor: Private school. Program: Certificate & diploma programs in Basic, Intermediate, & Superior levels for Cuisine & Pastry. Le Grande Diplome. Instruction in Spanish. Established: 2004. Curriculum: culinary.

COSTS: $4,025-$4,600/Cuisine certificate, $3,622-$4,255/Pastry certificate, $12,880/Cuisine diploma, $11,557/Pastry diploma, $24,387/Le Grand Diplome.

CONTACT: Luis Alvarez, Le Cordon Bleu Mexico, Havre 15, Col. Juárez, Mexico City, 5600 Mexico; E-mail lalvarez@cordonbleu.edu, URL http://www.lcbmexico.com.

MEXICAN HOME COOKING SCHOOL
Tlaxcala/Year-round

Sponsor: Private school. Program: 1- & 2-wk certificate courses individually structured to the needs of professional chefs & their staffs. Established: 1998. Admission dates: yr-round. Student to teacher ratio 3:1. Facilities: Fully-equipped 500-sq-ft kitchen with Talavera tile & view of volcanoes. Stove & adjacent work areas set below a 70-sq-ft skylight.

FACULTY: Estela Salas Silva served a classic apprenticeship from age 7 in the traditions of the Mexican kitchen.

COSTS: $1,000/1-wk resident course includes meals & lodging in hacienda-style country home.

CONTACT: Estela Salas-Silva, Owner, Mexican Home Cooking School, Apdo. 64, Tlaxcala, 90000 Mexico; (52) 246-46-809-78, Fax (52) 246-46-809-78, E-mail mexicanhomecooking@yahoo.com, URL http://mexicanhomecooking.com.

NEW ZEALAND

CENTRAL INSTITUTE OF TECHNOLOGY
Wellington/Year-round

Sponsor: Trade school. Program: 3-yr Bachelor's degree, 2-yr diploma, 1-yr certificate in Hotel Reception, 6 mo courses in cookery & food service. Established: 1978. Accredited by State. Calendar: semester. Curriculum: core. Admission dates: Feb & Jul. Total enrollment: 300. 90 each admission period. 50% of applicants accepted. 40% receive financial aid. Student to teacher ratio 14:1. 50% of graduates employed within 6 mos. Facilities: 3 kitchens, 20 classrooms, 2 restaurants. **FACULTY:** 18 full-time.

COSTS: In-country NZ$3,725, out-of-country NZ$17,200. On-campus housing cost NZ$160/wk. Admission requirements: HS diploma or equivalent & admission test.

CONTACT: Kay Nelson, Head of Department, Central Institute of Technology, Centre for Hospitality & Tourism Management, Private Bag 39803, Wellington, New Zealand; (64) (0)4-9202-620, Fax (64) (0)4-9202-628, E-mail kay.nelson@weltec.ac.nz, URL http://www.cit.ac.nz.

THE NEW ZEALAND SCHOOL OF FOOD AND WINE
Christchurch/Year-round

Sponsor: Proprietary institution. Program: 16-wk full-time certificate in Foundation Cookery Skills, which includes New Zealand certificate in wine; 22-wk full-time certificate in Restaurant-Cafe mgmt. Established: 1994. Accredited by New Zealand Qualifications Authority. Calendar: trimester. Curriculum: culinary. Admission dates: Jan, Feb, May, Jul, Aug. 12 each admission period. Student to teacher ratio 1:12. 90% of graduates employed within six months. Facilities: Include 1 demonstration kitchen with overhead mirrors & 1 practical kitchen with commercial equipment, computer & seminar rooms. **FACULTY:** 10 full-time and part-time tutors.

COSTS: ~NZ$4,650 (includes tax). Loans: yes.

CONTACT: Celia Hay, Director, The New Zealand School of Food and Wine, 63 Victoria St., Box 25217, Christchurch, So. Island, New Zealand; (64) (0)3-3797-501, Fax (64) (0)3-366-2302, E-mail celia@foodandwine.co.nz, URL http://www.foodandwine.co.nz.

TAI POUTINI POLYTECHNIC
Greymouth/February-November

Sponsor: Trade/technical school. Program: One-yr full-time (34 wks)London City & Guilds certificate and diplomaT.P.P. Certificate in Professional Culinary Arts. Established: 1988. Curriculum: culinary, core. Admission dates: Feb. Total enrollment: 20. 20 each admission period. 80% of applicants accepted. 90% receive financial aid. Student to teacher ratio 10:1. 100% of graduates employed within six months. Facilities: Modular training kitchen with the latest equipment. Classrooms with overheads, video. Student cafeteria & lounge. Library with Internet access.

COSTS: NZ$3,500 includes uniforms, knife & tool kit, field trip, qualification fees. Admission requirements: Good knowledge of English & mathematics. Scholarships: yes. Loans: yes.

CONTACT: Jos Wellman, Chef Tutor, Tai Poutini Polytechnic, Tainui St., Greymouth, SI, 3 New Zealand; (64) 3-7680411 x747, Fax (64) 3-7684503, E-mail jos.wellman@odin.taipoutini.ac.nz, URL http://www.tpp.ac.nz/taipoutini/qualifications.asp?id=4.

PANAMA

ACADEMIA DE ARTES CULINARIAS Y ETIQUETA
Panama/Year-round

Sponsor: Private culinary arts academy. Program: 9-mo diploma in Culinary Arts. Established: 2002. Calendar: semester. Curriculum: culinary. Admission dates: Jan, Jul. Total enrollment: 60. 16

each admission period. 95% of applicants accepted. Student to teacher ratio 1:16. Facilities: Fully-equipped professional kitchen, accomodating 16 students.

FACULTY: 3 full-time chef-instructors, all educated in Europe & the U.S. 10 part-time local chef-instructors.

COSTS: 6675. Admission requirements: HS diploma, health certificate. Scholarships: yes.

CONTACT: Elena Hernández, Director, Academia de Artes Culinarias y Etiqueta, Calle 51E y Federico Boyd, Casa #24, Local #3, Panama, Panama; 507-263-6083, Fax 507-263-6083, E-mail cocina@cwpanama.net.

PHILIPPINES

CENTER FOR CULINARY ARTS, MANILA
Quezon City/Year-round
Sponsor: Private school. Program: 2-yr diploma in Culinary Arts & Technology mgmt, 1-yr certificate in Baking & Pastry Arts. 5 terms of 2 mos/term. Established: 1995. Accredited by TESDA (Technical Education Skills Development Authority). Calendar: quinmester. Curriculum: culinary. Admission dates: Jun, Aug, Oct, Jan. Total enrollment: 191. 163 each admission period. 72% of applicants accepted. 2% receive financial aid. Student to teacher ratio 10:1. Facilities: Modern lecture & lab facilities for institutional & quantity cooking, baking lab, research center, computer facilities, restaurant outlet.

FACULTY: 20 instructors.

COSTS: ~$10,000 for diploma, $6,000 for baking, includes books, supplies/materials, ingredients, exams. Admission requirements: HS diploma, transcript of records, recommendation letter, interview, written exam, medical exam, attendance in discovery course. Scholarships: yes.

CONTACT: Lotees Dell Palacios, Marketing Officer, Center for Culinary Arts, Manila, 287 Katipunan Ave., Loyola Heights, Quezon City, 1102 Philippines; (632) 426-48-41 / 40 / 35 / 37 / 25, Fax (632) 426-48-36, E-mail marketing@cca-manila.com, URL http://www.cca-manila.com.

SCOTLAND

COLLEGE RESTAURANT
Edinburgh/September-June
Sponsor: Part of Edinburgh's Telford College. Program: Courses ranging from Basic Cookery to Professional Culinary Arts. Established: 1979. Accredited by Member of The International Consortium of Hospitality and Tourism Institutes. Calendar: trimester. Curriculum: culinary, core. Admission dates: yr-round. 16/class max each admission period. 80% of applicants accepted. 50% receive financial aid. 30% enrolled part-time. Student to teacher ratio 16:1. 90% of graduates employed within six months. Facilities: Include training restaurant, training cafe & a training bakery. 7 practical classroom/kitchens.

CONTACT: Colin McLaren, The College Restaurant, Edinburgh's Telford College, School of Leisure Industries, Crewe Toll, Edinburgh, EH4 2NZ Scotland; (44) (0)131 315 7373, Fax (44) (0)131 343 1218, E-mail info@collegerestaurant.com, URL http://www.collegerestaurant.com.

EDINBURGH SCHOOL OF FOOD AND WINE
Edinburgh/September-July
Sponsor: Private school. Program: 6-mo (2-sem) diploma in Food & Wine for career cooks, 5-wk Intensive for chalet & freelance cooks, recreational classes & courses. Established: 1987. Accredited by British Accreditation Council for Independent, Further & Higher Education. Calendar: semester. Curriculum: culinary. Admission dates: Jan for diploma course, yr-round for other courses. Total enrollment: 20/class. 20 each admission period. 90% of applicants accepted. 10% receive financial aid. 5% enrolled part-time. 100% of graduates employed within six months. Facilities: Full range of domestic & commercial equipment.

Faculty: Certificate/Diploma.

Costs: £8500/sem for diploma course. £2,500 for certificate course. Apartment £75/wk including utilities. Admission requirements: No formal qualifications. Loans: yes.

Contact: Jill Davidson, Managing Director, Edinburgh School of Food and Wine, The Coach House, Newliston, Edinburgh, EH29 9EB Scotland; (44) (0) 131 333 5001, Fax (44) (0) 131 335 3796, E-mail info@esfw.com, URL http://www.esfw.com.

TOP TIER SUGARCRAFT
Inverness/Year-round
Sponsor: Private school & mail order business. Program: 1-, 2-, & 3- wk demonstration & participation courses for beginners & experts. Established: 1985. Student to teacher ratio 1-8:1. Facilities: 600-sq-ft classroom with specialized equipment.

Faculty: Principal teacher Diana Turner, British Sugarcraft Guild member & judge.

Costs: 2-day (3-day, wk-long) course £300 (£450, £750).

Contact: Diana Turner, Top Tier Sugarcraft, 10 Meadow Rd., Balloch, Inverness, IV2 7JR Scotland; (44) (0)1463-790456, Fax (44) (0)1463-790456, E-mail toptier@btinternet.com.

SINGAPORE

AT-SUNRICE THE SINGAPORE COOKING SCHOOL & SPICE GARDEN
Singapore/Year-round
Sponsor: Center for pan-Asian culinary arts. Program: 2-yr Advanced Culinary Placement diploma (ACP) offered with Johnson & Wales Univ; 3-wk pan-Asian Culinary course (ACA) + optional internship; leisure classes. Established: 2001. Curriculum: culinary. Admission dates: Mar, Apr, Jun, Jul, Aug, Oct. Facilities: Industry-current kitchens, spice garden.

Faculty: Professional teaching chefs.

Costs: $3,600/3-wk course includes lodging, meals, 4 credits. $40,500/2-yr course. Admission requirements: ACA: completion of a basic culinary course. ACP: 3 yrs work experience or culinary school graduate. Scholarships: yes. Loans: yes.

Contact: Phyllis Ong, at-sunrice, The Singapore Cooking School & Spice Garden, Fort Canning Park, Fort Canning Centre, Singapore, 179618 Singapore; (65) 336 3307, Fax (65) 336 9353, E-mail academy@at-sunrice.com, URL http://www.at-sunrice.com.

SOUTH AFRICA

BARNES STREET CULINARY STUDIO
Johannesburg
Sponsor: Private school. Program: Certificate and diploma in Food Preparation & Cooking Principles & Practice. ~15 each admission period.

Faculty: Owner & principal Suzi Holzhausen, 15+ yrs as a professional chef & culinary lecturer.

Costs: R12,000, fees ~R,4,000. Admission requirements: Identification document, letter of intent, MD's letter attesting health.

Contact: Suzi Holzhausen,Barnes Street Culinary Studio, PO Box 579, Auckland Park, Johannesburg, 2006 South Africa; E-mail info@barnesculinary.co.za, URL http://www.barnesculinary.co.za.

CHRISTINA MARTIN SCHOOL OF FOOD AND WINE
Durban/February-November
Sponsor: Private culinary college, culinary professional. Program: 1-yr Intensive Diploma Chef's Course. Established: 1973. Accredited by THETA & SAQA Dept. of Education South Africa, City & Guilds Intl London. Calendar: semester. Curriculum: culinary, core. Admission dates: Feb. Total enrollment: 36. 36 each admission period. 80% of applicants accepted. 10% receive financial aid.

36% enrolled part-time. Student to teacher ratio 6:1. 100% of graduates employed within six months. Facilities: 4 industrial kitchens with latest equipment, auditorium, delicatessen, 60-seat restaurant, 80-seat conference venue, garden restaurant.

FACULTY: Christina Martin is a Maitre Chef de Cuisine.

COSTS: R63,756 for Intensive Diploma Course, ~R955 each for Cordon Bleu 1 & 2 courses. Casual day & evening courses ~R12,500. Admission requirements: Senior School leavers certificate (matric). Scholarships: yes.

CONTACT: Christina Martin, Principal and Owner, Christina Martin School of Food and Wine, PO Box 4601, Durban, 4000 South Africa; (27) (0)31-3032111, Fax (27) (0)31-312-3342, E-mail chrismar@iafrica.com, URL http://www.safarichef.com.

THE SILWOOD SCHOOL OF COOKERY
Rondebosch Cape/Year-round
Sponsor: Private school. Program: Three 1-yr culinary career courses: the certificate course, the diploma course, the Grande Diplome. Established: 1964. Accredited by Hospitality Industries Training Board. Calendar: quarter. Curriculum: core. Admission dates: Jan. Total enrollment: 48. 48, divided into groups of 12 each admission period. 60% of applicants accepted. Student to teacher ratio 12:1. 100% of graduates employed within six months. Facilities: 200-yr-old coachhouse converted into a demo & experimental kitchen, 3 add'l kitchens, demo hall, library.

FACULTY: 11-member faculty includes school principal Alicia Wilkinson.

COSTS: R28,300/certificate course, R12,500/diploma course, R1,200/Grande Diplome. Housing R1,000-R1,500/mo.

CONTACT: Mrs. Alicia Wilkinson, The Silwood School of Cookery, Silwood Rd., Rondebosch Cape, South Africa; (27) 21-686-4894/5, Fax (27) 21-686-5795, E-mail cooking@silwood.co.za, URL http://www.silwood.co.za.

SOUTH KOREA

LE CORDON BLEU – SOOKMYUNG ACADEMY
Seoul/Year-round   *(See display ad page 161)*
Sponsor: Private school in Sookmyung Women's University, Korea branch of Le Cordon Bleu. Program: 12-mo diploma programs in Initiation, Basic, Intermediate & Superior levels for Cuisine; 9-mo diploma programs in Basic, Intermediate & Superior levels for Pastry;6-mo certificate programs in Basic & Advanced for Bakery. Established: 2002. Calendar: quarter. Curriculum: culinary. Admission dates: qtrly. Student to teacher ratio 10:1. Facilities: Professionally-equipped kitchens, demo classrooms with slated mirrors & video equipment, individual work spaces with refrigerated marble tables, convection ovens, specialty appliances.

FACULTY: 6 full-time French Master Chefs from Michelin-star restaurants or competition winners.

COSTS: Cuisine: Initiation 6,298,000 won, Basic 5,328,000 won, Intermediate 5,418,000 won, Superior 5,922,000 won. Pastry: Basic 5,848,000 won, Intermediate 5,049,000 won, Superior Pastry 5,139,000 won, Bakery Basic 5,848,000 won, Advanced 5,049,000w on includi.

CONTACT: Jungyeon Choi, Student Service Manager, Le Cordon Bleu-Sookmyung Academy Korea, 53-12, Chungpa-dong2Ka, Youngsan-Ku, Seoul, 140-742 Korea (South); (82) 2 719 6961 x3, Fax (82) 2 719 7569, E-mail jchoi@cordonbleu.edu, URL http://www.cordonbleu.co.kr.

SPAIN

ACADEMY FOR FOOD STYLING
Mallorca
Sponsor: Private school. Program: 2-wk food styling program devoted to food & drinks, 3-day program for drinks, 3-day program for ice cream. Instruction in German. Established: 2002.

Costs: €7,800 for 2-wk program, €3,800 for each 3-day program includes airfare to/from Germany, lodging, breakfasts.

Contact: Manuel Van de Kerkhof, Food Stylist, Academy for Food Styling, Kaiserstrasse 138 D, Wuppertal, 42329 Germany; (41) 0202 87 01 085, E-mail manuel.van.de.kerkhof@foodeffects.com, URL http://www.foodeffects.com.

ESCUELA DE COCINA LUIS IRÍZAR
Basque Country/October-August

Sponsor: Private school. Program: 2-yr diploma with instruction in Spanish. Established: 1992. Curriculum: culinary. Admission dates: yr-round, selection in May. Total enrollment: 28/yr. 28 each admission period. 80% of applicants accepted. Student to teacher ratio 14:1. 100% of graduates employed within 6 mos. Facilities: Fully-equipped kitchen, separate classroom, TV & video.

Faculty: Founder Luis Irízar was chef in Spain's leading restaurants. Staff of 3 full-time instructors.

Contact: V. Irízar, Escuela de Cocina Luis Irízar, c/ Mari, #5, Bajo, San Sebastian, 20003 Spain; (34) 943-431540, Fax (34) 943-423553, E-mail cocina@escuelairizar.com, URL http://www.escuelairizar.com.

ESC.UNIV.HOST. I TURISME SANT POL DE MAR, BARCELONA
Barcelona/Year-round

Sponsor: Hotel school. Program: 3-yr technical Hosteleria-Cooking program. 16- or 32-wk postgraduate degree in Culinary Arts (150 lecture-hrs & 450 practical-hrs per sem). Established: 1966. Accredited by Diploma accredited by the EUHT Sant Pol, Univ of Girona & the Spanish Government. Calendar: quarter trimester semester. Curriculum: culinary, core. Total enrollment: 30. 25 each admission period. 50% of applicants accepted. 25% receive financial aid. Student to teacher ratio 7. 100% of graduates employed within six months. Facilities: 4 kitchens, kitchen-auditorium & hotel used as a practice laboratory.

Faculty: 35 university degrees, Ph.D., culinary school graduates. Michelin-star guest chefs.

Costs: $7,000-$14,000/yr includes housing, meals, books. Scholarships: yes. Loans: yes.

Contact: Lluis Serra, External Relations, Esc.Univ.Host. i Turisme Sant Pol de Mar, Barcelona, Hotel Gran Sol, Carrtera N-II s/n, Sant Pol de Mar, Barcelona, 8395 Spain; (34) 93-760 0051/0212, Fax (34) 93-760 0985, E-mail mail@euht-santpol.org, URL http://www.euht-santpol.org.

LA TAHONA DEL MAR
Barcelona/September-May

Sponsor: Bakery. Program: 1-wk (40-hr) courses in artisanal European breadmaking, Spanish & Catalan breads, pastries. Established: 1998. Curriculum: culinary. Admission dates: Spring & fall. Facilities: Modern culinary classroom attached to a working bakery.

Costs: 80,000 Spanish pesetas. Instruction is in Spanish. English interpretation is $200 add'l. Admission requirements: Professional experience or training in bread or pastry making.

Contact: Elizabeth Duran, English Language Representative, La Tahona del Mar, 605 W. 111th St., #63, New York, NY 10025; 212-222-9062, Fax 212-222-6613, E-mail eduran@pipeline.com, URL http://www.sinix.net/paginas/tahona/ingles.htm.

SPANISH CULINARY INSTITUTE
Valencia/Year-round

Sponsor: Valencia School of Hotel & Catering & Tourism, a 2-yr college. Program: Four wk-long (25-hour/wk) modules consisting of theoretical and practical courses in Spanish & Mediterranean cuisine. Established: 1991. Accredited by Ministerio del Turismo. Curriculum: culinary, core. Admission dates: Rolling. Total enrollment: 350. 10-15 each admission period. 90% of applicants accepted. Student to teacher ratio 15:1 max. 100% of graduates employed within six months. Facilities: 3 full kitchens & 3 full-menu restaurants.

Costs: $2,299/mo (4 modules) includes meals & lodging. Admission requirements: Students attending, graduating, or graduated from culinary schools, or 1 yr kitchen experience.

CONTACT: Jana O'Keefe, Director, USA Programs, Spanish Culinary Institute, 126 2nd Place, Brooklyn, NY 11231; 718-875-0547, Fax 718-875-5856, E-mail chefschoolintl@aol.com, URL http://www.ehtvalencia.com.

SWITZERLAND

DCT SWISS HOTEL & CULINARY ARTS SCHOOL
Vitznau-Lucerne/Year-round

Sponsor: Private school. Program: Three 11-wk courses: Foundation in European Cuisine, European Gourmet Cuisine, European Pastry & Chocolate, plus Swiss industry internship leading to advanced diploma in European Culinary mgmt. Established: 1992. Accredited by ACF, Swiss Hotel School Assn, ACBSP, HCIMA. Calendar: quarter. Curriculum: culinary, core. Admission dates: Jan, Apr, Jul, Oct. Total enrollment: 40. 20 each admission period. 75% of applicants accepted. Student to teacher ratio 10:1 max. 100% of graduates employed within six months.
Costs: Sfr. 9,500 (~$7,000, payable in Sfr.) for each 3-mo course includes tuition, rm & bd.
CONTACT: Dr. Joseph Gregg, Director, Americas Office, DCT Swiss Hotel & Culinary Arts School, Seestrasse, Vitznau-Lucerne, CH6354 Switzerland; (41) 41 399 00 00, Fax (41) 41 399 01 01, E-mail culinary@dct.ch, URL http://culinaryschool.ch.

TAIWAN

KAOHSIUNG HOSPITALITY COLLEGE (KHC)
Kaohsiung

Program: Programs in Western Culinary Arts, Chinese Culinary Arts, Baking & Pastry Arts, Food & Beverage mgmt, Hospitality mgmt. Facilities: Teaching kitchen with fully-equipped stations.
CONTACT: KHC College, 1 Sung-ho Rd. Hsiao-kang, Kaohsiung, Taiwan R.O.C.; (886) 07-8060505, Fax (886) 07-8061473, E-mail stone@mail.nkhc.edu.tw, URL http://www.nkhc.edu.tw/depart-new.htm.

THAILAND

ROYAL THAI SCHOOL OF CULINARY ARTS
Bang Saen/Year-round

Sponsor: Private school. Program: Ten 5-session courses in Royal & Regional Thai cuisine that lead to a Grand Diploma in Thai Cooking. Established: 1997. Accredited by Thai Ministry of Education. Admission dates: yr-round. Total enrollment: 160. 16 each admission period. 100% of applicants accepted. Student to teacher ratio 4:1. 50% of graduates employed within six months. Facilities: 2 professional kitchens, lounge, dining room & terrace overlooking the Gulf of Siam.
FACULTY: 5 instructors, 2 master fruit & vegetable carvers.
Costs: $1,200-$10,000 includes lodging & meals. Admission requirements: Basic kitchen & knife skills. Scholarships: yes.
CONTACT: Chris Kridakorn-Odbratt, Exec. Chef, Royal Thai School of Culinary Arts, 5 Thanon Rob Kau Sammuk; Bang Saen, T. Saen Suk; A. Muang, Chonburi, 20130 Thailand; (66) 1-867 9450, (66) 38-748 404, Fax (66) 38-748 405, E-mail rtsca@cscoms.com, URL http://www.gourmetthailand.com.

SAMUI INSTITUTE OF THAI CULINARY ARTS
Koh Samui/Year-round

Sponsor: Private institution. Program: 2-3 wk training programs for professionals that prepare non-Thais for a career in the Thai culinary arts or for opening a Thai restaurant overseas. Established: 1999. Curriculum: culinary. Admission dates: moly. Total enrollment: 5. 5 each admission period. Student to teacher ratio 3:1. Facilities: New 12-million baht 3-story, 300-sq-meter facility with 90-sq-meter instruction area, 10-burner teaching stove, gourmet restaurant with separate kitchen.

FACULTY: 3 instructors. Director Roongfa Sringam has 12 yrs experience preparing Thai cuisine.

COSTS: Thai baht equivalent of ~$2,440. Admission requirements: Basic kitchen experience, knowledge of food storage techniques & professional hygiene standards.

CONTACT: Martin Amada, Co-Director, Samui Institute of Thai Culinary Arts, 46/6 Moo 3 Chaweng Beach, Koh Samui, 84320 Thailand; (66) (77) 413-172, Fax (66) (77) 413-434, E-mail info@sitca.net, URL http://www.sitca.net/thai_cooking_school.htm.

VIRGIN ISLANDS

NEW ENGLAND CULINARY INSTITUTE AT H. LAVITY STOUTT CC
Road Town, Tortola/Year-round   *(See display ad above)*
Sponsor: New England Culinary Institute in partnership with H. Lavity Stoutt Community College (HLSCC). Program: 2-yr AOS in Culinary Arts. Students spend 6 mos on campus & 6 mos on paid internships each yr. Established: 2001. Accredited by ACCSCT. Calendar: sem. Curriculum: culinary. Admission dates: Aug & Feb. Total enrollment: 60. 21 each admission period. 40% receive financial aid. Student to teacher ratio 7:1. Facilities: Operating kitchens at a contemporary restaurant, the Road Town Bakery, & the cafeteria at HLSCC. Student housing available. Courses: Include baking, pastry, prepared foods, a la carte, catering, meat fabrication, garde manger.

COSTS: U.S. citizens $14,200/yr, Caribbean residents $11,360/yr, BVI residents $9,940/yr. Admission requirements: HS or college transcript, letter of reference, essay, application. Scholarships: yes. Loans: yes.

CONTACT: Director of Admissions, New England Culinary Institute at H. Lavity Stoutt CC, PO Box 3097, Road Town, Tortola, British Virgin Islands; 284-494-4994, Fax 284-494-4996, E-mail neci@HLSCC.edu.vg, URL http://www.hlscc.edu.vg.

2

Recreational Programs

ALABAMA

COOK'S GARDEN
Mobile
Sponsor: Restaurant. Programs: Series of hands-on & demo classes that cover a variety of topics. Established: 1970. Class/group size: 25 demo, 14 hands-on. 4 programs/yr. Facilities: Restaurant kitchen. Also featured: Full-service catering, culinary tours.
FACULTY: Local & guest chefs.
COSTS: $35-$85/class.
CONTACT: Priscilla Gold-Darby, CCP, Owner/Director, Cook's Garden, 306 Cottage Hill Rd., Mobile, AL 36606; 251-476-6184, Fax 251-432-2637.

CULINARD – THE CULINARY INSTITUTE OF VIRGINIA COLLEGE
Birmingham   *(See also page 1) (See display ad page 3)*
Sponsor: Private, proprietary institution of higher education. Programs: Series of programs, weekend & 1-day events on intermediate to advanced topics that include cooking, baking, wine appreciation. Established: 2000. Facilities: 7 instructional kitchens, full-service restaurant, full-service bakery, 10 lecture facilities.
FACULTY: Faculty selected for academic qualifications & real world business experience.
CONTACT: Toni Bishop, Receptionist, CULINARD The Culinary Institute of Virginia College, 195 Vulcan Rd., Birmingham, AL 35209; 205-271-8228, 877-429-CHEF (2433), Fax 205-271-8229, tbishop@vc.edu, www.culinard.com.

ARIZONA

ANDYFOOD, A CULINARY STUDIO
Scottsdale
Sponsor: Private school. Programs: Hands-on & demo classes, cooking class parties, corporate teambuilding classes. Established: 2003. Class/group size: 16 hands-on, 36 demo. 250+ programs/yr. Facilities: 1500-sq-ft space with Viking appliances & John Boos butcher block/steel work surfaces. Outdoor patio area. Also featured: Kids' & teens' summer cooking camps.
FACULTY: Primary instructor is Chef/Owner Andy Broder, honors graduate of Scottsdale Culinary Institute; part-time instructor Chris Green, graduate L'Academie de Cuisine; guest chefs.
COSTS: $50-$65/hands-on class, $25-$60/demo.
CONTACT: Andy Broder, AndyFood, A Culinary Studio, 7000 E. Shea Blvd., #1740, Scottsdale, AZ 85254; 480-951-2400, Fax 602-532-7271, Info@andyfood.com, www.andyfood.com/home.html.

THE BISBEE COOKING SCHOOL
Bisbee
Sponsor: Culinary professional. Programs: Hands-on half-day classes in classical & regional cuisines including New Southwest, Cajun, Provincial French. Established: 2001. Class/group size: 14 demo, 6 hands-on. 100+ programs/yr. Also featured: Wine appreciation classes, garden tours.
FACULTY: Helen Saul, former restaurant owner/chef, college culinary instructor, menu & wine advisor. She has trained with Paul Prudhomme & Marcella Hazan.
COSTS: $35-$40/class.
CONTACT: Helen Saul, Owner/chef, The Bisbee Cooking School, Box 541, Bisbee, AZ 85603; 520-432-3882, bisbeecookingschool@yahoo.com, www.geocities.com/bisbeecookingschool.

COOKING WITH CLASS, LTD.
Scottsdale
Sponsor: Private cooking school. Programs: Participation & demo cooking classes based on 3- or 4-course menus. Established: 1999. Class/group size: 16 hands-on, 24 demo. 250+ programs/yr.

Facilities: 1,900-sq-ft teaching facility with ~900-ft kitchen & 600-sq-ft dining area. Features Dacor professional style equipment. Also featured: Custom cooking parties, cooking clubs, corporate team building, cooking camp for kids, spouse programs, gift certificates.

FACULTY: Three full-time instructors: Beth Cole, Deb DeBrino, Maggie Thomasson, graduates of the Scottsdale Culinary Institute & members of the IACP.

COSTS: Average $65/participation class. Includes snack, beverages & 3- or 4-course meal.

CONTACT: Beth Cole, Director, Cooking with Class, Ltd., 14202 N. Scottsdale Rd., Suite 100, Scottsdale, AZ 85254; 480-607-7474, Fax 480-659-6821, info@cookingwithclass.com, www.cookingwithclass.com.

CULINARY CONCEPTS
Tucson

Sponsor: Cooking school & retail kitchenware store. Programs: Participation classes include a 9-wks certificate course, series for youngsters, dinner workshops, celebrity & local chefs. Established: 1994. Class/group size: 25 hands-on/40 demo. 400+ programs/yr. Facilities: 900-sq-ft teaching kitchen with 14 gas burners, 4 ovens, 2 kitchen aids, 4 cuisinart & 9 work tables. Also featured: Wine appreciation, private classes, bridal showers, corporate parties, bimonthly Fri. luncheons, team-building programs.

FACULTY: Proprietor Judith Berger, CCP; Marilyn Davison, CCP; Marianne Bane, CCP. Each 20+ yrs culinary experience. Suzan Gross studied at Natural Gourmet Institute.

COSTS: $45-$65/class.

CONTACT: Judith B. Berger, CCP, Owner/Founder, Culinary Concepts, 2930 N. Swan, #126, Tucson, AZ 85712; 520-321-0968, Fax 520-321-0375, culinaryconcept@theriver.com, www.culinaryconcepts.net. Maggie Dearborn.

ELDERWOOD, THE ART OF COOKING
Scottsdale

Sponsor: Culinary professional. Programs: Personalized demo & hands-on cooking classes for individuals or small groups. Culinary tours & week-long cooking classes in Europe. Established: 1996. Class/group size: 3-15. 6 programs/yr. Facilities: European kitchens. Personalized instruction in student's home. Also featured: Group classes, private instruction.

FACULTY: Founder Debbie J. Elder, associated with the culinary arts since 1980, planning meal functions, catered events, & group travel. Guest chefs from around the world.

COSTS: $55+/class. Tour costs vary.

CONTACT: Ms. Debbie J. Elder, CMP, Founder, Elderwood, the Art of Cooking, 9455 E. Raintree Drive, #2030, Scottsdale, AZ 85260; 480-551-9769, Fax 480-551-9603, debbiejelder@msn.com.

GANACHE THIS
Scottsdale

Sponsor: Wholesale bakery. Programs: Hands-on chocolate & dessert classes. Established: 2001. Class/group size: 10-20. 50 programs/yr. Facilities: Wholesale industrial bake shop.

FACULTY: Pastry chef Judy Palmer, a CIA honors graduate with 27 yrs experience, is Coordinating Pastry Chef at Cannes Film Festival & formerly instructor of Advanced Pastry Arts at SCI.

COSTS: $40-$50/class. Group & series discounts available.

CONTACT: Lorin or Judy, Ganache This, 2951 N. Scottsdale Rd., Scottsdale, AZ 85251; 480-947-6503, Fax 480-941-3886, ganachethis@qwest.net, www.GanacheThis.com.

THE HOUSE OF RICE STORE
Scottsdale

Sponsor: Retail store & school. Programs: Single-session participation classes. Established: 1977. Class/group size: 13. 130 programs/yr. Facilities: Kitchen with large U-shaped counter. Also featured: Private group classes.

FACULTY: Owner Kiyoko Goldhardt, Chau Liaw, Chef Santos Villarico (Scottsdale Culinary Inst), Salma Dutta O'Brien (Salma's Curry Club).

COSTS: $25-$45/class.

CONTACT: Kiyoko Goldhardt, Owner, The House of Rice Store, 3221 N. Hayden Rd., Scottsdale, AZ 85251; 480-949-9681/480-947-6698, Fax 480-947-0889, info@houserice.com, www.houserice.com.

LES GOURMETTES COOKING SCHOOL
Phoenix

Sponsor: Private school. Programs: Demo classes & series. Established: 1982. Class/group size: 15. 40-50 programs/yr. Facilities: Private home in central Phoenix. Also featured: Culinary travel.

FACULTY: School proprietor Barbara Fenzl, CCP, studied at Le Cordon Bleu & Ecole Lenotre. Guest instructors included Giuliano Bugialli, Hugh Carpenter, Lydie Marshall, Jacques Pepin, Anne Willan.

COSTS: $50-$125/class.

CONTACT: Barbara Fenzl, Owner, Les Gourmettes Cooking School, 6610 N. Central Ave., Phoenix, AZ 85012; 602-240-6767, Fax 602-266-2706, barbara.fenzl@cox.net.

LES PETITES GOURMETTES CHILDREN'S COOKING SCHOOL
Scottsdale

Sponsor: Culinary professional Linda Hopkins. Programs: 4- & 5-day hands-on courses for youngsters ages 8-17. Established: 1994. Class/group size: 10-12. 14-20 programs/yr. Facilities: Home kitchen.

FACULTY: Linda Hopkins has assisted for 15 yrs at Les Gourmettes in Phoenix & worked with such professionals as Jacques Pepin, Emeril Lagasse, Martin Yan.

COSTS: $140/4 days, $175/5 days.

CONTACT: Linda Hopkins, Owner/Teacher, Les Petites Gourmettes Children's Cooking School, 12007 N. 62nd Pl., Scottsdale, AZ 85254; 480-991-7648, Fax 480-991-4516, LPGourmett@aol.com, www.lespetitesgourmettes.com.

ONE MEAL AT A TIME
Phoenix, East Valley, West Valley

Sponsor: Private school. Programs: Private & group hands-on lessons, theme parties for special occasions, food & wine pairing. Established: 2003. Class/group size: 1-40. Facilities: Client's home kitchen.

FACULTY: Stacy Patel, graduate of Scottsdale Culinary Institute.

COSTS: $75-150/private class, $40+/group class.

CONTACT: Stacy Patel, Chef/Owner, One Meal At A Time, Chandler, AZ; 480-664-3545, stacy@OneMealAtATime.com, www.OneMealAtATime.com.

SWEET BASIL GOURMETWARE & COOKING SCHOOL
Scottsdale

Sponsor: Cookware store. Programs: Demo classes & 1- to 3-session participation courses. Established: 1993. Class/group size: 14 hands-on/26 demo. 250 programs/yr. Facilities: 600-sq-ft kitchen with 6 workspaces, gas & electric appliances. Also featured: Field trips to herbfarms & other food related sites.

FACULTY: 6 instructors include Amy Barnes, Chris Green, Linda Hunt-Smith, Jennifer Russo, Marcia Saldin, Ashly Young; local guest chefs.

COSTS: $20-$120/course.

CONTACT: Martha Sullivan, Owner, Sweet Basil Gourmetware & Cooking School, 10749 N. Scottsdale Rd., #101, Scottsdale, AZ 85260; 480-596-5628, Fax 480-367-1722, sweetbasil@sweetbasilgourmet.com, www.sweetbasilgourmet.com.

THAI GOURMET HOUSE COOKING SCHOOL
Scottsdale

Sponsor: Private specialty culinary school. Programs: Thai Cuisine & Basic Cooking Fundamentals & Technique. Established: 1989. Class/group size: 1-8. Facilities: Fully-equipped professional classroom kitchen with overhead mirror, individual work stations, & traditional outdoor Thai-style cooking facilities. Also featured: Specialty class: A simple & practical approach to healthy cooking for a modern lifestyle.

FACULTY: Director Praparat Sturlin, culinary professional, won national culinary competitions in Thailand & interned at The Oriental, The Ambassador & The Hyatt Regency hotels in Bangkok.
COSTS: $45-$195.
CONTACT: Praparat Sturlin, Director, Thai Gourmet House Cooking School, 8313 E. Monterosa St., Scottsdale, AZ 85251; 480-947-1258, thaigourmethouse@cox.net, www.thaigourmethouse.com.

ARKANSAS

COTTAGE INN RESTAURANT
Eureka Springs
Sponsor: Restaurant specializing in Mediterranean cuisine. Programs: 3-day hands-on cooking classes that cover the basics of a professional kitchen. Established: 1986. Class/group size: 8. 10 programs/yr. Facilities: Fully-equipped kitchen of a 100-seat operating restaurant. Work space for each student. Also featured: Art galleries, walking trails, antique shops, spa facilities, massage therapy.
FACULTY: Linda Hager, restaurant owner & chef for 20 years, studied in Paris & Madrid, apprenticed in kitchens in Austria & Crete.
COSTS: $350 includes 5 meals; optional onsite lodging available.
CONTACT: Linda Hager, Cottage Inn Restaurant, 450 West Van Buren, Eureka Springs, AR 72632; 501-253-5282, Fax 501-253-5232, lthager@ipa.net, www.cottageinneurekaspgs.com.

CALIFORNIA

ACADEMY OF COOKING – BEVERLY HILLS
Beverly Hills
Sponsor: Meredith's Marvelous Morsels catering firm. Programs: Participation classes. Established: 1990. Class/group size: 10. 12 programs/yr. Facilities: Restaurant kitchen with 10 work stations, or student's home (min 8 students). Also featured: Children's, private, corporate & group classes, culinary tours in southern California.
FACULTY: Meredith Jo Mischen studied with chefs at New York's Plaza & Waldorf-Astoria Hotels.
COSTS: $65/class.
CONTACT: Meredith Jo Mischen, Director, Academy of Cooking - Beverly Hills, 400 S. Beverly Dr., #214, Beverly Hills, CA 90212; 310-284-4940, meredith@acbh.com.

AMY MALONE SCHOOL OF CAKE DECORATING
La Mesa
Sponsor: Cake decorating professional Amy Malone. Programs: Morning & evening participation & demo classes. Established: 1977. Class/group size: 14 hands-on/30 demo. 150+ programs/yr.
FACULTY: Amy Malone is a graduate of the Wilton, Betty Newman May, John McNamara, & Frances Kuyper schools of cake decorating & was guest instructor at L'Academie de Cuisine.
COSTS: $15-$75/class.
CONTACT: Amy Malone, Amy Malone School of Cake Decorating, 4212 Camino Alegre, La Mesa, CA 91941; 619-660-1900, amymalone@aol.com, www.amymalone.com.

APRON STRINGS
San Francisco
Sponsor: Private school. Programs: Hands-on cooking classes for children, ages 10+. Established: 2001. Class/group size: 12. ~50 programs/yr. Facilities: Professional kitchen. Also featured: Birthday cooking parties, private lessons, culinary camps.
FACULTY: Chef Roberta DesBouillons, a CIA graduate with 20+ yrs experience.
COSTS: $55-$65/class, $325 for culinary camps.
CONTACT: Roberta DesBouillons, Owner, Apron Strings, Box 460824, San Francisco, CA 94146; 415-550-7976, Fax 415-648-6384, rdesbouillons@mindspring.com, www.apronstringssf.com.

THE ART OF THAI COOKING
Oakland; Thailand

Sponsor: Private cooking school. Programs: 4-wk, 4-session beginner, intermediate & advanced participation courses. 1-wk beginner & advanced intensive classes for out-of-towners. Established: 1985. Class/group size: 12. 20 programs/yr. Facilities: Fully-equipped private kitchen. Also featured: Private instruction, classes in private homes, food & cultural tours to Thailand.

FACULTY: Kasma Loha-unchit, a native of Thailand, has taught Thai cooking since 1985. She is author of 2 Thai cookbooks, including It Rains Fishes, winner of IACP award for Best International Cookbook.

COSTS: $150 for 4-wk, 4-session series. $500for wk-long intensives. $2,650-$3,450 for 18- to 27-day tours of Thailand, including airfare, meals, & lodging.

CONTACT: Kasma Loha-unchit, The Art of Thai Cooking, P.O. Box 21165, Oakland, CA 94620; 510-655-8900, kasma@thaifoodandtravel.com, www.thaifoodandtravel.com/.

AYURVEDIC COOKING & NUTRITION
Carlsbad

Sponsor: Organization created by Deepak Chopra, M.D. Programs: A holistic system of natural healing with emphasis on creating & cooking a well-balanced, personalized diet. 3 programs/yr.

FACULTY: Leanne Backer, Executive Chef of The Chopra Center for Well Being.

CONTACT: Leanne Backer, Executive Chef, The Chopra Center at La Costa Resort, 2013 Costa Del Mar Rd., Carlsbad, CA 92009; 888-424-6772, 760-931-7558, Fax 760-931-7563, info@chopra.com.

BE GOURMET!
Los Angeles

Sponsor: Private school. Programs: Participation classes, wine & food tastings, dessert making. Established: 2000. Class/group size: 2-8. Daily programs/yr. Facilities: Fully-equipped home kitchen. Also featured: Demo & participation cooking parties, catering.

FACULTY: Tim Ross, CAP graduate from Paris' Ecole Superieur de Cuisine Francaise. Catering & restaurant experience in the U.S. & France.

COSTS: $50-65/class.

CONTACT: Tim Ross, Chef, Be Gourmet!, 2419 Tesla Terrace, Los Angeles, CA 90039; 323-610-1082, begourmet@att.net, begourmet.home.att.net.

BERINGER MASTER SERIES ON FOOD & WINE
Napa Valley; Argentina; Australia; Chile; France; Italy; New Zealand; Spain

Sponsor: Beringer Vineyards. Programs: 1-day to 2-week wine & cooking programs. Established: 2001. Class/group size: 10-14. 10 programs/yr. Facilities: Private kitchens, cellars, & vintner homes of Beringer & other Napa Valley wineries. Also featured: Garden tours, croquet, spa treatments, wine- & food-related excursions.

FACULTY: Well-known chefs & vintners.

COSTS: Napa Valley programs from $175/1 day to $3,150/6 days; intl programs begin at $5,500.

CONTACT: David Mitchel, Director of Operations, Beringer Master Series on Food & Wine, PO Box 111, St. Helena, CA 94574; 707-967-4451, Fax 707-963-5521, david.mitchel@beringerblass.com, www.beringer.com.

BORDER GRILL
Los Angeles

Sponsor: Restaurant. Programs: Quarterly demo classes. Established: 1992. Class/group size: 65.

FACULTY: Susan Feniger & Mary Sue Milliken, chef-owners of the Border Grill & authors of City Cuisine, Mesa Mexicana, Cantina, & Cooking With Too Hot Tamales.

COSTS: $75/session includes full lunch & bar.

CONTACT: Jackee Ermansons, General Manager, Border Grill, 1445 Fourth St., Santa Monica, CA 90401; 310-451-1655, Fax 310-394-2049, bgsmman@bordergrill.com, www.bordergrill.com.

BRISTOL FARMS COOKING SCHOOL
Manhattan Beach

Sponsor: Gourmet specialty foods & cookware store. Programs: 1- to 6-session demo & participation courses. Established: 1985. Class/group size: 20 hands-on/40 demo. 200+ programs/yr. Facilities: Kitchen with 6-burner stove, grill, oven. Also featured: Children's & private classes, field trips, tours.
FACULTY: Director Grace-Marie Johnston. Guest instructors have included Graham Kerr, Paul Prudhomme, Stephen Pyles, Patricia Wells, Jacques Pepin, Tommy Tang.
COSTS: $40-$55/session.
CONTACT: Grace-Marie Johnston, Cooking School Director, Bristol Farms Cooking School, 1570 Rosecrans Ave., Manhattan Beach, CA 90266; 310-233-4752, gmjohnston@bristolfarms.com, www.bristolfarms.com/cookingschool/index.html.

CAKEBREAD CELLARS
Napa Valley

Sponsor: Winery. Programs: Demo & participation classes. Established: 1973. Class/group size: Demo 25, hands-on 16. 5 programs/yr. Facilities: Winery house & outdoor kitchens.
FACULTY: Resident chefs Brian Streeter & Richard Haake, both New England Culinary Institute graduates; guest chefs.
COSTS: $170/person.
CONTACT: George Knopp, Winery Events Coordinator, Cakebread Cellars, 8300 St. Helena Hwy., Box 216, Rutherford, CA 0; 707-963-5221 x230, Fax 707-963-1034, knopp@cakebread.com, www.cakebread.com. Additional contact: Pat Kincaid.

CALIFORNIA CULINARY ACADEMY
San Francisco   *(See also page 14) (See display ad page 13)*

Sponsor: Culinary career academy. Programs: Single topic culinary & baking & pastry classes, 5-part essentials series, food & wine pairing seminars, specialty & seasonal classes. Established: 1977. Class/group size: 15. 200+ programs/yr. Facilities: Commercial kitchens used for professional programs. Also featured: Private cooking classes.
FACULTY: Academy chef instructors, industry professionals.
COSTS: $175/class, $625 for essentials series.
CONTACT: Weekend Gourmet at the Academy, California Culinary Academy, 625 Polk St., San Francisco, CA 94102; 415-354-9198, Fax 415-292-8290, weekends@baychef.com, www.baychef.com.

CALIFORNIA SUSHI ACADEMY
Venice

Sponsor: Private school. Programs: Weekend 1-day sushi classes that include sushi rice, California, tuna & rainbow rolls, tempura, nigiri sushi, fish cutting. Professional certification programs. Established: 7. Class/group size: 14 max. 100+ programs/yr. Also featured: Private instruction, catering, business consultation.
COSTS: $80-$85/day.
CONTACT: Danielle Chase, Director, California Sushi Academy, 1611 Pacific Ave., Venice, CA 90291; 310-581-0213, Fax 310-306-2605, email@sushi-academy.com, www.sushi-academy.com.

CHEF ERIC'S CULINARY CLASSROOM
Los Angeles

Sponsor: Private professional & recreational cooking school. Programs: Participation courses & classes that cover basic to advanced cooking & individual topics. Established: 2003. Class/group size: 10-12. 200 programs/yr. Facilities: Classroom with display mirror area, professionally designed kitchen, dining area. Also featured: Parties, corporate team-building, private instruction.
FACULTY: Owner Chef Eric Jacques Crowley, an honors graduate of The CIA, taught at the Epicurean in LA & was a head chef with the catering division of Patina Restaurant Group. Chef Julia Stein has 3 years of culinary training.

Costs: $75/class, $250 for 4-session Culinary Basics course.
Contact: Eric Crowley, President, Chef Eric's Culinary Classroom, 2366 Pelham Ave., Los Angeles, CA 90064; 310-470-2640, Fax 310-470-2642, cheferic@culinaryclassroom.com, www.CulinaryClassroom.com.

CHEZ CHERIE COOKING CLASSES
La Canada (Los Angeles)
Sponsor: Private school & cooking supply store. Programs: Demo & hands-on classes & series. Established: 1999. Class/group size: 5-25. 36 programs/yr. Facilities: Full commercial demo kitchen, dining area, patio. Also featured: Field trips to gourmet purveyors, food related travel, corporate culinary team-building programs.
Faculty: Chef/owner Cherie Mercer Twohy, CCP, is a member of the IACP, AIWF & Women Chefs & Restaurateurs.
Costs: $50-$65/class.
Contact: Cherie Twohy, Chef-Owner, Chez Cherie Cooking Classes, 1401 Foothill Blvd., La Canada, CA 91011; 818-952-7217, cherie@chezcherie.com, www.chezcherie.com.

COOKS & BOOKS COOKING SCHOOL
Danville
Sponsor: Cooking school with chef's tools, chef wear, cookbooks, wine shop. Programs: Demo & participation courses, 4- & 5-part hands-on series, single topic classes, corporate team building. Established: 1991. Class/group size: 10-30. 100+ programs/yr. Facilities: 1,600-sq-ft teaching area & 600-sq-ft commercial kitchen. Also featured: Local shopping excursions, culinary tours.
Faculty: In-house instructors D.J. Rae, CCA graduate & Kent Nielsen. Other guest chef/instructors, culinary teachers & cookbook authors.
Costs: $45-$65/class.
Contact: D.J. Rae, Chef/Owner, Cooks & Books & Corks, 148 E. Prospect Ave., Danville, CA 94526; 925-831-0708, Fax 925-831-0741, ckbkcrk@silcon.com, www.cooksbookscorks.com.

COOKSONOMA
Healdsburg
Sponsor: Private school. Programs: Hands-on 1- to 4-day cooking courses with each day's session at a different winery or restaurant. Established: 2003. Class/group size: 10. 8 programs/yr. Facilities: Winery & restaurant cooking facilities. Also featured: Culinary travel programs to Italy.
Faculty: Gloria Demaria, who has studied cooking in Italy for 15 years; guest chefs.
Costs: $120/1 day, $875/3 days, $1,000/4 days.
Contact: Kathy Taylor, President, CookSonoma, 967 Jasmine Ct., Healdsburg, CA 94118; 707-473-9622, Fax 707-473-9642, kathy@cooksonoma.com, www.cooksonoma.com. gloria@cooksonoma.com.

COPIA: THE AMERICAN CENTER FOR WINE, FOOD & THE ARTS
Napa Valley
Sponsor: Cultural center devoted to wine, food & the arts in American culture. Programs: 60- to 90-min classes that cover wine & food pairing, ethnic & regional foods, seasonal cuisine, specific topics. Established: 2001. Class/group size: 50+. 100+ programs/yr. Facilities: 74-seat demo theatre with four 40' plasma monitors, commercial kitchen, 1,000-sq-ft vintage room for wine study. Also featured: Continuing ed & certificate courses in conjunction with the Univ of California-Davis & England's Wine & Spirit Education Trust.
Faculty: Chefs, authors, producers & farmers. Culinary Program Mgr Brigid Callinan, a graduate of New England Culinary Inst, co-authored the Mustards Grill Cookbook. Curator of wine is Peter Marks, MW.
Contact: Brigid Callinan, Culinary Program Manager, Copia: The American Center for Wine, Food & the Arts, 500 First St., Napa, CA 94559; 707-265-5929, 800-888-51-COPIA, bcallinan@copia.org, www.copia.org.

CULINARY ADVENTURES COOKING SCHOOL
San Diego
Sponsor: Culinary professional Janet Burgess. Programs: Theme classes & hands-on workshops for holidays, parties, gourmet groups; lower fat conversion, healthy cooking, food history. Established: 1998. Class/group size: 12 max. 40-50 programs/yr. Facilities: Private home or on-site. Also featured: Kids classes, private instruction, visits to markets, ethnic food producers & specialty shops.
FACULTY: Janet Burgess, cooking teacher, lecturer, food consultant, IACP-member, has attended cooking schools in Tuscany & the CIA, Greystone.
COSTS: $38-$60/class.
CONTACT: Janet Burgess, Owner/Teacher, Culinary Adventures Cooking School, PO Box 19601, San Diego, CA 92159; 619-589-6623, Fax 619-589-6623, jburgess911@cox.net.

THE CULINARY INSTITUTE OF AMERICA AT GREYSTONE
Napa Valley *(See also page 18, 90, 224) (See display ad page 89)*
Sponsor: The CIA's Greystone campus, a center for continuing education of food & wine professionals. Programs: Workshops for culinary professionals. Established: 1995. Class/group size: 18. 35 programs/yr. Facilities: 15,000-sq-ft open teaching kitchens. Also featured: Travel programs & conferences.
FACULTY: The CIA's chefs & instructors.
COSTS: Tuition ranges from $850/30 hrs of instruction to $5,000/travel program.
CONTACT: Susan Cussen, Director of Marketing, CE, The Culinary Institute of America, Continuing Education Dept., 2555 Main St., St. Helena, CA 94574; 800-888-7850, Fax 845-451-1066, ciachef@culinary.edu, www.ciachef.edu/.

DR. ALAN YOUNG WINE PROGRAMS
San Francisco
Sponsor: Wine professional. Programs: Home study programs, 3-day seminars & study tours. Established: 1975. Class/group size: 25.
FACULTY: Dr. Alan Young is an Australian wine consultant & author of 18 books, intl. faculty.
COSTS: Home study $197, 101 Secrets of Wine Tasting $120.
CONTACT: Dr. Alan Young, President, International Wine Academy, 38 Portola Dr., San Francisco, CA 0; 415-641-4767, 800-345-8466, Fax 415-641-7348, alanyoung@wineacademy.com, www.wineacademy.com.

DRAEGER'S COOKING SCHOOL
Menlo Park & San Mateo
Sponsor: Draeger's Market Place. Programs: Demo & hands-on classes on American & intl cuisines. Established: 1991. Class/group size: 16-40. 100+ programs/yr. Facilities: Professional kitchens with a-v equipment, Dacor, Subzero, Wolf ranges. Also featured: Wine tastings.
FACULTY: Culinary school graduates, certified chefs, cookbook authors.
COSTS: $35+/class.
CONTACT: Joshua Lent, Office & Online Administrator, Draeger's Cooking School, 222 E. Fourth Ave, San Mateo, CA 94401; 650-685-3704, Fax 650-685-3790, cookingschool@draegers.com, www.draegers.com/DCS/index.html.

EPICUREAN SCHOOL OF CULINARY ARTS
Los Angeles
Sponsor: Private school. Programs: Participation classes in fish, chicken, & other specialties. Established: 1985. Class/group size: 15. Facilities: Teaching kitchen with 5 work stations.
FACULTY: CIA & CCA graduates.
COSTS: $65/class.
CONTACT: Staci Jenkins, Epicurean School of Culinary Arts, 8759 Melrose Ave., Los Angeles, CA 90069; 310-659-5990, Fax 310-659-0302, epicurean5@aol.com, www.epicureanschool.com.

ERNA'S ELDERBERRY HOUSE COOKING SCHOOL
Oakhurst

Sponsor: The Château du Sureau (Estate by the Elderberries). Programs: Saturday classes & 3-day participation programs featuring 8 hrs daily cooking instruction devoted to preparing a 6-course menu. Wine pairing instruction. Established: 1984. Class/group size: 12. 7 programs/yr. Facilities: Erna's Elderberry Restaurant's full commercial kitchen, herb garden, local organic vegetable farm. Also featured: Bass fishing, golf, hiking, tennis, horseback riding, river rafting, rock climbing, visits to Yosemite Natl Park.

FACULTY: Chef-Proprietor Erna Kubin-Clanin has 30 yrs of culinary & restaurant experience together with Executive Chef James Overbaugh.

COSTS: $1,250 includes lunch & dinner. Ten 2-person guest rooms at Château du Sureau range from $350-$550 including breakfast. 2-room villa $2,800/night.

CONTACT: Erna Kubin-Clanin, Proprietor, Elderberry House Cooking School, 48688 Victoria Ln., Box 2413, Oakhurst, CA 93644; 559-683-6800, Fax 559-683-0800, chateau@chateausureau.com, www.elderberryhouse.com.

FRED McMILLIN WINE COURSES
San Francisco

Sponsor: Wine professional. Programs: Twelve 3-session courses/yr. Est: 1965. Class/group size: 15.

FACULTY: Northern California editor for American Wine on the Web, 2 degrees in chemical engineering, writes for 3 wine publications.

COSTS: $80-$100/course.

CONTACT: Fred McMillin, 2121 Broadway, San Francisco, CA 94115; 415-563-5712, Fax 415-567-4468.

GOURMET RETREATS AT CASALANA
Napa Valley

Sponsor: Private school. Programs: Single sessions, week-end retreats, & 3- & 5-day courses that cover a variety of topics, including essential skills, ethnic & seasonal cuisines, desserts, food & wine pairing. Established: 1996. Class/group size: Demo 20, hands-on 8. 40-50 programs/yr. Facilities: Mediterranean style B&B with a professionally equipped kitchen, over a half acre of fruit & vegetable gardens. Also featured: Visits to specialty & farmers' markets, food producers, winemaker.

FACULTY: Gourmet Retreats owner Lana Richardson, an honor graduate of the California Culinary Academy with catering experience; guest chefs & authors.

COSTS: From $60/3-hr session to $725/5-day course, includes up to 36 hrs of instruction & meals.

CONTACT: Lana Richardson, Gourmet Retreats at CasaLana, 1316 S. Oak St., Calistoga, CA 94515; 877-968-2665, 707-942-0615, Fax 707-942-0204, lana@casalana.com, www.GourmetRetreats.com.

THE GREAT CHEFS AT ROBERT MONDAVI WINERY
Oakville

Sponsor: Robert Mondavi Winery. Programs: 3-day weekend programs (followed by 1-day programs) that feature cooking demos by noted chefs, wine seminars, private winery tours, theme lunches & dinners. Established: 1976. Class/group size: 26. 2 programs/yr.

FACULTY: Nationally- & internationally-known chefs.

COSTS: $2,000 ($150 single supplement) for 3-day program includes lodging, lunches & dinners; $225 for 1-day programs.

CONTACT: Valerie Varachi, Event Coordinator, The Great Chefs at Robert Mondavi Winery, P.O. Box 106, Oakville, CA 94562; 707-968-2100, Fax 707-968-2174, valerie.varachi@robertmondavi.com, www.robertmondavi.com.

GREAT NEWS!
San Diego

Sponsor: Cookware store & cooking school. Programs: Hands-on & demo classes in basic techniques, ethnic cooking, individual subjects. Established: 1977. Class/group size: 32 hands-on, 52

demo. 500+ programs/yr. Facilities: Teaching kitchen with 7 big-screen TV monitors. Also featured: Market visits.
FACULTY: Local professional teachers & restaurant chefs.
COSTS: $29-$69/class.
CONTACT: Allison Sherwood, Cooking School Director, Great News!, 1788 Garnet, San Diego, CA 92109; 858-270-1582, ext. 3, Fax 858-270-6815, allison@great-news.com, www.great-news.com. Ron Eisenberg, owner, Shop Online at www.discountcooking.com.

HUGH CARPENTER'S CAMP NAPA CULINARY
Oakville, Napa Valley
Sponsor: Chef & cookbook author Hugh Carpenter. Programs: 6-day food & wine tours that feature participation classes. Established: 1992. Class/group size: 18. 8 programs/yr. Facilities: Cakebread Cellars Winery kitchen. Also featured: Dining in fine restaurants, private winery tours, seminars on food & wine pairing, croquet tournament. Hot-air ballooning, Calistoga spa, golf, tennis.
FACULTY: Hugh Carpenter is author of 13 cookbooks, including Pacific Flavors, Great Ribs, Fast Appetizers, Fast Entrees.
COSTS: $1,623, includes meals & planned itinerary. A list of recommended lodging is available.
CONTACT: Hugh Carpenter, Hugh Carpenter's Camp Napa Culinary, P.O. Box 114, Oakville, CA 94562; 707-944-9112, 888-999-4844, Fax 707-944-2221, hugh@hughcarpenter.com, www.hughcarpenter.com.

INGREDIENTS COOKING/LIFESTYLE SCHOOL
Danville
Sponsor: Cooking school sponsored by grocery market group. Programs: Hands-on classes that focus on professional techniques, guest chef demos, lunch sessions, children's classes. Established: 3. Class/group size: 16 hands-on, 36 demo. 160 + programs/yr. Facilities: Commercial kitchen with granite work station, cameras & mirror. Also featured: Private classes, winemaker dinners.
FACULTY: Bernhardt Chirent, executive chef of San Francisco's Fairmont Hotel, chef/instructor at Diablo Valley College; Bill Wavrin, executive chef of the Savory Inn & Cooking School in Vail, aurhor of Rancho la Puerta Cookbook.Guests chefs.
COSTS: $35-$95.
CONTACT: Karen Alvarez, Director, Ingredients Cooking/Lifestyle School, 345 Railroad Ave., Danville, CA 94526; 925-314-4362, Fax 925-855-8934, karen.alvarez@andronicos.com, www.andronicos.com.

THE JEAN BRADY COOKING SCHOOL
Santa Monica
Sponsor: Culinary professional Jean Brady. Programs: 7-session demo series; guest chef, hands-on & children's classes; 1-wk summer cooking camps for kids. Established: 1973. Class/group size: 12. Facilities: Commercially-equipped home kitchen featured in Bon Appétit. Local guest chefs' restaurant kitchens. Also featured: Culinary tours to Europe, local tours with ethnic experts, market visits, private group classes, business team building.
FACULTY: Jean Brady studied with Lydie Marshall, Jacques Pepin & Paula Wolfert & attended the Cordon Bleu & La Varenne. Guest & local chefs.
COSTS: Guest chef classes $60-$90. 7-session series $340.
CONTACT: Jean Brady, The Jean Brady Cooking School, 680 Brooktree Rd., Santa Monica, CA 90402; 310-454-4220, bradyrustic@yahoo.com.

LA BUONA FORCHETTA
Guerneville
Sponsor: Applewood Inn. Programs: Mini-culinary vacations offering demo & hands-on classes with field trips to Sonoma County farms, wineries & farmers markets. Dining & lodging at the inn. Established: 2003. Class/group size: 12 max. 12 programs/yr. Facilities: Kitchen & dining rooms of the inn's historic Belden House. Also featured: Hot-air balloon trips, massage, horseback

riding, canoeing, kayaking.

FACULTY: Chef/instructor Gabrielle Dery, Executive Chef of the Restaurant at Applewood. Guest chefs, vintners, farmers, cheese makers.

CONTACT: Darryl Notter, Owner, La Buona Forchetta, 13555 Highway #116, Guerneville, CA 95446; 707-869-9093, Fax 707-869-9170, stay@applewoodinn.com, www.applewoodinn.com.

LA CUCINA MUGNAINI
Watsonville
Sponsor: Cooking school dedicated to the use of wood-fired ovens. Programs: Classes & demos on wood-burning oven basics. Topics range from seafood to bread-baking, Italian favorites to Asian fusion. Established: 1995. Class/group size: 32 demo, 16 hands-on. 75-100 programs/yr. Facilities: 1,000-sq-ft kitchen with 4 Italian wood-burning ovens. Also featured: Teambuilding, private parties, event planning, filming location.

FACULTY: In-house instructors experienced in the use of wood-fired ovens; visiting chef instructors.

COSTS: $50-$210, includes refreshments & tasting of foods prepared in class. Nearby lodging available.

CONTACT: La Cucina Mugnaini, Mugnaini Imports, 11 Hangar Way, Watsonville, CA 95076; 888- 887-7206 (toll free), 831-761-1767, Fax 831-728-5570, mugnaini@mugnaini.com, www.mugnaini.com.

LA FOOD WORKS
West Hollywood
Sponsor: Private culinary facility. Programs: Hands-on cooking & wine classes. Established: 2003. Class/group size: 12-40. Facilities: Professional kitchen with Thermador & Viking appliances, John Boos workstations & marble pastry station; dining area & garden patio. Also featured: Parties, team-building events, children's cooking camps.

FACULTY: Head Chef Robbie Robb. Co-owners are Tabitha Kenney & Janelle Dreyfuss.

COSTS: $75-$125/class, $155-$165/class with meal & wine, $45-$65/catered event with demo.

CONTACT: Tabitha Kenney, Co-Owner, LA Food Works, 9045 Nemo St., West Hollywood, CA 90405; 310-288-0100, Fax 310-288-0125, info@lafoodworks.com, www.lafoodworks.com.

LAGUNA CULINARY ARTS
Laguna Beach
Sponsor: Private school. Programs: Hands-on weekend, evening, full- & half-day classes for the home chef. Topics include smoking & grilling, entertaining, seafood, Italian, hors d'oeuvres, sauces, comfort food, vegetarian, sushi. Established: 2001. Class/group size: 10-12 hands-on. 350+ programs/yr. Facilities: Ocean-view teaching kitchen equipped with the latest appliances & designed for the home chef, outdoor deck & herb garden. Also featured: Team building events, wine tastings, private cooking parties, painting lessons.

FACULTY: 6 full-time & ~6 local guest chefs.

COSTS: $65-$75/evening class, $165-$385/1- to 3-day classes, $95-$395/weekend classes.

CONTACT: Megan Rainnie, Director of Sales & Marketing, Laguna Culinary Arts, 550 South Coast Hwy., #7, Laguna Beach, CA 92651; 949-494-0745, 888-288-0745, Fax 949-494-0136, megan@lagunaculinaryarts.com, www.lagunaculinaryarts.com.

LET'S GET COOKIN'
Westlake Village
Sponsor: Private school. Programs: 1- to 6-session demo & participation classes. Class/group size: 10-35. 150+ programs/yr. Facilities: 1,500-sq-ft combination demonstration/participation facilities, cookware store. Also featured: Classes for young people, day trips, travel abroad.

FACULTY: Includes cookbook authors & guest chefs.

COSTS: $50-$85/session ($30 for children's classes).

CONTACT: Phyllis Vaccarelli, Owner/Director, Let's Get Cookin', 4643 Lakeview Canyon Rd., Westlake Village, CA 91361; 818-991-3940, Fax 805-495-2554, lgcookin@aol.com, www.letsgetcookin.com.

MARIAN W. BALDY WINE PROGRAMS
Chico
Sponsor: University. Programs: 45-session 3-credit university course. Established: 1972. Class/group size: 190. 1 programs/yr. Also featured: Winemaking.
FACULTY: Marian W. Baldy, Ph.D. has a doctorate degree in genetics, winemaker, CWE, author of The University Wine Course, Chair of the Education Committee & Board of Examiners of SWE.
COSTS: $500/course.
CONTACT: Marian W. Baldy, Ph.D., California State University, First & Normal Sts., School of Agriculture, Chico, CA 0; 530-898-6250, Fax 530-898-5845, mbaldy@csuchico.edu, www.csuchico.edu/agr/faculty/Mbaldy.shtml.

THE MASTER CHEF SERIES AT MONARCH BEACH
Dana Point
Sponsor: Resort hotel. Programs: 4-day program includes demos, seminars, Martini class.
FACULTY: The hotel's executive chefs, guest chefs & culinary experts.
COSTS: $3,250 for two includes lodging, some meals.
CONTACT: Matt Kasa, Leisure Sales Specialist, The St. Regis Monarch Beach, One Monarch Beach Resort, Dana Point, CA 92677; 800-722-1543, www.stregismb.com/masters_at_monarch_beach.shtml.

MEADOWOOD FOOD & WINE PROGRAMS
St. Helena
Sponsor: Country resort. Programs: Cooking classes & farmer's market excursions, 2-day guest chef programs that include hands-on instruction, winery tours & tastings. Class/group size: ~10. Also featured: Special events & programs devoted to health & wellness, the arts, music, sports & nature. Tennis, golf, croquet.
FACULTY: John Thoreen, Meadowood's Wine Center Director for 15 yrs. Guest chefs include Patricia Wells, cooking teacher, restaurant critic of the International Herald Tribune & author of 8 cookbooks.
COSTS: 2-day guest chef program $4,500/couple, including lodging & some meals.
CONTACT: Ann Marie Conover, Meadowood Food & Wine Programs, 900 Meadowood Lane, St. Helena, CA 94574; 800-458-8080, 707-963-3646, Fax 707-963-3532, aconover@meadowood.com, www.meadowood.com.

MICHAEL A. AMOROSE WINE CLASSES
San Francisco
Sponsor: Wine professional. Programs: Wine tasting classes. 9 wines tasted/session. Price range $10-$40/bottle, current vintages. Established: 1974. Class/group size: 40-50. 25 programs/yr.
FACULTY: Michael Amorose is author of 10 books on wine.
COSTS: $25-$50/class.
CONTACT: Michael A. Amorose Wine Classes, 555 California St., #1700, San Francisco, CA 94104; 415-951-3377, Fax 415-248-2101, michael.amorose@ey.com.

MICHAEL R. BOTWIN WINE COURSES
San Luis Obispo
Sponsor: Wine professional. Programs: Three 5-session courses/yr (California wines). Two 6-session courses/yr (European wines). Established: 1973. Class/group size: 20.
FACULTY: Michael Botwin is a member of AWS, chairman of AWS Luis Obispo.
COSTS: $145/5-session course, $175/6-session course.
CONTACT: Michael R. Botwin, 2566 Santa Clara, San Luis Obispo, CA 93401; 805-543-1200.

NAPA VALLEY COOKING SCHOOL
St. Helena *(See also page 22) (See display ad page 23)*
Sponsor: College. Programs: 1- to 4-session demo & participation courses. Established: 1990. Class/group size: 12-28. Facilities: New kitchen with 18 burners, 4 ovens, demonstration counter, outdoor dining area. Also featured: Wine & food classes, farmer's market visits, catering seminars.

FACULTY: Guest chefs have included: Bruce Aidells, Hubert Keller, Michael Chiarello, Gary Danko, Carlo Middione, John Ash, & Jeremiah Tower.
COSTS: $50-$75/session.
CONTACT: Barbara Alexander, Exec. Chef, Napa Valley College, 1088 College Ave., St. Helena, CA 94574; 707-967-2930, Fax 707-967-2909, balexander@napavalley.edu, www.napavalley.edu/cookingschool/.

THE NEW SCHOOL OF COOKING
Los Angeles
Sponsor: Private school. Programs: Recreational participation classes, demo classes, kid's camp, part-time professional chef & baking programs. Established: 2000. Class/group size: 16. Facilities: 1,400-sq-ft professional kitchen classroom with demo area & hands-on student work area. Also featured: Wine & food pairing classes, private parties, corporate team building.
FACULTY: Karen Hillenburg, Carol Thompson & Tracy Callahan, CCA graduates; May Parich, CIA graduate; Jet Tila, Le Cordon Bleu graduate; Neelam Batra, Indian chef & cookbook author.
COSTS: $75/hands-on class, $325/wk kid's camp.
CONTACT: Anne Smith, Director, The New School of Cooking, 8690 Washington Blvd., Culver City, CA 90323; 310-842-9702, annesmith@newschoolofcooking.com, www.newschoolofcooking.com.

RAMEKINS SONOMA VALLEY CULINARY SCHOOL
Sonoma
Sponsor: Wine country cooking school, Bed & Breakfast, cookbook store, restaurant. Programs: Half day cooking & baking classes that include basic & general cooking instruction, ethnic & skill or ingredient specific sessions, seasonal menus; culinary team-building & cooking parties. Established: 1998. Class/group size: 36 demo, 18 hands-on. 375 programs/yr. Facilities: Two teaching kitchens with the latest equipment: one primarily demo with TVs, mirrors & residential equipment, the other a full-service commercial kitchen. Also featured: Private team-building & dinner-party classes; culinary tours to markets, food producers, & wineries; wedding reception & meeting space.
FACULTY: 100+ instructors including celebrity chefs, cookbook authors, local restaurant chefs, & other culinary professionals.
COSTS: Demos $38-$55, hands-on classes $55-$75.
CONTACT: Bob Nemerovski, Culinary Director, Ramekins Sonoma Valley Culinary School, 450 West Spain St., Sonoma, CA 95476; 707-933-0450 x3, Fax 707-933-0451, info@ramekins.com, www.ramekins.com.

RELISH CULINARY SCHOOL
Healdsburg
Sponsor: Home chefs Teresa Brooks & Donna del Rey. Programs: Mostly demonostration cooking & wine classes. Established: 2003. Class/group size: 12-45. ~60 programs/yr. Facilities: Wineries, art galleries, private homes. Also featured: Cooking parties, corporate team-building programs.
FACULTY: Restaurant & private chefs, cookbook authors, caterers, wine experts, food purveyors.
COSTS: $25-$100/class.
CONTACT: Donna del Rey, Co-Founder, Relish Culinary School, P.O. Box 933, Healdsburg, CA 95448; 707-431-9999, Fax 707-431-8446, info@relishculinary.com, www.relishculinary.com.

RUTA'S KITCHEN – REGIONAL INDIAN COOKING CLASSES
Oakland, Berkeley & San Francisco Bay Area
Sponsor: Culinary professional. Programs: Hands-on regional Indian cooking classes. Established: 2000. Class/group size: 12. Weekly programs/yr. Also featured: Culinary tours to India.
FACULTY: Ruta Kahate is also a culinary instructor at Sur La Table, Draeger's & Ramekins & a TV guest chef.
COSTS: $65/class, $170/3 classes, $80/weekend workshops. From $3,300/2 wk culinary tour to India.
CONTACT: Ruta Kahate, Chef, Ruta's Kitchen - Regional Indian Cooking Classes, Oakland, CA; 415-225-7898, ruta@pacbell.net, www.rutaruta.com.

SAN FRANCISCO BAKING INSTITUTE
San Francisco

Sponsor: Private school. Programs: 5-day hands-on seminars on bread & pastries. Established: 1991. Class/group size: 12-15 max. 15-18 programs/yr. Facilities: Newly constructed production-sized training facility with up-to-date equipment.

FACULTY: Head Instructor Didier Rosada; Jeffrey Yankellow & Erin Quinn.

COSTS: $950/5 days.

CONTACT: Evelyne Suas, Administrator, San Francisco Baking Institute, 480 Grandview Dr., So. San Francisco, CA 94080; 650-589-5784, Fax 650-589-5729, contact@sfbi.com, www.sfbi.com.

SCUOLA DI CUCINA
Mill Valley, Marin County

Sponsor: Professional chef. Programs: Hands-on classes feature restaurant-style dishes, professional tips & techniques. Specific techniques series available. Established: 2002. 6 programs/yr. Facilities: Frantoio Ristorante kitchen, serving ~200 guests/day. Also featured: On-site professional olive oil co.

FACULTY: Duilio Valenti, chef of Frantoio Ristorante & Olive Oil Co. Frantoio is ranked among the top 100 Bay Area restaurants by San Francisco Chronicle's food critic.

COSTS: $90/class.

CONTACT: Liza Garfield, Manager, Scuola di Cucina, 152 Shoreline Highway, Mill Valley, CA 94941; 415-389-0755, lizagarfield@attbi.com, www.frantoio.com.

SPUN SUGAR CAKE & CANDY CLASSES & SUPPLIES
Berkeley

Sponsor: Retail store & school. Programs: Classes & courses that include American cake decorating, gum paste & rolled fondant, gingerbread houses, sugar skulls & eggs, truffles, candy. Established: 1996. Class/group size: 8-12 hands-on. 100+ programs/yr. Facilities: Working kitchen with seating & workspace for all students. Also featured: Party classes, custom designed cookies, sales of cake decorating & candy making supplies.

FACULTY: 30+ years of hands-on experience in the cake decorating & candy making fields.

COSTS: $30-$350.

CONTACT: Bettye Travis, Spun Sugar, 1611 University Ave., Berkeley, CA 94703; 510-843-9192, Fax 510-848-5790, bettye@spunsugar.com, spunsugar.com.

A STORE FOR COOKS
Laguna Niguel

Sponsor: Cookware store & school. Programs: Morning & evening demo classes & Lunch & Learn classes. Established: 1981. Class/group size: 25 demo. 100+ programs/yr. Also featured: Classes for private groups.

FACULTY: Proprietor & cookbook author Susan Vollmer, Hugh Carpenter, Phillis Carey, Kay Pastorius, George Geary, cookbook authors, & local chefs.

COSTS: Lunch & Learn classes $16; demonstrations $40-$75.

CONTACT: Susan Vollmer, Owner, A Store for Cooks, 30100 Town Center Dr., Ste. R, Laguna Niguel, CA 92677; 714-495-0445, Fax 714-495-2139, store4cook@aol.com.

TANTE MARIE'S COOKING SCHOOL
San Francisco

Sponsor: Small private school. Programs: 1-week, 3-day, weekend, 6-session, & single-session participation courses, afternoon & weekend demos. Established: 1979. Class/group size: 12-32. 800 programs/yr. Facilities: Store front with tile floors, wooden counters, 6 ovens, 20 burners. Also featured: 1-week courses that include shopping at the Farmer's Market, visits to bread bakeries & cheese makers, winery tours, & dining in fine restaurants.

FACULTY: Founder Mary Risley studied at Le Cordon Bleu & La Varenne; guest instructors.

COSTS: 1-week course $675, 1-week vacation course $800, weekend course $50-$350, 6-session

evening course $540, morning classes $95, demonstrations $50. Hotel lodging available.
CONTACT: Peggy Lynch, Admin. Director, Tante Marie's Cooking School, 271 Francisco St.., San Francisco, CA 94133; 415-788-6699, Fax 415-788-8924, peggy@tantemarie.com, www.tantemarie.com.

WEIR COOKING
Wine Country; Provence, France; Italy
Sponsor: Culinary professional Joanne Weir. Programs: 3-7 day participation courses. Established: 1989. Class/group size: 10-15. 4-6 programs/yr. Facilities: Villas, chateaus, wineries & cooking schools. Also featured: Private weeklong classes; visits to restaurants, wineries, markets.
FACULTY: Joanne Weir hosts her own PBS cooking show, cooked at Berkeley's Chez Panisse, received the Julia Child/IACP Cooking Teacher Award of Excellence.
COSTS: $1,500-$3,950.
CONTACT: Joanne Weir, Weir Cooking, 2107 Pine St., San Francisco, CA 94115; 415-262-0260, mariangela@joanneweir.com, www.joanneweir.com.

WINESPEAK
Northern cities
Sponsor: Wine professional. Programs: Customized food & wine classes on demand, educational wine itineraries & tours. Established: 1986. Class/group size: 5-500.
FACULTY: Betsy Fischer, CWE, has 24 yrs experience in the food, beverage & tourism industry.
COSTS: $25-$125.
CONTACT: Betsy Fischer, Winespeak, 10 Fourth St., Santa Rosa, CA 95401; 707-577-8358, Fax 707-577-8358, gofish@sonic.net.

WOK WIZ WALKING TOURS & COOKING CENTER
San Francisco
Sponsor: Private school. Programs: Weekend Walk 'n Wok Workshop, which includes demo cooking class. Established: 1986. Class/group size: 4-7. 100+ programs/yr. Facilities: 1,100-sq-ft, 2-story building with demo area. Also featured: Walking tours of Chinatown, custom tours & classes, epicurean tours to Hong Kong & Thailand; Singapore, China, Italy.
FACULTY: Shirley Fong-Torres, author of the Wok Wiz Chinatown Cookbook, In the Chinese Kitchen, & San Francisco Chinatown, A Walking Tour.
COSTS: Food shopping & cooking workshop $75.
CONTACT: Shirley Fong-Torres, Owner, Wok Wiz Walking Tours & Cooking Center, 654 Commercial St., San Francisco, CA; 415-981-8989 OR 650-355-9657, Fax 650-359-8999, wokwiz@aol.com, www.wokwiz.com.

WORLDCHEFS, INTERNATIONAL COOKING CLASSES
San Jose, Santa Clara & Sunnyvale
Sponsor: Chef Suzanne Vandyck. Programs: Group & private classes; teambuilding. Established: 2000. Class/group size: 25 max. Weekly programs/yr. Also featured: Catering, consulting, personal chef services.
FACULTY: Founder/owner Suzanne Vandyck is guest instructor at Cordon Bleu Culinary Inst, Florence. Chef Toussaint Potter received a Grand diploma from La Varenne. Chef Mai Ward is a graduate of California Culinary Academy.
COSTS: ~$50 per class + food fee.
CONTACT: Suzanne Vandyck, Culinary Instructor & Owner, Worldchefs, International Cooking Classes, Santa Clara, CA 95051; 408-247-7351, Fax 408-247-7351, info@worldchefs.net, www.worldchefs.net.

YOSEMITE CHEFS' & VINTNERS' HOLIDAYS
Yosemite National Park
Sponsor: Yosemite Concession Services Corporation. Programs: A series of 2- & 3-day vacation programs that feature cooking demos or wine seminars & a concluding banquet. Established:

1982. Class/group size: 180. ~15 programs/yr. Facilities: Great Lounge of The Ahwahnee Hotel.
FACULTY: Each program features noted chefs or wineries. Executive Chef Robert Anderson & his staff prepare the vintner's banquet, visiting chefs prepare the chefs' banquet.
COSTS: Packages range from $599-$950 ($280-$450) including shared lodging at The Ahwahnee.
CONTACT: Yosemite Reservations, 5410 East Home Ave., Fresno, CA 93727; 559-252-4848, Fax 559-372-1362, www.yosemitepark.com/content2col.cfm?SectionID=104&PageID=321.

ZOV'S BISTRO
Tustin
Sponsor: Bistro/bakery, cooking school, caterer. Programs: Demo classes on a variety of topics.
Established: 1987. Class/group size: 25-40. 19 programs/yr. Facilities: Front kitchen of Zov's Bistro.
FACULTY: Zov Karamardian, caterer & teacher for 20+ yrs; noted chefs, TV personalities, cookbook authors, including John Ash, Hugh Carpenter, Joyce Goldstein, Julie Sahni, Martin Yan.
COSTS: $50-$100/class.
CONTACT: Zov Karamardian, Chef/Owner, Zov's Bistro, 17440 E. 17th St., Tustin, CA 92780; 714-838-8855 x5, Fax 714-838-9926, zov@zovs.com, www.zovs.com.

COLORADO

BED & BANQUET RETREAT AT THE RED ROOSTER INN
Glenwood Springs
Sponsor: Bed & breakfast. Programs: Hands-on programs include 1-day classes (weekend package) with extended stay option. Established: 2002. Class/group size: 12 max. 12 programs/yr. Facilities: The Inn's kitchen. Also featured: Nearby hot springs spa, pool & vapor caves, horseback riding.
FACULTY: Visiting chefs.
COSTS: $350 per person/2 nights, $500 per person/5 nights includes private room in guest house, breakfasts, dinner party.
CONTACT: Gretchen Wroblewski, Owner, Red Rooster Inn, 4351 County Rd. 115, Glenwood Springs, CO 81601; 970-928-8293, Fax 970-928-8293, reservations@red-rooster-inn.com, www.red-rooster-inn.com/frames/bedbanquet.html.

COOK STREET SCHOOL OF FINE COOKING
Denver *(See also page 28) (See display ad page 28)*
Sponsor: Private culinary school. Programs: Short series & one-time classes. 3- & 6-mo professional Food & Wine Career Program. Established: 1999. Class/group size: 24 max. 40 programs/yr. Facilities: 3,000-sq-ft newly-remodeled teaching kitchen featuring commercial grade equipment. Also featured: Facility available for corporate & private parties, dinners & cooking parties.
FACULTY: Full-time staff of experienced professional chef-instructors, guest chefs.
COSTS: $50-$149/single classes, $389/short series.
CONTACT: Cook Street School of Fine Cooking, 1937 Market St., Denver, CO 80202; 303-308-9300, Fax 303-308-9400, info@cookstreet.com, www.cookstreet.com.

COOKING SCHOOL OF ASPEN
Aspen
Sponsor: Cooking school, tour operator, specialty food store & catalog. Programs: Daily hands-on & demo classes, culinary adventures abroad, multi-day workshops. Established: 1998. Class/group size: 12-20 max. 200+ programs/yr. Facilities: 12-person hands-on design, 20-person demo design. Also featured: Customized private events, children's classes.
FACULTY: Owner & guest chefs.
COSTS: $130-$275/class.
CONTACT: Rob Seideman, President, Cooking School of Aspen, 414 E. Hyman Ave., Aspen, CO 81611; 800-603-6004, 970-920-1879, Fax 970-920-2188, rob@cookingschoolofaspen.com, www.cookingschoolofaspen.com.

COOKING SCHOOL OF VAIL AT THE SAVORY INN
Vail

Sponsor: Private cooking school in a B&B inn. Programs: Hands-on day & evening courses, demos for larger groups, wine pairing by sommelier. Established: 2002. Class/group size: 6-15/day, 6-40/eve. Weekly programs/yr. Facilities: Commercial kitchen & dining room. Also featured: Corporate events, private parties.

FACULTY: In-house chef David Nowakowski. Local & guest chefs.

COSTS: Day classes $55+, eve classes $75+.

CONTACT: Nancy Hassett, InnKeeper, Cooking School of Vail located at the Savory Inn, 2405 Elliott Road, Vail, CO 81657; 970-476-1304, Fax 970-476-0433, info@savoryinn.com, www.savoryinn.com. David Nowakowski, Chef. david@savoryinn.com.

CULINARY SCHOOL OF THE ROCKIES
Boulder

Sponsor: Private school. Programs: Individual classes, short courses, & 5-day basic techniques cooking vacations that emphasize creativity, organization, & presentation. Established: 1991. Class/group size: 32 demos, 12-16 hand. Facilities: Modern, fully-equipped kitchen with overhead mirror. Also featured: Corporate training, private parties, bridal showers, retail cookware store, diploma/professional program.

FACULTY: Revolving visiting instructors program featuring local & national restaurant/bakery chefs, guest chefs, cookbook authors.

COSTS: Classes from $35-$75 each; intensives $475-$525. A list of B&Bs & lodgings is available.

CONTACT: Joan Brett, Director, Culinary School of the Rockies, 637 S. Broadway, Ste. H, Boulder, CO 80303; 303-494-7988, Fax 303-494-7999, csr@culinaryschoolrockies.com, www.culinaryschoolrockies.com.

FOOD & WINE MAGAZINE CLASSIC AT ASPEN
Aspen

Sponsor: Food & Wine Magazine. Programs: Annual 3-day weekend festival featuring events for food & wine enthusiasts & professionals. The 20-hr program offers 80+ lectures, demos, panels, tastings, a benefit auction & fine dining. Established: 1983. Class/group size: 70-800. 1 programs/yr. Facilities: Hotels & tented park area. Also featured: Winemaker dinners.

FACULTY: Has included Julia Child, Marcella Hazan, Jacques Pepin, Emeril Lagasse, Robert M. Parker, Jr., Frank Prial.

COSTS: 3-day tickets ~$635. Reserve tastings $110-$220 extra. Deluxe hotel & condos available.

CONTACT: Jennifer Albright, Special Event Manager, Food & Wine Magazine Classic at Aspen, 425 Rio Grande Plaza, Aspen, CO 0; 877-900-WINE, Fax 970-920-1173, acra@aspenchamber.org, www.foodandwine.com/ext/classic/.

THE GOURMET SPOON
Denver, Lafayette, Ft. Collins & Littleton

Sponsor: Culinary professional. Programs: Demo classes & participation workshops. Established: 1998. Also featured: Corporate teambuilding classes, private culinary parties.

FACULTY: Chef Dan Witherspoon.

COSTS: $35-$70.

CONTACT: Dan Witherspoon, The Gourmet Spoon, Denver, CO; 303-394-0167, chefdan@thegourmetspoon.com, www.thegourmetspoon.com.

KATHY SMITH'S COOKING SCHOOL
Greenwood Village

Sponsor: Private school. Programs: Demo, participation & private classes. Established: 1996. Class/group size: 18 demo/10 hands-on. 40-50 programs/yr. Facilities: In-home school with seating area for demos & large viewing mirror. Kitchen equipped with Viking gas stove, double ovens

& restaurant quality appliances. Also featured: Private instruction for adults & children. Instruction for elementary, middle & HS programs (Sept-May). **FACULTY:** Chef Kathy Smith trained with Mary Risley, Giuliano Bugialli; local guest chefs. **COSTS:** Demos $40-$50, participation $50. **CONTACT:** Kathy Smith, Kathy Smith's Cooking School, 4280 E. Plum Ct., Greenwood Village, CO 80121; 303-437-6882, Fax 303-740-6884, kathy@kathysmithcooks.com, www.kathysmithcooks.com.

NOW YOU'RE COOKIN'
Crested Butte
Sponsor: Private school. Programs: Hands-on classes. Class/group size: 8. Facilities: Private home with 8 individual prep & cooking stations. **FACULTY:** Includes Chef Bruno, Graham Ullrich, Stacee VanAernem, Tom Favor, Peter Vanags. **CONTACT:** Kristina St. George-Patten, Now You're Cookin', 505 Slate River Drive, PO Box 1970, Crested Butte, CO 81224; 970-349-2112, nyc@now-youre-cookin.com, now-youre-cookin.com.

PASSIONATEPALETTE
Englewood
Sponsor: Private school. Programs: Hands-on cooking classes. Established: 2003. Class/group size: 40. 100+ programs/yr. Also featured: Cooking parties. **FACULTY:** Chefs Ben Davis & Jenifer Suydam have 20+ yrs combined experience in food, service, cooking & teaching. **COSTS:** Each class averages to be $40.00 per student with the exception of exceptional events. **CONTACT:** Jenfer Suydam, Owner/Chef, PassionatePalette, 9623 E County Line Rd., Englewood, CO 80112; 303-754-0005, cooking@passionatepalette.com, www.passionatepalette.com.

SAVORY PALETTE GOURMET RETREATS
Lyons
Sponsor: Private retreat. Programs: Classes in culinary techniques from selected menus. Established: 1997. Class/group size: 12 max hands-on. 12 programs/yr. Facilities: Full professional kitchen, dining room, lounge with fireplace, sandstone terrace with hot tub. Also featured: Hiking, biking, snowshoeing, fireside reading, hot tub. **FACULTY:** Deborah DeBord, Ph.D., has taught & cooked in Latin America, Europe & Asia. She is a food writer & has published 3 cookbooks. **COSTS:** Weekend retreat $190, $315/couple; $1,234/wk. Includes meals & lodging in pvt queen bedroom/bath. **CONTACT:** Deborah DeBord, Proprietor, Savory Palette Gourmet Retreats, 81 Cree Ct., Lyons, CO 80540; 303-823-0530, Fax 303-823-0337, ddebord@indra.com, www.expressionretreats.com.

SCHOOL OF NATURAL COOKERY – THE MAIN COURSE
Boulder, Longmont & Denver; Albuquerque, NM; Seattle, WA
Sponsor: Vegetarian non-recipe cooking school. Programs: Intensives & weekly courses in preparing natural food, no recipes, hands-on, the language of chefs. Established: 1985. Class/group size: 4-15. Facilities: Vary from homestyle kitchen to simple apartments & elaborate commercial kitchens. Also featured: In Boulder, nearby activities incl mountain biking, hiking, skiing, music, dance, theater, festivals. **FACULTY:** Joanne Saltzman, founder/director, author Amazing Grains, Romancing The Bean, The Natural Cook; All Main Course teachers certified by The School of Natural Cookery. **COSTS:** Tuition & materials are $395 for Parts I & II, $350 for Part III & IV. Intensives are $1,600 for the full program & $800 for the Part I weekend, ingredients & workbooks included. Text books included for intensives. **CONTACT:** Joanne Saltzman, Director, School of Natural Cookery, PO Box 19466, Boulder, CO 80308; 303-444-8068, info@naturalcookery.com, www.naturalcookery.com. Longmont - Lisa Ehlers Seattle - Omid Roustaei 206-365-8654Albuquerque - Gwen McCloskey 505-281-6129.

CONNECTICUT

ANNHOWARD/APRICOTSCOOKING SCHOOL
Farmington

Sponsor: Culinary professional Ann Howard, owner of Apricots Restaurant. Programs: 4-session demo & hands-on cooking classes featuring seasonal & entertaining menus & international cuisines. Established: 1985. Class/group size: 30 demo, 12 hands-on. 8-25 programs/yr. Facilities: Demos: Garden Room at Apricots resturant. Hands-on classes: professional kitchen of Ann Howard. Also featured: Private classes, corporate team-building, gourmet dinner clubs, wine pairing.

FACULTY: Chef Jeff Gankin, Ann Howard & 4 assistants.

COSTS: $55-$75/class, $155-$250/4 sessions.

CONTACT: Ann Howard, AnnHoward/ApricotsCooking School, 24 Mountain Rd., Farmington, CT 06032; 860-409-0886 or 860-673-5405, Fax 860-674-9050, annhoward_fem@sbcglobal.net.

BELLA CUCINA
New Canaan; Provence, France; Florence, Sorrento, Venice, Rome, Italy

Sponsor: Culinary professional. Programs: 1- to 6-session courses that include basic techniques, seasonal & regional menus, fresh pasta, risotto, excursions to markets & restaurants. Established: 1996. Class/group size: 5-20. 15-20 programs/yr. Facilities: Owner's fully equipped home kitchen; professional kitchens in Italy. Also featured: Travel programs to Italy that combine cooking instruction, visits to art museums & historic sites, lectures, Italian language lessons.

FACULTY: Culinary professional, artist & educator Carol Borelli studied at Le Cordon Bleu; guest teachers from the US & abroad.

COSTS: Classes & courses are $45-$270. Trip is ~$3,400-$7,000 all inclusive.

CONTACT: Carol Borelli, Owner, Bella Cucina, P.O. Box 421, New Canaan, CT 06840; 203-966-4477, Fax 203-966-8781.

THE CONSCIOUS GOURMET COOKING RETREAT TRAVEL PROGRAM
Locations in the US, Canada & Europe

Sponsor: Culinary professional Diane Carlson. Programs: 5-day cooking retreat travel programs offering health-supportive classes & lecture/workshops that focus on whole grains, beans, vegetables, natural sweeteners, fish, organic animal protein. Established: 2000. Class/group size: 8-14. 6 programs/yr. Facilities: Retreat center kitchens. Also featured: Yoga, excursions.

FACULTY: Diane Carlson former Co-President & Director of the Natural Gourmet Cookery School/Institute for Food & Health for 10 yrs, instructor, private chef & caterer. Other instructors include authors Myra Kornfeld & Peter Berley.

COSTS: $1,425+.

CONTACT: Diane Carlson, Owner, Director, Instructor, The Conscious Gourmet Cooking Retreat Travel Program, P.O. Box 662, New Canaan, CT 06840; 203-966-3559, Fax 203-972-5937, dcarlsonsspirit@aol.com, www.theconsciousgourmet.com.

COOKING BY HEART
New Jersey, New York

Sponsor: Culinary professional. Programs: Private in-home cooking classes; guided chocolate tastings. Established: 2003. Class/group size: 1+. Facilities: Client's home, rental space, conf. room.

FACULTY: Dina Cheney, a graduate of the Institute of Culinary Education & Columbia Univ, is a member of the IACP & taught at Whole Foods Market & NYC's JCC.

COSTS: $350/class for 2 adults (+ $50 pp up to 6); tastings from $30.

CONTACT: Dina Cheney, Cooking Teacher, Cooking By Heart, Cos Cob, CT; 203-629-1831, dina@cookingbyheart.com, www.cookingbyheart.com.

CUCINA CASALINGA
Wilton; Italy

Sponsor: Italian cooking school. Programs: Hands-on day & evening classes, series for adults & children, 3 cooking tours to Italy/yr, Kids Cook Italian Camp in Aug. Established: 1981. Class/group size: 15 hands-on/25 demo. Facilities: Renovated home kitchen with Tuscan wood-burning pizza oven, featured in Home Magazine, Oct '02. Also featured: Private group & corporate classes, wine tastings, market tours of Arthur Ave. in the Bronx.

FACULTY: Sally Maraventano, owner/instructor, author of Festa del Giardino, studied at the U. of Florence, & learned to cook from her mother & Sicilian grandfather. Guest chefs from the US & Italy.

COSTS: Adult classes $100 (series $280), guest chef & Sat evening classes $125, children (age 11-16) $60. Kids 4-day summer camp $240. Italy tours ~3,600-$5,200 includes lodging, meals, excursions.

CONTACT: Sally Maraventano, Owner, Cucina Casalinga, 171 Drum Hill Rd., Wilton, CT 06897; 203-762-0768, Fax 203-762-0768, info@cucinacasalinga.com, www.cucinacasalinga.com.

FOURTEEN LINCOLN STREET B&B & CULINARY STUDIO
Niantic

Sponsor: Chef-owned B&B. Programs: Weekend culinary retreats featuring cooking demos. Established: 1997. Class/group size: 12. 10 programs/yr. Facilities: Fully-equipped commercial kitchen. Also featured: Private dinners & cooking classes.

FACULTY: Cheryl M. Jean, CIA-honors graduate, named a Great New England Cook by Yankee Magazine. Guest chefs may include Deedy Marble, Claude Martin, Debbie Gaspardi, Tina de Bellegarde, Akiko Hirano.

COSTS: $650-$750/couple includes most meals, lodging w/Jacuzzi bath.

CONTACT: Cheryl Jean, Chef, Fourteen Lincoln Street, 14 Lincoln Street, Niantic, CT 06357; 860-739-8180, 860-739-6327, Fourteenlincoln@aol.com, www.14linlcolnstreet.com.

MYSTIC COOKING SCHOOL
Old Mystic

Sponsor: Private school. Programs: Techniques, regional & ethnic cuisines, food & wine pairings, tea classes. Established: 1994. Class/group size: 16 hands-on, 25 demo. 60+ programs/yr. Facilities: Well-equipped new farmhouse-style building on 4 rural acres, near the ocean. Also featured: Occasional regional cooking tours, private classes.

FACULTY: Cookbook authors, restaurant & guest chefs including George Hirsch, Micol Negrin, Jack Leonardo, Chris Prosperi, Patrick Boisjot, Daniel Rosati.

COSTS: $45-$75/class.

CONTACT: Annice Estes, Owner, Mystic Cooking School, P.O. Box 611, Mystic, CT 06355; 860-536-6005, Fax 860-536-6117, mail@mysticcooking.com, www.mysticcooking.com.

PRUDENCE SLOANE'S COOKING SCHOOL
Hampton

Sponsor: Culinary professional Prudence Sloane. Programs: Participation workshops, demos. Established: 1993. Class/group size: 8-150. 30 programs/yr. Facilities: Well-equipped teaching kitchen. Also featured: Private party classes, knife skills, food & wine pairing.

FACULTY: Prudence Sloane was awarded the Blue Ribbon professional diploma from the Institute of Culinary Education & is a TV food show host.

COSTS: $65/session, $300-$800/intensive technique series.

CONTACT: Prudence Sloane, Prudence Sloane's Cooking School, 245 Main St., P.O. Box 41, Hampton, CT 06247; 860-455-0596, prudencesloane@aol.com, www.prudencesloane.com/htm/school.htm.

RONNIE FEIN SCHOOL OF CREATIVE COOKING
Stamford

Sponsor: Culinary professional. Programs: Hands-on classes that emphasize ingredients, techniques, & menus. Established: 1971. Class/group size: 4 hands-on. Facilities: Fully-equipped home teaching kitchen. Also featured: Children's classes, private instruction.

FACULTY: Ronnie Fein writes for food publications & attended the China Institute & Four Seasons Cooking School. She is author of The Complete Idiot's Guide to American Cooking.

COSTS: $250/session.

CONTACT: Ronnie Fein, Owner, Ronnie Fein School of Creative Cooking, 32 Heming Way, Stamford, CT 06903; 203-322-7114, Fax 203-329-3366, RonnieVFein@optonline.net.

SANDY'S BRAZILIAN & CONTINENTAL CUISINE
Waterbury; Ireland

Sponsor: Private school. Programs: Culinary tours to Ireland & classes in Connecticut. Established: 1987. Class/group size: 10. 2-4 programs/yr.

FACULTY: Sandra N. Allen Certified Member IACP, Member NYACT, CWCA, CHOC.

CONTACT: Sandra Allen, Director, Sandy's Brazilian & Continental Cuisine, 827 Oronoke Rd., # 8-3, Waterbury, CT 06708; 203-596-9685, Sandyna@juno.com.

SILO COOKING SCHOOL
New Milford

Sponsor: Silo/Hunt Hill Farm Trust. Programs: Demo & participation courses. Established: 1972. Class/group size: 14 hands-on/30 demo. 70 programs/yr. Facilities: Well-equipped teaching kitchen. Also featured: Custom group & children's classes, bridal showers.

FACULTY: Master chefs, authors, TV Food Network chefs, including Giuliano Bugialli, Rachael Ray, Michael Lomonaco, Nick Malgieri, Jacques Pepin, Betty Rosbottom.

COSTS: ~$80-$100.

CONTACT: Renee Frinder, Cooking School Director, Silo/Hunt Hill Farm Trust, 44 Upland Rd., New Milford, CT 06776; 860-355-0300, Fax 860-350-5495, sales@thesilo.com, www.thesilo.com.

TOURS FOR WINE LOVERS
Napa & Sonoma; Burgundy, Alsace, Champagne, France; Mosel & Rhine, Germany

Sponsor: Wine educator. Programs: 9-day tours that feature winery visits, gourmet meals, cultural activities. Established: 1982. Class/group size: 25 max. 4 programs/yr.

FACULTY: Dr. Vincent Marottoli, fluent in French, Spanish & Italian, is a member of SWE.

COSTS: $1,900-$2,400 includes deluxe lodging, breakfast & dinner daily, ground transportation, planned activities.

CONTACT: Vincent Marottoli, Owner, Tours for Wine Lovers, 1211 Quinnipiac Ave., New Haven, CT 06513; 800-256-0141, Fax 203-469-4935, wineluvint@aol.com, www.vintagetours.com.

A WINE TUTOR
Milford

Sponsor: Wine professional. Programs: Public wine appreciation classes & private wine tasting events for corporations & groups. Established: 1988. Class/group size: 20/public program.

FACULTY: Len Gulino, MBA; earned certificate at CIA Greystone; member of SWE, journalist, retailer.

COSTS: 5-session courses $75-$150.

CONTACT: Len Gulino, Owner, A Wine Tutor, 19 Derby Ave., Milford, CT 06460; 203-877-2884, len4wine@optonline.net, www.culinarymenus.com/lengulino.htm.

WINE WANDERINGS, INC.
Norwalk

Sponsor: Wine professionals. Programs: 5- to 6-session courses. Established: 1993. Class/group size: 36. 10-12 programs/yr. Facilities: Classroom or dining room style seating. Also featured: Wine education & tastings for corporations, nonprofit orgs, & private groups.

FACULTY: Lou Campoli & Cathi Carroll both have 15+ yrs wine education, enrolled in Master of Wine program, Board of CT chapter AIWF, member IACP, SWE & AWS, wine column journalists, 30+ yrs. corp. career.

COSTS: $30-$50/session.

CONTACT: Lou Campoli & Cathi Carroll, Co-Owners, Wine Wanderings, Inc., 192 Gillies Lane, Norwalk, CT 06854; 203-853-9550, Fax 203-853-9550, winew@attglobal.net.

DELAWARE

CELEBRITY KITCHENS
Wilmington

Sponsor: Private school. Programs: Hands-on & demo classes. Established: 2002. Class/group size: 12 hands-on, 24 demo. 350 programs/yr. Facilities: Renovated kitchen with granite countertops. Also featured: Corporate bonding programs, kids cook, private classes, intl. cooking tours.
FACULTY: Local & regional guest chefs.
CONTACT: Cindy Weiner, President, Celebrity Kitchens, 1601 Concord Pike, #33, Independence Mall, Wilmington, DE 19803; 302-427-2665, Fax 302-427-9060, icook@celebritykitchensinc.com, www.celebritykitchens.com.

WHAT'S COOKING AT THE KITCHEN SINK
Hockessin

Sponsor: Kitchenware & specialty store. Programs: Demo & hands-on classes. Established: 1991. Class/group size: 18 demo/6 hands-on. 120+ programs/yr. Facilities: Well-equipped professional kitchen with overhead mirror. Also featured: Children's workshops & private classes.
FACULTY: Michele DiVincenzo, director & IACP member, studied at the CIA. Local chefs, caterers & professionals such as Peter Fontaine, George Geary, Christina Pirello.
COSTS: $26-$45/class. For lodging, the school recommends The Inn at Montchanin Village.
CONTACT: Michele DiVincenzo, Director, What's Cooking at the Kitchen Sink, 425 Hockessin Corner, Hockessin, DE 19707; 302-239-7066, Fax 302-239-7665, info@thekitchensink.com, www.thekitchensink.com.

DISTRICT OF COLUMBIA

COMPANY'S COMING
Washington

Sponsor: Home-based program. Programs: Demo & participation classes that teach entertaining at home. Includes menu planning, cooking, presentation, food & wine pairing. Established: 1997. Class/group size: 8-16. 36 programs/yr. Facilities: Home-based demo kitchen. Also featured: Team building classes, customized classes for groups.
FACULTY: Jinny & Ed Fleischman have been entertaining together for 28+ yrs & attend cooking schools & classes. Noted in Harper's Bazaar as 'one of the best cooking schools in the US'.
COSTS: $65-$80/class.
CONTACT: Jinny Fleischman, Company's Coming, 3313 Ross Place NW, Washington, DC 20008; 202-966-3361, Fax 202-362-8409, veflei@aol.com, www.companycoming.com.

DELIZIOSO! COOKING SCHOOL
Washington

Programs: 4-sessions or single classes by special arrangement. Established: 1985. Class/group size: 5 seated. 4-6 programs/yr. Facilities: Professional residential kitchen or other suitable location. Also featured: Group or private instruction. Teens summer specials.
FACULTY: Director Eugenia Van Horn Wilkie, teacher & food writer, lived & studied cooking in Milan for 10 yrs.
COSTS: $300/4 classes, $100/group class, $250 private lesson.
CONTACT: Eugenia Van Horn Wilkie, Director, Delizioso! Cooking School, 3915 Ivy Terrace Ct., Washington, DC 20007; 202-338-6580, ewilkie@mindspring.com.

SOCIETY OF WINE EDUCATORS PROGRAMS
Washington

Sponsor: Nonprofit organization for wine educators & consumers. Programs: Annual 1-wk conference featuring 50+ wine education workshops; wine certification programs. Established: 1977. Also featured: Sponsor 2 professional certification programs, Certified Specialist of Wine & Certified Wine Educator, designed to test the knowledge of individuals within the wine industry. **FACULTY:** Wine experts.
CONTACT: Bonnie Fedchock, Executive Director, Society of Wine Educators, 1200 G St., NW, Ste. .360, Washington, DC 20005; 202-347-5677, Fax 202-347-5667, director@societyofwineeducators.org, www.wine.gurus.com.

WHAT'S COOKING!
Washington

Sponsor: Culinary professional Phyllis Frucht. Programs: Limited participation and/or hands-on classes on a variety of topics. Series include The International Gourmet, Asian Cooking, Techniques, Vegetarian, & Contemporary Cooking. Established: 1976. Class/group size: 16. Facilities: Newly renovated townhouse kitchen.
FACULTY: Phyllis Frucht has taught cooking 30+ yrs at home, in adult ed, & at the former What's Cooking! cookware store/cooking school in Rockville, MD, where she was chef/owner.
COSTS: $45 for single class, $200 for a series of 5.
CONTACT: Phyllis Frucht, Teacher, What's Cooking!, 1917 S Street NW, Washington, DC 20009; 202-483-7282, Fax 202-483-7284, whatsckng@aol.com.

FLORIDA

ARS MAGIRICA
Coral Gables

Sponsor: Recreational cooking school. Programs: Hands-on classes & 6- to 18-session courses. Topics include intl, regional & seasonal cuisines, techniques, entertaining, healthy cooking. Culinary programs for children & teens. Established: 2001. Class/group size: 6. 120+ programs/yr. Facilities: Professional kitchen. Also featured: Kids & teens cooking camp & party place; corporate team building; private chef services, home cook training, culinary store.
FACULTY: Founder/Director Lourdes Castro, former instructor at NYU & Johnson & Wales; Javier Nassar, Home Chef Director, graduate of Johnson & Wales; Melissa Diaz, Jr. Chef Director.
COSTS: $59/class, culinary series from $325-$895.
CONTACT: Lourdes Castro, Owner, Ars Magirica, 158 Almeria Ave., Coral Gables, FL 33134; 305-443-8303, Fax 305-443-8378, info@arsmagirica.com, www.ArsMagirica.com.

CHEF ALLEN'S
Aventura

Sponsor: Chef Allen Susser. Programs: Demo & participation classes; one-on-one sessions with student working along with restaurant staff. Established: 1986. Class/group size: 1-25. 12 programs/yr. Facilities: Chef Allen's restaurant.
FACULTY: Chef Susser, faculty of FIU School of Hospitality. Author of Allen Susser's New World Cuisine; studied at Le Cordon Bleu & was chef at Paris' Bristol Hotel & Le Cirque in NYC.
COSTS: Group classes $45, individual session $195.
CONTACT: Chef Allen Susser, Chef/Owner, Chef Allen's, 19088 N.E. 29th Ave., Aventura, FL 33180; 305-935-2900, Fax 305-935-9062, ChefAllen@aol.com, www.chefallen.com.

CHEF JEAN-PIERRE COOKING SCHOOL
Ft. Lauderdale

Sponsor: Chef Jean-Pierre Gourmet Foods. Programs: Morning, evening & week-long demo classes on a variety of topics with emphasis on fundamentals. Established: 1976. Class/group size: 20.

Facilities: Fully-equipped demonstration Poggen Pohl kitchen with overhead mirror. Also featured: Visits to markets & food producers.

FACULTY: School director Chef Jean-Pierre Brehier is the host of the internationally distributed cooking shows Sunshine Cuisine & Incredible Cuisine.

COSTS: $45/class, $38 for 3 classes purchased at the same time.

CONTACT: Chef Jean-Pierre Brehier, School Director, Chef Jean-Pierre Cooking School, 1436 N. Federal Hwy., Ft. Lauderdale, FL 33304; 954-563-2700, Fax 954-563-9009, jp@chefjp.com, www.chefjeanpierre.com.

GALAXY NUTRITIONAL FOODS' VEGGIE CULINARY SCHOOL
Orlando

Sponsor: Producer of cheese & dairy-related alternatives. Programs: Half-day Cooking with Veggie programs that cover nutrition & the use of food products that reduce the risk of diseases linked to the consumption of high fat, high cholesterol foods. Established: 2000. Class/group size: 4-6. 50+ programs/yr. Facilities: Galaxy Foods' culinary kitchen. Also featured: Customized group education, Soy Story, Build Your Lunch, Desserts Only.

FACULTY: Includes Tony Oust, MBA, RD, Kulbir Sabharwal, Ph.D.

COSTS: $75/class (dietitians), $50/class (general public).

CONTACT: Tony Oust, Director, Galaxy Nutritional Foods' Veggie Culinary School, 2441 Viscount Row, Orlando, FL 32809; 407-855-5500, Fax 407-855-7485, toust@galaxyfoods.com, www.galaxy-foods.com/culinary.html.

LA MAISON GOURMET
Dunedin

Sponsor: Cooking school for home chefs. Programs: 9-wk culinary skills & techniques course; individual classes for adults, couples & children; full-day workshops. Established: 1998. Class/group size: 12-56. 250 programs/yr. Facilities: 750-sq-ft kitchen with 2 gas cooktops, 13-ft center island & 2 convection ovens; 1,800-sq-ft private dining room. Also featured: Chef competitions, private & house parties, bridal showers, rehearsal dinners, personal chef services, corporate training, catering.

FACULTY: Executive Chef John Lewis, 35 yrs cooking experience. 8 part-time restaurant chefs.

COSTS: Individual classes $10-$50. 9-wk course $595. Lodging info available.

CONTACT: John Lewis, General Mgr., La Maison Gourmet, 471 Main St., Dunedin, FL 34698; 727-736-3070, Fax 727-733-8915, john_10245@msn.com, www.lamaisongourmet.com. Debbie McGiffin, Event Coordinator.

LE BISTRO RESTAURANT & COOKING SCHOOL
Lighthouse Point

Sponsor: Culinary professional & restaurant chef/owner. Programs: Classes that include classic cooking,kitchen basics, herbs & spices, ethnic flavors, healthful cuisine. Established: 2001. Class/group size: 6-45. 100+ programs/yr. Facilities: Fully-equipped restaurant facility. Also featured: Private classes.

FACULTY: Andy Trousdale, a Professional Culinary Educator at the Art Institute of Ft. Lauderdale, is a European 3-starMichelin-trained chef with 27 yrs professional experience. Guest chefs, specialty purveyors & wine specialists.

COSTS: Demonstration classes: $40, $75/couple, $175/5 classes. Hands-on classes also available.

CONTACT: Andy Trousdale, Chef/Owner, Le Bistro Restaurant & Cooking School, 4626 North Federal Highway, Lighthouse Point, FL; 954-946-9240, andyelin@bellsouth.net, www.lebistrorestaurant.com.

THE PALM BEACH SCHOOL OF COOKING, INC.
Boca Raton

Sponsor: Private school & cafe. Programs: 1/2-day workshops & multi-session courses that include Caribbean, Pacific Rim, sushi making, vegetarian dishes; Personal Chef Certificate program;

advanced training for professional chefs specializing in ethnic cuisines. Established: 1998. Class/group size: 10 hands-on, 20 demo. 200 programs/yr. Facilities: Professional cooking equipment, individual work stations. Also featured: Private parties, demos.
FACULTY: Professionally-trained experienced teachers.
COSTS: $60/class.
CONTACT: Doreen N. Moore, Director/Executive Chef, The Palm Beach School of Cooking, Inc., 2950 Olivewood Terr., #108, Boca Raton, FL 33431; 561-750-9529, cybrcook@hotmail.com.

REAL.LIFE.BASIC
Miami Beach
Sponsor: Gourmet cookware store. Programs: Demo & participation classes. 70+ programs/yr. Facilities: Demonstration kitchen with the latest equipment.
FACULTY: Local chefs.
COSTS: $45/class.
CONTACT: Simone Mayer, real.life.basic, 643 Lincoln Rd., Miami Beach, FL 33139; 305-604-1984, Fax 305-604-1994, realpeople@reallifebasic.com, www.reallifebasic.com.

THE RITZ-CARLTON, AMELIA ISLAND COOKING SCHOOL
Amelia Island,
Sponsor: The Ritz-Carlton, Amelia Island. Programs: Quarterly 2-day participation courses that focus on a theme. Established: 1994. Class/group size: 15. 4 programs/yr. Facilities: The Grill Kitchen. Also featured: Tour restaurant kitchens, pastry & butcher shop, garde manger; wine presentations; learn the responsibilities of the 45-chef team.
FACULTY: Scott Crawford, Chef de Cuisine of The Grill; the hotel's food & beverage staff.
COSTS: From $658/person, $938/couple includes 2 nights lodging, lunch with chef. $260/person without lodging.
CONTACT: Kathleen O'Brien, Director of Marketing & Public Relations, The Ritz-Carlton, Amelia Island, 4750 Amelia Island Pkwy, Amelia Island, FL 32034; 800-241-3333, 904-277-1100, Fax 904-277-1041, diane.svela@ritzcarlton.com, www.ritzcarlton.com.

TWO CHEFS
Miami
Sponsor: Restaurant. Programs: Hands-on cooking classes. Established: 1997. Class/group size: 8+. 48 programs/yr. Facilities: Fully-equipped restaurant kitchen. Also featured: Private group classes & events also offered.
FACULTY: Chefs Andres E. Alarcon & Jorge Montes.
COSTS: $45 average.
CONTACT: Michael-Anne Rauback, Two Chefs, 8287 S. Dixie Hwy., Miami, FL 33143; 305-663-2100, twochefsfl@yahoo.com.

GEORGIA

THE ART INSTITUTE OF ATLANTA – SCHOOL OF CULINARY ARTS
Atlanta, Georgia   *(See display ad page 11)*
Sponsor: Private college of creative professional studies. Programs: Hands-on programs include non-credit Saturday workshops, teen workshops & camp, certificate program in baking & pastry. Established: 1991. Class/group size: 10-15. 56 programs/yr. Facilities: Include 4 professional kitchens & 1 baking & pastry kitchen with industry-standard equipment. Also featured: Cooking & business mgmt skills; teaching-dining room, open to the community, for classical French cuisine.
FACULTY: 20+ professional chef instructors lead participation courses. All have bachelor's degree or higher & industry experience, many have professional credentials through the ACF.
COSTS: Saturday workshops $85, teen workshops $25-$50, teen 5-day camp $400, certificate program $850.

CONTACT: June Fischer, Director, Community Education, The Art Institute of Atlanta - School of Culinary Arts, 6600 Peachtree Dunwoody Rd., 100 Embassy Row, Atlanta, GA 30328; 800-275-4242 x2420, Fax 770-394-0008, fischerj@aii.edu, www.artinstitute.edu.

CHEF JOE RANDALL'S COOKING SCHOOL
Savannah
Sponsor: Professional Chef Joe Randall. Programs: Demo classes & series. Established: 2000. Class/group size: 20 demo. 52 programs/yr. Facilities: New well-equipped professional demo kitchen with overhead mirrors & audio system. Also featured: Catering, private classes & dinner parties.
FACULTY: Chef Joe Randall, proprietor, cookbook author, & food-service consultant with 30+ yrs industry experience. Guest & local chefs, cookbook authors.
COSTS: Demos $45-$95/session; 6-wk series $250.
CONTACT: Chef Joe Randall, Chef Joe Randall's Cooking School, 5409 Waters Ave., Savannah, GA 31404; 912-303-0409, Fax 912-303-0947, info@chefjoerandall.com, www.chefjoerandall.com.

COLUMBUS COOKS
Columbus
Sponsor: Private school & gourmet food store. Programs: Hands-on & demo classes. Established: 2002.
FACULTY: Chef/caterer Mark Festa; food writer/restaurant critic Gail Greenblatt; Stacy Varner, Exec Chef at Doctors Hospital; Maurice Martin, Exec Sous Chef at the CC of Columbus; Donna Reed, 23+ yrs foodservice experience.
COSTS: $28/demo class, $45/hands-on class.
CONTACT: Becky Catrett, Owner, Columbus Cooks, 1332 13th St., Columbus, GA 31901; 706-221-8723, columbuscooks@knology.net, www.columbuscooks.com.

COOKING UP A PARTY
Atlanta & Roswell
Sponsor: Private cooking school for children. Programs: 1-wk day camps for children ages 5-12 that teach cooking basics, table settings, napkin folding & garnishing. Established: 1996. 9 programs/yr. Also featured: Advanced camps for older children, after school cooking classes, cooking parties, catering, gingerbread workshops.
FACULTY: Owner Margaret Konigsmark has 20 yrs experience working with children & teaching cooking classes.
COSTS: $300/1 wk camp.
CONTACT: Margaret Konigsmark, Owner, Cooking Up A Party, 1072 Canton St., Roswell, GA 30075; 770-993-4911, Fax 678-445-3882, mkon@prodigy.net, www.cookingupaparty.com. Brent Richardson, Business & Mkt. Mgr.richardson.brent@cox.net.

THE COOK'S WAREHOUSE, INC.
Atlanta & Suwanee
Sponsor: Gourmet store & cooking school. Programs: 2-4 hr demo & hands-on classes include basics, seasonal & holiday recipes, ethnic cuisines, chef specialties. Established: 1995. Class/group size: 25 demo, 16 hands-on. ~500 programs/yr. Facilities: 3 kitchens with the latest equipment. Also featured: Private classes at The Cook's Warehouse or on-location.
FACULTY: ~150 restaurant chefs & other culinary professionals.
COSTS: $35-$95/class.
CONTACT: Mary Moore, Owner, The Cook's Warehouse, Inc., 549-1 Amsterdam Ave. NE, Atlanta, GA 30306; 404-815-4993, Fax 404-815-0543, cooley@cookswarehouse.com, www.cookswarehouse.com. Cooley Keep Fales, Cooking School Director cooley@cookswarehouse.com.

HERBERT F. SPASSER WINE PROGRAMS
Atlanta
Sponsor: Wine professional. Programs: 4-session courses that include slide lectures & tastings. Established: 1976. Class/group size: 14. 2 programs/yr.

FACULTY: Dr. Spasser, CWE, is an Officier/Commandeur of the Chaine des Rotisseurs & has been teaching since 1976.

COSTS: $215/course.

CONTACT: Herbert F. Spasser, D.D.S., Herbert F. Spasser Wine Programs, 2660 Peachtree Rd NW, Atlanta, GA 30305; 404-842-1651, jill-herb@2660Peachtree.com.

THE NICHOLAS LODGE SCHOOL OF CAKE DECORATING
Atlanta

Sponsor: Private school. Programs: 1- to 5-day hands-on classes on cake decorating techniques, wedding cakes, gumpaste flowers, rolled fondant & other sugar arts. Established: 1992. Class/group size: 16 max. ~30 programs/yr. Facilities: 1 work station/student. Also featured: Cake decorating tools & equipment available.

FACULTY: Nicholas Lodge, 20+ yrs cake decorating experience, has taught for 14 yrs in 26 countries. Guest teachers.

COSTS: $85/day, $180/2 days, $450/5 days includes lunch. Hotel lodging available nearby.

CONTACT: Scott Ewing, School Director, The Nicholas Lodge School of Cake Decorating & Sugar Arts, 6060 McDonough Drive, Suite F, Norcross, GA 0; 770-453-9449, Fax 770-448-9046, nicklodge1@aol.com, nicholaslodge.com.

URSULA'S COOKING SCHOOL, INC.
Atlanta

Sponsor: Culinary professional Ursula Knaeusel. Programs: 4-session demo courses. Established: 1966. Class/group size: 30-40. 3 programs/yr. Facilities: 3-level classroom with 18-ft mirror over a 22-ft granite counter. Also featured: Gingerbread house, cutting & decorating classes, couples classes.

FACULTY: Ursula Knaeusel, 50 yrs experience includes supervising kitchens, operating restaurants & teaching. She hosts PBS' Cooking With Ursula.

COSTS: $100/4-session course.

CONTACT: Ursula Knaeusel, President, Ursula's Cooking School, Inc., 1764 Cheshire Bridge Rd., N.E., Atlanta, GA 0; 404-876-7463, Fax 404-876-7467, Ursula@UrsulaCooks.com, UrsulaCooks.com.

ILLINOIS

CALPHALON CULINARY CENTER
Chicago

Sponsor: Cookware manufacturer. Programs: Demo & hands-on classes in basic techniques, applied skills, & specifictopics such as desserts & sauces, entertaining, & ethnic cuisines. Guest chef classes & market tours. Class/group size: 12 hands-on, 60 demo. 100+ programs/yr. Facilities: 8,000-sq-ft facility includes 3 teaching areas, lecture/demo hall seating ~60 persons, 12-station hands-on classroom with separate cooktops, commercial kitchen, wine cellar & private dining area.

COSTS: $50-$75/class.

CONTACT: Calphalon Culinary Center, 1000 W. Washington St., Chicago, IL 60607; 866-780-7799, 312-529-0100, Fax 866-623-2089, CCC.chicago@calphalon.com, www.calphalonculinarycenter.com.

CHEZ MADELAINE COOKING SCHOOL & TOURS TO FRANCE
Hinsdale; Haute Vienne (Limousin), Bordeaux & Provence, France

Sponsor: Culinary professional Madelaine Bullwinkel. Programs: 1- to 3-session hands-on classes, evening menu classes, corporate team-building. Established: 1977. Class/group size: 6-12/class, 12/tour. 40-50 programs/yr. Facilities: Restored 18th century Chateau de Sannat in the Limousin; hotel in Bordeaux; private home in Provence. Also featured: Three 7-day tours/yr with hands-on classes, restaurant cooking class, market visits; some include the art of porcelain (Limoges), cheese & foie gras artisans, mushroom picking, wine school, chateau visits, winery tours.

FACULTY: Madelaine Bullwinkel received the Diplome from L'Academie de Cuisine, is author of Gourmet Preserves & Chez Madelaine & is a member of Les Dames d'Escoffier. Guest instructors.

COSTS: Classes: $90. Tours: $2,800 ($3,200) incl shared (single) lodging, meals, ground transport.
CONTACT: Madelaine Bullwinkel, Chez Madeleine Cooking School & Tours, 425 Woodside Ave., Hinsdale, IL 60521; 630-325-4177, Fax 630-655-0355, chezmb@aol.com, www.chezm.com.

CHICAGO WINE SCHOOL
Chicago & suburbs
Sponsor: Wine school. Programs: 1-session evening seminars & 5-wk courses. Established: 1984. Class/group size: 6-42. 67 programs/yr. Facilities: Local retail & restaurant locations. Also featured: Private sessions.
FACULTY: Director Patrick W. Fegan.
COSTS: $55-$75/1-evening seminar, $160-$325/5-wk course.
CONTACT: Patrick W. Fegan, Director, Chicago Wine School, 2001 S. Halsted St., Chicago, IL 60608; 312-266-9463, Fax 312-266-9769, pwfegan@aol.com, www.wineschool.com.

THE CHOPPING BLOCK COOKING SCHOOL
Chicago
Sponsor: Private cooking school. Programs: Daily & weekend hands-on & demo classes for the home cook; technique-oriented Building Blocks series; wine classes. Established: 1997. Class/group size: 16 demo/12 hands-on. 425 programs/yr. Facilities: 2 locations with fully equipped, home-style kitchens. Also featured: Customized private classes, corporate team building, events & parties, kitchen store.
FACULTY: Owner/chef Shelley Young & staff of 12 professional chefs.
COSTS: Demo classes $50, hands-on classes $75, wine classes $60.
CONTACT: Shelley Young, Founder/Instructor, The Chopping Block Cooking School, 1324 W. Webster Ave., Chicago, IL 60614; 773-472-6700, Fax 773-472-6779, info@thechoppingblock.net, www.thechoppingblock.net. 2nd location: 4747 N Lincoln Ave.

COOKING WITH INSPIRATION
Chicago
Sponsor: Inspiration Corporation, a non-profit that provides supportive services for the homeless. Programs: Tuesday evening classes. Established: 1989. Class/group size: 30. 20+ programs/yr. Facilities: Inspiration Cafe, a 3,500-sq-ft space with commercial kitchen.
FACULTY: Chicago-area executive/professional chefs who donate their time.
COSTS: $40/class, $100/3 classes. $10 lab fee for wine classes. All proceeds benefit Inspiration Corp.
CONTACT: Jennifer Salopek, Development Manager, Cooking with Inspiration, 4554 N. Broadway, #207, Chicago, IL 60640; 773-878-0981 x223, Fax 773-878-3114, jsalopek@inspirationcorp.org, www.inspirationcorp.org/support_scheduled_classes.html. info@inspirationcorp.org.

CORNER COOKS, INC.
Winnetka
Sponsor: Private school. Programs: Demo & hands-on classes. Established: 1999. Class/group size: 6-30. ~175 programs/yr. Facilities: Granite counter with seating for ~16, additional seating for 50; professional kitchen with home touches. Also featured: Dinner parties, private parties, corporate team building, catering, take-out.
FACULTY: Owner/teacher Betsy Simson, who studied in Italy & Chicago; Larry Smith, an executive chef; visiting chefs & lecturers.
COSTS: Classes $45-$60.
CONTACT: Betsy Simson, Owner, Corner Cooks, Inc., 507 Chestnut St., Winnetka, IL 60093; 847-441-0134, Fax 847-441-9434, cornercook@aol.com, www.cornercooks.com.

CULINARY CAMP AT KENDALL COLLEGE
Evanston *(See also page 50) (See display ad page 49)*
Sponsor: Private liberal arts college. Programs: 5-day camps for HS students ages 14-18 include Culinary Camp, Baking & Pastry Camp & Advanced Culinary Camp. Camps conclude with a banquet prepared by students. Established: 1985. Class/group size: 16 max. Facilities: 7 kitchens on cam-

pus, including a student-run cafeteria & an open-to-the-public fine dining room run by the students. FACULTY: Kendall College culinary faculty. COSTS: $885 includes dormitory lodging & meals. Commuter rate $575. CONTACT: Kendall College Culinary Camp, c/o Office of Admissions, Evanston, IL 60201; 847-448-2304, Fax 847448-2120, culinarycamp@kendall.edu, www.kendall.edu.

FRENCH PASTRY SCHOOL AT CITY COLLEGES OF CHICAGO
Chicago

Sponsor: Pastry Chefs Sebastien Canonne & Jacquy Pfeiffer, in collaboration with the City Colleges of Chicago. Programs: 3- to 5-day hands-on dessert courses. Established: 1996. Class/group size: 16 max. 50+ programs/yr. Facilities: New teaching facility with latest equipment. FACULTY: Owner/instructor Jacquy Pfeiffer, 25+ yrs experience, named one of Top Ten Pastry Chefs in U.S. by Chocolatier & Pastry Art & Design magazines. COSTS: $600/3-day course, $750/5-day course. CONTACT: Rowena Frith, French Pastry School, 226 West Jackson Blvd. at City Colleges of Chicago, Chicago, IL 60606; 312-726-2419, Fax 312-726-2446, info@frenchpastryschool.com, www.frenchpastryschool.com.

HEAT & SPICE COOKING SCHOOL
Chicago

Sponsor: Chef Joseph Sochor. Programs: Programs in regional Mexican, Indian & Thai cooking. Established: 1997. Class/group size: 5 hands-on. 145 programs/yr. Facilities: Private kitchen for hands-on classes, commercial facilities for corporate functions. Also featured: Business classes, cooking class parties, kitchen coaching, group demos. FACULTY: Chef & caterer Joseph Sochor, a graduate of Cordon Bleu Chicago; guest chefs. COSTS: $50-$95/class. $150-$310/3- to 6-session courses. CONTACT: Joseph Sochor, Heat & Spice Cooking School, 925 W. Cullom Ave., Chicago, IL 60613; 773-742-2331, heatandspice@rcn.com.

JILL PRESCOTT CULINARY SCHOOL
Chicago   *(See display ad page 204)*

Sponsor: Private school. Programs: Week-long, weekend & consecutive 1-day courses in classic cuisine, bread, seafood, Italian, pastry, desserts. Established: 1988. Class/group size: 10 hands-on/25+ demo. 800 programs/yr. Facilities: The 7,000-sq-ft new facility includes 4 teaching kitchens, 3 participation kitchens & a demo kitchen also used for filming the TV series. Also featured: Corporate & private programs. Annual 8-day Food Tour of Paris with Jill Prescott features classes, market visits, Michelin-star restaurant dining, tours of food-related shops. FACULTY: Jill Prescott, professionally trained in Paris, is host of 2 nationally-syndicated PBS series & author of Jill Prescott's Ecole de Cuisine. Executive Chef Mark Weber has experience in France & Italy & is recipient of a DiRona award. COSTS: Hands-on: $150-$1,200 for a full-week course; demos $70-$85. CONTACT: Jill Prescott, Jill Prescott Culinary School, Suite 107 Merchandise Mart Plaza, Chicago, IL 60654; 312-822-8100, Fax 312-822-8108, questions@jillprescott.com, www.jillprescott.com/shaws.

LET'S GO BISTRO
Downers Grove

Sponsor: Private school & retail store. Programs: Hands-on & demo classes; 12-wk basic techniques series. Established: 2003. Class/group size: 20 demo, 10 hands-on. 300/yr programs/yr. Facilities: Kitchen with new commercial equipment, bar seating with TVs for close-up viewing. FACULTY: Exec Chef/Owner Mike Sodaro, a graduate of the Culinary School at Kendall College; Gen'l Mgr Liz Sodaro, trained at CHIC; area guest chefs. COSTS: Classes ~$50, 12-wk basics series $895. CONTACT: Michael Sodaro, Chef/Owner, Let's Go Bistro, 970 Warren Ave., Downers Grove, IL 60515; 630-795-0100, Fax 630-795-0102, info@letsgobistro.com, www.letsgobistro.com.

THE PREMIER CULINARY SCHOOL FOR HOME CHEFS

Now open in Chicago's Merchandise Mart, the Jill Prescott Culinary School is the premier school designed specifically for home chefs. Founded in 1988, it is modeled after the professional Parisian schools where Jill has studied.

This prestigious school features renowned French techniques using only the finest ingredients and cookware as well as four state-of-the-art kitchens. Jill is host of two nationally syndicated PBS series with a third now in production and her book "Jill Prescott Culinary School" is in its second printing.

After numerous trips to Europe gathering insight from fellow chefs and artisan food producers, Jill now shares these time-honored traditions and instructions with her students. She fine-tuned her years of experience and vast curriculum into a variety of intensive one week, weekend and one-day participation courses. Demonstration classes are also offered. Best of all, most participation classes end with a meal and complimentary wine. The school is also a perfect venue for a client or company event or social outing.

Experience the ultimate cooking school. Visit jillprescott.com for course descriptions and enroll today.

JILL PRESCOTT
CULINARY SCHOOL

Professional Cooking *for the* Home Chef
CHICAGO'S MERCHANDISE MART · 312.822.8100 · JILLPRESCOTT.COM

NORTHSHORE COOKERY
Highland Park

Sponsor: Recreational cooking school & cookware store. Programs: Hands-on & demo classes that include knife skills, sauteing & grilling, ethnic cuisines, appetizers, entertaining, breads, pastries. Established: 2003. Class/group size: 5-25. 200 programs/yr. Facilities: Full hands-on kitchen with 20 stove tops, multiple ovens. Also featured: Private parties, catering, personal chefs.
FACULTY: Chicago-area chefs & instructors.
COSTS: $50-$100.
CONTACT: Northshore Cookery, 600 Central Ave., #130, Highland Park, IL 60035; 847-432-2665, Fax 847-432-2606, info@northshorecookery.com, www.northshorecookery.com.

PRAIRIE KITCHENS COOKING SCHOOL
Chicago & suburbs

Sponsor: Private school. Programs: Hands-on 1- to 5-session classes that feature updated classical techniques, certification program covering basic techniques, seasonal, & ethnic foods. Established: 1989. Class/group size: 15-25. 50+ programs/yr. Facilities: Professional kitchens with work stations. Also featured: Children's classes, private instruction, visits to markets & food producers, sightseeing, dining in private homes, wine & food events for individuals & businesses.
FACULTY: Carolynn Friedman, chef, caterer & instructor, member of the IACP & AIWF.
COSTS: ~$50/session.
CONTACT: Carolynn Friedman, President, Prairie Kitchens Cooking School, PO Box 372, Morton Grove, IL 60053; 847-966-7574, Fax 847-966-7589.

WHAT'S COOKING
Hinsdale; China; Hong Kong; India; Indonesia; Malaysia; Singapore; Thailand

Sponsor: Cookbook author Ruth Law. Programs: Demo & participation courses & Far East tours that feature classes with professional chefs, gourmet dining, sightseeing, visits to food markets. Established: 1980. Class/group size: 15 hands-on.
FACULTY: Ruth Law is author of Julia Child Cookbook Award finalist Indian Light Cooking, Pacific Light Cooking, & The Southeast Asia Cookbook.
CONTACT: Ruth Law, What's Cooking, 7206 Chestnut Hills Dr., Burr Ridge, IL 60521; 630-986-1595, Fax 630-655-0912, lawcooks2@netscape.net.

WILTON SCHOOL OF CAKE DECORATING & CONFECTIONERY ART
Woodridge

Sponsor: Private school. Programs: 1-day to 2-week participation courses, daily workshops. Established: 1929. Class/group size: 15-20. Facilities: The 2,200-sq-ft school includes a classroom, teaching kitchen, student lounge, & retail store.
FACULTY: Includes Sandra Folsom, Susan Matusiak, Collette Peters, Mary Gavenda, Nancy Guerine, Lois Levine.
COSTS: Range from $80 for 1 day to $725 for a 10-day course.
CONTACT: School Coordinator, Wilton School of Cake Decorating & Confectionery Art, 2240 W. 75th St., Woodridge, IL 60517; 630-810-2211, Fax 630-963-7299, cweeditz@wilton.com, www.wilton.com.

INDIANA

COUNTRY KITCHEN, SWEETART, INC.
Fort Wayne

Sponsor: Private school. Programs: Basic to advanced cake decorating courses, demo & participation classes on candies, desserts. Established: 1964. Class/group size: 35 hands-on/60 demo. 30-40 programs/yr. Facilities: Multipurpose classroom with cakes & desserts on display. Also featured: Classes for groups, children's parties.
FACULTY: 10+ instructors.

COSTS: Cake decorating courses from $65-$70, demos from $10-$40.

CONTACT: Vi Whittington, Owner, Country Kitchen, SweetArt, Inc., 4621 Speedway Dr., Fort Wayne, IN 46825; 260-482-4835, Fax 260-483-4091, cntryktchn@aol.com, www.countrykitchen-sa.com/Index.htm.

KITCHEN AFFAIRS
Evansville
Sponsor: Cooking school, cookware & gourmet food store. Programs: Evening & weekend demo & participation classes. Established: 1987. Class/group size: 12 hands-on/20 demo. 125+ programs/yr. Facilities: 400-sq-ft kitchen with 4 work stations. Also featured: Children's classes, private classes.
FACULTY: Restaurant chefs, professional instructors, cookbook authors, & school owners Shelly & Mike Sackett. Many instructors are IACP members.
COSTS: $15-$60.
CONTACT: Shelly Sackett, Director, Kitchen Affairs, 4610 Vogel Rd., Evansville, IN 47715; 800-782-6762, sales@kitchenaffairs.com, www.kitchenaffairs.com.

IOWA

COOKING WITH LIZ CLARK
Keokuk
Sponsor: Culinary professional Liz Clark with Southeastern Community College. Programs: Demo & participation classes. Established: 1977. Class/group size: 12 hands-on/16 demo. 80 programs/yr. Facilities: Elizabeth Clark's renovated antebellum home, which also houses her restaurant. Also featured: Weekend & 5-day intensives that offer CEU's, culinary tours in the U.S. & abroad.
FACULTY: Liz Clark studied in Italy & France, received a diploma from La Varenne, studied at Moulin de Mougins with Roger Verge & The Oriental in Bangkok.
COSTS: $39-$80/class. B&B is located nearby.
CONTACT: Sandy Seabold, Coordinator, Southeastern Community College, 335 Messenger Rd., Box 6007, Keokuk, IA 0; 319-752-2731 x8411, Fax 319-524-8621, sseabold@secc.cc.ia.us, www.secc.cc.ia.us/.

THE CHEF'S TABLE
Clive
Sponsor: Private school. Programs: Demo & participation classes. Private cooking parties & team-building workshops available. Facilities: Professional demo kitchen.
FACULTY: Executive Chef Darrin Miller, Chef Rex Coble, guest chefs from area restaurants.
COSTS: $45-$60.
CONTACT: The Chef's Table, 9902 Swanson Blvd., Clive, IA 50325; 515-205-3838, chefstabledsm@msn.com, www.thechefstable.net.

KANSAS

COOKING AT BONNIE'S PLACE
Wichita
Sponsor: Cooking instructor Bonnie Aeschliman. Programs: Demos. Established: 1990. Class/group size: 25. 40-50 programs/yr. Facilities: Demo kitchen.
FACULTY: Bonnie Aeschliman, CCP, has a master's degreee in food & nutrition; Dr. Phil Aeschliman is a member of the IACP.
COSTS: $30/class.
CONTACT: Bonnie Aeschliman, Cooking at Bonnie's Place, 5900 E. 47th St., North, Wichita, KS 67220; 316-744-1981, paeschlima@aol.com.

KITCHEN CREATIONS
Olathe
Sponsor: Private school. Programs: Demo classes. Established: 1998. Class/group size: 14. 100 programs/yr. Facilities: Home kitchen with overhead mirror & dining room. Also featured: Private classes.
FACULTY: Joe Gottschall, professional chef for 15 yrs & member of ACF.
COSTS: $40/class.
CONTACT: Kathy Ales Miller, Kitchen Creations, 15032 W. 144th Terr., Olathe, KS 66062; 913-764-8790, Fax 913-768-8846, KitchenCreations@yahoo.com, www.geocities.com/kitchencreations.

KENTUCKY

KREMER'S MARKET
Crescent Springs
Sponsor: Specialty market. Programs: Demo classes. Established: 1991. Class/group size: 20 max. 12+ programs/yr. Facilities: Designated area in the market. Also featured: Dinner party classes, private group classes.
FACULTY: Chef Maggie Green, RD, a graduate of Sullivan Univ. Local & guest chefs.
COSTS: $45-65 for guest chefs/teachers, $30-$35 for other classes.
CONTACT: Warren or Sis Heist, Owners, Kremer's Market, 755 Buttermilk Pike, Crescent Springs, KY 41017; 859-341-1067, Fax 859-341-7008, office@kremersmarket.com, www.kremersmarket.com.

LOUISIANA

CHEF JOHN FOLSE CULINARY INSTITUTE
Thibodaux
Sponsor: University. Programs: 1/2-day to week-long demo/participation program. Established: 1994. Facilities: 2 newly-equipped teaching kitchens, 2 demo classrooms. Also featured: Market visits, dining in fine restaurants, sightseeing, tours of food producers.
FACULTY: Chef John Folse, CEC, AAC, executive chef & owner of Chef John Folse & Co., specializing in Cajun & Creole cuisine; Institute faculty.
CONTACT: Dr. Robert Harrington, Dean, Nicholls State University, 107 Gouaux Hall, PO Box 2099, Thibodaux, LA 70310; 985-449-7100, 877-NICHOLLS, Fax 985-449-7089, jfci-rjh@nicholls.edu, www.nicholls.edu/jfolse.

COOKIN' CAJUN COOKING SCHOOL
New Orleans
Sponsor: Creole Delicacies, a company specializing in Cajun & Creole gourmet items. Programs: Demo classes Monday-Sunday mornings. Established: 1988. Class/group size: 1-75. Facilities: Theater-style mirrored kitchen overlooking the Mississippi River. Also featured: Private classes, parties, fish classes for anglers.
FACULTY: Susan Murphy & other instructors.
COSTS: $20/class.
CONTACT: Lissette Sutton, Owner, Cookin' Cajun Cooking School, #1 Poydras, Store #116, New Orleans, LA 70130; 504-523-6425, Fax 504-523-4787, info@cookincajun.com, www.cookincajun.com.

FOODVACATION
Kemptville, NS, Canada; Alajuela Province, Costa Rica; Albaycin, Granada, Spain
Sponsor: Private company. Programs: Hotel-based culinary programs: Nova Scotia Seafood Cooking School, Granada Cooking School in Spain, & Tropical Creole Cooking School in Costa Rica. Established: 1999. Class/group size: 12 max. 20 programs/yr. Facilities: Full commercial kitchens & teaching facilities. Also featured: Tours, travel assistance, field trips.
FACULTY: Owners & culinary professionals Daniel G. Abel, Vaughn J. Perret, & Charles L. Leary, Ph.D. have worked as specialty food consultants, organic farmers, authors, chefs & restaurateurs.

COSTS: $675/3-day program in Nova Scotia, including lodging & meals; $750/3-day all-inclusive program in Costa Rica; $400-$500 for Granada.

CONTACT: Vaughn Perret, Managing Director, Abel Perret & Leary LLC, 723 Hillary St., New Orleans, LA 70118; 504-866-2931, Fax (504) 866-5903, info@foodvacation.com, www.foodvacation.com. 902-742-0980 (Nova Scotia), (34) 958 201 557 (Granada, Spain).

KAY EWING'S EVERYDAY GOURMET
Baton Rouge

Sponsor: Culinary professional Kay Ewing. Programs: Full participation classes. Established: 1985. Class/group size: 8. 8-10 programs/yr. Facilities: Fully equipped kitchen in The Royal Standard, a specialized gift & antiques store. Also featured: Summer classes for youngsters, ages 9-14. Yearly culinary adventures to various cities.

FACULTY: Kay Ewing is a member of the IACP & author of Kay Ewing's Cooking School Cookbook & Kay Ewing's Cooking School Cookbook...A Second Course.

COSTS: $40 for adults, $30 for children.

CONTACT: Kay Ewing, Owner, c/o The Royal Standard, 16016 Perkins Rd., Baton Rouge, LA 70810; 225-751-0698, 225-756-2039, kaymewing@cox.net, www.kayewing.com.

LOUISIANA SCHOOL OF COOKING & CAJUN STORE
St. Martinville

Sponsor: Private school. Programs: Classes focusing on Cajun & Creole cuisine, culinary adventures, programs for foodservice professionals, food & wine dinners. Established: 1999. Class/group size: 30-100. Facilities: Demo kitchen with overhead mirror. Also featured: Custom classes, wine tastings, children's classes, corporate & team building programs.

FACULTY: Chef/owner Patrick Mould is a cookbook author, TV personality, food columnist, & culinary consultant whose specialty is Cajun & Creole cuisine.

COSTS: $25-$75/class, cooking vacations start at $1,595.

CONTACT: Eva Hebert, Director of Guest Service, Louisiana School of Cooking, 112 South Main St., St. Martinville, LA 70587; 337-394-1710, Fax 337-394-1711, chefpat@louisianaschoolofcooking.com, www.louisianaschoolofcooking.com. Chef Patrick Mould 337-983-0896.

THE MARDI GRAS SCHOOL OF COOKING
New Orleans

Sponsor: Culinary professional Richard Bond. Programs: Full-day customized hands-on courses. Established: 1997. Class/group size: 2-12. Daily programs/yr. Facilities: Kitchens located in 140-yr-old home. Also featured: Private dinner parties, demo classes for up to 2,000, receptions, theme events, private group classes.

FACULTY: Richard Bond, past owner of 2 four-star New Orleans restaurants & former instructor at The New Orleans School of Cooking & House, Gardens & Gumbo.

COSTS: Full day $90. Includes wine, beer, soft drinks.

CONTACT: Chef Richard Bond, The Mardi Gras School of Cooking, 232 Bermuda St., Suite B, New Orleans, LA 70114; 504-362-5225, chefbond@att.net, www.gumbos.net.

THE NEW ORLEANS COOKING EXPERIENCE
New Orleans

Sponsor: Private vacation cooking school. Programs: 4- & 6-day programs featuring hands-on classes, visits to architectural sites, antiquing, dining in fine restaurants. Established: 2002. Class/group size: 10 max. 40 programs/yr. Facilities: Private kitchen, dining room & salon in a French Quarter residential setting. Also featured: Half-day classes for private groups.

COSTS: $2,000/4 days, $2,500/6 days.

CONTACT: Judy Jurisich, Director, The New Orleans Cooking Experience, 321 St. Charles Ave., 5th Flr., New Orleans, LA 70130; 504-522-4955, Fax 504-522-0538, judy@neworleanscookingexperience.com, www.neworleanscookingexperience.com.

THE SAVVY GOURMET
New Orleans
Sponsor: Private school founded by psychologist Aaron Wolfson. Programs: Demo & hands-on classes. Established: 2001. Class/group size: 8-40. 50-60 programs/yr. Facilities: Restaurant kitchens. Dedicated facilty planned. Also featured: In-home dinner parties, wine tastings, convention programs, corporate team building, children's parties.
FACULTY: Professional chefs with restaurant experience.
COSTS: $60/hands-on class, $40/demo.
CONTACT: Peter Menge, General Manager, The Savvy Gourmet, 3816 Bienville St., New Orleans, LA 70119; 504-482-3726, Fax 504-488-9863, info@savvy-gourmet.com, www.savvy-gourmet.com.

MARYLAND

CHEFPROFESSOR IN-HOME COOKING CLASSES
Mitchellville & Upper Marlboro
Sponsor: Professional executive chef & teacher. Programs: Personalized private classes & small group parties. Established: 1998. Facilities: Client's kitchen.
FACULTY: Owner Jack A. Batten, CEC, 30+ yrs culinary experience, has taught at Prince Georges CC & Anne Arundel CC.
COSTS: Private classes $250-$350; group parties (6 max) from $350.
CONTACT: Jack Batten, Chef, ChefWorks PCS Personal Classes, 7203 Havre Turn, Upper Marlboro, MD 20772; 301-627-4496, Fax 301-574-0816, jbatten@earthlink.net, www.chefprofessor.com.

CHEZ MOI COOKING INSTRUCTION AT HOME
Annapolis & Baltimore
Programs: At-home one-on-one cooking instruction. 11-session Comprehensive Cooking course covers classic French cooking. Established: 2001. Class/group size: 1-2. Facilities: Participant's home.
FACULTY: Culinary professionals who have worked in restaurants as chefs, taught cooking & have served as consultants.
COSTS: $1,150 tuition. Cooking equipment $0-$700. Food supplies ~$250.
CONTACT: Jordan Holtzman, Franchise Owner/Instructor, Chez Moi Cooking Instruction At Home, 618 Harborside Dr., Suite F, Joppa, MD 21085; 410-538-4600, info@chezmoicooking.com.

THE CHINESE COOKERY, INC.
Silver Spring
Sponsor: Culinary professional Joan Shih. Programs: 8 levels of participation & demo courses in Chinese cuisine. Established: 1975. Class/group size: 5. ~36-40 programs/yr. Facilities: Classroom/lab equipped for Chinese cooking, outdoor Chinese brick oven. Also featured: Japanese sushi class, classes for teenagers, private lessons for cooking professionals, market visits, restaurant kitchen tours, culinary tours to the Far East.
FACULTY: Joan Shih, a retired chemist from the NIH, received a certificate in Chinese cuisine in Taiwan, has taught Chinese & Japanese cooking & is author of The Art of Chinese Cookery.
COSTS: 5-session courses are $200, vegetarian is $205, sushi class is $70.
CONTACT: Joan Shih, President & Director, The Chinese Cookery, Inc., 14209 Sturtevant Rd., Silver Spring, MD 20905; 301-236-5311, joanshih@aol.com, www.thechinesecookery.com. chinesecookery@aol.com.

A COOK'S TABLE COOKING CLASSES
Baltimore
Sponsor: Cookware store & cooking school. Programs: Participation classes on topics that include seasonal & holiday foods, guest chef specialties, American regional & international cuisines. Established: 1996. Class/group size: 20. 150 programs/yr. Facilities: Professional cooking area with close-counter seating facing the chef & cooking area. Also featured: Private cooking lessons & par-

ties, cooking tours to Italy, market shopping tours.

FACULTY: Local & nationally known chefs, cookbook authors, TV chefs.

COSTS: $35-$75/class.

CONTACT: A Cook's Table Cooking Classes, 717 Light Street, Baltimore, MD 21230; 410-539-8600, Fax 410-539-6845, info@acookstable.com, www.acookstable.com.

L'ACADEMIE DE CUISINE
Bethesda

Sponsor: Proprietary vocational & recreational school. Programs: 1- to 4-session demo & participation courses. Established: 1976. Class/group size: 21-30. 1,000 programs/yr. Facilities: 21-station practice kitchen, 30-seat demo classroom. Also featured: Children's classes, private dinners, guest chef demos, 1-wk culinary/culture trips to France, team building programs, wine courses.

FACULTY: 4 full- & 15 part-time. School President Francois Dionot, graduate of L'Ecole Hoteliere de la Societe Suisse des Hoteliers & founder of the IACP; Amy White, Patrice Dionot, Marina Ross, Nancy Novak.

COSTS: $40-$75/session.

CONTACT: Amy White, Managing Director, L'Academie de Cuisine, 5021 Wilson Lane, Bethesda, MD 20814; 301-986-9490, Fax 301-652-7970, classes@lacademie.com, www.lacademie.com.

RONALDO'S OF POTOMAC
Gaithersburg

Sponsor: Private school. Programs: Hands-on classes & series that cover basic & advanced techniques, party planning, regional & ethnic specialties. Established: 2004. Class/group size: 20 max. 150 programs/yr. Facilities: Home grade appliances. Also featured: Cooking parties, dinners, programs for children & families.

FACULTY: Includes local restaurant chefs, personal chefs, dietitians.

COSTS: Start at $35/class.

CONTACT: Jill Bloomfield, Owner, Ronaldo's of Potomac, 251 Market St. West, 2nd Flr., The Kentlands, Gaithersburg, MD 20878; 301-977-8300, Fax 301-977-8300, jillcolella@earthlink.net, www.ronaldosofpotomac.com.

MASSACHUSETTS

BOSTON UNIVERSITY CULINARY ARTS
Boston

Sponsor: University. Programs: 1- to 5-session demo & participation courses. Established: 1986. Class/group size: 12-130. 50 programs/yr. Facilities: Demo & wine tasting room, 8 restaurant kitchens, wine library. Also featured: Children's classes, market visits, food & wine pairing, domestic & foreign tours hosted by a culinary historian familiar with the region's food & wine.

FACULTY: Includes Jacques Pepin, Julia Child, Jasper White, Jody Adams, Franco Romagnoli, Daniel Bruce, Sandy Block, Chris Schlesinger, Nina Simonds, Julie Sahni, Todd English, Clive Coates.

COSTS: Seminars $10-$125, full-day classes & 3-session courses $150-$300.

CONTACT: Rebecca Alssid, Director of Special Programs, Boston University Culinary Arts, 808 Commonwealth Ave., Boston, MA 2215; 617-353-9852, Fax 617-353-4130, ralssid@bu.edu, www.bu.edu/met/programs.

THE CAMBRIDGE SCHOOL OF CULINARY ARTS
Cambridge

Sponsor: Proprietary school. Programs: 1- to 5-session participation courses. Established: 1974. Class/group size: 12. Facilities: 3 kitchens & demonstration classrooms with gas & electric commercial appliances. Also featured: Celebrity chef demonstrations.

FACULTY: Diverse faculty include CSCA graduates & instructors & other industry professionals.

COSTS: $70 for single session classes, $300 for 5-session courses.

CONTACT: The Cambridge School of Culinary Arts, 2020 Massachusetts Ave., Cambridge, MA 2140; 617-354-2020, Fax 617-576-1963, info@cambridgeculinary.com, www.cambridgeculinary.com.

THE CAPTAIN FREEMAN INN
Brewster, Cape Cod

Sponsor: Historic seaside country inn. Programs: Weekend courses that feature a hands-on Saturday class, wine tasting & dinner. Established: 1993. Class/group size: 12-18. 8-10 programs/yr. Facilities: The inn's kitchen. Also featured: Beach, theater, golf & antiquing nearby.

FACULTY: Carol Edmondson, chef & cookbook author.

COSTS: $490-$610, which includes inn lodging, breakfasts, wine tasting & dinner for 2.

CONTACT: Carol Edmondson, Innkeeper, The Captain Freeman Inn, 15 Breakwater Rd., Brewster, Cape Cod, MA 2631; 800-843-4664, 508-896-7481, Fax 508-896-5618, visitus@capecod.net, www.capecodculinary.com.

DELPHIN'S GOURMANDISE & SCHOOL OF PASTRY
Marblehead

Sponsor: Private school. Programs: 1- to 3-day hands-on workshops, evening demos. Established: 2000. Class/group size: 6-8 students. 5 programs/yr. Facilities: Kitchen/classroom.

FACULTY: Master Pastry Chef Delphin Gomes, co-owner of Delphin's Gourmandise Fine French Patisserie, received the Best of Boston award from Boston Magazine.

COSTS: $295-$840/workshop, $85/class.

CONTACT: Tone Gomes, Delphin's Gourmandise & School of Pastry, 258 Washington St., Marblehead, MA 1945; 781-639-2311, Fax 781-631-2311, DGschoolofpastry@delphins.com, www.delphins.com.

HOME CHEESEMAKING 101
Ashfield

Sponsor: New England Cheesemaking Supply Co. Programs: 1-day hands-on class covers fresh mozzarella, whole milk ricotta, whey ricotta, farmhouse cheddar, queso blanco, fromage blanc, mascarpone, & creme fraiche. Established: 1978. Class/group size: 25. 6-10 programs/yr.

FACULTY: Owner Ricki Carroll, teaching since 1978, is author of Home Cheese Making.

COSTS: $100 includes lunch.

CONTACT: Ricki Carroll, Pres., Home Cheesemaking 101, PO Box 85, Main St., Ashfield, MA 1330; 413-628-3808, Fax 413-628-4061, info@cheesemaking.com, www.cheesemaking.com.

LE PETIT GOURMET COOKING SCHOOL
Wayland

Sponsor: Culinary professional Fran Rosenheim. Programs: 1- to 4-session demo/participation courses. Established: 1979. Class/group size: 1-2. Facilities: 330-sq-ft kitchen with two workspaces. Also featured: Private classes weekday mornings.

FACULTY: Fran Rosenheim studied with local chefs & at Le Cordon Bleu & La Varenne in Paris.

COSTS: $60/session.

CONTACT: Fran Rosenheim, Le Petit Gourmet Cooking School, 19 Charena Rd., Wayland, MA 1778; 508-358-4219, Fax 508-358-4291 (call 1st), frosenheim@aol.com.

RUBY CHARD COOKING & BAKING CLASSES
Quincy

Sponsor: Private school. Programs: One- & two-session hands-on & demo cooking & baking classes. Established: 2000. Class/group size: 14-22. 30 programs/yr. Facilities: Teaching kitchen with industry-current appliances & 4 working islands. Also featured: In-home private & group classes.

FACULTY: Chef Joan MacIsaac has owned a catering business for 8 yrs. Other instructors:pastry chefs Clare Garland & Heather Macdonald, wine consultant Peter Magyar.

COSTS: $36-$56/class.

CONTACT: Joan MacIsaac, Chef / Owner, Ruby Chard Cooking & Baking Classes, PO Box 180393, Boston, MA 2118; 617-325-6060, joan@rubychard.com, rubychard.com.

SUMMERFARE
North Truro (Cape Cod)

Sponsor: Commercial kitchen. Programs: Hands-on classes for all levels, weekend seminars, demos by visiting chefs, private classes. Established: 2000. Class/group size: 8 hands-on, 16 demo. Facilities: Full commercial kitchen, cookbook reference library, & vegetable, fruit & herb garden. Also featured: Growing & using herbs, food & wine pairing.
FACULTY: Owner/Director from Boston Culinary Arts Program, professional chef. Demos by visiting chefs, cookbook authors & culinary professionals.
COSTS: Classes $75, weekend seminars $125.
CONTACT: Eva A. N. Hartmann, Owner/Chef, SummerFare, PO Box 502, North Truro, MA 2652; 508-487-2387, Fax 508-487-4564, summerfare@capecod.net, www.summerfare.net.

TAMING OF THE STEW
Wellesley

Sponsor: Culinary professional Sally Larhette. Programs: 3 classes/wk that feature pre- & post-cooking discussions, shopping & preparation trips, historical perspective, hands-on class of a full menu. Established: 1998. Class/group size: 15 demo, 9 hands-on. 150 programs/yr. Facilities: Fully-equipped professionally-styled home kitchen. Also featured: Private instruction, classes for youngsters, market & winery visits, dining in private homes.
FACULTY: Sally Larhette, CCP, member of IACP, trained in French & Italian cuisines by Madeleiine Kamman, on Board of Directors of The Culinary Guild in New England.
COSTS: $35-$50/class.
CONTACT: Sally Larhette, School Director, Taming of the Stew, 619 C Washington St., Wellesley, MA 2181; 781-235-1792, Fax 781-235-7714, larhette@comcast.net.

TERENCE JANERICCO COOKING CLASSES
Boston

Sponsor: Cookbook author. Programs: 1- & 5-session demo & participation courses. Established: 1966. Class/group size: 6 hands-on/14 demo. 100+ programs/yr. Facilities: Home kitchen. Also featured: Private classes, special events, create your own class.
FACULTY: Terence Janericco has operated a catering firm for 35+ years & has taught education centers & schools in New England & Michigan. Author of 12 books, including The Book of Great Hors d'Oeuvres, & The Book of Great Desserts.
COSTS: 5-session course $400, single session $80.
CONTACT: Terence Janericco, Terence Janericco Cooking Classes, 42 Fayette St., Boston, MA 2116; 617-426-7458, Fax 617-426-7458, terencej@bellatlantic.net, www.terencejanericcocookingclasses.com.

MICHIGAN

CUISINE UNLIMITED, ACADEMIE DE CUISINE FRANCAIS
Whitehall; Biarritz, France; Spain

Sponsor: Chef Deborah Ward. Programs: Cooking & wine classes & courses that focus on the French classical method of instruction. Established: 1990. Class/group size: 12. 12 programs/yr. Facilities: Restaurant, bakery & pastry kitchen.
FACULTY: Director Deborah Ward was awarded the Merit et Devouement Gold Cross by the French Government & International Chaine de Rotisseurs. She was regional chair of a college hospitality program.
COSTS: $1,500-$3,000 for weekly or bi-weekly programs, $500 for daily programs, $4,000-6,000 for studies in France & Spain. Scholarships available in US.
CONTACT: Chef Deborah Ward, Director, Cuisine Unlimited, Academie de Cuisine Francais, PO Box 249, 115 N. Mears Ave., Whitehall, MI 49461; 231-893-5163, greatcooking@voyager.net, www.greatcooking.org. Satellite progam at Chez Moi in Pentwater, MI, 231-869-4522.

CULINARY SECRETS COOKING SCHOOL
Jackson

Sponsor: Gourmet kitchen shoppe & cooking school. Programs: Classes & courses ranging from vegetarian cuisine to traditional French cuisine; teens & kids programs; technical classes in pastry, knife skills, basic cooking techniques. Established: 1998. Class/group size: max 40. 150 programs/yr. Facilities: Gourmet kitchen with appliances provided by Viking. 18 burners, 5 ovens, a proofing oven, outdoor grill. Demonstration classes feature Bistro-style table & chairs. Also featured: Private parties, bridal showers, birthday parties, kids summer camp, off-site programs.
FACULTY: 6 in-store instructors, guest chefs.
COSTS: Classes with guest chefs & staff instructors begin at $28 (average $35). Celebrity chefs range from $45-$95. Diploma series are $300-$475.
CONTACT: Kathe Meade, School Director, Culinary Secrets Cooking School, 1821 Horton Rd., Jackson, MI 49203; 517-788-8840, 877-788-8840, Fax 517-788-8856, www.culinarysecrets.com.

LET ME COOK PERSONAL CHEF SERVICE & CULINARY CLASSES
Novi, So. Lyon, Huron Valley & Milford

Sponsor: Personal chef. Programs: Demo & hands-on classes. Established: 2002. Class/group size: 12. 75 programs/yr. Also featured: Private lessons, personal chef services, dinner parties.
FACULTY: Chef Chad Davis has 15 yrs culinary industry experience.
COSTS: $15-$20/class + $5-$10 materials fee.
CONTACT: Chad Davis, Chef, Let Me Cook Personal Chef Service & Culinary Classes, 534 Atlantic, Milford, MI 48381; 248-685-7581, chaddavis@peoplepc.com, www.LetMeCook.com.

MARSHALL FIELD'S KULINARY KIDS
Novi

Sponsor: Department store restaurant. Programs: Cooking classes for youngsters. Established: 2004. Class/group size: 10-20. Facilities: Full-service restaurant. Also featured: Business meetings, showers, tea parties.
FACULTY: Chef Peter Yiu, CEC, 40+ yrs restaurant & hotel experience; Jessica Gales, AOS Culinary Arts (CIA); guest instructors.
COSTS: From $13.
CONTACT: Jessica Gales, Asst. Restaurant Mgr., Marshall Field's Kulinary Kids, Twelve Oaks Mall, 27550 Novi Rd., Novi, MI 48377; 248-344-6985, Fax 248-344-7051, jessica.gales@target.com.

NELL BENEDICT COOKING CLASSES
Birmingham

Sponsor: Adult community center. Programs: Evening demo classes. Established: 1970. Class/group size: 40. 12 programs/yr. Facilities: Teaching kitchen. Also featured: Catering.
FACULTY: Nell Benedict studied at Le Cordon Bleu & La Varenne, with James Beard, Jacques Pepin & Roger Vergé & is author of Italian Recipes from Nell's Cucina.
COSTS: $18/session.
CONTACT: Nell Benedict, International Cuisine, Gourmet Cooking, The Community House, 380 S. Bates St., Birmingham, MI 48009; 248-644-5832, Fax 248-644-2476, info@communityhouse.com, www.communityhouse.com.

MINNESOTA

BYERLY'S SCHOOL OF CULINARY ARTS
St. Louis Park

Sponsor: School in upscale supermarket. Programs: 1-session demo & participation classes, limited series offerings. Established: 1980. Class/group size: 16 hands-on/25 demo. 200+ programs/yr. Facilities: Large teaching kitchen with overhead mirror. Also featured: Private & couple's classes, children's birthday classes, special events, team building.

FACULTY: Culinary Services Mgr Deidre Schipani has a diploma from L'Academie de Cuisine. Instructors incl CIA graduate Carol Brown, NPR host Lynne Rossetto Kasper, cookbook authors, guest chefs.

COSTS: ~$45-50/class.

CONTACT: Deidre Schipani, CCP, Manager of Culinary Services, Byerly's School of Culinary Arts, 3777 Park Center Blvd., St. Louis Park, MN 55416; 952-929-2492, Fax 952-929-7756, cooking.school@lfhi.com, www.Byerlys.com.

COOKS OF CROCUS HILL
St. Paul & Edina

Sponsor: Cooking school & gourmet retail store. Programs: 1-, 4-, & 5-session demo & participation courses. Established: 1976. Class/group size: 12 hands-on/30 demo. 450+ programs/yr. Facilities: 2 locations with modern, professional kitchens & capacity for 40 full-service dinner classes. Also featured: Private groups, corporate team-building classes.

FACULTY: 60 local, national & intl chefs & cooking instructors. Guest instructors include Diana Kennedy, Giulliano Hazan, Kasma Unchit, Deborah Madison, Hugh Carpenter, Martin Yan.

COSTS: 4-session course $250, 5-sessions $350. Classes $10-$75.

CONTACT: Kevin Wencel, Director, Cooks of Crocus Hill, 877 Grand Ave., St. Paul, MN 55105; 651-228-1333, Fax 651-228-9084, kwencel@cochmail.com, www.cooksofcrocushill.com. Also at 3925 W. 50th St., Edina, MN 55424.

FOOD ON FILM®
Minneapolis

Sponsor: Twin Cities Chapter of Home Economists in Business. Programs: 2-day food styling & food photography seminar that features 12 rotating demo classes + three 1-day hands-on workshops. Held in odd-numbered years. Established: 1982. Class/group size: 50-100. Facilities: Hilton Minneapolis. Also featured: Keynote & luncheon speakers, cookbook & equipment gallery, tours.

FACULTY: Changes each seminar. Includes food stylists & photographers, cooking instructors, chefs, food writers, other industry professionals.

COSTS: $525 early bird, $575 regular includes some meals. Lodging available at Hilton Minneapolis.

CONTACT: Rachel Pederson, Administrative Asst., Food on Film®, 13251 180th Ave NW, Elk River, MN 55330; 763-241-2104, Fax 763-241-8783, rachelpederson@charter.net, www.foodonfilm.com.

KITCHEN WINDOW
Minneapolis

Sponsor: Kitchenware store & culinary arts facility. Programs: Celebrated Chefs program offered in leading Twin Cities restaurants, Cooking School classes on site. Established: 1990. Class/group size: 30 max. 180+ programs/yr. Facilities: 1,300-sq-ft facility with the latest equipment & a 32-ft island. Video & sound system. Also featured: Team-building events, private parties, parent-child classes.

FACULTY: Includes restaurant chefs & cookbook authors.

COSTS: ~$45-$85/class.

CONTACT: Ann Nelson, Cooking School Director, Kitchen Window, 3001 Hennepin Ave., Minneapolis, MN 55408; 888-824-4417, 612-824-4417, Fax 612-824-9225, info@KitchenWindow.com, www.kitchenwindow.com/.

THE CHEFS GALLERY
Stillwater

Sponsor: Cooking school & gourmet cookware store. Programs: Demo & hands-on instruction. Established: 1999. Class/group size: 12-30. 90+ programs/yr. Facilities: Viking-equipped teaching kitchen with participation facilities for 15 people. Also featured: Private group functions, corporate team building events.

FACULTY: 30 local chefs & instructors.

COSTS: $25-$80/class.

CONTACT: Stephanie Jameson, Cooking School Director, The Chefs Gallery, Grand Garage, 324 N. Main St., Stillwater, MN 55082; 651-351-1144, Fax 651-351-2165, steph@thechefsgallery.com, www.TheChefsGallery.com.

THE WRITE COOK
Minneapolis; Paris & Provence, France
Sponsor: Culinary professional. Programs: Hands-on cooking classes in Minneapolis during fall, winter & spring; food tours to Paris & Provence. Established: 1999. Class/group size: 10. Facilities: Minneapolis: home teaching kitchen. Provence: village home.
FACULTY: Classes in Minneapolis taught by cookbook author, food & travel writer Mary Ellen Evans with occasional guest instructors. Food tours conducted by Mary & Hallie Harron.
COSTS: $55/home class, tours from ~$1,500-$2,800.
CONTACT: Mary Evans, Owner/Operator, The Write Cook, 4844 Colfax Ave. South, Minneapolis, MN 55409; 612-822-6114, Fax 612-822-0274, info@thewritecook.com, www.thewritecook.com.

MISSISSIPPI

THE EVERYDAY GOURMET
Jackson
Sponsor: Schools in 2 Jackson cookware stores. Programs: Demo & participation classes. Established: 1981. Class/group size: 12 hands-on/36 demo. 100+ programs/yr. Also featured: Guest chefs, lunch sessions, classes for children, tour groups.
FACULTY: School director Chan Patterson.
COSTS: $25-$60; children's classes are $20.
CONTACT: Director, The Everyday Gourmet, Inc., 2905 Old Canton Rd., Jackson, MS 39216; 800-898-0122, Fax 601-981-3266, info@theeverydaygourmet.com, www.theeverydaygourmet.com.

MISSOURI

DIERBERGS SCHOOL OF COOKING
Four locations
Sponsor: Cooking school with 4 locations in retail grocery stores. Programs: 1-session demo & participation courses. Established: 1978. Class/group size: 18. 800+ programs/yr. Facilities: Sound-proof enclosures in Dierbergs Supermarkets. Also featured: Classes for adults, couples, children, parent-child teams, corporate teams.
FACULTY: 30+ faculty of home economists & cooking instructors; guest teachers, including industry spokespersons, restaurateurs, traveling chefs, cookbook authors.
COSTS: Adult classes $28-$32, guest classes $35-$50.
CONTACT: Barbara Ridenhour, Director of Consumer Affairs, Dierbergs School of Cooking, P.O. Box 1070, Chesterfield, MO 63006; 636-812-1330, Fax 636-537-2559, ridenhou@dierbergs.com, www.dierbergs.com. 636-812-1336 from MO, or 612-622-5353 from IL.

JASPER'S
Kansas City
Sponsor: Restaurant. Programs: Demo & holiday luncheon classes. Established: 1954. Class/group size: 45 demo. 25 programs/yr. Also featured: Private classes for groups of 20+, children's & couples' classes, wine classes.
FACULTY: Executive Chef Jasper J. Mirabile, Jr., studied at La Varenne & the Gritti Palace & has cooked at the James Beard House. Jasper's received the Dirona, Travel/Holiday, Mobil 4-Star & the AAA 4-Diamond awards.
COSTS: $45/class.
CONTACT: Jasper J. Mirabile, Jr., Chef/owner, Jasper's, 1201 W. 103rd, Kansas City, MO 64114; 816-941-6600, Fax 816-941-4346, jasperjr@aol.com, www.jasperskc.com.

KITCHEN CONSERVATORY
St. Louis

Sponsor: Cooking school in a gourmet shop. Programs: Demo & participation classes. Established: 1984. Class/group size: 18. 400+ programs/yr. Facilities: Modern kitchen with front-row seats for all students. Also featured: Day trips to restaurants & shops, classes for children.

FACULTY: Local chefs, restaurateurs, caterers, IACP members. Guest instructors have included Hugh Carpenter, Martin Yan, Joanne Weir, Paula Wolfert.

COSTS: $34-$75/class.

CONTACT: Anne Cori, Owner, Kitchen Conservatory, 8021 Clayton Rd., St. Louis, MO 63117; 314-862-COOK, 866-862-CHEF (toll free), Fax 314-862-2110, chef@kitchenconservatory.com, www.kitchenconservatory.com.

MONTANA

WHITEFISH COOKS
Whitefish

Sponsor: Private cooking school. Programs: Morning, afternoon & evening classes for beginner to advanced. Established: 1999. Class/group size: 8 max.

FACULTY: Chef Brian Cannavaro & host Joanna King.

COSTS: $50/workshop.

CONTACT: Joanna King, Whitefish Cooks, P.O. Box 4366, Whitefish, MT 59937; 406-862-5879, 406-756-8852, joanna@whitefishcooks.com, www.whitefishcooks.com/.

NEBRASKA

THE CLASSY GOURMET CULINARY ART CENTER
Omaha

Sponsor: Recreational cooking school. Programs: Demo & hands-on cooking classes, wine education programs. Topics include basics, regional, ethnic & seasonal cuisines, guest chef specialties. Established: 2002. Class/group size: Hands-on 20, demo 30. 200+ programs/yr. Facilities: 2,000-sq-ft professional Viking kitchen, full wine bar. Also featured: Private dinner parties & classes, personal chefs, corporate team building events.

FACULTY: Executive Chef Cory Guyer, owner Colleen Cleek, Chef Katie Kiviranta. Restaurant chefs include Brian O'Malley, Chris Meyer & Brad Benson.

COSTS: $25-$195/class (average $40).

CONTACT: Colleen Cleek, Owner, The Classy Gourmet, 721 N. 98th St., Omaha, NE 68114; 402-955-COOK (2665), Fax 402-932-2634, cook@theclassygourmet.com, www.theclassygourmet.com.

NEVADA

CREATIVE COOKING SCHOOL OF LAS VEGAS
Las Vegas

Sponsor: Private culinary school with a Viking appliance & retail store. Programs: Hands-on & demo classes, Intl Wine Sommelier Guild classes, Pro Chef program. Established: 2001. Class/group size: 30 demo, 16 hands-on. 300 programs/yr. Facilities: 2,000 sq-ft kitchen with the latest equipment. Also featured: Celebrity chef classes, classes for kids, corporate team-building, banquet & catering, private & special events.

FACULTY: 4 CECs, CCEs, CCPs, celebrity chefs.

COSTS: $75-$99.

CONTACT: Catherine Margles, President/Founder, Creative Cooking School of Las Vegas, 7385 W. Sahara Ave., Las Vegas, NV 0; 702-562-3900, Fax 702-562-3939, info@creativecookingschool.com, www.creativecookingschool.com. catherine@creativecookingschool.com.

NOTHING TO IT! CULINARY CENTER
Reno

Sponsor: Cookware store & gourmet take-out cafe. Programs: Classes that cover techniques & a variety of cuisines. Established: 1995. Class/group size: 55 demo, 16 hands-on. 200 programs/yr. Facilities: Culinary center with retail cafe. Also featured: Classes for youngsters, private instruction. **FACULTY:** 2 chefs on staff; nationally-known guest chefs.
COSTS: $40-$125/class.
CONTACT: Jennifer Bushman, Owner/Culinary Instructor, Nothing To It! Culinary Center, 255 Crummer Ln., Reno, NV 89502; 775-826-2628, jennifer@nothingtoit.com, www.nothingtoit.com.

NEW HAMPSHIRE

COOKING 'INN' STYLE
Manchester; Lower Waterford, VT

Sponsor: 3 New England country inns. Programs: 3-day theme cooking series that focus on seasonal menus, food & wine pairing, culinary tips & preparation techniques. Themes include Holiday Sweets & Treats, New England Comfort Food, & Summer Grilling. Established: 2002. Class/group size: 12. 3 programs/yr. Facilities: Inn kitchens. Also featured: Shopping, antiquing, historic sites, local attractions & seasonal outdoor recreation.
FACULTY: Award-winning, AAA Four-Diamond Executive & Pastry Chefs.
COSTS: $999/couple includes 1 night lodging at each inn, breakfasts, dinners & afternoon teas.
CONTACT: Mary Ellen Shields, Innkeeper, Cooking 'Inn' Style, Route 3, Holderness, NH 03245; 800-545-2141, Fax 603-968-2116, info@manorongoldenpond.com, www.cookinginnstyle.com.

A TASTE OF THE MOUNTAINS COOKING SCHOOL
Glen

Sponsor: Private cooking school at the Bernerhof Inn. Programs: Spring, winter, fall classes & weekend courses for novice & intermediate cooks; 3-hr Thursday guest chef classes in winter. Established: 1980. Class/group size: 10 hands-on. Facilities: Bernerhof Inn restaurant kitchen. Also featured: Custom seminars for groups of 7+.
FACULTY: Owner/Chef Scott Stearns of The Rare Bear at the Bernerhof Inn; northern New England area guest chefs.
COSTS: Weekend courses $479-$549, including shared lodging & meals; day rate $339 for the weekend; class rate $60.
CONTACT: Sharon Wroblewski, Owner, A Taste of the Mountains Cooking School, Box 240, Glen, NH 03838; 603-383-9132/800-548-8007, Fax 603-383-0809, stay@bernerhofinn.com, www.virtualcities.com/tastemt.htm. Other contact: Bernerhof Inn, http://www.bernerhofinn.com.

WHITE MOUNTAIN COOKING SCHOOL
Snowville

Sponsor: Snowvillage Inn. Programs: Weekend hands-on cooking programs. Customized programs for groups available. Established: 1994. Class/group size: 8. 12 programs/yr. Also featured: Swimming, canoeing, hiking, biking.
FACULTY: Inn owner/operator Kevin Flynn & Chef Laurel Tessier, executive chef at the Snowvillage Inn since 1998.
COSTS: $349 includes shared lodging & most meals.
CONTACT: Kevin Flynn, White Mountain Cooking School at The Snowvillage Inn, PO Box 68, Snowville, NH 03832; 603-447-2818, 800-447-4345, Fax 603-447-5268, info@snowvillageinn.com, www.snowvillageinn.com/cooking.htm.

NEW JERSEY

ADVENTURES IN COOKING
Wayne

Sponsor: Cooking school & cookware store. Programs: Demo & participation classes. Guest chef classes. Established: 1976. 80+ programs/yr. Also featured: Private classes.

FACULTY: Arlene Ward, a member of the IACP & NY Assn. of Cooking Teachers, has been a food stylist for professional photographers & food co's. Other instructors are IACP members. Guest instructors include Giuliano Bugialli & Rick Moonen.

COSTS: $45-$60/class.

CONTACT: Arlene Ward, Proprietor, Adventures in Cooking, 12 Legion Place, Wayne, NJ; 973-305-1114, Fax 973-305-4810, Arlene@adventuresincooking.com, www.adventuresincooking.com.

ALFREDO'S CUCINA E CULTURA
Milltown; Rome & other locations, Italy

Sponsor: Chef Alfredo de Bonis & Hotel Alimandi. Programs: 5-day hands-on cooking vacations in Rome that include market visits, sightseeing, restaurant dining; 1- to 3-wk culinary tours of Italy; 4-session courses in NJ. Established: 1990. Class/group size: 4-10. 12 programs/yr. Facilities: Italy: remodeled kitchen at Hotel Alimandi. NJ: chef's home kitchen, high school facilities.

FACULTY: Alfredo de Bonis, a chef/restaurateur for 25+ yrs, now owns & operates Bravo Alfredo Catering, teaches at North Brunswick HS.

COSTS: Italy: $1,995 incl shared lodging at Hotel Alimandi, meals, planned activities. NJ: $45/class, $140/4-sessions.

CONTACT: Alfredo de Bonis, Alfredo's Cucina & Cultura at Alimandi Rome, 375 Tremont Ave., Milltown, NJ; 732-828-8460, Fax 732-828-0858, adbonis@aol.com, www.alfredotoursitaly.com.

ATLANTIC CAPE COMMUNITY ACADEMY OF CULINARY ARTS
Mays Landing

Sponsor: 2-yr college. Programs: 1-day themed workshops covering a variety of cooking topics. Established: 1981. Class/group size: 30 demo, 16 hands-on. 10 programs/yr. Facilities: Academy of Culinary Arts instructional kitchens. Also featured: Kids College summer cooking program for children.

FACULTY: Academy of Culinary Arts faculty.

CONTACT: Rachel Wettstein, Program Developer, Academy of Culinary Arts, Atlantic Cape Community College, 5100 Black Horse Pike, Mays Landing, NJ 08330; 609-343-4829, Fax 609-343-4823, rwettste@atlantic.edu, www.atlantic.edu.

CHEF & SOMMELIER FOR A DAY
Short Hills

Sponsor: Hilton Short Hills. Programs: Thursday programs for 1-2 persons who plan & help prepare dinner + wine selection, & then dine with up to 6 guests. Established: 1997. Class/group size: 1-2. ~50 programs/yr. Facilities: Restaurant kitchen of the Hilton Hotel. Also featured: Food & wine tasting, discussion with sommelier.

FACULTY: Hilton Executive Chef Walter Leffler & Sommelier Isaac Alexander.

COSTS: $175 for guest chefs, $150 for dining companions.

CONTACT: George Staikos, Sommelier, Director of Food & Beverage, Chef & Sommelier for a Day, 41 JFK Parkway, Short Hills, NJ 07078; 973-379-0100 #7980, Fax 973-379-1153, www.hiltonshorthills.com/dinningroom.html.

CONNIE FOWLER WINE PROGRAMS
Summit; New York, NY

Sponsor: Wine professional. Programs: 3- to 6-session courses & custom wine tasting events. Established: 1995. Class/group size: 35. ~6 programs/yr.

FACULTY: Connie Fowler, member of SWE, WSET Diploma, 14+ yrs wine industry experience.
CONTACT: Connie Fowler, Let's Have a Taste, 16 Sherman Ave., Summit, NJ 07901; 908-277-4330, Fax 908-277-1348, connie@letshaveataste.com, www.letshaveataste.com.

COOKTIQUE
Tenafly
Sponsor: Cooking school, gourmet & housewares shop. Programs: Day & evening demo & participation sessions. Established: 1976. Class/group size: 20 hands-on/30 demo. 150 programs/yr. Facilities: 400-sq-ft demo kitchen with overhead mirror & latest equipment. Also featured: Children's classes, birthday parties, private group events.
FACULTY: Culinary professionals & master chefs. Guest chefs have included Guiliano Bugialli, Marcella Hazan, Nicholas Malgieri, Lorenza de'Medici, Arthur Schwartz, Jaques Pepin.
COSTS: From $35; guest chef classes $50-$100.
CONTACT: Cathy McCauley, CCP, Director, Cooktique, 9 W. Railroad Ave., Tenafly, NJ 07670; 201-568-7990, Fax 201-568-6480, cooktique@msn.com, www.cooktique.com.

GINGERCREEK COOKING SCHOOL
Stewartsville
Sponsor: Culinary professional. Programs: Regional, seasonal & holiday classes for adults. Kids Culinary College participation classes. Established: 1987. Class/group size: 12. 60 programs/yr. Facilities: English cottage, rural setting.
FACULTY: Nancy L. Wyant, owner & instructor.
COSTS: $50/class.
CONTACT: Nancy Wyant, Owner/instructor, Gingercreek Cooking School, 304 Rt. 173, Stewartsville, NJ 08886; 908-479-6062, gingercreek@hotmail.com.

GREEN GABLES RESTAURANT & INN
Beach Haven
Sponsor: Chef-owned restaurant & inn. Programs: Culinary classes. Class/group size: Limited. Facilities: Restored Victorian-era house.
FACULTY: Chef/owner Adolfo de'Martino.
COSTS: $45/class.
CONTACT: Adolfo de'Martino, Chef/Owner, Green Gables Restaurant & Inn, 212 Centre St., Beach Haven, NJ ; 609-492-3553, Fax 609-492-2507, greengableslbi@aol.com, www.lbinet.com/greengables/.

KINGS COOKING STUDIO
Short Hills, Bedminster, Verona & Hillsdale
Sponsor: Cooking school in Kings Super Markets. Programs: Single & multi-session demo & participation classes, includes techniques, single subjects & full menus. Established: 1983. Class/group size: ~25/demo, ~15/partic. 150+ programs/yr. Facilities: Fully-equipped enclosed kitchens, overhead mirrors. Also featured: Celebrity chef demos, classes for couples & children, wine tours.
FACULTY: 15+ resident faculty includes Carole Walter, Jean Yueh, Kathleen Sanderson. Guest chefs include Nick Malgieri, Julia Child, Andre Soltner, Rick Moonan.
COSTS: Principles of Cooking series $55-$65/session. Individual classes from $35-$85. Children's classes $35-$45.
CONTACT: Manager, Kings cooking studio, 700 Lanidex Plaza, Parsippany, NJ 07054; 973-463-6500, Fax 973-575-6518, cookingstudio@kingssm.com, www.kingscookingstudio.com.

ON THE MARK COOKING CLASSES
Bedminster, Short Hills & Verona
Sponsor: Professional chef. Programs: In-home & on-site cooking classes. Established: 2000. Class/group size: 1-20. 24 programs/yr. Facilities: Client's home kitchen or Kings Cooking Studios classrooms. Also featured: Corporate team building classes, personal chef services, catering.
FACULTY: Chef Mark Darragh, graduate of the US Personal Chef Institute, Global Wine

Edcuation Program, teaches at Kings Cooking Studios & Whole Foods Markets. **Costs:** $100/hr, 2-hr min. Individual instruction $300/4-hr class + ingredients. **Contact:** Mark Darragh, Chef, On The Mark Cooking Classes, 727 South Ave. West, Westfield, NJ 07090; 908-789-3239, markdchef@starchefs.com, www.onthemarkpcs.com. Susan Spadone, Director of Marketingsaspadone@comcast.net.

VIVA THE CHEF
Morristown

Sponsor: Private school. Programs: Classes for youngsters that cover the basics, kitchen procedures, nutrition, presentation, advanced concepts. Established: 2003. Class/group size: 10 min.
Faculty: Chef Gina learned to cook at her grandfather's Cuban restaurant in Miami.
Costs: ~$40/class, $190/6-week session.
Contact: Chef Gina, Viva the Chef, 16 Pine St., Morristown, NJ 07960; 866-KID-CHEF, 973-359-0600, ChefGina@VivatheChef.com, www.vivathechef.com.

NEW MEXICO

THE CANYON RESTAURANT
Santa Fe; Alamos & Oaxaca, Mexico

Sponsor: Culinary professional Vikki Nulman. Programs: 1-wk cooking tours, 1-day cooking classes. Established: 1997. Also featured: Wine tastings.
Faculty: Chef Vikki Nulman is a graduate of the French Culinary Institute & Le Cordon Bleu Paris, a professional caterer, & studied in Venice with Marcella Hazan.
Costs: Santa Fe, $25/day. Mexico trips from $2,000.
Contact: Vikki Nulman, Chef, The Canyon Restaurant, 731 Canyon Rd., Santa Fe, NM 87501; 505-984-3270, chefvikki@aol.com, www.thecanyonrestaurant.com/tours.htm.

COOKING AT VILLA FONTANA/RIO GRANDE COOKING SCHOOL
Taos

Sponsor: Restaurant Villa Fontana. Programs: 3- & 5-day classes in classical Northern Italian cuisine. Established: 2002. Class/group size: 10 max. ~20 programs/yr. Facilities: Cooking island in a marquis, overlooking the garden, with views of the Taos Mountain. Also featured: Welcome reception, farewell dinner, wine tasting.
Faculty: Chef Carlo Gislimberti was born in Italy, studied in Europe, & has been a restaurant owner since 1982. Villa Fontana is rated by Luigi Veronelli as one of the top 10 Italian restaurants in the US.
Costs: $250-$900.
Contact: Siobhan or Carlo Gislimberti, Owners, Cooking at Villa Fontana, PO Box 2872, Taos, NM 87571; 505-758-5800, Fax 505-758-0301, villafon@newmex.com, www.villafontanataos.com.

JANE BUTEL'S SOUTHWESTERN COOKING VACATIONS
Albuquerque

Sponsor: Culinary professional Jane Butel. Programs: 5-day & weekend full participation courses, group programs, 3-hour classes, culinary tours. Established: 1983. Class/group size: 45 demo/18 hands-on. 20+ demos programs/yr. Facilities: Southwestern 2,000-sq-ft tiled kitchen with 6 work stations equipped with the latest home cooking equipment, demo area, overhead mirror. Also featured: Advanced & private group lessons, team-building classes, sightseeing, ballooning, visits to markets & wineries. Tours of New Mexico, Mexico, Spain.
Faculty: Jane Butel, author of 16 cookbooks, including Jane Butel's Southwestern Kitchen, Chili Madness, & Fiesta; founder of Pecos Valley Spice Co.
Costs: $2,100/week & $1,100/weekend includes most meals & shared lodging at La Posada de Albuquerque Hotel. Demos ~$40-$55 each.

CONTACT: Jane Butel, Owner, Jane Butel's Southwestern Cooking School, c/o La Posada de Albuquerque Hotel, 125 Second St. NW, Albuquerque, NM 87102; 800-472-8229, 505-314-0787, Fax 505-247-1719, info@janebutel.com, www.janebutel.com. Tamara Bolek, Mgr.

LAS COSAS KITCHEN SHOPPE & COOKING SCHOOL
Santa Fe

Sponsor: Cookware store & gourmet food shop. Programs: Cooking classes on a variety of topics for professional & non-professional cooks. Established: 1998. Class/group size: 20 demo, 12 hands-on. 300 programs/yr. Facilities: Up-to-date home kitchen setting with the latest equipment. Also featured: Farmer's Market trips, guest chefs, private classes.

FACULTY: Director John Vollertsen has taught cooking in New York & Sydney, Australia, & worked with Jane Butel at her Southwestern Cooking School in Albuquerque.

COSTS: $45-$75; private classes from $60/student.

CONTACT: John Vollertsen, Director of Cooking School, Las Cosas Kitchen Shoppe & Cooking School, 181 Paseo de Peralta, DeVargas Center, Santa Fe, NM 87501; 505-988-3394, Fax 505-983-5587, lascosas@lascosascooking.com, www.lascosascooking.com.

MUY SABROSA AT THE INN ON THE ALAMEDA
Santa Fe

Sponsor: The Inn on the Alameda, a small hotel in Old Santa Fe. Programs: 2-night package that features 1 demo cooking class. Established: 1996. Class/group size: 44. 40 programs/yr. Facilities: Demo kitchen of The Santa Fe School of Cooking.

FACULTY: Cooking instructors of The Santa Fe School of Cooking.

COSTS: $340-$540 includes continental breakfast, shared lodging.

CONTACT: Judith Moir, Marketing Director, Muy Sabrosa at Inn on the Alameda, 303 East Alameda, Santa Fe, NM 87501; 800-289-2122, Fax 505-986-8325, info@inn-alameda.com, www.innonthealameda.com.

SANTA FE SCHOOL OF COOKING
Santa Fe

Sponsor: School, food market, mail order catalog. Programs: Demo classes & smaller hands-on classes that include shopping at the Farmer's Market. Established: 1989. Class/group size: 15 hands-on/44 demo. Facilities: Santa Fe-style kitchen with overhead mirrors. Also featured: Private classes, shopping trips to the Farmer's Market, culinary tours of northern New Mexico.

FACULTY: Cookbook authors & chefs from Santa Fe's top restaurants, guest celebrities including Cheryl Alters Jamison & Deborah Madison.

COSTS: Classes from $45-$90; tours are ~$800-$1,600 & include some meals, field trips, lodging.

CONTACT: Susan Curtis & Nicole Ammerman, Owner & Manager, Santa Fe School of Cooking, 116 W. San Francisco St., Santa Fe, NM 87501; 505-983-4511, Fax 505-983-7540, cookin@nets.com, www.santafeschoolofcooking.com.

NEW YORK

THE ACADEMY OF CAKE ART
New York, New York

Sponsor: Cake & sugar artist Scott Clark Woolley. Programs: Demos & hands-on classes in cake decorating & gum paste sugar flowers. Established: 1991. Class/group size: 7 max. 20+ programs/yr. Facilities: Woolley's studio. Also featured: Private one-on-one classes.

FACULTY: Scott Woolley is author of Cakes by Design. His cakes have appeared in Bride's mag & Martha Stewart's Weddings. Clients include President G. W. Bush, Christie Brinkley, Maria Shriver.

COSTS: $150-$250 for group classes, $100/hr for private classes.

CONTACT: Scott Woolley, Owner, The Academy of Cake Art, 171 W. 73rd St., #9, New York, NY 10023; 212-362-5374, scw@cakesbydesign.cc, www.cakesbydesign.cc/academy_of_cake_art.html.

ALICE ROSS HEARTH STUDIOS
Smithtown

Sponsor: Culinary historian Dr. Alice Ross. Programs: Hands-on classes in culinary history & traditional methods, Native American & Civil War cookery, game butchery & prep, baking using hearth & brick ovens. Established: 1988. Class/group size: 3-15. 35 programs/yr. Facilities: Converted carriage house with open hearth & wood stove, outdoor wood-fired oven, water pump, smoke house. Also featured: Custom classes.

FACULTY: Dr. Alice Ross is co-founder of Culinary Historians of NY, teaches at CCNY, served as consultant to Colonial Williamsburg & Lowell Natl Historic Park.

COSTS: $125/day.

CONTACT: Dr. Alice Ross, Alice Ross Hearth Studios, 15 Prospect St., Smithtown, NY 11787; 631-265-9335, aross@binome.com, aliceross.com.

ALTAMONT WINE SCHOOL
Altamont

Sponsor: Wine professional. Programs: 10-12 wine sessions/yr; guided NY wine/vineyard tours by appointment, dinner tastings, winemaking class. Established: 1987. Class/group size: 20.

FACULTY: Greg Giorgio is a wine educator, writer, consultant.

COSTS: $20/session.

CONTACT: Greg Giorgio, Altamont Wine School, PO Box 74, Altamont, NY 12009; 518-861-5627.

ANNA TERESA CALLEN ITALIAN COOKING SCHOOL
New York

Sponsor: Culinary professional Anna Teresa Callen. Programs: 5-session participation & demo courses. Established: 1978. Class/group size: 6. 10 programs/yr. Facilities: Efficient home kitchen. Also featured: Culinary tours to Italy.

FACULTY: IACP-member Anna Teresa Callen is author of Quiches & Savory Pies, Anna Teresa Callen's Menus for Pasta & Food & Memories of Abruzzo. She teaches at the Institute of Culinary Education & NYU.

COSTS: $675/course.

CONTACT: Anna Teresa Callen, Anna Teresa Callen Italian Cooking School, 59 W. 12th St., New York, NY 10011; 212-929-5640.

CAKES UNIQUELY YOURS SCHOOL OF CONFECTIONERY ARTS
New York

Sponsor: Ajike Williams, instructor & sugar artist. Programs: 1- to 12 session certificate programs Wilton Method, marzipan, gumpaste, advanced fondant, designer cookies, sugar craft, baking. Wedding cake development workshops. Established: 1996. Class/group size: 1-2. 18 courses programs/yr. Facilities: Modern home kitchen. Also featured: Wedding cake consultation, private lessons, customized intensives, off-site instruction for groups.

FACULTY: Ajike Williams received Gold & Silvermedals from Soc. Culinaire Philanthropique, attended Peter Kump's NY Cooking School, is a Wilton Method instructor & teaches classes for the NYC Bd. of Ed.

COSTS: $50-85/single session, $150-$350/4-session classes.

CONTACT: Ajike Williams, Instructor-Sugar Artist, Cakes Uniquely Yours School of Confectionery Arts, 1348 Noble Ave., Bronx, NY 10472; 718 861-7850, Fax 718-861-7850, AjikeW@aol.com.

CAROL'S CUISINE, INC.
Staten Island

Sponsor: Culinary professional. Programs: 1- to 6-session demo & participation courses. Established: 1972. Class/group size: 18. 90 programs/yr. Facilities: Fully-equipped professional teaching kitchen with overhead mirror. Also featured: Private lessons, wine classes.

FACULTY: Owner/Director Carol Frazzetta, IACP, advanced certificate from Le Cordon Bleu, stud-

ied at CIA, Wilton School of Cake Decorating, Marcella Hazan's School, L'Academie de Cuisine. Leonard Pickell, wine consultant.
Costs: $65-$125/session.
Contact: Carol Frazzetta, Owner, Chef, Cooking Teacher, Carol's Cuisine, Inc., 1571 Richmond Rd., Staten Island, NY 10304; 718-979-5600, Fax 718-987-4509, carolscuisine@aol.com, www.CarolsCafe.com.

CHINA INSTITUTE'S CHINESE COOKING SCHOOL
New York
Sponsor: Non-profit educational & cultural institution. Programs: 3-session course that focuses on a total of 12 traditional Chinese regional dishes. Class/group size: 15 max. Also featured: Chinese language & calligraphy classes, classroom teaching & seminars, art exhibitions, teacher education & curriculum development, lectures & symposia.
Faculty: Cooking teacher & food consultant Eileen Yin-Fei Lo is author of The Chinese Kitchen, The Dim Sum Book & The Chinese Banquet Cookbook.
Costs: $325 members, $350 non-members, $80 materials. Membership starts at $55/yr.
Contact: France Pepper, Associate Director, Public Programs, China Institute's Chinese Cooking School, 125 E. 65th St, New York, NY 10021; 212-744-8181, x143, Fax 212-628-4159, fpepper@chinainstitute.org, www.chinainstitute.org.

CITY ADVENTURES
New York
Sponsor: Specialty travel company. Programs: Culinary vacation programs that include cooking classes. Established: 1995. Class/group size: 12. Facilities: Local culinary schools. Also featured: Art, garden travel.
Faculty: Professional chefs.
Contact: Norma Greenwood, City Adventures, 32 Union Sq. E., #507, New York, NY 10003; 718-457-0672, greenwood@cityadventures.com, www.cityadventures.com.

COOKING BY THE BOOK, INC.
New York
Sponsor: Suzen & Brian O'Rourke. Programs: Corporate culinary team building, private culinary parties. Established: 1989. Class/group size: 12-40 guests. Facilities: Fully-equipped 650-sq-ft kitchen with 5 work stations & 600-sq-ft dining room. Also featured: Recipe testing, chef demos.
Faculty: Suzen & Brian O'Rourke; authors regularly present; 30 part-time employees.
Costs: $155 pp (12 person min.) + $300 admin. fee & 18% gratuity.
Contact: Suzen O'Rourke, Owner, Cooking by the Book, Inc., 11 Worth St., New York, NY 10013; 212-966-9799, Fax 212-925-1074, info@cookingbythebook.com, www.cookingbythebook.com.

COOKING THERAPY
Albany
Sponsor: Private school. Programs: Hands-on cooking classes & personal growth experiences using cooking as the activity. Established: 2002. Class/group size: 6-8. 24-36 programs/yr. Facilities: Professional kitchen in private home. Equipment includes convection ovens, Garland stove & oven.
Faculty: Primary instructor Katherine Wardle, Ph.D., is a licensed psychologist in private practice with an associate degree in the culinary arts. Guest chefs.
Costs: ~$45/class.
Contact: Dr. Katherine Wardle, Chef/owner, Cooking Therapy, 70 Nott Rd., Rexford, NY 12148; 518-384-3407, Fax 518-783-1051, chef@cookingtherapy.com, www.cookingtherapy.com.

COOKING WITH CLASS, INC.
New York; Perigord Noir, France; Tecate, Mexico
Sponsor: Culinary professional. Programs: Hands-on, semi-private cooking classes; topics include menus for dinner parties, gatherings & buffets. Established: 1975. Class/group size: 4. Facilities:

Corporate kitchen with commercial equipment. Also featured: Culinary travel programs, catering, team building, private in home instruction.

FACULTY: Janeen Sarlin, author of 7 cookbooks & writer of weekly cooking column.

COSTS: $110/class, $305/3 classes, $630/6 classes.

CONTACT: Janeen Sarlin, Cooking With Class, Inc., 110 East End Ave., New York, NY 10028; 212-517-8514, Fax 212-737-5227, sarlin@sarlincookingwithclass.com, www.sarlincookingwithclass.com.

THE CULINARY INSTITUTE OF AMERICA
Hyde Park; Asia; Europe *(See also page 18, 90, 182) (See display ad page 89)*

Sponsor: The CIA's continuing education department. Programs: 1- to 2-day & week-long demo & hands-on programs for food enthusiasts. Worlds of Flavor culinary travel programs. Established: 1946. Class/group size: 15. ~40 programs/yr. Facilities: Includes 38 teaching kitchens, library, student recreation center & 5 public student-staffed restaurants.

FACULTY: The CIA's chefs & instructors.

COSTS: On-campus programs from $160-$2,000.

CONTACT: Susan Cussen, Director of Marketing, CE, The Culinary Institute of America, 1946 Campus Dr., Hyde Park, NY 0; 800-888-7850, Fax 845-451-1066, ciachef@culinary.edu, www.ciachef.edu/. http://www.worldsofflavor.com.

DE GUSTIBUS AT MACY'S
New York

Sponsor: Independent school in Macy's department store operated by Arlene Feltman Sailhac. Programs: Demos & on-location classes, hands-on, knife skills. Established: 1980. Class/group size: 70 demo. 120 programs/yr. Facilities: Professionally-equipped teaching kitchen. Also featured: Wine seminars, private events, gourmet trip.

FACULTY: Guest chefs & cookbook authors include David Bouley, Mario Batali, Michael Romano, Tom Colicchio, Alain Sailhac.

COSTS: From $85/cooking session to $480/6 sessions, $95/wine clas.

CONTACT: Arlene Feltman Sailhac, Owner/Director, De Gustibus at Macy's, 343 E. 74th Street, Apt. 14A, New York, NY 10021; 212-439-1714, Fax 212-439-1716, grtcooks@aol.com, www.degustibusinc.com.

DINNER PARTY CHEF
New York

Sponsor: Culinary professional. Programs: Hands-on dinner party programs. Class/group size: 4-12. Facilities: Students' home kitchen.

FACULTY: Owner/Chef Jamie Sydney, a graduate of The French Culinary Institute, also studied at the CIA & Divina Cucina Culinary School in Florence.

COSTS: $80-$150.

CONTACT: Jamie Sydney, Owner, Dinner Party Chef, New York, NY; 718-935-1057, jamie@dinnerpartychef.com, www.dinnerpartychef.com.

EVENTS@DISH
New York

Sponsor: Restaurant with separate instructional kitchen. Programs: Hands-on cooking classes on a variety of topics. Established: 2002. Class/group size: 10-40. Facilities: Full professional kitchen with tree-lined deck & 2 skylights. Also featured: Catering, special events, party & corporate building cooking classes.

FACULTY: 20 professional chefs & instructors.

COSTS: $85-$125/class.

CONTACT: Nancy Evans, Event Coordinator, Events@Dish, 165 Allen St., New York, NY 10002; 212-253-8845, Fax 212-253-8872, events@dish165.com, www.dish165.com. Cell: 646-299-6656.

THE FRENCH CULINARY INSTITUTE
New York *(See also page 92) (See display ad page 91)*

Sponsor: Proprietary institution for aspiring professionals & serious amateur cooks. Programs: La Technique, a 22-session overview of classical French techniques; La Technique II, a 12-session course on menu development, seasonality, plate composition. Essentials of Pastry, a 20-session intro to pastry & confectionary. Established: 1984. Class/group size: 22. 12 programs/yr. Facilities: 30,000-sq-ft facility with newly-equipped pastry & bread kitchens, demo amphitheater, L'Ecole open-to-the-public restaurant. Also featured: Cooking with Marcella, essentials of Italian cooking; Artisanal Bread Baking, 1-wk intro to European bread baking; La Technique for serious amateurs; Essentials of Pastry, intro to pastry arts; Culinary Business courses in catering, restaurant mgmt & wine.

FACULTY: 41 teachers & culinary staff, including Dean of Studies Alain Sailhac, Dean of Special Programs Jacques Pépin, Master Chef André Soltner, Dean of Pastry Arts Jacques Torres, Dean of Wine Studies Andrea Immer, Visiting Dean Alice Waters, Marcella Hazen.

COSTS: Tuition (includes knife set, tools, application, uniform): $5,675 for La Technique I, $2,075 for La Technique II, $5,100 for Essentials of Pastry, $1,950 for Cooking with Marcella, $895 for Fundamentals of Wine & Great Wine & Food Made Simple.

CONTACT: David Waggoner, Dean of Enrollment, The French Culinary Institute, 462 Broadway, New York, NY 10013; 888-FCI-CHEF/212-219-8890, Fax 212-431-3054, admission@frenchculinary.com, www.frenchculinary.com/subpages/amateur/amateur.html.

GRANDMA'S SECRETS
New York

Sponsor: Custom-made desserts company. Programs: In-home, one-on-one instruction in pie making. Established: 1995. Class/group size: 5. Facilities: Students' home. Also featured: Specialize in occasion cakes: wedding, birthday, baby & bridal shower; pies, dietetic desserts, vegetarian cakes.
FACULTY: Regina McRae, founder.
COSTS: $125/2 hrs.
CONTACT: Regina McRae, Grandma's Secrets, 640 W. 138th St., New York, NY 10031; 212-862-8117, classes@grandmasecrets.com, www.grandmasecrets.com.

HARRIET LEMBECK, CWE
New York

Sponsor: Wine professional. Programs: Two 10-session courses/yr, 4-session spirits course in fall, 30+ 1- to 4-session courses/yr through New School University. Established: 1975. Class/group size: 30.
FACULTY: Harriet Lembeck is author of Grossman's Guide to Wines, Beers, & Spirits, 6th & 7th Eds; Director of New School University wine program; Charter Director SWE; CWE.
COSTS: $800/10-session course, $1,000 with spirits ($300 spirits alone), $81-$315/course through New School University.
CONTACT: Harriet Lembeck, CWE, Wine & Spirits Program, Inc., 54 Continental Ave., Forest Hills, NY 11375; 718-263-3134, Fax 718-263-3750, hlembeck@mindspring.com.

HARVARD LYMAN WINE PROGRAM AT SUNY-STONY BROOK
Stony Brook

Sponsor: University. Programs: 14-session course. Established: 1972. Class/group size: 25-30.
FACULTY: Harvard Lyman is a member of AWS & SWE.
COSTS: $270/three credits plus $40-$45 lab fee; $90/one credit option.
CONTACT: Harvard Lyman, Harvard Lyman Wine Program at SUNY-Stony Brook, Biochemistry Dept., Stony Brook, NY 0; 516-632-8534, Fax 516-632-9780, hlyman@notes.cc.sunysb.edu.

HOME COOKING
Greater NYC area

Sponsor: Culinary professional. Programs: Private cooking classes & parties. Established: 2002. Class/group size: 1-20.

FACULTY: Jennifer Clair teaches at The New School, JCC of Manhattan & City Harvest. She graduated from the Institute of Culinary Education & was a food editor at Martha Stewart Living.
COSTS: $195/2 people, $75 pp additional. Cost of ingredients ~$20 pp.
CONTACT: Jennifer Clair, Chef-Instructor, Home Cooking, ,; 718-783-0048, jennifer@homecookingny.com, www.homecookingny.com.

THE INSTITUTE OF CULINARY EDUCATION
New York City *(See also page 94) (See display ad above & pages 93, 94)*
Sponsor: Private school, formerly Peter Kump's New York Cooking School. Programs: Hands-on courses & workshops include the 5-session, 25-hour Techniques of Fine Cooking series, offered over 70 times a year, frequently on a Monday-Friday schedule. Established: 1975. Class/group size: 12 hands-on, 30+ dem. 1,000+ programs/yr. Facilities: 27,000-sq-ft facility opened in 1999 includes 9 kitchens, wine studies center, confectionery lab. Also featured: Other Techniques series: spa cuisine, Italian cooking, pastry & baking, cake decorating. Other courses: Japanese, Thai, Latino, Moroccan, Spanish cuisines, chocolate, vegetarian, fish & shellfish, grilling, knife skills, walking tours.
FACULTY: 15 staff chef-instructors & 30+ visiting guest chefs.
COSTS: Hands-on classes from $85-$520.
CONTACT: The Institute of Culinary Education, 50 W. 23rd St., New York, NY 10010; 800-522-4610, 212-847-0770, Fax 212-847-0722, marie@iceculinary.com, www.iceculinary.com.

ITALIAN CULINARY INSTITUTE, INC.
New York
Sponsor: Italian Cooking & Living magazine. Programs: Cooking demos, dinners, wine tastings & classes. Established: 1999. Class/group size: 24. 50+ programs/yr. Facilities: Open kitchen with modern equipment & a café setting. Also featured: Olive oil tastings, seminars.
FACULTY: Guest chefs, the magazine's editorial & test kitchen staff.
COSTS: $65 for basic courses, $75 for guest chef classes. Discounts for a package of classes. All include dinner.
CONTACT: Salvatore Rizzo, Center Manager, Italian Culinary Institute, Inc., 230 Fifth Avenue, Suite 1100, New York, NY 10001; 212-725-8764 x25, 212-889-9057, Fax 212-889-5057, rizzo@italiancookingandliving.com, www.italiancookingandliving.com. For trips, call Anna Canepa at Ariston Tours 212-725-8764 x16.

JCC MANHATTAN – CULINARY ARTS
New York
Sponsor: The Jewish Community Center, a private organization. Programs: Hands-on & demo cooking classes, private cooking parties. Facilities: Professional culinary studio.
FACULTY: Includes Jennifer Abadi, Megan Brenn-White, David Glickman, Andrea Klein, Myra Kornfeld, Jacob Pine, Emily Stulman.
COSTS: 1-day classes & demos $65 ($75 nonmembers), 2-session classes $130 ($150), 6-session classes $350 ($420), couples class $140 ($160).

CONTACT: Julie Negrin, Director, JCC Manhattan, 334 Amsterdam Ave. @ 76th St., New York, NY 10023; 646-505-5713, jnegrin@jccmanhattan.org, www.jccmanhattan.org/category.asp?c=1016.

JOSIE'S COOKING CLASSES
New York

Sponsor: Restaurant group. Programs: Monthly classes that focus on healthful cuisine, including low carb, organic, vegetarian, & dairy-free. Established: 2001. Class/group size: 80 max. 10 programs/yr. Facilities: Citrus Restaurant, which features 2 large screen TVs & a cooking stage with demonstration mirror.

FACULTY: Louis Lanza, executive chef & owner of Josie's & Better Burger, owner of Citrus & Josephina, author of Totally Dairy Free Cooking. Assisted by nutritionist Stephanie Field.

COSTS: $50.

CONTACT: Marketing & Events Dept., Josie's Cooking Classes, 20 W. 64th St., #29U, New York, NY 10023; 212-362-0852, josiesmarketing@aol.com, www.josiesnyc.com.

JULIE SAHNI'S SCHOOL OF INDIAN COOKING
Brooklyn Heights; India

Sponsor: Cookbook author Julie Sahni. Programs: NY: two 3-day hands-on courses (3 students max) are Indian Cooking & Understanding Spices & Herbs. Include shopping in an Indian/spice market. India: 16-day cultural & culinary tours that include visits to farm kitchens & cooking demos. Established: 1973. 2 trips to India programs/yr. Facilities: Specially-designed teaching kitchen in Ms. Sahni's studio. Also featured: 3-day courses can be taught anywhere in USA as a 1-day intro for 6 students. India trips (Feb & Oct) also include visits to spice & tea plantations, markets & bazaars, private receptions.

FACULTY: Julie Sahni is author of Classic Indian Cooking, Indian Vegetarian Cooking, & Savoring Spices & Herbs. She is a member of the IACP & Les Dames D'Escoffier & has degrees in Architecture & Classical Dance.

COSTS: 3-day course: $985/person. Trip: $4,975, includes shared lodging (single supplement $1,475), most meals, ground transport, planned activities. Lodging in deluxe hotels or best available.

CONTACT: Julie Sahni, Director, Julie Sahni's School of Indian Cooking, 101 Clark St., #13A, Brooklyn Heights, NY 11201; 718-625-3958, Fax 718-625-3456, jsicooking@aol.com.

KAREN LEE IMAGINATIVE COOKING CLASSES & CATERING
New York City & Amagansett

Sponsor: Culinary professional Karen Lee. Programs: 4-session participation courses, single session classes, 5-day vacation courses. Established: 1972. Class/group size: 10 hands-on.

FACULTY: Owner/caterer Karen Lee apprenticed with Madame Grace Zia Chu & is author of The Occasional Vegetarian; Nouvelle Chinese Cooking; Soup, Salad, & Pasta Innovations; & Chinese Cooking for the American Kitchen.

COSTS: $520/4-session course, $140/class.

CONTACT: Karen Lee Imaginative Cooking Classes & Catering, 142 West End Ave., #30V, New York, NY 10023; 212-787-2227, Fax 212-496-8178, foodnow@rcn.com, www.karenleecooking.com. In July & Aug: PO Box 1998, Amagansett, NY 11930; 631-267-3653, Fax 631-267-3114.

LA CUISINE SANS PEUR
New York

Sponsor: Chef-de-Cuisine Henri-Etienne Lévy. Programs: 5- & 6-session demo courses include the 2-part 6-session basic course, 3-part 5-session intermediate, advanced, & baking courses. Specialty classes include desserts, fish, game, vegetables & seasonal. Established: 1978. Class/group size: 4. 25+ programs/yr. Facilities: Traditional French well-equipped home kitchen. Also featured: 1-wk culinary vacations in Provence & Alsace in Sept.

FACULTY: Chef & proprietor Henri-Etienne Lévy trained & worked in restaurant kitchens in France & Germany for 15 yrs.

COSTS: $500/course.

CONTACT: Henri-Etienne Lévy, Chef/Proprietor, La Cuisine Sans Peur, 216 W. 89 St., New York, NY 10024; 212-362-0638, www.lacuisinesanspeur.com.

LOOK WHO'S COOKING, INC.
Oyster Bay
Sponsor: Culinary professional Barbara Sheridan. Programs: 1- to 4-session demo & participation courses. Established: 1994. Class/group size: 20 demo/12 hands-on. 200+ programs/yr. Facilities: 800-sq-ft well-equipped Viking kitchen with 12 workspaces. Also featured: Catering, instruction for private & nonprofit organizations, afternoon teas.
FACULTY: Barbara Sheridan, graduate of N.Y. Institute of Technology Culinary Arts, attended Peter Kump's NY School & Le Cordon Bleu.
COSTS: $75/session; 6-wk technique classes $450.
CONTACT: Barbara M. Sheridan, Chef/Owner, Look Who's Cooking, Inc., 7 W. Main St., Oyster Bay, NY 11771; 516-922-2400, Fax 516-379-6067, lookwhsckn@aol.com, www.lookwhoscooking.com.

MARY BETH CLARK
New York; Bologna, Italy
Sponsor: Chef & cookbook author Mary Beth Clark. Programs: 3-hour custom-designed, full-participation private lessons in Italian cuisine. Student brings home 3-4 dishes from the class. Established: 1977. Class/group size: 1-2.
FACULTY: Cookbook author Mary Beth Clark operates the International Cooking School Of Italian Food & Wine week-long cooking courses in Bologna, Italy (May-July, Sept-Oct).
COSTS: $500/session plus ingredients, payable in advance, refundable a week prior.
CONTACT: Mary Beth Clark, 201 E. 28th St., #15B, New York, NY 0; 212-779-1921, Fax 212-779-3248, marybethclark@worldnet.att.net, www.marybethclark.com.

MEDIUM RARE
Westchester County
Sponsor: Culinary professional Liv Grey. Programs: Private classes that cover such topics as knife skills, holiday meals, quick cuisine, healthy recipes, foods for kids. Established: 2003. Class/group size: 1-12. Facilities: Student's home kitchen.
FACULTY: Liv Grey is a graduate of the French Culinary Institute, has worked in restaurants in France & NY & at Martha Stewart Living.
COSTS: From $180/2-$500/7+ students. Ingredients~$20 pp.
CONTACT: Liv Grey, Medium Rare, 19 Jochum Ave., Larchmont, NY 10538; 914-834-1326, liv@livgrey.com, livgrey.com/mediumrare/classes.html.

MIETTE CULINARY STUDIO
New York
Sponsor: Miette Culinary Studio. Programs: Hands-on classes meet Mondays & Thursdays. Established: 1995. Class/group size: 14 max. Also featured: Cooking parties, corporate team-building, cook-ins, wine tastings.
FACULTY: Chef Paul Vandewoude & his assistant Mariette Bermowitz.
COSTS: $65/session.
CONTACT: Mariette Bermowitz, Miette Culinary Studio, 109 MacDougal Street, Suite #2, New York, NY 10012; 212-460-9322, Fax 212-460-9579, msmiette@aol.com.

THE MIXING BOWL
New York
Sponsor: Private school. Programs: Weekly classes for children ages 2-1/2 & older that cover kitchen safety, hygiene, healthy snacks, breakfast treats, dinners & desserts. Also includes storytime or creative food projects, personalized cookbooks. Also featured: Theme kitchen parties.
FACULTY: Meredith Berman is a former nursery school teacher.
COSTS: $40/class, $140-$672/course.

CONTACT: Meredith Berman, The Mixing Bowl, 243 E. 82nd St., New York, NY 10028; 212-585-2433, Fax 212-585-2401, info@kidsinthekitchenNYC.com, www.kidsinthekitchennyc.com.

THE NATURAL GOURMET INSTITUTE FOR FOOD & HEALTH
New York   *(See also page 96) (See display ad page 97)*

Sponsor: Private trade school devoted to healthy cooking. Programs: Demo & participation programs: evening & weekend classes & series. Intensives include Basic Techniques, Pastry Arts, Food & Healing. Established: 1977. Class/group size: 8-25. 120+ programs/yr. Facilities: Include 2 kitchens, classroom, bookstore. Also featured: Classes for adults & youngsters; beginning, advanced cooking & theory.

FACULTY: 10 faculty, incl founder Annemarie Colbin, MA, Certified Health Education Specialist, author of Food & Healing, The Book of Whole Meals, The Natural Gourmet; Co-Presidents/Directors Diane Carlson & Jenny Matthau, graduates of the school.

COSTS: Summer intensives $697/wk, classes & series $40-$75/session. Lodging at local hotels, hostels, B&Bs.

CONTACT: Susan Kaufman, Registration Mgr., The Natural Gourmet Institute for Food & Health, 48 W. 21st St., 2nd Floor, New York, NY 10010; 212-645-5170 #106, Fax 212-989-1493, info@naturalgourmetschool.com, www.naturalgourmetschool.com. Other contact: Diane Carlson.

NEW SCHOOL CULINARY ARTS
New York

Sponsor: New School University. Programs: 1- to 8-session demo & participation courses, weekend workshops. Established: 1919. Class/group size: 12-14. 300+ programs/yr. Facilities: B&B new instructional kitchen equipped with professional & high-end home equipment. Also featured: On-site restaurant chef demos, lectures on culture & cuisine, classes for youngsters, wine courses.

FACULTY: 50+ faculty headed by Gary Goldberg, co-founder Martin Johner, incl Bruce Beck, Miriam Brickman, James Chew, Richard Glavin, Arlyn Hackett, Micheal Krondl, Harriet Lembeck, Lisa Montenegro, Robert Posch, Dan Rosati.

COSTS: $65-$85 (+ materials fee)/session, $40 for youngsters, $15 for lectures, $325 for weekend workshops, $45-$65 for wine classes.

CONTACT: Gary A. Goldberg, Executive Director, New School Culinary Arts, 131 West 23rd St., New York, NY 10011; 212-255-414], 800-544-1978, Fax 212-229-5648, NSCulArts@aol.com, www.nsu.newschool.edu/culinary.

NEW YORK UNIVERSITY
New York   *(See also page 99) (See display ad page 98)*

Sponsor: Dept. of Nutrition & Food Studies, NYU's School of Education. Programs: Lecture & demo courses for food professionals, career changers, & nutritionists. Established: 1986. Class/group size: 10-35. 60 programs/yr. Facilities: New teaching kitchen & library, computer, academic resources.

FACULTY: Foodservice & industry professionals, historians, authors.

COSTS: ~$50-$200/session.

CONTACT: Carol Guber, Director of Food Programs, New York Univ., 35 W. 4th St., 10th Fl., New York, NY 10012; 212-998-5588, Fax 212-995-4194, nutrition@nyu.edu, www.education.nyu.edu/nutrition/.

NYC WINE CLASS
New York

Sponsor: Wine professional. Programs: Single & multiple session classes. Established: 2002. Class/group size: 16-28. Also featured: Wine & private dinners, cheese tastings, corporate functions.

FACULTY: Andrew Harwood was a winemaker in Hungary, France & California, masters degree Cornell Univ, Asst Beverage Director for Cornell wine program.

COSTS: $45-$325.

CONTACT: Andrew Harwood, NYC Wine Class, 67 E. 2nd St., Apt. #23, New York, NY 10003; 917-838-8591, andrew@nycwineclass.com, www.nycwineclass.com.

RONALD A. KAPON WINE PROGRAMS
New York

Sponsor: Wine professional. Programs: dinners & 1-session courses. Established: 1969. Class/group size: 20-100. 40 programs/yr. Also featured: Private wine dinners, tastings, corporate events. **FACULTY:** Ronald Kapon, Ph.D., grad. German Wine Acad; member SWE; VP/co-dir. Tasters Guild Intl, NY; prof. FDU Hotel, Rest. & Tourism School; radio host; wine columnist. **COSTS:** $50-$130/dinners & tastings. **CONTACT:** Ronald A. Kapon, Ronald A. Kapon Wine Programs, 230 W. 79th St., #42N, New York, NY 0; 212-799-6311, ron@tastersguildny.com, www.tastersguildny.com.

RUSTICO COOKING
New York

Sponsor: Cookbook author Micol Negrin. Programs: Hands-on classes in Italian cooking. Established: 2002. Class/group size: 6-16. 90+ programs/yr. Facilities: Grace's Marketplace kitchen has 2 gas stoves, 6 ovens, 1 full-size grill & 3 work stations. Also featured: Private cooking parties, team-building events, wine tastings, theme evenings. **FACULTY:** Micol Negrin, author of Rustico: Regional Italian Country Cooking, which was nominated for a James Beard award. She was an editor of The Magazine of La Cucina Italiana. **COSTS:** $95/class. **CONTACT:** Micol Negrin, Rustico Cooking; 917-602-1519, micol@rusticocooking.com, www.rusticocooking.com.

SAVORY SOJOURNS, LTD.
New York, New York

Sponsor: Culinary tour provider Addie Tomei. Programs: 1-day tours of NYC neighborhoods; customized multi-day tours that combine cooking classes, fine restaurant dining, market & store visits, tastings, chef demos, other food events. Established: 1997. Class/group size: 2-30+. Facilities: Institute of Culinary Education & other teaching facilities including private homes. Also featured: Spousal & incentive programs, corporate & family events, fashion, art, jazz, historic, & cultural tours. **COSTS:** Day tours from $70-$250. **CONTACT:** Addie Tomei, President, Savory Sojourns, Ltd., 155 W. 13th St., New York, NY 10011; 212-691-7314, 888-9-SAVORY, Fax 212-367-0984, Addie@savorysojourns.com, www.savorysojourns.com.

SILVI FORREST WINE COURSES
Connecticut; New Jersey; New York

Sponsor: Wine professional. Programs: Wine classes & dinners for professional organizations, corporate groups, graduate students. Established: 1982. Class/group size: 20-30. **FACULTY:** Silvi Forrest is a member of SWE & writer of food & wine articles. **CONTACT:** Silvi Forrest Wine Courses, 303 W. 66th St., New York, NY 10023; 212-874-0683.

SPOLETO COOKING SCHOOL
Spoleto, Italy

Sponsor: The Spoleto Arts Symposia. Programs: 1-wk hands-on courses that include dining & demos at fine restaurants, excursions, truffle hunting & visits to a truffle factory, olive oil production, & Lungharotti wine makers, shopping at local food market. Established: 1997. Class/group size: 10 max. 2 programs/yr. Facilities: Professional kitchens at La Scuola Alberghiero, featuring individual professional-level work stations. Also featured: Italian language class with culinary focus, interaction with opera master class, writers' workshop, improv workshop. **FACULTY:** Master chef from La Scuola Alberghiero di Spoleto, a national chef's training school; restaurant owners & chefs. **COSTS:** $2,200, includes most meals, lodging at a 4-star hotel, planned activities. **CONTACT:** Clinton J. Everett III, Exec. Director, Spoleto Cooking School, 760 West End Ave. #3A, New York, NY 10025; 212-663-4440, Fax 212-663-4440, clintoneve@aol.com, www.spoletoarts.com.

TO GRANDMOTHER'S HOUSE WE GO COOKING TOURS
New York; Sicily, Italy; Oaxaca, Mexico

Sponsor: Culinary tour operator. Programs: Cooking/cultural tours that include informal classes with local cooks & visits to craftspersons & cultural sites. Established: 1995. Class/group size: 10-12. 2 programs/yr.

FACULTY: Susan Baldassano, Director of Education at The Natural Gourmet Cookery School, is a graduate of the Institute for Culinary Education.

COSTS: $1,800 - $2,350 for tours.

CONTACT: Susan Baldassano, To Grandmother's House We Go, 471-17th St., #1, Brooklyn, NY 11215; 718-768-4662, 212-645-5170 x111, grancooks@earthlink.net, www.tograndmothershousewego.com.

VINTAGE HUDSON VALLEY COOKING VACATIONS & SEMINARS
Hudson Valley

Sponsor: 12 country inns & Diners Club. Programs: 10-session cooking vacations at different inns on 3 consecutive days, seminars on summer dishes, special occasion recipes, heritage cookery, celebrity chef & food arts seminars. Established: 1994. Class/group size: 12. 20 programs/yr. Facilities: Kitchens of the country inns & historic homes. Also featured: Dining in country inns, visits to markets, food producers & wineries, summer theater packages, arts & crafts vacations.

FACULTY: The inn's CIA-trained chefs.

COSTS: $125-$525.

CONTACT: Maren Rudolph, President, Vintage Hudson Valley Cooking Vacations & Seminars, P.O. Box 288, Irvington, NY 10533; 914-591-4503, Fax 914-591-4510, vintagehudsn@earthlink.com, www.vintagehudsonvalley.com. maren@vintagehudsonvalley.com.

THE WINE SCHOOL AT WINDOWS ON THE WORLD
New York

Sponsor: Wine professional. Programs: 8-session course covering the regions of US, France, Italy, Spain, Germany. Established: 1976. Class/group size: 125. 4 programs/yr.

FACULTY: Kevin Zraly, author of Windows on the World Complete Wine Course, 1993 James Beard Wine & Spirits Professional of the Year, 2002 European Wine Council Lifetime Achievement award.

COSTS: $895/course.

CONTACT: Kevin Charles Zraly, The Wine School at Windows on the World, 16 Woodstock Ln., New Paltz, NY 12561; 845-255-1456, Fax 845-255-2041, kevinz@netstep.net, www.wowws.com.

WINE SPECTATOR SCHOOL
Internet

Sponsor: Wine Spectator magazine. Programs: Introductory & intermediate on-line, interactive wine education courses.

FACULTY: Wine Spectator magazine editorial & educational staff members.

COSTS: 3-class introductory course $39, 10-class intermediate course $195.

CONTACT: Gloria Maroti, Director of Education, Wine Spectator School, 387 Park Ave. South, New York, NY 10016; 212-481-8610, x302, winespectatorschool@mshanken.com, www.winespectatorschool.com/wineschool.

WINES FOR FOOD
New York

Sponsor: Wine professional. Programs: 1- & 5-session wine classes. Established: 1977. Class/group size: 40-50. 10 programs/yr. Facilities: Hotel meeting room, classroom-style seating.

FACULTY: Willie Glückstern has written wine lists for 200 Manhattan restaurants, teaches at NYC's Institute of Culinary Education, is author of The Wine Avenger.

COSTS: $65/class, $250/series of 5. Friends can attend for $50 each.

CONTACT: Willie Glückstern, Wines for Food, 158 W. 76th St., New York, NY 10023; 212-724-3030, Fax 212-501-0717, willie@winesforfood.com, www.winesforfood.com.

ZOË RESTAURANT
New York

Sponsor: Contemporary American restaurant. Programs: Cooking classes featuring chef demos. Established: 1992. Class/group size: 12. 10-12 programs/yr. Facilities: Counter overlooking open display kitchen with woodburning oven, grill & rotisserie. Also featured: Lunch, dinner, weekend brunch; dining at the chef's counter; winemaker dinners; walking tours of SoHo.
FACULTY: Exec. Chef Tim Kelley, Wine Director Scott Lawrence, owners Thalia & Stephen Loffredo.
COSTS: $65-$95/class.
CONTACT: Zoë Restaurant, 90 Prince St., New York, NY 10012; 212-966-6722, Fax 212-966-6718, zoerest@aol.com, www.zoerestaurant.com.

NORTH CAROLINA

C'EST SI BON! COOKING SCHOOL
Chapel Hill

Sponsor: Recreational cooking school. Programs: Hands-on cooking classes; some include food shopping at ethnic markets. Established: 1997. Class/group size: 1-25. 15-20 programs/yr. Facilities: 800-sq-ft studio de la cuisine & old-fashioned veranda, heirloom vegetable gardens. Also featured: European culinary tours, kid-chef culinary camps, corporate team building programs, wine education & regional tastings.
FACULTY: CIA-trained chef & certified sommelier.
COSTS: From $65/class.
CONTACT: C'est si Bon! Cooking School, dorette@cestsibon.net, www.cestsibon.net.

CHEZ BAY GOURMET COOKING SCHOOL
Raleigh-Durham-Chapel Hill

Sponsor: Avocational cooking school. Programs: Beginner & intermediate techniques, baking & pastry, kid's classes, cooking camps, wine tasting, nutrition. Established: 2001. Class/group size: Hands-on: 30 max. 300+ programs/yr. Facilities: 1,500-sq-ft culinary arts center with prep area & 6 cooking stations. Also featured: Cookbook writing seminars, continuing ed, field trips, corporate team building, cooking software training.
FACULTY: Chef/owner & restaurateur Joel Goldfarb, IACP & AIWF, trained at Paul Bocuse's Ecole Des Arts; culinary instructor John Bowser.
COSTS: Classes from $45; $300/4-session series; camps $375/week.
CONTACT: Joel Goldfarb, Chef & Owner, Chez Bay Gourmet, 1921 North Pointe Plaza, Durham, NC 27705; 919-477-7878, 800-477-7857, Fax 919-882-9129, info@chezbaygourmet.com, www.chezbaygourmet.com.

A SOUTHERN SEASON
Chapel Hill

Sponsor: Retail cookware store & marketplace. Programs: Demo classes, wine tasting courses. Established: 1975. Also featured: Private & corporate team building programs.
FACULTY: Local culinary experts & visiting chefs.
COSTS: Classes $35-$65, wine courses $12-$45.
CONTACT: A Southern Season, Hwy 15-501 @ Estes Dr., University Mall, Chapel Hill, NC 27514; 877-929-7133, 919-929-7133, class@southernseason.com, www.southernseason.com.

OHIO

BUEHLER'S FOOD MARKETS
4 locations

Sponsor: Food market. Programs: Demo & participation classes. Established: 1983. Class/group size: 30 demo/12 hands-on. Facilities: Teaching areas with theater-type seating & overhead mir-

rors. Also featured: Child, teen, & parent-child classes.
FACULTY: Staff home economists & guest instructors.
COSTS: $7-$20/session.
CONTACT: Mary McMillen, Director of Consumer Affairs, Buehler's Food Markets, P.O. Box 196, 1401 Old Mansfield Rd., Wooster, OH 44691; 330-264-4355 #256, Fax 330-264-0874, mmcmillen@buehlers.com, www.buehlers.com.

COLUMBUS STATE CULINARY ACADEMY
Columbus
Sponsor: Division of Columbus State Community College. Programs: Demo & participation classes for adults & children. Established: 1995. Class/group size: 18-30. 160 programs/yr. Facilities: 2 professionally-equipped kitchens.
COSTS: $50 for demos, $70 for hands-on classes.
CONTACT: Carolyn Claycomb, Program Coordinator, Columbus State Culinary Academy, 550 E. Spring St., P.O. Box 1609, Columbus, OH 43216; 614-287-5126, Fax 614-287-5973, CClaycom@cscc.edu, www.cscc.edu.

COOKING SCHOOL AT JUNGLE JIM'S
Fairfield
Sponsor: Gourmet market & cooking school. Programs: Demo & hands-on classes on a variety of topics. Class/group size: 35 demo; 15 hands-on. 100+ programs/yr. Facilities: Features the latest equipment. Also featured: Culinary travel programs.
FACULTY: Includes school director Carol Tabone, Kathy Baker, Glenn Rinsky, Paul Teal, John Bostick, Janet Hontanosas, & Steve Lee. Visiting instructors & guest chefs.
COSTS: $38-$60/class.
CONTACT: Carole Tabone, School Director, The Cooking School at Jungle Jim's, 5440 Dixie Hwy., Fairfield, OH 45014; 513-829-1919 x3, Fax 513-829-1512, cookingschool@junglejims.com, www.junglejims.com.

COOKS'WARES CULINARY CLASSES
Cincinnati & Springboro
Sponsor: Kitchenware store. Programs: Demo & participation classes. Established: 1992. Class/group size: 28 demo/16 hands-on. 275 programs/yr. Facilities: 450-sq-ft teaching kitchens with overhead mirror. Also featured: Private group classes, children's & teen classes.
FACULTY: Includes Marilyn Harris & chefsJean-Robert de Cavel, Helen Chen, David Cooke, George Geary, Meg Galvin, Steve Hellmich.
COSTS: From $35-$65, $25 for youngsters.
CONTACT: Nancy Pigg, Director, Cooks'Wares Culinary Classes, 11344 Montgomery Rd., Cincinnati, OH 45249; 513-489-6400, Fax 513-489-1211, cookswares@aol.com, www.cookswaresonline.com. Nancy Rau, 746 Main St., Springboro, OH 45066; 937-748-4540, Fax 937-748-9060.

DOROTHY LANE MARKET'S SCHOOL OF COOKING
Dayton
Sponsor: Upscale supermarket & cooking school. Programs: Demo & participation classes for the home cook. Established: 1984. Class/group size: 36 demo/12 hands-on. 80-100 programs/yr. Facilities: 1,200-sq-ft teaching kitchen with overhead mirror. Also featured: Private, corporate, & team-building classes.
FACULTY: Chefs, caterers, cookbook authors, home economists. Celebrity chefs include David Rosengarten, Hugh Carpenter, Nick Malgieri, Pam Anderson, Judith Fertig, Shirley Corriher.
COSTS: Adult classes from $50-$95, teen classes $45, kid's classes $35.
CONTACT: Deb Lackey, School of Cooking Director, Dorothy Lane Market's School of Cooking, 6161 Far Hills Avenue, Dayton, OH 45459; 937-434-1294 exr. 22269, Fax 937-434-1299, cooking@dorothylane.com, www.dorothylane.com. dlackey@dorothylane.com.

HANDKE'S CUISINE COOKING CLASS
Columbus
Sponsor: Restaurant. Programs: Demos & private classes year-round for groups of 20 or more. Established: 1991. Class/group size: 32.
FACULTY: Hartmut Handke, CMC.
COSTS: 39.
CONTACT: Margot Handke, Handke's Cuisine Cooking Class, 520 S. Front St., Columbus, OH 43215; 614-621-2500, Fax 614-621-2626, finedining@chefhandke.com, www.chefhandke.com/index.html.

LAUREL RUN COOKING SCHOOL
Vermilion
Sponsor: Culinary professional Marcia DePalma. Programs: Basic to advanced demo or hands-on classes. Established: 1996. Class/group size: 18 hands-on/30 demo. 100-125 programs/yr. Facilities: Remodeled 1600 sq-ft school includes demo counter with mirrors, prep kitchen, herb garden. Also featured: Wine tastings, jr. chefs, field trips to markets, hands-on herb classes in the herb garden, private group classes.
FACULTY: Owner/instructor Marcia DePalma, 25 yrs experience growing/cooking with herbs, trained under Zona Spray, guest appearances on local TV & radio. 3 staff instructors; visiting local chefs.
COSTS: $35-$45/demo, $40-$65/hands-on class.
CONTACT: Marcia DePalma, Laurel Run Cooking School, 2600 North Ridge Rd., Vermilion, OH 44089; 440-984-5727, Fax 440-984-5727, LRCS@hbr.net, laurelruncookingschool.com.

THE LORETTA PAGANINI SCHOOL OF COOKING
Chesterland
Sponsor: Private school affiliated with Lakeland Community College. Programs: 1- to 4-session demo & participation courses. Established: 1981. Class/group size: 28 demo/12 hands-on. 400+ programs/yr. Facilities: Large professional kitchen with overhead mirror, professional equipment. Also featured: Couples & young gourmet classes, gastronomic tours/cruises to Italy, local trips, wk-long series in Sanibel, Florida.
FACULTY: Owner/director Loretta Paganini, culinary consultant, food writer, cookbook author & guest chef on local TV. Guest faculty includes local chefs, teachers & visiting professionals.
COSTS: $25-$45/session. Tour/cruise prices from $2,450-$4,850, including airfare, lodging, meals, excursions.
CONTACT: Loretta Paganini, Owner/Director, The Loretta Paganini School of Cooking, 8613 Mayfield Rd., Chesterland, OH 44026; 440-729-1110, Fax 440-729-6459, lpsc@lpscinc.com, www.lpscinc.com.

OKLAHOMA

THE STOCK POT SCHOOL OF COOKING
Tulsa
Sponsor: Gourmet food & cooking supply store. Programs: 2-hour demo classes. Established: 2002. Class/group size: 25. 200+ programs/yr. Facilities: Modern household-style equipment, 2 video monitors, digital cameras.
FACULTY: Chef Mark Hall, a culinary professional for 20+ years, was Executive Chef for Catering by Rosemary & Hilton Hotels & taught continuing ed classes at the U. of Texas. Guest chefs.
COSTS: $35-$50/class.
CONTACT: Jill Gillen, Director of Culinary Events, The Stock Pot School of Cooking, 7227 E. 41st Street, Tulsa, OK 74145; 918-627-1146, Fax 918-622-5804, chefmark@thestockpots.com, www.the-stockpots.com.

OREGON

ALL ABOUT WINE
Eugene
Sponsor: Wine professional. Programs: Wine education courses. Established: 1988. Class/group size: 20. Also featured: Wine tastings, food/wine programs.
FACULTY: Rick Ross is a member of SWE with 25+ yrs of study.
CONTACT: Rick Ross, Director, All About Wine, 40934 Highway 228, Sweet Home, OR; E-mail redwine5@earthlink.net.

CAPRIAL & JOHN'S KITCHEN
Portland
Sponsor: Cooking school. Programs: Cooking classes. Established: 2001. Class/group size: 16-40. 280 programs/yr. Also featured: Private classes.
FACULTY: Caprial & John Pence, resident chef Spence Lack, local & national guest chefs.
COSTS: $50-$135.
CONTACT: Caprial or John Pence, Owners, Caprial's Bistro & Wine, 7015 S.E. Milwaukie, Portland, OR 97202; 503-236-6457, Fax 503-238-8554, caprial@caprial.com, www.caprialand-johnskitchen.com.

CARL'S CUISINE, INC.
Salem
Sponsor: Culinary professional Carl Meisel. Programs: Demo classes. Established: 1978. Class/group size: 12.
FACULTY: Proprietor Carl Meisel has traveled & studied in Europe, Thailand, & the U.S. He is a consultant on menu planning, travel, & kitchen design.
COSTS: $30/class.
CONTACT: Carl Meisel, President, Carl's Cuisine, Inc., 333 Chemeketa St. NE, Salem, OR 97301; 503-363-1612, Fax 503-363-5014.

IN GOOD TASTE COOKING SCHOOL
Portland
Sponsor: Private cooking school & gourmet shop. Programs: Demo & hands-on cooking & wine classes. Established: 1998. Class/group size: Demo 16, hands-on 14. 360 programs/yr. Also featured: Team building classes, corporate private events, catering.
FACULTY: Professionally trained instructors.
COSTS: $35-$350.
CONTACT: In Good Taste Cooking School, 231 NW 11th Ave., Portland, Or 97209; 503-248-2015, Fax 503-248-2015, cook4fun@igtoregon.com, www.ingoodtastestore.com.

INSTITUTE FOR CULINARY AWAKENING
Eugene
Sponsor: Culinary professional. Programs: 5- & 12-day vegan culinary arts programs. Format is part lecture & mostly hands-on. Established: 1991. Class/group size: 12 max. Facilities: The chef's kitchen or the client's site/facility.
FACULTY: Founder/Director Chef Al Chase is a graduate of The CIA. Marketing Director Donna Benjamin is a graduate of Syracuse Univ.
COSTS: From $750-$1,400.
CONTACT: Chef Al Chase, Founder & Culinary Director, Institute for Culinary Awakening, 1292 High St., #171, Eugene, OR 97401; 541-686-8443, chefal@chefal.org, www.chefal.org.

LAYERS OF FLAVOR
Bend

Sponsor: Culinary professional. Programs: Custom individual & group classes. Established: 1993. Class/group size: 1-30. Facilities: 450-sq-ft modern kitchen, 12-ft island with commercial cooktop, stadium-type seating. Also featured: Private parties, team building, bridal & baby showers.

FACULTY: Chef/owner Deborah Middleton, CHE, has 14 yrs experience; 2 sous chefs assist.

COSTS: Classes $60-$200; workshops from $250/day.

CONTACT: Deborah Middleton, Layers of Flavor, 66592 E. Cascade, Bend, OR 97701; 541-318-5042, Fax 541-318-5042, LayersofFlavor@starband.net, LayersofFlavor.com. Mobile: 541-948-1804.

PENNSYLVANIA

CHARLOTTE-ANN ALBERTSON'S COOKING SCHOOL
Philadelphia; Florida; Europe

Sponsor: Culinary professional Charlotte-Ann Albertson. Programs: 1- to 4-session demo & some participation courses. Established: 1973. Class/group size: 25 demo/15 hands-on. 75 programs/yr. Also featured: Market tours, children's classes, wine seminars & dinners, wine & cheese pairing, European culinary vacations, winter classes in Florida.

FACULTY: Charlotte-Ann Albertson, IACP-member & certified teacher, studied at La Varenne & Le Cordon Bleu. CIA-trained Philadelphia chefs, caterers & experts.

COSTS: $40-$80/class. All Profits to Ronald McDonald House. Trips $80-$4,000 incl bus transport or airfare from Philadelphia, hotel lodging, most meals, planned excursions.

CONTACT: Charlotte-Ann Albertson's Cooking School, PO Box 27, Wynnewood, PA; 610-649-9290, Fax 610-649-2939, cookline99@aol.com, www.albertsoncookingschool.com.

COOKING AT TURTLE POND
Quakertown

Sponsor: Corporate chef Una Maderson. Programs: Demo & hands-on classes, weekend vacation courses. Private dinner classes, gift certificates. Established: 2000. Class/group size: 4-14. Facilities: Purpose-built large country home kitchen with cookbook library at Turtle Pond, a 23-acre wildlife protected area with a 2-acre pond.

FACULTY: Una Maderson, a professional chef with a degree in hotel & restaurant mgmt.

COSTS: $55/class. Weekend cooking vacations by arrangement.

CONTACT: Una Maderson, Turtle Pond, 210 Axehandle Rd., Quakertown, PA 0; 215-538-2564, Fax 215-538-2564, turtlepond@erols.com, www.turtlepondcooking.com.

COUNTRY WINES
Pittsburgh

Sponsor: Wine store. Programs: 3-session courses. Established: 1972. Class/group size: 5-20. 2 programs/yr. Also featured: Beermaking course.

FACULTY: Alexis Hartung, AWS-certified judge & a graduate of Carnegie-Mellon Univ.

COSTS: $30/course.

CONTACT: Alexis Hartung, Country Wines, 3333 Babcock Blvd., Pittsburgh, PA 0; 412-366-0151, Fax 412-366-9809, info@countrywines.com, www.countrywines.com.

CRATE
Pittsburgh

Sponsor: Cooking school & retail kitchenware store. Programs: Day & evening demo & participation courses & tours. Established: 1978. Class/group size: 40 demo/15 hands-on. 200+ programs/yr. Facilities: Demo kitchen with 10 burners, convection & microwave ovens, overhead mirror. Professional kitchen for hands-on classes. Also featured: Knife sharpenings, cookbook signings.

FACULTY: Chefs & owners of top local retaurants, culinary professionals, business owners, caterers.

COSTS: $18-$75/class, series ~$400.

CONTACT: Linda Wernikoff, Owner, Crate, 1960 Greentree Rd., Pittsburgh, PA 15220; 412-341-5700, Fax 412-341-6231, cratecook1@aol.com, www.cratecook.com.

FOOD FEST
Tannersville; Morgantown, WV

Sponsor: Publicist Gail Guggenheim. Programs: Cooking school get-away weekends that feature cooking classes, seminars, tastings. Established: 1984. 4 programs/yr. Facilities: Complete kitchen with overhead mirrors set up on a stage; closed-circuit monitors. Also featured: Hotel amenities.
FACULTY: Area chefs & cooking teachers, food authorities.
COSTS: $299-$325/couple for 2 nights includes continental breakfasts.
CONTACT: Gail Guggenheim, President, Food Fest, Inc., 125 Country Lane, Highland Park, IL 60035; 847-831-4265, Fax 847-831-4266, foodfest1@aol.com.

JULIAN KRINSKY COOKING SCHOOL
Haverford & Radnor

Programs: 2- & 3-wk summer culinary camp for teenagers ages 12-17 featuring cooking classes, celebrity chef demos, day-trips to markets & restaurants, weekend trips, camp activities. Established: 1978. Class/group size: 4-6:1. 6 programs/yr. Facilities: Air-conditioned demo kitchens. Also featured: Includes art, music, tennis, golf, fitness, business.
FACULTY: Tina Krinsky, Culinary Director. Chef instructors & assistants.
COSTS: ~$1,100/wk residential, ~$390/wk day camp. Includes private dorm lodging, meals & trips.
CONTACT: Tina Krinsky, Owner, Julian Krinsky Cooking School, P.O. Box 333, Haverford, PA 0; 866-TRY-JKCP, 610-265-9401, Fax 610-265-3678, julian@JKCP.com, www.jkcp.com/.

THE KITCHEN SHOPPE INC. & COOKING SCHOOL
Carlisle

Sponsor: Kitchenware, gift & gourmet store. Programs: Demo & hands-on classes. Established: 1974. Class/group size: 36 demo/15 hands-on. 150 programs/yr. Facilities: Well-equipped professional kitchen with 6 work stations, overhead mirrors, audio system. Also featured: Classes for youngsters & private groups.
FACULTY: Proprietor Suzanne Hoffman, IACP; instructors Amber Sunday, Jim Lupia, Diana Povis. Guest chefs include Hugh Carpenter, George Geary, Joanne Weir.
COSTS: $40-$60/session; children's classes $20-$40.
CONTACT: Amber Sunday, Cooking School Director, The Kitchen Shoppe Inc. & Cooking School, 101 Shady Lane, Carlisle, PA 17013; 800-391-COOK/717-243-0906, Fax 717-258-5162, kshoppe@pa.net, www.kitchenshoppe.com.

RANIA'S COOKING SCHOOL
Pittsburgh

Sponsor: Restaurant. Programs: 20+ demos each season. Established: 1984. Class/group size: 24. 48 programs/yr. Also featured: Children's classes, wine instruction, private classes.
FACULTY: Proprietor Rania Harris & chefs Tony Pias (Baum Vivant), Joe Nolan (Cafe Allegro), Bill Fuller (Casbah), Stuart Marks (Rania's Catering); Joe Och, beer tasting.
COSTS: $40/class, children's class is $25.
CONTACT: Rania Harris, Rania's Cooking School, 100 Central Sq., Pittsburgh, PA 15228; 412-531-2222, Fax 412-531-7242, rania@rania.com, www.rania.com.

THE RESTAURANT SCHOOL AT WALNUT HILL COLLEGE
Philadelphia   *(See also page 120) (See display ad page 122)*

Sponsor: 4-year private college. Programs: Hands-on & demo classes in a variety of culinary & pastry arts disciplines. Established: 1974. Class/group size: 24-85. 200+ programs/yr. Facilities: Include 5 classroom kitchens, two 75-seat demonstration kitchens, 3 classrooms, pastry shop, wine lab & multi-style dining complex. Also featured: The Wine Academy.
FACULTY: The 12-member professional faculty, internationally-known guest chefs & cookbook authors.

Costs: $35-$50/class.

Contact: GiGi Sheppard, Community Educ. Administrator, The Restaurant School at Walnut Hill College, 4207 Walnut St., Philadelphia, PA 19104; 877-925-6884, 215-222-4200 #3067, Fax 215-222-4219, info@walnuthillcollege.com, www.walnuthillcollege.com. gsheppard@walnuthillcollege.com.

SEWICKLEY COOKING STUDIO
Sewickley

Sponsor: Private school. Programs: 3- to 5-session hands-on courses, evening & weekend classes. Established: 1994. Class/group size: Max 12. 100 programs/yr. Also featured: Couples evenings, kids classes, dinner party courses, catering, corporate team building, recipe testing.

Faculty: School Director Gaynor Grant, formerly director of Peter Kump's NY Cooking School, is an IACP member.

Costs: Courses $250-$375; theme classes $75, $100/couple.

Contact: Gaynor Grant, Director, Sewickley Culinary, 443 Walnut St., Sewickley, PA 15143; 412-741-8671, Fax 412-749-1400, info@sewickleyculinary.com, www.sewickleycookingstudio.com.

SYLVIA SCHRAFF WINE PROGRAMS
Altoona

Sponsor: Wine professional. Programs: 4-session course. Established: 1989. Class/group size: 30.

Faculty: Sylvia Schraff has a Masters degree in Nursing, Certified Wine Judge.

Costs: $45/course.

Contact: Sylvia Schraff, Oak Spring Winery, R.D. 1, Box 612, Altoona, PA 16601; 814-946-3799, Fax 814-946-4245, oakspring@keyconn.net, www.oakspringwinery.com.

TORTE KNOX
Hawley   *(See display ad page 238)*
Sponsor: Culinary professional & TV chef Sheelah Kaye-Stepkin. Programs: Hands-on classes & series. Established: 1993. 100+ programs/yr. Facilities: Kitchen studio & cookbook library in a turn-of-the-century bank. Baking studio with sugar artistry arena, dining room/tasting room inside the vault. Also featured: Private instruction available year-round.
FACULTY: Founder Sheelah Kaye-Stepkin & guest chefs from NYC & surrounding area.
COSTS: $75-$150/session + food cost, weekly courses from $750 + food.
CONTACT: Sheelah Kaye-Stepkin, Torte Knox, 301 Main Ave., Hawley, PA 18428; 570-226-8200, 866-U-CAN-COOK, Fax 570-226-8201, mary@torteknox.com, www.torteknox.com.

THE WINE SCHOOL OF PHILADELPHIA
Manayunk & Philadelphia
Sponsor: Private school. Programs: Wine education certification programs for consumers & professionals; sensory education for consumers & academic courses for professionals. Established: 1999. Class/group size: 20. 10 programs/yr. Facilities: Classrooms. Also featured: Weekly wine tastings, corporate training seminars, private events.
FACULTY: 10 instructors, all with a minimum of 5 years in the wine industry.
COSTS: Wine Basics Certificate $285, Advanced Wine Program $450, Master of Vinology $1,400.
CONTACT: Keith Wallace, The Wine School of Philadelphia, 6124 Greene St., Philadelphia, PA 19144; 267-307-9220, keith@winelust.com, www.winelust.com.

PUERTO RICO

RUTAS GASTRONOMICAS PORTA DEL SOL – WESTERN REGION
Porta del Sol & Western Region
Sponsor: Puerto Rico Tourism Co. Programs: 1-day to wk-long culinary programs that include chef demos, hands-on classes, & tours to historical landmarks, farmers, markets. Established: 2003. Class/group size: 6 min. Facilities: Restaurants, mesones gastronomicos facilities/kitchens. Some artisanal food product factories, small farms & bakeries. Also featured: Optional extensions, custom tours, gastronomic events.
FACULTY: Chef Norma Llop, a bi-lingual graduate of the CIA & Univ of Puerto Rico. Part-time tour-chefs available.
COSTS: Group programs $900-$1,600 (seasonal), including deluxe hotel lodging, most meals, ground transport, 2 or more cooking classes.
CONTACT: Norma Llop, Chef &Culinary Product Development Officer, Rutas Gastronómicas Porta del Sol- Western Region, P.O. Box 902-3960, Old San Juan Station, San Juan, PR 0; 787-722-1604, Fax 787-721-3884, nllop@prtourism.com, www.gotopuertorico.com.

RHODE ISLAND

FLOUR BUDS, LLC
Newport
Sponsor: Culinary professional. Programs: Classes on the basics, quick cuisine, kitchen tool techniques, food safety, nutrition. Established: 2002. Class/group size: 8-10. 50+ programs/yr. Also featured: Table setting, menu planning, etiquette, personal chef, theme parties, kids' classes.
FACULTY: Jennifer Gower is a self-taught chef, owned a gourmet luncheonette, held chef positions on yachts.
COSTS: $25-$60/class.
CONTACT: Jennifer Gower, Cooking Instuctor, Flour Buds, 59 Burnside Ave., Newport, RI 02840; 401-849-3202, jnjy5@yahoo.com.

SAKONNET MASTER CHEFS SERIES
Little Compton
Sponsor: Sakonnet Vineyards. Programs: Full-day demo & participation classes. Established: 1980. Class/group size: 12. 10 programs/yr. Facilities: Kitchen with chopping block work table & counter that can serve as individual work areas.
FACULTY: Has included Johanne Killeen, George Germon, Jasper White, Todd English, Michael Schlow, Casey Riley, Joe Simone.
COSTS: $80-$100. Lodging can be arranged.
CONTACT: Susan Samson, Sakonnet Vineyards, P.O. Box 197, Little Compton, RI 02837; 401-635-8486, Fax 401-635-2101, SakonnetRI@aol.com, www.sakonnetwine.com.

SOUTH CAROLINA

BOBBI COOKS II
Hilton Head Island
Sponsor: Culinary professional Bobbi Leavitt. Programs: Demo & participation classes. Established: 1993. Class/group size: 10 hands-on/15 demo. 30 programs/yr. Facilities: Large fully-equipped home kitchen. Also featured: Classes for youngsters, wine & food pairing, couples' classes, private instruction.
FACULTY: Bobbi Leavitt studied at Johnson & Wales, Master Chefs Inst, Michael James French Chefs School, La Varenne, France; past president NYACT, member IACP, AIWF. Guest instructors.
COSTS: $30-$40/class.
CONTACT: Bobbi Leavitt, Owner, Bobbi Cooks II, 9 Baynard Pk., Hilton Head Island, SC 29928; 843-671-5902, Fax 843-671-5902, BobbiCooksatHHI@juno.com.

IN GOOD TASTE
Charleston
Sponsor: Gourmet shop. Programs: 5-day hands-on MacroBalanced Series. Wine classes, generally 4 in a series. Private classes available. Established: 1982. Class/group size: 8-14. Facilities: Well-equipped teaching kitchen.
FACULTY: Owner Jacki Boyd, local guest chefs & Kushi Institute Certified Guide, Roxanne Koteles.
COSTS: $30-$200/session. Reduced fee for whole series.
CONTACT: Jacki Boyd, In Good Taste, 1901 Ashley River Rd., Charleston, SC 29407; 843-763-5597, jackiboyd1@prodigy.net.

TENNESSEE

BLACKBERRY FARM FOOD & WINE HAPPENINGS
Walland
Sponsor: Resort hotel. Programs: 3-day vacation programs that include cooking demos & wine tastings. Established: 1995. Class/group size: 24. 17 programs/yr. Facilities: Demo kitchen of proprietors' private home. Also featured: Fly fishing, horseback riding, hiking, tennis, mountain biking, spa.
FACULTY: Blackberry Farm's Executive Chef John Fleer; guest chefs include Chef Rick Tramonto, Suzanne Goin, Charlie Trotter, Joel Antunes, Allen Susser; guest vintners, culinary experts.
COSTS: $400 includes some meals; lodging additional.
CONTACT: Sarah Elder, Blackberry Farm Food & Wine Happenings, 1471 W. Millers Cove Rd., Walland, TN 37886; 800-557-8864, Fax 865-977-4012, foodandwine@blackberryfarm.com, www.blackberryfarm.com.

VIKING CULINARY ARTS & HOMECHEF CENTERS
Atlanta, GA; Bryn Mawr, PA; Memphis & Nashville, TN; Dallas, TX
Sponsor: Cooking school & culinary retail store. Programs: Demo classes on a variety of topics; 12-week Essential Cooking Series; 1- to 3-day Techniques of Cooking hands-on courses.

Established: 1999. Class/group size: 12 hands-on; 40 demo. 800 programs/yr. Facilities: Teaching participation kitchen & demo theater equipped with Viking Range Corp. product line. Also featured: Corporate team-building programs.

FACULTY: Chan Patterson, Corporate Cooking School Director. Local & national guest chef instructors.

COSTS: $35-$50 for demos, $125-$375 for techniques classes.

CONTACT: Chan Patterson, Corporate Cooking School Director, Viking Culinary Arts Center, 1052 Highland Colony Parkway, #125, Ridgeland, MS 39157; 601-898-2778 x-6607, Fax 601-898-7947, cpatters@vikingrange.com, www.vikingrange.com. Also homechefinfo@vikingrange.com.

TEXAS

BATTER UP KIDS COOKING SCHOOL
Austin
Sponsor: Culinary professional Barbara Beery. Programs: Hands-on cooking classes, birthday parties & summer camps for 4- to 10-year-olds. Established: 1991. Class/group size: 10-20. Facilities: French country kitchen with central work area.

FACULTY: Founder Barbara Beery earned a bachelors degree in elementary education, is author of Batter Up Kids: Delicious Desserts, & has 25 years teaching experience.

COSTS: $30/class, $160/5-day camp.

CONTACT: Barbara Beery, Founder/Owner, Batter Up Kids Cooking School, 4403 CanyonsideTrail, Austin, TX 78731; 512-342-8682, 866 -345-8682, Fax 512-343-8810, barbara@batterupkids.com, batterupkids.com.

BLAIR HOUSE COOKING SCHOOL
Wimberley
Sponsor: Country inn. Programs: 3-day hands-on cooking vacations that focus on a specific theme, such as holiday baking, seasonal or intl cuisines with an emphasis on French. Established: 1992. Class/group size: 10. 15 programs/yr. Facilities: Commercial kitchen with open circular floor plan. Also featured: Massage, art gallery, hiking trail, library.

FACULTY: Exec. Chef Christopher Stonesifer. Innkeepers/owners Mike & Vickie Schneider. Blair House was named 1 of the Top 25 B&B/Country Inns by Arrington's Bed & Breakfast Journal.

COSTS: $450/2 nights includes lodging, meals, beverages.

CONTACT: Angel Bacon, Director/Public Relations, Blair House Cooking School, 100 Spoke Hill Ln., Wimberley, TX 78676; 877-549-5450, Fax 512-847-8820, info@blairhouseinn.com, www.blairhouseinn.com.

CENTRAL MARKET COOKING SCHOOLS
Austin, Dallas, Ft. Worth, Houston, Plano
Sponsor: Specialty foods markets. Programs: Basic & advanced cooking, intl cuisines, guest chef specialties. Established: 1994. Class/group size: 20 hands-on, 36 demo. 350+ programs/yr. Facilities: Modern culinary classroom. Also featured: Shop the market classes, hands-on, childrens activity programs.

FACULTY: National & regional guest chefs & cookbook authors, Central Market culinary staff.

COSTS: $25-$125/class.

CONTACT: Shelley Grieshaber, Cooking School Coordinator, Central Market Cooking School, 4001 N. Lamar Blvd., Austin, TX 78756; 512-458-3068, Fax 512-206-1009, grieshaber.shelley@heb.com, www.centralmarket.com.

CREATING CULINARY OPPORTUNITIES
Houston
Sponsor: Culinary professional Ann Iverson. Programs: 1- & 2-day hands-on courses in Italian & occasionally other European cuisines. Established: 1993. Class/group size: 12-16. 4-6 programs/yr.

Facilities: 340-sq-ft private kitchen with 12 work areas. Also featured: Special food tastings. **FACULTY:** Ann Iverson studied with Giuliano Bugialli, Mary Beth Clark, Marcella & Victor Hazan, Giuliano Hazan, Lorenza di Medici. Guest chefs & authors such as Giuliano Hazan. **COSTS:** $150-400/session. **CONTACT:** Ann Iverson, Owner, Creating Culinary Opportunities, 2902 West Lane Dr., Unit E, Houston, TX 77027; 713-622-6936, Fax 713-622-2924, annci@sbcglobal.net.

CUISINE CONCEPTS
Fort Worth
Sponsor: Author & food stylist Renie Steves. Programs: Private wine & cooking instruction designed to the student's requests. Established: 1979. Class/group size: 1-3:1. 10-20 programs/yr. Facilities: Kitchen in a private home. Also featured: Group classes, hands-on classes for 9 max. **FACULTY:** Owner Renie Steves, CCP, past chair of the IACP Foundation, past president Les Dames d'Escoffier, studied with Madeleine Kamman, James Beard, Julia Child, Nick Malgieri, & the Hazans. **COSTS:** $100/hr for 1 student, $125 for 2, + $10/hr asst fee; each class is 4-hr minimum. **CONTACT:** Renie Steves, Owner/Teacher, Cuisine Concepts, 1406 Thomas Pl., Ft. Worth, TX 0; 817-732-4758, Fax 817-732-3247, RenieSteves@msn.com.

CULINARY ACADEMY OF AUSTIN
Austin
Sponsor: Private career school. Programs: Classes that include intl & American regional cuisines, pastries & desserts, wine appreciation. Established: 1998. Class/group size: 8-15. 200+ programs/yr. Facilities: 2-story building contains commercial kitchen with demo cooking stations, classrooms, dining room, media room. Also featured: Team building programs. **FACULTY:** 2 pastry chefs, 3 culinary chefs. **COSTS:** ~$40-$125. **CONTACT:** Jimmy Henig, Director of Admissions, Culinary Academy of Austin, Inc., 2823 Hancock Dr., Austin, TX 78731; 512-451-5743, Fax 512-467-9120, jhenig@culinaryacademy-ofaustin.com, www.culinaryacademyofaustin.com.

CULINARY INSTITUTE ALAIN & MARIE LENÔTRE
Houston   *(See also page 128) (See display ad page 128)*
Sponsor: Proprietary institution with French curriculum. Programs: Chef's Club hands-on culinary & wine classes. Established: 1998. Class/group size: 8-15 hands-on. 50 programs/yr. Facilities: 14,000-sq-ft newly-equipped kitchens. Also featured: Summer camps, programs for youngsters, private instruction, travel programs, team building. **FACULTY:** Technical Director Alain LeNôtre, French & European chefs. **COSTS:** $69/cooking class, $35/wine class, $300/wk for teen summer camp, $400/week for adult summer camp. **CONTACT:** Alain LeNôtre, President & CEO, Culinary Institute Alain & Marie LeNôtre, 7070 Allensby St., Houston, TX 0; 888-LeNotre, 713-692-0077, Fax 713-692-7399, lenotre@wt.net, www.lenotre-alain-marie.com.

DESIGNER EVENTS COOKING SCHOOL
Bryan
Sponsor: Culinary professional Merrill Bonarrigo. Programs: Quarterly hands-on cooking classes & food & wine pairing seminars provided by Messina Hof Winery & Resort. Established: 1992. Class/group size: 20-30. 4 programs/yr. Facilities: Restaurant settings. Also featured: Wine tastings, festivals, vintner dinners. **FACULTY:** Executive Chef Terry Howry & Maitre d' Klaus Elfeldt of the Vintage House at Messina Hof. **COSTS:** $29.95/class. Lodging available at The Villa B&B on the estate. **CONTACT:** Merrill Bonarrigo, Owner, Designer Events Cooking School, 4545 Old Reliance Rd., Bryan, TX 77808; 979-778-9463 x34, Fax 979-778-1729, event@messinahof.com, www.messinahof.com.

HUDSON'S ON THE BEND COOKING SCHOOL
Austin

Sponsor: Restaurant. Programs: Demo/participation classes in the chef's restaurant & home. Established: 1993. Class/group size: 20-25. 12 programs/yr. Facilities: Hudson's on the Bend restaurant kitchen, Chef Blank's home kitchen. Also featured: Sightseeing.

FACULTY: Executive Chef Jay Moore, a CIA graduate, & Owner/Chef Jeff Blank, creators of Hudson's on the Bend Gourmet Sauces.

COSTS: $90/session.

CONTACT: Shanny Lott, Hudson's on the Bend, 3509 Highway 620, Austin, TX 78734; 512-266-1369/800-996-7655, Fax 512-266-3518, jeffreyblank@austin.rr.com, hudsons.citysearch.com/1.html.

INTERNATIONAL FOODWORKS
Hill County; Santa Fe, NM; Oaxaca & Jalisco, Mexico

Sponsor: Nonprofit organization. Programs: Hands-on classes that include intl & American regional cuisines, cheese making, pastries, desserts, wine appreciation. Established: 1999. Class/group size: 12. 50 programs/yr. Facilities: Free-standing newly-renovated building with commercial kitchen, air-conditioned classrooms. Also featured: Food research & consulting, foreign language culinary training, culinary culture & travel seminars, food library, Historic Foodways Group of Austin.

FACULTY: Ken Rubin, Carmen Quijano, Glenn Mack, Chefs Javier Montesinos, Matthew Shipman & Ped Phommavong.

COSTS: $60/class.

CONTACT: Ken Rubin, Program Director, International FoodWorks, 815-A Brazos, PMB 152, Austin, TX 78701; 512-619-3916, Fax 512-832-5945, info@i-foodworks.org, URL www.i-foodworks.org, kmr@i-foodworks.org.

KITCHEN FRIENDS
Duncanville (near Dallas)

Sponsor: Culinary professional. Programs: Hands-on morning & evening classes. Established: 1999. Class/group size: 12 max. 25 programs/yr.

FACULTY: K.A. Tieszen taught classes in Dallas/Ft. Worth, worked with top local chefs, attended cooking school in France & completed a 1-wk program at the 3-star Troisgros restaurant in Roanne.

COSTS: $40/class, children's classes are $25.

CONTACT: K.A. Tieszen, Chef/Owner, Kitchen Friends, Duncanville, TX 75137; 972-298-5427, Fax 972-283-8408, chefkat@kitchen-friends.com, www.kitchen-friends.com.

THE KITCHEN SHOP AT THE GREEN BEANERY
Beaumont, Texas

Sponsor: Cafe & cookware store. Programs: Demon & limited participation classes. Established: 1992. Class/group size: 30 demo/15 hands-on. 20 programs/yr. Facilities: 20-seat demo kitchen area. Also featured: Culinary tours.

FACULTY: Glenn Watz, chef/owner of the Green Beanery Cafe for 25 years; local & visiting instructors, cookbook authors.

COSTS: $25-$35/class.

CONTACT: Carolyn Wood, Owner, The Kitchen Shop at the Green Beanery, 2121 McFaddin Ave., Beaumont, TX 77701; 409-832-9738, Fax 409-833-5134.

LAKE AUSTIN SPA RESORT
Austin

Sponsor: Lake Austin Spa Resort. Programs: 3-, 4-, & 7-night packages that include cooking classes, spa treatments, fitness & discovery programs. Established: 1997. Class/group size: 65 max. Facilities: Fully-equipped demo kitchen & fitness facility, 25,000-sq-ft new spa building. Also featured: Yoga, kayaking, Nia, Pilates, hiking, spinning, meditation.

FACULTY: Chef Terry Conlan, author of Fresh: Healthy Cooking & Living from Lake Austin Spa Resort, a finalist in the 2004 IACP cookbook awards & Lean Star Cuisine, has 30+ yrs restaurant experience & appeared on TV food shows; celebrity guest chefs.
COSTS: 3-day packages from $1,430 includes lodging, meals, classes, spa treatments.
CONTACT: Reservations, Lake Austin Spa Resort, 1705 S. Quinlan Park Rd., Austin, TX 78732; 512-372-7360, 800-847-5637, Fax 512-372-7280, info@lakeaustin.com, www.lakeaustin.com.

THE MAIN COURSE
Plano

Sponsor: Chef Sue Boyer. Programs: Hands-on classes covering appetizers to desserts. Established: 2003. Class/group size: 6-8. 100 programs/yr. Facilities: Home kitchen. Also featured: Cooking parties, competitions, team building.
FACULTY: Sue Boyer graduated from New Zealand's Wellington Polytechnic School of Fashion & Food. She is a caterer to realtor & title company functions.
COSTS: $25-$55/class.
CONTACT: Sue Boyer, Chef, The Main Course, 6805 Thorncliff Trail, Plano, TX 75023; 214-680-1914, maincoursecooking@yahoo.com, www.maincoursecooking.com.

THE MANSION ON TURTLE CREEK
Dallas

Sponsor: Mobil 5-star, AAA 5-diamond hotel & restaurant. Programs: A demo class, special dinner, or both each month. Established: 1994. Class/group size: 10-150. 5 programs/yr. Also featured: Chef for a Day, Cookiing Class & Dining Etiquette for Children.
FACULTY: Chef Dean Fearing co-hosts the classes. Guest chefs have included Wolfgang Puck, Julia Child, Jacques Pepin, Emeril Lagasse, Norman Van Aken.
COSTS: $100-$225/class, $1,600/person for Chef for a Day.
CONTACT: Rebecca Swartz, The Mansion on Turtle Creek, 2821 Turtle Creek Blvd., Dallas, TX 75219; 214-559-2100, Fax 214-871-3245, rswartz@rosewoodhotels.com, www.mansiononturtlecreek.com/.

LE PANIER
Houston

Sponsor: Private cooking school. Programs: Demo & participation classes. Established: 1980. Class/group size: 45 demo/15 hands-on. 200 programs/yr. Facilities: Well-equipped teaching area with theater seating, overhead mirror, cooking & work spaces. Also featured: Classes for youngsters, basic techniques series, catering courses.
FACULTY: Owner/Director LaVerl Daily teaches basics. Other classes taught by guest chefs, teachers, & cookbook authors, including Giuliano Bugialli, Giuliano Hazan, Nicholas Malgieri, Hugh Carpenter.
COSTS: $35-$60/session, children's classes $20.
CONTACT: LaVerl Daily, Director, Le Panier, 7275 Brompton Rd., Houston, TX 77025; 713-664-9848, Fax 713-666-2037, ldaily8673@aol.com.

SOPHIE'S KITCHEN COOKING SCHOOL AT FITNESS SOLUTIONS
Pearland

Sponsor: Private school. Programs: Demo & hands-on classes for adults & children that emphasize healthy cuisine & nutrition. Established: 2003. Class/group size: 6-30. 40-50 programs/yr. Facilities: Industry-current kitchen & classroom. Also featured: Private classes, parties, team building, catering.
FACULTY: Norie Berndt, a professional chef with teaching experience; registered dietitians Cassie Dimmick & Gaye Koenning have masters degrees in nutrition.
COSTS: $40-$65/class.
CONTACT: Norie Berndt, Chef, Sophie's Kitchen Cooking School at Fitness Solutions, 9330 W. Broadway, #104, Pearland, TX 77584; 832-736-9700, Fax 832-736-9955, Kitchen@fitnesssolutions.net, www.fitnesssolutions.net.

UTAH

LOVE TO COOK!
Logan
Sponsor: Retail kitchenware store & cooking school. Programs: Demo & hands-on cooking classes.
FACULTY: Includes Bryan Woolley, Kristin Trevino, Jadene Denniston, John Simpson, Ed Quinlan, Julie Stenquist, Bob Calloway, Nancy Beykirch, Margurite Henderson.
COSTS: $10-$45/session.
CONTACT: Love to Cook!, 1211 N. Main, Logan, UT 84321; 888-GADGET9/435-752-9220, questions@luvtocook.com, www.luvtocook.com/.

VERMONT

ARTISANAL CHEESEMAKING
Warren
Sponsor: Dr. Larry & Linda Faillace, owners of Three Shepherds' farmstead dairy. Programs: 1- & 3-day hands-on cheesemaking courses using sheep, goat & cow milk. Established: 1997. Class/group size: 10 max. 7+ programs/yr. Facilities: Ag-Innovations' farmstead cheesemaking facility.
FACULTY: Linda & Larry Faillace, Ph.D. & their daughter Jackie; Freddie Michiels, owner of a farmstead dairy in northern Belgium.
COSTS: $500 includes lunches & farmstead dinner.
CONTACT: Dr. Larry & Linda Faillace, Ag-Innovations, Inc., 108 Roxbury Mountain Rd., Warren, VT 05674; 802-496-3998, 802-496-4559, Fax 802-496-4096, localfood@msn.com.

CULINARY MAGIC COOKING SEMINARS
Ludlow
Sponsor: The Governor's Inn. Programs: 2-day cooking vacations featuring morning hands-on theme cooking classes & wine pairing. Established: 1992. Class/group size: 4. 9 programs/yr. Facilities: Commercial kitchen facilities of The Governor's Inn. Also featured: Shopping & sightseeing.
FACULTY: Cathy Kubec, chef, innkeeper, & graduate of the Connecticut Culinary Institute.
COSTS: $825/couple includes 2 nights shared lodging with both guests taking course, $525 single.
CONTACT: Chef Cathy Kubec, Innkeeper, Culinary Educator, Culinary Magic Cooking Seminars, The Governor's Inn, 86 Main St., Ludlow, VT 05149; 800-468-3766, Fax 802-228-2961, thegovinn@adelphia.net, www.thegovernorsinn.com.

DEBORAH KRASNER'S CULINARY VACATIONS
Putney; Amelia, Umbria, Italy
Sponsor: Culinary professional & cookbook author. Programs: 3- & 6-day vacation cooking programs that include visits to food artisans, craftsmen, gardens. Travel programs to Italy. Established: 2004. Class/group size: 5-10. 9 programs/yr. Facilities: Modern kitchen, 10-foot marble island, wood-fired pizza oven. Also featured: Private concert, mushroom hunt, sightseeing.
FACULTY: Deborah Krasner received a James Beard Award for The Flavors of Olive Oil & was a finalist for the Julia Child Award & the Jacob's Creek Intl Food Media Award.
COSTS: $2,650 includes lodging, meals, planned activities, airport pickup/return, ground transport.
CONTACT: Deborah Krasner, Deborah Krasner's Culinary Vacations, 192 Taylor Rd., Westminster West, Putney, VT 05346; 802-387-6610, Fax 802-387-2846, dkrasner@sover.net, www.deborahkrasnersvermont.com. madiinitaly@yahoo.com.

POND HOUSE INN NORTHERN ITALIAN COOKING WORKSHOPS
Brownsvillle
Sponsor: B & B inn. Programs: 2-day hands-on cooking programs with a visit to a producer of organic Italian-style cheeses. Established: 2002. Class/group size: 6. 9 programs/yr. Facilities: The

Inn's Italian-style kitchen. Also featured: Swimming, hiking, biking, croquet.
FACULTY: Chef/owner Gretel Schuck trained in Paris & Italy.
COSTS: $750/couple includes lodging, meals, excursion.
CONTACT: Gretel Schuck, Pond House Inn, PO Box #234, Brownsville, VT 05037; 802-484-0011, pondhouse0011@yahoo.com, www.pondhouseinn.com.

VERMONT CULINARY VACATION
Middlebury
Sponsor: Henry Sheldon Museum of Vermont History & the Swift House Inn. Programs: 4-day cooking vacation that includes 16 hrs of hands-on cooking classes, tours to local organic & artisan food producers. Swift House Inn in Middlebury, Vermont. Established: 2004. Class/group size: 8. 2 programs/yr. Facilities: Recently renovated commercial kitchen facilities of the Swift House Inn. Also featured: Seasonal outdoor recreation, galleries, shops, museums, historic sites within walking distance.
FACULTY: Bonnie Moore, Executive Chef of FoodFit.com.
COSTS: $2,000 ($3,500, $3,000) includes single lodging (double lodging for 2 students, double lodging for 1 student & 1 guest) at the Swift House Inn, some meals, planned activities.
CONTACT: Dan Brown, Innkeeper, Swift House Inn, 25 Stewart Lane, Middlebury, VT 05753; 802-388-9925, cooking@henrysheldonmuseum.org, www.henrysheldonmuseum.org.

VIRGINIA

THE ACCIDENTAL CHEF
Richmond, Charlottesville, Goochland & Tidewater
Sponsor: Culinary professional Kendra Bailey Morris. Programs: Hands-on/demo cooking & wine parties for groups of 2+. Classes for children. Established: 2003. 40+ programs/yr. Facilities: The client's home or a well-equipped, off-site kitchen. Also featured: Private instruction, corporate team building, catering.
FACULTY: Kendra Bailey Morris, MFA, managed a cooking school & is a food writer & restaurant critic. She has worked in restaurants, country clubs & catering firms.
COSTS: From $45.
CONTACT: Kendra Bailey Morris, Chef/Owner, The Accidental Chef, Richmond, VA; E-mail info@theaccidentalchef.net, www.theaccidentalchef.net.

BOAR'S HEAD INN
Charlottesville
Sponsor: Resort at The University of Virginia & Cuisine International. Programs: 3-day hands-on cooking vacations that include a wine seminar, winery tour, & vintner dinners. Established: 2001. Facilities: Boar's Head Inn kitchens. Also featured: Spa, 18-hole golf course, sports club.
FACULTY: Boar's Head Inn Executive Chef Alex Montiel, Mexico City native who trained under five Michelin-star chefs.
COSTS: $1,400 ($300 single supplement) includes lodging, two dinner, planned excursions.
CONTACT: Cuisine International, P.O. Box 25228, Dallas, TX 75225; 214-373-1161, Fax 214-373-1162, CuisineInt@aol.com, www.cuisineinternational.com/us/boarshead/index.html.

CULINARY UNIVERSITY
Leesburg
Sponsor: Lansdowne Resort & Conference Center. Programs: Cooking demos featuring seasonal theme-based menus. Food & Wine Camp weekends that combine demos, garden & winery tour, aroma class. Established: 1982. Class/group size: 75 classes, 18 camp. 16 programs/yr. Facilities: Amphitheater & ballrooms with seating. Portable kitchen equipment. Also featured: Golf, spa, tennis, racquetball, trails, indoor & outdoor swimming pool.
FACULTY: Konrad Meier, Executive Chef; Andrew Reh, Executive Sous Chef; Mary Watson-DeLauder, Sommelier.

Costs: Demo classes $60-$75. Food & Wine Camps $925/couple, includes 2-night deluxe lodging. **Contact:** Cricket Manjarrez, Executive Club Manager, Culinary University, 44050 Woodridge Parkway, Lansdowne, VA 20176; 703-858-2107, Fax 703-858- 2101, CManjarrez@benchmarkmanagement.com, www.lansdowneresort.com/events/culinaryuniversity.cfm.

THE INN AT MEANDER PLANTATION COOKING SCHOOL
Locust Dale
Sponsor: Private school in a country inn. Programs: 1- & 2-day hands-on cooking programs. Topics change monthly & include theme & holiday menus, grilling, fish, herbs & baking. Established: 1999. Class/group size: 18. 12 programs/yr. Facilities: Country B&B with professional kitchen & classrooms. Also featured: Field trip to local producers, biking, wine tasting.
Faculty: Chef/owner Suzie Blanchard, former food writer & columinist; Head Chef Paul Deigl & Pastry Chef Sarah Deigl.
Costs: $125/day, $225/2 days. 2-day B&B package $750 ($525) includes shared (single) lodging, meals.
Contact: Suzie Blanchard, Chef/owner, The Inn at Meander Plantation Cooking School, 2333 N. James Madison Hwy., Locust Dale, VA 22948; 800-385-4936, 540-672-4912, Fax 540-672-0405, inn@meander.net, www.meander.net.

JUDY HARRIS COOKING SCHOOL
Alexandria
Sponsor: Culinary professional Judy Harris. Programs: Classes in international cuisines including Italian, French, Spanish, American Regional, Mexican, Indian & Thai. Established: 1978. Class/group size: 12 hands-on/20 demo. 65 programs/yr. Facilities: Well-equipped kitchen, culinary herb & vegetable gardens. Also featured: Private group classes, culinary tours, restaurant trips.
Faculty: Judy Harris studied at La Varenne in Paris. Well-known guest chefs, teachers, & cookbook authors include Hugh Carpenter, Jacques Blanc, & Jacques Haeringer.
Costs: $42-$75/session.
Contact: Judy Harris, Judy Harris Cooking School, 2402 Nordok Place, Alexandria, VA 22306; 703-768-3767, judy@judyharris.com, judyharris.com.

SAVORING THYME GOURMET COOKING CLASSES
Richmond area
Sponsor: Personal chef. Programs: Hands-on & demo in-home cooking classes. Established: 2001. Class/group size: 1-30. 25+ programs/yr. Facilities: Client's home or professional kitchen. Also featured: Private or group instruction, interactive dinner parties, children's classes.
Faculty: Paige Kerr, graduate US Personal Chef Institute, trained at George Brown College.
Costs: From $40.
Contact: Paige Kerr, Savoring Thyme Gourmet Cooking Classes, 12411 Creek Mill Ct., Glen Allen, VA 23059; 804-218-3319, savoringthyme@comcast.net, www.uspca.net/va/pkerr.

STRATFORD UNIVERSITY
Falls Church
Sponsor: Private career institution. Programs: Demo & participation classes that cover basic techniques, special occasion menus, & international cuisines. Classes for couples, singles, & youngsters. Established: 1990. 40+ programs/yr. Facilities: Kitchens with the latest equipment.
Faculty: Stratford University culinary faculty.
Costs: $50/class.
Contact: Short Course Coordinator, Stratford University, 7777 Leesburg Pike, Falls Church, VA 22043; 703-734-5307, shortcourse@stratford.edu, www.stratford.edu.

VIRGINIA GOURMET COOKING SCHOOL
Richmond
Sponsor: Private school. Programs: Hands-on classes & series ranging from the basics to specific subjects. Established: 2002. Class/group size: 16-30. 200+ programs/yr. Facilities: Fully equipped

900-sq-ft kitchen. Also featured: Private parties, wine classes, corporate team-building seminars. **FACULTY:** Local chefs, including Michelle Williams & Thomas Sears. **COSTS:** $35-$45/class. Series classes offered at reduced rate. **CONTACT:** Kendra Bailey, Manager of Culinary Division, Virginia Gourmet Cooking School, 11400 West Huguenot Rd., #109, Richmond, VA 23113; 804-897-3710 x12, Fax 804-897-5311, kbailey@vagourmet.org, www.vagourmet.org.

WASHINGTON

BLUE RIBBON COOKING SCHOOL
Seattle
Sponsor: Private cooking school. Programs: Hands-on classes. Established: 1973. Class/group size: 20. Weekly programs/yr. Facilities: Teaching kitchen with the latest equipment in a 1907 Craftsman-style home. Also featured: Private & kids classes, corporate team-building, summer camps. **FACULTY:** Owner Virginia Duppenthaler, CCP, Le Corden Bleu, Paris; Gastronomic Institute, Vienna. Owner Mike Duppenthaler, BBQ specialist. Suzanne Hunter, CCP, Iole Aguero, Jamil Johnson. **COSTS:** ~$65/class. **CONTACT:** Mike & Virginia Duppenthaler, Proprietors, Blue Ribbon Cooking School, 1611 McGilvra Blvd. East, Seattle, WA; 206-328-2442, Fax 206-328-2863, mike@blueribboncooking.com, www.blueribboncooking.com.

THE COMPLEAT COOK
Bellevue
Sponsor: Kitchen & giftware store. Programs: Classes cover such topics as appetizers, table decorating, meal planning, quick & easy meals, roasting, Asian noodles, vegetarian gourmet, baking. Established: 1990. Class/group size: 24 max. Also featured: Corporate parties & team building. **FACULTY:** Local restaurant & private chefs. **COSTS:** ~$45/class. **CONTACT:** The Compleat Cook, Crossroads Shopping Ctr., 15600 NE 8th St., # K-10, Bellevue, WA 98008; 425-746-9201, Fax 425-746-2491, info@compleatcook.com, www.compleatcook.com.

COOK'S WORLD COOKING SCHOOL
Seattle
Sponsor: Cookware store. Programs: Demo & participation courses. Established: 1990. Class/group size: 20 demo/12 hands-on. 200+ programs/yr. Facilities: 400-sq-ft professionally-designed instructional kitchen with overhead mirrors, large teaching classroom. Also featured: Private classes, team-building seminars. **FACULTY:** Nancie Brecher, IACP member, who studied at the CIA, Peter Kump's, & La Varenne; local chefs & professional food experts. **COSTS:** $38-$45/3-hr class. 20% discount on merchandise. **CONTACT:** Nancie Brecher, Director, Cook's World, 2900 NE Blakeley St., Seattle, WA 98105; 206-528-8192, cooksworld@aol.com, www.cooksworld.net.

CULINARY COMMUNION
Seattle
Sponsor: Private school. Programs: Hands-on classes & 6-session series covering techniques, American & international cuisines, baking; wine education; culinary vacations. Established: 1999. Class/group size: 8-10. 50+ programs/yr. Facilities: Private home with well-equipped kitchen. **FACULTY:** Gabriel Claycamp, owner & former sous chef at The Tasting Room in NYC; Scott Samuel, owner/chef of Simply Brilliant; Kären Jurgensen, executive chef of Baci Catering. **COSTS:** $360/6-session series. **CONTACT:** Heidi Kenyon, Culinary Communion, Seattle, WA 98119; 206-284-8687, Fax 425-650-9887, info@culinarycommunion.com, www.culinarycommunion.com. scott@chefscottsamuel.com.

THE KITCHEN DOOR
Langley

Sponsor: Private recreational cooking school. Programs: Hands-on programs for the home cook; some advanced classes. Established: 2000. Class/group size: 8-10 hands-on. 36 programs/yr. Facilities: Private home kitchens. Also featured: Private group or individual classes, corporate team building, field trips.

FACULTY: Owner Shirlee Read also instructs at Sur la Table & other Seattle area cooking schools. Guest chefs, lecturers & demonstrators from the Pacific NW.

COSTS: $85-$95/class; guest chef classes $125.

CONTACT: Shirlee Read, Owner, The Kitchen Door, PO Box 422, Langley, WA 98260; 360-730-2322, shirlee@thekitchendoor.net, www.thekitchendoor.net.

SOOK ENTERPRISES
Seattle & nearby locations

Sponsor: Professional chef/sushi chef. Programs: Hands-on classes that include Korean & Thai cuisine, Asian wraps & rolls, sushi, noodles, sauces. Established: 2000.

FACULTY: Owner/chef Kris Drew trained as a sushi chef in Seattle.

COSTS: $42-$65/class.

CONTACT: Kris Drew, Owner, Sook Enterprises, Seattle, WA; 206-241-2158, kris@sookfood.com, www.sookfood.com.

SUR LA TABLE
Arizona, Illinois, New York, Ohio, Oregon, Texas, Utah, Virginia, Washington

Sponsor: Cookware store. Programs: Hands-on & demo classes that include ethnic themes, basic to advanced skills & techniques, chef specialties. Established: 1972. Class/group size: 16-34. 200 programs/yr. Facilities: Full demo kitchens with TV monitors & overhead mirrors above teaching islands, hands-on tables. Also featured: Professional & corporate team-building classes, culinary walking tours, market visits, programs for youngsters & spouses.

FACULTY: Professional chefs, restaurateurs & cookbook authors.

COSTS: $45-$100/class.

CONTACT: Sur La Table, Inc. Corporate Headquarters, 5701 Sixth Ave. South, Ste. 486, Seattle, WA 98108; 866-328-5412, culinary@surlatable.com, www.surlatable.com/cooking.

WEST VIRGINIA

THE GREENBRIER CULINARY ARTS PROGRAM
White Sulphur Springs

Sponsor: The Greenbrier. Programs: 3- & 5-day demo programs & optional hands-on classes; children's classes. Established: 1990. 50+ programs/yr. Facilities: The Greenbrier Culinary Arts Center. Also featured: Includes golf, tennis, spa, horseback riding, Land Rover Driving School, Falconry Academy, indoor & outdoor pools.

FACULTY: Greenbrier chefs, guest chefs & instructors.

CONTACT: Eve Cohen, Cooking School Director, The Greenbrier, 300 West Main St., White Sulphur Springs, WV 24986; 800-228-5049, 304-536-7863, Fax 304-536-7754, cookingschool@greenbrier.com, www.greenbrier.com.

WISCONSIN

THE COOKING SCHOOL AT KRISTOFER'S
Sister Bay

Sponsor: The Inn at Kristofer's Restaurant. Programs: Participation & demo classes. Established: 1994. Class/group size: 8-24. 20 programs/yr. Facilities: Professional cooking classroom & the restaurant's kitchen.

FACULTY: Chef Terri Milligan, a graduate of the Postillion School of Culinary Arts, has been featured in Good Housekeeping, Midwest Living & the TV Food Network.

COSTS: $40-$45/demo class, $125-$135/participation class.

CONTACT: Terri Milligan, Chef & Co-Owner, The Cooking School at Kristofer's, 734 Bay Shore Dr., P.O. Box 619, Sister Bay, WI 54234; 920-854-9419, Fax 920-854-7149, milligan@dcwis.com, www.innatkristofers.com.

ORANGE TREE IMPORTS COOKING SCHOOL
Madison

Sponsor: Cookware store. Programs: Single session evening classes on a variety of topics. Established: 1981. Class/group size: 10 demo & hands-on. Facilities: Classroom kitchen in gourmet store.

FACULTY: Experienced staff of local chefs & cooking experts.

COSTS: $35/class.

CONTACT: Dean Schroeder, Co-owner, Orange Tree Imports Cooking School, 1721 Monroe St., Madison, WI 53711; 608-255-8211, Fax 608-255-8404, info@orangetreeimports.com, www.orangetreeimports.com.

ASIA

ABSOLUTE ASIA
Over 35 destinations

Sponsor: Travel company. Programs: Customized private gourmet tours that emphasize regional cuisine throughout Asia & the South Pacific. Established: 1989. Class/group size: 1-15. Daily programs/yr. Facilities: Private homes, major hotels & established cooking schools in Asia. Also featured: Market tours, gourmet meals, visits to private homes, wine certification courses, special lectures, regional sightseeing.

FACULTY: Prominent culinary professionals.

COSTS: Tours start at $2,000, which includes deluxe lodging, meals, touring, & regional airfare.

CONTACT: Absolute Asia, 180 Varick St., 16th floor, New York, NY 10014; 800-736-8187, 212-627-1950, Fax 212-627-4090, info@absoluteasia.com, www.absoluteasia.com.

ARTISANS OF LEISURE
Asia, Australia, Europe, New Zealand

Sponsor: Luxury travel company offering private, customized tours. Programs: Culinary tours that include hands-on classes, fine dining, sightseeing, visits to markets, gourmet shops, & private homes. Established: 2003. Class/group size: 1-15. 20 programs/yr. Facilities: Cooking schools, restaurants, hotels, private homes.

FACULTY: Chefs at cooking schools, restaurants, hotels, & private homes.

COSTS: From $4,490 including shared luxury lodging.

CONTACT: Ashley Ganz, President, Artisans of Leisure, 18 E. 16th St., #301, New York, NY 10003; 800-214-8144/212-243-3239, Fax 212-243-4798, info@artisansofleisure.com, www.artisansofleisure.com.

ASIAN FOODTOURS.COM & THE GLOBETROTTING GOURMET®
Asia, Australia

Sponsor: Asian cookbook author. Programs: Focus on food & its origins. Tours include demo & hands-on cooking classes & visits to markets & food producers. Class/group size: 16 max. 2 programs/yr. Facilities: Commercial hotel kitchens to street hawker stands. Also featured: Cultural stops in craft villages: weaving, pottery, carving; local museums.

FACULTY: American-born TV food stylist & author Robert Carmack (Thai Home Cooking, Vietnamese Home Cooking, Fondue); Australian-born textile expert Morrison Polkinghorne.

COSTS: $2995-$3995 includes deluxe lodging, most meals, ground transport, planned activities.

CONTACT: Robert Carmack, The Globetrotting Gourmet®, robert@globetrottinggourmet.com, www.asianfoodtours.com. Morrison Polkinghorne, morrison@globetrottinggourmet.com.

AUSTRALIA

AMANO
Perth
Sponsor: Cookware store. Programs: 2- to 3-session demo & participation courses. Established: 1982. Class/group size: 14 hands-on/30 demo. 60+ programs/yr. Facilities: Teaching kitchen with overhead mirror & individual work areas. Also featured: Culinary tours to France, Bali, & Italy.
FACULTY: School director is IACP-member Beverley Sprague. Instructors are prominent Australian & intl culinary professionals.
COSTS: A$55-A$90/session.
CONTACT: Beverley Sprague, Director, Amano, 12 Station St., Cottesloe, Perth, WA, 6011 Australia; (61) 8-(0)9384-0378, Fax (61) 8-(0)9385-0379, bmsamano@echidna.id.au, www.amano.com.au/.

BAN SABAI THAI COOKING SCHOOL
Brisbane; Bangkok & Phuket, Thailand
Sponsor: Thai cooking school. Programs: Culinary tours & hands-on Thai cooking classes. Annual professional course. Established: 2000. Class/group size: 6-12. Weekly programs/yr. Also featured: Home teaching & private catering available.
FACULTY: Owner Raymund Venzin.
COSTS: $85/class, min. 5 students required; complimentary for the host if held in host's home.
CONTACT: Raymund Venzin, Ban Sabai Thai Cooking School, 27 Empire Vista Ormiston, Brisbane, Qld, 4160 Australia; (61) (0)7 3821 4460, (61) (0)409 069 161 (mobile), raymund@venzin.com.au, www.venzin.com.au/thai.

BEVERLEY SUTHERLAND SMITH COOKING SCHOOL
Mt. Waverley
Sponsor: Cookbook author Beverley Sutherland Smith. Programs: 1- to 2-session demo courses. Established: 1967. Class/group size: 20 demos 10 hands on. 15-20 programs/yr. Facilities: Mirrored teaching kitchen that overlooks garden, pool & fountain. Also featured: Tours of the show gardens, potager vegetable gardens.
FACULTY: Beverley Sutherland Smith, Bailli Regional de Victoria magazine & newspaper food writer, authored 29 books & won the Australian Gold Book award.
COSTS: From A$60, GST included.
CONTACT: Beverley Sutherland Smith, Beverley Sutherland Smith Cooking School, 29 Regent St., Mt. Waverley, Victoria, 3149 Australia; (61) 3-9802-5544, Fax (61) 39-802-7683, beverley@gu.com.au.

COUNCIL OF ADULT EDUCATION
Melbourne
Sponsor: Educational organization. Programs: 2- to 6-session cooking & catering courses; full-day classes. Class/group size: 18. 70 programs/yr. Facilities: Demo kitchen. Also featured: Workshops & travel programs.
FACULTY: Cooking instructors & guest chefs.
COSTS: Nonrefundable tuition from A$20-A$40/course session & from A$80-A$85/full-day class. Discounts for seniors & pensioners.
CONTACT: Alex Moraitis, Program Mgr., Council of Adult Education, 256 Flinders St., Melbourne, Victoria, 3000 Australia; (61) 3-9652-0624, Fax (61) 3-9652-0799, alexm@cae.edu.au, www.cae.edu.au.

ELISE PASCOE COOKING SCHOOL
Sydney, Jamberoo
Sponsor: Private cooking school run by culinary professional Elise Pascoe. Programs: 1- to 3-day classes. Established: 1975. Class/group size: 20. 50 programs/yr. Facilities: Purpose-designed building.

Faculty: Elise Pascoe, 29 yrs teaching worldwide including cookbooks, TV programs & food editor of newspapers & magazines.
Costs: A$135-A$165/day.
Contact: Ms. Elise Pascoe, Elise Pascoe Cooking School, PO Box 170, Jamberoo, NSW, 2533 Australia; (61) 2 4236-1666, Fax (61) 2 4236-1777, elisepascoe@cookingschool.com.au, www.cookingschool.com.au.

FACES OF FOOD, THE COOKING SCHOOL
Sydney; La Drome, France; Tokyo, Japan
Sponsor: Culinary professional. Programs: Beginner to advanced classes. Established: 1999. Class/group size: 5-10. Facilities: Include professional cooking room, hotel & restaurant kitchens, private homes. Also featured: Food tours, recipe & cookbook writing, food & chef consulting.
Faculty: Angela Nahas, chef, cooking teacher, food consultant, contributor to 30+ cookbooks; has worked in Australia, Paris, London & Japan. Guest chefs & teachers.
Costs: Demo classes JPY5,000, A$50. Hands-on classes JPY6,000, A$60.
Contact: Angela Nahas, Faces of Food, The Cooking School, 57 Mountain View Dr., Woongarrah, NSW, 2259 Australia; (61) 40 227 3939, Fax (61) 2 4393 9648, whatscooking@facesoffood.com, www.facesoffood.com.

HOWQUA-DALE GOURMET RETREAT
Mansfield; France; Indonesia
Sponsor: Howqua-Dale Country House-Hotel resort. Programs: Weekend hands-on courses, 6-day gourmet cycling tours of Australia's wine regions, gastronomic tours abroad. Established: 1977. Class/group size: 12. 10 programs/yr. Facilities: Horse-shoe shaped pavilion with specialized equipment. Also featured: Fishing, skiing, swimming, horseback riding, bird-watching, bushwalking.
Faculty: Food writer & cooking demonstrator Marieke Brugman conducts classes. Her partner Sarah Stegley teaches wine selection. Noted Australian guest chefs.
Costs: All-inclusive fee ~$A1,100 for weekend course & A$3,750 for wine tours, excluding airfare.
Contact: Marieke Brugman, Director/Chef, Howqua-Dale Gourmet Retreat, P.O. Box 379, Mansfield, Victoria, 3722 Australia; (61) 35-777-3503, Fax (61) 35-777-3896, howqua@mansfield.net.au, www.gtoa.com.au.

LE CORDON BLEU – SYDNEY
Sydney   *(See also page 146) (See display ad page 161)*
Sponsor: Private school. Programs: 10-wk Classic Cycle programs of Basic, Intermediate & Superior Cuisine & Patisserie. Established: 1996. Class/group size: ~12:1. 6 programs/yr. Facilities: Classrooms designed to resemble professional working kitchens. Individual workspaces, demo kitchen.
Faculty: French & Australian master chefs, international staff.
Costs: Basic Cuisine A$7,200, Intermediate Cuisine A$7,400, Superior Cuisine A$9,000. Basic Patisserie A$7,200, Intermediate Patisserie A$7,400, Superior Patisserie A$8,000.
Contact: Julie Ladic, Admission Manager, Le Cordon Bleu Australia, Days Road, Regency Park, Adelaide, SA, 5010 Australia; (61) 8 8346.3700, Fax (61) 8 346.3755, australia@cordonbleu.net, www.lecordonbleu.com.au. In U.S. & Canada: 800-457-CHEF.

MARCEA WEBER'S COOKING SCHOOL – HEALTHY SECRETS
Faulconbridge
Sponsor: Culinary professional Marcea Weber. Programs: demo & hands-on classes. Established: 1980. Class/group size: 10-12. Facilities: Private home, large modern kitchen. Also featured: Women's workshops including hands-on Food as Medicine.
Faculty: Nutritionist Marcea Weber.
Costs: A$35-A$40/class.
Contact: Marcea Weber, Director, Marcea Weber's Cooking School - Healthy Secrets, 56 St. George's Crescent, Faulconbridge, NSW, 2776 Australia; (61) (02) 4751-1680, marceaweber@hotmail.com.

MATTERS OF TASTE
Bicton

Sponsor: Private school. Programs: Evening, lunchtime & individual classes; 3-session & seasonal courses; Christmas class. Established: 1997. Class/group size: 12. 84+ programs/yr. Facilities: Well-equipped domestic-style kitchen.

FACULTY: Proprietor Tracey Cotterell has a Tech Diploma in Hotel Catering & Institutional Mgmt & is a culinary professional with 20+ yrs experience.

COSTS: A$60/class, A$175/course.

CONTACT: Tracey Cotterell, Matters Of Taste, 103 Harris St., Bicton, WA, 6157 Australia; (61)(8) 9319-1097, Fax (61)(8) 9339-0697, info@mattersoftaste.com.au, www.mattersoftaste.com.au.

THE OLIVE & THE GRAPE
Hunter Valley, Sydney

Programs: Hands-on pasta making classes at a boutique winery, includes local olive oil & wine tastings. Established: 2002. Class/group size: 12 max. Facilities: Sandalyn Estate winery.

FACULTY: Jane Thomson, Francesca Robinson, Helen Topp, Simon Payne.

COSTS: A$89, includes GST.

CONTACT: The Olive & The Grape, Australia; (61) 2 9590 9531, bookings@theoliveandthegrape.com, www.theoliveandthegrape.com. www.theoliveandthegrape.com.

PARIS INTERNATIONAL COOKING SCHOOL
Sydney (Stanmore)

Sponsor: Culinary professional. Programs: 9- & 10-session courses, 1-wk residential course, half-day workshops. Established: 1994. Class/group size: 16 demo, 10 hands-on. 240+ programs/yr. Facilities: Fully-equipped demo kitchen with mirrors & practical kitchen for 20 students. Small Application restaurant open 3 days/wk where students prepare meals for guests. Also featured: Classes for teenagers, tour of Sydney market, seasonal workshops, residential cooking tours.

FACULTY: French native Laurent Villoing trained at Ecole Lenotre, has 25 yrs experience as hotel chef, lectured at London catering colleges & in Sydney, appears on TV shows.

COSTS: A$49-A$80/half-day workshop, A$130-A$200/9-wk class, A$570/10-wk hospitality course, A$900/wk + lodging for residential course.

CONTACT: Laurent Villoing, Paris International Cooking School, 216 Parramatta Rd., Stanmore, NSW, 2048 Australia; (02) 9518 1066, Fax (02) 9518 1077, Laurent4@bigpond.com.au.

SYDNEY SEAFOOD SCHOOL
Pyrmont, Sydney

Sponsor: Sydney Fish Market Pty. Ltd. Programs: Hands-on courses in seafood cookery. Established: 1989. Class/group size: 40. 200+ programs/yr. Facilities: Practical kitchen & 66-seat demo auditorium with tiered seating & overhead mirror. Also featured: Exclusive classes for corporate groups, social clubs.

FACULTY: Qualified seafood educators & guest chefs from Sydney's top restaurants.

COSTS: Non-refundable tuition payable in advance, from A$70-A$125/course.

CONTACT: Roberta Muir, Mgr., Sydney Seafood School, Locked Bag 247, Pyrmont, NSW, 2009 Australia; (61) 2 9004 1111, Fax (61) 2 9004 1177, sss@sydneyfishmarket.com.au, www.sydneyfishmarket.com.au.

TAMARA'S KITCHEN
Melbourne

Sponsor: Culinary professional Tamara Milstein. Programs: Classes in breadmaking, pasta, risotto, modern Jewish menus, fish, European desserts. Established: 1989. Facilities: Varies with host school.

FACULTY: Tamara Milstein.

COSTS: A$120-A$220/course.

CONTACT: Tamara Milstein, Owner, Tamara's Kitchen, 2 Garden St., Hawthorn East, VIC, 3123 Australia; (61) 3-9882 4906, Fax (61) 3-9882 3436, tamara@iaa.com.au, www.tamaraskitchen.com.au.

TEAM COOKING AT SEA LEGGS
Melbourne

Sponsor: Dockland Sailing School's corporate team-building facility. Programs: Customized group programs in which participants work together to produce meals using unfamiliar techniques & ingredients. Established: 1984. Class/group size: 20 max. Facilities: 8 training kitchens including a specialist Asian kitchen, 4 training bakeries & 3 restaurants.

FACULTY: Professionals trained in cooking, hospitality & hotel management, conference & event management, workplace psychology, leadership coaching, workplace training & assessment.

CONTACT: Tony Legg, Director/Chief Instructor, Team Cooking At SEA LEGGS, Victoria Harbour - Melbourne Docklands, Melbourne, Victoria, 3002 Australia; (61) 394190925, tonyslegg@docklandsailingschool.com.au, www.docklandsailingschool.com.au/team_building_cooking.html.

TOUR DE FORKS – AN EPICUREAN ADVENTURE DOWN UNDER
Melbourne & Sydney

Sponsor: Australian culinary tour provider. Programs: Chef-led tours featuring cooking classes & demos, tasting menus with matching wines at restaurants, visits to artisanal producers. Established: 2001. Class/group size: 12. 2 programs/yr.

FACULTY: Meera Freeman, food consultant, cooking demonstrator, writer, tour group leader; George Biron, chef, writer, owner of Sunnybrae Restaurant.

COSTS: $8,000 includes LA/Sydney round trip airfare, hotel lodging, meals, wines, ground transport.

CONTACT: Melissa Joachim, Tour de Forks-An Epicurean Adventure Down Under, 108 East 38th St, #710, New York, NY 10016; 212-447-9640, tourdeforks@earthlink.net, www.tourdeforks.com.

WHOLEFOOD VEGETARIAN, MACROBIOTIC & JAPANESE COOKING
Malvern (Melbourne)

Sponsor: Private school. Programs: Hands-on classes in wholefood organic, macrobiotic-style, dairy-, wheat- & sugar-free, low fat; traditional Japanese cooking. Established: 1986. Class/group size: 5-15. 10-15 programs/yr. Facilities: Private kitchen. Also featured: Personal food training programs, nutritional counselling, kids classes.

FACULTY: Sandra Dubs, founder of the Melbourne Vegetarian & Japanese Cooking School, nutritionist & author of the cooking video, Sandra's Whole Cuisine.

COSTS: A$70-A$80/class.

CONTACT: Sandra Dubs, Wholefood Vegetarian & Japanese, PO Box 523, Malvern, Victoria, 3144 Australia; (61) (0)407-360323, sandra@wholecookingvideo.com.au, www.wholecookingvideo.com.au.

AUSTRIA

HERZERL TOURS 'A TASTE OF VIENNA'
Vienna, Austria

Programs: 1-wk trips that include 3 classes at Vienna's Am Judenplatz cooking school & one at the haute cuisine restaurant Drei Husaren. Established: 1994. Class/group size: 18. 3 programs/yr. Also featured: Market visit, winery tour & tasting, trip to tableware displays in the Imperial Palace, sightseeing on foot & per coach, dinners in gourmet restaurants, concert.

COSTS: $2,550 includes airfare from NYC, lodging, buffet breakfast, some meals, planned activities.

CONTACT: Susanne Servin, Owner, Herzerl Tours, P.O. Box 217, Tuckahoe, NY 10707; 800-684-8488, 914-771-8558, Fax 914-771-5844, sms@herzerltours.com, www.herzerltours.com.

BRAZIL

BRAZILIAN ACADEMY OF COOKING & OTHER PLEASURES
Ouro Preto, Brazil

Sponsor: Brazilian culinarian Yara Castro Roberts. Programs: 1-wk vacation programs that feature hands-on classes in Brazilian cuisine, including the regional dishes of Amazon, Bahia, & Minas

Gerais. Established: 1996. Class/group size: 8-12. 10 programs/yr. Facilities: Professional kitchens of 5-star hotels. Also featured: Sugar cane distillery, coffee plantation, underground gold mine, market visits, cultural activities, dancing, craft workshops.

FACULTY: Founder Yara Castro Roberts, Emmy Award nominee host for a PBS cooking series & graduate of Boston U. Culinary Arts program; Dr. Moacyr Laterza, a Brazilian history professor; local chefs & food artisans.

COSTS: $2,250 includes shared lodging, meals, planned activities.

CONTACT: Yara Castro Roberts, Director/Instructor, Academy of Cooking & Other Pleasures, Brazil, 256 Marlborough St., Boston, MA 2116; 617-262-8455, Fax 617-267-0786, yara@cookingnpleasures.com, www.cookingnpleasures.com.

CANADA

ACCOUNTING FOR TASTE
Ottawa, ON

Sponsor: Wine professional. Programs: 4-session wine courses. Established: 1996. Class/group size: 25. 4 programs/yr. Also featured: Tastings, seminars, dinners.

FACULTY: Michael Botner is Governor & co-founder of National Capital Sommelier Guild, writer, chair of the Cellars of the World International Wine Competition, member SWE.

COSTS: $150/course, $275/series.

CONTACT: Michael Botner, Accounting for Taste, 195 Rodney Crescent, Ottawa, ON, Canada; 613-523-3389, Fax 613-523-3397, michael@accountingfortaste.ca, www.accountingfortaste.ca.

AU BON GOÛT
Montreal, QB

Sponsor: Culinary professional Sandra M. Carmichael. Programs: One-week Italian & French cookery school holidays that feature local specialties, special occasion menus, & quick dishes. Established: 1996. Class/group size: 4-12. 10+ programs/yr. Facilities: Include local trattoria. Also featured: Shopping for specialties.

FACULTY: Trained cook & teacher.

CONTACT: Sandra M Carmichael, President, Au Bon Goût, 369 52nd Ave., Lachine, Quebec,Canada; 514-637-0740, Fax 514-637-1642, abg@aubongout.com, www.aubongout.com.

BONNIE STERN SCHOOL OF COOKING
Toronto, ON

Sponsor: Private school. Programs: Demo & participation classes for corporate & private group functions. Established: 1973. Class/group size: 30 demo/15 hands-on. 50 programs/yr. Facilities: Interchangeable demo/participation area with overhead mirror & closed circuit TV.

FACULTY: Bonnie Stern, a George Brown College graduate, studied with Simone Beck & Marcella Hazan & authored 9 cookbooks, including Simply Heartsmart Cooking; TV cooking show host, newspaper columnist.

CONTACT: Bonnie Stern, Founder, Bonnie Stern School of Cooking, 6 Erskine Ave., Toronto, ON,Canada; 416-484-4810, Fax 416-484-4820, bonnie@bonniestern.com, www.bonniestern.com.

BRYANNA'S VEGAN COOKING VACATIONS
Denman Island, BC

Sponsor: Vegan specialist & cookbook author. Programs: 5 afternoon vegan cooking classes that include ethnic specialties, bread, seitan recipes, desserts. Established: 2003. Class/group size: 6-12. 1-3 programs/yr. Facilities: Private kitchen. Also featured: Bodywork session, pottery class, yoga, herbal walks, outdoor activities; optional visits to traditional miso maker, vegan chocolate factory.

FACULTY: Bryanna Clark Grogan, author of 8 vegan cookbooks, moderator of New Veggies forum on vegsource.com, author of online newsletter, The Vegan Feast.

COSTS: C$600 includes lunch & dinner. B&B lodging additional.

CONTACT: Bryanna Grogan, Bryanna's Vegan Cooking Vacations, 1721 Scott Rd., Denman Island, BC,Canada; 250-335-0814, Fax 250-335-2433, bryanna@bryannaclarkgrogan.com, www.bryannaclarkgrogan.com/page/page/593346.htm.

BUTTERNUT INN GOURMET GETAWAY WEEKEND
Port Hope, ON

Sponsor: Butternut Inn B&B. Programs: Gourmet hands-on cooking classes for guests that include 2-night stay in the Butternut Inn, breakfasts & 4-5 course dinners. Established: 1996. Class/group size: 8 hands-on. 16-20 programs/yr. Facilities: Large kitchen with an island, or BBQ cooking in the garden. Also featured: Hiking, shopping, golfing, fishing.

FACULTY: Chef/instructor Linda Stephen, trained at Ryerson, worked with Bonnie Stern & other established chefs, & has led cooking tours to Thailand.

COSTS: C$549/couple, all inclusive.

CONTACT: Bonnie Harrison, Innkeeper, Butternut Inn Bed & Breakfast's Gourmet Getaway Weekend, 36 North St., Port Hope, ON,Canada; 800-218-6670, 905-885-4318, Fax 905-885-5464, info@butternutinn.com, www.butternutinn.com.

CATERING BY LARKELL
Creemore, ON

Sponsor: Chef & caterer. Programs: Hands-on evening & weekend classes in meal preparation & baking skills. Established: 2002. Class/group size: 6-8. 10-15 programs/yr. Facilities: Studio kitchen, professional equipment. Also featured: Personal chef, event planner, caterer.

FACULTY: Larkell Bradley, Le Cordon Bleu-trained catering chef.

COSTS: C$85/class.

CONTACT: Larkell Bradley, Owner, Larkell's Sweet Sensations & Fine Cuisine, 15 Elizabeth St. W., Creemore, ON,Canada; 705-466-6315, toona@infinity.net.

CHEZ SOLEIL
Stratford, ON

Sponsor: Cooking school with B&B facilities. Programs: Hands-on cooking weekends & classes. Harvest to Table Cooking Week. Established: 1996. Class/group size: 6. Facilities: Commercial kitchen in a residential setting. Also featured: Cooking tours in Canada & abroad.

FACULTY: Liz Mountain, 20 yrs professional cooking experience, graduate of George Brown College; Janet Sinclair, instructor of restaurant design at Stratford Chefs School.

COSTS: C$428/weekend includes 2 nights lodging at an English Tudor cottage B&B. C$2,000/cooking wk.

CONTACT: Janet Sinclair, Chez Soleil Cooking School, 120 Brunswick St., Stratford, ON,Canada; 519-271-7404, Fax 519-271-7404, cooking@chezsoleil.com, www.chezsoleil.com.

CINNABAR CULINARY DELIGHTS
Toronto, ON

Sponsor: Culinary professional. Programs: In-home cooking classes for individuals or small groups; corporate team-building cooking events. Established: 1998. Class/group size: 35 max.

FACULTY: Chef Paul Mesbur, an honors graduate of the Stratford Chefs School, has 10 yrs. experience in the restaurant, hotel & catering trade.

COSTS: $75/person.

CONTACT: Paul Mesbur, Cinnabar Culinary Delights, 400 Walmer Rd., #1012, Toronto, ON,Canada; 416-963-9675, cinnabarculinarydelights@rogers.com, cinnabar10.tripod.com.

COOKING AT THE HARVEST KITCHEN
Oakville, ON

Sponsor: Recreational cooking school. Programs: Demo classes with hands-on components for public, corporate entertaining & team-building. Established: 1979. Class/group size: 18. 25+ programs/yr. Facilities: Demo country kitchen in a 160 year-old home with herb garden. Also fea-

tured: Private chef's tables, birthday cooking parties, gourmet trips to local food & wine festivals & to Italy & France.
FACULTY: Gurth Pretty, past Canadian culinary consultant for Emeril Live! & a graduate of George Brown College's Culinary Mgmt program, writes food columns & has worked professionally.
COSTS: C$80-C$95/class.
CONTACT: Gurth M. Pretty, Culinary Director, Harvest Kitchen Cookery School, 134 Thomas St., Oakville, ON,Canada; 416-760-9504, Fax 416-760-0150, info@epicureanexpeditions.com, www.epicureanexpeditions.com.

THE COOKING STUDIO
Winnipeg
Sponsor: Private school. Programs: Hands-on & demo classes. Established: 1994. Class/group size: 14-24. 100 programs/yr. Facilities: 1,200-sq-ft professional kitchen with Miele, Garland & Dacor equipment. Also featured: Private dinning room & catering.
FACULTY: Owner Marisa Curatolo, Dubrulle French Culinary School, Ecole LeNotre.
COSTS: Hands-on classes C$75, demos C$45, children's classes C$25.
CONTACT: Marisa Curatolo, Owner, The Cooking Studio, 3200 Roblin Blvd., Winnipeg, MB,Canada; 204-896-5174, Fax 204-888-0628, cookingstudio@mts.net, www.thecookingstudio.ca.

COOKING WORKSHOP
Toronto, ON
Sponsor: Private school. Programs: Weekend hands-on workshops, evening workshops/demos. Established: 1985. Class/group size: 8-12. Facilities: Industrial kitchen of Dufflet Pastries, a cafe/bakery equipped with skylights & double ovens; a private home kitchen, & large cooking labs. Also featured: Wine-tastings, private group classes, culinary tours to Italy & Toronto.
FACULTY: Maria Pace, author of The Little Italy Cookbook, studied at La Varenne with Marcella Hazan. Baker Paula Bambrick trained at George Brown College. Doris Eisen creates bread & pastry recipes. Chef Steve Jukic, European trained, leads culinary events.
COSTS: C$75-C$90. Group rates available.
CONTACT: Maria Pace, Owner, The Cooking Workshop, 10 Beaconsfield Ave., Ste. 2, Toronto, ON, Canada; 416-588-1954, Fax 416-588-1954, marypace@enoreo.on.ca.

COOKSCHOOL AT THE COOKSHOP
Vancouver, BC
Sponsor: Cookware store. Programs: Demo & participation classes, 2 classes/day, 6 days/wk. Established: 1992. Class/group size: 8-20. Facilities: 1,000-square-foot area with overhead mirror. Also featured: Private lessons/functions, wine pairing, nutrition counseling, cookbook author signings, guided tours of wineries & other facilities.
FACULTY: School director, restaurateur, & teacher Nathan Hyam; 60 local guest chefs.
COSTS: From C$19-C$199/class. Payment in advance. Good hotels within 5 min walk.
CONTACT: Peter Haseltine, Cookschool at the Cookshop, 3-555 W. 12th Ave., Vancouver, BC,Canada; 604-873-5683, Fax 604-876-4391, info@cookshoponline.com, www.cookshoponline.com.

THE COOKWORKS
Toronto, ON
Sponsor: Private cooking school operated in conjunction with Mildred Pierce Restaurant. Programs: Evening & weekend classes on a variety of topics. Established: 1997. Class/group size: 14 hands-on. 100 programs/yr. Facilities: The studio kitchen next to Mildred Pierce Restaurant is equipped with professional cooking equipment & individual work stations. Also featured: Corporate hands-on cooking classes for groups.
FACULTY: 3 full-time chef-instructors, Mildred Pierce Restaurant & local restaurant chefs.
COSTS: ~$135/class.
CONTACT: Donna Dooher, Director, The Cookworks, 99 Sudbury St., Ste. 8, Toronto, ON,Canada; 416-537-6464, Fax 416-537-2653, cook@thecookworks.com, www.thecookworks.com.

COOPER'S COVE GUESTHOUSE & ANGELO'S COOKING SCHOOL
Sooke, BC

Sponsor: B&B inn. Programs: 1- & 3-day hands-on cooking programs. Established: 1994. Class/group size: 8 max. Weekly programs/yr. Facilities: Well-equipped private kitchen with granite island seating 8. Also featured: Hiking, kayaking, fishing, whale watching.

FACULTY: Professional chef trained on Vancouver Island. Past member of Culinary Team Canada.

COSTS: $458-$895 high season for 2-3 nights includes breakfasts & dinners.

CONTACT: Angelo Prosperi-Porta, Chef/co-owner, Cooper's Cove Guesthouse & Angelo's Cooking School, 5301 Sooke Rd., Sooke, BC,Canada; 250-642-5727 or 877-642-5727, Fax 250-642-5749, info@cooperscove.com, www.cooperscove.com.

DISH COOKING STUDIO
Toronto, ON

Sponsor: Chef-owned school. Programs: Hands-on & demo classes. Established: 2000. Class/group size: 12-24+. 150 programs/yr. Facilities: Modern, casual kitchen with counter seating for 16 & high-top counter for 6. Also featured: Private, children's, corporate team-building classes, field trips, dishBasix classes.

FACULTY: 11 professional resident teachers/chefs, visiting & celebrity guest chefs including Ted Reader, Massimo Capra.

COSTS: $75-$150/class, Gourmet brunch $65, Core or Celebrity Chef classes $125 or $550/5.

CONTACT: Trish Magwood, Owner, dish cooking studio, 390 Dupont St, Toronto, ON,Canada; 416-920-5559, Fax 416-920-6469, trish@dishcookingstudio.com, www.dishcookingstudio.com.

FLAVOURS SCHOOL OF COOKING
Thornton, ON

Sponsor: Private cooking school. Programs: Hands-on cooking & baking classes. Also featured: Kid's classes, culinary team building, gourmet nights.

FACULTY: Executive chef/owner Kurt Meierhans, 35 yrs experience, recipe developer for Swiss Movenpick Restaurant chain.

COSTS: ~C$49-C$68/class.

CONTACT: Kurt Meierhans, Flavours School of Cooking, 8288 11th Line, Thornton, ON,Canada; 705-737-4769, info@flavourscooking.com, www.flavourscooking.com/.

THE GOOD EARTH COOKING SCHOOL
Beamsville, ON

Sponsor: Private school. Programs: Hands-on & demo classes focusing on techniques & seasonal products, wine education dinners. Class/group size: 12 max. ~ 50 programs/yr. Also featured: Corporate events, private functions, catering.

FACULTY: Resident chefs Eric Miller & Lisa Rollo; top chefs from local restaurants.

COSTS: Demos C$135, hands-on C$175.

CONTACT: Nicolette Novak, Proprietor, The Good Earth, 4556 Lincoln Ave., Beamsville, ON,Canada; 800-308-5124, 905-563-7856, Fax 905-563-9143, info@goodearthcooking.com, www.goodearthcooking.com.

GREAT COOKS & THE TEA SPOT
Toronto, ON

Sponsor: Cooking school. Programs: Afternoon & evening demo & hands-on classes. Established: 1989. Class/group size: 10 - 70. 60+ programs/yr. Facilities: 600-sq-ft modern kitchen, similar to a chef's table. Larger facility for corporate groups. Also featured: Wine tastings, corporate classes, culinary trips, tours of Toronto markets, dining in top restaurants.

FACULTY: 30+ Toronto chefs, including Massimo Capra, Jean Pierre Challet, Marc Picone, Jason Barato, Albino Silva, Anthony Walsh.

COSTS: C$80-C$110/class.

CONTACT: Esther Benaim, Proprietor/Director, Great Cooks, 176 Yonge St, Lower Level, Toronto, ON,Canada; 416-861-4727, Fax 416-861-9762, cook@greatcooks.ca, www.greatcooks.ca.

HEALTHY GOURMET INDIAN COOKING
Oakville, ON

Sponsor: Private school. Programs: Hands-on Indian, Ayurvedic, Thai, Malaysian & Mexican cooking classes; 6-wk Indian beginner's series. Established: 1993. Class/group size: 8+. 100+ programs/yr. Facilities: Well-equiped kitchen; separate, sit-in formal dining area. Also featured: Culinary trips to India, field trips & tours; cooking parties.
FACULTY: Arvinda Chauhan, owner/instructor, recipe developer, cookbook author.
COSTS: $50-$65/class; $160/6-wk series, includes field trip to Toronto's Little India bazaar.
CONTACT: Arvinda Chauhan, Cooking Instructor, Healthy Gourmet Indian Cooking, 1334 Creekside Dr., Oakville, ON,Canada; 905-842-3215, info@hgic.ca, www.hgic.ca.

LE CORDON BLEU PARIS OTTAWA CULINARY ARTS INSTITUTE
Ottawa, ON *(See also page 150) (See display ad page 161)*

Sponsor: Private school. Programs: Specialized short courses, gourmet sessions, day & evening demo classes. Established: 1988. Class/group size: 16:1 max. Facilities: Include demo room, fully-equipped pastry & cuisine kitchens with individual work spaces, specialized equipment.
FACULTY: Classically-trained professional master French chefs.
COSTS: C$40/demo, C$565/short courses, C$190/gourmet sessions.
CONTACT: Sylvie Sofi, Campus Coordinator, Le Cordon Bleu Ottawa Culinary Arts Institute, 453 Laurier Ave. East, Ottawa, Ontario,Canada; 613-236-CHEF, Fax 613-236-2460, ottawa@cordonbleu.edu, lcbottawa.com.

MY PLACE FOR DINNER
Toronto, ON

Sponsor: Culinary professional. Programs: Hands-on cooking classes: scheduled, private group, corporate entertaining & team-building. Established: 1996. Class/group size: 8-24. Facilities: Kitchen & dining room. Classes can be held in student's home if within 2 hrs of central Toronto.
FACULTY: Debbie Diament, cookbook writer, recipe tester & developer.
COSTS: $85/workshop.
CONTACT: Debbie Diament, My Place for Dinner, 56 Arundel Avenue, Toronto, ON,Canada; 416-465-7112, Fax 416-465-7112, mpfd@idirect.com, www.myplacefordinner.com.

NIAGARA GOURMET
St. Catharines, ON

Sponsor: Personal chef. Programs: Hands-on cooking lessons. Established: 1999. Class/group size: 6-12. 10 programs/yr. Also featured: Personal chef services, catering, winery tours, local excursions.
FACULTY: Chef David Paquet.
CONTACT: David Paquet, Chef, Niagara Gourmet, 70 Maple St., St. Catharines, ON,Canada; 905-682-0184, david@niagaragourmet.com, www.niagaragourmet.com.

RICHMOND HILL CULINARY ARTS CENTRE
Richmond Hill, ON

Sponsor: Private cooking school & banquet facility. Programs: Hands-on 5-session techniques course, topical classes, jr. cooking camp, culinary tours. Facilities: Fully equipped kitchen & classroom facility. Also featured: Corporate cooking classes, catering, Demo & Dine program.
FACULTY: Includes Chef Frederick Oh, a graduate of Culinary Arts & Baking Technology; Vinesh Saxena, certified Food Service Manager; Jacques Marie, intl wine judge, Master in Food & Wine Technology, Master Chef; Claude Gambin, certified chef.
COSTS: C$35/jr workshop, C$75-$85/hands-on program, C$450/5-session series, C$395/jr camp.
CONTACT: Richmond Hill Culinary Arts Centre, 1550 16th Ave., Unit 1, Bldg. A, Richmond Hill, ON, Canada; 905-508-2665, Fax 905-508-2666, NotifyMe@CulinaryArts.ca, www.culinaryarts.ca.

SILVER SPRINGS CULINARY RETREAT
Flesherton, ON

Sponsor: Private & corporate conference & retreat center. Programs: Culinary weekend retreats feature hands-on & demo classes, wine education, Asian ingredients seminar. Established: 1999. Class/group size: 8-10. Also featured: Include guided hiking, fly-fishing, swimming, cycling, skiing, snowshoeing, yoga, Thai Chi, meditation, spa, area tours.

FACULTY: Chef Greg Couillard & hosts Sue & Derek Tennant.

COSTS: C$650 (C$799) includes shared (single) lodging, some meals.

CONTACT: Sue Tennant, Owner/Director, Silver Springs Culinary Retreats, R.R. #4, Flesherton, ON,Canada; 800-546-5601, Fax 519-922-1136, stennant@georgian.net, www.silverspringsretreat.com. michele@silverspringsretreat.com.

SIMPLY INDONESIAN
Toronto, ON

Sponsor: Private cooking school & caterer. Programs: Classes on Indonesian cuisine, workshops for youngsters. Established: 2002. Class/group size: 6 hands-on. 80+ programs/yr. Facilities: Kitchen with home professional cooking equipment. Also featured: Catering, cooking at clients' homes, culinary adventure tour.

FACULTY: Owner/teacher Linda Clarke, an Indonesian, is also a recipe developer.

COSTS: $45-$85/class.

CONTACT: Linda Clarke, Owner, Simply Indonesian, 33 Triller Ave., Toronto, ON,Canada; 416-523-6875, info@simplyindonesian.com, www.simplyindonesian.com. 416-535-9191.

TRAVEL WITH TASTE
Victoria, Vancouver Island

Sponsor: Kathy McAree. Programs: 1-, 4- & 7-day culinary & wine tours that include chef demos, wine tastings, visits to food producers. Established: 2003. Class/group size: 4-24. Facilities: Restaurant kitchens.

FACULTY: Vintners, chefs, microbrewers.

COSTS: C$150/1-day wine tour, C$1,699/4-day tour.

CONTACT: Kathy McAree, Owner, Travel With Taste Tours Ltd., 356 Simcoe St., #1, Victoria, BC,Canada; 250-385-1527, kathy@travelwithtaste.com, travelwithtaste.com.

TRAVELS WITH CHEF MANUEL
Vancouver, BC; Mexico City & San Miguel de Allende, Mexico

Sponsor: Culinary professional. Programs: Cooking classes; culinary & cultural tours to Mexico that include cooking classes, meals prepared by executive chefs, visits to restaurants. Established: 1998. Class/group size: 14. 4 tours programs/yr.

FACULTY: Manuel Otero, a graduate of the Pacific Institute of Culinary Arts, teaches Mexican cooking at Dubrulle.

COSTS: $1,890 includes lodging & most meals.

CONTACT: Manuel Otero, Travels with Chef Manuel to Mexico, # 205-525 Wheelhuose Sq., Vancouver, BC,Canada; 604-876-2099, Fax 604-876-9040, contact@chefmanuel.com, chefmanuel.com.

WINE COUNTRY COOKING SCHOOL
Niagara-on-the-Lake

Sponsor: Strewn estate winery. Programs: Hands-on 1- & 2-day culinary weekends, week-long culinary vacations focusing on food, wine & seasonal ingredients. Established: 1997. Class/group size: 16 hands-on. 30 programs/yr. Facilities: An estate winery, includes a teaching kitchen, demo classroom, private dining room & patio. Also featured: Field trips to producers, tutored wine tastings, meals at top Niagara restaurants, corporate team-building events.

FACULTY: Jane Langdon, proprietor/chief instructor, food writer, charter member of Cuisine Canada, & IACP member. Her husband is winemaker/president of Strewn estate winery. Other instructors incl food writers & cookbook authors.

Costs: Weekend hands-on classes: 2-day C$350; 1-day C$195; couples 1-day classes C$300. 5-day Culinary Vacations C$1,450.

Contact: Jane Langdon, Owner, Wine Country Cooking School, General Delivery, 1339 Lakeshore Rd., Niagara-on-the-Lake, ON, Canada; 905-468-8304, Fax 905-468-8305, info@winecountrycooking.com, www.winecountrycooking.com.

CHINA

ASIAN CULINARY JOURNEYS
Asia; China; India; Macau; Thailand; Viet Nam

Sponsor: Specialty travel company. Programs: 8- to 15-day culinary journeys that include demo & hands-on cooking classes, market visits, cultural activities. Established: 2003. Class/group size: 24 max. 8-10 programs/yr. Facilities: Hotel & private cooking schools. Also featured: Intros to Thai Buddhism, Traditional Chinese Medicine, Tai Chi.

Faculty: Culinary professionals.

Costs: China (15 days) from $3,400, Thailand (8 days) from $1,680, Vietnam (13 days) from $2,800, Vietnam & Thailand (14 days) from $3,425. Single supplements available.

Contact: David Allardice, Asian Culinary Journeys by Eastern Journeys, 603 Grosvenor House, 120 Macdonnell Rd., Hong Kong SAR, China; E-mail david@easternjourneys.com, www.eastern-journeys.com/tastesofasia/tasteofasia/index.htm.

CHOPSTICKS COOKING CENTRE
Kowloon, Hong Kong

Sponsor: Private trade school. Programs: 1-day to 4-wk individual & group programs that cover Chinese culinary culture & regional cooking techniques. Established: 1971. Class/group size: 15 max. Ongoing programs/yr. Facilities: Fully-equipped kitchen. Also featured: Kitchen & market visits.

Faculty: Cecilia J. Au-Yang, proprietor, with 40+ yrs experience; Caroline Au-Yeung, graduate of hotel mgmt school, with 15+ yrs experience; other culinary professionals.

Costs: Group classes from $400/2-hr demo session, from $500/1- to 2-day customized course. Individual classes from $60-$100. Local lodging $400+/wk.

Contact: Cecilia Au-Yang, Chopsticks Cooking Centre, 8A Soares Ave., Ground Floor, Kowloon, Hong Kong, China; (852) 2336-8433, Fax (852) 2338-1462, chopsticks1971@netvigator.com.

THE PENINSULA ACADEMY CULINARY EXPERIENCE
Hong Kong

Sponsor: The Peninsula Hotel, Hong Kong. Programs: The Culinary Experience features chef's welcome dinner, tour of hotel kitchens, cooking classes & luncheons. Established: 1997. Class/group size: 10-15. 6-8 programs/yr. Facilities: Hotel kitchens, restaurants & function rooms. Also featured: Includes Tai Chi, dim-sum prep, market tour, Chinese meals.

Faculty: Chefs of the hotel's restaurants.

Costs: 4 classes from HK$16,600/1 guest or HK$20,600/2 guests; includes 4 nights lodging in a Jr. Suite, welcome dinner, 1 afternoon tea, daily breakfast & lunch, Rolls-Royce transfers.

Contact: Co-ordinator, The Peninsula Academy, The Peninsula Hong Kong, Salisbury Rd., Tsim Sha Tsui, Kowloon, Hong Kong, China; (852) 2315 3150, Fax (852) 2315 3147, academy.pen@peninsula.com, www.peninsula.com.

ENGLAND

ACORN ACTIVITIES
Herefordshire

Sponsor: Activity holiday provider. Programs: 2-day gourmet cooking course. Established: 1989. Class/group size: 12. Facilities: Well-equipped kitchen with individual work areas & cookers. Also

featured: Study tours, courses, & recreational programs.
FACULTY: A professional chef who has appeared on the BBC2 Food & Drink program.
COSTS: Tuition is £100. Lodging, including breakfast, ranges from farmhouses & cottages at £20/night to luxury hotels at £95/night.
CONTACT: Derren Hotchkiss, Accounts Mgr., Acorn Activities, P.O. Box 120, Hereford, England; (44) (0)8707 40 50 55, Fax (44) (0)1432-830110, info@acornactivities.co.uk, www.acornactivities.co.uk.

AGA WORKSHOP
Buckinghamshire
Sponsor: Culinary professional Mary Berry. Programs: 1- & 2-day Aga demo workshops. Established: 1990. Class/group size: 20. 50 programs/yr. Facilities: Watercroft, Mary Berry's home. Also featured: Occasional gardening days.
FACULTY: Mary Berry studied at the Paris Cordon Bleu & Bath College of Home Ec & has a City & Guilds teaching qualification. She is author of 40+ cookbooks, presenter for TV series & contributes to BBC Radio.
COSTS: 1-day (2-day) workshop £115 (£223). Group bookings, 4 or more, £109/person/day.
CONTACT: Lucy Young, Asst. to Mary Berry, Aga Workshop, Watercroft, Church Rd., Penn, Buckinghamshire, England; (44) 1494-816535, Fax (44) 1494-816535, agawshop@maryberry.co.uk, www.maryberry.co.uk.

THE ALDEBURGH COOKERY SCHOOL
Aldeburgh, Suffolk
Sponsor: Private school. Programs: Day & weekend hands-on courses on a variety of topics, single-subject master classes. Established: 1999. Class/group size: 10 max. ~100 programs/yr. Facilities: 2 demo rooms, sitting & dining room. Also featured: Corporate programs.
FACULTY: Co-owners Thane Prince, journalist, TV cook, author of 7 books; Sara Fox, chef/proprietor of the Lighthouse Restaurant in Aldeburgh.
COSTS: £110/day or masterclass, £125/fish, shellfish class, £425/weekend includes lunch & dinner.
CONTACT: Thane Prince & Sara Fox, The Aldeburgh Cookery School, 84 High St., Aldeburgh, Suffolk, England; (44) 01728-454039, Fax (44) 01728-454039, info@aldeburghcookeryschool.fsnet.co.uk, www.aldeburghcookeryschool.com.

ANNETTE GIBBONS COOKERY & CUMBRIA ON A PLATE
Mawbray, Cumbria
Sponsor: Culinary professional. Programs: Cooking demos, gourmet day tours of regional food producers. Established: 1996. Class/group size: 8-10. 50-100 programs/yr. Facilities: Converted stable kitchen, dining room, organic kitchen garden.
FACULTY: Annette Gibbons, Certificate in Education, City & Guilds Advanced Cooking.
COSTS: ~£20 for classes includes lunch.
CONTACT: Annette Gibbons, Annette Gibbons Cookery, Ostle House, Mawbray, Maryport, Cumbria, England; (44) 1900 881356, Fax (44) 1900 881356, annette@ostlehouse.fsnet.co.uk, www.cumbriaonaplate.co.uk.

BOOKS FOR COOKS COOKING SCHOOL
London
Sponsor: Specialty cookbook store. Programs: 3-day hands-on courses, half-day demos, hands-on children's classes. Established: 1987. Class/group size: 8-22. 150+ programs/yr. Facilities: Purpose-built demo kitchen with overhead mirror. Also featured: Gourmet & food & wine evenings, Italian days.
FACULTY: Includes cookbook authors Eric Treuillé, Ursula Ferrigno, Kimiko Barber, Jennifer Joyce, Nada Saleh, Tom Kime, Olivia Greco, Monisha Bharadwaj, Sophie Braimbridge.
COSTS: £25 for demos to £170 for 3-day courses.
CONTACT: Eric Treuillé, Workshops, Books for Cooks Cooking School, 4 Blenheim Crescent, London, England; (44) (0)20-7221-1992, Fax (44) (0)20-7221-1517, info@booksforcooks.com, www.booksforcooks.com.

BREAD MATTERS – BREADMAKING COURSES
Melmerby, Penrith

Sponsor: Organic artisan baker Andrew Whitley. Programs: Bread basics, including mixing, fermenting, shaping, proving & baking. Specialist options include sourdoughs, yeasted pastries & gluten-free baking. Established: 1976. Class/group size: 12. 20 programs/yr. Facilities: The Village Bakery, which has a separate workstation for each person & a seminar room/library. Also featured: Meals in the Village Bakery Organic Restaurant, which include a dinner & discussion, visits to the adjacent Lake District & Pennine hills.

FACULTY: Andrew Whitley, founder of The Village Bakery, assisted by a fellow master baker.

COSTS: £315 (£595) for 2-day (5-day) course includes meals in the organic restaurant & materials. Lodging available at extra cost in local bed & breakfasts.

CONTACT: Andrew Whitley, Breadmatters Ltd, The Tower House, Melmerby, Penrith, Cumbria, England; (44) (0) 1768 881899, Fax (44) (0) 1768 889146, andrew@breadmatters.com, www.breadmatters.com.

BRIGHTON WINE SCHOOL
Brighton

Sponsor: Wine school. Programs: 3-session wine tasting courses, 2-hr classes. Established: 2000. Class/group size: 10-20. 10 programs/yr. Also featured: Wine dinners, home & corporate tastings.

FACULTY: Vintners Henry Butler & Richard Piggott.

COSTS: £40/class, £105-£130/course.

CONTACT: Ella Macpherson, Director, Brighton Wine School, 9 Foundry St., Brighton, England; (44) 1273 672525, info@brightonwineschool.co.uk, www.brightonwineschool.co.uk.

CAROLINE HOLMES
London, Ipswich, Portsmouth & West Country; Paris & Loire region, France

Sponsor: Culinary professional Caroline Holmes. Programs: 1-day courses at Hintlesham Hall, 5-day tours that visit food producers & herb gardens in UK & France. Established: 1983. Class/group size: 10 min. 10 programs/yr. Also featured: Tailored itineraries for groups.

FACULTY: Caroline Holmes holds a Certificate in Gourmet Cookery & City & Guilds Horticulture. She works with the Museum of Garden History, Hintlesham Hall, Hilton Hotels.

COSTS: 1-day courses from £60; 5-day tours £200; French-based from £600; UK weekends from £200. Lodging is 4-star.

CONTACT: Caroline Holmes, Gardens Millenium to Millenium, Denham, Bury St. Edmunds, Suffolk, England; (44) (0)1284-810653, Fax (44) (0)1284-811753, cholmesgmm@aol.com.

CONFIDENT COOKING
Wiltshire

Sponsor: Private school. Programs: Monthly demos & residential weekend hands-on courses that include market visits, visits to food producers, mushroom forays. Established: 1996. Class/group size: 8 hands-on, 25 demo. 36 programs/yr. Facilities: High-tech professional kitchen with overhead mirror. Also featured: Children's classes, private instruction, men-only classes.

FACULTY: Cook, author, & food consultant Caroline Yates & guest chefs.

COSTS: £30-£35/class, £315 for weekend courses, includes meals, lodging & planned activities.

CONTACT: Caroline Yates, Confident Cooking, PO Box 841, Devizes, Wiltshire, England; (44) (0)1380-812846, cyates@confidentcooking.com, www.confidentcooking.com.

CONSTANCE SPRY COOKERY DEMONSTRATIONS & WORKSHOPS
Farnham Surrey

Sponsor: Private school. Programs: Demos & hands-on workshops devoted to specialties of the season. Established: 1928. Class/group size: 6-40. Facilities: Demon hall, teaching kitchen, 4 classrooms. Also featured: 4- to 20-week professional courses.

FACULTY: Includes Francesca Fenwick, Annie Grubb, & Elizabeth Bowyer.

Costs: £36.50 for demos, £56.50 for workshops.
Contact: Mrs. Martine Frost, Constance Spry, Ltd., Moor Park House, Moor Park Lane, Farnham Surrey, England; (44) 1252-734477, Fax (44) 1252-712011, info@constancespry.com, www.constancespry.com.

COOKERY AT THE GRANGE
Frome
Sponsor: Private school. Programs: 5-day hands-on course in addition to certificate program. Established: 1981. Class/group size: 16-24. 8 programs/yr. Facilities: Main kitchen, cold kitchen, herb garden. Also featured: Wine instruction, basic food hygiene certificate.
Faculty: Jane & William Averill (Grange-trained) & teaching staff.
Costs: All-inclusive rates from £790 for 5-day program to £2,390-£2,790 for certificate program.
Contact: Jane & William Averill, Cookery at The Grange, Whatley, Frome, Somerset, England; (44) (0)1373-836579, Fax (44) (0)1373-836579, info@cookery-grange.co.uk, www.cookery-grange.co.uk.

COOKERY SCHOOL AT LITTLE PORTLAND STREET
London
Sponsor: Private school. Programs: Courses for adults & children, lunchtime classes, evening demos. Class/group size: 15 max. Facilities: Custom-designed premises. Also featured: Tastings, corporate events, cooking parties.
Faculty: Rosalind Rathouse, a professional cook & culinary teacher; demos by visting cooks.
Costs: £40/session, £210/6-session adult course, £150/4-session childrens' course, lunch classes £150/4 or £210/6.
Contact: Rosalind Rathouse, Cookery School at Little Portland Street, 15B Little Portland St., London, England; (44) (0) 20 7631 4590, information@cookeryschool.co.uk, www.cookeryschool.co.uk.

COOKING WITH CLASS
Herefordshire
Sponsor: Professional chef. Programs: demos & hands-on classes. Established: 1981. Class/group size: 22 demo/10 hands-on. Facilities: Modernized home kitchen. Also featured: Classes for men, children, teens.
Faculty: Victoria O'Neill, 25 yrs professional chef, trained at Le Cordon Bleu London. Guest chefs.
Costs: £35-£55/class, £25/children's class. B&B lodging £65/night, £175-£350/wk.
Contact: Victoria O'Neill, Cooking with Class, Ltd., Pyon House, Canon Pyon, Herefordshire, England; (44) (0)1432 830122/830185, Fax (44) (0)1432 830499, sales@cookingwithclass.co.uk, www.cookingwithclass.co.uk.

THE COOKING EXPERIENCE LTD
Hadleigh, Suffolk
Sponsor: Private school. Programs: 1-day, 2-day & weekend residential hands-on courses. Established: 2001. Class/group size: 8. 100+ programs/yr. Facilities: Includes 2 range cookers & cooking utensils. Also featured: Weekend courses include visits to local food producers & vineyards.
Faculty: Mark David, whose background includes chef, caterer, restaurant mgr, hotel/restaurant inspector, radio guest.
Costs: Day course £99 incl lunch. Evening class £55 incl supper. Residential course from £399 incl meals, 2 nights lodging.
Contact: Mark David, The Mark David Cooking Experience, 9 High Street, Hadleigh, Ipswich, Suffolk, England; (44) (0) 1473 827568, Fax (44) (0) 1473 828523, info@mdcookeryschool.co.uk, cookingexperience.co.uk.

CORDON VERT COOKERY SCHOOL
Altrincham, Cheshire
Sponsor: The Vegetarian Society UK, a registered charity. Programs: Weekend & day courses on a variety of vegetarian topics in addition to the 4-week diploma course & 1-week Cordon Vert cer-

tificate course. Established: 1982. Class/group size: 12 maximum. 40 programs/yr.

FACULTY: Lyn Weller, Principal, & 10 part-time tutors.

COSTS: Weekend residential (non-residential) courses range from £250 (£200); day courses are £65, which includes lunch. Local hotel/motel lodging.

CONTACT: Mureen Surgey, Cooking School Administrator, Cordon Vert Cookery School, Parkdale, Dunham Road, Altrincham, Cheshire, England; (44) (0) 161-925-2000, Fax (44) (0) 161-926-9182, cordonvert@vegsoc.org, www.vegsoc.org/cordonvert/.

DENISE'S KITCHEN
London

Sponsor: Private cookery school. Programs: Jewish cooking demos. Established: 1998. Class/group size: 22-100. Facilities: Mirrors & equipment designed for demonstrations.

FACULTY: Denise Phillips, caterer, author of Modern Jewish Cooking with Style, writer of cookery columns for London & USA weekly, Prue Leith Advanced Course Food & Wine graduate.

COSTS: £50 includes lunch.

CONTACT: Denise's Kitchen, PO Box 83, Northwood, Middlesex, England; (44) (0) 1923 836 456, Fax (44) (0) 1923 826 180, denise@jewishcookery.com, www.jewishcookery.com.

EARNLEY CONCOURSE
Sussex, near Chichester

Sponsor: Resident center for courses founded by the Earnley Trust, Ltd. educational charity. Programs: Weekend demo & participation courses. Established: 1975. Class/group size: 12. 15 programs/yr. Facilities: Fully-equipped kitchen workshop with demo & dining areas. Amenities include art & craft studios, computer room, heated pool, gardens.

FACULTY: Includes Deh-Ta Hsiung, Steven Page, Mary Whiting, & Lucy Shaw-Baker.

COSTS: From £142/course, including lodging & meals. Nonresident tuition £98, including lunch. Cost of ingredients additional.

CONTACT: Owain Roberts, Earnley Concourse, Earnley, Chichester, West Sussex, England; (44) (0)1243-670392, Fax (44) (0)1243-670832, info@earnley.co.uk, www.earnley.co.uk/.

EGGLESTON HALL COOKERY SCHOOL
Barnard Castle, County Durham

Sponsor: Private school. Programs: 4-week hands-on courses, men-only cookery weekends, one-day cookery demos. Established: 2002. Class/group size: 8-100. 6 programs/yr. Facilities: Fully-equipped kitchen with 4 cookers & Aga. Also featured: Flower arranging courses & demos.

FACULTY: In-house instructors & guest chefs.

COSTS: From £38 for one-day demos, £345 for men-only weekends, £1,850 for 4-week course.

CONTACT: Lorraine Vine, Eggleston Hall Cookery School, Eggleston Hall, Barnard Castle, Co. Durham, England; (44) 01833 650553, Fax (44) 01833 650553, info@egglestonhall.co.uk, www.egglestonhall.co.uk.

FOOD OF COURSE
Sutton, Somerset

Sponsor: Professional cook. Programs: 4-wk residential foundation cookery course; 5-day course emphasizing new foods, recipes & tips; 1-day refresher course on advanced prep & easy entertaining. Established: 2000. Facilities: Farmhouse kitchen with modern appliances. Also featured: Visits to local markets & suppliers.

FACULTY: Lou Hutton, professional cook with 14+ yrs teaching experience, was principal instructor at The Grange for 4 yrs; guest chefs, wine experts &suppliers.

COSTS: Foundation Course £2,450; 5-day New Food Course £720; 1-day Refresher Course £85; 1-day Young Chefs Course £55.

CONTACT: Louise Hutton, Food of Course, Middle Farm House, Sutton, Somerset, England; (44) (0)1749 860116, Fax (44) (0)1749 860765, louise.hutton@foodofcourse.co.uk, www.foodof-course.co.uk.

GREEN CUISINE LTD
Kington, Herefordshire

Sponsor: Private school. Programs: 2- to 5-day residential courses include Food & Health, Women's Health, Seeds of Change (weight control), Pregnancy & Babycare. Established: 1995. Class/group size: 6-12. 20 programs/yr. Facilities: Penrhos, a 700-yr-old manor farm. Also featured: Yoga, aromatherapy, walking.

FACULTY: Proprietor Daphne Lambert, nutritionist, chef, author & organic gardener; practitioners.

COSTS: £240-£265/2 days, £295/3 days, includes lodging & meals.

CONTACT: Daphne Lambert, Head of Studies, Green Cuisine Ltd, Penrhos Court, Kington, Herefordshire, England; (44) 01544 230720, Fax (44) 01544 230754, daphne@greencuisine.org, www.greencuisine.org.

HAVE YOUR CAKE & EAT IT
New Longton

Sponsor: Cake decorator. Programs: 1-day classes & 6-session cake decorating courses.

FACULTY: Carol has decorated cakes for 20+ yrs & creates custom wedding cakes.

COSTS: £16/workshop, £45/course.

CONTACT: Carol , Have Your Cake & Eat It, Preston, Lancashire, England; (44) 01772 628 798, haveyourcakeandeatit@lineone.net, www.haveyourcakeandeatit.org.

HAZLEWOOD CASTLE
North Yorkshire

Sponsor: Hotel. Programs: Cookery demos & hands-on Masterclasses. Class/group size: 20/cookery. Facilities: Fully-equipped demo kitchen.

FACULTY: Professional chefs.

COSTS: £45/cookery demo, £55/Masterclass.

CONTACT: Hazlewood Castle, Paradise Lane, Hazlewood, Tadcaster, Near York & Leeds, North Yorkshire, England; (44) (0)1937-535353, Fax (44) (0)1937 530630, info@hazlewood-castle.co.uk, www.hazlewood-castle.co.uk.

INSPIRED TO LOVE COOKING
Rutland

Sponsor: Cooking school. Programs: Inspired to Love Cooking course for young people. Chalet Cooks course preparatory to ski season. Established: 1978. Class/group size: 6. Facilities: Country house kitchen in a converted old school. Also featured: Sailboarding, bird watching, cycling, golf.

FACULTY: Miranda Hall, a former teacher/examiner at London's Cordon Bleu Cooking School, studied at the Cordon Bleu in Paris & has a teaching diploma in Home Economics.

COSTS: Inspired to Love Cooking course, non-residential, £285. Chalet Cooks course, residential, £495.

CONTACT: Miranda Hall, Inspired to Love Cooking, Old School House Hambleton, Rutland, England; 44-01572723576, miranda@hall.vispa.com.

ITALIAN SECRETS
Beaconsfield, Bucks; Capo d'Orlando, Sicily, Italy

Sponsor: Private school. Programs: UK: Demo & hands-on 1- to 5-day programs in Italian cuisine. Sicily: 1-wk gastronomic holidays. Established: 1995. Class/group size: 18 demo, 12 hands-on. 40 programs/yr. Facilities: High tech kitchens accommodating 12 students. Also featured: Private instruction.

FACULTY: Anna Venturi, raised in Milan, learned to cook from grandmother & family cook.

COSTS: UK: £80-£250. Sicily: £1280 includes lodging, meals, ground transport, excursions.

CONTACT: Anna Venturi, Owner, Italian Secrets, 13 The Broadway, Penn Rd., Beaconsfield, Bucks, England; (44) 1494 676136, Fax (44) 1494 681704, enquiries@italiansecrets.co.uk, www.italiansecrets.co.uk.

KILBURY MANOR COOKERY COURSES
Devon

Sponsor: Private school. Programs: Short hands-on courses for beginners to professionals. Established: 1995. Class/group size: 1-4. Facilities: Refurbished farmhouse kitchen.

FACULTY: Suzanne Lewis is a home economist with Advanced City & Guilds training, Qualified Teacher & Trainer, former restaurateur, caterer with experience in the food industry.

COSTS: £150-£195 for 1-day course & lodging with meals; £295 [one-on-one] for 2 night's lodging & 3 half-day classes; 2 pers: £225; 3 pers: £200; 4 pers: £185 [2002].

CONTACT: Suzanne Lewis, Kilbury Manor Cookery Courses, Kilbury Manor Farm, Colston Road, Buckfastleigh, Devon, England; (44) (0) 1364 644079, Fax (44) (0) 1364 644059, suzanne@kilbury.co.uk, www.kilbury.co.uk.

LE CORDON BLEU – LONDON
London *(See also page 156) (See display ad page 161)*

Sponsor: Private school, sister school of Le Cordon Bleu-Paris. Programs: Daily half-day demos, 1- to 5-day gourmet hands-on sessions, evening classes, 1-month courses. Established: 1933. Class/group size: 10. 50 programs/yr. Facilities: Professionally equipped kitchens; individual workspaces with refrigerated marble tops; demonstration rooms with video & tilted mirror. Also featured: Children's workshops, guest chef demonstrations, First Certificate in Food Safety.

FACULTY: All staff full time. Chefs all professionally qualified with experience in Michelin-starred & fine quality culinary establishments.

COSTS: Range from £15-£395.

CONTACT: Richard O'Leary, Sales & Promotions Executive, Le Cordon Bleu, 114 Marylebone Lane, London, England; (44) 20-7-935-3503, Fax (44) 20-7-935-7621, london@cordonbleu.edu, cordonbleu.edu. Toll free in U.S. & Canada: 800-457-CHEF.

LEITHS SCHOOL OF FOOD & WINE
London

Sponsor: Private school with cooking agency. Programs: 1- & 4-wk holiday courses, 1-wk fish, healthy eating, Oriental cooking, dinner party, & holiday cooking courses; 10-session beginner to advanced courses, Saturday demos, 5-session Certificate in Wine. Established: 1975. Class/group size: 48 demo, 16 hands-on. Facilities: Demo theatre, 3 kitchens, prep kitchen, library, changing room. Also featured: Private instruction.

FACULTY: 13 full-, 2 part-time. School founder & cookbook author Prue Leith is former Veuve Cliquot Business Woman of the Year. Principal is Caroline Waldegrave, vice-principal is A. Cavaliero.

COSTS: 10-session evening courses £500, Wine Certificate course £265. Housing list provided.

CONTACT: Judy Wilkinson, Registrar, Leiths School of Food & Wine, 21 St. Alban's Grove, London, England; (44) 020 72290177, Fax (44) 020 79375257, info@leiths.com, www.leiths.com.

THE MANOR SCHOOL OF FINE CUISINE
Widmerpool

Sponsor: Private school. Programs: 5-day Foundation course, 4-day Entertaining course, theme weekends, & day & evening courses. Established: 1988. Class/group size: 12. 40 programs/yr. Facilities: Residential school in Georgian manor house with purpose-built kitchens & demonstration theatre. Also featured: Water sports, clay pigeon shooting, horseback riding, golf.

FACULTY: Cordon Bleu diploma, head chef of noted restaurants. Member of Cookery & Food Assoc., Craft Guild of Chefs, Chef & Cooks Circle.

COSTS: Inclusive of VAT, tuition is £390 resident (£295 nonresident) for Foundation course, £330 (£285) for Entertaining course, £130 for weekend courses. Lodging at the Manor.

CONTACT: Claire Tuttey, The Manor School of Fine Cuisine, Old Melton Road, Widmerpool, Nottinghamshire, England; (44) (0)1949-81371.

MOSIMANN'S ACADEMY
London
Sponsor: Private school. Programs: Half- & one-day demos & courses that focus on intl cuisine, fine dining & wines, chocolate & pastry arts, specialized food presentation, food & flowers. Established: 1996. Class/group size: 60. 50 programs/yr. Facilities: New seminar & demo theater, library of Anton Mosimann's 6,000 cookery books. Also featured: Tailor-made corporate courses. **FACULTY:** Academy chef & mgr. Simon Boyle, assisted by 2 full- & 2 part-time staff. Anton Mosimann & guest chefs Shaun Hill, Brian Turner, Jean-Christophe Novelli & Jamie Oliver regularly appear. **COSTS:** £125 for demo & lunch at Mosimann's Dining Club in Belgravia, £65 demo only. **CONTACT:** Simon Boyle, Academy Chef & Manager, Mosimann's Academy, 5 William Blake House, The Lanterns, Bridge Lane, London, England; (44) (0) 20 7326 8366, Fax (44) (0) 20 7326 8360, academy@mosimann.com, www.mosimann.com.

PADSTOW SEAFOOD SCHOOL
Padstow
Sponsor: Established by the BBC TV chef Rick Stein. Programs: Residential & non-residential 1-, 2-, & 4-day hands-on/demo seafood courses designed around a daily lunch menu; 1-day fish filleting courses. Established: 2000. Class/group size: 16. 142 programs/yr. Facilities: Purpose-built facility features with the latest equipment & dining area overlooking the Camel Estuary. Also featured: Cliff walks, beaches, water sports, golf courses, fishing trips, local visits, trips to Newlyn Fish Market. **FACULTY:** Paul Sellars, 25+ yrs restaurant experience including sous chef at Rick Stein's Seafood Restaurant & running his own fish restaurant. **COSTS:** £155-£615/1- to 4-day non-residential courses include lunch; £615-£1,395/2- to 4-day residential courses includes meals, lodging, VAT. Participants' guests stay on B&B basis. **CONTACT:** Jo Greengass, Marketing Manager, Padstow Seafood School, Riverside, Padstow, England; (44) (0) 1841 532700, Fax (44) (0) 1841 532942, seafoodschool@rickstein.com, www.rickstein.com.

PAUL HEATHCOTE'S SCHOOL OF EXCELLENCE
Manchester
Sponsor: Private school. Programs: demos & hands-on classes on a variety of topics. Established: 1997. Class/group size: 12 hands-on, 40 demo. Facilities: Professionally-equipped kitchen with 6 individual work spaces, demonstration auditorium with projector & screen. **FACULTY:** Paul Heathcote, chef & owner of four restaurants, & his staff of instructors. **CONTACT:** Marketing Director, Paul Heathcote's School of Excellence, Jackson Row, Deansgate, Manchester, England; (44) (0)161-839-5898, Fax (44) (0)161-839-5897, cookeryschool@heathcotes.co.uk, www.heathcotes.co.uk.

RAYMOND BLANC'S ECOLE DE CUISINE
Oxford
Sponsor: Le Manoir, 12th century manor house. Programs: 5-day cooking vacations that feature hands-on stage 1, 2, & 3 classes; 1-2 day courses including fusion, nutrition, & la cuisine moderne. Established: 1991. Class/group size: 10. Year-round programs/yr. Facilities: Individual work areas in the restaurant kitchen. Also featured: Themed courses include vegetarian, fish & shellfish, Christmas, 1-day dinner parties, nutrition. **FACULTY:** Chef Raymond Blanc owns & operates Le Manoir. Stephen Bulmer, director of L'Ecole. **COSTS:** From £550 for 1-day courses to £1,775. Includes all meals & luxury lodging at Le Manoir aux Quat' Saisons, which has the highest classification of Relais & Chateaux. Lodging free for non-cooking guests. **CONTACT:** Raymond Blanc, Chef Patron, Le Manoir aux Quat' Saisons, Great Milton, Oxford, England; (44) (0)1-844-278-881, Fax (44) (0)1-844-278-847, lemanoir@blanc.co.uk, www.manoir.com. In the U.S.: Judy Ebrey, Cuisine International Inc., P.O. Box 25228, Dallas, TX 75225; 214-373-1161, Fax 214-373-1162, Email CuisineInt@aol.com, www.cuisineinternational.com.

REAL ENGLAND – WORCESTERSHIRE COOKERY
Worcestershire

Sponsor: Specialty tour company. Programs: Dining in private homes, excursions including cookery schools, gardens. Established: 1989. Class/group size: 8-16. 2-5 programs/yr. Facilities: Modern purpose-built kitchen with work stations & overhead mirror. Also featured: Individual visits to food related venues.

FACULTY: Professional cooks & teachers. Tour leaders Tina Boughey & Jenny Mills trained in college for 5 yrs.

COSTS: £895/week includes bed & breakfast lodging, most meals, excursions.

CONTACT: Tina Boughey & Jenny Mills, Real England, Pudding Bag, Elm Hill, Sinton Green, Worcestershire, England; (44) 01905-640126, (44) 01905-26529, Fax (44) 01905-640126, (44) 01905-26529.

RED EPICURUS
London

Sponsor: Gourmet & culinary organization. Programs: Demo & participation classes that focus on a selected cookbook or chef menu. Established: 2002. Class/group size: 8-15. 24+ programs/yr. Also featured: Wine & spirits tastings, culinary tours, food & wine pairing.

FACULTY: 15+ rotating faculty, all experienced in their fields.

COSTS: £25+/class.

CONTACT: Karey Butterworth, Director, Red Epicurus, PO Box 31601, London, England; (44) (0) 7900691632, karey@redepicurus.com, www.redepicurus.com/calendar.html.

ROB REES & THE COUNTRY ELEPHANT
Bisley, Gloucestershire

Sponsor: Chef, food consultant & restaurateur. Programs: Cooking classes. Established: 1994.

FACULTY: Rob Rees, chef for the Country Elephant restaurant & Stroud Farmers' Market, finalist for BBC Radio 4 Best Food Educator, Pathfinder Achievement Award, former Michelin, AA & Good Good guide.

CONTACT: Robert Rees, Director/Chef, Robert Rees & The Country Elephant, Norwich House, High St., Bisley, Gloucestershire, England; (44) (0)1452770872, Fax (44) (0)1452770872, robertrees@btopenworld.com, www.robrees.com.

ROSEMARY SHRAGER'S COOKERY COURSES AT SWINTON PARK
Masham, Ripon, North Yorkshire

Sponsor: Castle hotel. Programs: 1- to 4-day demo & hands-on cooking courses, including back to basics, fish, French & Italian, bread, sauces. Established: 2003. Class/group size: 14 max. 40 programs/yr. Facilities: Demo kitchen & dining room housed in converted Georgian stables. 4-acre garden provides fresh ingredients. Also featured: Local excursions, fishing, walking, riding, shooting, golf, falconry, massage.

FACULTY: Rosemary Shrager, a professional chef for 20+ yrs, has 2 TV series. She worked for Pierre Koffman at Tante Claire & for Jean-Christophe Novelli.

COSTS: £560/2 days, £1,100/4 days includes meals & shared lodging in the 30-bedroom castle hotel. Single supplement £50/day. Day courses £95, hotel lodging available from £50.

CONTACT: Reception Manager, Rosemary Shrager's Cookery Courses at Swinton Park, Swinton Park, Masham, Ripon, North Yorkshire, England; (44) (0)1765 680900, Fax (44) (0)1765 680901, enquiries@swintonpark.com, www.swintonpark.co.uk.

SQUIRES KITCHEN INTERNATIONAL SCHOOL OF SUGARCRAFT
Farnham, Surrey

Sponsor: Private school. Programs: 1-hour to 3-day demo & participation courses. Established: 1987. Class/group size: 12 hands-on/35 demo. 74+ programs/yr. Facilities: A kitchen with specialized equipment & materials. Also featured: Classes for youngsters, private instruction.

FACULTY: 17 full- & part-time. Members of the British Sugarcraft Guild. Guest tutors include Eddie Spence, Alan Dunn, Toribi Peck.
CONTACT: Course Coordinator, Squires Kitchen, Int'l School of Sugarcraft & Cake Decorating, 3 Waverley Lane, Farnham, Surrey, England; (44) (0)1252-734309, Fax (44) (0)1252-714714, school@squires-group.co.uk, www.squires-group.co.uk.

A TABLE
Richmond, Surrey
Programs: Hands-on cooking courses consisting of 4 evening or morning classes once a week. 1-day theme classes also available. Established: 2000. Class/group size: 7-9. Facilities: Martina's kitchen, purpose-built for instructing. Also featured: Catering services.
FACULTY: Martina Lessing.
COSTS: ~£95 for 4-class course, £25-£30 for single class.
CONTACT: Martina Lessing, A Table Cooking Classes & Catering, 7 Arlington Road, Richmond, Surrey, England; (44) 0208 940 9910, martina@lessing.freeserve.co.uk.

TANTE MARIE SCHOOL OF COOKERY
Surrey
Sponsor: Private school. Programs: Certificate courses thrice yearly, 3- to 5-day hands-on courses, 1-day theme demos. Established: 1954. Class/group size: 12/group max. 3 programs/yr. Facilities: Include 5 modern teaching kitchens, a mirrored demo theatre, & a lecture room. Also featured: Wine instruction, private group demos.
FACULTY: 12 full- & part-time. Qualified to teach adult ed. Many have held catering positions. Well-known TV cookery demonstrators, a noted wine expert, & local tradesmen also present.
COSTS: From £3,650 including all food.
CONTACT: Marcella O'Donovan, Principal, Tante Marie School of Cookery, Woodham House, Carlton Rd., Woking, Surrey, England; (44) (0)1483-726957, Fax (44) (0)1483-724173, info@tantemarie.co.uk, www.tantemarie.co.uk.

TWO BABES FROM BRITAIN
Essex
Sponsor: Caterers Alyson Cook & Maxine Martens. Programs: 1-wk culinary tour based in English country mansion that combines cooking classes, visits to local markets, cheesemakers & food producers, sightseeing & dining in fine restaurants. Established: 1996. Class/group size: 16. 2 programs/yr.
FACULTY: Alyson Cook & Maxine Martens, 30 yrs combined catering experience. Cook graduated from Le Cordon Bleu & cooked for the royal family. Martens has been a Hollywood caterer for 10+ yrs.
COSTS: $4,999 includes airfare from NYC, lodging, meals, planned activities.
CONTACT: Alyson Cook, Partner, Two Babes From Britain, P.O. Box 40281, Pasadena, CA 91114; 626-791-9757, 818-784-8274, Fax 626-791-9698, 818-784-8463, alysoncook@earthlink.net.

THE VEGETARIAN COOKERY SCHOOL
Bath
Sponsor: Private but allied to Demuths Vegetarian Restaurant in Bath. Programs: Hands-on 1- to 3-day vegetarian cooking courses including international, breadmaking, spices & herbs, gluten-free. Established: 1999. Class/group size: 8 max. ~75 programs/yr.
FACULTY: Rachel Demuth, Jan Berridge, Nick Troup.
COSTS: £45-£225.
CONTACT: The Vegetarian Cookery School, 30 Belgrave Crescent, Bath, England; (44) (0)1225 789682, us@vegetariancookeryschool.com, www.vegetariancookeryschool.com.

WOODEND COOKERY
Woodend, Egremont, Cumbria
Sponsor: Culinary professional. Programs: Informal cookery demos that cover traditional & modern techniques with emphasis on the use of seasonal & local produce. Facilities: Home kitchen.

FACULTY: Grainne Jakobson.

COSTS: £30/session.

CONTACT: Grainne Jakobson, Woodend Cookery, Woodend House, Woodend, Egremont, Cumbria, England; 01946 813017, gmjakobson@aol.com, www.woodendcookery.50megs.com.

FINLAND

HELSINKI CULINARY INSTITUTE
Helsinki & Mustio Manor
Sponsor: Owner/Chef Gero Hottinger. Programs: Individualized 1-day, hands-on theme workshops. Instruction in Finnish, Swedish, German, English. Established: 1994. Class/group size: 10-18. Facilities: Teaching kitchen, conference & dining room.

FACULTY: Chef de Cuisine Gero Hottinger, Pia Wahlberg, visiting chefs from Finland & Europe.

COSTS: $80-$220.

CONTACT: Pia Wahlberg, Sales Manager, Helsinki Culinary Institute, Uudenmaankatu 7 B, Helsinki, 120 Finland; (358) 9-68117212, Fax (358) 9-68117213, toimisto@kulinaarineninstituutti.com, kulinaarineninstituutti.com.

EUROPE

ARTE DI VIVERE
France; Italy
Sponsor: Tour guide operating food & wine tours for 20+ yrs. Programs: Weekend to week-long tours featuring cooking lessons from local chefs in their restaurants, tours of private villas & castles, wine tastings, excursions into the Italian Alps. Established: 1999. Class/group size: 8-12. 4-6 programs/yr. Facilities: Range from small professionally equipped kitchens to home kitchens. Also featured: Visits to local artisans & wine makers, tours of private castles & gardens, dinners & cooking lessons in private homes, boating excursions.

FACULTY: Owners of well-known restaurants, sommeliers, private chefs.

COSTS: $650/weekend to $3,095/wk includes shared lodging in 3- & 4-star country inns, small hotels & villas (single supplement $300-$500), most meals, local transportation, planned activities.

CONTACT: Claudia Harris, Owner, Arte di Vivere, 4208 West Pine Blvd., St Louis, MO 63108; 314-534-1826, Fax 314-534-1826, forketta@earthlink.net.

ART OF LIVING – CULINARY & LIFE STYLE TOURS WITH SARA MONICK
Provence, Paris, Burgundy, France; Venice & Veneto, Italy; Morocco; Barcelona, Spain
Sponsor: Culinary & travel professional Sara Monick. Programs: 5- to 11-day culinary tours that include hands-on & demo classes. Established: 1986. Class/group size: 8-14. Also featured: Visits to markets, food producers, wineries, private homes & gardens; dining at fine restaurants; sightseeing; language classes; custom tours for private groups.

FACULTY: Tour escort Sara Monick, a cooking instructor since 1977 & Certified Member of the IACP, owns The Cookery in Minneapolis. She studied with Madeleine Kamman, Jacques Pepin, Nicholas Malgieri & Giuliano Bugialli. Local chefs.

COSTS: $2,300-$4,000, which includes double occupancy lodging, most meals & planned excursions. Lodging in first-class hotels or private homes.

CONTACT: Sara Monick, Hilliard & Olander Ltd., 226 East Myrtle, Stillwater, MN 55082; 651-275 8960, 800-229-8407, Fax 651-275-8962, Diane@hilliardolander.com, www.hilliardolander.com.

BEV GRUBER'S EVERYDAY GOURMET TRAVELER
France; Italy; United States
Sponsor: Culinary professional Beverly Gruber. Programs: Small group culinary tours that feature visits with local artisan food producers. Established: 1988. Class/group size: 4-12. 6-8 programs/yr. Also featured: Trip planning services in Italy for individuals desiring independent travel.

FACULTY: Beverly Gruber, professional chef & culinary guide, has led international tours since 1988, working with professional colleagues in Italy, France & US.

COSTS: $1,500-$2,900 includes shared lodging.10% discount on select trips.

CONTACT: Beverly Gruber, Owner, Everyday GOURMET TRAVELER, 5053 NE 178th St., Seattle, WA 98155; 206-363-1602, 888-636-1602, Fax 206-363-1602, gourmetravel@aol.com, www.gourmetravel.com.

BIKE RIDERS
Burgundy & Provence, France; Umbria, Sicily, Tuscany, Italy

Sponsor: Travel company. Programs: 1-week tours to Italy & France that combine hands-on cooking classes & 15-40 miles biking/day with guest chefs. Established: 1990. Class/group size: 16 max. 14 programs/yr. Facilities: Inn & restaurant kitchens. Also featured: Market visits, wine classes, winery tours, olive oil tastings.

FACULTY: Chefs of well-known restaurants.

COSTS: $2,980/Umbria; $3,080/Burgundy, Provence, Tuscany & Sicily. Includes support van, lodging (villas & 4- & 5-star inns), most meals, planned activities. Bike rental $150. Single supplement $420-$480.

CONTACT: Eileen E. Holland, Director, Bike Riders, P.O. Box 130254, Boston, MA 2113; 800-473-7040, 617-723-2354, Fax 617-723-2355, info@bikeriderstours.com, www.bikeriderstours.com.

CLASSIC JOURNEYS
Provence, France; Naples, Florence, Italy

Sponsor: Tour provider. Programs: Week-long tours featuring hands-on cooking instruction, walks, & visits to cultural sites, wineries, olive oil mills, local markets. Established: 1995. Class/group size: ~10 (max 18). 25 programs/yr. Facilities: Cooking instruction in chateaux, local homes & restaurants. Also featured: Walking, cultural & natural history tours available.

FACULTY: Local chefs & guides knowledgeable about the regional history & culture.

COSTS: ~$2,500/wk includes shared lodging, ground transport, most meals.

CONTACT: Hilary Achauer, Communications Director, Classic Journeys, 5580 La Jolla Blvd., #104, La Jolla, CA 92037; 800-200-3887, Fax 858-454-5770, moreinfo@classicjourneys.com, www.classicjourneys.com.

COOKEURO
Provence, France; Emilia Romagna, Tuscany & Umbria, Italy

Sponsor: Travel company. Programs: 1-wk hands-on culinary vacations: l'Amore di Cucina Italiana in Italy, La Cuisine de Provence in France. Include visits to wineries, markets, food producers, dining in fine restaurants, cultural evenings. Established: 1992. Class/group size: 12. 9 programs/yr. Facilities: Italy: kitchens of Locanda di Praticino (Tuscany), Il Rotolone (Umbria) & Locanda dei Cinque Cerri (Emilia Romagna). France: kitchen of Domaine de la Fontaine. Also featured: Customized programs, one-day classes.

FACULTY: Cristina Blasi, Gabriella Mari, own Scuola di Arte Culinaria Cordon Bleu; Silvia Maccari, author; Eros Patrizi, chef, Trattoria del Festival; Marcello Dall'Aglio, chef, Locanda del Castello. Jean-Claude Aubertin, member Academie Culinaire de France.

COSTS: $2,495 includes meals, shared lodging, planned activities. Single supplement $400, non-cook/guest $2,295.

CONTACT: Ralph P. Slone, Inland Services, Inc., 708 Third Ave., 13th flr., New York, NY 10017; 212-687-9898, incook@earthlink.net, www.cookeuro.com.

A COOK'S TOUR
Provence, France; Cinque Terre, Piedmonte, Tuscany, Veneto, Italy; Cape, South Africa

Sponsor: Culinary tour operator. Programs: Guided culinary tours that feature hands-on cooking lessons taught by local chefs. Established: 2000. Class/group size: ~12. ~15 programs/yr. Also featured: Visits to local wineries & food production facilities, cultural excursions, restaurant dining.

FACULTY: Provence: Marie-Claude Ricard; Northern Italy & the Veneto: Rinaldo Biraldi; Tuscany: Gianluca Pardini; Mediterranean: Paolo Monti; Tuscany: Marcello Crimini.

COSTS: From $2,160 includes meals, lodging, planned activities.

CONTACT: Patty LeDonne, Partner, A Cook's Tour, 221 214th NE, Sammamish, WA 98053; 800-726-6388, Fax 425-557-9906, patty@acookstour.com, www.acookstour.com.

CUISINE INTERNATIONAL INC.
Charlottesville, Virginia; Brazil; England; France; Ikaria Island, Greece; Italy; Portugal

Sponsor: Tour operator specializing in culinary vacations. Programs: Cooking schools & culinary tours. Established: 1987. Class/group size: 8-20. Facilities: Hotel & restaurant kitchens, private homes, castles, monasteries. Also featured: Excursions to food-related & historical sites; winery visits, tastings, shopping.

FACULTY: Owner Judy Ebrey, CCP.

COSTS: $2,250-$4,700/week including lodging, meals, planned activities, ground transport.

CONTACT: Judy Ebrey, Owner, Cuisine International, P.O. Box 25228, Dallas, TX 75225; 214-373-1161, Fax 214-373-1162, info@cuisineinternational.com, www.cuisineinternational.com.

CULINARY JOURNEYS
Argentina, Cambodia, England, France, Greece, Indonesia, Ireland, Italy, Mexico, Morocco

Sponsor: Specialty tour organizer. Programs: 6- & 7-day culinary vacations that include hands-on cooking classes & excursions. Established: 2003. Class/group size: 8-12. 25 programs/yr. Facilities: Well-equipped kitchens. Also featured: Include hiking, cycling, swimming, golf, tennis, mountaineering, spa treatments, horseback riding, fly fishing, art & language instruction, eco-adventures, visits to private art collections, sightseeing.

COSTS: $2,695-$4,995 includes meals & luxurylodging,ground transport, planned excursions.

CONTACT: Mary Ann Albright, Cultivator, Culinary Journeys, 2911 Turtle Creek Blvd., #300, Dallas, TX 0; 214-599-8325, Fax 214-523-9001, maryann@culinaryjourneys.com, www.culinaryjourneys.com.

CULINARY TOURS
France; Italy; New Zealand; Spain; Thailand; United States

Sponsor: Culinary professional Glenn Watz. Programs: International food-focused tours featuring demo classes, market tours, wine tastings & restaurant meals. Established: 1994. Class/group size: 12-25. 12 programs/yr. Facilities: Hotels, restaurants, chateaux & villas. Also featured: Sightseeing, visits to food producers.

FACULTY: Glenn Watz, professional chef for 23 yrs, & other chefs in destination cities.

COSTS: $1,195-$2,295 includes shared lodging, most meals, tours.

CONTACT: Glenn Watz, Owner, Culinary Tours, 2450 Gladys Ave., Beaumont, TX 77702; 409-832-4929, Fax 409-833-5134, grwatz@earthlink.net, www.culinarytours.net. Carolyn Wood 409-832-9738, Pat Klein, Unlimited Travel 800-766-5725.

CULINARY VACATIONS, INC.
Normandy & Provence, France; Tuscany, Italy

Sponsor: Chef John Wilson. Programs: 6-day cooking vacations & vineyard tours that feature daily cooking classes & excursions to monuments, villages, wineries, food producers, & shopping venues. Established: 1998. 15+ programs/yr. Facilities: Inn kitchens.

FACULTY: Chef John Wilson is a certified chef, graduate of The CIA, director of the Culinary Arts Program at Clayton College & State University & teaches for Kroger School of Cooking.

COSTS: $1,800-$2,500 includes shared lodging, meals, planned activities.

CONTACT: John Wilson, Owner, Culinary Vacations, Inc., P.O. Box 747, Roswell, GA 0; 888-636-2073 or 770-998-2073, Fax 770-998-2073, ChefJohnWilson@hotmail.com, www.culinaryvacationsinc.com/.

321 E. Washington Ave. • Lake Bluff, Ill. 60044
E-Mail: info@epiculinary.com • Web Site: www.epiculinary.com • Fax: 847.295.5371

CALL US TODAY AT 888.380.9010 OR 847.295.5363

EPICULINARY INC.
United States, France, Italy, Mexico, Spain   *(See display ad above)*
Sponsor: Tour company specializing in cooking vacations to Italy, France, Spain, Mexico, Canada & the U.S. Programs: 2- to 14-night cooking vacations featuring cooking lessons, excursions, & wine tastings. Established: 1999. Class/group size: 2-8. 100+ programs/yr. Facilities: Cooking schools, restaurant kitchens, country villa kitchens. Also featured: Customized group travel, individual itineraries, specialized tours.
FACULTY: Restaurant chefs, cooking school instructors, regional culinary experts.
COSTS: $550-$3,000 includes lodging (from 5-star hotels like Villa d'Este to country farmhouses), meals, wine tastings, & excursions.
CONTACT: Catherine Merrill, Owner/President, Epiculinary Inc., 321 E. Washington Ave., Lake Bluff, IL 60044; 888-380-9010, 847-295-5363, Fax 847-295-5371, info@epiculinary.com, www.epiculinary.com.

FOOD & WINE TRAILS
Napa & Sonoma; France; Italy; New Zealand; Spain
Sponsor: HMS Travel Group. Programs: 5- to 12-day cooking vacation programs that feature hands-on classes, winery tours, visits to food-related sites, & cultural activities. Established: 1983. Class/group size: 20-25. 10+ programs/yr.
FACULTY: Culinary & wine experts including chefs, cookbook authors, wine judges.
COSTS: $2,200-$3,300 includes lodging, most meals, planned activities.
CONTACT: Food & Wine Trails, 707-A Fourth St., Santa Rosa, CA 95404; 800-367-5348, 707-526-2922, Fax 707-526-6949, info@foodandwinetrails.com, www.foodandwinetrails.com.

GOURMET ON TOUR
Europe, Asia, Australia, US
Sponsor: Travel company specializing in gourmet,cooking, & wine tours. Programs: 1-day to 1-week culinary experiences with hands-on cooking courses & wine appreciation. Established: 2000. Class/group size: 1-18. 80 programs/yr. Facilities: Professionally-equipped hotel & restaurant kitchens, private villas, chateaus, farmhouses. Also featured: Truffle & mushroom hunts, spa treatments, cycling tours, corporate events, master classes, team building.
FACULTY: Restaurant chefs, cookbook authors, wine experts.
COSTS: $100-$3,900 ranging from day classes to packages that include deluxe or private lodging, meals & excursions.
CONTACT: Judith von Prockl-Palmer, Managing Director, Gourmet On Tour, Berkeley Square House, 2 Fl, Berkeley Square, Mayfair, London, England; UK: (44) 20-7396-5550, US: 800-504-9842, Fax (44) 20-7900-1527, info@gourmetontour.com, www.gourmetontour.com.

THE INTERNATIONAL KITCHEN
6 cities & regions, France; 21 cities & regions, Italy
Sponsor: Travel company specializing in culinary tours. Programs: 1-day classes, & week-long & shorter vacations that include hands-on instruction in the regional cuisine, market visits, winery

tours, visits to food producers, fine dining, cultural excursions. Established: 1994. Class/group size: 2-12. 70 programs/yr. Facilities: Restaurant, home, villa & farmhouse kitchens. Also featured: Some programs include walking, bicycling, European spa treatments, or truffle hunting. FACULTY: Restaurant chefs, regional experts, cooking school instructors. COSTS: France: $2,250-$3,290 includes B&B to deluxe lodging, meals, planned activities. Italy: $1,660-$3,950 includes farmhouse to deluxe lodging, meals, planned activities. CONTACT: Karen Herbst, The International Kitchen, Inc., One IBM Plaza, 330 N. Wabash, Ste. 3005, Chicago, IL 60611; 800-945-8606, Fax 312-803-1593, info@theinternationalkitchen.com, www.theinternationalkitchen.com.

JC FOOD & WINE TOURS
Napa Valley, Asia, England, France, Italy, Spain
Sponsor: Special interest tour operator. Programs: Customized itineraries to Italy, France, Napa Valley. Occasional trips to other countries in the UK, Europe, southeast Asia. Established: 1992. Class/group size: 6-18. Also featured: Small group tours to visit wineries, private villas, agritourismos, markets, food/wine producers; dining at fine restaurants, truffle hunts, sightseeing. FACULTY: Winemakers, food producers, chefs, restaurateurs, culinary consultants. Joyce Capece, a 30-yr travel professional, specializes in food & wine tours & special interest travel. COSTS: Rates are based on countries, regions, seasons, & length of program, usually 7-12 days. CONTACT: Joyce Capece, CTC, DS, JC Food & Wine Tours, 2101 Golden Rain Rd., #7, Walnut Creek, CA 94595; 925-938-9635, Fax 925-938-5692.

L'ECOLE DES CHEFS RELAIS & CHATEAUX
United States, Belgium, Canada, Denmark, France, Germany
Sponsor: Relais & Chateaux. Programs: 2- & 5-day internship programs at Michelin- & Mobil-starred Relais Gourmands restaurants. Open to amateur cooks. Certificate upon completion. Established: 1998. Class/group size: 1:1. Facilities: The kitchens of participating Relais Gourmands restaurants. Also featured: Internships for 2 people available at some locations. FACULTY: Michelin- & Mobil-starred chefs, including Patrick O'Connell, Thomas Keller, Gary Danko, Rick Tramonto, Michel Troisgros, Alain Passard, Michel Rostang. COSTS: 2-day (5-day) programs $1,100-$1,400 ($1,900-$2,950). Does not include travel or lodging. Must submit application with non-refundable $25 fee. ~80% of applicants accepted. CONTACT: L'Ecole des Chefs Relais & Chateaux, 11 E. 44th St., #707, New York, NY 10017; 877-334-6464, Fax 212-856-0193, info@ecoledeschefs.com, www.ecoledeschefs.com.

PROVENCAL GETAWAY VACATIONS
Provence, France; Tuscany, Italy
Sponsor: Cooking instructor Eileen Dwillies. Programs: Open-ended participation vacations in a restored 17th century house, B&B format. Established: 1994. Class/group size: 4-5. 7 programs/yr. Facilities: Home-style kitchen. Also featured: Daily tours of outdoor markets, vintners caves, artists' workshops, olive mills. FACULTY: Eileen Dwillies, author of 9 cookbooks, has taught cooking for 20 yrs & is a former food editor & TV show host. COSTS: $250/day, all inclusive. $50/day for B&B with optional cooking classes, each $60. CONTACT: Eileen Dwillies, Provencal Getaway Vacations, 12768 Blackstock St., Maple Ridge, B.C., Canada; 604-467-8424, Fax 604-467-8424, edwillies@hotmail.com.

PROVENCE ON YOUR PLATE
Burgundy, Périgord, Provence, France; Tuscany & Umbria, Italy
Sponsor: Culinary professional Connie Barney. Programs: 7- to 10-day culinary vacation programs that include classes in contemporary & traditional dishes, winery tours, dining in fine restaurants & private homes, visits to markets & food producers, sightseeing. Established: 1993. Class/group size: 6-16. 10-12 programs/yr. Facilities: Fully-equipped kitchens in venues ranging from farmhouses to luxury hotels. Also featured: Food artisan visits, hand-made crafts.

FACULTY: Connie Barney, CCP, holder of Grand Diplome from La Varenne, former director of Roger Vergé's cooking school in Mougins, recipe consultant for Markets of Provence.
COSTS: From $2,250/8 days in a country inn to $5,250/10 days in a luxury hotel. Includes shared lodging, most meals, ground transport, planned activities.
CONTACT: Connie Barney Wilson & Andrew Wilson, Owners/Directors, Provence on Your Plate, 915 E. Blithedale, #10, Mill Valley, CA 94941; 800-449-2111, 415-389-0736, Fax 415-389-0736, connie@provenceonyourplate.com, www.provenceonyourplate.com.

RHODE SCHOOL OF CUISINE
Theoule sur Mer, France; Vorno near Lucca, Tuscany, Italy; Marrakech, Morocco
Sponsor: Private school. Programs: 7-day hands-on cooking vacation programs. Established: 1996. Class/group size: 10-14. ~45 programs/yr. Facilities: Villas with full demo kitchen, dining facilities. Also featured: Cultural excursions, dining at Michelin-star restaurants, market visits, mushroom hunting in season, activities for non-cooking guests.
FACULTY: Chefs of the regions:Frederick Riviere (France/Morocco),Giancarlo Talericco (Italy).
COSTS: $1,995-$2,995 includes lodging, meals, ground transport, planned excursions. Non-cook rate $1,795-$2,495. Luxury suites available in Tuscany.
CONTACT: Beverley Ellis, Client Services Director, Rhode School of Cuisine c/o Luxury Destinations Ltd., 3 The Street, Frensham, Surrey, England; 888-254-1070, (44) (0) 1252 790 222, Fax (44) (0) 1252 794 499, info@rhodeschoolofcuisine.com, www.rhodeschoolofcuisine.com.

TASTE OF EUROPE
Provence, France; Tuscany, Italy
Sponsor: Teachers' Travel, a travel agency focusing on special interest vacations. Programs: Five- to seven-day hands-on cooking holidays in Provence & Tuscany that focus on preparing food the old-fashioned way. Established: 1994. Class/group size: 8 max. 40 programs/yr. Facilities: Teaching kitchens with specialized cooking & baking equipment (wood-fired baking oven). Also featured: Market visits, sightseeing excursions, wine-tasting.
FACULTY: Signora Rener of La Chiusa, René Bérard of Hostellerie Bérard, Sylvie Lallemand of Les Mégalithes. All are English-speaking chefs.
COSTS: $769-$950 includes lodging, breakfast & dinner plus cooking classes.
CONTACT: Cathy Kinloch, Tour specialist, Taste of Europe, 21 St. Clair Ave. East #1003, Toronto, ON, Canada; 800-268-7229, 416-922-2232, Fax 416-922-8410, teacherstravel@cs.com, www.taste-of-europe.com.

TASTING PLACES
France, Greece, Italy, Spain, Thailand, UK
Sponsor: Culinary travel company. Programs: 1-wk hands-on cookery courses & holidays focusing on regional cuisine. Master classes at notable London restaurants. Food & wine tours. Established: 1992. Class/group size: 12-16. 30+ programs/yr. Facilities: Stately homes, Palazzi, country houses with well-equipped kitchens, including pizza ovens & open fire cooking. Restaurant kitchens in London. Also featured: Wine tastings, visits to markets, vineyards & fine restaurants, customized trips.
FACULTY: Restaurateurs, chefs & cookery writers Alastair Little, Carla Tomasi, Maxine Clark, Thane Prince, Hugo Arnold, Franco Taruschio, Peter Gordon. Notable London restaurant chefs.
COSTS: Trips from £1,200 ($1,650), which includes lodging, meals, wine, excursions. London master classes £120-£200.
CONTACT: Sara Schwartz or Sarah Robson, Tasting Places, Unit 108, Buspace Studios, Conlan St., London, England; (44) (0) 207-460-0077, Fax (44) (0) 207-460-0029, ss@tastingplaces.com, www.tastingplaces.com. USA: 877-695-2469.

TRAVELS WITH TASTE
France; Great Britain; Italy; Spain
Sponsor: Travel professional Mariann Vandenberg. Programs: Personalized trip planning with emphasis on cuisine, the arts & gardens. Established: 1998. Class/group size: 10. 4 programs/yr.

FACULTY: Mariann Vandenberg, CTC, has 20 yrs experience planning group travel for art, garden, & culinary groups. Local cooking instructors.

COSTS: $2,500+.

CONTACT: Mariann Vandenberg, CTC, Travels With Taste, 5921 W. 88th Terr., Overland Park, KS 66207; 913-648-0858, Fax 913-649-2288, Travelberg@aol.com, Travels-With-Taste.com.

VANTAGGIO TOURS
Cannes, France; Chianti, Tuscany, S. Pietro Felletto, Italy; Marrakech, Morocco

Sponsor: Travel company. Programs: 1-week travel programs that feature cooking classes, visits to markets, wineries, farms, churches, cultural sites. Established: 1998. Class/group size: 12 max. Facilities: Restaurant kitchens & Il Faè Cooking Center. Also featured: Hands-on classes.

FACULTY: Marco Fatorell, chef for Il Faè.

COSTS: $1400-$2,850/wk, includes shared first-class lodging or bed/breakfast inn.

CONTACT: Margot Cushing, CTC, Principal, Vantaggio Tours c/o Linden Travel Bureau, 41 E. 57th St., New York, NY 10022; 800-808-6237 x259, 212-784-0259, Fax 212-421-2790, mcushing@lindentravel.com, www.vantaggio.com.

FRANCE

A LA BONNE COCOTTE EN PROVENCE
Provence

Sponsor: Culinary professional Lydie Marshall. Programs: 5-day cooking vacations that include classes & sightseeing. Established: 1971. Class/group size: 6-8. 6 programs/yr. Facilities: Large country kitchen, outdoor terrace for dining. Also featured: B&B facilities.

FACULTY: Lydie Marshall, author of Cooking with Lydie Marshall, Passion for my Provence (chez Nous), & Braises & Casseroles.

COSTS: $2,200 including lodging in Lydie Marshall's small chateau.

CONTACT: Lydie P. Marshall, A La Bonne Cocotte en Provence, Chateau Feodal, Nyons, 26110 France; (33) 475-26-45-31, Fax (33) 475-26-09-31, ciboulette@juno.com, www.Lydiemarshall.com.

ABM FRENCH COOKING COURSES
Montpellier

Sponsor: Private education institution & vocational training company. Programs: 7-day cooking vacation program featuring 4 cooking classes & culinary excursions; 7-day wine program with 12 hrs of wine courses & wine excursions. Established: 1996. Class/group size: 6-8. 6 programs/yr. Facilities: Professional kitchen in an inn close to Montpellier. Professional wine tasting equipment. Also featured: French language courses may be combined with cooking or wine classes.

FACULTY: Chefs, restaurateurs, oenologists, wine growers.

COSTS: Cooking course €810, wine course €700.Lodging available in a 3- or 2-star hotel or residential hotel (one-room flat or apartment).

CONTACT: Anaïs Baurens, Director, ABM, 23 avenue Saint Lazare, Parc des Roses D, Montpellier, 34000 France; (33) 4 67 02 75 00, Fax (33) 4 67 02 76 00, info@abm-france.com, www.abm-france.com.

THE ASSOCIATION CUISINE & TRADITION (ACT)
Arles

Sponsor: Private school. Programs: Evening, full-day, weekend, half- & full-week hands-on programs that feature seasonal ingredients. Established: 1996. Class/group size: 4-8. 12 programs/yr. Facilities: Traditional Provencal kitchen outfitted with professional equipment for teaching. Also featured: Half- & full-wk programs include excursions such as market visits, winery tours, herb collecting, visits to an olive oil mill, cheese maker, honey collector & bakery.

FACULTY: Erick Vedel, author of l'Archeologie de la Cuisine, member IACP; Madeleine Vedel.

COSTS: €100/eve class, €180/full-day, €750/4 days, €1,200/full wk. Lodging at school available, €65/night; hotels within walking distance.

CONTACT: Madeleine Vedel, Co-owner, The Association Cuisine & Tradition, 30, rue Pierre Euzeby, Arles, 13200 France; (33) (0)4-90-49-69-20, Fax (33) (0)4-90-49-69-20, actvedel@wanadoo.fr, www.cuisineprovencale.com.

BASQUE CUISINE
Biarritz
Sponsor: Private school. Programs: 3- to 6-day cooking vacations that feature hands-on cookery sessions, trips to local markets, vineyards, cheese producers & culinary landmarks. Established: 2001. Class/group size: 2-8. 38 programs/yr. Facilities: Well-equipped new kitchen. Also featured: Golf, surfing, walks in the Pyrenees, horseback riding, white water rafting, fishing, sightseeing, tennis. FACULTY: Cordon Bleu-trained chef with 20+ yrs experience & an intl chef with 30+ yrs experience. COSTS: €900/3 days, €1,800/6 days includes meals & planned activities. CONTACT: Stephen & Carolyn Harrington, Basque Cuisine, 551 Chemin D'Aguerria, Ahetze, 64210 France; (33) 559 418187, info@basquecuisine.com, www.basquecuisine.com.

CHATEAU COUNTRY COOKING COURSE
Montbazon-en-Touraine
Sponsor: Denise Olivereau-Capron & her children. Programs: 6-day participation courses. Established: 1986. Class/group size: 8-12. 3-6 programs/yr. Facilities: The chateau's renovated kitchen, dining rooms, 15-hectare park, swimming pool, tennis court. Also featured: Dining at fine restaurants & visits to chateaux, goat cheese farm, Chinon market, caves of Vouvray with wine tasting. FACULTY: Chef Freddy LeFebvre. COSTS: Course fee of 12,500 FF single, 11,500 FF double, includes chateau lodging, meals, wine tastings, planned excursions. Complimentary stay for 8 paying guests. CONTACT: Denise, Anne & Xavier Olivereau-Capron, Owners, Chateau Country Cooking Course, Montbazon en Touraine, 37250 France; (33) (0)247-34-35-00, Fax (33) (0)247-65-95-70, domaine.tortiniere@wanadoo.fr, www.tortiniere.com. Additional contact: Xavier Olivereau, Mona Augis.

CHATEAU MEYRE COOKING SCHOOL
Bordeaux
Programs: 5-day Masterchef Adventures featuring French cooking classes, food & wine pairing, vineyard tours & tastings, fine dining. Class/group size: 10 max. Also featured: Wine tour programs. FACULTY: Well-known local chef. COSTS: $2,500. Includes 5 days lodging at Chateau Meyre. Single supplement $200. CONTACT: Sophie Viterale, Chateau Meyre Cooking School, 908B, Lippo Centre, Tower 2, 89 Queensway, Hong Kong; (852) 2918 9492, Fax (852) 2521 2626, michael@winebond.com, www.winebond.com.

CHOCOLATE WALKS PARIS
Paris
Sponsor: Pastry chef, chocolatier & tour guide. Programs: Full-day custom tours concentrating on chocolate, confectionery & pastry shops in Paris. May include visits to restaurant equipment & pastry supply shops. Established: 2001. Class/group size: 1-12. Also featured: Includes 1-wk culinary tours with Anne Block of Take My Mother Please. FACULTY: David Lebovitz, author of Room for Dessert & The Great Book of Chocolate, attended Callebaut College in Belgium & Ecole Lenôtre in Paris. Former Chez Panisse pastry chef. COSTS: €150/day. CONTACT: David Lebovitz, Chocolate Walks Paris, Paris, France; E-mail david@davidlebovitz.com, www.davidlebovitz.com.

COOK IN FRANCE WITH LES LIAISONS DELICIEUSES
France, Canada, Morocco
Sponsor: Culinary tour company. Programs: 1-wk vacations in different provinces that include 12 hrs of hands-on cooking instruction. Established: 1994. Class/group size: 8-10. 10-20 programs/yr.

Facilities: Hotel & restaurant kitchens with individual workspaces. Also featured: Visits to wineries, food producers, markets, & restaurants, sightseeing, hiking & biking. Custom trips.
FACULTY: Founder Patricia Ravenscroft is tour director & translator. Classes are taught by Michelin-star restaurant chefs & proprietors.
COSTS: $1,790-$4,990, includes lodging, meals. Lodging: Hotel Les Pyrenees (Basque), L'Auberge de la Truffe (Dordogne), Auberge La Feniere (Provence), Chateau d-Amondans (Jura), Chateau St. Paterne (Normandy), Bastide St. Antoine (Côte d'Azur).
CONTACT: Patricia R. Ravenscroft, Program Founder & Director, Cook in France with Les Liaisons Delicieuses, 4710 - 30th St. N.W., Washington, DC 20008; 877-966-1810, 202-966-1810, Fax 202-966-4091, info@cookfrance.com, www.cookfrance.com.

COOKERY LESSONS IN THE SOUTH-WEST OF FRANCE
Bordeaux & Saint Emilion
Sponsor: French chef Stéphane Brieff. Programs: French cooking lessons of a few hours to gastronomic holidays up to one week. Holidays feature wine-tasting, market visits & excursions. Class/group size: 2-12. Facilities: The Châteaux's traditional family kitchens. Also featured: Swimming, fishing, forest walks. Vineyards, wineries, golf course & horseback riding nearby.
FACULTY: Stéphane Brieff, French chef with 10 yrs experience. Classes available in English & French.
COSTS: €700-€2,000 includes lodging, meals, planned activities.
CONTACT: Stéphane Brieff, Cookery Lessons in the South West of France, 1 Chemin des Bouvreuils, Saint Médard d'Eyrans, 33650 France; (33) 05 56 72 68 09, stephane.brieff@wanadoo.fr, www.classicfrenchcookinginbordeaux.com.

COOKERY LESSONS & TOURAINE VISIT
Brehemont
Sponsor: Maxime & Eliane Rochereau in the 18th-century Le Castel de Bray et Monts. Programs: 1-wk hands-on vacation programs that include morning instruction & afternoon tours of chateaux, visits to wineries, shopping excursions. Established: 1983. Class/group size: 2-8. 32 programs/yr. Facilities: The manor's restaurant kitchen.
FACULTY: Chef Maxime Rochereau, former executive chef at the Ritz Carlton in Chicago.
COSTS: $1,660 includes lodging at the manor, meals, wine, planned activities.
CONTACT: Maxime Rochereau, Cookery Lessons & Touraine Visit, Brehemont, Langeais, 37130 France; (33) (0)247-96-70-47, Fax (33) (0)247-96-57-36, cooking-class-infrance@wanadoo.fr, www.cooking-class-infrance.com.

COOKINFRANCE
Sarlat
Sponsor: Culinary professional Fred Fisher. Programs: 1- & 2-day classes & 5-day cooking vacations that focus on classic & contemporary French & international cuisines. Includes visits to chateaux & food related venues. Established: 2002. Class/group size: 8. 30 programs/yr. Facilities: Fully equipped kitchen with workstations & central island for food prep. Also featured: Visits to chateaux, food-related venues, wine caves & distilleries.
FACULTY: Chef Fred Fisher has appeared on BBC Masterchef & worked with TV chefs Rick Stein, Alastair Little & Tony Tobin. He ran Wine&Dine, which provided home dinners, wine tastings & cooking demos.
COSTS: £645 (€975/$1,165)/5-day course includes lodging & some meals.
CONTACT: Fred Fisher, Cookinfrance, Bombel, St. Amand de Coly, Montignac, 24290 France; (33) 553 302405, enquiries@cookinfrance.com, www.cookinfrance.com.

COOKING AT THE ABBEY
Salon-de-Provence
Sponsor: The Hostellerie Abbaye de Sainte Croix resort. Programs: 3-, 4-, & 7-day vacation participation courses; afternoon classes on request. Established: 1987. Class/group size: 6-12. Facilities: Restaurant kitchen with 4 ovens & 12 work stations. Also featured: Sightseeing, vineyard visits.

FACULTY: Chef P. Morel of the Abbey's Michelin 1-star restaurant.

COSTS: €1,042/4 days, €2,020/7 days, includes most meals, lodging in the 12th-century Abbey's Roman-style rooms, planned activities. Additional afternoon class €116.

CONTACT: Catherine Bossard, Director, Cooking at the Abbey, Abbaye de Sainte Croix, Route Val-de Cuech, Salon-de-Provence, 13300 France; (33) (0)490-56-24-55, Fax (33) (0)490-56-31-12, saintecroix@relaischateaux.fr, www.relaischateaux.fr/saintecroix. US Contact: Michael Giammarella, EMI Int., Box 640713, Oakland Gardens, NY 11364-0713; 800-484-1235, #0096; 718-631-0096; Fax 718-631-0316.

COOKING COURSES IN BURGUNDY
Grancey le Chateau

Sponsor: Private cookery school & tour organizer. Programs: Hands-on short cooking courses & 1-wk gastronomic holidays featuring visits to the vineyards of Burgundy & Champagne, cultural & culinary excursions. Established: 1994. Class/group size: 10 max. 12 programs/yr. Facilities: 200-yr-old converted farmhouse with modern facilities. Also featured: Gourmet weekends in Burgundy for private groups; 1- & 2-day short courses near Canterbury, England.

FACULTY: Michel Robolin, an English-speaking French chef who ran restaurants in France, taught in the UK, France, & USA, & consults for restaurants in the UK. Penny Easton trained in England.

COSTS: From £395/4-day course including lodging, meals & planned activities, to £975/1-wk gastronomic holiday including lodging, meals, & tours to Burgundy, Champagne, Chablis, Alsace, Jura.

CONTACT: Penny Easton, Burgundy Encounters, Ltd., Garden House, Chillenden, Canterbury, Kent,England; (44) 1304-841136, cell (44) 077-88414927, Fax (44) 1304-841136, info@cookingcourses.co.uk, www.cookingcourses.co.uk.

COOKING FRANCE
Beaumont-en-Veron, Loire Valley

Sponsor: Private culinary tour company. Programs: 7-day culinary travel program that features daily cooking classes & excursions, including visits to wineries, mushroom caves, food producers, markets, sightseeing & dining in local restaurants. Established: 2003. Class/group size: 8-12. 8-10 programs/yr. Facilities: Classes & lodging are in the restored 15th Century Chateau de Tilly. Also featured: Golf, tennis, cycling, horseback riding, boating, swimming.

FACULTY: French Chef Sebastian Girardeau, who has worked in Michelin-starred restaurants & is part of his family's catering business.

COSTS: $3,395 includes lodging, most meals, & planned activities.

CONTACT: Howard or Carol Wertheim, Directors, Cooking France, P.O. Box 7963, Newport Beach, CA 92658; 949-435-4000 or 800-705-6040, Fax 949-717-7554, cookingfrance@cox.net, www.cookingfrance.com.

COOKING WITH FRIENDS IN FRANCE
Chateauneuf de Grasse *(See display ad page 281)*

Sponsor: Vacation school on the property once shared by Julia Child & Simone Beck. Programs: 6-day participation courses. Established: 1993. Class/group size: 8. 28-30 programs/yr. Also featured: Visits to the Forville Market, a butcher shop, cheese ripener, cutlery shop, & Michelin 2-star restaurant kitchens; demo by a French chef.

FACULTY: Proprietor/instructor Kathie Alex apprenticed at Roger Vergé's Le Moulin de Mougins, assisted well-known chefs at the Robert Mondavi Winery, studied catering at Ecole Lenotre, & studied with & assisted Simone Beck at her school.

COSTS: ~$2,350 includes shared lodging (most with pvt baths), breakfasts, lunches, cheese tastings, planned excursions (car required). Lodging at La Pitchoune or La Campanette, private homes formerly owned by Julia Child & Simone Bec.

CONTACT: Kathie Alex, Owner, Cooking with Friends in France, 696 San Ramon Valley Blvd., #102, Danville, CA 0; 800-236-9067 (US), (33) 493-60-10-56 (France), Fax (33) 493-60-05-56, info@cookingwithfriends.com, www.cookingwithfriends.com.

Cooking with Friends in France

Come cook with us in Julia Child's former Provence kitchen! This week-long cultural immersion includes classes in English given by French chefs, most meals, market/village tours, restaurant visits, and accommodations. Afternoons free to explore the French Riviera.

(800) 236.9067 • *www.cookingwithfriends.com*

COOKING IN PROVENCE
Crillon le Brave

Sponsor: Hostellerie de Crillon le Brave, member of Relais & Chateaux. Programs: 5-day/6 night hands-on cooking vacation courses. Established: 1992. Class/group size: 8. 4 programs/yr. Facilities: The hotel's restaurant kitchen. Also featured: Market visits, winery tour, truffle hunting, visits to Avignon & other Provence sites, dining at the hotel & fine restaurants, golf, tennis, cycling, hiking.

FACULTY: Chef de Cuisine Philippe Monti, a native of Provence, trained at Pic, l'Esperance, Auberge de l'Ill, & Taillevent, plus 2 other members of his brigade. Classes taught in English.

COSTS: $2,800 ($3,200) includes meals, shared (single) lodging at Hostellerie de Crillon le Brave, planned excursions; supplement for non-cooking partners is $1,300.

CONTACT: Valérie Mansis, Cooking in Provence, Place de l'Eglise, Crillon le Brave, 84410 France; (33) (0)490-65-61-61, Fax (33) (0)490-65-62-86, crillonbrave@relaischateaux.fr, www.crillonlebrave.com.

DISCOVER FRANCE
France

Sponsor: Tour operator specializing in activity tours in France. Programs: 5- to 8-day cooking programs that feature regional cooking classes, restaurant dining, market visits. Some offer optional truffle hunt. 7-day Bordeaux wine tour. Established: 1994. Class/group size: 6-10. 5-10 programs/yr. Facilities: French manors with teaching kitchens. Wine programs held in wineries & wine houses. Also featured: Bicycling, walking, sightseeing, historical visits, countryside drives.

FACULTY: Master Chefs & Certified Wine Experts.

COSTS: $750-$2,000 includes lodging & breakfast; some may include lunch or dinner.

CONTACT: K Moore, Sales, Discover France, 8690 E. Via de Ventura, S-220, Scottsdale, AZ 85258; 480-905-1235, 800-960-2221 (toll-free within U.S.), Fax 480-905-1307, sales@discoverfrance.com, www.discoverfrance.com.

ÉCOLE LENÔTRE
Plaisir Cedex

Sponsor: French gastronomy school. Programs: 2- to 4-day participation courses for amateur cooks. Established: 1970. Class/group size: 12.

FACULTY: 4 instructors are recipients of the Meilleur Ouvrier de France. Founded by Gaston Lenôtre & managed by Marcel Derrien, Meilleur Ouvrier de France in pastry-confectionery.

CONTACT: Marie-Anne Dufeu, École Lenôtre, 40, rue Pierre Curie-BP 6, Plaisir Cedex, 787373 France; (33) (0)1-30-81-46-34, Fax (33) (0)1-30-54-73-70, ecole@lenotre.fr, www.lenotre.fr.

ÉCOLE RITZ-ESCOFFIER
Paris

Sponsor: Private school in the Ritz Paris. Programs: 1-week hands-on theme & pastry courses, half-day workshops, demos Monday & Thursday afternoons. Established: 1988. Class/group size: 10 hands-on/40 demo. Facilities: 2,000-sq-ft custom-designed facility includes a main kitchen, pastry kitchen, conference room/library, changing rooms. Also featured: Wine tastings, children's

courses, custom-designed programs for groups.
FACULTY: 4 full-time. School Director Jean-Philippe Zahm.
COSTS: Demos 45.75€, themed courses start at 488€/3 days, Art of French Pastry course 885€/wk, César Ritz course 915€/wk, César Ritz Escoffier course 5336€/6 wks. Lodging packages available.
CONTACT: M. Jean-Philippe Zahm, Director, Ecole Ritz-Escoffier, 15, Place Vendôme, Paris Cedex 01, 75041 France; (33) (0)143-16-30-50, Fax (33) (0)1-43-16-31-50, ecole@ritzparis.com, www.ritzparis.com.

ÉCOLE DES TROIS PONTS
Roanne *(See display ad above)*
Sponsor: French cooking & language institute in a château. Programs: 1-wk courses include: French Country Cooking courses in English, French Pastry, French & Cooking, Wine & Gastronomy. Features 4 afternoon hands-on cooking or pastry classes, 3 morning market visits with guided excursion, optional wine course. Established: 1991. Class/group size: 10. 14 programs/yr. Facilities: Classes, meals & lodging in the Château. Also featured: Cooking-only option (instruction in English), French & Cooking option. AlsoGeneral, Intensive & Private French instruction.
FACULTY: Chef Jean-Marc Villard for French Country Cooking, Meilleur Ouvrier de France Chef Alain Berne for Pastry. Wine grower Simon Hawkins for Wine.
COSTS: €1,190-€1,340 for Cooking or Pastry course, €1,390-€1,540 for Cooking or Pastry & French course. Includes single or twin room with private facilities &meals. Pool, tennis, equestrian center nearby.
CONTACT: Mr. René Dorel, Ms. Valérie Perez, Director & Course Coordinator, Ecole des Trois Ponts, Château de Mâtel, Roanne, 42300 France; (33) 477-71-53-00, Fax (33) 477-70-80-01, info@3ponts.edu, www.3ponts.edu.

FAMOUS PROVENCE
Goult, Luberon
Sponsor: Chef Patrick Payet. Programs: One-week cooking vacations that include daily hands-on classes preparing 3-course menus, guided tours, visits to markets & food producers. Established: 1998. Class/group size: 4-6. ~15 programs/yr. Facilities: Restaurant kitchen.
FACULTY: Patrick Payet, owner-chef of Restaurant 'Le Tonneau'.
COSTS: $1,900 includes continental breakfasts & 6-course dinners, lodging in an 18th-century house restored by Patrick Payet, & daily guided tours.
CONTACT: Patrick Payet, Owner, Famous Provence, Place de l'Ancienne Mairie, Goult, 84220 France; (33) (0)4-90-72-22-35, Fax (33) (0)4-90-72-22-35, famous.provence@wanadoo.fr, www.famous-provence.com.

A FOOD & WINE LOVERS TOUR OF FRANCE
Seven regions; Rioja & Ribera del Duero, Spain
Sponsor: Travel company specializing in wine & gourmet food tours. Programs: 1-2 week vacations that feature private tastings at wineries, cooking classes, visits to artisanal food producers,

dining at Michelin-star restaurants, winemaker dinners. Established: 1978. Class/group size: 14. 1 programs/yr. Facilities: Michelin-star restaurants, professional kitchens, wineries. Also featured: Visits to historical & cultural sites, outdoor food markets, tours of celebrity chefs' kitchens. **FACULTY:** Dr. June Forkner-Dunn & Toby Dunn, members of the SWE & AIWF. June has guided groups to Europe since 1978, taught wine classes at the Univ of London & American Embassy in Paris. Toby is a wine collector. **COSTS:** $3,189-$4,179 includes lodging in chateaux, villas & castle hotels, meals, planned activities. **CONTACT:** June Forkner-Dunn, Wine-Knows Travel, 4382 Bridgeview Dr., Oakland, CA 94602; 510-336-0303, Fax 510-336-0303, dunn@wineknowstravel.com, www.wineknowstravel.com.

FRANCE CRUISES
Paris, Burgundy & Provence
Sponsor: Provider of French barge vacations. Programs: 1-wk canal barge cruises featuring wine & cooking instruction. Established: 2000. Class/group size: 6-14. 10 programs/yr. Facilities: The Hotel Barge La Luciole. Also featured: Wine tastings, excursions, cooking class at the Michelin 3-star Cote Saint Jacques restaurant, 2 nights at the 3-star Hotel des Tuileries in Paris. **COSTS:** $3,200 includes lodging, meals, excursions. **CONTACT:** Jean Dabrowski, France Cruises, 5700 Collins Ave., #16N, Miami Beach, FL 33140; 866-498-3920, Fax 707-215-6811, info@francecruises.com, www.francecruises.com/Culinary.htm.

FRANCE THROUGH THE KITCHEN DOOR
Chinon; Skagit Valley, WA
Sponsor: Chef Sally McArthur. Programs: Week-long culinary programs at a Loire Valley chateau that include 5 hands-on cooking classes. French-themed cooking courses in Washington state. Established: 2004. Class/group size: 12. 4 in Loire programs/yr. Facilities: The 15th century Chateau du Rivau's newly restored kitchen & remodelled facilities. Also featured: Include bistro & restaurant dining, excursions to local food market, asparagus farm, walnut mill, chateaus, patisseries & ceramic atelier. **FACULTY:** Sally McArthur, formerly exec chef for noted Seattle restaurants, is an Intl Director of les Dames d'Escoffier. She was selected to cook for President Clinton & his re-election team & represented Washington State at NYC's James Beard House. **COSTS:** $2,950 includes shared lodging at the Chateau, meals, excursions. **CONTACT:** Sally McArthur, France Through the Kitchen Door, P.O. Box 15618, Seattle, WA 98115; 206-522-8678, sally@frenchchefsally.com, www.frenchchefsally.com. jood@frenchchefsally.com.

FRANÇOISE MEUNIER'S KITCHEN
Paris
Sponsor: Culinary professional. Programs: Hands-on classes featuring preparation of French meal; diploma after 20 classes. Established: 1997. Class/group size: 8-10. Facilities: Modern, purpose-designed kitchen. Also featured: Demos for groups of 12-15, visits to food markets, young people's workshops, private lessons. **FACULTY:** Françoise Meunier worked in luxury hotel kitchens. She teaches in French & English. **COSTS:** €90/class, €400/5 classes. **CONTACT:** Françoise Meunier's Kitchen, 7, rue Paul-Lelong, Paris, 75002 France; 33 (0) 1 40 26 14 00, Fax 33 (0) 1 40 26 14 08, cuisine@fmeunier.com, www.fmeunier.com.

FRENCH COOKING CLASSES – A WEEK IN PROVENCE
Nyons, Provence
Sponsor: Private owners. Programs: 5-day cooking vacations featuring hands-on classes, cultural excursions, meal with French family, wine tour/tasting, visits to artisans/craftsmen & open air market. Established: 1999. Class/group size: 10 max. 4 programs/yr. Facilities: Restored & fully-equipped Provencal farm kitchen with 6 burner gas stove, work tables with bar stools. Also featured: Hiking, cycling, swimming, horseback riding. **FACULTY:** Chef Daniel Bonnot, trained in France. Experience includes London's Savoy Hotel, Chef

Saucier at La Caravelleat in Guadeloupe. His Bizou was named one of the 10 Best New Restaurants in the U.S. by Esquire magazine.
Costs: $2,400 includes shared lodging at the farmhouse, most meals. $200 for optional pick-up/return to Montelimar.
Contact: Anne Reinauer, Owner, French Cooking Classes - A Week in Provence, 813 Shell Beach Dr., Lake Charles, LA 70601; 337-436-4422, Fax 337-310-3726, david@lakecharlescommercial.com, FrenchCookingClasses.com.

THE FRENCH KITCHEN IN GASCONY
Gascony
Sponsor: Culinary professional Kate Hill. Programs: 5-day cooking vacation programs that include hands-on classes in the cuisine of Southwest France, wine tastings, market shopping & culinary excursions. Established: 1987. Class/group size: 8 max. 30+ programs/yr. Facilities: 18th-century stone farmhouse kitchen/atelier, traditional French cooking equipment.
Faculty: Kate Hill, author of A Culinary Journey in Gascony, has lived in Southwest France since 1988. Local chef instructors include Madame Pompele of Creperie Vetou.
Costs: €2,450-€3,250 (payable in dollars) includes lodging with private bath, meals, local transport, planned activities.
Contact: Kate Hill, The French Kitchen Cooking School at Camont, 5 Ledgewood Way, #6, Peabody, MA 1960; 800-852-2625, 978-535-5738, Fax 978-535-5738, info@thefrenchkitchen.com, www.thefrenchkitchen.com. In France: 'Camont', 47310 Ste. Colombe-en-Bruilhois, Laplume, France.

FRENCH WINE EXPLORERS
Avignon
Sponsor: American wine & culinary tour company operating in France. Programs: Week-long program that includes hands-on Provençal cooking classes, wine & food pairing, winery visits, & wine, cheese & olive oil tastings. Established: 1998. Class/group size: 12 max. 2+ private programs/yr. Facilities: Professional kitchen/classroom. Also featured: Antiquing, shopping, sightseeing, dinners at fine local restaurants.
Faculty: Chef Edouard Loubet, chef & restaurant-owner Raoul Reichrath & Robert Brunel, certified sommeliers Jean-Pierre Sollin & Lauriann Greene-Sollin.
Costs: $3,995 includes 7 nights lodging, most meals, local transport, tastings, sightseeing.
Contact: Lauriann Greene-Sollin, Sommelier-Conseil, Company President, French Wine Explorers, 4799 Coconut Creek Pkwy, #112, Coconut Creek, FL 33063; 877-261-1500, Fax 253-423-5316, info@cooking-wine-provence.com, www.cooking-wine-provence.com. www.wine-tours-france.com, info@wine-tours-france.com.

FUGUES EN FRANCE
Burgundy, Bordeaux, Champagne, Provence, Alsace
Sponsor: French specialty tour operator. Programs: 1- to 15-day customized gourmet & French vineyard wine tours. Established: 1994. 20 programs/yr. Facilities: Wineries & cooking schools. Also featured: Corporate programs.
Faculty: Wine experts & noted chefs.
Contact: Catherine Thevenin, Director, Fugues En France, 11 square Jean Cocteau, St Germain Les Corbeil, 91250 France; (33) (0) 1 60 75 89 16, Fax (33) (0) 1 60 75 89 16, fugues@club-internet.fr, www.bonappetit-france.com.

GEORGEANNE BRENNAN'S HAUTE PROVENCE
Aups
Sponsor: Culinary professional Georgeanne Brennan. Programs: 1-wk culinary vacations that include daily hands-on instruction, visits to local markets, artisan cheese makers, honey makers, wineries & market gardens. Established: 2000. Class/group size: 7. 8 programs/yr. Facilities: The farm kitchen of a restored 17th-century convent. Also featured: Herb & vegetable gathering, private Provencal music concerts, visit to eco-museum of Haute Provence & the Museum of

Prehistory of the Gorge du Verdon, sightseeing, visit to potter's studio.
FACULTY: Teacher & cookbook author Georgeanne Brennan is recipient of a James Beard, Julia Child, & International Versailles Cookbook Award & has had a home in Provence for 30 yrs. She is a jury member of Slow Food & a member of the IACP.
COSTS: $2,750 includes lodging in the convent, all meals, accompanied trips, pick-up & return to Nice, ground transport.
CONTACT: Georgeanne Brennan, Georgeanne Brennan's Haute Provence, PO Box 502, Winters, CA 95694; 530-795-3043, Fax 530-795-4190, gbrennan@yolo.com, www.georgeannebrennan.com.

A GOURMET CONNECTION
Morance
Sponsor: Cookery school. Programs: 6-day program in France featuring hands-on cookery classes, wine tasting, visits near Lyon/Beaujolais. Established: 2001. Class/group size: 4-12. 10 programs/yr. Facilities: Chateau kitchen facilities.
FACULTY: Guy Chanudet has worked in Michelin-starred restaurants & as a hotel Executive Chef.
COSTS: $2,570 ($2,870) includes shared (single) lodging, meals, ground transport, visits.
CONTACT: Guy Chanudet, Chef/Owner, A Gourmet Connection, L'etang, St Etienne Sur Chalaronne, France; (33) (0)4 74 24 04 76, Fax (33) (0)4 74 24 05 31, contact@agourmetconnection.com, www.agourmetconnection.com.

HOLIDAYS IN THE SUN IN THE SOUTH OF FRANCE
Gordes
Sponsor: Les Megalithes school in a private country home. Programs: 1-wk participation courses with instruction in English, French, & German. Established: 1980. Class/group size: 6. 17 programs/yr. Facilities: Indoor & outdoor home kitchen. Also featured: Market visits, horseback & bicycle riding, handicraft shopping, visits to museums & historic sites.
FACULTY: Sylvie Lallemand, president/founder of Assn des amis de la cuisine, learned to cook from her mother & studied with Roger Vergé; author of Enchanted Provence.
COSTS: €670 includes lodging & most meals.
CONTACT: Sylvie Lallemand, Les Megalithes, Gordes, 84220 France; (33) (0)490-72-23-41.

AT HOME WITH PATRICIA WELLS
Provence & Paris
Sponsor: Author Patricia Wells. Programs: 5-day hands-on cooking vacations. 4-day truffle workshops. Established: 1995. Group size: 6-10. Facilities: Darmhouse kitchen with wood-fired oven. Paris cooking studio with the latest equipment. Also featured: Visits to markets & food-related sites.
FACULTY: Patricia Wells has lived in France since 1980, is restaurant critic of The International Herald Tribune, & author of 9 books, including Bistro Cooking & The Provence Cookbook.
COSTS: $3,500 includes meals & planned activities
CONTACT: Judith Jones, At Home with Patricia Wells, 708 Sandown Pl., Raleigh, NC 27615; Fax 919-845-9031, cookingclasses@patriciawells.com, www.patriciawells.com.

LA COMBE EN PÉRIGORD
Dordogne
Sponsor: Private cooking school at La Combe, an 18th-century French manor house. Programs: 8-day cooking programs include hands-on classes, visits to farmers' markets, vineyards, & food artisans; dining in restaurants ranging from farmhouse cuisine to Michelin 2-star. Established: 1998. Class/group size: 8. 18 programs/yr. Facilities: 400 sq-ft French country kitchen with imported American & European appliances. Seating & work spaces for 12. Also featured: Antiqueing, canoeing, cycling, horseback riding, shopping for housewares, visiting historic caves & castles.
FACULTY: Noted culinary professionals including Stephanie Alexander, Catherine Bell, Lora Brody, Marieke Brugman, Barbara Pool Fenzl, Diane Holuigue, Cheryl Jamison, Paula Lambert, Louise Lamensdorf, Sara Monick, Betty Rosbottom, Marie Simmons, Beverley Sprague.
COSTS: $3,000-$3,500 includes shared lodging, meals, scheduled activities, ground transport.

CONTACT: La Combe en Périgord, 3450 Sacramento St., #436, San Francisco, CA 94118; 888-LACOMBE (415-673-0429), Fax 888-522-6623, 415-673-0429, info@lacombe-perigord.com, www.lacombe-perigord.com. In France: Wendely Harvey, La Combe, 24620 Les Eyzies, France; (33) 5-53-35-17-61, Fax (33) 5-53-35-25-64, wendelyh@ctanet.fr.

LA CUISINE DE MARIE-BLANCHE
Paris

Sponsor: Culinary professional Marie-Blanche de Broglie (formerly Princess Ere 2001). Programs: 1- to 4-week participation courses with instruction in French, English, or Spanish. Established: 1975. Class/group size: 6-8. 10 programs/yr. Facilities: 50-sq-meter kitchen, 40 sq-meter lecture room for slides. Also featured: Discovering French Style for groups; French Cheeses, French Pastry & Tasting. A Gastronomic Tour of France: French wines, table setting, candlelight dinner, visit to a Parisian market.

FACULTY: Marie-Blanche de Broglie, founder & director, is author of The Cuisine of Normandy & A La Table des Rois.

COSTS: 1 class 760FF, 5 classes 3,010FF, 10 classes 5,510FF, 3 pastry classes 1,760FF, The Little Pastry Chef 150FF, 1-wk course in (Cooking) l'Art de Vivre (5,500FF) 4,500FF, 1 class 1,500FF, Grand Diplome 19,500FF, Le Diplome 45,000FF.

CONTACT: Marie-Blanche de Broglie, La Cuisine de Marie-Blanche, 18 Ave. de la Motte-Picquet, Paris, 75007 France; (33) (0)145-51-36-34, Fax (33) (0)145-51-90-19, infocmb@CuisineMB.com, www.CuisineMB.com/index.htm.

LA CUISINE DE SAVOIE
Albertville

Sponsor: Hotel Restaurant Million. Programs: 6-day participation courses featuring cooking lessons, visits to market, escargot farm, foie gras & cheese producers, vineyards; wine tastings, dinners in homes & restaurants, local trips. Established: 1999. Class/group size: 8. 4-8 programs/yr. Facilities: Professional restaurant kitchen. Also featured: Custom-designed programs including cycling tours, wine tours, artists' & photography groups.

FACULTY: Chef Jose DeAnacleto, Betsy Jane Clary, Ph.D., professional staff of Restaurant Million.

COSTS: $2,295 ($2,495) includes shared (single) lodging at Hotel Million, meals, planned excursions. Supplement for non-cooking partner is $1,295 & includes lodging & meals.

CONTACT: La Cuisine de Savoie, P.O. Box 21570, Charleston, SC 29413; Fax 843-577-2720, cuisinesavoie@att.net, www.lacuisinedesavoie.com. In France: Hotel Million, 8 Place de la Liberte, 73200 Albertville, FR; http://www.hotelmillion.com.

LA VARENNE
Burgundy; White Sulphur Springs, WV

Sponsor: Private school. Programs: 5-day Master Class program (hands-on, demo, celebrity chef, wine & cheese tastings). Class/group size: 12. Facilities: The restored 17th-century Château du Feÿ, a registered historic monument owned by founder Anne Willan. Also featured: Daily excursions include wine growing regions, market & vineyard tours, dining at Michelin-starred restaurants.

FACULTY: Cookbook author Anne Willan & French guest chefs.

COSTS: $3,245 includes transport from Paris, meals, shared lodging at Château du Feÿ, planned activities. Single supplement $400.

CONTACT: La Varenne, PO Box 5840, Austin, TX 78763; 800-537-6486, info@lavarenne.com, www.lavarenne.com.

LATITUDE CULTURAL CENTER
La Toulzanie

Sponsor: Non-profit association, organized under the Loi de 1901 in France. Programs: Week-long summer culinary adventures in French & English. Course also offered in cooking French dinners. Established: 1998. Class/group size: 18 max. 10-15 programs/yr. Facilities: 14th century mill, converted tobacco hangar, pool, gardens, motor boat. Also featured: Free evening conferences on such

topics as local Quercy history, world affairs, Freud's theories. Swimming pool, fishing.
FACULTY: U.S. & French college professors & local experts, including CNRS researchers, cheese &
wine maker.
COSTS: $1,000-$1,200/wk includes lodging, most meals. Special rate for full-time students.
CONTACT: E. Barbara Phillips, Director, Latitude Cultural Center, 1043 Oxford St., Berkeley, CA
94707; 510-525-8436, barbara@latitude.org, www.latitude.org. May-Sept: LatitudeLa Toulzanie,
46330 St. Martin Labouval, France.

LE BAOU D'INFER COOKERY SCHOOL
La Mole
Programs: Five-day cookery courses with daily themes that include pasta, bread & Provençal clas-
sics. Established: 1999. Class/group size: 6 max. 10 programs/yr. Facilities: Air-conditioned studio
with demonstration area & 3 fully-equipped work stations. Also featured: Wine tasting at nearby
producers, country walks, swimming.
FACULTY: Alex Mackay, 5 yrs sous chef & director of the cookery school at Raymond Blancs Le
Manoir aux Quat Saisons; chef in Michelin-starred kitchens in France, Italy, Germany; TV series,
cookery writer.
COSTS: £1,185-£1,860 includes lodging, meals, visit to a local restaurant.
CONTACT: Peter & Diana Knab, Le Baou D'Infer Cookery School, 63 Campden Street,
London,England; (44) 2077270997, Fax (44) 2077270997, alex@lebaou.com, www.lebaou.com.

LE CORDON BLEU – PARIS
Paris   *(See also page 160) (See display ad page 161)*
Sponsor: Private school. Programs: 1/2-day to 4-day courses in French cuisine, pastry & bread-
baking, daily demos, market tours, wine seminars. (Basic, Intermediate, & Superior levels).
Established: 1895. Class/group size: 8-14 hands-on. 60+ programs/yr. Facilities: Professionally
equipped kitchens, demo rooms with video & overhead mirrors.
FACULTY: 10 full-time French Master Chefs from Michelin-starred restaurants & fine hotels.
International staff. Wine lecturers Patricia Gastaud-Gallagher & Jean-Michel Deluc.
COSTS: €29 for a half-day class, €39 for daily demos, €849-€1,200 (Food & Wine Pairing).
CONTACT: Director of Admissions, Le Cordon Bleu, 8, rue Leon Delhomme, Paris, 75015 France;
800-457-CHEF (USA & Canada), (33) (0)1-53-68-22-50, Fax (33) (0)1-48-56-03-96, paris@cor-
donbleu.edu, cordonbleu.edu.

LE MARMITON – COOKING IN PROVENCE
Avignon
Sponsor: Hotel-restaurant. Programs: 1- & 5-day participation courses. Established: 1994.
Class/group size: 12. Facilities: Restored 19th century kitchen with its original wood-fired cast-iron
stove & restored counters. Also featured: Visit to wineries, markets, sightseeing, special itineraries
can be arranged through concierge.
FACULTY: Christian Etienne, Robert Brunel, Jean-Claude Aubertin, Daniel Hébet, Frédérique Féraud.
COSTS: € 95(€ 70, €115) for an AM (PM, evening) class, €2,510 for 6 days double occupancy.
CONTACT: Martin Stein, Artist Director, Le Marmiton-Cooking in Provence, 4, place de La
Mirande, Avignon, 84000 France; (33) (0)490-85-93-93, Fax (33) (0)490-86-26-85, mirande@la-
mirande.fr, www.la-mirande.fr.

L'ECOLE DE CUISINE DU DOMAINE D'ESPERANCE
La Bastide d'Armagnac
Sponsor: 18th-century country house. Programs: 1-wk hands-on vacations that include theoretical instruction in the mornings & preparation of the evening meal in the afternoons. Established:
1993. Class/group size: 9. 6 programs/yr. Facilities: Country kitchen with 8 work areas. Also featured: Market trip, visits to nearby wine cellars.
FACULTY: Natalia Arizmendi, recipient of the Cordon Bleu Grand Diplome, has taught cooking &
pastry for 15+ yrs.She is tri-lingual in French, English, & Spanish.

Costs: $2,000 double, $2,200 single includes meals & lodging at the Domaine. Amenities include outdoor swimming pool & tennis court.

Contact: Claire de Montesquiou, L'Ecole de Cuisine du Domaine d'Esperance, Mauvezin d'Armagnac, La Bastide d'Armagnac, 40240 France; (33) (0) 558-44-85-33, Fax (33) (0) 558-44-85-33, info@esperance.fr, www.esperance.fr. In the U.S.: Judy Ebrey, Cuisine International, P.O. Box 25228, Dallas, TX 75225; 214-373-1161, Fax 214-373-1162, Email CuisineInt@aol.com, URL www.cuisineinternational.com.

L'OLMO
Catania, Sicily, Italy

Sponsor: Private estate. Programs: 7-day vacation programs that include cooking classes, dining in fine restaurants, visits to wineries & private estates. Established: 2003. Class/group size: 12-14. Facilities: The kitchen of l'Olmo. Also featured: Cultural activities, excursions to Mt. Etna, archaeological sites, & nearby cities, boat & fishing trips, water-skiing, sailing.

Faculty: Giuliana Spadaro di Passanitello, author of Notebook of Joy, a collection of Sicilian recipes, & articles on Sicilian history & culinary art.

Costs: $3,150 includes lodging, meals & planned excursions.

Contact: Alexis Magarò, l'Olmo, 11, rue Chapon, Paris, 75003 France; (33) (0) 1 48 04 54 29, Fax (33) (0) 1 48 04 54 29, alexis.magaro@mageos.com, www.lolmo.it.

LES DEUX COPINES COOKING SCHOOL
Thomirey

Sponsor: Recreational cooking school. Programs: 5-day program that includes hands-on classes in French & Burgundian cooking, wine pairings, restaurant kitchen demos. Established: 2004. Class/group size: 6. 4 programs/yr. Facilities: B&B kitchen at La Monastille. Also featured: Visits to food & wine artisans, outdoor market shopping, wine tastings, restaurant dining.

Faculty: 3 professional chefs, guest instructors.

Costs: $2,100 includes meals, lodging, local transport, excursions.

Contact: Summer Whitford, President, Chez Vous Productions, Inc./Les Deux Copines Cooking School, 9205 Weathervane Pl., Montgomery Village, MD 20886; 301-216-1182, Fax 301-216-1184, summerwhitford@msn.com, lesdeuxcopines.com.

LES PETITS FARCIS
Nice

Sponsor: Culinary professional Rosa Jackson. Programs: Half- & full-day programs that feature a market tour, hands-on cooking class & gourmet food tour. Established: 2004. Class/group size: 6 max. Year-round programs/yr. Facilities: Home kitchen in a renovated 17th-century apartment. Also featured: Food excursions to other parts of the Côte d'Azur & the back country.

Faculty: Cookbook author & Le Cordon Bleu-trained cook Rosa Jackson is bilingual (French/English), has lived in France for 10 yrs, & has been a restaurant critic & food writer for 13 yrs.

Costs: €200/half day (market tour, cooking class, lunch), €290/full day.

Contact: Rosa Jackson, Les Petits Farcis, 7 rue du Jésus, Nice, 6300 France; (33) 6 8167 4122, rosa.jackson@free.fr, www.petitsfarcis.com.

MARGUERITE'S ELEGANT HOME COOKING
Suresnes (Paris)

Sponsor: Culinary professional Muriel-Marguerite Foucher. Programs: Half-day programs featuring optional market visit, hands-on French cooking lesson, lunch. Established: 2003. Class/group size: 6 max. Year round programs/yr. Facilities: Professionally-equipped cooking station for each participant. Also featured: Team-building sessions, gourmet week-ends.

Costs: From €80.

Contact: Muriel-Marguerite Foucher, Marguerite's Elegant Home Cooking, 35 rue Rouget de Lisle, Suresnes, 92150 France; (33) (0)1 42 04 74 00, Fax (33) (0)1 42 04 74 00, marguerite@elegantcooking.com, www.elegantcooking.com.

MAS DE CORNUD
St. Remy-de-Provence

Sponsor: David & Nitockrees Carpita's cooking school in their private 18th-century Provençal farmhouse/country inn. Programs: Home Cooking in Provence, offers 5 days of participation classes, market shopping & visits to regional artisans. Established: 1993. Class/group size: 10. 2 programs/yr. Facilities: Indoor & outdoor professional teaching kitchens, wood-burning oven & grill, herb & vegetable garden, boules court, swimming pool, private property. Also featured: Wine tastings, open air village market trips, walks & shopping.

FACULTY: Nitockrees Tadros Carpita, CCP, member IACP, trained in France. She teaches in the US at Draegers, Viking & private homes.

COSTS: $2,700 includes shared lodging ($2,500 non-participant) at the 4-star Mas de Cornud, most meals, ground transport, outings. Single sessions from $130-$150.

CONTACT: David Carpita, School Administrator, Mas de Cornud, Route de Mas Blanc, St. Remy-de-Provence, 13210 France; (33) 490-92-39-32, Fax (33) 490-92-55-99, mascornud@compuserve.com, www.mascornud.com.

ON RUE TATIN, COOKING IN FRANCE WITH SUSAN LOOMIS
Louviers, Normandy

Sponsor: Culinary professional Susan Herrmann Loomis. Programs: Five-day cooking vacation program featuring hands-on cooking classes, visits to farmers markets, artisanal food producers & nearby villages. Three-day wine programs. Established: 2000. Class/group size: 8 max. 8 programs/yr. Facilities: Fully-equipped modern kitchen in a restored 15th-century convent. Also featured: Links with regional tour guides, French country lunches for groups of 6+.

FACULTY: Susan Herrmann Loomis, owner/chief instructor who has lived in France for 10 yrs, & 2 assistants, each with 7+ yrs experience in professional kitchens.

COSTS: $2,000/5-day ($1,800/3-day) cooking (wine) course includes most meals. Mother-daughter weeks $2,300/person.

CONTACT: Laiko Bahrs, U.S. Director, On Rue Tatin, 1424 Jones St. A, San Francisco, CA 94109; 415-673-4292, Fax 415-673-4292, cookingclasses@onruetatin.com, www.onruetatin.com.

PAULE CAILLAT'S PROMENADES GOURMANDES
Paris

Sponsor: Culinary professional Paule Caillat. Programs: Classes in French cuisine include visits to the food market, butcher, bakery, Dehillerin cookware store, & a spice shop. Class/group size: 7 max. Facilities: Professional-quality equipment in a home kitchen.

FACULTY: Paule Caillat is a Paris native who attended college in U.S.

COSTS: From $200 for a half-day session to $537 for two full days. Bookings a month in advance.

CONTACT: Paule Caillat, Paule Caillat's Promenades Gourmandes, 187 rue du Temple, Paris, 75003 France; (33) 1-48-04-56-84, Fax (33) 1-42-78-59-77, paule.caillat@wanadoo.fr, www.theinternationalkitchen.com/promen.htm. In the USA: The International Kitchen, Inc., 55 E. Monroe, #2840, Chicago, IL 60603; 800-945-8606, Fax 847-945-0820, info@intl-kitchen.com, http://www.intl-kitchen.com.

PROVENCAL COOKING AT LES TUILLIÈRES
Pont de Barret, Drôme Provençale *(See display ad page 290)*

Sponsor: Guest house in 17th-century mas provençal. Programs: 5-day cooking classes (M-F), advanced course in spring & fall. Established: 1995. Class/group size: 3-6. 16 programs/yr. Facilities: Newly refurbished farmhouse kitchen with up-to-date equipment, cookbook library, vegetable & herb gardens, heated pool, 40 acres of woodland & fields with stream & nature path. Also featured: Excursions to markets, wineries, goat cheese farm, potteries, medieval villages.

FACULTY: Owner Hermann Jenny, trained chef with Swiss diploma in classical French cooking, career in managing luxury hotels.

COSTS: $1,500 ($1,650, $1,200)/wk, includes double (single, triple) occupancy lodging, meals, excursions; $2,000/wk for couple with only one partner cooking. One complimentary night's stay is offered before or after cooking session.

CONTACT: Hermann & Susan Jenny, Provencal Cooking at Les Tuillieres, Les Tuillières, Pont de Barret, 26160 France; (33) 475 90 43 91, Fax (33) 475 90 43 91, h.jen@infonie.fr, www.guideweb.com/provence/gastronomie/tuillieres/indexa.html.

Cuisine Provençale

Spend a week in France in the charming setting of Hermann & Susan Jenny's Les Tuillières, a 17th-century farmhouse where you'll learn new skills in Provençale cooking. April-October, except August.

For info call/fax +33 475 90 43 91 or e-mail h.jen@infonie.fr

---

PROVENCE BONJOUR!
Grasse

Sponsor: Private family villa. Programs: 5- to 7-day theme programs, some of which include cooking lessons. Established: 2002. Class/group size: 8. 12 programs/yr. Also featured: Concerts, tastings, restaurant dining, local excursions, market visits.

FACULTY: Josette Andre, a Provence native.

COSTS: $2,800-$3,200 includes meals & lodging in a Provençal villa.

CONTACT: Josette Andre, Provence Bonjour!, 402 Washington St., Wellesley, MA 2481; 781-239-1101 or 866-PROVENCE, info@provencebonjour.com, www.provencebonjour.com.

RESTAURANT HOTEL LA COTE SAINT JACQUES
Joigny, Burgundy

Sponsor: Michelin 2-star restaurant. Programs: 3-day demo programs that feature French cuisine, market visit, wine tasting, dining in the restaurant. Some programs taught in English, others in French. Established: 1948. Class/group size: 8-15. 10 programs/yr. Also featured: Boat rides, indoor swimming pool, sauna, tennis, golf, vineyard visits.

FACULTY: Jean Michel Lorain, Chef of La Cote Saint Jacques.

COSTS: €705/wk (€865) or €765/wk-end (€940) incl standard (superior) lodging & half-board at Hotel La Cote Saint Jacques, a member of Relais & Chateaux. €165 for non-participant guest.

CONTACT: Jean-Michel Lorain, Hotel Restaurant La Côte Saint Jacques, 14, Faubourg de Paris, Joigny, 89300 France; (33) (0)3-86-62-09-70, Fax (33) (0)3-86-91-49-70, lorain@relaischateaux.fr, www.cotesaintjacques.com.

ROBERT ASH AT RUE DU LAC
Mâcon

Sponsor: Chef Robert Ash. Programs: 5-day cooking vacations that include daily classes, visits to markets & wineries, wining & dining in fine restaurants. Established: 2003. Class/group size: 6 max. 8 programs/yr. Facilities: Well-equipped teaching kitchen in a converted farmhouse. Also featured: Golf, horse-riding, canoeing, ballooning, fishing, microlight flights.

FACULTY: Robert Ash, chef-patron of London's Blythe Road Restaurant, won the Observer MasterChef competition in 1989.

COSTS: $1,660 includes meals & lodging. Non-participant guest $1,420, single supplement $775.

CONTACT: Roger Pring, Director, Robert Ash at rue du Lac, Rue du Lac, les Chalendons, St Symphorien d'Ancelles, Mâcon, 71570 France; France during courses (33) 3 85 33 86 69, info@cuisinecourse.com, www.cuisinecourse.com/. Press materials:http://www.cuisinecourse.com/press.html.

ROGER VERGÉ COOKING SCHOOL
Mougins
Sponsor: Restaurant l'Amandier. Programs: 2-hour demos from Tuesday through Saturday. Established: 1984. Class/group size: 20. 12 programs/yr. Facilities: Restaurant kitchen specially designed for classes.
FACULTY: Serge Chollet & other chefs from the Moulin de Mougins restaurant.
COSTS: €51/class, €230/5 classes.
CONTACT: Sylvie Charbit, Manager, Roger Vergé Cooking School, Restaurant l'Amandier, Mougins Village, 6250 France; (33) (0)493-75-35-70, Fax (33) (0)493-90-18-55, info@moulin-mougins.com, www.moulin-mougins.com.

ROUTAS EN PROVENCE
Chateauvert, Provence
Sponsor: Chateau in a working vineyard. Programs: One-week cooking vacation programs that include trips to local markets & villages & French language instruction. Established: 1993. Class/group size: 12 max. 2 programs/yr. Facilities: The chateau kitchen. Also featured: Visits to local markets, hiking on the property, swimming.
FACULTY: Frances Wilson, Routas Culinary Director & cooking teacher in the San Francisco Bay Area. Anne Le Masson, native French speaker & teacher at the Alliance Francais in Berkeley, CA.
COSTS: $2,500-$3,000 includes chateau lodging, meals, & planned activities.
CONTACT: Frances Wilson, Culinary Director, Routas en Provence, 1814 Addison St., Berkeley, CA 94703; 510-848-2654, ferw@onebox.com, www.franceswilson.net. In France: Rouviere Plane Sarl, Chateauvert, Bras, 83149 France; (33) 04 94 69 96 41.

SAVOUR OF FRANCE
Burgundy, Provence, Alsace, Champagne, Bordeaux; Tuscany, Italy
Sponsor: Specialty travel company. Programs: 6-day cooking & wine-tasting tours that include chateau lodging, private winery tours, dining at Michelin 3-star restaurants, visits to local producers. Established: 1995. Class/group size: 12. 15 programs/yr. Facilities: Professional chateau kitchen in Burgundy, home-style kitchen in Provence. Also featured: Mediterranean day cruise, Rhine cruise, Burgundy Canal barging, ballooning.
FACULTY: Local French chefs including Chef Vignaud of the Michelin-star Hostellerie des Clos, Burgundy; Collette Aron in Provence.
COSTS: $2,495-$3,495 includes lodging, meals, wines, ground transport, planned activities.
CONTACT: David Geen, Director, Villas & Voyages, 2450 Iroquois Ave., Detroit, MI 48214; 800-827-4635, Fax 313-331-1915, dgeen1@aol.com, www.savourfrance.com.

A TASTE OF FRANCE
Loire Valley, Paris, Provence; Tuscany, Italy; Marrakech, Morocco
Programs: 1-wk programs that include hands-on cooking classes, Michelin-star restaurant dining, market visits & excursions. Established: 1998. Class/group size: 12. Also featured: Tennis, golf, bicycling, excursions to St. Tropez, Cannes, Nice.
FACULTY: Guest Chefs include Jacques Pepin, Reine Sammut, Jean-Andre Charial, Christian Etienne, Daniel Hébet, Jean-Michael Minguella, Nito Carpita.
COSTS: $2,900-$4,900 includes lodging, meals, ground transport, excursions.
CONTACT: Kathryn Copeland, A Taste of France, 201 E. City Hall Ave., Ste. 610, Norfolk, VA 23510; 757-216-2662, Fax 757-216-2663, desiree@thetasteoffrance.com, www.thetasteoffrance.com.

A TASTE OF PROVENCE
Le Bar sur Loup *(See display ad page 290)*
Sponsor: Private cooking program. Programs: Hands-on culinary vacations in a private farmhouse in Provence. Includes a class at Roger Vergé cooking school, market visits, winery tours, sightseeing, visits to food producers & private homes. Established: 1994. Class/group size: 8. 12

programs/yr. Facilities: Provençal kitchen, swimming pool, grounds with orchards & olive groves. Also featured: Special programs on olives & olive oil, wine & food pairings; 1 day gourmet tours of Nice; 1 day market/cooking class/lunch.

FACULTY: Tricia Robinson, IACP, owner; Jeanette Locker, M.S., CFCS, professor in nutrition dept at CSU, San Luis Obispo; Jonathan Waters, sommelier of Chez Panisse restaurant in Berkeley; Nella Opperman, decorative artist.

COSTS: $2,400 includes lodging, most meals, planned activities; $350 single supplement. Special programs & guest chef weeks are higher. 1 day courses from $150.

CONTACT: Tricia Robinson, Owner, A Taste of Provence, 925 Vernal Ave., Mill Valley, CA 94941; 415-383-9439, Fax 415-383-6186, info@tasteofprovence.com, www.tasteofprovence.com.

TWO BORDELAIS
Basque country, Bordeaux & Normandy

Sponsor: Culinary professionals. Programs: 4- to 7-day culinary participation vacations. Established: 1988. Class/group size: 8-12. 6 programs/yr. Facilities: Professional kitchen of Chateau La Louviere & a small farmhouse kitchen with grilling fireplace. Also featured: Visits to chateaux, wine estates, markets, cheese shops, medieval villages, oyster beds, regional inns, local artisans.

FACULTY: Jean-Pierre Moulle, graduate of Ecole Hoteliere in Toulouse, is head chef at Chez Panisse, restaurant consultant. Bordeaux native Denise Moulle markets her family's French chateau wines in the US. Ken Hom, authority on Oriental cooking.

COSTS: $2,400-$3,400 includes lodging, meals, excursions, ground transport for classes.

CONTACT: Denise Lurton-Moulle, Owner, A Week in Bordeaux, P.O. Box 8191, Berkeley, CA 0; 510-848-8741, Fax (33) 5 57 74 98 59, jdmoulle@pacbell.net, www.twobordelais.com.

VINEYARDS & KITCHENS IN FRANCE
Provence, Burgundy, Rhone Valley, Cote d'Azur

Sponsor: Travel company specializing in culinary & vineyard programs in France. Programs: One-week culinary & wine programs that include cooking classes, vineyard visits, dining in fine restaurants. Established: 2002. Class/group size: 8-12 min. 10 programs/yr.

FACULTY: Owner/director Chuck Hornsby is a food & wine writer/educator & creator of vineyard & culinary theme programs in France.

COSTS: $2,680-$2,780 land only, all-inclusive except for two meals.

CONTACT: Chuck Hornsby, Owner/Director, Vineyards & Kitchens in France, PO Box 1151, Brattleboro, VT 05302; 866-200-8394, 802-251-6044, Fax 802-254-4436, info@vineyardsand kitchensinfrance.com, www.vineyardsandkitchensinfrance.com.

WALNUT GROVE COOKERY
Mayenne region

Sponsor: Chefs Maynard Harvey & Benedict Haines. Programs: 5-day hands-on cooking holidays in the Loire Valley. Established: 2002. Class/group size: 8. 30 programs/yr. Facilities: Professionally-equipped kitchen across the courtyard from the farmhouse; stainless steel work surfaces & oven. Also featured: 4-day stays for up to 8 people that include 6-course dinners & the services of a personal butler. Custom programs on request.

FACULTY: Maynard Harvey was chef/owner of Seland Newydd restaurant & has won gold medals in national competitions; Benedict Haines was head chef at hotel Tyddyn Llan in Snowdonia National Park.

COSTS: £895 includes shared lodging, meals, planned excursions. Single room supplement available. Non-participant guest £425.

CONTACT: Freya Harvey, Proprieter, Walnut Grove Cookery, Le Hunaudiere, Livre la Touche, Mayenne, 53400 France; (33) 2 43 98 50 02, Fax (33) 2 43 98 50 02, walnutgrovecookery@tiscali.fr, www.walnutgrovecookery.com.

A WEEK IN THE HEART OF THE BORDEAUX WINE COUNTRY
Gauriac
Sponsor: Winemaker Pascal Méli & food & wine expert Michèle Rousseau. Programs: One-week cooking & wine appreciation vacations that include visits to wineries of the Bordeaux region. Established: 1999. Class/group size: 6. 20 programs/yr. Facilities: Chateau Bujan, a 42-acre vineyard. Lodging at La Maison des Vignes, a restored 17th century home in the estate. Also featured: Swimming, hiking, biking.
FACULTY: Pascal Méli, agricultural engineer, winemaker & owner of Château Bujan; Michèle Rousseau, admin director of a Bordeaux wine Controlled Appellation for the last 9 yrs.
COSTS: $2,100 ($250 single supplement) includes lodging, most meals, daily excursions, wine tastings.
CONTACT: Michèle Rousseau & Pascal Méli, Château Bujan, Gauriac, 33710 France; (33) 557 64 86 56, Fax (33) 557 64 93 96, pmeli@maison-des-vignes.fr, www.maison-des-vignes.fr. In the US: Lenora Ammon-Rousseau, 212-772-3590, ammon-rousseau@nyc.rr.com. In Tokyo: Keiko Nishimura, (81) 3 3834 1767,keiko-n@qb3.so-net.ne.jp.

A WEEK IN PROVENCE WITH SARAH & MICHAEL BROWN
Gordes
Sponsor: Cultural & culinary specialists Sarah & Michael Brown. Programs: Week-long vacation programs, scheduled every other week in spring & fall, that include daily hands-on cooking demos, art & architectural tours, visits to markets in Provence, lectures. Established: 1996. Class/group size: 6. 16 programs/yr. Facilities: 6-bedroom family home with library, sitting rooms, dining room, & kitchen overlooking the Luberon Valley. Also featured: Swimming, tennis, golf, hiking, biking, riding.
FACULTY: Sarah Ferguson Brown, a Ph.D. in Medieval Art History, has been cooking since she was 8, & has lived in the region on & off for 40+ years. Michael Brown represented food interests in Washington, DC, & exports wines to the U.S.
COSTS: $2,000 includes lodging in the Brown's converted farmhouse, 7 breakfasts & dinners, lectures.
CONTACT: Sarah & Michael Brown, A Week in Provence, Les Martins, Gordes, 84220 France; (33) (0)490-72-26-56, Fax (33) (0)490-72-23-83, lesmartins@compuserve.com, www.week-in-provence.com. In the US: Sheppard Ferguson, 4700 Connecticut Ave. NW, #304, Washington, DC 20008; 202-537-7202, shepferg@ix.netcom.com.

GREECE

AEGEAN HARVEST
Athens, Peloponnese, Santorini, the Islands, Greece
Sponsor: Culinary tour operator. Programs: Mediterranean food, wine & cultural programs. Custom group & independent travel culinary programs. Established: 1999. Class/group size: 20. 4+ programs/yr. Facilities: Private villa near ancient Venetian port of Nafplio. Also featured: Visits to wineries, markets & artisanal food producers, food demos, tours of ancient ruins & historic sites.
FACULTY: In-country experts on Greek cuisine & wines.
COSTS: $2,995-$3,595.
CONTACT: Lisa Meyer, Aegean Harvest, 251 Cokesbury Rd., Lebanon, NJ 08833; 877-330-3648, aegeanharvest@hotmail.com.

COOKING WITH STAVROS
Symi, Greece
Sponsor: Specialty travel company. Programs: 5 half-day Mediterranean-style cooking classes featuring such chef specialties as feta mousse, squid in basil sauce & sea food filo. Established: 2001. Class/group size: 10. 4 programs/yr. Facilities: Restaurant kitchen. Also featured: Gardening courses, painting & walking holidays.
FACULTY: Stavros Gogios, owner/chef of the harborside Mythos restaurant.
COSTS: £220 includes lunch.

CONTACT: Laskarina Holidays, St. Marys Gate, Wirksworth, Derbyshire,England; (44) 01629 822203, Fax (44) 01629 822205, info@laskarina.co.uk, www.laskarina.co.uk/cooking.html.

CRETE'S CULINARY SANCTUARIES
Heraklio, Crete & surrounding area, Greece

Sponsor: Culinary professional Nikki Rose. Programs: Culinary classes & cultural tours covering ingredients, cooking techniques, menu planning & nutrition, organic farming, wine. Established: 1994. Class/group size: 4-10. 15 programs/yr. Facilities: Hotels, tavernas, vineyards, archeological & production sites. Also featured: Cultural-culinary research, sustainable agriculture.

FACULTY: Professional chef-guides from 4-star hotels & village tavernas, home cooks, farmers & fishermen. Nikki Rose, a Greek-American pro chef, food writer/historian & CIA graduate.

COSTS: $100-$2,200 for 1- to 5-day classes, includes lodging in mountain village, some meals, tours. **CONTACT:** Nikki Rose, Director, Crete's Culinary Sanctuaries, T.K. 72053, Elounda, Crete, Greece; 415-835-9923 (USA), info@cookingincrete.com, www.cookingincrete.com. USA Contact: 1207 Montgomery St., #3, San Francisco, CA 94133.

KEA ARTISANAL
Kea, Cyclades, Greece

Sponsor: Private company. Programs: One-week cooking vacation programs that include hands-on classes & dining in the homes of island cooks, herb foraging, visits to food producers, cultural & nature excursions. Established: 2004. Class/group size: 6-10. 6+ programs/yr. Facilities: Aglaia Kremezi's country home kitchen & other cook's villas. Also featured: Boating, fishing, swimming in Kea, cultural & food tour in Athens.

FACULTY: Aglaia Kremezi's four cookbooks include The Foods of the Greek Islands & Julia Child Award winner The Foods of Greece. She is a food columnist & contributing writer for the Los Angeles Times, Gourmet, Food & Wine & other publications.

COSTS: $2,795 includes shared villa lodging, most meals, ground transport, planned excursions. Custom programs available.

CONTACT: Kostis Maroulis, Co-founder, Kea Artisanal, PO Box 24, Kea Cyclades, 84002 Greece; (30) 2 28-802-1346, peggysotirhos@yahoo.com, www.keartisanal.com. USA contact: Peggy Sotirhos, 212-929-1248. Greece contact: marulis@otenet.gr.

NUTRITION & CULTURE AT THE MOUTH OF SANTORINI VOLCANO
Santorini, Greece

Sponsor: Magma, a division of Heliotopos Inc., a destination management company in Greece. Programs: 4-day program focusing on nutrition & culture. Established: 1985. Class/group size: 6-14. 4 programs/yr. Facilities: Hotel Heliotopos, overlooking the volcano, the sea, & the neighboring islands. Also featured: Geological tours.

FACULTY: Dr Connie Phillipson, prehistoric archeologist, nutritionist, Greek food columnist of Athens News, president of the Institute of Paleonutrition.

COSTS: €1,150 (€305) includes shared (single) lodging.

CONTACT: Yiota Aidoni, Manager, Santorini Cultural & Culinary Holidays, Magma, Imerovigli, Santorini, 84700 Greece; (30) 2286 024758, Fax (30) 2286 023867, magma@heliotopos.net, e-magma.santorini.net/index.php?brink.

ZANTE FEAST FOOD DISCOVERY HOLIDAYS
Zakynthos, Greece

Sponsor: Non-profit group dedicated to the preservation of agro-tourism & family farming on the Island of Zakynthos. Programs: One-week vacations that feature hands-on cooking lessons in the traditional specialties of the Greek Ionian Islands. Class/group size: 8-10. 4 programs/yr. Also featured: Excursions to markets, artisanal food producers, nearby locales.

FACULTY: Sotiris Kitrilakis, founder, received bachelor's & master's degrees from MIT & worked on the N.A.S.A. Space Program. For the past 20 yrs he has worked at introducing authentic Greek foods to the American market.

Costs: €1,955 includes most meals & shared lodging in Leeda's Village, a group of homes that are examples of Zakynthian stone masonry. €200 single supplement.
Contact: Sotiris Kitrilakis, Founder, Zante Feast Food Discovery Holidays, Lithakia T.K., Zakynthos, 29092 Greece; (30) 26950 24224 or (30) 6944 563677 (mobile), Fax (30) 26950 24264, info@zante-feast.org, www.zante-feast.org.

IRELAND

BALLYMALOE COOKERY SCHOOL
Midleton, County Cork
Sponsor: Private cookery school. Programs: 12-wk Certificate course, 1-to-5-day hands-on vacation programs. Established: 1983. Class/group size: 56 hands-on/70 demo. 30 programs/yr. Facilities: Include a purpose-built kitchen with gas & electric cookers, mirrored demo area with TV monitors, gardens that supply fresh produce. Also featured: Fishing, walking & golf.
Faculty: 9 full time teachers. Includes Principal Darina Allen, IACP-certified teacher, food professional, author of Irish Traditional Cooking, presented the Ballymaloe Cookery Course on TV; Rory O'Connell & Rachel Allen; featured guest chefs.
Costs: 1-day courses €195, weekend courses €425, 5-day courses €720. Lodging in schools's self-catering cottages during short courses €25/night shared, €32/night single.
Contact: Darina Allen, Owner, Ballymaloe Cookery School, Kinoith, Shanagarry, County Cork, Ireland; (353) 21-4646785, Fax (353) 21-4646909, enquiries@ballymaloe-cookery-school.ie, www.ballymaloe-cookery-school.ie.

BELLE ISLE SCHOOL OF COOKERY
Enniskillen, Co. Fermanagh
Sponsor: Private residential cooking school. Programs: 1-day to 4-wk hands-on cooking courses that emphasize seasonal ingredients & holiday menus; wine courses, evening demos. Established: 2002. Class/group size: 10 max. 50+ programs/yr. Facilities: Modern, fully-equipped kitchen with 1 cooking island for 2 guests. Also featured: Angling & game fishing, water recreation, tennis, golf, historic homes, garden tours.
Faculty: Chef Liz Moore & 2 staff assisants.
Costs: £320/weekend, £775/5 days, £2,000/4 wks includes meals & lodging; £75/1-day non-residential.
Contact: Liz Moore, Master Chef, Belle Isle School of Cookery, Lisbellaw, Enniskillen, Co. Fermanagh, Ireland; (44) 28 6638 7231, Fax (44) 28 6638 7261, accommodation@belleisle-estate.com, www.irishcookeryschool.com.

BERRY LODGE COOKERY SCHOOL
County Clare
Sponsor: Cooking school in a country guest house. Programs: 2- & 3-day residential & 1-day non-residential cooking programs. Includes holiday & pub cookery, basic techniques, entertaining, vegetarian, team development. Established: 1994. Class/group size: 10. 15 programs/yr. Facilities: Modernized 18th-century Victorian family home, restaurant & kitchen. Also featured: Golf, walking, fishing, swimming.
Faculty: Rita Meade, chef, home economist & teacher of food programs for 30+ yrs.
Costs: €185/2 days, €365/3 days includes lodging, dinner. Non-residential €75. Team development €80 pp/day.
Contact: Rita Meade, Berry Lodge, Annagh, Miltown Malbay, Co. Clare, Ireland; (353) 65 708 7022, Fax (353) 65 708 7011, info@berrylodge.com, www.berrylodge.com.

CARLINGFORD COOKERY SCHOOL
Carlingford
Sponsor: Ghan House restaurant. Programs: Guest chef & head chef cookery demos; half- to 2-day hands-on courses. Established: 1991. Also featured: Private & corporate group lessons.

FACULTY: Guest chefs include TV/radio Paula McIntyre, cookbook author Ursula Ferrigno, artisan baker Paul Merry.
COSTS: From €40/guest chef demo, from €250/2-day course. Shared B&B lodging €75-€90.
CONTACT: Carlingford Cookery School, ;; (353) (0) 42 937 3682, Fax (353) (0) 42 937 3772, ghanhouse@eircom.net, www.ghanhouse.com/index1.htm.

THE GOURMET SOLUTION
Ennis, Co. Clare
Sponsor: Private school. Demo & hands-on 6-session courses in Irish & contemporary cuisine.
FACULTY: Proprietor James Hunt has worked in 4- & 5-star establishments in Ireland & fine restaurants in London, Paris, Munich & Sydney, incl 7 yrs in 1- & 2-star Michelin restaurants.
COSTS: €110-€180/course.
CONTACT: James Hunt, Owner, The Gourmet Solution, 31 Maiville, Ennis, Co. Clare, Ireland; (353) (0)65 6864743, jahunt@eircom.net.

ITALY

A TAVOLA CON LO CHEF
Rome
Sponsor: Private school. Programs: Amateur & professional training courses include basic & advanced cooking, confectionery, pizza, fish, specific themes, hands-on or demo courses. Established: 1992. Class/group size: 15 hands-on, 25 demo. Facilities: 3 well-equipped professional kitchens. Also featured: Children's programs, private group instruction, market visits.
FACULTY: Antonio Sciullo, Alberto Ciarla, Leonardo Di Carlo, Nazzareno Lavini, Salvo Leanza, Gianni Alicino, Agata Parisella Caraccio, Salvatore Tassa.
COSTS: $90/$120 for each 3/4-hour lesson.
CONTACT: Maria Teresa Meloni, Fiorella D'Agnano, A Tavola con lo Chef, Via dei Gracchi 60, Rome, 192 Italy; (39) 06-32 22 096, Fax (39) 06-320 34 02, atavola@pronet.it, www.atavolaconlochef.it.

ABBONDANZA TOSCANA
Tuscany
Sponsor: Private school. Programs: Hands-on cooking classes, wine & olive oil tours, cheese & art excursions, nature walks, intro to regional restaurants. Established: 1999. Class/group size: 12. 16 programs/yr. Facilities: Professional kitchen with modern equipment in adedicated space; woodburning oven. Also featured: Watercolor workshop, cultural excursions, language classes, shopping tours, visits to Italian gardens, markets, regional artisans, dining al fresco.
FACULTY: 3 chef-instructors: Emanuela Dini, local chef; Davide Botta, owner L'Artigliere; Claudio Laurentino, owner Gaudemus; Eduardo Dalcin, pizzaiola; Ken Inglis, sommelier.
COSTS: €1,700-€1,900 includes meals, lodging at Selva, a restored 16th-century farmhouse on a 1000-acre wine & olive oil working estate, ground transport, planned excursions. Custom & group courses.
CONTACT: Abbondanza Toscana, Italy; E-mail serendipity@abbondanzatoscana.com, www.abbondanzatoscana.com.

ADVENTURES IN TUSCANY
Siena
Sponsor: Azienda Agrituristica, Vittorio Cambria. Programs: 5 different Sunday-Saturday programs that focus on Tuscan cuisine. Includes daily classes & culinary & cultural excursions. Established: 1997. Class/group size: 6-16. 22 programs/yr. Facilities: Professional kitchen, woodburning oven, herb & vegetable garden, outdoor dining with view. Also featured: Private tours for groups. Walking, cultural & cooking holidays for 8 or more.
FACULTY: Chef Giancarlo Giannelli, chef-owner of L'oste Poeta Restaurant in Tocchi, cookbook author; anthropologist Vittorio Cambria, an expert on the culture of the region; Sergio Villani, Ph.D. in Art History.

Costs: $2,300-$3,100 all-inclusive for land portion. Lodging in a restored 1,000-year-old castello. **Contact:** Ann Dunne, Program Director, Adventures in Tuscany, P.O. Box 644, Solana Beach, CA 92075; 619-989-9416, Fax 858-258-1474, ann_dunne@attglobal.net, www.tuscany-adventures.com. In Italy: Dott. Vittorio Cambria, Azienda Agrituristica, 53010 Tocchi, Monticiano, Siena, Italy. Fax (39) (0)577 757 100.

AOLMAIA TUSCANY SOCIETY
San Miniato, Tuscany
Sponsor: Italian language & culture school. Programs: Italian cuisine cooking classes & courses. Tuscany wine tours. Established: 1997. Class/group size: 8 max. 24 programs/yr. Facilities: Restaurant & private home kitchens, family-run exclusive lodgings. Also featured: Cultural activities, customized tours & vacations.
Faculty: Restaurant chefs, home cooks, professional sommelier, English speaking Italian guides.
Costs: $200-$300/day includes meals, lodging, tours, local transportation.
Contact: Pierpaolo Chiartosini, Coordinator, Aolmaia Tuscany Service Sas, Via Cafaggio 12, San Miniato - Pisa, 56027 Italy; (39) 0571-408038, Fax (39) 0571-408038, countrypost@aolmaia.com, www.aolmaia.com/tours.html.

APICIUS – THE CULINARY INSTITUTE OF FLORENCE
Florence   *(See also page 163) (See display ad page 163)*
Sponsor: Private school. Programs: 10-day food/wine/culture programs, 1-mo language/cooking/wine courses, wine & cooking classes, 1-yr diploma programs. Established: 1973. Class/group size: 15 max. 15 programs/yr. Facilities: New facility consisting of 2 kitchens with individual workstations, wine tasting room, conference room, reading room & lounge. Also featured: Market tour, wine tastings, gastronomic walking tours, culinary lectures.
Faculty: Chefs, restaurateurs, culinary professionals, incl founder/director Gabriella Ganugi, author of The Four Seasons of the Tuscan Table.
Costs: Programs that combine private & group cooking classes, wine tasting, Italian language, & gastronomic walking tours from €790.
Contact: Dr. Gabriella Ganugi, Director, Apicius - The Culinary Institute of Florence, Via Guelfa 85, Florence, 50129 Italy; (39) 0552658135, Fax (39) 0552656689, info@apicius.it, www.apicius.it.

ARTE E MESTIERI
Montopoli in Val d'Arno
Sponsor: Cultural association. Programs: 1-day, weekly & week-end programs that include 4 cooking classes, wine tasting, & the use of plants in phytoterapy. Established: 2000. Class/group size: 6:1. 4 programs/yr. Facilities: Restored kitchen in Villa Belvedere country house with garden & swimming pool. Also featured: Workshops in stained glass, mosaic art, ceramics, decoupage, fresco, & paintings; archeological excursion, mountain biking, swimming.
Faculty: Anna Ciampolini & Cesare Ciurli (cooking), Cesare Ciurli (wine), Gianna (art tours), Marcella Cuccu (art teacher).
Costs: $900-$2,000 includes meals & shared lodging in Villa Belvedere & apts., planned activities.
Contact: Anna Maria Ciampolini, Artist, Arte e Mestieri, Via Guicciardini 50, Montopoli in Val d'Arno, Pisa, 56020 Italy; (39) 0571 466937, Fax (39) 0571 466937, info@arteemestieri.com, www.arteemestieri.com.

ARTEMISIA HOLIDAYS GASTRONOMIA
Garfagnana, Tuscany
Sponsor: Specialty travel company. Programs: One-week cooking & wine programs that include visits to artisan food & wine producers. Established: 2004. Class/group size: 8-10. 14 programs/yr. Facilities: Professional restaurant kitchen.
Faculty: Rita has been owner/chef of a Tuscan restaurant for 18 yrs. Wine guides are professionally trained & employed by Tuscan wine estates.
Costs: £845/culinary program, £895/wine program includes lodging, most meals, field trips.

CONTACT: Lorraine McAvoy, Artemisia Holidays Gastronomia, PO Box 7504, Glasgow, Scotland; (44) (0) 141 424 0958, Fax (44) (0) 141 424 0958, lorraine@mcavoymail.freeserve.co.uk, www.artemisia-holidays.com.

ARTISANAL COOKING
Montelama, Tuscany
Programs: Weekend hands-on classes in Viennese pastry, Moroccan cooking or Lunigiana specialties that cover basic recipes & techniques. Established: 1997. Class/group size: 1-3 preferred. Facilities: Indoor & outdoor kitchen facilities including grill, stove, oven & tables. Also featured: Visits to local farmers' market & traditional trattorias.
FACULTY: Christine Berl, pastry chef & author of The Classic Art of Viennese Pastry, & her husband, Chef Hamid, specialist in Moroccan Berber cuisine.
COSTS: $300/weekend class. Lodging available with bedrooms for up to 4 people.
CONTACT: Christine Berl, Pastry Chef, Artisanal Cooking, Montelama, 54020 Italy; (39) 335 649 5827, cinqueterreetc@yahoo.com.

BADIA A COLTIBUONO
Tuscany
Sponsor: Badia a Coltibuono, a medieval abbey, Tuscan wine estate & villa. Programs: Residential 3- or 5-day vacation courses (usually Mon-Sat) that include participation cooking classes, wine & olive oil tastings, gastronomic & cultural visits. Established: 1985. Class/group size: 16. 8 programs/yr. Facilities: Large teaching kitchen in an 11th-century abbey. Also featured: Visits to food producers, wineries & castles; trip to the Palio horse race (July).
FACULTY: Chef Paolo Pancotti & Guide John Meis.
COSTS: Land cost is $1,300 double, $1,500 single for 3 day program; $3,300 double, $3,900 single, for 5 day program; includes lodging at Badia a Coltibuono; $500 supplement for Palio week.
CONTACT: Louise Owens, Badia a Coltibuono, 3128 Purdue, Dallas, TX 75225; 214-739-2846, Fax 214-691-7996, coltibuono@charter.net, www.coltibuono.com.

BEI RICORDI – A ROAD THROUGH TUSCANY & UMBRIA
Orvieto, Tuscany & Umbria
Sponsor: Private culinary company. Programs: Seasonal programs that include cooking classes, cultural tours, & visits to markets, winemakers, cheese makers & bakers. Established: 1997. Class/group size: 3-7. 12 programs/yr. Also featured: Truffle searches, pheasant & wild boar hunts, olive & grape harvests, baking classes, language lessons.
FACULTY: Marlena DeBlasi, a chef & cooking teacher, has authored 3 books on the regional foods of Italy, including 1000 Days in Venice.
COSTS: $3,500 includes 5 nights lodging & meals.
CONTACT: Marlena & Fernando de Blasi, Bei Ricordi, 34 via del Duomo, Orvieto, 5018 Italy; 011-39-0763-393-549, Fax 011-39-0763-341-718, join-us@beiricordi.com, www.beiricordi.com. US contact: Lia Huber, 800-340-9610, lia@beiricordi.com.

BOOKS FOR COOKS IN TUSCANY, THE ITALIAN COOKING SCHOOL
Tuscany
Sponsor: Heidi Lascelles, founder of Books for Cooks in London. Programs: Customized 1- & 2-day cooking courses, weekend & week-long culinary vacations with daily hands-on classes. Established: 1998. Class/group size: 8 max. ~6 programs/yr. Facilities: Kitchens with open fireplaces, wood-burning ovens. Also featured: Seasonal grape & olive picking, well-being weeks with healthy cooking classes.
FACULTY: Principal tutor Olivia Greco.
COSTS: €100-€120/day, €500/weekend, €2,000/week includes lodging & meals.
CONTACT: Heidi Lascelles, Books for Cooks in Tuscany, The Italian Cooking School, Strada della Paneretta 11, Barberino V.E. (Fi.), 50021 Italy; (39) 055-8072231/(39) 348 773 0009, Fax (39) 055-8072231, heidi.lascelles@libero.it, www.booksforcooks.com.

CAMILLA IN CUCINA
Florence

Sponsor: Private school. Programs: Classes for individuals or small groups, includes S. Lorenzo market visit. Established: 1998. Class/group size: 1-12. Facilities: Fully-equipped kitchen in a private home (up to 4 people), professional kitchen for larger groups. Also featured: Florence & Chianti guided tour, wine tasting.
FACULTY: Silvia Maccari, Cordon Bleu, gastronome, cook book author, TV food show host.
COSTS: From $190/single class.
CONTACT: Silvia Maccari, Owner, Camilla in Cucina, Via Atto Vannucci 3, Florence, 50134 Italy; (39) 055-461-381, Fax (39) 055-461-381, smaccari@iol.it.

CAPRI DOLCE VITA
Capri

Sponsor: Culinary vacation company. Programs: 1/2-, 3-, 4- & 8-day Capri vacation programs that include hands-on cooking lessons, wine, grappa & cheese tastings. Programs offered in English & Italian. Established: 2002. Class/group size: 10 max. 15 programs/yr. Facilities: Family farm equipped with both modern & traditional kitchen facilities. Also featured: Include guided walks, excursions, boat trips, nightlife.
FACULTY: Executive Chef Renato De Gregorio, Maitre Cuisinier, Chaine des Rotisseurs, Assoc. mondiale de la gastronomie. Activities are led by Capri Dolce Vita's owners Massimo & Elisabeth.
COSTS: From €145 includes meals, activities, shared 4-star hotel lodging, transfers from Naples.
CONTACT: Massimo & Elisabeth Catuogno, Owners, Capri Dolce Vita, via Tito Minitti, 9, Anacapri, 80071 Italy; (39) 334 367 2794, info@capridolcevita.com, www.capridolcevita.com.

CHIANTI IN TUSCANY – TOSCANA MIA
Gaiole in Chianti & Florence

Sponsor: Private school. Programs: 1- to 5-day hands-on cooking & wine programs that focus on Tuscan & Italian recipes. Established: 1986. Class/group size: 6-10 hands-on. 24 programs/yr. Facilities: Chianti: Podere Le Rose, a 13th-century restored Tuscan farmhouse, which is also Marquis de' Mari's private home. Florence: private homes. Also featured: Food, olives & wine intinerary, 1-day market visit, Italian language & art history programs, customized group programs.
FACULTY: Sisters Paola & Simonetta de' Mari, assisted by a Tuscan chef.
COSTS: $750/5-day cooking course.
CONTACT: Simonetta de'Mari di Altamura, Toscana Mia, Poggio S. Polo 2, Gaiole in Chianti (SI), 53013 Italy; (39) 0577-746152, Fax (39) 0577-746132, info@welcometuscany.com, www.welcometuscany.com.

THE CLASSIC ART OF VIENNESE PASTRY
Pontremoli, Tuscany

Sponsor: Culinary professional Christine Berl. Programs: Courses on classic Viennese pastry including tortes & Austrian specialties. Established: 1998. Class/group size: 15. Facilities: Professional kitchen.
FACULTY: Christine Berl is daughter of a Viennese pastry Chef, author of The Classic Art of Viennese Pastry. & has taught at The CIA, ICE, & Cordon Bleu Florence.
COSTS: $300/one- or two-day course.
CONTACT: Christine Berl, The Classic Art of Viennese Pastry, Pontremoli, 54020 Italy; (39) 0187 447 136, annemarierimal@yahoo.com.

COOK ITALY
Italy

Sponsor: Private cooking school. Programs: Classes in authentic Italian food that is quick & simple to prepare. Established: 1999. Class/group size: 4-8. 25 programs/yr. Facilities: Italian family homes. Lucca: converted stable block with pool; Florence: villa with pool; Cortona: country villa; Arezzo: country house with pool; Siracusa: small hotel. Also featured: Market shopping tours, wine & olive oil tastings, cheese & olive oil producer vists, dining at fine restaurants, demos by chefs & in private homes.

FACULTY: Culinary expert, cook & gastronome Carmelita Caruana; local bread & pizza chefs & expert pasta makers. Restaurant chef demos on request.

COSTS: From $850/3-day classes, from $1,400- $2,050/week includes shared lodging, meals, food trip. 1-day custom lessons from $200, weekend custom tour from $750.

CONTACT: Carmelita Caruana, Cook Italy, Via Bellombra 10, Bologna, 40136 Italy; (39) 051-644-86-12, Fax (39) 051-644-8612, carmelita@cookitaly.com, www.cookitaly.com.

COOK WITH PASSION
Florence

Sponsor: Private school. Programs: Half-day hands-on cooking classes, Italian wine tasting & olive oil classes, Tuscan wine tours. Established: 2003. Class/group size: 10.

FACULTY: Florentine/Tuscan woman.

COSTS: Cooking class €165, wine class €55, Tuscan wine tour €65-€200, olive oil class €35.

CONTACT: David Johnstone, Owner, Cook With Passion, Via San Gallo, 26R, Box 253, Florence, 50129 Italy; (39) 320-413-2892, Fax 270-588-6938 (U.S.), ClassInfo_Shaw@CookWithPassion.com, www.CookWithPassion.com.

COOK AT SELIANO
Paestum, Naples & Salerno

Sponsor: Cookbook author Arthur Schwartz. Programs: 5-day program that includes 3 half-day Neapolitan cooking classes, visits to a mozzarella di bufala producer, intro to regional wines, dining in local restaurants, visits to private homes. Established: 2002. Class/group size: 16 max for hands-on. 4 programs/yr. Facilities: New kitchen classroom. Tenuta Seliano, a vegetable farm, & Masseria Eliseo, a water buffalo farm, have modern rooms with private baths. Also featured: Tours to Naples & Salerno, a visit to the Greek temples of Paestum with an archaeologist, pottery shopping, swimming pool, horseback riding.

FACULTY: Arthur Schwartz, New York radio program host, cookbook author & experienced cooking teacher, & Baronessa Cecilia Bellelli Baratta; assistants include Iris Carulli, an American who lives in Italy, & local women.

COSTS: $3,350 includes shared lodging, meals, local transportation; $450 single supplement.

CONTACT: Arthur Schwartz, Cook At Seliano, 718-783-2626, Fax 718-783-4242, CookAtSeliano@aol.com, www.arthurschwartz.com.

COOKING CLASSES IN ELBA ISLAND
Elba Island

Sponsor: Villa San Giovanni Residenza Hotel. Programs: 5-day food & wine courses featuring daily half-day hands-on classes, farm visits, wine tastings. Established: 1959. Class/group size: 6-16. 24 programs/yr. Facilities: The hotel kitchen. Also featured: Sports (trekking, biking, golf, tennis), ceramics, wellness.

FACULTY: Marco di Nenno & Pio Dapra, chefs at Tuscan Villa San Giovanni.

COSTS: Include shared villa lodging & half board. Amenities include private beach, pool, garden.

CONTACT: Alex Galvani, Manager, Cooking Classes in Elba Island, Villa San Giovanni Residenza Hotel, San Giovanni 202, Portoferraio, 57037 Italy; (39) 565-914460, Fax (39) 565-945950, info@hotelvillasangiovanni.com, www.hotelvillasangiovanni.com.

COOKING WITH GIULIANO HAZAN AT VILLA GIONA
Verona

Sponsor: Cookbook author Giuliano Hazan & the Allegrini Winery. Programs: Hands-on classes & field trips that include the Allegrini winery (producer of Amarone), a risotto mill, an olive oil frantoio, a maker of Parmigiano-Reggiano, food markets, the Lake of Garda, fine restaurants. Established: 2000. Class/group size: 12. 4-6 programs/yr. Facilities: Modern teaching kitchen in the newly restored Villa Giona.

FACULTY: Giuliano Hazan, author of The Classic Pasta Cookbook & Every Night Italian.
COSTS: $3,775-$4,175 includes deluxe lodging at the Villa Giona, most meals, planned excursions, ground transport.
CONTACT: Giuliano Hazan, Cooking With Giuliano Hazan at Villa Giona, 4471 S. Shade Ave., Sarasota, FL 34231; 941-923-1333, Fax 941-923-1335, giuliano@giulianohazan.com, www.giulianohazan.com/school.

COOKING SECRETS
Venice
Sponsor: Private school. Programs: 3-day courses that include hands-on classes in the 2 instructors' home & a trip to the Rialto market Established: 2003. Class/group size: 8. Facilities: Teaching kitchen in 18th-century Venetian palazzo. Also featured: Visits to food producers & local workshops.
FACULTY: Chef Alessandra & Chef Francesca.
COSTS: €450 for 3-day course.
CONTACT: Francesca Boggio, Cooking Secrets, Fax (44) 870 4292024, cooking@fineitalianrentals.com, www.fineitalianrentals.com.

COOKING IN TUSCANY
Sinalunga
Sponsor: Vacation villa. Programs: Weekend & 1-week hands-on Tuscan cooking vacations that feature home-grown vegetables & home-bred poultry. Established: 2001. Class/group size: 2-8. Also featured: Swimming pool, regional excursions, shopping in Florence, winery & market visits.
FACULTY: Donna Annunziata, an experienced Tuscan trattoria cook.
COSTS: €680-€780 (€1,200-€1,400)/weekend (1-week) includes lodging & meals.
CONTACT: Cooking in Tuscany, info@cookingtuscany.com, www.cookingtuscany.com.

COOKING VACATIONS INTERNATIONAL
Sorrento
Sponsor: Private cooking school. Programs: 1-week culinary vacations that include 3 cooking classes. Established: 2004. Class/group size: 8-10. 52 programs/yr. Facilities: Italian villas, B&B. Also featured: Include visits to markets, local butcher, cheese shop, wine bottega, mozzarella & olive oil maker; cultural & gastronomic day trips.
FACULTY: Teachers range from self-taught to Michelin-trained chefs.
COSTS: $500-$2,500.
CONTACT: Lauren Birmingham, Owner, Cooking Vacations International, 115 Newbury St., Boston, MA 2116; 617-247-4112, Fax 617-247-4850, cookingvacations@aol.com, www.cookingvacations.com.

COOKING AT THE VILLA
Verona; Boston, MA
Sponsor: Chef Luisa Zecchinato. Programs: 6-day culinary tour of Verona that includes 3 cooking classes, visit to wineries, cheese, prosciutto & balsamic vinegar factories, restaurant dining, sightseeing. Established: 1996. Class/group size: 4-8. 3 programs/yr. Also featured: Cooking classes in Boston & Providence.
FACULTY: Luisa Zecchinato, a native of Verona; Leena Cagnoni, executive chef of Hobby & Food.
COSTS: $2,325/6 days includes 4-star hotel lodging, most meals, ground transport, planned activities.
CONTACT: M. Luisa Zecchinato, Chef &Teacher, Cooking At The Villa, P.O. Box 106, Mashpee, MA 2649; (+39) 045 7971312, zecchinato@cooking-at-the-villa.com, www.cooking-at-the-villa.com. Italy address: via Cadellora 15/a Alpo (Vr) Verona, Italy.

COOKING & WINE TASTING IN ETRUSCANS LAND
Monti della Tolfa (near Rome)
Sponsor: Italian family-run cooking & wine tasting courses. Programs: 5-8 day cooking vacations featuring hands-on classes using home-grown products, visits to food producers, tutored wine, olive

oil & grappa tastings. Established: 1998. Class/group size: 2-8. 100 programs/yr. Facilities: Large furnished kitchen & a wood fired oven on the terrace. Also featured: Horse riding, Italian language classes, pottery, archaeology, mountain biking, trekking, sightseeing, free climbing, painting. **FACULTY:** Local cooks.
COSTS: €1,428/week, €820/5 days includes lodging, meals, excursions; €92/1 day includes lunch & wine tasting.
CONTACT: Assuntina Antonacci, Owner, Cookery in Etruscans Land, Fontana del papa, Tolfa, 59 Italy; (39) 766 93455, (39) 328 9463763, Fax (39) 766 93455, info@fontanadelpapa.it, www.cookitaly.it. (39) 3331092556.

COSELLI SCHOOL OF TUSCAN CUISINE
Coselli, Lucca, Tuscany
Sponsor: Private school affiliated with La Famiglia Tuscan restaurant in London & Italian cheese producer Alival/Mandara. Programs: 4- & 6-day Tuscan hands-on cooking vacations with cultural program. Established: 1966. Class/group size: 10-16. Facilities: Purpose-built cooking school kitchen. Also featured: Visits to Lucca, Pisa, Chianti vineyards, wineries, a distillery, markets; pizza, chocolate & truffle making; olive oil & balsamic vinegar tastings.
FACULTY: Professional Italian chef Alvaro Maccioni, owner of La Famiglia restaurant & author of Mamma Toscana cookbook, sommelier/master of wine Raoul Ferrari.
COSTS: 4-day (6-day) course €2,200-€2,500 (€2,900-€3,200) includes lodging, meals, ground transport, planned excursions. Lodging at Borgo Bernardini, a restored historic property.
CONTACT: Borgo Bernardini, Via di Coselli 77/79, Lucca, Tuscany, 55060 Italy; (39) 0583 94404, Fax (39) 0583 947681, info@coselli.com, www.coselli.com. Cuisine International, PO Box 25228, Dallas, TX 75225. 214-373-1161, Fax:214-373-1162, Email:CuisineInt@aol.com, http://www.CuisineInternational.comInternational Kitchen, 55 East Monroe, Suite 2840, Chicago, IL 60603. 800-945-8606, Fax:312-803-1593, Email.

CUCINA CON MIA
Coldigioco
Sponsor: Culinary professional. Programs: Week-long hands-on cooking vacations that include visits to artisan food producers, markets & wineries, & dining in private homes & fine restaurants. Established: 2000. Class/group size: 4-10. 3-4 programs/yr. Facilities: Professional kitchen, wood-burning oven, organic vegetable garden.
FACULTY: Mia Chambers, program director & California Culinary Academy graduate; local Italian artisans, chefs, & home-cooks.
COSTS: $1,850-$2,000/wk includes lodging in restored farmhouses, meals, planned excursions, ground & airport transport.
CONTACT: Chef Mia Chambers, Cucina con Mia, 4096 Piedmont Avenue #263, Oakland, CA 0; 510-814-0758, Chefmiachambers@aol.com, www.cucinaconmia.com.

CUCINA MEDIEVAL IN ITALY
Viterbo
Sponsor: Special interest tour company. Programs: Hands-on programs that focus on nutrition & Mediterranean diet, with emphasis on kitchen-tested recipes of the 12th-14th centuries. Established: 1993. Class/group size: 10-12. 24 programs/yr. Facilities: Professional kitchen in the Villa Ex convente of Cistercian (Villa Citerno). Also featured: Winery tours, visits to markets & food producers, dinner in private homes, spa, 1-day sightseeing trips to Rome & Florence.
FACULTY: Giovanna Scapucci, owner of Il Richiastro restaurant.
COSTS: $1,400 ($2,200) includes all meals & 5 (7) days shared lodging at Villa Citerno. $200 single supplement, $1,800 non-cook friend.
CONTACT: Iolanda Alexander Davidov, President, Aquilanti Viaggi S.R.L., Via Marzio 46, Vitorchiano (Viterbo), 1030 Italy; (39) 0761-370210, Fax (39) 0761-371240, aquilantiviaggi@libero.it, www.aquilantiviaggi.com/.

CUCINA CON VISTA IN FLORENCE
Florence

Sponsor: Private cooking school. Programs: 1- to 4-day cooking courses based on traditional Tuscan & Florentine cooking. Established: 2001. Class/group size: 1-16. 20 programs/yr. Facilities: Modern farmhouse kitchen & dining room. Also featured: Guided tour of the Sant'Ambrogio market, wine tour through the Chianti Hills, promenades in Florence.
FACULTY: Elena Mattei, owner/chef of La Baraonda Restaurant in Florence.
COSTS: Cooking classes: ~€200/day. Cooking packages (cooking classes + activities): €350-€600. Farmhouse lodging available.
CONTACT: Elena Mattei, Owner, Cucina con Vista, via delle Cinque Vie 4, Florence, 50125 Italy; (39) 347-210-1677, Fax (39) 06-233-237-227, jacopo@cucinaconvista.it, www.cucinaconvista.it.

CUCINA MONDIALE
Florence countryside

Sponsor: Private cooking school. Programs: 1-wk regional culinary tours that include hands-on cooking, wine tasting, cheese making, visits to kitchens, markets, & ceramic producers, restaurant dining. Established: 1999. Class/group size: 8. 4 programs/yr. Facilities: The kitchens of a 650-acre working farm/estate that produces cheese & wine. Features woodburning ovens & fireplace. Also featured: Guided walking tours, art tours.
FACULTY: Timothy Bartling trained at the California Culinary Acad, was a chef at Zuni Cafe & works privately in NY & Italy. 4 local chefs present demos. Hostess Andrea Blum has lived in Italy for 10+ yrs.
COSTS: $2,500 includes 6 nights shared lodging in restored 500-yr-old villa (single supplement available), meals, planned activities.
CONTACT: Andrea Blum, Owner, Cucina Mondiale, 166 Carl Street, San Francisco, CA 94117; 415-731-2429, Fax 415-731-2429, cucinamondiale@earthlink.net.

CUCINA TOSCANA
Florence

Sponsor: Culinary travel service, culinary professional. Programs: Customized 1-day to 1-mo gastronomic excursions in Italy & cooking classes. Established: 1983. Facilities: Gourmet kitchen in private home. Also featured: Wine tastings, regional food producers, walking tours of Florence, shopping, special interest tours.
FACULTY: Owner Faith H. Willinger, author of Red, White & Greens: The Italian Way with Vegetables & Eating in Italy. She is a featured chef on PBS-TV & columnist for Epicurious.com.
COSTS: Itinerary planning from $75/day/person; exclusive cooking lessons $450/day/person (6 max).
CONTACT: Faith Heller Willinger, Cucina Toscana, via della Chiesa, 7, Florence, 50125 Italy; (39) 055-2337014, Fax (39) 055-2337014, fwillinger@dinonet.it.

CULINARY TOUR OF TUSCANY
Tuscany

Sponsor: The Clown, wine cellar, art gallery, & retail shop. Programs: Week-long culinary vacation in Tuscany featuring cooking classes, wine tastings, cultural & shopping trips. Established: 1999. Class/group size: 8-10. 10-15 programs/yr. Facilities: 2 well-equipped kitchens. Also featured: Visits to restaurants, vineyards & historic sights.
FACULTY: Tom Gutow, chef at Trattoria Delia in Burlington, VT.
COSTS: $2,500 includes shared lodging ($600 single supplement).
CONTACT: THE CLOWN, 123 Middle St., Portland, ME 4101; 207-756-7399, Fax 207-828-1549, workshops@the-clown.com, www.the-clown.com/tc-lists/mod.php?mod=userpage&menu=23&page_id=12.

DIANE SEED'S ROMAN KITCHEN & CULINARY ADVENTURES
Rome, Amalfi Coast & Naples, Puglia

Sponsor: Culinary professional Diane Seed. Programs: 6-day cooking vacations that include hands-on classes & excursions. Established: 1996. Class/group size: 12. 12 programs/yr. Facilities:

Rome: Purpose-designed kitchen in 17th-century Doria Pamphili palace. Amalfi coast: kitchens in local trattorias. Puglia: historic fortified farmhouse, now a Rerlais Chateaux hotel. Also featured: Market visits, fine dining, wine, olive oil & balsamic vinegar tastings, pizza making.
FACULTY: Diane Seed, British cooking teacher & author, who has lived in Rome for 30 years.
COSTS: Rome: $1,200 includes some meals. List of small hotels supplied. Amalfi coast: $2,400 includes lodging, meals, ground transport, day Naples trip. Puglia $2,800 all-inclusive from Brindisi airport.
CONTACT: Diane Seed, Diane Seed's Roman Kitchen, Via del Plebiscito 112, Rome, 186 Italy; (39) 06-6797-103, Fax (39) 06-6797-109, dianeseed@compuserve.com, www.italiangourmet.com.

DISCOVER FRIULI
Friuli-Venezia Giulia
Sponsor: Special interest travel company. Programs: Hands-on cooking holidays & wine appreciation classes. Established: 2000. Class/group size: 2-10. 15+ programs/yr. Facilities: Well-equipped kitchens at castles, country inns & farmhouses. Also featured: Visits to cheese makers & farms, market & winery tours, cultural excursions, Italian language & culture classes, customized tours.
FACULTY: Restaurant chefs, professional & experienced instructors, wine experts.
COSTS: €920-€2,500 includes lodging, meals, excursions.
CONTACT: Sonia Cos, Mrs., Discover Friuli, Via Manzoni 28, Cividale del Friuli (UD), 33043 Italy; (39) 0432-732882 or (39) 339-7245055, Fax (39) 0432-734386, info@discoverfriuli.com, www.discoverfriuli.com.

DIVINA CUCINA
Florence
Sponsor: Judy Witts Francini, IACP member & Certified Culinary Professional. Programs: Shopping in the Central Market & hands-on cooking classes (offered Tues-Thurs); food-lover's walking tours of Florence; tours of the Chianti wine region (offered daily). Established: 1984. Class/group size: 4-8 hands-on courses. 100+ programs/yr. Facilities: Fully-equipped apartment kitchen overlooking Florence's Mercato Centrale. Also featured: Winery tours, day trips, private instruction, visits to markets & food producers, dining in fine restaurants & private homes, sightseeing, visits to Italian artisans.
FACULTY: Judy Witts Francini, CCP.
COSTS: 3-day cooking session $750; 1-day cooking class $300; half-day walking tour of Florence with lunch, prices on request; 1-day Chianti tour, prices on request.
CONTACT: Judy Witts Francini, Owner, Divina Cucina, Via Taddea, 31, Florence, 50123 Italy; (39) 055-29-25-78, Fax (39) 055-29-25-78, info@divinacucina.com, www.divinacucina.com.

ESPERIENZE ITALIANE
Tuscany, Veneto, Umbria, Piedmont, Sicily
Sponsor: Lidia Bastianich, co-owner of Felidia Ristorante. Programs: 7- to 10-day trips that feature cooking demos, dining in fine restaurants, art tours, meetings with wine producers, chefs, & Italian artists, visits to wine estates. Established: 1997. Class/group size: 15-20. 4 programs/yr. Also featured: Custom-designed group trips.
FACULTY: Lidia Bastianich, author of Lidia's Italian Table & star of PBS series; Burton Anderson, author of The Wine Atlas of Italy; art historians Tanya Bastianich & Shelly Burgess.
COSTS: $3,800-$4,100, includes 4- & 5-star shared hotel lodging, most meals, planned excursions, ground transport.
CONTACT: Shelly Burgess Nicotra, Program Director, Esperienze Italiane Travel c/o Felidia Ristorante, 243 E 58th St., New York, NY 10022; 212-758-1488, 800-480-2426, Fax 212-935-7687, shelly@lidiasitaly.com, www.lidiasitaly.com.

FLAVOURS COOKERY HOLIDAYS
Bologna, Puglia & Rome
Sponsor: Cookery holiday operator. Programs: Hands-on cookery holidays in Italy. Weekly courses & short breaks. Established: 1998. Class/group size: 8 max. 26 programs/yr. Facilities: Private luxury villas with fully-equipped kitchen. Also featured: Excursions to local food producers (wine, olive oil, cheese, honey) & other places of interest.
FACULTY: Professional local cooks.
COSTS: £1,049/8 days, £599/5 days includes lodging, meals, excursions, airport transfers.
CONTACT: Lorne Blyth, Flavours of Italy Ltd., PO Box 525, Broxburn, West Lothian,Scotland; (44) (0)1506 854621, Fax (44) (0)1526 854102, info@flavoursholidays.com, www.flavours-foodiehols.co.uk.

FOOD LOVERS' ADVENTURES IN EMILIA ROMAGNA
Emilia-Romagna towns
Sponsor: Travel company specializing in Italian culinary vacations. Programs: 7-day programs that include hands-on classes in restaurants & private homes, visits & tastings with producers of parmesan cheese, balsamic vinegar, prosciutto, olive oil, wines. Established: 1996. Class/group size: 2-8+. Monthly programs/yr. Facilities: Restaurant & private home kitchens. Also featured: Excursions to markets, herb garden, ceramic studio, castle, mosaics in Ravenna, Bologna shops, truffle hunting, spa, golf.
FACULTY: Restaurant & family chefs.
COSTS: $2,750 includes shared lodging, meals, planned excursions.
CONTACT: Marcello & Raffaella Tori, Owners, Bluone Tour Operator, Via Parigi, 11, Bologna, 40121 Italy; (39) 051-263546, Fax (39) 051-267774, info@bluone.com, www.bluone.com. In North America: Margaret Cowan, 101-1184 Denman St., #310, Vancouver, BC, Canada V6G 2M9; 800-557-0370 or 604-681-4074, Fax 604-681-4909URL http://www.italycookingtours.com/.

GOURMET GETAWAYS
Italy
Sponsor: Travel company specializing in culinary tours to Italy. Programs: Four different 5- to 6-night cooking programs combined with sightseeing trips to nearby towns. Established: 1998. Class/group size: 4-9. 10 programs/yr. Facilities: Hotel kitchens.
FACULTY: Chef Giancarlo with the Excelsior Vittorio hotel in Sorrento. Chef Massimo Infarati at Castello Dell'Oscano in Perugia.
COSTS: $2,400 includes shared lodging for 5-6 nights. Single supplement extra.
CONTACT: Marlene Iaciofano, Pres., Gourmet Getaways, 45 Eagle Nest Rd., Morristown, NJ 07960; 973-644-0906, 888-95-Italy, Fax 973-644-0907, getaways@optonline.net, www.gourmetget.com.

GIULIANO BUGIALLI'S COOKING IN FLORENCE
Florence *(See display ad page 306)*
Sponsor: Cookbook author Giuliano Bugialli. Programs: 1-wk hands-on vacation programs. Established: 1973. Class/group size: 18. 4 programs/yr. Facilities: Large newly-equipped kitchens in a Chianti villa, wood-burning brick oven & hearth. Also featured: Dining in fine restaurants & trattorias, gastronomic & oenologic trips, tastings.
FACULTY: Giuliano Bugialli is author of The Fine Art of Italian Cooking, Tastemaker Award winners Giuliano Bugialli's Classic Techniques of Italian Cooking, Giuliano Bugialli's Foods of Italy, Julia Child Award winner Foods of Sicily & Sardinia.
COSTS: $4,000 includes most meals, planned excursions, & first class or superior hotel lodging in central Florence.
CONTACT: Giuliano Bugialli's Cooking in Florence, 252 Seventh Ave., #7R, New York, NY 10001; 646-638-0883, 646-638-1099, Fax 646-638-0381, bugialli@aol.com, www.bugialli.com.

IL CHIOSTRO
Vagliagli, Siena

Sponsor: Private school. Programs: Hands-on 1-wk or 10-day (June & October) traditional Tuscan country cooking courses in Italy, featuring visits to olive oil, vinegar, grappa, & honey producers, butchers, bakers. Established: 1995. Class/group size: 4-12. 2 programs/yr. Facilities: Authentic Tuscan country villa or inn at 900-yr-old Chianti winery, with pool. Also featured: Excursions to Tuscan hilltowns, day trips to Florence, walking tour of Siena, winery & sommelier tours, private entree to castle & gardens, local artisans.

FACULTY: Chef Michael Vignapiano from New York Restaurant School, Chef Linda Mironti.

COSTS: $1,400-$2,000 includes meals, lodging, planned activities, transfers from Siena.

CONTACT: Michael Mele, Director, Il Chiostro Inc., 241 W. 97th St., #13N, New York, NY 10025; 800-990-3506, Fax 212-666-3506, ilchiostro@hotmail.com, www.ilchiostro.com.

IL FAÈ COOKING COURSES
San Pietro di Feletto, Veneto

Sponsor: Il Faè B&B. Programs: 5-day cooking classes on traditional Italian cuisine. Courses for professionals on blast chiller application & vacuum system. Class/group size: 5 min. Facilities: Kitchen of Il Faè. Also featured: Gluten-free & private cooking classes on request.

FACULTY: Chef Marco Fattorel, member of Fed'n of Italian Cooks; Chef Nicola Michieletto, specialist in Mediterranean & natural cuisine.

CONTACT: Salvatore Valerio, Il Faè Cooking Courses, via faè 1, San Pietro di Feletto, Veneto, 31020 Italy; (39) 0438 787117, Fax (39) 0438 787818, mail@ilfae.com, www.ilfae.com/. In the US: mcushing@lindentravel.com.

IL TESTIMONIO TUSCAN VACATION
Tuscany
Sponsor: Maria Teresa Sardella. Programs: At least 4 days of regional cooking lessons, cultural trips to art sites & lesser known Tuscan locales. Established: 1996. Class/group size: 8. 10 programs/yr. Facilities: 18th-century farmhouse. Also featured: Aesthetic & shiatsu massage, Italian language lessons.
FACULTY: Maria Teresa Sardella, MA in Sociology, Slowfood Sommelier Certificate; Isabella Ferrari, MA in Foreign Languages; Norberto Perosino, MA in Medicine & Psychiatry, Italian art & culture expert; Mario Luridiana, physiotherapist.
COSTS: €80/day (€60-€70/day) includes single (double) room, breakfast & dinner. Half-day cooking lesson €30. Cultural trip €50-€70.
CONTACT: Maria Teresa Sardella, Owner, Il Testimonio Tuscan Vacation, Bagnano - Certaldo, Florence, 50052 Italy; (39) 0571-660045, Fax (39) 0571-660045, sardellamt@libero.it, www.iltestimonio.it. Isabella Ferrari isaferrar@yahoo.it.

INTERNATIONAL COOKING SCHOOL OF ITALIAN FOOD & WINE
Bologna, Piedmont, Tuscany
Sponsor: Private school established by chef & author Mary Beth Clark. Programs: Hands-on courses include: 4-day Taste of Emilia-Romagna, 6-day Basics of Great Italian Cooking, 7-day Savoring Emilia-Romagna & Tuscany & October Truffle Festival. Established: 1987. Class/group size: 12. 11 programs/yr. Facilities: Modern professional kitchen with individual work stations in a Renaissance palazzo. Also featured: Visits to food producers & outdoor food markets, regional olive oiltastings, private winery tours, truffle hunt, dining in Michelin-star restaurants with private demos.
FACULTY: Chef Mary Beth Clark, cooking teacher & cookbook author; a pasta chef; a Neapolitan pizza chef; Michelin-star Italian chef.
COSTS: $1,895-$3,725 includes most meals, first-class to deluxe lodging, ground transport, excursions, Michelin-star dining.
CONTACT: Mary Beth Clark, Owner, International Cooking School Of Italian Food & Wine, 201 E. 28th St., #15B, New York, NY 0; 212-779-1921, Fax 212-779-3248, contact@marybethclark.com, www.internationalcookingschool.com.

ISTITUTO VENEZIA
Venice
Sponsor: Private school offering courses in Italian language, culture & cooking. Established: 1995. Class/group size: 8. Facilities: Private apartments or residences. Also featured: Custom group programs.
CONTACT: Matteo Savini, Director, Istituto Venezia, Dorsoduro 3116/A (Camp S. Margherita), Venice, 30123 Italy; (39) 041-5224331, Fax (39) 041-5285628, info@istitutovenezia.com, www.istitutovenezia.com.

ITALIAN ART & COOKING
Siena, Tuscany
Sponsor: Private Italian cooking & language school. Programs: 1- to 4-wk intensive seasonal Italian cooking courses for groups & individuals. Established: 1979. Class/group size: 5-12. 10 programs/yr. Facilities: New fully-equipped professional kitchen & frescoed dining room. Established language school. Also featured: Italian language & cultural courses, excursions to vineyards & sites of interest.
FACULTY: Professional cooking school instructors Mario Neri, Serena Massari; sommeliers & specialized chefs.
COSTS: Amateur: $465/1 wk, $715/2 wks.Professional: $800/2 wks, $1,350/4 wks.
CONTACT: Sonia Di Centa, Executive Director, Soc. Dante Alighieri - Siena, Via Tommaso Pendola, 37, Siena, 53100 Italy; (39) 0577 49533, Fax (39) 0577 270646, marketing@dantealighieri.com, www.dantealighieri.com.

ITALIAN COOKERY COURSE
Italy

Sponsor: Private school. Programs: 6-day hands-on Italian cookery course featuring antipasti, primi, secondi, contorni e dolce. Established: 2001. Class/group size: 8-10. 2 programs/yr. Facilities: Hotel kitchen. Also featured: Seasonal hunting for & cooking wild mushrooms. Mountain walks for trekkers, with guides available.
FACULTY: 3 professional chef/teachers. Head chef Elena Vecchio.
COSTS: €750 includes 5 nights 3-star hotel lodging & meals.
CONTACT: Gary Vincent, Chef/Teacher, Italian Cookery Course, Albergo Alpino, Via Cantoniera 7, Colere, (Bg), 24020 Italy; (39) 34631103, Fax (39) 34638770, albalp@tin.it.

ITALIAN COOKERY IN TUSCANY WITH URSULA FERRIGNO
Lucca, Tuscany

Sponsor: Private school. Programs: 4- & 7-day residential cookery programs featuring hands-on classes, & excursions to Lucca & Florence, & to wineries of the Lucchese Hills. Established: 1996. Class/group size: 10-14. 5-6 programs/yr. Facilities: Tuscan farmhouse kitchen. Traditional wood-burning oven for pizza & bread-making. Also featured: Art & architectural visits. Swimming, horseback riding, tennis.
FACULTY: Ursula Ferrigno, cookbook author, TV/radio guest; plus her assistant.
COSTS: 4-day program: £585/£625. 7-day program: £985. Includes shared lodging, meals with wine, ground transport, wine tastings, excursions.
CONTACT: Berenice Bonallack, Italian Cookery in Tuscany with Ursula Ferrigno, Box 15, London,England; (44) 20 7680 1377, Fax (44) 20 7680 1377, tours@vallicorte.com, www.vallicorte.com.

ITALIAN COOKERY WEEKS LTD
Amalfi Coast, & Umbrian/Tuscan border

Sponsor: Culinary professional Susanna Gelmetti. Programs: 7-day gastronomic holidays that include regional cookery instruction & excursions to local sites of cultural & historical interest. Established: 1990. Class/group size: 20. 10 programs/yr.
FACULTY: Professional Italian chefs.
COSTS: £1,399 includes 7 nights shared lodging, meals, excursions.
CONTACT: Susanna Gelmetti, Italian Cookery Weeks Ltd, PO Box 2482, London,England; (44) (020) 8208-0112, Fax (44) (020) 7627 8467, info@italian-cookery-weeks.co.uk, www.italian-cookery-weeks.co.uk. http://www.cuisineinternational.com.

ITALIAN CUISINE IN FLORENCE
Florence

Sponsor: Culinary professional Masha Innocenti. Programs: 3- to 5-day hands-on courses. Special 1- or 2-day demo classes for larger groups with travel agencies. Established: 1983. Class/group size: 8 hands-on/18 demo. 11 programs/yr. Facilities: 300-sq-ft kitchen with modern equipment. Also featured: Private instruction, food lectures.
FACULTY: Masha Innocenti, CCP, IACP, diploma from Scuola di Arte Culinaria Cordon Bleu, a member of the Assoc Italiana Sommeliers & Commanderie des Cordons Bleus de France.
COSTS: $780/5-day gourmet cuisine courses, $470/3-day intensive course, includes meals. Private classes $165/day.
CONTACT: Masha Innocenti, Italian Cuisine in Florence, Via Trieste 1, Florence, 50139 Italy; (39) 055-499503, Fax (39) 055-480041. US Contact: William Grossi, 182 Four Corners Rd., Ancramdale, NY 12503, 518-329-1141.

ITALIAN CULINARY INSTITUTE FOR FOREIGNERS
Costigliole d'Asti, Torino

Sponsor: Professional cooking school in Italy. Programs: 3-, 4-, & 7-day hands-on culinary & enology courses. Established: 1991. Class/group size: 10. 8 programs/yr. Facilities: New high-tech facili-

ties include Modulari stainless steel equipment. Wine cellar & olive oil tasting room, with 200+ labels. Also featured: Market visit. Custom tours, including airfare.
FACULTY: Chef Pietro Baldi has 30+ yrs experience in Italian cuisine & wine making. Sergio Zanetti has worked in major European hotels & presented Italian cuisine in the Far East & S. America. Regional guest chefs.
COSTS: $799-$1,799 includes meals, lodging in mini-apartments, airport transportation.
CONTACT: Enrico Bazzoni, Director, ICIF-USA, 126 2nd Place, Brooklyn, NY 11231; 718-875-0547, Fax 718-875-5856, Eabchef@aol.com, www.icif.com.

ITALIAN FOOD ARTISANS
Tuscany, Emilia-Romagna, Campania & Piemonte
Sponsor: Pamela Sheldon Johns, culinary professional & cookbook author. Programs: Week-long excursions with emphasis on regional artisan products. 1-day workshops for small groups. Established: 1994. Class/group size: 8 max. 15 programs/yr. Facilities: Restaurants, cooking schools, & farms. Also featured: Hands-on cooking classes, wine tastings, visits to markets & artisan food producers, dining in fine restaurants & private homes.
FACULTY: Director Pamela Sheldon Johns is author of 12 cookbooks including Italian Food Artisans, Parmigiano!, Pasta!, & Pizza Napoletana!. She oversees the local Italian chef/instructors.
COSTS: €2,650/wk for Tuscany, Campania, & Emilia-Romagna. €2,850 for Piemonte includes all land costs: shared lodging in a villa or 4-star hotel, meals, ground transport, planned excursions.
CONTACT: Pamela Sheldon Johns, Director, Italian Food Artisans, 27 W. Anapamu St., #427, Santa Barbara, CA 93101; 805-963-7289, Fax 928-222-3935, Pamela@FoodArtisans.com, www.FoodArtisans.com. In Italy:Poggio Etrusco,Via del Pelago 1153045 Montepulciano (Siena) Italy;Tel/Fax (39) 0578 798 370.

ITALIAN GOURMET COOKING CLASSES IN PORTOVENERE
Multiple locations
Sponsor: Grand Hotel Portovenere - Chef Paolo Monti's Northern Culinary Program. Programs: 7-day courses covering fish, vegetables, antipasti, sauces, soups, salads, pasta, main dishes, desserts. Established: 1994. Class/group size: 6-12. 8-10 programs/yr. Facilities: Hands on Cooking class kitchen with overhead mirror & audio system. Also featured: Visit to vineyards, olive oil mill, Parma, Cinque Terre. Shorter courses & 1-day classes available. Instruction in English, French, German. Wine tasting & wine tours.
FACULTY: Grand Hotel Portovenere's Chef Paolo Monti & his kitchen team.
COSTS: €2,090 includes lodging at the 4-star Grand Hotel Portovenere (single room supplement €400), meals, wines & excursions.
CONTACT: Paolo Monti, Chef, Chef Paolo Monti's Culinary Program, Via Garibaldi, 5, Portovenere, 19025 Italy; (39) 0187-79-26-10, Fax (39) 0187-79-06-61, paolomonti@cucina-italiana.com, www.cucina-italiana.com. For information in the USA & Canada: 1-800-557-0370.

ITALIAN & MEDITERRANEAN COOKING VACATIONS AT CASA OMBUTO
Tuscany *(See display ad page 310)*
Sponsor: Casa Ombuto. Programs: 1-wk hands-on culinary vacations that offer an Italian & a Mediterranean cookery course. Both include visits to wineries, olive oil & cheese producers. Established: 2000. Class/group size: 8-12. 20 programs/yr. Facilities: Professional kitchen designed for cooking lessons in an old Tuscan cantina. Also featured: Shopping in Arezzo & dining at local restaurant. Hiking, day trip to Florence, golf course nearby.
FACULTY: Italian chef Paola Baccetti runs the Italian course & international chef Sylvie Pragout runs the Mediterranean course.
COSTS: €1,950 (€2,350)/wk includes shared (single) lodging at the luxury villa Casa Ombuto, most meals, use of facilities including heated pool. Non-cooking guest €1,300/wk.
CONTACT: Pippa Ward-Smith, Casa Ombuto, Larniano 21, Poppi, AR, 52014 Italy; (39) 3487363864, Fax (31) 35 5334607, info@italiancookerycourse.com, www.italiancookingvacation.com.

ITALIAN RIVIERA COOKS
Cinque Terre
Sponsor: Mother & daughter team Lori Boyd & Karen Haas. Programs: 1-wk cooking vacation programs. Established: 2003. Class/group size: 10. 12 programs/yr. Facilities: Villa kitchen. Also featured: Shopping, Central Market tour, food market visits.
FACULTY: Local Italian mothers & grandmothers.
COSTS: $2,500, all inclusive.
CONTACT: Lori Boyd, Owner, Italian Riviera Cooks, 1029 Ponderosa Ridge, Little Elm, TX 75068; 469-438-0772, Fax 972-294-8766, lori@italianrivieracooks.com, www.italianrivieracooks.com.

LA CORNUCOPIA ITALIA
Tuscany, Umbria, Liguria, Sicily & Piedmont
Sponsor: American wine tour operator based near Siena. Programs: 1-, 3- & 8-day wine tours that include cooking classes, fine dining, visits to artisans' workshops, & cultural excursions. Established: 2000. Class/group size: 15-20.
FACULTY: Steven R. Kronenberg studied art history at the Italian university in Florence & completed the professional course for sommeliers; Elvira H.A. Ackermann is a certified sommelier.
CONTACT: Steven Kronenberg, Owner, La Cornucopia Italia, Podere Casaini / Via di Tolle 174, Scrofiano (SI), 53040 Italy; (39) 0577 660290, Fax (39) 0577 660290, info@lacornucopiaitalia.com, www.lacornucopiaitalia.com.

LA DOLCE VITA WINE TOURS
Piedmont, Tuscany, Sicily, Cinque Terre, Veneto
Sponsor: Specialty tour operator. Programs: Week-long wine tours in Italy. Tastings & winemaker talks on production, history & trends, food & wine pairings. Established: 1999. Class/group size: 2-16. 17 programs/yr. Facilities: Vineyards, castles, villas, hotels. Also featured: Some itineraries include hiking or biking.
FACULTY: Owners/guides Claudio Bisio, a native of Piedmont, & Patricia Thomson, a wine writer for Tastes of Italia & Gastronomica.
COSTS: $2,295-$2,795 includes 3- or 4-star lodging, tastings, most meals, local transportation.
CONTACT: Pat Thomson, President, La Dolce Vita Wine Tours, 576 Fifth St., Brooklyn, NY 11215; 888-746-0022, Fax 718-499-2618, info@dolcetours.com, www.dolcetours.com. www.dolcetours.com.

LA NOSTRA TOSCANA
Pisa, Lucca, Florence, Greve in Chianti, Siena
Sponsor: Sommelier Fabrizio Ferruzzi & his wife Cathy. Programs: 4-day food & wine tour with hands-on cooking classes preparing lunch. Afternoons devoted to escorted Tuscan city tours & fine dining. Established: 1999. Class/group size: 5-8. 5 programs/yr. Facilities: Corte di Valle, a renovated villa with modern kitchen. Also featured: Wine & olive oil tastings.
FACULTY: Tuscan gourmet/sommelier Fabrizio Ferruzzi, founder of Arte degli Oliandoli; Cathy Fabrizio, 20+ yrs experience with Tuscan cooking; Tuscan chef Beppe Ceserali.

Costs: $2,900/4-days includes meals, lodging, ground transport, activities.

Contact: Mary Frances Sheffield, General Manager, La Nostra Toscana, 3045 West Ardmore, Chicago, IL 60659; 773-275-6903, Fax 773-275-6985, Theshefs@aol.com.

LA PENTOLA DELLE MERAVIGLIE
Florence
Sponsor: Culinary professional. Programs: 1- to 10-session courses on a variety of topics.
Faculty: Barbara Desderi.
Costs: €45/session.
Contact: Barbara Desderi, Owner, La Pentola delle Meraviglie, Via Aretina, 118 r, Florence, 50136 Italy; (39) 055670205, Fax (39) 055670205, info@lapentoladellemeraviglie.it, www.lapentoladellemeraviglie.it.

LA VILLA CUCINA
Umbria & Tuscany
Sponsor: Culinary travel provider. Programs: 1-wk vacations that combine a villa holiday & cooking school vacation, including hands-on classes, visits to markets, wineries, olive oil & artisan food producers, sightseeing, restaurant dining. Established: 1998. Class/group size: 12. 3+ programs/yr. Facilities: Professional kitchen. Also featured: Private instruction.
Faculty: Daniel Rosati has been a cooking instructor at The New School in NYC 12+ yrs, was teaching assistant to Giuliano Bugialli, & received the Auguste Escoffier gold medal.
Costs: Programs start at $3,450 including shared lodging at Il Poggio degli Olivi in Umbria & at Tenuta la Bandita in western Tuscany, both restored 17th-century villas & working agricultural complexes, meals, ground transport, planned activities.
Contact: Daniel Rosati, Owner, La Villa Cucina, 14 Wilson Ave., 3rd Floor, Newark, NJ 07103; 973-344-7577, info@lavillacucina.com, www.lavillacucina.com.

LUNA CONVENTO COOKING CLASSES WITH ENRICO FRANZESE
Amalfi
Sponsor: Luna Convento Hotel. Programs: 1-wk culinary vacations that include 4 morning demo & participation classes. Established: 1991. Class/group size: 12-18. 8 programs/yr. Facilities: Luna Convento Hotel's Saracen Tower, overlooking the sea. Also featured: Guided excursions to Sorrento, Ravello, Pompeii, & Amalfi; dinner at Don Alfonso, a Michelin 3-star restaurant owned by Alfonso & Livio Iccharino.
Faculty: Enrico Franzese, trained at the Cipriani in Venice & Rome's Hassler, won the 1990 Parma Ham Chef's Competition in Bologna & appears on Italian TV; interpreter Rosemary Anastasio.
Costs: $2,700 ($3,000) includes meals, planned excursions, transportation from Salerno, & first class double (single) occupancy lodging & private bath at the 4-star Luna Convento Hotel, a restored 13th-century convent.
Contact: Rosemary Anastasio, School Director, Luna Convento, Amalfi, SA, 84011 Italy; (39) 089-830-130, info@cuisineinternational.com, www.cuisineinternational.com. In the U.S.: Judy Ebrey, Cuisine International, Inc. P.O. Box 25228, Dallas, TX 75225; 214-373-1161, Fax 214-373-1162.

MAMA MARGARET & FRIENDS' COOKING ADVENTURES IN ITALY
Piedmont, Tuscany, Umbria, Emilia-Romagna, Amalfi
Sponsor: Margaret Cowan Direct Ltd. & specialty tour operators in Italy. Programs: 3- to 8-day cooking holidays with cooking classes in fine restaurants, winery visits & tastings, winemakers' dinners, food producer visits. Established: 1995. Class/group size: 2-7. 60 programs/yr. Facilities: Restaurant kitchens. Also featured: Custom designed tours.
Faculty: Restaurant chefs. A farm family in Tuscany.
Costs: $1,200-$3,095, all-inclusive.
Contact: Margaret Cowan, Mama Margaret & Friends' Cooking Adventures in Italy, 310 101-1184 Denman St., Vancouver, BC,Canada; 800-557-0370/604-681-4074, Fax 604-681-4909, margaret@italycookingschools.com, www.italycookingtours.com.

MAMI CAMILLA COOKING CLASS ITALY
Sorrento

Sponsor: Private cooking school. Programs: 3- to 7-session courses that focus on the food, techniques, culinary traditions & artisan products of the south of Italy; individual classes. Established: 2002. Class/group size: 5 max. Facilities: Country-style home with kitchen & classroom. Also featured: Visits to cheese factories, pasta & olive oil producers, wine cellars, San Marzano tomato factory.
FACULTY: Biagio, the lead native Italian chef, has 30 years of international culinary experience.
COSTS: €100-€2,000.
CONTACT: Mami Camilla Cooking Class Italy, Via Cocumella 4, 80065 S. Agnello di Sorrento, Naples, Italy; (39) 081 878 20 67, Fax (39) 081 878 20 67, info@mamicamilla.com, www.mamicamilla.com.

MAMMA AGATA COOKING CLASSES
Ravello

Sponsor: Travel company owned by Chiara Lima, daughter of Mamma Agata. Programs: AM cooking classes, wine tastings. Established: 1997. Class/group size: 8 max. Facilities: Mamma Agata's simple, well-equipped kitchen in her cliff-top home with terraces & gardens. Also featured: Visits to cheese & lemon factories, boat excursion, sightseeing.
FACULTY: Mama Agata has cooked for Humphrey Bogart, Audrey Hepburn, Jacqueline Kennedy & Gore Vidal.
COSTS: €200/day includes lunch.
CONTACT: Chiara Lima, Proprietor, Mamma Agata Cooking Classes, Via San Cosma, 9, Ravello, Salerno, 84010 Italy; (39) 089-857019, (39) 089 858432, Fax (39) 089-858432, info@mammaagata.com, www.mammaagata.com.

MARIA BATTAGLIA – LA CUCINA ITALIANA, INC.
Italy

Sponsor: Culinary professional. Programs: 9-day demo cooking vacation courses. 5 programs/yr. Also featured: Sightseeing, dining in fine restaurants, shopping, visits to nearby towns.
FACULTY: Maria Battaglia has conducted seminars on food, wine & culture of Italy for 15+ yrs. She was national spokesperson for Contadina Foods.
COSTS: $3,250-$4,260 includes air-fare, lodging, meals, planned activities.
CONTACT: Maria Battaglia, Maria Battaglia - La Cucina Italiana, Inc., P.O. Box 6528, Evanston, IL 60204; 847-933-0077, Fax 847-933-0088, mbcucina@aol.com, www.la-cucina-italiana.com.

MEDITERRANEAN LIFE
Bari, Brindisi, Lecce, Taranto

Sponsor: Tour operator specializing in Apulia & Southern Italy. Programs: Culinary tours featuring lessons on traditional Apulian recipes, wine, olive oil, architecture, history, heritage. Includes excursions to orchards, citrus groves, oil-mill, olive tree farm. Established: 1992. Class/group size: 4-12. 12 programs/yr. Facilities: Farmhouse or hotel kitchens.
FACULTY: Local chefs or experts in Mediterranean cooking.
CONTACT: Rossana Muolo, Owner, Itinerant Course of Mediterranean Cooking, SS.379 Savelletri - Torre Canne Loc. Forcatella Piccola, Savelletri di Fasano , BR, 72010 Italy; (39) 080 48 29 421, Fax (39) 080 48 28 036, info@mediterraneanlife.com, www.mediterraneanlife.com.

PALAZZO TERRANOVA
Umbria

Sponsor: Bed & breakfast hotel. Programs: Cooking weekends in November during the Porcini & Truffle festival. Truffle hunting, Umbrian cooking classes; visits to markets, farms, food producers & vineyards; olive oil, balsamic vinegar & wine tastings; local excursions. Class/group size: 6 min. 5 programs/yr. Facilities: Hotel kitchen including wood fired oven. Also featured: Courses on wine, art, art history. Swimming pool, boules, horseback, trekking, golf, hot air ballooning, tennis, archery, cultural tours.

FACULTY: Hotel owner Sarah Townsend.

COSTS: From €200/day including lunch. Lodging €685/night including breakfast.

CONTACT: Sarah Townsend, Palazzo Terranova Srl, Loc. Ronti Morra, Perugia, 6010 Italy; (39) 075 8570083, Fax (39) 075 8570014, bookings@palazzoterranova.com, www.palazzoterranova.com.

PEGGY MARKEL'S CULINARY ADVENTURES
Tuscany, Elba & Sicily; Morocco

Sponsor: Culinary tour provider Peggy Markel. Programs: 5-, 7- & 10-day hands-on culinary vacations: La Cucina al Focolare, Rustic Mediterranean Island Cooking, A Different Italy, A Feast for the Senses. Weekend summer & winter intensives in the US. Established: 1991. Class/group size: 16 max. 15+ programs/yr. Facilities: Professional kitchens with the latest equipment, including wood-burning oven, individual work stations. Also featured: Visits to bakery, artisan cheese maker & herb farm, market & winery tour, dining in fine restaurants, cultural excursions.

FACULTY: Program founder Peggy Markel; Piero Ferrini, chef-professor; Luciano Casini, chef/owner of Il Chiasso, Elba; author/cook Anna Tasca Lanza, women chefs of Morocco. Mr. Pat, Thailand. Chefs of Laos.

COSTS: $2,500-$4,195 includes lodging, meals, excursions, ground transport.

CONTACT: Peggy Markel, Director, Peggy Markel's Culinary Adventures, P.O. Box 54, Boulder, CO; 800-988-2851, 303-413-1289, Fax 303-440-8598, info@cookinitaly.com, www.cookinitaly.com.

ROBERTO'S ITALIAN TABLE
Venice

Sponsor: Culinary professional Robert Wilk. Programs: 1-week culinary & cultural holiday that includes cooking lessons at the Hotel Cipriani, cultural activities, visits to private palaces. Established: 1995. Class/group size: 1-20. Daily programs/yr. Facilities: Kitchens of Hotel Cipriani, Roberto's home kitchen in the 15th-century Palazzo Michiel Berlendis. Also featured: Tours of countryside, wineries & vineyards, dining in fine restaurants & private homes, sightseeing.

FACULTY: Chefs Renato Piccoloto & Roberto Gatto (Hotel Cipriani), Cultural Director Dr. Joseph A. Precker, Host/Cooking Teacher Roberto Wilk.

COSTS: $4,950/1-wk program includes 5-star hotel lodging, most meals, planned activities. $550/1-day program ($450 for each additional person).

CONTACT: Robert Wilk, Roberto's Italian Table, Dorsoduro 3441, Venice, 30123 Italy; Fax (39) 041-714-571, roberto@italiantable.com, www.italiantable.com.

ROMANTICA COOKING TOURS
Italy

Sponsor: Tour operator specializing in vacations in Italy. Offices in U.S. & Italy. Programs: Vacations that include cooking classes, wine, cheese & olive oil tastings, vinery tours, sightseeing & excursions. Established: 1985. Class/group size: 1-50. 150+ programs/yr. Facilities: Cooking schools, restaurant kitchens, country villa & home kitchens. Also featured: Customized group & individual travel. Itineraries & tours with overnight in small boutique hotels. Private boat rental.

FACULTY: Restaurant chefs, regional experts.

COSTS: $200-$3,460 includes hotel lodging, most meals, tastings, excursions, sightseeing.

CONTACT: Aldo Caronia, Dir. of USA Operations, Romantica Tours, 580 Roger Williams Ave., Highland Park, IL 60035; 847-433-7560, Fax 847-433-7561, info@romanticatours.com, www.romanticatours.com. Italy Office (Rome): Damiana Bianchi, V.P/Dir. of Italy Operations Via Asconio Pediano, 24 00175 Rome, Italy; dbianchi@romanticatours.com; (39) 067142017; fax(39) 067142039.

SAVOR ITALIA!
Sicily, Tuscany, Veneto

Sponsor: Culinary professional Renee Restivo. Programs: One-week culinary tours that include cooking lessons, wine tastings, walking tours, visits to markets & food producers, cultural excursions. Established: 2004. Class/group size: 12-13. 10 programs/yr. Facilities: Food producers, villas, restaurants. Also featured: Fresco painting & Italian language lessons.

FACULTY: Renee Restivo, cooking instructor at Toscana Saporita Cooking School, former chef/recipe tester for La Cucina Italiana magazine, food writer.
COSTS: $2,600 includes lodging, most meals, ground transport, planned activities.
CONTACT: Renee Restivo, President, Savor Italia!, ,; 201-437-9460, tuscanchef@hotmail.com.

SAY ITALY!™
Messina, Sicily
Sponsor: Specialty travel company. Programs: 1-wk culinary & cultural tours that include hands-on cooking classes & visits to markets, winemakers, museums & nearby towns. Established: 2002. Class/group size: 10-16. ~5 programs/yr. Also featured: Horseback, tennis, swimming, excursions.
FACULTY: Elena Feminò & other native Italian cooks.
COSTS: $1,600 includes shared apartment lodging, meals, excursions.
CONTACT: Jackie Hendrix, Owner, Say Italy!™, P. O. Box 1600, Houston, TX 0; 866-621-6676, 713-621-6676, Fax 713-552-9512, info@sayitaly.com, www.sayitaly.com.

SCUOLA DI ARTE CULINARIA 'CORDON BLEU'
Florence, Tuscany
Sponsor: Private school. Programs: 4-session courses & 7-day cooking, wine, art, culture programs. Established: 1985. Class/group size: 15 max. 12 programs/yr. Facilities: 40-sq-meter teaching kitchen. Also featured: Wine tasting, guided excursions & tours, market visit.
FACULTY: 2 full- & 2 part-time instructors. Cristina Blasi & Gabriella Mari, 18 yrs teaching experience, sommeliers & olive oil experts, authored books on ancient Roman cooking, members Commanderie des Cordon Bleus de France, IACP.
COSTS: Classes from €60; 4-session course €360 including VAT & insurance; 7-day program €750 including one 5-session course, 3 dinners, planned activities.
CONTACT: Emilia Onesti, Secretary, Scuola di Arte Culinaria 'Cordon Bleu', Via di Mezzo, 55/R, Florence, 50121 Italy; (39) 055-2345468, Fax (39) 055-2345468, info@cordonbleu-it.com, www.cordonbleu-it.com.

SCUOLA LEONARDO DA VINCI
Rome, Florence & Siena
Sponsor: Private school. Programs: Hands-on Italian cooking & Italian wine courses held 1 evening weekly for a 2-wk or 4-wk session. Established: 1977. Class/group size: 10-15. ~40 programs/yr. Facilities: Fully-equipped professional kitchen. Also featured: Italian language & culture courses, excursions to vineyards & other places of interest.
FACULTY: Professional cooking school instructors & sommeliers.
COSTS: Italian cooking or wine course 2 evenings over 2 wks €95; 4 evenings over 4 wks €150.
CONTACT: Niccolò Villiger, Co-webmaster, Italian Cuisine & Wine Courses in Florence, Rome, Siena, Via Brunelleschi 4, Florence, 50123 Italy; (39) 055-290305, Fax (39) 055-290396, info@scuolaleonardo.com, www.scuolaleonardo.com.

SCUOLA DI ARTE CULINARIA CORDON BLEU, PERUGIA
Ponte Vallecceppi, Umbria
Sponsor: Private school. Programs: 1- to 9-session courses on basic to advanced cooking plus specific topics from appetizers to desserts. 3- to 5-day programs in collaboration with wineries, restaurants & food producers. Established: 1997. Class/group size: 8-12. 25+ programs/yr. Facilities: 16th century estate with a home kitchen.
FACULTY: Andrea Sposini & Roberto Menichetti, who both studied at the Cordon Bleu School of Culinary Arts in Rome.
COSTS: €60/session, $600-$1,000 for multi-day programs.
CONTACT: Sheila Santolamazza, Scuola di Arte Culinaria Cordon Bleu Perugia, viale Ponte Nestore, 23, Marsciano, 6055 Italy; (39) 333 9813695, Fax (39) 075 874 1690, Sheila@gestionecupido.com, www.gestionecupido.com/ENG/corsi/default.htm. Andrea Sposini, (39) 338 392 8335, Fax (39) 075 874 8316, Chef@gestionecupido.com.

SICILIAN ODYSSEY
Sicily

Sponsor: Culinary travel company. Programs: 7 night culinary & sightseeing program that features cooking with 2 well-known Sicilian chefs. Established: 1998. Class/group size: 4-10. 2 programs/yr. Also featured: Visits to the major tourist sites on Sicily, wine tasting, visits to food artisans, dinners in private homes.

FACULTY: Jack Bruno, president of the Sicilian Chef's Org & owner/chef of the restaurant Villa Albanese Rubicon. Signora Giuliana Condorelli & her husband are experts in ancient cuisine of the Sicilian nobility.

COSTS: $2,500 includes 4-star hotel lodging, most meals, transfers, planned excursions.

CONTACT: Roberta Barbagallo, Sicilian Odyssey, Via Cesare Vivante, 28, Catania, Italy; (39) (0)95-552725, Fax (39) (0)95-446628, info@intl-kitchen.com, www.theinternationalkitchen.com/sicily.htm. Local Contact: The International Kitchen, Email: info@intl-kitchen.com; Toll-free: 800-945-8606; Local: 312-726-4525, Fax: 312-803-1593.

SIENA CULTURE COOKING
Siena

Sponsor: Private school. Programs: 3-hr Italian cooking classes offered daily or weekly. Established: 1990. Class/group size: 6 max. Facilities: Kitchen with Tuscan furniture restored by Marco. Also featured: Italian language classes, wine instruction, visits to local farms.

FACULTY: Elisabetta, her husband Marco, & staff. Elisabetta has 10+ yrs teaching foreign students, & holds a degree in English Lit. Marco works in the wine & olive oil industry.

CONTACT: Elisabetta Ungaro, Siena Culture Cooking, Via Pian D'ovile - 21, Siena, 53100 Italy; (39) 0577 920451, cell 3337526246, sienaculturacucina@libero.it, www.sienaculturecooking.it.

SIMPLY SICILY COOKING TOURS
Sicily

Sponsor: Sole Blu Sicilia travel company. Programs: 8-day cooking & wine tours that feature 3 cooking classes, dining in fine restaurants, visits to open air markets, wineries, historic homes, farms. Established: 1995. Class/group size: 6-12. 5 programs/yr. Facilities: Kitchens are located in historic homes. Also featured: Custom tours for cooking schools & other groups, wine tours, general culinary tours.

FACULTY: Cooking experts & authors.

COSTS: ~$2,300/person includes shared 4-star hotel lodging, most meals, planned activities.

CONTACT: Margherita Perricone, President, Simply Sicily - Sole Blu Sicilia, Via M. Stabile 10, Palermo, 90141 Italy; (39) 091323064, Fax (39) 091306584, info@worldsisland.com, www.worldsisland.com/cooking.htm.

SORRENTO COOKING SCHOOL BY LAURA NICCOLAI
Sant'Agnello, Sorrento

Sponsor: Culinary professional Laura Niccolai. Programs: 4- & 8-day programs (3 & 6 classes) based on traditional Italian regional cuisine. Established: 2004. Class/group size: 6-20. Facilities: Well-equipped professional kitchen. Also featured: Include restaurant dinners, visits to Limoncello liqueur, mozzarella cheese & Sorrento Intarsio factories, visit to Capri or Pompeii.

FACULTY: IACP-member Laura Niccolai studied with Michelin 3-star chef Gualtiero Marchesi & French pastry chef Jain Bellouet.

COSTS: €800-€1,200/4 days, €1,400-€2,000/8 days includes shared hotel lodging, some meals, local transfers, planned activities.

CONTACT: Raffaella D'Esposito, Managing Director, Sorrento Cooking School by Laura Niccolai, Viale dei Pini 52, Sant'Agnello, Sorrento, 80065 Italy; (39) 081-878- 3255, Fax (39) 081-878-5022, info@esperidi.com, www.sorrentocookingschool.com.

SPA & COOKING IN THE VENETO
Veneto

Sponsor: Culinary tour company. Programs: Six-night program that combines an Italian spa with hands-on cooking lessons & excursions. Established: 1998. Class/group size: 2-8. 4 programs/yr. Facilities: Villa kitchen. Also featured: Spa treatments, market visit, excursion to Lake Garda & Verona, grappa tasting, dinner cruise on the Venetian lagoon.
FACULTY: Sergio Torresini has taught cooking at Abano's hotel management school for ten years.
COSTS: $2,550 includes six nights lodging in a 4-star spa hotel, meals, excursions, spa treatments.
CONTACT: Lino Barillari, Spa & Cooking in the Veneto, Via Monteortone, 19, Abano Terme, Italy; (39) (0)49-8669990, Fax (39) (0)49-667549, info@intl-kitchen.com, www.theinternationalkitchen.com/abano.htm. The International Kitchen, Email: info@intl-kitchen.com, Toll-free: 800-945-8606,Local: 312-726-4525,Fax: 312-803-1593.

SUSAN SCHIAVON'S VENETIAN EXPERIENCE
Venice

Sponsor: Culinary professional Susan Schiavon. Programs: 5-day hands-on Italian/Venetian cookery vacations that include 3 classes, shopping at Rialto market, boat trip, visit to Murano & Veneto countryside. Established: 1996. Class/group size: 7. 5-6 programs/yr.
COSTS: $2,000/5 days includes full board & lodging in a luxury home in central Venice, ground transport, planned activities.
CONTACT: Susan Schiavon, Susan Schiavon's Venetian Experience, Calle Zanardi 4133, Cannaregio, Venice, 30121 Italy; (39) 0415237194, Fax (39) 0415212705, susan.venice@iol.it. London Office: Liz Heavenstone, 188, Regent's Park Rd., London NW1 8XP, England; (44) 020 7722 5060, Fax (44) 020 7586 3004, Heavenstone@btinternet.com.

TASTE THE LIFE OF TUSCANY
Chiusi

Sponsor: Private school. Programs: 1-wk vacation programs that feature cooking classes, fine dining, cultural & historical trips. Class/group size: 12 max. 2 programs/yr. Facilities: Hotel & inn kitchens.
FACULTY: Linda Grossman, former restaurant owner & caterer, has taken classes at The CIA.
COSTS: $3,600 includes scheduled meals, lodging, planned excursions.
CONTACT: Taste The Life of Tuscany, 822 South 67th St., Omaha, NE 68106; Fax 402-552-0739, info@lifeoftuscany.com, www.tuscanycookingschools.com.

TASTE A PLACE
Tuscany

Sponsor: Specialty travel company. Programs: Weekend & one-week cooking vacation programs that feature instruction by either a professional chef or a regional native home cook. Established: 2004. Class/group size: 5. 15 programs/yr. Also featured: Culinary excursions, shopping & spa trips, restaurant visits.
FACULTY: Chef Paolo Gronchi owns a restaurant in Montecatini; Franca Scarpato is a native Tuscan home cook.
COSTS: £695-£1,495 includes luxury villa lodging, some meals, planned excursions.
CONTACT: Keri Cook, Director, Taste A Place, 25 Chiswick Rd., London,England; (44) 020 8994 7707, info@tasteaplace.com, www.tasteaplace.com.

A TASTE OF SICILY
Noto, Sicily

Sponsor: Percorsi, a Sicilian cultural services agency. Programs: 8-day program that includes three cooking lessons, wine & oil tastings. Established: 2004. Class/group size: 12 max. 25 programs/yr. Facilities: Include holiday farms, rural hotels, historic houses & villas. Also featured: Archeological visits, Italian language courses, Sicilian ceramic & music courses, trekking, cultural & nature programs.
FACULTY: Local chefs.

COSTS: From $1,650 includes shared lodging with half-board, local transfers.
CONTACT: Mariangela Gioacchini, Percorsi Sicilia, Vico Lucio Bonfanti 24, Noto, 96017 Italy; (39) 0931 574748, Fax (39) 0931 574748, info@percorsisicilia.com, www.percorsisicilia.com.

TASTES OF ITALY LTD
Venice, Verona, Bologna, Florence
Sponsor: Italian gourmet travel company, based in London. Programs: Feature fine dining, gourmet visits, cooking demos, cultural activities, vineyards & wine. Established: 2000. Class/group size: 8-16. 15 programs/yr. Facilities: Restaurant kitchens or country villas.
FACULTY: Includes restaurateurs Giancarlo Gianelli (Tuscany), Giancarlo Gioco (Verona), Bonifacio Brass, grandson of Giuseppe Cipriani (Venice), Nico Costa (Bologna).
COSTS: £300-£1,000 for a 3- to 5-day program includes deluxe lodging, meals, planned activities.
CONTACT: William Goodacre, Director, Tastes of Italy Ltd, PO Box 31799, London,England; (44) 20 87882337, Fax (44) 870 169 5324, info@tastesofitaly.co.uk, www.tastesofitaly.co.uk.

TASTY TUSCANY
Agliati (Pisa) & Tuscany
Sponsor: Private school. Programs: Weekly 1- & 2-wk hands-on cooking vacation programs that include wine tastings, tour of chianti producers, dining with local families, truffle hunting, cultural events. Established: 1995. Class/group size: 2-10. 5 programs/yr. Facilities: Kitchen of a restored 16th-century country house with marble working stations, garden & patio facing the Tuscan hills. Also featured: Art excursions, archaeological hiking, horseback riding, mountain biking, swimming, ceramic making, basket weaving, painting, yoga & massage workshops.
FACULTY: Includes Patrizia d'Intino & Paolo Vecchia (cooking), Steve Armstrong (wine), Giovanni Corrieri (archaeology), Grazia Bodino & Luciano Dallapè (art tours).
COSTS: €1,980-€2,150/wk (€1,200-€1,540 for non-cooking guest) includes shared villa lodging, meals, planned activities. 2- to 3-day courses also available.
CONTACT: Patrizia d'Intino, Culinary Artist, Tasty Tuscany, Via Agliati, 123, Località Agliati - Palaia (Pisa), 56036 Italy; (39) 0587 622186, (39) 0587 621784, cell phone (39) 335 569 5678, Fax (39) 0587 621784, patrizia@tastytuscany.com, www.tastytuscany.com.

TAVERNA DEL LUPO CULINARY ARTS SCHOOL
Gubbio, Umbria
Sponsor: Taverna de Lupo restaurant. Programs: Five-day culinary vacations that feature cooking classes, a truffle hunt, visits to wineries & food producers, dining in fine restaurants, cultural excursions. Established: 1997. Class/group size: 10. 50 programs/yr. Facilities: A medieval room next door to the Hotel Relais Ducale.
FACULTY: Chef Claudio of the 14th century restaurant Taverna del Lupo.
COSTS: €850-€900 includes lodging at Hotel Relais Ducale.
CONTACT: Rodolfo Mencarelli, Patron, Taverna del Lupo Culinary Arts School, via Ansidei 21, Gubbio, PG, 6024 Italy; (39) 075-9274368, Fax (39) 075-9271269, sales@mencarelligroup.com, www.mencarelligroup.com.

TOSCANA AMERICANA
Cortona
Sponsor: Special interest travel provider. Programs: One-week culinary travel programs that include Tuscan cooking classes, visits to food producers, museum excursions, wine tastings, shopping, sightseeing. Established: 2000. Class/group size: 4-8. 10+ programs/yr. Facilities: From kitchens in villas & privates homes to restaurant kitchens.
FACULTY: Tuscan chefs, restaurant owners, farmers, wine & olive oil producers.
COSTS: From $2400.
CONTACT: Patrick Mahoney, Producing Director, Toscana Americana, 367 West Broadway, Gardner, MA 1440; 508-254-8265, Italy: (39) 329-07-77-215, infotuscany@aol.com, hometown.aol.com/upcoevents/workshopintropage.html.

TOSCANA SAPORITA TUSCAN COOKING SCHOOL
Massarosa, Lucca, Tuscany
Sponsor: Culinary professional Sandra Lotti. Programs: Include 6-day traditional Tuscan cuisine. Each features 17-20 hrs of hands-on instruction & afternoon tours. Established: 1995. Class/group size: 8-12. 24 programs/yr. Facilities: Professional, modern kitchen housed in a 15th-century villa with a wood-beamed dining room, antique furniture, modern plumbing & electricity. Also featured: Market shopping, fine dining, tours of Lucca, Portovenere, Pietrasanta, Viareggio, Pisa.
FACULTY: Sandra Lotti (author of Sapore di Maremma, L'Anno Toscano, & Zuppe Toscane), cousin of the late Anne Bianchi (author of From The Tables of Tuscan Women, Zuppa!, Solo Verdura, Italian Festival Food). Both co-authored Dolci Toscani. 2-3 assistants.
COSTS: $2,050-$2,450 incl meals, ground transport, tours, & lodging at Toscana Saporita.
CONTACT: Toscana Saporita, P.O. Box 686, Prince St. Station, New York, NY 10012; 212-219-8791, Fax 212-925-0827, toscana@compuserve.com, www.toscanasaporita.com.

TOSCANAINBOCCA
Florence
Sponsor: Private school. Programs: 1- to 5-day courses in Tuscan cuisine. Established: 1998. Class/group size: 2-12. Also featured: Visits to specialty shops & craftsmen, sightseeing.
FACULTY: Anna has a degree in literature & manages a school for children. Gloria is an art historian & lived in the US.
COSTS: 5-day course €750, 3-day course € 460, 1-day course € 300/couple, €160/person.
CONTACT: Gloria Marinelli, Toscana in Bocca, Via Cimatori, 5, Florence, 50122 Italy; (39) 055 2678149, Fax (39) 055 2678149, toscanainbocca@yahoo.it, www.toscanainbocca.it.

THE TUSCAN CHEF
Lucca
Sponsor: Private culinary school. Programs: 6-day residential hands-on cooking courses that include regional tours. Established: 1997. Class/group size: 8-12. 12+ programs/yr. Facilities: Fully-equipped Tuscan kitchen & dining room. Also featured: Vineyard & market visits; wine, olive oil & balsamic vinegar tastings; pastry, chocolate, & truffle courses.
FACULTY: Professional Italian chef & sommelier Valter Roman.
COSTS: €2,400-€2,700 includes villa lodging, meals, ground transport, planned excursions.
CONTACT: Valter Roman, The Tuscan Chef, Via del Folle Manzi 8, 55060 Italy; (39) 348 4406367, (39) 320 6066859, (39) 0583 971464, info@thetuscanchef.com, www.thetuscanchef.com. valter.julia@cln.it.

THE TUSCAN TURTLE
Tuscany & Florence
Sponsor: Caterer & private school. Programs: Full & half-day cooking classes, market tours, wine estate tours, porcini mushroom hunting, olive harvesting, customized programs. Established: 1998. Class/group size: 4+. Also featured: Food Lovers' Tours of Florence, meal service for home renters featuring a discussion of local food customs & traditions.
FACULTY: Florentine D.O.C.G. chefs.
COSTS: Cooking lessons start at $150, including meal. Market tour ~$75 flat fee (8 people max).
CONTACT: Jennifer Schwartz & Leonardo Tirinnanzi, Owners, The Tuscan Turtle, 127 Blackfriars Circle, Doylestown, PA 18901; (39) 055-436-8108, cell: (39) 0347-766-8262, jelcora@dinonet.it.

TUSCAN WAY – LA VIA DEI SENSI
Tuscany
Sponsor: Country estates Casa Innocenti, Villa Gaia & Villa Castelletti. Programs: 1-week & 1/2-week hands-on Tuscan cuisine culinary vacations that feature daily classes & excursions. Established: 1999. Class/group size: 4-8. 30+ programs/yr. Facilities: Historic kitchens equipped with stoves & a wood-burning oven. Also featured: Wine tastings, grape harvest tours, excursions

to small villages of Northern & Southern Tuscany. Lunches at local restaurants.
FACULTY: Carlo Innocenti, chef-owner of Casa Innocenti; Isabel Innocenti, program founder/director. Linda Sorgiovanni, hostess of Villa Castelletti.
COSTS: $2,790 ($1,690) for 7 days (4 days) includes shared lodging in Casa Innocenti, meals, excursions. Single $3,190 ($1,890).
CONTACT: Isabel Innocenti, Director, Tuscan Way - La Via dei Sensi, 2829 Bird Ave., Suite 5, PMB 242, Coconut Grove, FL 33133; 800-766-2390, 305-598-8368, Fax 305-598-8369, Isabel@tuscanway.com, www.tuscanway.com. In Italy: Casa Innocenti, 12 Piazza del Cassero, Arcidosso (GR), Italy.

TUSCAN WOMEN COOK
Montefollonico, Tuscany
Sponsor: Specialty travel company. Programs: 1-day, 3-day & week-long culinary & cultural vacation programs that feature morning hands-on cooking classes & afternoon visits to food-related sites. Established: 1998. Class/group size: 12. 9 programs/yr. Facilities: Kitchens in Tuscan country homes & restaurants. Also featured: Fine dining, trekking, cycling, hot air ballooning, outlet shopping, excursions to historic Tuscan cities.
FACULTY: Local Tuscan women who use fresh local ingredients & prepare family recipes.
COSTS: $2,350 includes 7 nights shared first class lodging at Hotel La Costa, a 14th-century restored farmhouse, most meals, planned activities. $350 single supplement.
CONTACT: Bill & Patty Sutherland, Owners, Tuscan Women Cook, Podere Poggio Castagni, Montefollonico (SI), 53040 Italy; (39) 0577 669 444, Fax (39) 0577 668 707, info@tuscanwomen-cook.com, www.tuscanwomencook.com. Philip Cecchettinipolenta@pacbell.net.

VENETIAN COOKING IN A VENETIAN PALACE
Venice
Sponsor: Culinary professional Fulvia Sesani. Programs: Cooking classes in her 13th-century Venetian palace. Established: 1984. Class/group size: 10. Facilities: Modern, fully-equipped kitchen. Also featured: Shopping in the Rialto market, visits to the Ducal palace, museums, & private homes, dinner at Harry's Bar, & the Palazzo Morosini. Also available: day classes & private lessons.
FACULTY: Fulvia Sesani.
CONTACT: Fulvia Sesani, Venetian Cooking in a Venetian Palace, Castello 6140, Venezia, 30122 Italy; (39) 041-522-8923. In the U.S.: Judy Ebrey, Cuisine International Inc., P.O. Box 25228, Dallas, TX 75225; 214-373-1161, Fax 214-373-1162, Email CuisineInt@aol.com, www.cuisineinternational.com.

VENICE VENETO GOURMET
Venice
Sponsor: Art & gastronomy historian Sara Cossiga. Programs: History of gastronomy & food product tours, cooking classes, wine tastings. Established: 2003. Class/group size: 2-15.
FACULTY: Sara Cossiga, art historian, graduate of Ca' Foscari University of Venice, tour guide, & professional wine taster. Cooking classes are taught by 3 professionals (Italian Culinary Academy).
COSTS: €200/gastronomic tour, €85-€190/cooking class, €110/wine tasting.
CONTACT: Sara Cossiga, Venice Veneto Gourmet, S. Polo 2308, Venice, 30125 Italy; E-mail info@venicevenetogourmet.com, www.venicevenetogourmet.com. sara.cossiga@flashnet.it.

VERBENA BLU VIAGGI – COOKING CLASSES IN SIENA
Siena & Florence, Tuscany
Sponsor: Cultural & culinary specialists. Programs: Cooking classes & gourmet tours. Visits to Tuscany countryside, Chianti wine & olive oil tastings. Established: 1999. Class/group size: 8. 24 programs/yr. Facilities: Kitchen-classroom. Also featured: Walking, biking, wine & customized tours.
FACULTY: Culinary professionals.
COSTS: From $2,000 including lodging, most meals, escorted tours, ground transport.
CONTACT: Franco Battista, Verbena Blu Viaggi - Cooking in Siena, V.le Toselli, 35, Siena, 53100 Italy; (39) 0577 226691, Fax (39) 0577 221051, info@verbenabluviaggi.com, www.verbenabluviaggi.com.

VILLA CROCIALONI COOKING SCHOOL
Fucecchio, Tuscany
Sponsor: Private villa on 35 acres. Programs: 5-day programs every other week include hands-on classes daily & an excursion to Viareggio (seashore) fish market & Central Market in Florence. Established: 1996. Class/group size: ~4-8. 25 programs/yr. Facilities: Family kitchen with large oven & 6 burners, wood burning oven. The villa produces olive oil, vegetables, herbs, & raises farm animals. Also featured: Pool, jogging, visits to Santa Croce leather factories, & to Lucca, on request. B&B stays available between cooking courses.
FACULTY: Buncky Pezzini, who trained in New York City, has 47 yrs experience in Italian cuisine.
COSTS: $2,800 includes lodging at the villa, meals, excursions, ground transport; single supplement $350. Airport transfers additional.
CONTACT: Patricia (Buncky) Pezzini, Cook/Owner, Villa Crocialoni Cooking School, Via Delle Cerbaie #60, Fucecchio, Florence, 50054 Italy; (39) 0571-296237, Fax (39) 0571-296237, villacrocialoni@leonet.it. In the U.S.: Judy Ebrey, Cuisine International Inc., P.O. Box 25228, Dallas, TX 75225; 214-373-1161, Fax 214-373-1162, Email CuisineInt@aol.com, www.cuisineinternational.com.

VILLA DELIA HOTEL & TUSCANY COOKING SCHOOL
Ripoli di Lari
Sponsor: Tuscan villa hotel & cooking school. Programs: 10-day vacation packages that include 7 hands-on cooking classes. Established: 1995. Class/group size: 22. 18 programs/yr. Facilities: 16th century restored Tuscan villa on 80 acres of olive groves & vineyards; swimming pool & tennis courts. Also featured: Wine & private instruction, day trips, market visits, wine & olive oil tastings, fine restaurant dining, cultural sightseeing.
FACULTY: Resident chef Marietta. Umberto Menghi teaches some spring & fall classes.
COSTS: $4,700 double, $5,200 single occupancy. Includes meals, excursions, Pisa airport transfers & deluxe lodging with private bath.
CONTACT: Kim Lloyd, Director of Sales, Umberto Management Ltd., 1376 Hornby St., Vancouver, BC,Canada; 604-669-3732, Fax 604-669-9723, inquire@umberto.com, www.umberto.com.

VILLA LUCIA – THE BED & BREAKFAST OF TUSCANY
Tuscany
Sponsor: Culinary professional Lucia Luhan. Programs: 1-wk & half-day cooking courses that include oil pressing, bread making & cheese making. Established: 1985. Class/group size: 4+. 6-8 programs/yr. Facilities: Ms. Luhan's family farm/B&B has a kitchen with individual work areas. Also featured: Sightseeing, tours & shopping.
FACULTY: Restaurateur/caterer Lucia Ana Luhan studied in Europe & S. America & owns a restaurant in California.
COSTS: $1,500/1-wk includes lodging & most meals.
CONTACT: Food & Wine Appreciation Program-Luhan Corp., ,; 714-546-9600, Fax 714-546-5899, villalucia@yahoo.com, www.bboftuscany.com. In Italy: Via Bronzoli 1443, 51015 Montevettolini (PT), Italy, (39) 0572 617790, Fax (39) 0572 628817.

VILLA RIGNANA
Florence
Sponsor: Private villa in Tuscany. Programs: 1-wk & 3-day weekend programs that include demos of Tuscan cuisine, lectures on wine & culture. Established: 2003. Class/group size: 6-12. 12 programs/yr. Facilities: Purpose-built indoor & outdoor kitchens, modern appliances. Also featured: Riding, tennis, golf, walks, classic car tours.
FACULTY: Up to 4 professional chefs.
COSTS: €1,250/wk includes lodging, most meals; €550/3 days.
CONTACT: Alessandra Bianchini, Contessa, Villa Rignana, via di Rignana 7, Greve in Chianti, Florence, 50022; (39) 055 85 21 37, Fax (39) 055 85 22 05, book@villarignana.com, www.villarignana.com.

VILLA UBALDINI
Florence

Sponsor: Villa originally built in the 13th century. Programs: 1-wk hands-on programs devoted to kitchen-tested recipes of Italian cuisine, nutrition & the Mediterranean diet. Established: 1995. Class/group size: 16. 10 programs/yr. Facilities: Large teaching kitchen. Also featured: Visits to food producers, winery & guided tours of lesser known Tuscany, dining in private homes & Villa Ubaldini, cultural activities.

FACULTY: Margherita Vitali, mgr of the courses & a founder of the Italian Assn. of Cooking Teachers, & Chef Janet Hansen, author of Medieval Fires...Renaissance Stoves.

COSTS: $2,900-$3,500, includes shared lodging at Villa Ubaldini, private bath, most meals, planned excursions. Amenities: pool, billiards. Golf, horses, gliders at additional cost.

CONTACT: Margherita Vitale, Villa Ubaldini, via Genova 10, Grosseto, 58100 Italy; (39) 335 6543530, Fax (39) 055 8428998.

VILLA RENTALS & COOKING SCHOOLS IN TUSCANY
Tuscany

Sponsor: Tour operator in Italy specializing in cookery schools & villa rentals. Programs: 1-day to 1-week cooking vacations that include hands-on lessons, visits to wineries, dining in fine restaurants, sightseeing. Established: 2003. Class/group size: 2- 8. 10 programs/yr.

COSTS: €150/day including meals to €2,700/wk including lodging, some meals, planned excursions.

CONTACT: Elisa Biagini, Villa & Vacation Srl, Viale Giotto 7, Arezzo (AR), 52100 Italy; (39) 0575 40 32 63, Fax (39) 0575 40 79 86, info@villa-and-vacation.com, www.villa-and-vacation.com.

VINARIUM
Italy

Sponsor: Vinarium special interest tour operator. Programs: 1-wk cooking & wine programs, 1- & 2-wk programs that combine optional Italian language instruction with cooking & wine classes, private & group cooking classes. Established: 1994. Class/group size: 10 max. 23 programs/yr. Facilities: Historical buildings & farmhouses. Also featured: Visits to markets, food producers, & farms, winery tours.

FACULTY: Andrea Moradei, Ph.D., owner & Tuscan food & wine expert. Chef/instructors include Gino Noci, Concetta, Francesca Nustrini, & Valentina Lami.

COSTS: €170/private lesson, €55/group lesson, €490/Maremma 1-wk course, $1,450/Chianti 1-wk course includes lodging & most meals, 1,050 (€585) with language instruction, €735 (€410) without language instruction for 2 (1) wks.

CONTACT: Andrea Moradei, Owner, Vinarium Travel Agency, Via de' Pepi 56 red, Florence, 50122 Italy; (39) (0)55-213881, Fax (39) (0)55-216949, info@vinaio.com, www.vinaio.com. Koinè Center, Via Pandolfini 27, 50122 Florence, Italy; (39)055213881, Fax (39)055 216949.

WINE & TASTE TOURS
Treviso

Sponsor: Park Hotel Bolognese. Programs: Customized culinary, wine, & cultural tours. Established: 1985. Class/group size: 8-20. Facilities: Local wine cellars, the hotel kitchen. Also featured: Contact with regional wine cellars for business opportunities.

FACULTY: Chef of the Park Hotel Bolognese's restaurant, Villa Pace, & an oenologist.

CONTACT: Livio Zoppas, Wine & Taste Tours, Int.O.C., Viale Verdi 21, Treviso, 31100 Italy; (39) 0422 419890, Fax (39) 0422 598676, info@intoc.com, www.hotelbolognese.com/en/wine_tours.html.

WINE TOURS & COOKING COURSES ON THE AMALFI COAST
Amalfi Coast

Sponsor: Tour company specializing in regional wine & cooking vacations in Italy. Programs: 3-14 day vacations featuring cooking lessons, excursions & wine tastings; wine tours. Established: 2003. Class/group size: 2-20. 50+ programs/yr. Also featured: Specialized tours, regional excursions.

FACULTY: Local chefs.

COSTS: $590 -$ 3,000 includes lodging, dinners, excursions.

CONTACT: Carlo de Filippo, Manager, Wine Tours & Cooking Course on the Amalfi Coast, Via S. Botteghelle, 5, Furore, Amalfi Coast, 84010 Italy; (39) 3288815393, carlodefilippo@tiscali.it, www.dfconsulting.biz.

ZIBIBBO COOKING SCHOOL
Florence
Sponsor: Trattoria Zibibbo restaurant. Programs: Week-long apprenticeship for up to 2 students or 4 consecutive Saturday classes limited to 6 students. Established: 1999. Class/group size: 2-6. 20 programs/yr. Facilities: The classes take place in Zibibbo's kitchen, alongside the cooks. Also featured: Sightseeing excursions can be arranged.

FACULTY: Chef-Instructor Benedetta Vitali is co-founder & former chef of Cibreo restaurant, chef-owner of Tratorria Zibibbo, & author of Soffritto.

COSTS: €660/week-long program, €385/4 Saturdays includes breakfast, lunch & wine tasting.

CONTACT: Benedetta Vitali, Chef, Zibibbo Cooking School, Via di Terzollina, 3/R, Florence, 50129 Italy; (39) 055 433 383, Fax (39) 055 428 9070, zibibbofirenze@hotmail.com, www.zibibbonline.com.

JAPAN

KONISHI JAPANESE COOKING CLASS
Tokyo
Sponsor: Culinary professional Kiyoko Konishi. Programs: Hands-on classes with flexible schedule. Home-style Japanese dishes/decorative cutting also included. Established: 1969. Class/group size: 4-7. 42 programs/yr. Facilities: 300-sq-ft kitchen with Japanese & Chinese utensils & Japanese tableware. Also featured: Classes for youngsters, fish market & supermarket visits, private lessons.

FACULTY: Kiyoko Konishi has taught foreigners in English for 32 yrs & is author of Japanese Cooking for Health & Fitness, Entertaining with a Japanese Flavor, & 3 bilingual cooking videos.

COSTS: 4,000 yen/class includes tax. List of nearby hotels is available.

CONTACT: Kiyoko Konishi, Principal, Konishi Japanese Cooking Class, 3-1-7-1405, Meguro, Meguro-ku, Tokyo,Japan; (81) 3-3714-8859, Fax (81) 3-3714-8859, kikonishi@aol.com, www.seiko-osp.com/kjcc.

LE CORDON BLEU – JAPAN
Tokyo (Daikanyama district), Yokohama & Kobe   *(See display ad page 161)*
Sponsor: Private school, sister school of Le Cordon Bleu Paris. Programs: Half-day to 1-yr courses, daily demos, gourmet sessions, cuisine & pastry courses, Introduction to Cuisine, Pastry & Bread Baking. Established: 1991. Class/group size: 8-16. 10-20 programs/yr. Facilities: Professionally-equipped kitchens; individual work spaces with refrigerated marble tables, convection ovens; specialty appliances. Also featured: Guest chef demos.

FACULTY: 15 full-time French & Japanese Master Chefs from Michelin-star restaurants & hotels.

COSTS: From 5,250 yen (2-hr demo) to 696,150 yen (12-wk Cuisine Superior course).

CONTACT: Taeko Okabe, Students Services & Sales Mgr., Le Cordon Bleu Japan, ROOB-1, 28-13 Sarugaku-cho, Daikanyama, Shibuya-ku, Tokyo,Japan; (81) 3 5489 0141, Fax (81) 3 5489 0145, tokyo@cordonbleu.edu, www.cordonbleu.co.jp. Toll free in the U.S. & Canada: 800-457-CHEF. http://www.cordonbleu.edu.

A TASTE OF CULTURE
Tokyo
Sponsor: Culinary professional Elizabeth Andoh. Programs: Participation classes that focus on a specific theme, tasting programs devoted to traditional Japanese ingredients, Tokyo neighborhood market tours. Established: 1970. Class/group size: 6. 25-30 programs/yr. Facilities: Home kitchen fully equipped for teaching Japanese cooking. Also featured: Customized market tours & workshops.

FACULTY: Elizabeth Andoh trained at Yanagihara Kinsaryu School of Traditional Japanese Cuisine, Tokyo. She contributes to The NY Times & is Gourmet magazine's Japan correspondent. **COSTS:** $75/tour, $85/thematic workshop, $95/tasting session. **CONTACT:** Elizabeth Andoh, Director & Instructor, A Taste of Culture, 1-22-18-401 Seta, Setagaya-ku, Tokyo,Japan; (81) 3-5716-5751, Fax (81) 3-5716-5751, andoh@tasteofculture.com, www.tasteofculture.com.

MEXICO

ADVENTURES IN PERSPECTIVE
Tulum, Yucatan Peninsula
Sponsor: Adventure travel company. Programs: 1-wk cooking vacation focusing on Mayan & Mexican cuisine. Established: 1996. Class/group size: 6-10. 1 programs/yr. Facilities: Indoor & outdoor beach-side kitchens, area restaurants. Also featured: Snorkeling, kayaking, visit to Mayan ruin. **FACULTY:** James Foley, executive chef of Tejas restaurant in Edina, MN; Leydy Sausedo, who specializes in Mexican cuisine; local chefs. **COSTS:** $1,450 includes lodging, ground transport, most meals, sea kayaking equipment. **CONTACT:** Gail Green, Director, Adventures In Perspective, P.O. Box 874, Bayfield, WI 54814; 715-779-9503, Fax 715-779-5605, info@livingadventure.com, www.livingadventure.com/acooking.html.

ARCOS MEXICAN COOKING VACATION IN SAN MIGUEL ALLENDE
San Miguel de Allende
Sponsor: Culinary professional. Programs: 1-wk culinary vacation featuring daily Mexican cooking classes, market excursion, visits to a restaurant kitchen & Queretaro Culinary Institute. Established: 2002. Class/group size: 7 max. 8 programs/yr. Facilities: Traditional clay & steel cooking utensils. Also featured: Evening activities, classes for non-cooking companions. **FACULTY:** Patricia Merrill Marquez, 35 yrs experience Mexican cooking. Guest Instructor Maria Marquez, taught Mexican cooking in León. Other native guest instructors. **COSTS:** $1,500-$1,700 includes lodging at Arcos Del Atascadero B&B, meals, airport & ground transport, planned activities. **CONTACT:** Patricia Merrill Marquez, Lead Instructor, Mexican Cooking Vacation in San Miguel Allende, Callejon Atascadero # 5B, San Miguel de Allende, GT, 37700 Mexico; (52) 415 152 5299 or 2276, Fax (52) 415 152 5299, congusto@cybermatsa.com.mx, www.mexicancookingvacation.com.

CABO CASA COOKING
Los Cabos
Sponsor: Travel consultant/agency. Programs: 3- to 5-day seafood cooking programs with opportunities to catch & cook fish. Class/group size: 10 max. 10 programs/yr. Facilities: 13,500-s-ft villa with new kitchen & home-style equipment. Also featured: Guided or self-guided tours, fishing, golf, scuba, snorkling, shopping, night life. **FACULTY:** Top local Mexican chefs. **COSTS:** From $150/day including airport pickup, shared lodging, transportation to/from classes. **CONTACT:** Marion Snyder, Owner, Cabo Casa Cooking, Plaza Nautica, Los Cabos, 23140 Mexico; (52) 1435872, Fax (52) 1435872, cabocasa@juno.com.

CASA DEL ANGEL COOKING SCHOOL
Mexico City & Cuernavaca
Sponsor: Chef. Programs: Customized classes by appointment. Established: 2004. Class/group size: 6-40. 52 programs/yr. Facilities: Professional-style kitchens. Also featured: Market, restaurant & cultural tours. **FACULTY:** Chef/host Billy Cross, co-founder of the Great Chefs of France Cooking School at the Robert Mondavi Winery. **COSTS:** $75/class. Guest house lodging available.

CONTACT: Billy Cross, Chef Instructor, Casa del Angel Cooking School, Calle Ciltlatepec No. 39, Colonia Las Palmas, Cuernavaca, Morelos, c.p. 62050, Mexico; (52) 777-310-3841, mexicochef@yahoo.com, www.hotelangelmexico.com. Rio Guadalquivir No. 57, Piso 7, Colonia Cuauhtemoc, Mexico City, c.p. 06500 Mexico; (52) 555-525-5314.

CHEF'S TOUR
Oaxaca, Huatulco, Puebla, Merida
Sponsor: Chef & cooking instructor. Programs: 4-day to 3-week culinary adventure tours with cooking classes & cultural activities. Established: 2000. Class/group size: 8-24. 12 programs/yr.
FACULTY: Chef with 25 yrs experience teamed with local guides & experts.
COSTS: $2,300 for 10 days, all inclusive.
CONTACT: Daniel Hoyer, Chef/tour leader, Chef's Tour, Box 2-d, Pilar Route, Embudo, NM 87531; 505-751-4611, hoyer@laplaza.org, www.freeyellow.com/members8/cooks-tour/index.html.

CHOCOLATE CHILIES & COCONUTS
Puerto Vallarta
Sponsor: The Center for World Indigenous Studies. Programs: Food & cooking of indigenous peoples of Mexico, study with native cooks & healers, traditional medicine, ethnobotany, intl relations, cultural history. Established: 1977. Class/group size: 20 max. 5 programs/yr. Also featured: Swimming, scuba, snorkeling, massage, bodywork, exercise, yoga, horseback riding, mountain treks.
FACULTY: Leslie Korn, Ph.D. lived & worked in Mexico 25 yrs; former Harvard Medical school faculty Dr. Rudolph Ryser, Ph.D., a cross-cultural historian & chef; Alisia Rodriguez, a chef who specializes in foods of indigenous cultures.
COSTS: $1,949/wk includes shared lodging & meals. Professional development univ. credit available.
CONTACT: Dr. Leslie Korn, Director of Education, Chocolate Chilies & Coconuts, 1001 Cooper Pt. Rd. SW, Ste. 140-214, Olympia, WA 0; 360-754-1990, Fax 360-786-5034, usaoffice@cwis.org, www.cwis.org/seminars/tmsem195a.html.

COCINAR MEXICANO
Tepoztlán
Sponsor: Under the Volcano International. Programs: 1-wk classes in classical & contemporary Mexican cuisine featuring daily hands-on workshops, visits to local kitchens, bartending, wine-tasting, dining in fine restaurants. NYC workshops in 2005. Established: 2003. Class/group size: 12 max. 4-6 programs/yr. Facilities: Fully-equipped kitchen/classroom, 4-star hotel, kitchens of local restaurants & homes. Also featured: Excursions to archaeological ruins & museums, pyramid climb, village fiestas, optional Spanish classes, massage, swimming, hiking, horseback riding.
FACULTY: Guest chefs from noted Mexican restaurants: Patricia Quintana of Izote, Martha Ortiz of Aguila y Sol, Gabriela Cámara of Contramar. Lecturers in culinary history & Mexican culture.
COSTS: $2,295 includes shared lodging at the 4-star Posada del Tepozteco, most meals, ground transport, planned activities.
CONTACT: Cocinar Mexicano; E-mail info@cocinarmexicano.com, www.cocinarmexicano.com.

COOKING WITH MARIA
San Miguel de Allende
Sponsor: Private school. Programs: Hands-on & demo classes in traditional Mexican cooking, including salsas, adobos, pipianes, moles, tamales, pozole, & chiles rellenos. Established: 1992. Class/group size: 7 max. Facilities: Kitchen classroom equipped with stove, tortilla pans, copper & clay pots, grinding stone bowls & boards. Also featured: Shopping in the Farmer's Market.
FACULTY: María Laura Ricaud Solórzano, featured in Texas Monthly, who uses family recipes passed down for 200+ years.
COSTS: $40-$50/class.
CONTACT: Maria Ricaud, Chef, Cooking with Maria, Calle La Luz 12, Colonia San Antonio, San Miguel de Allende, 37750 Mexico; (52) 415-152-4376, cocimari@hotmail.com. Holly Yasui, 2a Privada de Animas #21,San Miguel de Allende, Gto Mexico CP 377700;hyasui@cybermatsa.com.mx.

CULINARY ADVENTURES OF MEXICO
San Miguel de Allende
Sponsor: Culinary travel company. Programs: 1-wk culinary tours that include hands-on classes, market visits, sightseeing, 2-day trips, optional language classes. Established: 1996. Class/group size: 4-10. 5 programs/yr. Also featured: Spa treatments, yoga, salsa dance classes.
FACULTY: Local prominent chefs.
COSTS: $1,650 includes luxury lodging, meals, ground transport, planned activities. $400 single suppl.
CONTACT: Kristen Rudolph, Director, Culinary Adventures of Mexico, Jesus 23, San Miguel de Allende, 37700 Mexico; 0-11-52-(4)-154-4825, Fax 0-11-52-(4)-154-4825, culadv@unisono.net.mx, www.mexicocooks.com.

FLAVORS OF MEXICO – CULINARY ADVENTURES, INC.
Various regions
Sponsor: Marilyn Tausend's Culinary Adventures. Programs: 7- to 10-day regional cooking vacations to Mexico. Established: 1988. Class/group size: 8-18. 4-5 programs/yr. Facilities: Home & restaurant kitchens. Also featured: Visits to food markets & artisans' workshops, meals & demos in local cooks' homes, tours of historical & archaeological sites.
FACULTY: Marilyn Tausend, author of Cocina de la Familia; Chef/owner Rick Bayless & Ricardo Munoz Zurita; Culinary Director Roberto Santibanez (Rosa Mexicano); Ana Elena Martinez.
COSTS: ~$2,750-$2,950 includes meals, shared lodging, excursions, local transport. Lodging in small hotels popular with Mexican families.
CONTACT: Marilyn Tausend, Culinary Adventures, Inc., 6023 Reid Dr. N.W., Gig Harbor, WA 98335; 253-851-7676, Fax 253-851-9532, cul_adv_inc@attglobal.net, www.marilyntausend.com.

ILUMINADO TOURS – COOKING ADVENTURES IN THE YUCATAN
Merida, Yucatan
Sponsor: Specialty tour company. Programs: One-week cooking & cultural tours that include market visits, & excursions to archeological sites & colonial cities. Established: 2003. Class/group size: 4-10. 5-8 programs/yr. Facilities: Modern kitchen in a renovated colonial home.
FACULTY: Chef David Sterling.
COSTS: $1,250-$1,450 includes lodging, ground transport, & some meals.
CONTACT: Trudy Woodcock, Tour Guide, Iluminado Yucatan Cooking Tour; In Canada: 905-337-3104, 866-212-4644; info@iluminado-tours.com, www.iluminado-tours.com/tour6-focus-on-food.asp.

LA CASA DE MIS RECUERDOS COOKING CLASSES
Oaxaca
Programs: 1-day classes & 10-day cooking class package. All are demo/hands-on & include market tour. Established: 1985. Class/group size: 4-10. 24 programs/yr. Facilities: B&B kitchen, with both traditional & modern equipment. Also featured: Cooking classes in nearby villages, cheese making demo, tours to local cultural & archeological sites.
FACULTY: Nora Gutierrez, who was taught traditional Oaxaqueno cooking by her mother & grandmother; both have been featured in A Cooks Tour of Mexico cookbook.
COSTS: $65/class. $1,199/10 days includes B&B lodging, some meals, tours, local transportation.
CONTACT: William Gutierrez, Innkeeper, La Casa de Mis Recuerdos, Pino Suarez 508, Oaxaca, 68000 Mexico; (52) 951-51-5645, Fax (52) 951-51 5645, misrecue@prodigy.net.mx, www.misrecuerdos.net/new%20cooking%20class.htm.

LA VILLA BONITA SCHOOL OF MEXICAN CUISINE
Cuernavaca
Sponsor: Chef Ana Garcia, co-owner of La Villa Bonita. Programs: 4- & 7-night hands-on culinary vacation programs that cover traditional & nouvelle Mexican dishes, salsas, condiments, beverages. Vegan, vegetarian, parent-child, healthy Mexican available. Established: 2000. Class/group size: 6. 40-44 programs/yr. Facilities: Kitchen of a 16th-century mansion, one of the first Spanish colonial

structures in the Americas. Also featured: Shopping at local markets, visits to regional villages.
FACULTY: Chef Ana Garcia, owner of La Villa Bonita & her restaurant Reposado in Cuernavaca. Native cooks assist.
COSTS: $1,550 ($1,850)/7 nights or $1,050 ($1,350)/4 nights + tax includes meals, shared (single) lodging at La Villa Bonita, airport transportation. Non-participant guest $750/7 nights, $450/4 nights.
CONTACT: Robb Anderson, La Villa Bonita School of Mexican Cuisine, Netzahualcoyotl #33, Colonia Centro, Cuernavaca, 62000 Mexico; 800-505-3084, Fax 800-505-3084, reservations@lavillabonita.com, www.lavillabonita.com.

LOS DOS COOKING SCHOOL
Merida
Sponsor: Private school. Programs: 1- to 3-day classes that include shopping at local market. Established: 2003. Class/group size: 8 max. 60 programs/yr. Facilities: Private kitchen in a restored colonial home. Also featured: Tours to Mayan ruins, ex-haciendas & colonial cities can be arranged.
FACULTY: Chef David Sterling holds an MFA in design from Cranbrook Academy of Art & lived in New York City for 25 years. He has studied Mexican cuisine since 1972.
COSTS: $75-$300.
CONTACT: David Sterling, Chef, Los Dos Cooking School, Calle 68 #517 x 65 y 67, Merida, 97000 Mexico; (52) 999-928-1116, Fax (52) 999-928-1157, info@los-dos.com, www.los-dos.com.

MEXICAN COOKING COURSE/LEARNING HOLIDAYS
Cancun
Sponsor: Hotel Cancun Suites 'El Patio'. Programs: 1-week cooking course featuring 5 Mexican cooking lessons & an archaeological site tour. For organized groups of 6 minimum. Established: 1995. Class/group size: 6-10. Varies programs/yr. Facilities: Fully-equipped kitchen & restaurant. Also featured: Spanish lessons, Mayan culture excursions.Healing holidays, osteopathy treatments, chelation therapy, diabetes mellitus treatments.
FACULTY: Mexican chefs.
COSTS: $470 includes 7 nights shared lodging at the Mexican colonial Cancun Inn Suites 'El Patio', breakfast & lunch, archaeological site tour, airport transportation.
CONTACT: El Patio-Reservations, Mexican Cooking Course, Learning Holidays, Bonampak 51 SM 2A, corner of Cereza, Cancun, Q. Roo, 77500 Mexico; (52) (9) 8 84 35 00, Fax (52) (9) 8 84 35 40, lia2001@mail.com, www.cancun-links.com/cooking.htm.

MEXICAN CULINARY TOURS WITH NANCY ZASLAVSKY
San Miguel de Allende & Oaxaca
Sponsor: Culinary professional Nancy Zaslavsky. Programs: One-week tours that include cooking classes, visits to markets, food producers, archaeological sites & museums, & dining in fine restaurants. Established: 1994. Class/group size: 10 max. 2-3 programs/yr.
FACULTY: Nancy Zaslavsky is author of A Cook's Tour of Mexico (a James Beard Foundation Award nominee) & Meatless Mexican Home Cooking. She has traveled in Mexico since 1970.
COSTS: $1,950-$2,150 includes meals, lodging & planned activities.
CONTACT: Nancy Zaslavsky, Owner, Mexican Culinary Tours with Nancy Zaslavsky, 4061 Mandeville Canyon Rd., Los Angeles, CA 90049; 310-440-8877, Fax 310-471-0163, nancy@nancyzaslavsky.com, www.nancyzaslavsky.com.

MEXICAN HOME COOKING
Tlaxcala
Sponsor: Culinary professional Estela Salas Silva. Programs: 7-day & customized hands-on cooking vacations. Periodic special menus, cultural events or holiday weeks. Established: 1996. Class/group size: 4 max. Facilities: Fully-equipped 500-sq-ft kitchen with stove & adjacent work areas set below a 70-sq-ft skylight. Also featured: Visits to market, pulquerias, sightseeing.Optional trips to Puebla, archaeological sites at Cacaxtla, Xochitécatl, Cholula; pool & tennis at 4-star hotel in Tlaxcala.

FACULTY: Estela Salas Silva, chef in Mexico City & San Francisco since 1974; local guest cooks.

COSTS: $1,200 includes meals & lodging in the Silva family home.

CONTACT: Estela Salas Silva, Owner, Mexican Home Cooking, Apartado 64, Tlaxcala, Tlaxcala, 90000 Mexico; (52) 246-46-809-78, Fax (52) 246-46-809-78, mexicanhomecooking@yahoo.com, mexicanhomecooking.com.

SEASONS OF MY HEART COOKING SCHOOL
Oaxaca

Sponsor: Private school. Programs: Hands-on 1-wk & 4- to 5-day weekend courses, day classes, 7- to 10-day regional culinary tours. Established: 1993. Class/group size: 4-28. Facilities: 12-station Mexican kitchen, outdoor kitchen with wood-fire adobe oven & pre-Hispanic cooking utensils. Also featured: Visits to corn & chocolate mills, mezcal factory, markets, archaeological sites, farms, local artisans.

FACULTY: Susana Trilling, TV host, lecturer, chef, caterer, IACP-member; part-time teachers; cheese & chocolate makers, bread bakers, herbal healers.

COSTS: Day classes from $75; 4-day/5-day weekend course $950/$1,200. 1-wk course $1,695/$1,895, culinary tours $950-$2,300 include meals, lodging, planned activities.

CONTACT: Cheryl Camp, Adminstrative Manager, Seasons of My Heart Cooking School, Apdo. 42, Admon 3, Oaxaca, Oaxaca, CP, 68101 Mexico; (52) 951-518-7726/(52)951-508-0044, Fax (52)951-518-7726, seasons@spersaoaxaca.com.mx, www.seasonsofmyheart.com/.

TRADITIONAL MEXICAN COOKING SCHOOL
San Miguel de Allende

Sponsor: Culinary professional. Programs: Basic techniques classes cover salsas, adobos, pipianes, moles, tamales, pozoles, main dishes, soups, rice.Custom Classes in Traditional Mexican Menus. Established: 1996. Class/group size: 1-7. Facilities: Kitchen with traditional family cooking utensils. Also featured: Market tours, custom classes.

FACULTY: María Solórzano has cooked traditional family recipes from Oaxaca, Michoacán & other parts of Mexico for 30+ yrs. Her grandmothers & aunts were culinary professionals in private clubs.

COSTS: $40/class.

CONTACT: María Solórzano, Traditional Mexican Cooking School, La Luz 12, San Miguel de Allende, 37700 Mexico; (52) 415 152 4376, cocimari@hotmail.com, www.cocimari.com.

XILONEN: MEXICO CULINARY VACATIONS
Jalisco

Sponsor: Bed & breakfast. Programs: One-week courses in traditional Mexican cuisine & seasonal specialities. Established: 2004. Class/group size: 10 max. 12 programs/yr. Also featured: Excursions to Guadalajara, artisans workshops, cultural activities.

FACULTY: Chef/proprietor Rose Marie Plaschinski.

COSTS: $1,850 includes lodging, most meals, planned excursions.

CONTACT: Rose Marie Plaschinski, Proprietor, Xilonen: Mexico Culinary Vacations, informes@xilonen.com.mx, www.xilonen.com.mx.

MOROCCO

COOKING AT THE KASBAH
Morocco

Sponsor: Cookbook author Kitty Morse. Programs: 2-wk tour emphasizing local cuisine & culture, including cooking demo with Kitty Morse & local experts. Established: 1983. Class/group size: 15 max. 1 programs/yr. Facilities: Morse's home, a restored pasha's residence; private & hotel kitchens. Also featured: Visits with friends, excursions to historic locales, marketplaces, working farms; special events; golf & tennis available.

FACULTY: Native of Casablanca, Kitty Morse is author of Cooking at the Kasbah, Couscous, & The Scent of Orange Blossoms: Sephardic Cooking from Morocco.

COSTS: ~$4,800 includes land transport, most meals, planned activities, shared lodging in first class or deluxe hotels.

CONTACT: Kitty Morse, Box 433, Vista, CA 92085; E-mail kmorse@adnc.com, www.kittymorse.com.

EAT SMART CULINARY TOURS
Morocco; Poland; Turkey

Sponsor: Author of culinary travel guides. Programs: 10-day to 2-wk vacations that focus on the country's cuisine & include classes, visits to markets, wineries & other culinary venues. Established: 1998. Class/group size: 15 max. Facilities: Restaurants & private homes. **FACULTY:** Joan Peterson, Ph.D., was a biochemist at the Univ. of Wisconsin & is author of the Eat Smart series of culinary travel guides to Brazil, Turkey, Indonesia, Mexico & Poland. **COSTS:** $2,395-$3,300 includes shared lodging in 4- & 5-star hotels, most meals, regional transportation, planned activities. **CONTACT:** Dr. Joan Peterson, Eat Smart Culinary Tour to Poland, PO Box 5346, Madison, WI 53705; 608-233-5488, Fax 608-233-0053, joanp@ginkgopress.com, www.ginkgopress.com/tours.html.

NETHERLANDS

LA CUISINE FRANCAISE
Amsterdam, Netherlands

Sponsor: Culinary professional Patricia I. van den Wall Bake-Thompson. Programs: 1- & 4-session demo & participation courses. Established: 1980. Class/group size: 25 demo/16 hands-on. 60 programs/yr. Facilities: 90-sq-meter kitchen rebuilt in 1994, private dining room in 1647 canal house. Also featured: Sessions in English for groups, private classes, market visits. **FACULTY:** School owner & instructor Patricia I. van den Wall Bake-Thompson was born in Great Britain & studied home ec at Harrow Technical College. She is a consultant to food companies. **COSTS:** Cooking session from €55. Lodging by arrangement in nearby hotels. **CONTACT:** Pat van den Wall Bake-Thompson, La Cuisine Francaise, Herengracht 314, Amsterdam CD, 1016 Netherlands; (31) 20-627-8725, Fax (31) 20-620-3491, info@lacuisinefrancaise.nl, www.lacuisinefrancaise.nl.

MMMMM COOKING HOLIDAYS
Tarn

Sponsor: Mmmmm catering service. Programs: 7-day cooking holiday featuring daily classes & visits to wineries & markets. Established: 2001. Class/group size: 10 max. 10 programs/yr. Facilities: Fully-equipped kitchen, vegetable & herb garden. Also featured: Afternoon children's cooking courses, seasonal classes, sausage making. **FACULTY:** Professional cook with experience in Dutch restaurants & on a sailing vessel; assistant & host. **COSTS:** $ 1,200 includes shared lodging, most meals, airport transfer, excursions. **CONTACT:** C. T. Deys, Mmmmm Cooking Courses, Teniersstraat 5-3, Amsterdam,Netherlands; E-mail info@mmmmm.net, www.mmmmm.net.

NETHERLANDS ANTILLES

ABSOLUTECARIBBEANCUISINE
Willemstad, Curaçao

Sponsor: Specialty travel company. Programs: 10-day vacation programs that include cooking classes, culinary & cultural excursions, fine dining. Established: 2002. Class/group size: 12 max. 4 programs/yr. Facilities: Angelique's kitchen in a renovated house. Also featured: Swimming with dolphins, diving, golf, windsurfing, sailing,hiking, horseback riding. **FACULTY:** Angelique Schoop, a native Antillean; restaurant chefs. **COSTS:** $2,165 includes deluxe oceanfront lodging, meals, planned activities.

CONTACT: Ulla Strandberg, Managing Director, AbsoluteCaribbean, Kaminda Hofi Abou # 65, Willemstad, Curaçao, Netherlands Antilles; (599) 986-43320, Fax (599) 8644020, info@absolute-caribbean.com, www.absolutecaribbean.com/cuisine.html.

ANGELICA'S KITCHEN
Willemstad, Curaçao

Sponsor: Culinary professional. Programs: Hands-on classes & courses in Caribbean cuisine, 1-, 2- or 4-day cooking sessions, 4- & 7-day cooking vacations. Established: 2000. Class/group size: 8-14. 10 programs/yr. Facilities: 19th-century restored colonial house with 550-sq-ft kitchen. Also featured: Golf, scuba diving, sailing, sightseeing.

FACULTY: Angelique Schoop, a pharmacist & chef, studied at The Institute of Culinary Education in NY & at La Varenne, France.

COSTS: $45 walking tour includes lunch. 4-day/7-day culinary vacation $1,600/$2,450 includes 5-star hotel lodging, meals, sightseeing.

CONTACT: Angelique Schoop, Angelica's Kitchen, Hoogstraat 49, Willemstad, Curaçao, Netherlands Antilles; (599) 9 5623699, Fax (599) 9 8696582, (599) 9 8890554, info@angelicas-kitchen.com, www.angelicas-kitchen.com.

NEW ZEALAND

EPICUREAN WORKSHOP
Auckland

Sponsor: Cookware store & cooking school/espresso bar. Programs: Demo & participation classes, 1-hr Gourmet on the Run classes 3 times/wk. Established: 1989. Class/group size: 10-40. 200-250+ programs/yr. Facilities: Teaching kitchen with overhead mirrors. Also featured: Tailor-made Taste of New Zealand classes for visitors, private classes, corporate events, team-building.

FACULTY: Director Catherine Bell, CCP is a graduate of Leith's School in London & an IACP member. Local chefs & cookbook authors include Ray McVinnie, Greg Heffernan, Julie le Clerc.

COSTS: Demos NZ$22-NZ$85, hands-on classes from NZ$200.

CONTACT: Catherine Bell, Epicurean Workshop, 6 Morrow St., P.O. Box 9255, Newmarket, Auckland, New Zealand; (64) 9 524-0906, Fax (64) 9-524-2017, info@epicurean.co.nz, www.epicurean.co.nz.

HERZOG'S WINERY & RESTAURANT COOKING CLASSES
Blenheim

Sponsor: Herzog's Winery & Restaurant. Programs: 1/2-day hands-on workshops, wine education classes. Established: 2000. Class/group size: 12. 25 programs/yr. Facilities: Herzog's Restaurant kitchen.

FACULTY: Head chef Louis Schindler from former Michelin-star restaurant Taggenberg in Switzerland & his team of chefs.

COSTS: From NZ$170.

CONTACT: Louis Schindler, Head Chef, Herzog's Winery & Restaurant, 81 Jeffries Rd., RD2, Blenheim, 7301 New Zealand; (64) 3 572 8770, Fax (64) 3 572 8730, info@herzog.co.nz, www.herzog.co.nz.

LONGHOUSE ISLAND RETREAT NEW ZEALAND
Auckland

Sponsor: Private culinary school. Programs: 5 to 7-day cooking & wine-matching vacations. demo classes, visits to vineyards, olive groves, local village & restaurants. Established: 2001. Class/group size: 8-10. 12 programs/yr. Facilities: Purpose-built teaching facility with commercial demonstration kitchen, outdoor wood-fired bread oven & the latest stainless steel appliances. Dining area with ocean views. Also featured: Visits to art studios, charter fishing, sailing & sea kyaking, swimming, coastal & beach walks & horse trekking. Excursions to Auckland city.

FACULTY: Local & international guest chefs offering modern cuisine.

COSTS: NZ$2,750-NZ$3,500 includes shared lodging, island transfers, tours & specified meals.

CONTACT: Longhouse Island Retreat, 155 Nick Johnstone Drive, RD1 Waiheke, Auckland, New Zealand; (64) 09 3729619, Fax (64) 09 3722537, molly@longhousenz.com, longhousenz.com.

RUTH PRETTY COOKING SCHOOL
Te Horo, Kapiti Coast
Sponsor: Ruth Pretty Catering. Programs: Full-day weekend classes. Established: 1994. Class/group size: 32 demo, 10 hands-on. 40 programs/yr. Facilities: Commercial catering kitchen. Also featured: Group classes that include a talk & focus on such topics as gardening or wine (no cooking), wine tastings, company dinners.
FACULTY: Caterer Ruth Pretty & a variety of New Zealand & overseas instructors.
COSTS: NZ$155/class.
CONTACT: Ruth Pretty, Ruth Pretty Cooking School, P.O. Box 41, Te Horo, Kapiti Coast, 5560 New Zealand; (64) (0)6-3643161, Fax (64) (0)6-3643262, ruth@ruthpretty.co.nz, www.ruthpretty.co.nz.

PHILIPPINES

HENY SISON CULINARY SCHOOL
Quezon City
Sponsor: Private culinary school. Programs: 20-day Essential Cooking Series;10-day Master Course in Cake Decorating; 5-day Advanced Gumpaste/Foreign Methods Cake Decorating. Short term & specialty courses. Established: 1985. Class/group size: 40 demo, 25 hands-on. 300 programs/yr. Facilities: Air-conditioned lecture room with the latest baking & cake decorating equipment. Also featured: Design & production of cakes for special occasions.
FACULTY: Heny Sison & experienced guest chef-lecturers.
COSTS: $40-$1,200.
CONTACT: Heny Sison, Proprietress, Heny Sison Culinary School, 33 Bonnie Serrano Avenue, corner Sunrise Drive, Crame, Quezon City, Metro Manila, Philippines; 632-726-5316, 632-412-7792, Fax 632-412-7792, henysison@pacific.net.ph, www.henysison.com.

PORTUGAL

REFUGIO DA VILA HOTEL & COOKING SCHOOL
Portel, Alentejo
Sponsor: Resort hotel. Programs: 7-day hands-on cooking vacations. Established: 1997. ~30 programs/yr. Facilities: Specially-designed teaching kitchen with a fireplace for baking Portuguese breads & curing sausages. Also featured: Wine, art, & cultural excursions.
FACULTY: Chef António Miguel Amaral.
COSTS: $2,195 includes lodging, meals, planned activities.
CONTACT: Refugio da Vila Rural Hotel, Largo Dr. Miguel Bombarda, 8, Portel, Alentejo,Portugal; (351) 266 619010, Fax (351) 266 619011, refugiodavila@iname.com, www.refugiodavila.com/. In the U.S.: Judy Ebrey, Cuisine International, P.O. Box 25228, Dallas, TX 75225; 214-373-1161, Fax 214-373-1162, Email CuisineInt@aol.com, www.cuisineinternational.com.

SCOTLAND

THE COOKERY SCHOOL AT GLASGOW
Glasgow
Sponsor: Private school. Programs: Hands-on classes & courses that cover Scottish cookery, appetizers to desserts, entertaining menus, international cuisines, & specific topics. Established: 2003. Class/group size: 12. 200 programs/yr. Facilities: Individual cooking stoves, ovens, mixers & other kitchen equipment. Also featured: Team-building workshops, cooking parties, individual tuition.
FACULTY: John Quinn, former executive head chef at The Corinthian in Glasgow. Cake courses by Rhona Wilson of Creative Cakes in Glasgow.

Costs: £25/class, £80/4-session course, £80/one day, £150/wkend, £350/wk.
Contact: Brian Hannan, Chief Executive, The Cookery School, 65 Glassford St., Glasgow,Scotland; (44) (0) 141 552 5239, bhkhannan@aol.com, www.thecookeryschool.org.

EDINBURGH SCHOOL OF FOOD & WINE
Edinburgh
Sponsor: Private school. Programs: 1- to 5-day programs include demo & hands-on classes, short courses & master classes. 1- & 5-wk intensive certficate courses & 6-mo Diploma in Food & Wine. Established: 1987. Class/group size: 20 max. Facilities: Full range of domestic & commercial equipment. Costs: From £25-£8,500.
Contact: Jill Davidson, School Director, Edinburgh School of Food & Wine, The Coach House, Newliston, Edinburgh,Scotland; (44) (0) 131 333 5001, Fax (44) (0) 131 335 3796, info@esfw.com, www.esfw.com/.

NAIRNS COOK SCHOOL
Stirling
Sponsor: Private school. Programs: 1-day classes, 5-day master classes, guest chef classes. 200+ programs/yr. Also featured: Private classes.
Faculty: Michelin-star chef John Webber, who was head chef at Gidliegh Park Hotel in Devon & Kinnaird Country House in Perthshire. Guest & celebrity chefs.
Costs: £120-£200/1-day class, £540/5-day master class.
Contact: Nairns Cook School, Port of Menteith, Stirling,Scotland; (44) 01877 385603, Fax (44) 01877 385643, info@nairnscookschool.com, www.nairnscookschool.com.

SINGAPORE

AT-SUNRICE THE SINGAPORE COOKING SCHOOL & SPICE GARDEN
Singapore
Sponsor: at-sunrice, a center for Asian food, culinary skills & craftware. Programs: Demo & hands-on classes, chef courses, baking classes for children, teens culinary camp, course with internship, culinary adventure. Established: 2001. Class/group size: 20. Also featured: Corporate team building, spice garden walks, farmers market.
Faculty: Professional chefs.
Costs: S$60-S$80/evening class, S$30-S$40/children's, S$450/week teen camp. US$2,500/2-wk course + internship includes lodging & meals. Singapore/Bali adventure US$2,800 includes shared lodging, meals, spa treatment, excursions, ground transport.
Contact: Angie Lim, Marketing & Communications, at-sunrice The Singapore Cooking School & Spice Garden, at-sunrice, Fort Canning Park, Fort Canning Centre, Singapore, 179618 Singapore; (65) 336 3307, Fax (65) 336 9353, angie@at-sunrice.com, www.at-sunrice.com. zeke@at-sunrice.com.

COOKERY MAGIC
Katong
Sponsor: Culinary professional Ruqxana Vasanwala. Programs: Classes that cover asian & intl cuisines, chocolates, cakes, desserts, pastries. Established: 2002. Class/group size: 1-10. 50-100 programs/yr. Facilities: Well-equipped home kitchen. Also featured: Harvesting, cooking & dining at an eco-farm, Kids Kan Kook classes for children, market tours.
Faculty: Ruqxana was an engineer & has been cooking for 33 yrs. Her specialty is 3D children's birthday cakes.
Costs: S$50-S$150/class.
Contact: Ruqxana Vasanwala, Cookery Magic, Haig Rd., Katong, East Coast, 438779 Singapore; (65) 63489667, Fax (65) 63489667, classes@cookerymagic.com, www.cookerymagic.com.

CORIANDER LEAF – THE NEW ASIAN FOOD HUB
Singapore
Sponsor: Asian Food Hub - bistro, shop, cooking school. Programs: Courses featuring traditional & interpreted dishes from the cuisines of the Middle East, South Asia, South East Asia & the Orient. Established: 2001. Class/group size: 6-10. 50 programs/yr. Facilities: Domestic home appliances. Also featured: Corporate team building, wine tastings & wine pairings, private dining. **FACULTY:** Culinary professionals. **COSTS:** S$75-S$125.

CONTACT: Samia Ahad, Director, Coriander Leaf - The New Asian Food Hub, 76 Robertson Quay #02-01, The Gallery Evason, Singapore, 238254 Singapore; (65) 732-3354, Fax (65) 732-3374, info@corianderleaf.com, www.corianderleaf.com.

EPICUREAN WORLD
Singapore
Sponsor: Culinary professional Devagi Sanmugam. Programs: Demo & hands-on cooking classes. Established: 1990. Class/group size: 10-24. 20 programs/yr. Facilities: Home-based well-equipped air-conditioned cooking studio. Also featured: Workshops, market & spice tours, kids' cooking classes.
FACULTY: School Director Devagi Sanmugam is a food columnist, consultant & cooking teacher with 21+ yrs experience; author of 8 cookbooks, including Great Bakes No Eggs & South Indian Cookbook.
COSTS: $50/class or $350/hr.
CONTACT: Devagi Sanmugam, Culinary Consultant, Epicurean World, 52 Jalan Leban, 577589 Singapore; (65) 458 0572, (65) 456 3014, Fax (65) 6457 3650, sandegi@pacific.net.sg, www.epicureanworld.com.sg.

RAFFLES CULINARY ACADEMY
Singapore
Sponsor: Raffles Hotel, Singapore. Programs: 1-2 classes daily, both demo & hands-on. Established: 1995. Class/group size: 24. Facilities: Well-equipped residential-type kitchen with demo area. Also featured: Wine instruction, classes for youngsters, dessert & pastry classes.
FACULTY: Raffles Hotel chefs, including Executive Chef Jean Paul Naquin & Executive Deputy Chef Gregoire Simonin.
COSTS: $60-$100/class. Suites range from $650/night at the 103-suite Raffles Hotel, which has 18 restaurants & bars, a Victorian-style playhouse, & a 40-shop arcade.
CONTACT: Raffles Culinary Academy Executives, 1 Beach Rd., 189673 Singapore; (65) 6412-1256, Fax (65) 6339-7013, rca@raffles.com, www.raffleshotel.com/facilities/culinary/culinary.htm.

SOUTH AFRICA

CHRISTINA MARTIN SCHOOL OF FOOD & WINE
Durban
Sponsor: Private school. Programs: Cordon Bleu 6-session courses, theme classes. Established: 1988. 30+ programs/yr. Facilities: Auditorium, delicatessen, 60-seat restaurant, 80-seat conference venue, garden restaurant.
FACULTY: Christina Martin is a Maitre Chef de Cuisine & Commandeur Associé de la Commanderie des Cordons Bleus de France. Instructors include vice-principal Michelle Barry, Chef de Cuisine; Sous Chefs Janet Sawkins, Debbie Earle, Amanda van Rooyen.
COSTS: R1270.50/Cordon Bleu course, R170/class.
CONTACT: Christina Martin, Principal & Owner, Christina Martin School of Food & Wine, PO Box 4601, Durban, 4000 South Africa; (27) (0)31-3032111, Fax (27) (0)31-312-3342, chrismar@iafrica.com, www.safarichef.com.

CAPE WINELAND TOURS
South Africa

Sponsor: Tour operator. Programs: Educational food & wine tours of South Africa, featuring introductory lecture by industry professional & winemaker-hosted tastings at 10-15 wine estates. Established: 1996. Class/group size: 6-15 max. 8 programs/yr. Facilities: Hotels, inns, restaurants. Also featured: Visit to Hermanus (whale-watching), Cape Town, safari extensions.
FACULTY: South African winemakers, wine guides, chefs, other food & wine experts.
COSTS: $3,200-$3,900 includes luxury lodging, most meals, ground transport.
CONTACT: Lisa Hough, President, Cape Wineland Tours, 3263 Juniper Lane, Falls Church, VA 22044; 888-868-7706, 703-532-8817, Fax 703-532-8820, info@capewinetours.com, www.capewinetours.com. Lisa Hough, President;Robin Fetsch, VP Operations.

SILVER PLATE COOKERY ACADEMY OF SOUTH AFRICA
Pretoria

Sponsor: Private school. Programs: 1-day intro to South African cooking, weekly hobbyist workshops, 1- or 2-day themed hostess workshops, 10-session intro to fine cooking. Classes incorporate theory & application. Established: 1999. Class/group size: 10-15. ~ 8 programs/yr. Facilities: Fully-equipped demo kitchen. Also featured: Sampling of South African food & wine.
FACULTY: Ilze van der Merwe trained at the Cordon Bleu Cookery School, South Africa; Marita Pieterse, trained at the Prue Leith Cookery School, London.
CONTACT: Ilze van der Merwe, Silver Plate Cookery Academy of South Africa, 93 Gardenia St., Lynnwood Ridge, Pretoria, 81 South Africa; (27) (0)83-656-7830, Fax (27) (0)12-361-7267, ilzev@btinternet.com, www.angelfire.com/il/silverplate/.

THE SILWOOD SCHOOL OF COOKERY
Rondebosch Cape

Sponsor: Career school. Programs: Guest chef demos, part-time cooking courses. Established: 1964. Class/group size: 4 groups of 10 stude. 6 programs/yr. Facilities: A 200-yr-old coach-house converted into a demo & experimental kitchen, 3 additional kitchens, demo hall & library. Also featured: 1-wk hands-on classes for children twice yearly, weekly participation classes.
FACULTY: 11-member faculty, includes principal Alicia Wilkinson, Rene Larsen, Alisa Smith, Louise Faull, Carianne Wilkinson, Lara DuToit, Gaie Gaag, Toinet Brink, Liz Bell.
COSTS: R225/part-time lesson.
CONTACT: Mrs. Alicia Wilkinson, The Silwood Kitchen School of Cookery, Silwood Rd., Rondebosch Cape, South Africa; (27) 21-686-4894/5, Fax (27) 21-686-5795, cooking@silwood.co.za, www.silwood.co.za.

WICKEDFOOD COOKING SCHOOL
Fourways, Sandton, South Africa

Sponsor: Private school. Programs: Hands-on beginner to advanced series, single classes on specific topics. Class/group size: 16 max. Facilities: Purpose built cooking studio in Fourways. Also featured: Group, corporate & team-building classes.
FACULTY: Mike & Cilla Crewe-Brown, editors of food & travel related books & magazines & founding editors of BonVivant food & travel, have traveled & attended cooking schools in Asia, Australia, Africa, USA & Europe & served as restaurant judges.
COSTS: ~R240/class.
CONTACT: wickedfood Cooking School, PO Box 846, Fourways, 2055 South Africa; (27) 11 705-2616, info@wickedfood.co.za, www.wickedfood.co.za.

SPAIN

CASA CANELA COOKING SCHOOL HOLIDAYS
Estremoz

Sponsor: Private cooking school. Programs: 5- & 7-day demo & hands-on classes, visits to private estates, olive oil mills, cheese factories, markets. Established: 1978. Class/group size: 12. 10 programs/yr. Facilities: Country kitchen, outside barbeque, modern facilities. Lodging available for 6 couples or 12 sharing. Also featured: Include golf, biking, horseback riding, boating, shooting, fishing, sightseeing.

FACULTY: Susanna Redman, has catered to embassies in Lisbon & cooked for heads of state & members of the European royal families.

COSTS: €2.380 sharing, all-inclusive.

CONTACT: Susanna Redman, Casa Canela Cooking School Holidays, Rua do Serrado, Sintra, Portugal; (351) 21 924 2438, cell (351) 91 409 6464, Fax (351) 21 924 4891 Attn SMR, redman_pt@yahoo.com.

CATACURIAN
El Masroig   *(See display ad above)*

Sponsor: Privately owned 4th-generation family home. Programs: 3-, 7-, & 9-day cooking vacation programs that include classes in Catalan cuisine, Priorat wines & olive oils. 9-day programs include grape or olive-picking sessions. Christmas session is 10-days. Established: 2002. Class/group size: 6. 44 programs/yr. Facilities: Private hotel with fully-equipped kitchen, prep area, fireplace; wine cellar & wine tasting room; outdoor barbecue. Also featured: Visits to Priorat villages, wine producers & museum, olive oil presses, historical sites. Priorat wine & olive oil tastings.

FACULTY: Alicia Juanpere Artigas studied at the Terra d'Éscudella & Bell-Art chef schools in Barcelona & has worked in the kitchens of the Restaurante Julian Tomas. An oenologist teaches Priorat wines.

COSTS: 3 days/7 days/9 days €1,000/€2,000/€2,700 (€1,150/€2,300/€3,150) includes shared (single) lodging, meals, ground transport, planned activities. 10-day Christmas program €3,100 (€3,650).

CONTACT: Vicki Austin, US Manager, Catacurian, PO Box 245, Palmetto, FL 0; 800-601 5008, 941-723 7588, Fax 941-723 7876, info@catacurian.com, www.catacurian.com. Alicia Juanpere,Carrer del Progrès 2, 43736 El Masroig, Tarragona, Spain (34) 977-825341.

CELLAR TOURS GOURMET WINE VACATIONS IN SPAIN & PORTUGAL
Spain & Portugal

Sponsor: Specialty travel company. Programs: 4- to 6-day programs that include vineyard tours, port & wine tastings, cooking & wine classes, private estate visits, fine dining, cultural excursions. Established: 2003. Class/group size: 15 max. 6 programs/yr. Facilities: Cooking schools, professional chefs' private homes.

FACULTY: Genevieve McCarthy, owner & founder of Cellar Tours, worked in wine importing in Ireland, wine consulting in Spain, a winery in Italy & received all WEST wine credentials. Professional chefs, sommeliers & food & wine specialty guides.
COSTS: €2,700-€3,500 includes luxury lodging, most meals, planned activities. Customized 1-day wine tours from €400.
CONTACT: Genevieve McCarthy, Owner, Cellar Tours Wine Tours in Spain & Portugal, c/ Ribera del Manzanares, n. 1, 8A, Madrid, 28008 Spain; (34) 91 547 7568, Fax (34) 91 559 9918, info@cellartours.com, www.cellartours.com.

CULINARY DISCOVERIES
Castilla, Cordoba, Granada
Sponsor: Jose Antonio (Tony) Sierra, a native of Spain, & his wife, Lisa. Programs: 5- to 7-day culinary tours of Spain's regions that include winery visits, trips to markets, tapas & olive oil tastings, cultural excursions. Established: 2003. Class/group size: 4-10. 27 programs/yr. Facilities: Restaurant kitchens & cooking schools.
FACULTY: Professional chefs in Spain.
COSTS: $2,750-$3,000/7 days includes shared lodging, most meals, ground transport, planned excursions.
CONTACT: Lisa Sierra, Culinary Discoveries, 755 Cleveland St., #B, Woodland, CA 95695; 530-383-3196, 530-383-0919, info@culinarydiscoveries.com, www.culinarydiscoveries.com.

ESCUELA DE COCINA LUIS IRIZAR
Basque Country
Sponsor: Private school. Programs: 1-wk courses for professionals & amateurs (4 hrs/day). Instruction in Spanish, English-speaking courses available. Optional visits to markets & food producers, winery tours, sightseeing, dining in Michelin-star restaurants. Established: 1992. Class/group size: 10-15. 8 programs/yr. Facilities: Fully-equipped kitchen, separate classroom, TV & video.
FACULTY: Founder Luis Irizar has served as chef in Spain's leading restaurants. Staff includes 3 full-time instructors & part-time teachers for continuing ed.
CONTACT: V. Irizar, Escuela de Cocina Luis Irizar, c/ Mari, #5, Bajo, San Sebastian, 20003 Spain; (34) 943-431540, Fax (34) 943-423553, cocina@escuelairizar.com, www.escuelairizar.com.

LA SERRANIA RETREATS
Pollensa, Mallorca
Sponsor: Private retreat center. Programs: Hands-on morning sessions & pre-dinner sessions including demos, talks & some hands-on involvement. Established: 1999. Class/group size: 6-12. 3 programs/yr. Facilities: All teaching takes place in the large kitchen with ample working space. Also featured: Walks in the country or visits to local market towns, massages.
FACULTY: Margalida Colomar & Martina Singer, experienced chefs, have been with La Serranía cooking since opening in 1999.
COSTS: €700 (+€180 single) includes lodging w/pvt bath & meals. La Serrania features a swimming pool, terrace, living/room library.
CONTACT: La Serrania Retreats, Apartado 211, Pollensa, Mallorca, 7460 Spain; (34) 639 306 432, Fax (34) 971 182 144, retreats@laserrania.com, www.laserrania.com.

A QUESTION OF TASTE
Seville
Sponsor: Tour provider emphasizing Spanish food & wine. Programs: 3- & 6-night gastronomic breaks. Includes cooking classes, visits to markets, wineries, olive oil mill, & ham factory, wine & olive oil tastings, tapas tour & meals in local restaurants. Established: 2002. Class/group size: 4-8. 12 programs/yr. Facilities: Fully-equipped kitchen with prep area for 8 students. Meals served on a balcony overlooking Seville's cathedral & Giralda. Also featured: 1-day food & wine excursions, group tapas tours & wine-tastings, customized regional gastronomic tours of Spain.
FACULTY: Tour guide Roger Davies has lived in Spain since 1987 & worked in Spanish wine industry.

Cooking instructor Ruth Roberts has 20+ yrs professional experience in Spain. Local professionals.
COSTS: €700/3-night break, €1,750/6-night break, shared lodging.
CONTACT: Roger Davies, A Question of Taste, Calle Alcazar, 12, Espartinas, Seville, 41807 Spain; (34) 954713710, enquiries@aqot.com, www.aqot.com. Mobile phone (34) 661620033.

QUIXOTE'S KITCHEN
Six regions
Sponsor: Private school. Programs: Week-long hands-on cooking vacations. Established: 2001. Class/group size: 6-12. 10 programs/yr. Facilities: Modern professional kitchens with individual work stations. Also featured: Visit to the fish market, dinners at Michelin-star restaurants, field trips to producers of wine, olive oil, marzipan, jamon serrano, & cheese.
FACULTY: Chef & Mediterranean food expert, Isabel Sanchez (native of Spain); Michelin star Chefs of the regions visited.
COSTS: €3,000-€3,500 includes shared luxury lodging, most meals, ground transport, planned activities.
CONTACT: Clara Garcia, Marketing Mgr., Quixote's Kitchen, Oakridge Centre, North Tower, 650 W 41st Ave., #567, Vancouver, BC,Canada; Fax 604-267-0291, clara.garcia@quixoteskitchen.com, www.quixoteskitchen.com. C/ Orellana 5, 1 Centro Izquierda Madrid, 28004 Spain.

SPANISH JOURNEYS
Barcelona, Catalonia
Sponsor: Specialty travel company. Programs: 1-week culinary vacations that include hands-on cooking lessons, cultural excursions, fine dining, visits to wineries, markets, artisans. Established: 2003. Class/group size: 16 max. 4 programs/yr.
FACULTY: Tour guide Teresa Parker trained as a chef in Barcelona. Catalonia-based chef &restaurateur Jaume Vidal provides cooking instruction.
COSTS: $3,195-$3,695/7- to 8-days includes luxury lodging, planned excursions, most ground transport.
CONTACT: Teresa Parker, Director, Spanish Journeys, 805 Long Pond Rd., Wellfleet, MA 2667; 508-349-9769, teresa@spanishjourneys.com, www.spanishjourneys.com.

SPANISH & MEDITERRANEAN COOKING WITH JEANNIE AT BUENVINO
Aracena Nature Park
Sponsor: Buenvino, a family-run B&B inn & cookery school. Programs: 1-wk hands-on cookery courses focusing on Andalucian & Mediterranean/North African cooking. Sherry tasting. 4-day tapas courses & private group courses also offered. Established: 1985. Class/group size: 6-8. 16 programs/yr. Facilities: Well-equipped family kitchen with marble-topped work table & outside kitchen courtyard. Also featured: Walking in the nature reserve, visit to a goat farm & Jerez winery, sightseeing trip to Sevilla.
FACULTY: Jeannie Chesterton trained at the Cordon Bleu School, cooked in Hong Kong, London & Scotland & has lived in Spain for 18 yrs. runningBuenvino with her husband.
COSTS: €900 includes 6 nights shared lodging, most meals, transport from Seville, excursion to Jerez. Single supplement €25/night. Non-cooking partners €95/night.
CONTACT: Jeannie Chesterton, Cooking with Jeannie at Buenvino, Finca Buenvino, Los Marines, Huelva, 21293 Spain; (34) 959 12 40 34 (10am-9pm central European time), Fax (34) 959 50 10 29, buenvino@facilnet.es, www.fincabuenvino.com. Sam Chesterton.

VINTAGE SPAIN – RUTAS DE VINO
Wine regions
Sponsor: Specialty travel company. Programs: 1- to 6-day wine tasting tours that combine wine & food with culture, art & history. Established: 2002. Class/group size: 14 max. 12 programs/yr. Facilities: Wineries, hotels, restaurants, cooking schools. Also featured: Cooking classes, hiking, biking, golf, custom programs.
FACULTY: Cristina Alonso & Javier Alonso, Spanish natives from the Rioja & Ribera del Duero

regions; professional instructors.

Costs: €170/1 day to €1750/6 days includes lodging, meals, ground transport, planned activities.

Contact: Cristina Alonso, Owner, Vintage Spain - Rutas de Vino, C/ Burgos 9 - 4 B, Miranda de Ebro, 9200 Spain; (34) 699246534, Fax (34) 947320066, info@vintagespain.com, www.vintagespain.com.

WINE PLEASURES WINE TASTING TOURS
Costa Brava, Empordà, Barcelona, Penedès & Priorat

Sponsor: Specialty travel company. Programs: 2- to 6-day winery tours that include grape cultivation & harvesting, guided wine tastings. Established: 2003. Class/group size: 6-15. 12 programs/yr. Facilities: Tasting rooms. Also featured: Biking & golf.

Faculty: Instructors have been employed in the wine business &/or are educators.

Costs: From €122 for a weekend.

Contact: Anthony Swift, Wine Pleasures, C/Vino y Sol, 1, La Llacuna, Barcelona, 8779 Spain; (34) 93 897 70 48, Fax (34) 93 897 60 16, info@winepleasures.com, www.winepleasures.com. Mobile (34) 687 34 57 44.

THAILAND

CREATIVE PHUKET
Phuket

Sponsor: Holiday workshop organizer. Programs: One-week Thai cooking workshops including hands-on classes & market visits. Class/group size: 6 max. Facilities: Open walled Thai style kitchen set in tropical gardens of fruits & herbs.

Faculty: Executive Chef Khun Sirikarn.

Costs: $380 ($420) includes shared (single) lodging, daily breakfast & dinner.

Contact: Creative Phuket, PO Box 103, Patong Beach, Phuket, 83150 Thailand; (66) 189 224 19, Fax (66) 76 385 168, kirjon@samart.co.th, www.phuket.net.

ROYAL THAI SCHOOL OF CULINARY ARTS
Bang Saen

Sponsor: Private cooking school specializing in Thai cuisine. Programs: Ten 5-session courses in Royal & Regional Thai cuisine that can be taken individually or as a 3-, 5- or 10-wk intensive. Other courses include vegetarian & contemporary Thai cooking. Established: 1997. Class/group size: 8. 30+ programs/yr. Facilities: 2 professional kitchens, beachfront swimming pool, lounge, dining room & terrace overlooking the Gulf of Siam. Also featured: Optional weekend culinary tours.

Faculty: 5 instructors, 2 master fruit & vegetable carvers.

Costs: $1,200-$10,000.

Contact: Chris Kridakorn-Odbratt, Exec. Chef, Royal Thai School of Culinary Arts, 5 Thanon Rob Kau Sammuk; Bang Saen, T. Saen Suk; A. Muang, Chonburi, 20130 Thailand; (66) 1-867 9450, (66) 38-748 404, Fax (66) 38-748 405, rtsca@cscoms.com, www.gourmetthailand.com.

SAFFRON 59
(Burma), Myanmar

Sponsor: Caterer/event planner. Programs: Culinary tours to Asia featuring regional cooking classes, market visits, tastings of local delicacies, & sightseeing. Class/group size: 15. 1 programs/yr. Facilities: Classes held in restaurants & local homes.

Faculty: Director/chef Irene Khin Wong, is on the faculty of the New School for Culinary Arts, is a board member of the Asian Culinary Society & has appeared on the TV Food Network.

Costs: 14-day Burma/Cambodia tour $4,500, includes shared hotel lodging ($899 single supplement), some meals, domestic travel within Indochina.

Contact: Saffron 59, 59 Fourth Ave., New York, NY 10003; 212-253-1343, Fax 212-253-0477, saffron59@juno.com, www.saffron59.com. www.snowlion.com.

SAMUI INSTITUTE OF THAI CULINARY ARTS
Koh Samui

Sponsor: Private institute. Programs: Twice daily Thai cooking classes, 3-day courses in decorative fruit & vegetable carving. Established: 1998. Class/group size: 5-10. 52 programs/yr. Facilities: Modern, fully-equipped 90-sq-meter teaching facility with individual cooking stations. Fine dining restaurant. Also featured: 3-4 wk professional training programs.

FACULTY: Director Roongfa Sringam has 10+ yrs experience in the kitchens of 5-star hotels & is a master fruit & vegetable carver. 2 addt'l instructors.

COSTS: $25-$35/class, $75/3-day carving course.

CONTACT: Roongfa Sringam, Institute Director, Samui Institute of Thai Culinary Arts, 46/26 Moo 3, Chaweng Beach, Koh Samui, 84320 Thailand; (66) 77-413172, Fax (66) 77-413172, info@sitca.net, www.sitca.net.

THAI COOKING CLASSES & HOLIDAYS
Chiang Mai & Bangkok

Sponsor: Private cookery school & travel co. Programs: 1-5 day hands-on cooking programs using fresh ingredients. Includes techniques, vegetable carving, curry pastes. Established: 2000. Class/group size: 1-16. Daily programs/yr. Facilities: Fully equiped individual work stations with gas cookers, classrooms. Also featured: Food market shopping, trip extensions to Laos, Cambodia, southern Thai beaches.

FACULTY: English-speaking Thai cooks.

COSTS: Chiang Mai: $20/day; $300/5-day course includes hotel lodging, some meals, domestic flight to Chiang Mai. Bangkok: from $50/course.

CONTACT: Thai Cooking Holidays, ,; (66) 2 6286721, Fax (66) 2 2812534, info@thaicookingholidays.co.uk, www.thaicookingholidays.co.uk.

THAI COOKING SCHOOL AT THE ORIENTAL, BANGKOK
Bangkok

Sponsor: The Oriental, Bangkok. Programs: Lecture & demo classes (Mon-Thurs), hands-on classes (Fri & Sat). Established: 1986. Class/group size: 15. Facilities: Classroom, participation/demo room, kitchen, dining area.

COSTS: $120/class; ~$2,200 (~$1,600)/6 days includes shared (single) lodging, some meals, 4 classes, airport transfers.

CONTACT: Tanika Peerakum, Mgr., Thai Cooking School at The Oriental, Bangkok, 48 Oriental Ave., Bangkok, 10500 Thailand; (662) 437-6211, (662) 437-3080, Fax (662) 439-7587, TanikaP@mohg.com, URL www.mandarinoriental.com. USA: Mandarin Hotel Group, 800-526-6566.

THE THAI HOUSE COOKING SCHOOL
Nontaburi

Sponsor: Private school. Programs: 1-, 2- & 3-day courses that include lectures, preparation of ingredients, hands-on cooking. Established: 1991. Class/group size: 2-10. Facilities: Open-air kitchen, farm & orchard. Also featured: 2- & 3-day courses include an excursion to an open-air market.

FACULTY: Pip Fargrajang.

COSTS: $100 for 1-day course. 2- (3-) day courses $255 ($475) including lodging at Thai House. Price includes transport from/to Bangkok.

CONTACT: Pip Fargrajang, The Thai House Cooking School, 3 2/4 Moo 8 Tambol Bangmuang, Ampur Bangyai, Nonthaburi, 11140 Thailand; (662) 9039611, 9475161, Fax (662) 9039354, pip_thaihouse@hotmail.com, newsroom.tat.or.th/article/thai_cuisine.html.

TIME FOR LIME CREATIVE THAI COOKING WORKSHOPS
Saladan, Koh Lanta, Krabi

Sponsor: Thai cooking school. Programs: 1-, 2- & 3-day hands-on workshops that concentrate on seafood & vegetables. Established: 2003. Class/group size: 10-16. Year-round programs/yr.

Facilities: Specially designed Thai-temple buildingwith 8 woks, chopping & eating tables. Also featured: Group workshops can be arranged.

FACULTY: Junie Kovacs, a graphic, conceptual & food designer; Naum, an experienced Thai chef who has worked in resorts & restaurants.

COSTS: 1,500-1,600 Baht/day; 4,400-4,500 Baht/3 day course.

CONTACT: Junie Kovacs, Instructor, 20 moo 3, Klong Dao Beach, Saladan, Koh Lanta, Krabi, 81150 Thailand; (66) 75 697 069/(66) 99 675 017, info@timeforlime.net, www.timeforlime.net.

ZOLOTRIPS
Bangkok & Chiang Mai
Sponsor: Travel company specializing in adventure, holistic & cultural trips. Programs: 1- to 2-wk trips that include hands-on cooking classes & market visits. Established: 1996. Class/group size: 5-12. 30 programs/yr. Facilities: Hotels & private homes or kitchens.

FACULTY: Local expert chefs.

COSTS: $150-$200/day.

CONTACT: Adam Zolot, Co-Founder, ZOLOtrips, 101 Baker St., San Francisco, CA 94117; 415-255-9520, Fax 415-680-1522, info@zolotrips.com, www.zolotrips.com. AOL Instant Messenger: ZOLOtrips.

TURKEY

COOKING IN TURKEY
Kalkan
Sponsor: Small country hotel. Programs: 1-wk course that combines daily hands-on cooking lessons & demos of such traditional skills as bread, grape molasses & yogurt making. Established: 2004. Class/group size: 8 max. 4 programs/yr. Facilities: Owlsland, a 150-yr-old restored traditional farmhouse with fully-fitted kitchen. Also featured: Guided walks, market visits, excursions, boat trip.

FACULTY: Local chef, 15 yrs experience; local artisans.

COSTS: £635/week includes lodging, meals, excursions.

CONTACT: Pauline Salvarli, Cooking in Turkey, Owlsland, Bezirgan Village, Kalkan, 7963 Turkey; (90) 242 8375214, owlsland@superonline.com, www.owlsland.com/cooking.htm.

CULINARY ADVENTURE IN TURKEY
Istanbul
Sponsor: Culinary travel company. Programs: 10-day program includes 5 cooking classes in different regions of Turkey, cooking & dining with locals. Final dinner on a Bosphorus cruise. Established: 1990. Class/group size: 6-12. 4 programs/yr. Facilities: Fully-equipped cooking school in Istanbul, hotel kitchens in some regions, facilities of a ranch in the country. Also featured: Private culinary tours in Turkey.

FACULTY: Turkish wine/dine magazine, cooks of 5-star hotels.

COSTS: $1,800-$2,400 includes shared lodging.

CONTACT: Asli Mutlu, Owner, Culinary Adventure in Turkey, 7319 Croy Lane, Dublin, CA 94568; 800-434-1989, 925-556-1278, Fax 925-556-0371, info@tourag.com, www.tourag.com.

CULINARY EXPEDITIONS IN TURKEY
Turkey
Sponsor: Kathleen O'Neill, culinary historian, foodresearcher & Turkey resident. Programs: Culinary land programs & cruises featuring traditional Turkish foodways, local harvests, dining with local families, informal classes with home cooks & noted chefs. Established: 1996. Class/group size: 6-12. Year-round programs/yr. Facilities: Home & professional restaurant kitchens. Also featured: Cultural & archaeological site visits, private gulet charters, custom itineraries.

FACULTY: Kathleen O'Neill; local chefs & home cooks.

COSTS: $2,200-$2,850, includes meals, lodging, planned activities, internal transport.

CONTACT: Kathleen O'Neill, Culinary Expeditions in Turkey, P.O. Box 1913, Sausalito, CA 94966; 415-437-5700, Fax 925-210-1337, info@turkishfoodandtravel.com, www.turkishfoodandtravel.com.

VIETNAM

DISCOVER VIETNAM
3 historical cities
Sponsor: Travel company specializing in cycling, culinary & custom adventure tours of Vietnam. Programs: 16-day tours that feature classes in the cuisine of three regions of Vietnam. Established: 1997. Class/group size: 15. Facilities: Hotel restaurant. Also featured: Lectures on the country's history & culture, dining in fine restaurants, sightseeing.
FACULTY: Master chef Nguyen Thi Hanh of the Huong Giang Hotel in Hue.
COSTS: $2,895 incl luxury hotel lodging, meals, ground transport, planned activities.
CONTACT: Hans Krausche, Discover Vietnam, 1088 Clarendon Crescent, PO Box 10096, Oakland, CA 94610; 510-839-4019.

WEST INDIES

ANNE-MARIE'S CARIBBEAN KITCHEN
Bridgetown, Barbados
Sponsor: Native Treasures, Inc., manufacturer of Caribbean condiments. Programs: 7-day cooking holiday featuring participation & demo classes in Caribbean cuisine & culture. Established: 1996. Class/group size: 15 hands-on, 25 demo. 9 programs/yr. Facilities: 5 work stations, demo kitchen with overhead mirrors. Also featured: Island tour, Calypso dancing instruction, party cruise, beach picnic, Atlantis submarine tour.
FACULTY: Anne-Marie Whittaker, author of Treasures of My Caribbean Kitchen & owner of Native Treasures, Inc.; guest chefs.
COSTS: $2,100 includes hotel lodging & activities, $1,200 for nonparticipants.
CONTACT: Anne-Marie Whittaker, Director Native Treasures Inc., Anne-Marie's Caribbean Kitchen, Unit #1, Food Complex, Wildey Industrial Park, St. Michael, Barbados, West Indies; (246) 228-5837, (246) 427-0532, Fax (246) 427-6278, annemarie@native-treasures.com.

3

Index

INDEX OF ADVERTISERS

Cooking School Index

D

M

N

O

P

Q

R